The Pocket Modern Welsh Dictionary

The Pocket Modern Welsh Dictionary

A guide to the living language

Edited by Gareth King

OXFORD
UNIVERSITY PRESS

OXFORD
UNIVERSITY PRESS

Great Clarendon Street, Oxford OX2 6DP

Oxford University Press is a department of the University of Oxford.
It furthers the University's objective of excellence in research, scholarship,
and education by publishing worldwide in

Oxford New York
Auckland Cape Town Dar es Salaam Hong Kong Karachi Kuala Lumpur
Madrid Melbourne Mexico City Nairobi New Delhi Shanghai Taipei Toronto

With offices in
Argentina Austria Brazil Chile Czech Republic France Greece
Guatemala Hungary Italy Japan South Korea Poland Portugal
Singapore Switzerland Thailand Turkey Ukraine Vietnam

Oxford is a registered trade mark of Oxford University Press
in the UK and in certain other countries

Published in the United States
by Oxford University Press Inc., New York

British Library Cataloguing in Publication Data

Data available

Library of Congress Cataloging in Publication Data

Data available

ISBN 978-0-19-864531-3
ISBN 0-19-864531-7

7

Designed by George Hammond Designs
Typeset in Swift and Arial
by Alliance Phototypesetters, India
Printed in Great Britain by
Clays Ltd, Bungay Suffolk

Preface

This dictionary is intended for the growing number of learners of modern Welsh in all walks of life, and is designed with their needs in mind.

It represents a departure from traditional dictionaries which, particularly for Welsh, have confined themselves to more or less word-for-word entries without explanation. A notable feature of the present dictionary is the provision in the Welsh-English side of numerous illustrative examples taken from actual native speech and writing. I hope that this feature alone will greatly enhance the value of the book to its users by allowing them to see the language in its true context as a vibrant and lively medium of everyday communication.

Another innovation concerns the consonant mutations—all instances of mutation (except fossilized/fixed mutation) are explicitly indicated by special typographical signs throughout the dictionary on both sides. This is to make the system of mutations and their patterns of occurrence transparent, and therefore no longer a matter of guesswork for the inexperienced student.

I have tried to keep the principle of user-friendliness very much to the fore during the compilation of the present work, and for this reason I have included explanations of usage wherever it seemed to me that a word

warranted it. Irregular pronunciations have been similarly pointed out on the Welsh-English side. Some particularly important or difficult aspects of Welsh grammar and usage are discussed at greater length in separate half-page or full-page boxes. In addition, a summary of the grammatical structures and mechanisms of Welsh is given in the Grammar Reference section.

Every dictionary, of whatever type and for whatever language, owes an immeasurable and inevitable debt to its forerunners, and the present one is no exception. Throughout its compilation I have been particularly fortunate to have at my side the *Welsh Academy English-Welsh Dictionary* by Bruce Griffiths and Dafydd Glyn Jones —a mammoth work whose sheer scope and thoroughness have made it an indispensable aid.

For his unstinting support and encouragement right from the start of this project I thank my friend Dewi Rhys-Jones. I am indebted also to the many people at Oxford University Press whose help and expertise have smoothed the way for me. Last but not least I owe a great debt of gratitude to Jonquil, Adam, and Liam for being there to help me keep things in perspective.

Gareth King

Note on Proprietary Status

This dictionary includes some words which have, or are asserted to have, proprietary status as trade marks or otherwise. Their inclusion does not imply that they have acquired for legal purposes a non-proprietary or general significance, nor any other judgement concerning their legal status. In cases where the editorial staff have some evidence that a word has proprietary status, this is indicated in the entry for that word by the abbreviation ®, but no judgement concerning the legal status of such words is made or implied thereby.

Contents

How to use the dictionary

■ Where to look for a word

In the Welsh-English half of the dictionary, the order of the Welsh alphabet is followed:

a b c ch d dd e f ff g ng h i j l ll m n o p ph r rh s t th u w y

This means that, for example, **fi** (f-i) will appear before **ffa** (ff-a); **ynganu** (y-ng-a...) before **ymlaen** (y-m-l...); and **lori** (l-o-r-i) before **llaw** (ll-a-w), and so on.

In the English-Welsh half of the dictionary, British English spellings are used for headwords, but specifically US terms are also included. Translations are given for both British and US senses of a word where these differ. Entries are listed in strict alphabetical order, with the exception of phrasal verbs, which are entered under their root noun.

Vowel changes

A significant number of commonly occurring nouns in Welsh form their plural by changing one or more vowels—e.g. **corff** 'body' > **cyrff** 'bodies'; **carreg** 'stone' > **cerrig** 'stones'; or by a vowel change plus addition of an ending—e.g. **nant** 'brook' > **nentydd** 'brooks'; **chwaer** 'sister' > **chwiorydd** 'sisters'. These plurals, which would otherwise be hard to find in the dictionary, are listed as headwords in their own right with a cross-reference to the singular noun:

cerrig *plural of*
⇨**carreg**

Vowel alterations of various kinds occur elsewhere throughout the Welsh grammatical system, though not as frequently as with noun plurals. Space constraints preclude inclusion of every instance in the dictionary. Awareness of these alterations can therefore help identify apparently problematic words. The most common alterations are:

a	>	**e**
aw	>	**o**
o	>	**y**
w	>	**o**
w	>	**y**
ai	>	**ei**

For example:

trymach 'heavier' is from **trwm** 'heavy'

cron 'round' is the feminine form of **crwn**

tlota 'poorest' is from **tlawd** 'poor'

saf- is the stem of **sefyll** 'stand'

gwrandaw- is the stem of **gwrando** 'listen'

Looking up mutated forms of Welsh words

The initial consonants of words in Welsh can change under certain circumstances, and in various ways. These ways of changing are termed the mutations—three types are recognized in the standard written language: soft mutation, aspirate mutation and nasal mutation. Their causes and effects are set out in more detail below in the section on MUTATIONS. Words are entered in the Welsh-English side of the dictionary in their radical (unmutated) form, so when looking up a word it should always be borne in mind that the initial consonant of the word you are trying to find may be a mutated form and that you will need to search for the radical form. In some cases there is more than one possibility, and you may need to check in several places before finding the radical form you require.

Soft mutation

Soft mutation of a consonant is shown by the symbol °. At the beginning of a word it indicates that the initial consonant has been mutated—so, for example °**drafod** shows that the radical form of this word is **trafod**. Note that:

°**f-** can represent the soft mutation of radical **b-** or **m-**

°**l-** can represent the soft mutation of radical **gl-** or **ll-**

°**r-** can represent the soft mutation of radical **gr-** or **rh-**

radical **g-** disappears under soft mutation, so words beginning °[vowel] should be sought under **g-**:

°**ardd** represents radical **gardd**

°**orsaf** represents radical **gorsaf**

Although words beginning **dd-**, **f-** are unambiguously already mutated (i.e. no native radical word begins with these letters), and those in **l-** and **r-** virtually so, the mutation is indicated all the same in order to highlight mutation patterns within sentences.

The symbol ° at the *end* of a word indicates that this word causes soft mutation of the initial consonant immediately following—so, for example, **neu°** ('or') means that 'tea or coffee' will be **te neu °goffi**.

In the illustrative examples, the soft mutation sign is generally used at the beginning of words, while the end-of-word use is largely confined to headwords. But instances of fixed (i.e. permanent) soft mutation, such as

with words like (°)**fyth**, i (°)**gyd** and (°)**gartre** are not shown, since there is no need ever to derive a radical form from them.

Soft mutation is not indicated in cases where the corresponding radical is not normally used. So, for example, °**wneud** 'do, make' is tagged throughout (because the radical of the verbnoun, **gwneud**, is also in common use), while the preterite **nes**, **naeth** etc is not—the theoretically possible radical forms **gwnes**, **gwnaeth** etc are hardly ever encountered in the modern spoken language, and the soft mutation has in this case taken on, to all intents and purposes, the status of a fixed mutation.

Nasal mutation

Nasal mutation is indicated by [n] on the same principles as soft mutation—so [n]**nillad** indicates that the radical form is **dillad**; **pum** [n]**mlynedd** that this represents underlying **pum + blynedd**. It should be borne in mind that many speakers use this mutation inconsistently at best, and often not at all except in set phrases. A detailed discussion can be found under the two headwords associated with this mutation: **fy**[n] and **yn**[n].

Aspirate mutation

Aspirate mutation is similarly indicated by [h]. After headwords, [h] is used to indicate that the word causes aspirate mutation, and [h]/° to indicate words where either aspirate or soft mutation is possible in the modern spoken language.

While the theoretical presence of aspirate mutation is indicated for those few words that are associated with it, the illustrative examples generally reflect normal spoken usage in not applying this mutation

consistently to words beginning **t-**
and **p-**. So, for example, although
tua is associated with the aspirate
mutation and is therefore listed as
tua[h], the examples will show **tua
[h]chant** but **tua tri** (not **tua **[h]**thri** which
is technically required in formal styles
but sounds affected in speech). In these
cases the user must decide what degree
of formality is appropriate in any given
instance.

■ Regional and stylistic variants

Words and expressions showing
identifiably northern or southern
characteristics of language or
phrasing are labelled (*North*) or
(*South*). These labels have been used
very sparingly, since the differences
between North and South lie mainly
in the field of pronunciation, while
formal differences are confined
largely to commonly-occurring parts
of the verb **bod** 'to be' and a very
limited number of other items.
Sometimes two words are listed,
but only one indicated for region—
for example at the English-Welsh
entry for

> **out** *adverb*
> = allan; mas (*South*)

shows that the Northern word **allan**
is also the accepted standard in
most formal and written styles.
Examples of formal usage accepted as
part of everyday language are almost
entirely restricted to the common
use of the impersonal verb forms in
-ir (non-past) and **-wyd** (past)
throughout the media. These have not
been labelled (*formal*), since it is safe
to assume that any illustration
containing such a form is taken from
this register.

■ Parts of speech and grammatical information

Parts of speech are indicated for all
headwords in both Welsh-English and
English-Welsh halves. Different parts of
speech are separated by numbers, e.g.:

gerllaw
1 *preposition*
> = near
> **o'n i'n aros mewn gwesty gerllaw'r
> afon ar y pryd** = I was staying in a
> hotel near the river at the time

2 *adverb*
> = nearby
> **ceir cyfoeth o atyniadau gerllaw** =
> there is a wealth of attractions
> nearby

fall
1 *noun*
• (*action*)
> = cwymp (*plural* -au) *masculine*
• (*US: autumn*)
> = hydre(f) *masculine*
> **in the fall** = yn yr hydre

2 *verb*
> = syrthio, cwympo (*South*)

Grammatical information is given
systematically for each headword
on the Welsh-English side of the
dictionary, including irregular verb
forms, comparative forms of adjectives,
and conjugated prepositions. When
looking for a translation for items
such as verbs and prepositions in the
English-Welsh half of the dictionary it
is therefore important to check the
word in the Welsh-English half to find
out how it might change its form.

Nouns

Noun plurals are given on both sides of
the dictionary, but only where these
are in normal use. Gender is indicated
for all singular nouns on both sides of
the dictionary.

Collective nouns, which generally

translate as English plurals, are listed as headwords if in common use in their collective form, with a cross-reference to the corresponding singular form— so not only is **deilen** 'leaf' a headword, but also the collective base-form **dail** 'leaves; foliage'.

Masculine agent nouns ending in **-(i)wr**, plural **-wyr**, are very common, and a less commonly used feminine form can be derived from them as follows:

(masculine) **cyfreith|iwr**, plural **cyfreith|wyr**

(feminine) **cyfreith|wraig**, plural **cyfreith|wragedd**

In this dictionary, for reasons of space, these derived feminine forms are not consistently listed, and all masculine agent nouns in **-(i)wr** should be taken to include the feminine variant.

Note also that agent nouns ending in **-ydd**, though grammatically masculine, may often also be used where the sex of the individual is unspecified:

cadeirydd = chairman *or* chairperson

cadeiryddes = chairwoman

Verbs

Welsh verbs are given in the base form, which is in fact the verbnoun. All verbnouns in Welsh can be used as true nouns, so for example, **cydweithio** can mean not only 'collaborate', but also, as context requires, 'collaboration'. The noun translation is given only where it is thought to be at least as common as the verbal.

Verbnouns which convey *state* rather than dynamic action are indicated by an asterisk *—this is to remind the user, among other things, that such a verb cannot form a preterite (which by definition in Welsh indicates completed dynamic action). The stem of the verb is given if it is not predictable from the verbnoun, i.e. if it

is not formed by deletion of a final vowel (eg verbnoun **talu**, stem **tal-**) or, in the case of consonant-ending verbnouns, is not the same as the verbnoun (e.g. verbnoun **agor**, stem **agor-**). Non-predictable stems are not included, however, if they are not in normal use. Irregular or anomalous forms are listed after the headword, except for **bod** 'to be' and **gwybod** 'to know' which have their own boxes.

Adjectives

Adjectives that form their comparative and superlative forms with the endings **-ach** and **-a(f)** are so indicated. Where there is no indication, this means that **mwy** and **mwya** are used instead.

....

■ Senses

Different senses of a headword are introduced by •, e.g.:

defnydd (*plural* **-iau**) *noun, masculine*
• = material
canllawiau ar gyfer cludo defnyddiau hylosg = guidelines for the transport of flammable materials
• = use
°**driwn ni °wneud defnydd da o'r** °**wybodaeth 'ma** = we'll try and make good use of this information

bank *noun*
• (*financial institution*)
= banc (*plural* -iau) *masculine*
• (*side of river*)
= glan (*plural* -nau) *feminine*

....

■ Translations

Translations are given only for frequently-used senses falling within

the scope of a keyword dictionary—
lesser-used meanings are omitted; for
example, **athro** is given as 'teacher'—
by far its most common meaning—
while its other meaning 'professor'
is not.

On the Welsh-English side
alternative translations are separated
by a comma, a semicolon, or 'or', as
appropriate for clarity.

On the English-Welsh side of the
dictionary synonymous translations
are separated by commas or 'or'.
Where two or more non-synonymous
translations are given, the difference in
usage is explained.

cheek *noun*
- (*part of face*)
  = boch (*plural* -au) *feminine*
- (*insolence*)
  = haerllugrwydd *masculine*

■ Cross-references

Cross-references are indicated by an
arrow ⇨ to words, or by *see* to articles
or related usage points

Headwords that are connected either
by form, meaning, or use are cross-
referenced in the Welsh-English
section with ⇨. So, for example,
annioddefol 'insufferable' also directs
the user to the root word ⇨ **diodde(f)**
'suffer'; while the entry for the
conjunction **achos** 'because' includes
a cross-reference to the compound
preposition ⇨ **o achos** 'because of',
and vice versa. Sometimes a cross-
reference will refer the user to a word
that can be confused in use or meaning
with the headword. So, for example,
o flaen 'before' (= in front of) has a

cross-reference to **cyn** 'before' (time)—
these words are in no way
interchangeable in Welsh, but they can
cause confusion to speakers of English.
In all cases, *cross-references should not be
taken as synonyms*, but should be
followed up.

The many forms of the verb **bod** 'to
be' in Welsh are all cross-referenced to
a single article.

■ 'you'

Both main Welsh words for 'you' (**ti**
and **chi**) occur throughout the
illustrative examples on the Welsh-
English side. No attempt is made to
indicate where the two are
interchangeable and where not—the
user is referred to the headword **you**
for an explanation of the sense and
context criteria for determining this in
each case.

■ Usage notes

Usage notes on both sides of the
dictionary give additional information
on grammar, usage or pronunciation of
the headword or related words:

yr Alban *noun, feminine*
= Scotland

> **!** *This noun is always used with the
> definite article in Welsh*

In the Welsh-English half of the
dictionary the notes are generally
fuller. Where appropriate, cross-
references in the English-Welsh half
also guide the user to these boxes.

Guide to pronunciation

Welsh spelling is largely phonetic. Note the order of the Welsh alphabet, which comprises 29 letters, some of them digraphs:

a b c ch d dd e f ff g ng h i j l ll m n o p ph r rh s t th u w y

....

■ Vowels

a as in Welsh English m*a*n (i.e. slightly more open than in English m*a*n),

â longer version of **a**

e as in English m*e*n

ê longer version of **e**, like Welsh English g*a*me (i.e. without diphthongization)

i as in English p*i*n

î longer version of **i**, like mach*i*ne

o as in English h*o*t

ô longer version of **o**, as in Welsh English h*o*le (i.e. without diphthongization)

u in the North, like French u, German ü, but with unrounded lips; in the South, the same as **i** above

û longer version of **u**

w as in English b*oo*k

ŵ longer version of **w**, as in Welsh English p*oo*l (i.e. without diphthongization)

y 1) in one-syllable words—like **u** above

   2) in the last syllable of words of more than one syllable—like **u** above

   3) everywhere else—like the second vowel in English sof*a*, butt*er* (there are a few exceptions to this rule)

ŷ same as **û** above

....

■ Consonants

b as in English *b*ook

c always a '*k*' sound, as in English *c*all; NEVER pronounced as *s*

ch as a Scottish English lo*ch* or German Ba*ch* (NOT as in English chur*ch*)

d as in English *d*amp

dd *th* as in English *th*is (NOT as in English *th*ink)

f as in English *v*an

ff as in English *f*an

g always a '*g*' sound, as in English *g*irl; NEVER pronounced as '*j*'

ng as in English si*ng*er (NOT as in fi*ng*er)—can occur at the start of a word

h as in English *h*at—always sounded in Welsh

j as in English *j*am (loanwords only)

l as in English *l*amp (NOT as in English mi*l*k)

ll aspirated version of **l**—articulated in the same way but with breath instead of voice

m as in English *m*other

n as in English *n*ow

p as in English *p*ark

ph as in English *ph*iloso*ph*y (but quite rare in Welsh)

r rolled or flapped *r* as in Welsh and

Scottish English

rh h followed by **r**

s 1) as in English s*it*; NEVER
      pronounced as 'z'

   2) **si** + vowel is used for '*sh*'

t as in English *t*art

th as in English *th*ink (NOT as English
      *th*is)

In addition, **i** and **w** can be used as
consonants—**i** like English *y*, **w** like
English *w*.

....

■ Diphthongs

ae generally like the English word *eye*

ai generally like the English word *eye*

au generally like the English word *eye*,
      except: as a plural marker **-au** on
      nouns, where it is pronounced as
      -a in the North, and **-e** in the South

aw as in English d*ow*n

ei a combination of **y** (3 above) + **i**;

but note the word **ei** (and related
words) has a special pronunciation
(see dictionary)

eu as **ei** above; note that the word **eu**
      has a special pronunciation (see
      dictionary)

ew **e+w**—NOT like English n*ew*

iw as in English n*ew*, but with more
      emphasis on the first sound

oe as in English b*oy*

ou as in English b*oy* (but rare)

ow **o+w**—NOT as in English d*ow*n

uw as in English n*ew*, but with more
      emphasis on the first sound

wy generally like English g*ooey*

yw as in English n*ew*, but with more
      emphasis on the first sound

Word stress in Welsh nearly always
falls on the penultimate syllable—the
only exceptions to this among native
words are certain adverbs that were
originally two words, e.g. **ymlaen** (from
yn + **blaen**), and certain verbnouns
ending in **-au**, e.g. **sicrhau**.

Mutations

Welsh words can change at the beginning under certain circumstances, and in different ways. For example, **cath** 'cat' can appear as **gath**, **chath** and **nghath**. This change is called mutation, and there are three types in Welsh—*soft*, *nasal*, and *aspirate*. Some letters can be affected by all three (for example **c**, **p** and **t**), others by only soft and nasal (for example **g**, **b** and **d**), and others by only soft (for example **ll**, **rh** and **m**).

Vowels are not affected by any of these mutations, and consonants not included in the following tables are similarly immune.

....

■ Soft mutation

The soft mutation, indicated ° in this dictionary, has the following effects:

B-	> °F-	bara	> °fara
C-	> °G-	cath	> °gath
D-	> °DD-	darn	> °ddarn
G	> °(disappears)	gardd	> °ardd
LL-	> °L-	llawr	> °lawr
M-	> °F-	merch	> °ferch
P-	> °B-	pysgod	> °bysgod
RH-	> °R-	rhosyn	> °rosyn
T-	> °D-	tegan	> °degan

This mutation is by far the most commonly occurring in Welsh, and the only one of the three that is consistently applied over all Welsh-speaking regions. It occurs in the following situations:

1. after the grammatical or notional subject of the sentence:
   fe °welodd Sioned °gath =
   Sioned saw a cat
   (Sioned is the actual subject of the sentence)

   rhaid i Dafydd °fynd =
   Dafydd has to go
   (Dafydd is the notional, though not grammatical, subject of the sentence)

2. after a feminine singular noun, or after the feminine singular definite article:
   merch °fach = a little girl
   (but **merched bach** = little girls)
   y °ferch °fach = the little girl
   (but **y merched bach** = the little girls)

3. after most monosyllabic prepositions, e.g.:
   bwrdd = table
   ar °fwrdd = on a table
   Caerdydd = Cardiff
   i °Gaerdydd = to Cardiff
   Lloegr = England
   o °Loegr = from England

4. after the following miscellaneous words, many of them very common:
   dau = two *masculine*
   dwy° = two *feminine*
   dacw° = there is ...
   dyma° = here is ...
   dyna° = there is ...
   dy° = your *singular*
   ei° = his
   fe° = *affirmative particle*
   go° = fairly, quite
   mi° = *affirmative particle*
   mor° = so (+ *adjective*)
   (does not mutate **ll-** or **rh-**)
   neu° = or
   pa° = which
   pan° = when
   pur° = very
   pwy° = which (*South*)
   rhy° = too
   un° = one *feminine*

y° = the *feminine singular*
yn° = before nouns and adjectives
(does not mutate **ll-** or **rh-**)

5. on verbs with personal endings generally in the spoken language:
(**talu** = pay) **°dales i** = I paid

6. on adverbs of time saying when something happened:
(**blwyddyn** = a year)
°flwyddyn yn ôl = a year ago
(**dydd Llun** = Monday)
°ddydd Llun = on Monday

7. on the second of two words joined together as a compound:
prif = main + **dinas** = city
prifddinas = capital

8. after prefixes, eg:

ym- + golchi	ymolchi
af- + llwyddiannus	aflwyddiannus
di- + gwaith	diwaith
gwrth + taro	gwrthdaro

■ Nasal mutation

The nasal mutation, indicated [n] in this dictionary, affects six letters:

B- > [n]M-	bara	>	[n]mara
C- > [n]NGH-	cath	>	[n]nghath
D- > [n]N-	darn	>	[n]narn
G- > [n]NG-	gardd	>	[n]ngardd
P- > [n]MH-	pysgod	>	[n]mhysgod
T- > [n]NH-	tegan	>	[n]nhegan

This mutation is used only in certain regions in speech, but is the norm in writing. It is found in only two circumstances:

1. on nouns to indicate 'my…' sometimes with a preceding '**y…**', or (mostly in the written language) **fy…**:
plant = children

[n]mhlant (i) = my children
(written: **fy mhlant**)
car = car
[n]nghar (i) = my car
(written: **fy nghar**)

2. after the preposition **yn[n]** 'in', with some spelling changes (see entry in Welsh-English section):

Dolgellau	**yn [n]Nolgellau**
Cymru	**yng [n]Nghymru**

■ Aspirate mutation

The aspirate mutation, indicated [h] in this dictionary, affects only three letters:

C	> [h]CH	cath	>	[h]chath
P	> [h]PH	pysgod	>	[h]physgod
T	> [h]TH	tegan	>	[h]thegan

Of these, only the change C > [h]CH is applied with any consistency in the modern spoken language, though all three are the norm in writing.

This mutation occurs in the following circumstances:

1. after the following miscellaneous words:
a[h] = and
â[h] = with
chwe[h] = six
ei[h] = her *possessive*
gyda[h] = with
tri[h] = three *masculine*
tua[h] = about, towards

2. in some regions only, on a negative verb with personal endings:
(**colli** = lose)
[h]cholles i °ddim = I didn't lose
(**talu** = pay)
[h]thala i °ddim = I won't pay

Grammar reference

This summary confines itself to the grammar of the modern language, and does not refer to Literary Welsh, which has marked differences in the verb system and other areas of grammar.

....

■ Word order

The normal word order in the Welsh sentence is verb–subject–object:

agorodd   **y dyn**   **y drws**
[opened]   [the man]   [the door]
the man opened the door

But the verb can be displaced by something singled out for special focus:

y dyn   **agorodd**   **y drws**
[the man]   [opened]   [the door]
(it was) the man (who) opened the door
(i.e. not anyone else)

....

■ Nouns

Nouns in Welsh are either masculine or feminine—in most cases the gender is not predictable, and should therefore be learnt for each noun. Gender is shown for all nouns in this dictionary.

Feminine nouns differ from masculine nouns in that:

1. in the singular they undergo soft mutation after the definite article:

bwrdd (*masculine*) = table
bwydlen (*feminine*) = menu
y bwrdd = the table
but
y °fwydlen = the menu

2. in the singular they cause soft mutation of a following adjective:

ci (*masculine*) = dog
cath (*feminine*) = cat
ci mawr = a big dog
but
cath °fawr = a big cat

Plurals of nouns are formed in a wide variety of ways, and therefore the plural must be learnt with each noun. All noun plurals in common use are indicated in this dictionary. Most nouns form their plural by the addition of an ending—the most common plural endings are **-au**, **-iau**, **-on** and **-ion**:

llyfr = book
llyfrau = books
defnydd = material
defnyddiau = materials
geiriadur = dictionary
geiriaduron = dictionaries
dyn = man
dynion = men

Some nouns form their plural by internal vowel change:

troed = foot
traed = feet
oen = lamb
ŵyn = lambs
carreg = stone
cerrig = stones

Some nouns form their plural by ending and vowel change:

braich = arm
breichiau = arms
cwrs = course
cyrsiau = courses
saer = carpenter
seiri = carpenters

Some nouns form their plural by removing an ending:

coeden = tree
coed = trees

....

■ Pronouns

None of the personal pronouns make any distinction between subject and object, but several of them have variant forms depending on how they are used:

i/mi/fi	I/me
ti/di/chdi	you
e/fe/o/fo	he/him
hi	she/her
ni	we/us
chi	you
nhw	they/them

These differing usages are explained in the dictionary.

A set of extended pronouns also exists, mainly used for emphasis and contrast:

innau/minnau/finnau	I/me
tithau/dithau	you
yntau/fothau	he/him
hithau	she/her
ninnau	we/us
chithau	you
nhwthau	they/them

....

■ Adjectives

In Welsh the adjective follows the noun it refers to:
llyfr = a book
llyfr trwm = a heavy book
stafell = a room
stafell °fawr = a big room

There are a few exceptions to this rule, e.g.
llyfr = a book
hen °lyfr = an old book

These exceptions are indicated in the dictionary.

There are two ways of forming the comparative and superlative of adjectives:

SHORT ADJECTIVES (one or two syllables) add the endings **-ach** and **-a(f)**:
ysgafn = light
ysgafnach = lighter
ysgafna(f) = lightest
hapus = happy
hapusach = happier
hapusa(f) = happiest
doniol = funny
doniolach = funnier
doniola(f) = funniest
hardd = beautiful
harddach = more beautiful
hardda(f) = most beautiful

In some cases the addition of these syllables changes the word itself slightly in the process:
trwm = heavy
trymach = heavier
tryma(f) = heaviest
tlawd = poor
tlotach = poorer
tlota(f) = poorest
rhad = cheap
rhatach = cheaper
rhata(f) = cheapest
gwlyb = wet
gwlypach = wetter
gwlypa(f) = wettest
teg = fair
tecach = fairer
teca(f) = fairest

These changes are indicated in the dictionary.

LONGER ADJECTIVES (two or more syllables) use **mwy** = more and **mwya(f)** = most instead of endings:
doniol = funny
mwy doniol = funnier
mwya(f) doniol = funniest

(two-syllable adjectives can often use either method)
cyfforddus = comfortable
mwy cyfforddus = more comfortable,

mwya(f) cyfforddus = most comfortable
diddorol = interesting
mwy diddorol = more interesting
mwya(f) diddorol = most interesting

A few adjectives have irregular comparatives and superlatives—these are indicated in the dictionary.

■ Verbs

The basic form of every verb is the verbnoun—this is the form cited in dictionaries.

From the verbnoun the stem of the verb is formed either by removal of a final vowel, or by leaving it unchanged, or by another method:

verbnoun   stem

canu   **can-** (removal of final vowel)
agor   **agor-** (no change)
rhedeg **rhed-**
sibrwd **sibryd-**

Unpredictable stems are indicated in the dictionary.

Most of the tenses of the Welsh verb are formed by using the appropriate tense of the verb **bod** 'to be' in conjunction with the verbnoun. In other words, the verbnoun conveys the meaning of the action, while the verb **bod** 'to be' indicates the tense. So:

mae'r dyn yn rhedeg =
the man is running
roedd y dyn yn rhedeg =
the man was running
bydd y dyn yn rhedeg =
the man will run
basai'r dyn yn rhedeg =
the man would run

Changing **yn** to **wedi** gives a further four tenses:

mae'r dyn wedi rhedeg =
the man has run

roedd y dyn wedi rhedeg =
the man had run
bydd y dyn wedi rhedeg =
the man will have run
basai'r dyn wedi rhedeg =
the man would have run

■ Verb endings

One tense, however—the preterite (completed action in the past)—does not use the [**bod** 'to be' + verbnoun] pattern. Instead a set of endings is added to the stem of the verb itself:

-es i   I …
-est ti   you …
-odd e/hi he/she …
-on ni   we …
-och chi   you …
-on nhw   they …

So 'the man ran' would be: **rhedodd y dyn** (stem **rhed-** + ending **-odd**)

There is also a set of future tense endings that work the same way:

-a i
-i di
-ith e/hi
-wn ni
-wch chi
-an nhw

Therefore there are two future tenses in Welsh—one using the verb 'to be', and the other using endings. By and large they are interchangeable.

bydd yn dyn yn rhedeg
or
rhedith y dyn = the man will run

In addition, the verb **gwneud** 'do' can be used as an auxiliary to form preterite and future tenses:

nes i °redeg = I ran (= **rhedes i**)
na i °redeg = I'll run (= **rheda i**)

In the North, yet another auxiliary **ddaru**—is used to form the preterite:

ddaru mi °redeg = I ran

Examples of all these uses are given in the dictionary.

A third set of endings, denoting hypothetical or unreal events, is confined to the verb **bod** 'to be' and a few other verbs:

-wn i
-et ti
-ai fe/hi
-en ni
-ech chi
-en nhw

So, for example:

baswn i = I would be
hoffwn i = I would like
gallwn i = I could
dylwn i = I should

Verbs with endings in positive sentences can optionally be preceded by particles **fe°** or **mi°** that indicate that a statement (and not a question or negative) is involved. So:

rhedodd y dyn

or

fe °redodd y dyn

or

mi °redodd y dyn = the man ran

In some regions of Wales, the particle is not used, but the mutation remains:

°redodd y dyn

Generally, statements are turned into questions by simply using the mutated form of the verb. Compare:

rhedodd y dyn =
the man ran
°redodd y dyn? =
did the man run?
talan nhw =
they'll pay
°dalan nhw? =
will they pay?
dylwn i °fynd =
I should go
°ddylwn i °fynd? =
should I go?

basen ni'n hwyr =
we'd be late
°fasen ni'n hwyr? =
would we be late?

Negatives generally use the soft mutated form, and add **°ddim** after the subject:

°redodd y dyn? =
did the man run?
°redodd y dyn °ddim =
the man didn't run
°dalan nhw? =
will they pay?
°dalan nhw °ddim =
they won't pay
°ddylwn i °fynd? =
should I go?
°ddylwn i °ddim mynd =
I shouldn't go
°fasen ni'n hwyr? =
would we be late?
°fasen ni °ddim yn hwyr =
we wouldn't be late

But verbs beginning **c-** optionally have aspirate mutation in the negative:

collodd e = he lost
°gollodd e? = did he lose?
°gollodd e °ddim (or **ʰchollodd e °ddim**) = he didn't lose

In more formal language this option is extended to verbs beginning **p-** and **t-**:

talodd e = he paid
°dalodd e? = did he pay?
°dalodd e °ddim (or formal **ʰthalodd e °ddim**) = he didn't pay

....

■ Imperative

The imperative or command form of the verb is made by adding endings to the stem.

If the stem is formed by dropping a vowel or other element from the verbnoun, then **-a** (*singular*) and **-wch** (*plural*) are added:

verbnoun	talu	rhedeg
stem	tal-	rhed-
imperatives	tala!	rheda!
	talwch!	rhedwch!

If the last letter of the stem is the same as that of the verbnoun, then generally the singular imperative is the same as the verbnoun, while -wch is added to the stem as usual for the plural:

verbnoun	agor	aros
stem	agor-	arhos-
imperatives	agor!	aros!
	agorwch!	arhoswch!

■ Irregular verbs

Apart from the verb **bod** 'to be' (very irregular—see special box in dictionary), there are only four irregular verbs in Welsh: **mynd** 'go', **dod** 'come', **gwneud** 'do/make' and **cael** 'get'. And these four are irregular only in the preterite, the inflected future and certain other less common forms. All are indicated in the dictionary.

■ Adverbs

Adverbs of manner ('quickly', 'bravely', 'quietly' etc) are formed by placing **yn°** in front of the corresponding adjective:

cyflym = quick **yn °gyflym** = quickly
dewr = brave **yn °ddewr** = bravely
tawel = quiet **yn °dawel** = quietly

Adverbs of time and place must be learnt individually.

■ Prepositions

Most simple (one-syllable) prepositions cause soft mutation of a following word. This is indicated in the dictionary.

Most simple prepositions 'conjugate' rather like verbs when used with pronouns. For example:

ar = on
ar y bwrdd = on the table
but
arna i = on me
arnat ti = on you
arno fe = on him
arni hi = on her
arnon ni = on us
arnoch chi = on you
arnyn nhw = on them

All personal forms of simple prepositions are given in the dictionary.

Compound prepositions also have similar special personal forms. For example:

o °flaen = in front of
o °flaen yr adeilad = in front of the building
but
o °mlaen i = in front of me
o dy °flaen di = in front of you
o'i °flaen e = in front of him
o'i blaen hi = in front of her
o'n blaen ni = in front of us
o'ch blaen chi = in front of you
o'u blaen nhw = in front of them

All personal forms of compound prepositions are given in the dictionary.

■ Reported Speech

Turning neutral sentences into reported speech in Welsh involves using **bod/°fod** etc. or the conjunction **y**, and the choice of which to use depends on what type of verb begins the speech to be reported.

Broadly, there are four choices:

1. speech to be reported begins with present (occasionally also imperfect) tense of the verb **bod**;

2. speech to be reported begins with any verb in the preterite tense;

3. speech to be reported begins with any other tense of **bod**, or any other verb in any other tense;

4. speech to be reported begins with something that is not a verb (this includes verbnouns, which are grammatically nouns).

Examples of each of the four choices:

1. **bod/°fod** etc:
   '**mae'r tywydd yn °dda**' = 'the weather is good'
   dw i'n meddwl °fod y tywydd yn °dda = I think that the weather is good
   '**maen nhw'n mynd nawr**' = 'they're going now'
   maen nhw'n dweud bod nhw'n mynd nawr = they say that they're going now

2. **i°**
   '**glaniodd yr awyren bore 'ma**' = 'the plane landed this morning'
   maen nhw'n dweud i'r awyren °lanio bore 'ma = they say that the plane landed this morning

3. **y:**
   '**byddwn ni'n hwyr**' = 'we'll be late'
   dw i'n meddwl y byddwn ni'n hwyr = I think that we'll be late
   '**dylech chi °fynd**' = 'you ought to go'
   maen nhw'n dweud y dylech chi °fynd = they say that you ought to go

4. **mai (/taw/na):**
   '**Sioned ydy'r un °orau**' = 'Sioned is the best'
   dw i'n meddwl mai Sioned ydy'r un °orau = I think that Sioned is the best

'**gwaethygu mae'r sefyllfa**' = 'the situation is worsening'
maen nhw'n dweud mai gwaethygu mae'r sefyllfa = they say that the situation is worsening

(for further information on choice 4, see FOCUS below).

....

■ Focus

Focusing is a technique in Welsh whereby a particular element in a sentence is singled out (or focused) for emphasis by being repositioned at the start of the sentence. Thus, what English achieves by intonation, Welsh achieves by word order, as can be seen in the following pairs of neutral and focused sentences in the two languages:

[*neutral*] they live in Cardiff
[*focused*] they live in <u>Cardiff</u> (i.e. not Swansea)
[*neutral*] **maen nhw'n byw yng ⁿGhaerdydd**
[*focused*] **yng ⁿGhaerdydd maen nhw'n byw**

This leaves a sentence which begins with an element (in this case **yng ⁿGhaerdydd**) which is not the verb, an abnormal situation in a language like Welsh where the verb usually has the first main position in the sentence reserved for it.

Turning neutral sentences into reported speech in Welsh usually involves using **bod/°fod** etc or the conjunction **y**, and the choice of which to use depends on what type of verb begins the speech to be reported (see REPORTED SPEECH above). But when we wish to turn focused sentences into reported speech this question does not arise, because focused sentences by definition in Welsh do not have a verb at the start. Here Welsh simply uses the conjunction **mai** (or **taw** or **na** in some areas) and leaves the rest of the reported speech unaltered. This is the essence of **mai**, and since focused sentences can start with practically any of the main parts of speech (because any important idea can be emphasised), it follows that the word or phrase directly after **mai** can be anything other than a verb (since sentences with the verb at the front are not focused). But note that the verbnoun is not grammatically a verb (even if it is in meaning), and can be focused by placing it in the verb position just like any other non-verb element—in other words, the verb in the neutral sentence **mae'r sefyllfa'n gwaethygu** 'the situation is worsening' is **mae** (it must be—it is in the first slot in the sentence), while **gwaethygu** merely carries the meaning of 'worsen'. This latter is a noun, albeit of verbal meaning, and can be focused in the usual way. So, if we want to emphasize the worsening of the situation (for example, if we want to contrast it with opposite expectations), then we can say **gwaethygu mae'r sefyllfa** 'the situation is worsening' (and not improving at all, as we had all expected); from there we can turn this

into reported speech with **mai: maen nhw'n dweud mai gwaethygu mae'r sefyllfa** 'they say that the situation is worsening'; compare this with the neutral reported version: **maen nhw'n dweud °fod y sefyllfa'n gwaethygu.**

Further examples:

wedodd e mai Ioan °dorrodd y ffenest = he said that (it was) Ioan (that) broke the window

mae ofnau mai dyfnhau mae'r argyfwng yn Bosnia = there are fears that the crisis in Bosnia is deepening

rhaid i mi'ch atgoffa chi mai chi'n sy'n °gyfrifol am hyn = I must remind you that (it is) you (who) are responsible for this

efallai mai chi °fydd hi! = it could be you!

Note that the last example requires **mai** because **efallai** (and other words for 'perhaps') need a conjunction ('that') to join them to a following statement.

mae'n °debyg mai nhw biau nhw = they're probably theirs

o'n i'n meddwl mai yfory o'n nhw'n bwriadu dod = I thought they were planning to come tomorrow

Glossary of grammatical terms

abbreviation a shortened form of a word or phrase

active in active sentences, the SUBJECT of the verb performs the action, e.g. the man bought a book = **mi °brynodd y dyn °lyfr** (as opposed to the PASSIVE construction the book was bought by the man = **mi °gafodd y llyfr ei °brynu gan y dyn**; compare PASSIVE)

adjective a word that decribes a NOUN, e.g. a *big* room = **stafell °fawr**; a *Welsh* dictionary = **geiriadur Cymraeg**

adverb 1) a word that describes a VERB; in English most adverbs end in *-ly*, in Welsh most begin with **yn°**: he works *quickly* = **mae e'n gweithio'n °gyflym**
2) a word or phrase that describes when or where an action takes place, e.g. here = **fan hyn**, every year = **°bob blwyddyn**

aspirate mutation one of the three MUTATIONS in Welsh

auxiliary verb a verb, for example be, do, have, or **bod, ddaru, gwneud**, used to form a particular TENSE of another verb, or—in English—also to form a negative, or a question, or imperative, e.g. he *is* reading, *do* you like fish? we *didn't* go, *don't* be late; **mae e'n darllen, ddaru ni °fynd, naethoch chi °weld?**

clause a self-contained section of a sentence that contains a SUBJECT and a VERB

closed conditions a CONDITIONAL sentence where the action or incident referred to is regarded as hypothetical and not real or even possible, e.g. *if I were you*, I'd leave now; *if James came*, he'd tell you (but he's not coming); compare OPEN CONDITIONS

collective noun in Welsh, one of a relatively small group of nouns whose basic form denotes the plural, often viewed collectively, and from which the singular is derived by means of a suffix, e.g. **dail** 'leaves, foliage', singular **deilen** 'leaf'.

comparative the form of an ADJECTIVE or ADVERB that makes it 'more' or 'less', e.g. more interesting = **mwy diddorol**; heavier = **trymach**; compare SUPERLATIVE

compound noun a NOUN formed from two or more separate words, e.g. bus stop = **safle bysiau**, stepmother = **llysfam**

conditional the form of a VERB that expresses what might happen if something else occurred, e.g. they would come = **basen nhw'n dod**, I would have paid = **byddwn i wedi talu**

conjugated preposition in Welsh, a PREPOSITION that takes personal endings for use with pronouns, e.g **ar** 'on' + **hi** 'her'—**arni hi** = 'on her'. Many simple prepositions have this characteristic in Welsh.

conjunction a word used to join CLAUSES or SENTENCES together, e.g. and = **a**, because = **achos**, although = **er**

consonant a letter representing a sound that can only be used together with a vowel, e.g. b, c, d, f, g in English, **b, c, ch, d, dd, f, ff, g** in Welsh

definite article the word the in English, **y, yr** or **'r** in Welsh

dynamic used to describe VERBS that express an action rather than a state, e.g. run, make, photocopy, analyse. The majority of verbs in English and Welsh are dynamic; compare STATIVE

ending the letters added to the STEMS of VERBS in Welsh to show TENSE and PERSON, or to NOUNS to show PLURAL, to ADJECTIVES to show COMPARATIVE and SUPERLATIVE, and to PREPOSITIONS to show PERSON.

equative the form of an ADJECTIVE or ADVERB in Welsh that conveys the idea of 'as... (as...)', e.g. **cystal** = as good (as)

feminine one of the two genders of nouns in Welsh

focus emphasizing a particular element in a Welsh sentence by placing it at the beginning. See GRAMMAR REFERENCE section.

future the tense of the VERB used to express what will happen in the future, e.g. I'll call tomorrow = **bydda i'n galw yfory** or **galwa i yfory** or **na i °alw yfory**—there is more than one future tense in Welsh

gender a classification of nouns into two groups in Welsh—masculine and feminine

genitive relationship a special construction in Welsh to denote possession or belonging, e.g. Dafydd's car = **car Dafydd**, the centre of the city = **canol y °ddinas**

imperfect the term for the usual past TENSE of the verb **bod** 'to be' in Welsh, and for the TENSE of other verbs for which it is the AUXILIARY verb, e.g. **o'n i** = I was, **o'n i'n mynd** = I was going

indefinite article the word 'a' or 'an' in English; there is no equivalent in Welsh

inflected used to describe a word that includes ENDINGS

inflected future one of the FUTURE tenses in Welsh, which uses ENDINGS attached to the STEM

masculine one of the two genders of nouns in Welsh

mutation a system of sound changes in Welsh whereby certain initial consonants of words can change in sound and writing, e.g. cat = **cath**, **gath**, **chath** or **nghath**. See 'How to use the dictionary' and MUTATION box for details

nasal mutation one of the three MUTATIONS in Welsh

noun a word that names a person or thing, e.g. David = **Dafydd**, book = **llyfr**, Swansea = **Abertawe**, hope = **gobaith**

numeral a word for a number, e.g. two = **dau** or **dwy**, a hundred = **cant**

object the noun or pronoun affected by the action of the verb; in 'the man saw the cat' the cat is the OBJECT, while the man is the SUBJECT

open conditions a CONDITIONAL sentence where the action or incident referred to is regarded as possible, although the speaker does not know either way, e.g. if James comes, I'll have a word with him (but I don't know if he is coming or not); compare CLOSED CONDITIONS

particle in Welsh, one of a small number of short words that often have no direct translation in English, but perform a grammatical function, e.g. the affirmative markers **fe°** and **mi°**

passive in passive sentences, the subject of the verb experiences the action rather than performs it; in English the passive is expressed by the verb 'to be' + past participle; in Welsh it is expressed by the verb **cael** + verbnoun, e.g. the bridge was built last year = **cafodd y °bont ei ʰchodi llynedd**

perfect in Welsh, the traditional name for the TENSE of the verb formed by the present tense of the verb **bod** 'to be' + **wedi** + VERBNOUN, and corresponding to English 'have/has (done)', e.g. **mae'r plant wedi gorffen** = the children have finished

periphrastic used to describe a TENSE of the verb in Welsh which uses an AUXILIARY VERB rather than ENDINGS. Most tenses in Welsh are formed periphrastically

person each of three categories used for pronouns and verbs; the first person = I (*singular*), we (*plural*), the second person = you (*singular and plural*), the third person = he/she/it (*singular*), they (*plural*)

pluperfect in Welsh, the traditional name for the TENSE of the verb formed by the imperfect tense of the verb **bod** 'to be' + **wedi** + VERBNOUN, and corresponding to English 'had (done)', e.g. **roedd y plant wedi gorffen** = the children had finished

possessive adjective the words used with NOUNS to express possession or ownership, e.g. what is *your* name? = **beth ydy'ch enw chi?**

possessive pronoun the word used to express possession or ownership when the NOUN itself is not stated, e.g. is this *yours*? = **'ch un chi ydy hwn?** these are *mine* = **'n rhai i yw'r rhain**

prefix a syllable or word added to the beginning of another word, e.g. successful—*un*successful, **llwyddiannus—af*lwyddiannus**

preposition a word used in front of a noun or pronoun and relating it to another word or phrase. It often describes position or direction of movement of something (e.g. on, in, into, towards, under) or the time at which something happens (e.g. at, during, after)

present the TENSE of the verb used to express something that is happening now, or that is habitual, or that will happen in the immediate future, e.g. I am reading = **dw i'n darllen**, I work in London = **dw i'n gweithio yn Llundain**, I'm going to Wales next week = **dw i'n mynd i °Gymru wythnos nesa**

preterite the past tense in Welsh formed by adding ENDINGS to the stem of the verb, or by the AUXILIARY VERBS **ddaru** or **gwneud**, e.g. they phoned yesterday = **ffonion nhw ddoe** or **ddaru nhw ffonio ddoe** or **naethon nhw ffonio ddoe**—it denotes completed action in the past, and cannot be used with STATIVE verbs

pronoun a word that is used instead of a NOUN already mentioned or known, e.g. English I, me, you, he, him, we, us, Welsh **ti, chi, nhw, ni**

pronunciation the way in which words are pronounced or spoken

radical the basic form of a Welsh word, as opposed to any of its possible variants under MUTATION; **cath** 'cat' is the radical, °**gath**, ʰ**chath** and ⁿ**nghath** are not

sentence a sequence of words, with a SUBJECT and a VERB, that can stand alone to make a statement, ask a question, or give a command

short future another term for the INFLECTED FUTURE

soft mutation one of the three MUTATIONS in Welsh

stative used to describe a verb that expresses a continuing state of mind or situation, rather than an action, e.g. hope, think, belong, know; stative verbs in English cannot generally be used in the present continuous, and in Welsh cannot generally form a PRETERITE; compare DYNAMIC

stem the form of the verb in Welsh to which ENDINGS are added; it can be identical to the VERBNOUN, but more often differs in some way. If the verbnoun ends in a vowel, then the stem is nearly always found by removing this vowel (e.g. verbnoun **talu**, stem **tal-**); otherwise, the stem usually has to be learnt

subject the subject of a sentence or clause is the noun or pronoun that carries out the action of the verb. In 'the man saw the cat' *the man* is the SUBJECT, while *the cat* is the OBJECT. In passive constructions, the subject is the person or thing to which the action is done, e.g. *the man* was arrested by the police = **cafodd *y dyn* ei arestio gan yr heddlu**

subjunctive in Welsh and English, a special form of the verb that is used to express actions or situations that are not real, or are wished for, and which is confined mostly to set phrases

superlative the form of an ADJECTIVE that makes it 'most' or 'least', e.g. most interesting = **mwya diddorol**, heaviest = **tryma**; compare COMPARATIVE

syllable part of a word that forms a spoken unit, usually a vowel sound with consonants before or after

tag a short word or phrase added to the end of a statement or question to elicit an answer, e.g. it's cold, *isn't it?* = **mae'n oer, *on'd ydy?***, they left, *didn't they?* = **naethon nhw °adael, *on'do?***

tense the form of a VERB that tells when the action takes place in relation to the speaker, e.g. present, past, future

***that*-clause** a type of clause introduced by 'that...' in English, and by various equivalents in Welsh. In English that-clauses are mostly used for reported speech, while in Welsh they are also very common after CONJUNCTIONS

unreality used to describe a special set of ENDINGS attached to certain verbs in Welsh when the action referred to is regarded as unreal or hypothetical, e.g. **dyl*wn* i** = I ought to, **gall*ai* hi** = she *could*

verb a word that expresses an action or state of affairs, e.g. John *ran* home, John *knows* a lot, John *is* tall

verbnoun the basic, or dictionary, form of the verb in Welsh; it names the action or state without reference to who does it or when—these two pieces of information are supplied by AUXILIARY VERBS or ENDINGS when it is used in a sentence. Grammatically the verbnoun is a noun, and can be used as such.

vowel a letter representing a sound that can be spoken by itself. The English vowels are a, e, i, o, u; the Welsh vowels are **a, e, i, o, u, w, y**

Aa

a[h] (*before vowels* **ac**) *conjunction*
= and
  cathod a [h]**chŵn** = cats and dogs
  bydd angen meddwl am °**gwestiynau
  a sefyllfaoedd chwarae rôl** = you will
  need to think about questions and
  role-playing situations

> **!** *Although the aspirate mutation is
> specified after this word in
> prescriptive grammars, it is only with
> words beginning* **c-** *that this is
> applied with anything approaching
> consistency in the modern natural
> language. So, for example, while* **bws
> a char** *sounds natural enough,* **bws a
> thacsi** *certainly does not. But it is
> normal in certain set phrases, like*
> **halen a phupur** *salt and pepper
> although even here* **halen a pupur** *is
> nothing out of the ordinary.*

⇒**ac**

(a)° *particle*
= who; which; that
  dyna'r °**ddynes (a) oedd yn chwilio
  amdanat ti** = there's the woman who
  was looking for you
  dw i eisiau siarad â'r dyn (a) °**ddaeth â
  hwn i mewn** = I want to speak to the
  man who brought this in
  rhaid nodi pa °**lyfr a** °**ddefnyddiwyd** =
  you must note which book was used

> **!** *An important use of this particle is
> to mark the subject before a following
> verb. This occurs in focus sentences
> where a non-verbal element is
> highlighted as new information by
> placing it in the 'first idea' slot
> normally reserved in a Welsh
> sentence for the verb. But even here it
> is normal for only the mutation to be
> heard, and this accounts for many
> instances of the the most wide-
> reaching grammatical use of the soft
> mutation—namely that the subject or
> notional subject of the Welsh
> sentence is followed by soft mutation*
> **torrodd Iwan y ffenest** (*neutral
> sentence*) = Iwan broke the window

  Iwan (a) °**dorrodd y ffenest** (*focused
  sentence*) = it was Iwan that broke the
  window

> *The same double use is found with
> the special verb form* **sy** *or* **sydd**,
> *which really stands for* **[a**° **+ mae]** —
> **mae** *alone of all verb forms in Welsh
> cannot be preceded by the usual
> particles that can appear before
> verbs.*
>   **dyna'r** °**ddynes sy'n chwilio
>   amdanat ti** = there's the woman who
>   is looking for you
>   **mae Iwan yn torri'r ffenest** = Iwan is
>   breaking the window
>   **Iwan sy'n torri'r ffenest** = it is Iwan
>   that is breaking the window

(a)° *interrogative particle*
  (a) oedd pawb yn °**bresennol?** = was
  everybody present?
  (a) °**allwch chi** °**ddod â'r plant i'r ysgol
  erbyn hanner awr wedi tri?** = can you
  bring the children to the school by
  half past three?
  (a) °**fyddai'n** °**bosib inni** °**drafod hyn
  nes ymlaen?** = would it be possible for
  us to discuss this later?
  oedd y syniad yn un da, neu a
  °**fedrwch chi** °**feddwl am un gwell?** =
  was the idea a good one, or can you
  think of a better one?

> **!** *This particle indicates that the
> following verb is asking a question. In
> normal speech it is usually not heard,
> but the following mutation is.*

(a)° *conjunction*
= whether; if (*where this* = *whether*)
  cer i °**ofyn (a) ydyn nhw'n** °**barod** = go
  and ask if *or* whether they're ready
  tybed (a) °**fydden nhw'n** °**fodlon
  helpu?** = I wonder if *or* whether they
  would be willing to help?

> **!** *The brackets indicate that this
> conjunction is not normally heard in
> speech except in rather formal
> registers or deliberately careful
> enunciation, but the following*

mutation is, as in the second example.

This conjunction usually translates as if *in informal English. There are two other words in Welsh corresponding to* if: ⇒**os** *and* ⇒**pe**. *But if English* if *can be replaced by* whether *with no change in meaning, then the conjunction* (a)° *is required.*

â^h *preposition (before vowels* **ag**)
• = with; by means of
nes i agor 'y ⁿmys â ^hchyllell fara = I cut my finger with a breadknife
• (*with comparatives*) = as
mor °ddu â'r °frân = as black as a crow
ewch mor °bell ag y medrwch chi ar y ffordd 'ma = go as far as you can on this road
cyn °gynted ag y bo modd, cyn gynted â ^hphosib = as soon as possible

> ❗ *In* 'as...as...' *expressions, only the second* 'as' *is translated by* **â^h/ag** *in Welsh, while the first one is either* ⇒**mor°** *or* ⇒**cyn°**.
> *Note that* **â**, *and not* **ag**, *is used before* **ei, ein, eich** *and* **eu**, *giving* **â'i, â'n, â'ch** *and* **â'u**.

absennol *adjective*
= absent
pwy sy'n absennol heddiw? = who is absent today?

absenoldeb *noun, masculine*
= absence

ac *conjunction*
= and
Sbaeneg ac Eidaleg = Spanish and Italian
mae disgybl newydd yn cyrraedd y dosbarth ac eraill yn ei holi = a new pupil arrives in class and others ask him/her questions

> ❗ **ac** *is used instead of* **a** *not only before vowels, but also with the following common words: the affirmative markers* ⇒**fe°**, ⇒**mi°**; *parts of the verb* **bod** 'to be' ⇒**mae, sy(dd),** ⇒**roedd** *etc.; and miscellaneous words* ⇒**fel,** ⇒**felly,** ⇒**mai** *and* ⇒**mewn**.

⇒**a^h**

ac eithrio *preposition*
= except, apart from
dim cŵn ac eithrio cŵn y deillion = no dogs except guide dogs
⇒**ar wahân i°,** ⇒**heblaw**

acw *adverb*
• = there (*distant from the speaker, but still in sight—corresponds to archaic English* yon, yonder)
pwy sy'n byw acw, 'te? = who lives (over) there, then?
• (*with definite article*) = that..., those...
mae 'na aur yn y mynyddoedd acw = there is gold in those hills
• (*North*) = at our home, at our place
galwch acw! = call round!
⇒**dacw°,** ⇒**fan 'cw**

achlysur (*plural* **-on**) *noun, masculine*
= occasion
anrhegion a ^hchardiau at °bob achlysur = presents and cards for every occasion

achlysurol *adjective*
= occasional
yn achlysurol = occasionally

achos (*plural* **-ion**)
1 *noun, masculine*
• = case
ond, yn achos y glowyr, gwahanol iawn oedd y canlyniad = but, in the case of the miners, the outcome was very different
fe °welwyd cynnydd yn y nifer o achosion o'r °frech °goch llynedd = a rise in the number of cases of measles was seen last year
• = cause
yr arian i gyd i °fynd at achosion da = all the money to go to good causes
2 *conjunction*
= because
°fydd Dewi °ddim yma heddiw achos °fod e'n sâl = Dewi won't be here today because he's ill
aethon ni °ddim yn y diwedd achos nad oedd digon o amser 'da ni = we didn't go in the end because we didn't have enough time

> ❗ **achos** *is generally followed by a* 'that' *clause in most native varieties of Welsh*

⇒**oherwydd,** ⇒**o achos**

achosi *verbnoun*
= cause

achub *verbnoun*
= save, rescue
mae hofrennydd wedi achub tri dyn o'r môr ger y Borth prynhawn 'ma = a helicopter has rescued three men from the sea near Borth this afternoon
yr hen °orsaf bad achub = the old lifeboat station
⇨**arbed**

achwyn *verbnoun*
= complain
mae gormod o achwyn wedi bod fan hyn yn °ddiweddar = there's been too much complaining round here lately
⇨**cwyno**

adar *plural noun*
⇨**aderyn**

adeg (*plural* **-au**)
1 *noun, feminine*
= time
fe °geisiwn ni °ddod yn ôl yr un adeg wythnos i heddiw = we'll try and come back the same time a week today
doedd neb yn gwybod am y troseddau 'ma adeg (hyn)ny = no-one knew about these crimes at that time
dw i'n teimlo'n °wan ar adegau = I feel weak at times
2 *adverb*
= at the time of
roedd y °fath agwedd yn °gyffredin iawn adeg y Streic °Gyffredinol = such an attitude was very common at the time of the General Strike

! *There are a number of words for* time *in Welsh—***adeg** *can indicate either a point in time, or have a more general use, and indeed the most general word for* time, ⇨**amser**, *can often be substituted, as in the first three examples above.*

adeilad (*plural* **-au**) *noun, masculine or feminine*
= building
dw i'n credu °fod yr adeilad 'ma'n °warth = I think this building is a disgrace

adeiladu *verbnoun*
= build, construct

rhaid adeiladu ar ein llwyddiannau diweddar = we must build on our recent successes
bydd cwmnïau adeiladu o °Loegr hefyd yn cystadlu am y gwaith = construction companies from England will also be competing for the work
⇨**codi**

aderyn (*plural* **adar**) *noun, masculine*
= bird

adlewyrchu *verbnoun*
= reflect
dydy hyn °ddim yn adlewyrchu'r °duedd °genedlaethol = this does not reflect the national trend

adloniant *noun, masculine*
= entertainment
bwyd ac adloniant am °ddim = food and entertainment free

adnabod (*stem* **adnabydd-**) *verbnoun*
= recognise
ydych chi'n adnabod y dyn yn y llun 'ma? = do you recognise the man in this picture?
doedd ei °deulu hyd yn oed °ddim yn adnabod e pan °ddaeth e yn ôl = even his family didn't recognise him when he came back

! *In the literary language this verb tends to mean* know *(a person), for which the living language uses* ⇨**nabod**

adnabyddus *adjective*
= famous, well-known

adnewyddu *verbnoun*
= renew
°ga i adnewyddu'r llyfrau 'ma os gwelwch yn °dda? = can I renew these books please?
⇨**newydd**

adnoddau *plural noun*
= resources
bydd angen mwy o adnoddau dwyieithog y °ganrif nesa = more bilingual resources will be needed for the next century

adran (*plural* **-nau**) *noun, feminine*
= department

sawl adran sy yn y °brifysgol 'ma? = how many departments are there in this university?

adre(f) *adverb*
= home (*motion*)
dw i eisiau mynd adre = I want to go home

> **!** *Officially,* **adre(f)** *means 'towards home' while* ⇒**gartre(f)** *means 'at home', but in practice this distinction is not made, with many speakers using either word for both meanings. So usages like* °**fydda i adre yfory** I'll be (at) home tomorrow *and* **mae pawb wedi mynd gartre** everyone's gone home *are normal.*

adrodd *verbnoun*
= report

adroddiad (*plural* **-au**) *noun, masculine*
= report
dyma adroddiad nawr gan Dafydd Rhys = here is a report now from Dafydd Rhys
mae disgwyl mai siomedig iawn °fydd adroddiad blynyddol y cwmni eleni = the company's annual report is expected to be a very disappointing one this year

addas *adjective*
= suitable
dyw'r ffordd 'ma °ddim yn addas i °gerbydau nwyddau trwm = this road is not suitable for heavy goods vehicles

addasiad (*plural* **-au**) *noun, masculine*
= adaptation

addasu *verbnoun*
= adapt
drama wedi'i haddasu ar °gyfer y radio = a play adapted for radio

addawol *adjective*
= promising

addewid (*plural* **-ion**) *noun, masculine or feminine*
= promise

addo (*stem* **addaw-**) *verbnoun*
= promise

maen nhw wedi addo dod = they have promised to come

addysg *noun, feminine*
= education
ein bwriad yw sicrhau addysg °ddwyieithog i °bob plentyn yng ⁿNghymru = our intention is to ensure a bilingual education for every child in Wales

aelod (*plural* **-au**) *noun, masculine*
= member
dw i'n cael bwyta fan hyn er nad ydw i'n aelod = I'm allowed to eat here even though I'm not a member
aelodau'r clwb sboncen yn unig = squash club members only
Aelod Cynulliad (AC) = Assembly Member (AM)
Aelod Seneddol (AS) (*plural* **Aelodau Seneddol**) = Member of Parliament (MP)

aelodaeth *noun, feminine*
= membership
aelodaeth o'r clwb = membership of the club
mae'ch tâl aelodaeth yn °ddyledus = your membership fee is due
amgaeaf eich cerdyn aelodaeth a ʰchopi o °gyfansoddiad y °gymdeithas = I enclose your membership card and a copy of the society's constitution

aelwyd (*plural* **-ydd**) *noun, feminine*
= hearth; home (*emphasis on the home environment*)
eistedd wrth yr aelwyd = to sit by the hearth
plant o aelwydydd di-°Gymraeg = children from non-Welsh-speaking homes
⇒**cartre(f)**

af-° *prefix*
= un-

> **!** *This prefix, which reverses the sense of both nouns and adjectives, is used instead of* ⇒**an-** *with words beginning with (consonantal)* **i-, gl-, ll-** *and* **rh-** *So* **llwyddiannus** successful, **aflwyddiannus** unsuccessful; **iach** healthy, **afiach** unhealthy.

afal (*plural* **-au**) *noun, masculine*
= apple

aflonyddu *verbnoun*
= disturb
peidiwch ag aflonyddu = do not disturb
ffilm yw hon a °fydd yn aflonyddu'r gwyliwr = this is a disturbing film

aflwyddiannus *adjective*
= unsuccessful
yn anffodus, roedd eich cais yn aflwyddiannus y tro yma = unfortunately your application was unsuccessful this time

afon (*plural* **-ydd**) *noun, feminine*
= river
afonydd a mynyddoedd Cymru = the rivers and mountains of Wales

ag
⇨**âʰ**

agor *verbnoun*
• = open
newch chi agor y drws i mi? = will you open the door for me?
pwy agorodd y bocs 'ma? = who opened this box?
• = cut (*injure*)
nes i agor 'y ⁿmys â ʰchyllell °fara = I cut my finger with a bread-knife

agored *adjective*
= open

> **!** *This word often, but not necessarily, indicates a inherent quality rather than a temporary state, cf ⇨**ar agor**. And the adverb 'openly' can only be translated with* **agored**.

mae'n gwneud lles i'r plant °fod yn yr awyr agored am awr neu °ddwy = it does the children good to be in the open air for an hour or two
man a man inni siarad yn agored = we might as well speak openly
⇨**ar agor**

agoriad (*plural* **-au**) *noun, masculine*
= key
°fedra i °ddim ffeindio'r agoriad = I can't find the key

> **!** *This Northern word for 'key' is often heard as* **goriad,** *with this being*

regarded as the base form. From this then is formed °**oriad** etc: **gormod o** °**oriadau** too many keys. *The standard language, however, insists on* **agoriad**.

⇨**allwedd**

agos *adjective* (*comparative* **agosach** *or* **nes**, *superlative* **agosa(f)** *or* **nesa(f)**)
= near, close (**at°** *or* **i°** to)
= nearby
ydy'r banc yn agos? = is the bank nearby?
oedden ni am °fyw'n agosach i'r °dre = we wanted to live closer to town
wedi'r rhyfel cartre roedd ysbytai'r °wlad yn agos at °fynd i'r wal = after the civil war the country's hospitals were close to going to the wall
dewch yn nes er mwyn i mi °glywed yn iawn = come closer so I can hear properly

> **!** *The choice of whether to use* **at°** *or* **i°** *when saying* 'close to' *something is sometimes a difficult one—there are many instances where both sound acceptable to native speakers. One criterion is that* **at°** *is more definitely associated with movement, so many speakers say* **eisteddwch yn agosach i'r bwrdd** sit closer to the table, *but* **dewch yn agosach at y bwrdd** come closer to the table. *Even so, proper names often seem to prefer* **i°**: **dewch yn agosach ato fe** come closer to him, *but* **dewch yn agosach i Dylan** come closer to Dylan. *On another level,* **i°** *tends to be used when a particular person or place is in mind (see, for example, the second example), while* **at°** *is preferred with non-concrete ideas or concepts (as in the third example).*

agosáu *verbnoun*
= approach; get nearer

agwedd (*plural* **-au**) *noun, feminine*
• = aspect
agwedd arall o °waith y Fforwm yw diogelu'r °dafodiaith °leol = another aspect of the Forum's work is safeguarding the local dialect

• = attitude

beth yw eu hagwedd nhwthau tuag at yr ymgyrch? = what is *their* attitude towards the campaign?

angen (*plural* **anghenion**)

1 *noun, masculine*

= need; want

beth am anghenion y plant? = what about the children's needs?

oes angen paratoi'r bwyd ymlaen llaw? = do we need to prepare the food in advance?

bydd angen cywiro'r camgymeriadau = the mistakes will have to be corrected

2 *functioning as verbnoun*

= need

dych chi angen help? = do you need help?

pwy oedd angen y geiriadur? = who needed the dictionary?

! *Although a noun, this word behaves very much like a verb in the modern language, in that it can be used in conjunction with the verb* **bod** (*though without the 'linking' particle* **yn**) *to express the English verb* need. *An alternative construction treats it as the noun it is, using* **arº**—*compare:*

wyt ti angen arian?

or: **oes angen arian arnat ti?** = ('*Is there a need of money on you?*') = do you need money?

oes *is heard in many parts of Wales as the answer 'yes' to 'Do you need…?' questions even when they are phrased verbally—so:*

Dych chi angen hwn?—Oes = Do you need this?—Yes

⇨**eisiau**, ⇨**rhaid**

---

anghofio *verbnoun*

= forget

anghofiwch am y gwaith papur am nawr! = forget about the paperwork for now!

oedd bron iawn i mi anghofio = I almost forgot

anghwrtais *adjective*

= impolite; rude

oedd ei ºlythyr yn un anghwrtais braidd = his letter was rather rude

anghyfarwydd *adjective*

= unfamiliar

mae 'na nifer o ºeiriau anghyfarwydd yn y darn 'ma = there are a number of unfamiliar words in this piece

⇨**cyfarwydd**

anghyfeillgar *adjective*

= unfriendly

⇨**cyfeillgar**

anghyffredin *adjective*

= uncommon, unusual

profiad go anghyffredin oedd e = it was a pretty unusual experience

⇨**cyffredin**

anghyfreithlon *adjective*

= illegal, unlawful

defnydd anghyfreithlon o adnoddau = illegal use of resources

dw i ºddim eisiau parcio 'n anghyfreithlon yn y ºdre 'ma = I don't want to park illegally in this town

⇨**cyfraith**

anghyfrifol *adjective*

= irresponsible

⇨**cyfrifol**

anghytuno *verbnoun*

= disagree (**âʰ** with)

rhaid i mi anghytuno â chi fan'na = I have to disagree with you there

⇨**cytuno**

anghywir *adjective*

= wrong; incorrect

oedd ei atebion i gyd yn hollol anghywir = all his answers were completely wrong

dyw hi ºddim yn ffasiynol i ºwneud jôcs gwleidyddol anghywir = it's not fashionable to make politically incorrect jokes

⇨**cywir**

ai *interrogative particle*

ai Iwan ºdorrodd y ffenest 'ma? = did *Iwan* break this window? (was it Iwan that broke this window?)

ai chi sy'n ºgyfrifol am hyn? = are *you* responsible for this? (is it you that is responsible for this?)

ai yfory maen nhw'n bwriadu dod? = are they planning to come *tomorrow*? (is it tomorrow that they're planning to come?)

o'n i ºddim yn gwybod ai y fo oedd o = I didn't know whether it was *him*

ai dyma'r diwedd? = is this the end?

! *This particle corresponds to the verbal interrogative particle* ⇒**(a)°**, *and is used to query a non-verbal element, usually in a focused question or clause. Compare the following pairs:*
(a) °**dorrodd Iwan y ffenest 'ma?** = did Iwan break this window? (or didn't he?) (*neutral question*)
ai Iwan °**dorrodd y ffenest 'ma?** = did *Iwan* break this window? (or was it someone else?) (*focused question*)
o'n i °**ddim yn gwybod (a) oedd e'n** °**gyfrifol** = I didn't know whether he was responsible (or not) (*neutral question*)
o'n i °**ddim yn gwybod ai y fe oedd yn** °**gyfrifol** = I didn't know whether *he* was responsible (or someone else) (*focused question*)

⇒**ifê**

ail° *adjective*
= second (*precedes noun*)
dyma'r ail °**dro i mi** °**glywed hynny heddiw** = this is the second time I've heard that today
yn °**gynta, dw i** °**ddim yn nabod e, ac yn ail, dw i** °**ddim eisiau nabod e** = in the first place, I don't know him, and in the second place, I don't wish to know him
dyma °**bortread heb ei ail o** °**fywyd y glowyr yn y tridegau** = this is a first-class portrait of miners' lives in the thirties

ail°- *prefix*
= re-
aildoi reroof, **ailgloriannu** reappraise, reassess, **ailsefyll** resit (*exam*), **ailwifro** rewire, **ailwneud** redo, **ailysgrifennu** rewrite
See others listed separately

ailadrodd *verbnoun*
= repeat (*words*)
newch chi ailadrodd os gwelwch yn °**dda?** = will you repeat (that) please?
⇒**adrodd**

ailagor *verbnoun*
= reopen
fe °**gafodd y ffordd rhwng Lledrod a Llanilar ei hailagor prynhawn 'ma** = the road between Lledrod and Llanilar was reopened this afternoon

⇒**agor**

ailddarlledu *verbnoun*
= rebroadcast, repeat (*programme*)
fe °**fydd y rhaglen 'na'n cael ei hailddarlledu Nos** °**Wener am wyth** = that programme will be repeated on Friday night at eight
⇒**darlledu**

ailddechrau (*stem* **ailddechreu-**) *verbnoun*
= recommence, resume, restart
bydd y °**wers 'ma'n ailddechrau ar ôl cinio** = this lesson will recommence after lunch
ailddechreuir ar y gwaith y mis nesa = work will resume next month
⇒**dechrau**

ailfeddwl *verbnoun*
– have second thoughts; change one's mind; think again
wedi ailfeddwl dw i ers hynny = I've changed my mind since then
bydd rhaid iddyn nhw ailfeddwl, on'd bydd? = they'll have to think again, won't they?
⇒**meddwl**

ail-law *adjective*
= second-hand
oes 'na siop °**lyfrau ail-law yn y** °**dre 'ma?** = is there a second-hand bookshop in this town?
⇒**ail°**, ⇒**llaw**

yr Alban *noun, feminine*
= Scotland

! *This noun is always used with the definite article in Welsh.*

mae Cymru'n chwarae yn erbyn yr Alban yng ⁿ**Nghaerdydd heddiw** = Wales are playing Scotland in Cardiff today

Albanes (*plural* **-au**) *noun, feminine*
= Scotswoman

Albanwr (*plural* **Albanwyr**) *noun, masculine*
= Scotsman

yr Almaen *noun, feminine*
= Germany

! *This noun is always used with the definite article in Welsh.*

buon ni yn yr Almaen am °bythefnos =
we were in Germany for a fortnight

°fuoch chi erioed yn yr Almaen? =
have you ever been to Germany?

Almaeneg *noun, feminine*
= German (language)

Almaenes (*plural* **-au**) *noun, feminine*
= German (woman)

Almaenwr (*plural* **Almaenwyr**) *noun,*
masculine
= German (man)

allan *adverb*
= out

dewch allan! = come out!

mae pedwar allan o °bob deg bellach
yn °ddiwaith = four out of every ten are
now unemployed

beth am °fynd allan heno? = how
about going out tonight?

⇒**mas,** ⇒**tu allan**

allanfa (*plural* **allanfeydd**) *noun,*
feminine
= exit, way out

faint o allanfeydd sy yn yr adeilad
'ma? = how many exits has this
building got?

⇒**mynedfa**

allanfa °dân
= fire exit

allanol *adjective*
= external

allwedd (*plural* **-i, -au**) *noun, feminine*
= key

lle °roddest ti'r allweddi? = where did
you put the keys?

bydd allwedd y °broblem yn anoddach
i'w ffeindio = the key to the problem
will be harder to find

⇒**agoriad**

allweddol *adjective*
= key, crucial

mae hyn yn °bwynt allweddol, cofiwch
= this is a crucial point, remember

chwiliwch am y geiriau allweddol gan
anwybyddu'r lleill i gyd am y tro =
look for the key words and ignore all
the others for now

am° *preposition*
personal forms: **amdana i, amdanat ti,**
amdano fe, amdani hi, amdanon ni,
amdanoch chi, amdanyn nhw

• (*in exchange*) = for

faint °dalest ti am y sgidiau 'na? = how
much did you pay for those shoes?

diolch yn °fawr am eich cymorth =
thanks very much for your help

• (*referring to length—time or space*) = for

bydd y ffenestri 'na'n para am
°flynyddoedd = those windows will
last for years

mae'r ffordd yn mynd yn syth am
°ddwy °filltir = the road runs straight
for two miles

am faint mae'r °ŵyl yn para? = how
long does the festival go on?

carchar am oes = life imprisonment

• (*time of the day*) = at

fe °ddown ni yn ôl am °dri o'r °gloch =
we'll come back at three o'clock

• (*concerning*) = about

beth yw eich barn chi am hyn? = what
is your opinion about this?

⇒**ynglŷn â**[h]**, ynghylch**

• (*enclosing*) = (a)round

rhowch °rwymyn am ei ben o = put a
bandage round his head

⇒**o amgylch,** ⇒**o °gwmpas**

• (*expressing a desire*)

ydych chi am °roi gwybod i'r
awdurdodau? = do you want to
inform the authorities?

o'n i am °gael gair bach â chi = I
wanted to have a quick word with you

os ydych am °ddisgrifiad manylach o'r
dyletswyddau, cysylltwch â ni = if you
want a more detailed description of
the duties, contact us

⇒**eisiau,** ⇒**moyn**

• (*in exclamations*) = What (a)...!

am °ddiwrnod! = what a day!

am sbort! = what fun!

• (*idiomatic expressions*)

ewch amdani! = go for it!

does dim dwywaith amdani... = there's
no two ways about it...

y gwir amdani yw... = the truth of it is...

! *common verbs governing* **am°** *are:*
anghofio am° = forget about
aros am° = wait for
breuddwydio am° = dream about
cofio am° = remember about
chwilio am° = look for
disgwyl am° = wait for, expect
galw am° = call for
gobeithio am° = hope for

gofalu am° = look after, care for
gofyn am° = ask for/about
meddwl am° = think of/about
poeni am° = worry about
pryderu am° = worry about
siarad am° = talk about
sôn am° = talk about
ysu am° = yearn to...

am (°fod) *conjunction*
= since, because
am °fod y bwyd mor hallt, byddan nhw °bob amser yn sychedig iawn = since the food is so salty, they are always very thirsty
fe °ohiriwyd y cyfarfod am °fod cynlleied o °bobol wedi dod = the meeting was postponed because so few people had come

amau (*stem* amheu-) *verbnoun*
• = suspect
mae'r heddlu'n amau °fod y tri wedi'u llofruddio = the police suspect that the three have been murdered
• = doubt
dw i °ddim yn amau = I don't doubt (it)

ambell° *adjective* (*precedes the noun*)
= occasional
mae'n °fater o °bobol eisiau ennill ambell °bunt yn ychwanegol = it's a question of people wanting to win an occasional extra pound

amcan (*plural* -ion) *noun, masculine*
• = aim, purpose
beth ydy prif amcan y cynllun 'ma? = what is the main aim of this scheme?
• = guess; idea
oes gynnoch chi °ryw amcan lle gallen nhw °fod? = have you any idea where they could be?

amcangyfri(f)
1 *noun, masculine* (*plural* amcangyfrifon)
= estimate
2 *verbnoun*
= estimate

amddifadu *verbnoun*
= deprive
y peryg yw y bydd y °bobol 'ma'n cael eu hamddifadu o'u hawliau dynol = the danger is that these people will be deprived of their human rights

amddiffyn *verbnoun*
= defend
mae'r llywodraeth wedi amddiffyn y penderfyniad = the government has defended the decision

Americanaidd *adjective*
= American

Americanes (*plural* -au) *noun, feminine*
= American (woman)
Americanes yw'ch gwraig, 'te? = so your wife is an American?

Americanwr (*plural* Americanwyr) *noun, masculine*
= American
mae'r Americanwyr yn hoff o siarad â'u therapyddion = the Americans like talking to their therapists

amgaeedig *adjective*
= enclosed
gweler y ffurflen amgaeedig = see the enclosed form

amgau (*stem* amgae-) *verbnoun*
= enclose
amgaeaf °fanylion y swydd y buoch yn holi amdani = I enclose the details of the job you enquired about

amgueddfa (*plural* amgueddfeydd) *noun, feminine*
= museum
beth am °daith i'r Amgueddfa °Werin yfory? = what about a trip to the Folk Museum tomorrow?

amgylch *in* o amgylch *preposition*
= (a)round
wedyn aeth y °ddwy am °dro o amgylch y pentre = then the two of them went for a walk round the village
⇒**o amgylch,** ⇒**o °gwmpas,** ⇒**am°**

amgylchedd *noun, masculine*
= environment
sut mae llygru'r amgylchedd yn effeithio arnon ni? = how does pollution of the environment affect us?

amhosib *adjective*
= impossible
mae'n amhosib rhoi ateb pendant ar hyn o °bryd = it's impossible to give a definite answer at the moment
⇒**posib**

aml *adjective* (*comparative* **amlach**, *superlative* **amla(f)**)
= often, frequent
pa mor aml dych chi'n mynd am °dro gyda'r plant? = how often do you go for a walk with the children?
'na beth dw i'n °glywed amla = that's what I hear most often
dyn ni'n mynd i'r sinema rhan amla = mostly we go to the cinema
yn amlach na heb = more often than not
⇒**mynych**, ⇒**anaml**

amlen (*plural* **-ni**) *noun, feminine*
= envelope

amlwg *adjective* (*comparative* **amlycach**, *superlative* **amlyca(f)**)
• = obvious
mae'n °gwbwl amlwg °fod rhywbeth o'i °le fan hyn = it's quite obvious that something is wrong here
• = clear
mi °ddaw'n amlycach cyn bo hir = it will soon become clearer

amlygu *verbnoun*
= make clear

amod (*plural* **-au**) *noun, masculine or feminine*
= condition (*not physical*)
mi °gewch chi'r rhain ar yr amod bod chi'n rhannu nhw gyda'r lleill = you can have these on condition that you share them with the others
⇒**cyflwr**

amryw (**o°** + *plural*) *adverb*
= several; some
mae amryw o °bobol y pentre yn erbyn y syniad = some of the people of the village are against the idea

amrywio *verbnoun*
= vary
bydd y trefniadau'n amrywio yn ôl yr ardal = the arrangements will vary according to region

amrywiol *adjective*
= various

amser (*plural* **-au**, **-oedd**) *noun, masculine*
= time

°fydd digon o amser 'da nhw, ti'n meddwl? = will they have enough time, do you think?
mae'n amser inni °fynd = it's time for us to go
mae'r amseroedd wedi newid, ac mae diwydiant trwm wedi diflannu °fwy na °lai = times have changed, and heavy industry has more or less disappeared

! *The most general term for time, used to express the concept or resource. It can often be substituted for other, more specialised terms.*

amserlen (*plural* **-ni**) *noun, feminine*
= timetable
mae'r cwmni bellach yn gweithredu amserlen °ddiwygiedig = the company is now operating a revised timetable

amynedd *noun, masculine*
= patience
amynedd yw mam pob doethineb (*proverb*) = patience is the mother of all wisdom

amyneddgar *adjective*
= patient

an- (an°-, anⁿ-) *prefix*
= un-; in-; dis-

! *This prefix reverses the meaning of nouns and adjectives. It causes soft mutation of* **b-**, **g-** *and* **m-**. *So* **bwriadol** *intentional,* **anfwriadol** *unintentional;* **gwybodaeth** *knowledge,* **anwybodaeth** *ignorance;* **mantais** *advantage,* **anfantais** *disadvantage. It causes nasal mutation of* **c-**, **d-**, **p-** *and* **t-**, *with the following complications:* **an + c-** *gives* **angh-**, *so* **cyson** *consistent,* **anghyson** *inconsistent;* **an + d-** *gives* **ann-**, *so* **digonol** *sufficient,* **annigonol** *insufficient,* **an + p-** *gives* **amh-**, *so* **personol** *personal,* **amhersonol** *impersonal;* **an + t-** *gives* **annh-**, *but* **an + tr-** *gives* **anhr-**, *so* **teg** *fair,* **annheg** *unfair, but* **trefnus** *organised, tidy,* **anhrefnus** *disorganised, untidy. Words beginning with consonantal* **i**, **gl-**, **ll-** *and (with a very few exceptions)* **rh-** *take the prefix* ⇒**af°-**.

anabl *adjective*
= disabled
llefydd parcio i'r anabl yn unig = parking spaces for the disabled only

anabledd *noun, masculine*
= disability

anad
• **yn anad dim** = more than anything; above all
ond yn anad dim dw i eisiau i chi °fod yn hapus fan hyn = but above all I want you to be happy here
• **yn anad neb** = more than anyone
Siwan, yn anad neb, °ddylai °wybod am hynny = Siwan, more than anyone, should know about that

anadlu *verbnoun*
= breathe
°alla i °ddim anadlu'n iawn = I can't breathe properly

anafiad (*plural* **-au**) *noun, masculine*
= injury
mae'r dyn arall yn dioddef o anafiadau difrifol i'w °goesau = the other man is suffering from serious injuries to his legs

anafu *verbnoun*
= injure
dyn ni °ddim eisiau i neb °gael ei anafu wrth °wneud y gwaith 'ma = we don't want anyone to get injured doing this work

anaml *adjective*
= infrequent; rare; seldom
yn anaml iawn dyn ni'n gweld nhw dyddiau 'ma = we very seldom see them these days
⇒**aml**

andros (**o°** + *adjective or noun*) *noun, masculine, functioning as intensifier* (*North*)
= awfully ..., incredibly ...; hell of a...
mae'n andros o °drwm, °wyddost ti = it's awfully heavy, you know
mi oedd o'n andros o °beth = it was a hell of a thing
⇒**hynod o°** *adverb*

anelu *verbnoun*
= aim (**at°** at)
mae'r cynllun 'ma wedi'i anelu'n °bennaf at °ddysgwyr rhugl = this scheme is aimed mainly at fluent learners
anelir at °ddarparu profiad o °ddefnyddio cyfrifiaduron i °bob plentyn yn yr ysgol = the aim is to provide every child in the school with computer experience

anfantais (*plural* **anfanteision**) *noun, feminine*
= disadvantage
tybed a oes anfanteision yn y ffordd 'ma o °weithredu? = I wonder if there are disadvantages in doing things this way?
mae nifer o °blant 'da ni yma o °deuluoedd dan anfantais = we have a number of children here from disadvantaged families

anferth *adjective*
= enormous, huge
pentwr anferth o hen °ddillad = a huge pile of old clothes

anfodlon *adjective*
= unwilling
os bydd hi'n anfodlon siarad am y peth, nawn ni °ofyn i Sara = if she's unwilling to talk about it, we'll ask Sara
⇒**bodlon**

anfoddhaol *adjective*
= unsatisfactory

anfon *verbnoun*
= send
a °fyddech chi °gystal ag anfon y manylion ata i? = would you be so good as to send me the details?
⇒**danfon**, ⇒**hala**

anfwriadol *adjective*
= unintentional; not on purpose
mi nes i hynny'n anfwriadol = I did that unintentionally
⇒**bwriad**, ⇒**bwriadol**

anffawd (*plural* **anffodion**) *noun, feminine*
= mishap, misfortune; accident
fe °gaeth hi anffawd yn ei ʰchar ar y ffordd i'r °dre = she had an accident in her car on the way to town

anffodus *adjective*
= unfortunate

mi oedd hi'n °gyd-ddigwyddiad
anffodus, 'na i gyd = it was an
unfortunate coincidence, that's all
yn anffodus, roedd eich cais yn
aflwyddiannus y tro yma =
unfortunately your application was
unsuccessful this time

------

ang-
words beginning **ang-** are listed
according to Welsh alphabetical order
immediately following **ag-**

------

anhawster (*plural* **anawsterau**) *noun,
masculine*
= difficulty, problem
os °gei di anawsterau, ffonia fi'n syth
= if you have any problems, phone me
straight away
⇒**anodd**

anhrefnus *adjective*
= disorganised; untidy

anhygoel *adjective*
= incredible
mae hynny'n anhygoel! = that's
incredible!
⇒**coel, coelio**

anifail (*plural* **anifeiliaid**) *noun,
masculine*
= animal

anifail anwes (*plural* **anifeiliaid
anwes**)
= pet

anlwc *noun, masculine*
= bad luck, misfortune
anlwc oedd e = it was (a piece of) bad
luck
⇒**lwc**

anlwcus *adjective*
= unlucky
oeddet ti'n anlwcus fan'na = you were
unlucky there
⇒**lwcus**

annhebyg *adjective*
= unlikely
**annhebyg iawn y byddai'ch
cymdogion yn cytuno** = (it's) very
unlikely that your neighbours would
agree
⇒**tebyg**

annheg *adjective*
= unfair

dyn ni °ddim eisiau bod yn annheg â
neb = we don't want to be unfair to
anyone
⇒**teg**

annibyniaeth *noun, feminine*
= independence
⇒**dibynnu**

annibynnol *adjective*
= independent
**mae Estonia bellach yn °gwlad
annibynnol** = Estonia is now an
independent country
**ymholiad annibynnol sy eisiau, a
hynny ar °fyrder** = what is needed, and
urgently, is an independent enquiry

annifyr *adjective*
• = miserable
• = embarrassed
o'n i'n teimlo tipyn bach yn annifyr = I
felt a bit embarrassed
⇒**difyr**

annigonol *adjective*
= insufficient; not enough
mae'r arian a neilltuwyd yn annigonol
= the money set aside is insufficient
⇒**digon**, ⇒**digonol**

annioddefol *adjective*
= insufferable, unbearable
mae'r dyn 'na'n annioddefol! = that
man is insufferable!
⇒**diodde(f)**

annwyd *noun, masculine*
= cold (*illness*)

> **!** *This term indicating a temporary
> state of health is used with* ⇒**ar°**
> *when a person is stated*

**mae annwyd trwm arna i ar hyn o
°bryd** = I've got a heavy cold at the
moment
oes annwyd arnat ti? = have you got a
cold?

annwyl *adjective*
• = dear; endearing
**maen nhw'n °greaduriaid bach
annwyl, on'd ydyn nhw?** = they're
sweet/dear little things, aren't they?
• = nice (*personality*)
**dw i'n cofio'ch mab fel bachgen
annwyl** = I remember your son as a
nice boy

! *Used as a formal mode of address in letters,* **annwyl°** *precedes the noun, but mutates only titles, not names, which are generally not susceptible to mutation.*
Annwyl °Olygydd, ... = Dear Editor, ...
Annwyl °Brifathro, ... = Dear Headmaster, ...
but: **Annwyl Dafydd, ...** = Dear Dafydd, ...

• *idiomatic phrases:*
  °Bobol annwyl!, Tad annwyl!, Esgob annwyl! = Goodness gracious!

annymunol *adjective*
= unpleasant, disagreeable
mi oedd hynny'n °brofiad annymunol iawn = that was a very unpleasant experience
⇨**dymunol**

anobeithiol *adjective*
= hopeless
mae hyn yn anobeithiol! = this is hopeless!
⇨**gobaith**

anodd *adjective (comparative* **anoddach** *or* **mwy anodd** *or (rarer)* **anos**, *superlative* **anodda(f)** *or* **mwya anodd)*
= difficult, hard
mae'n anodd dweud = it's hard to say
ydy'r iaith °Gymraeg yn anoddach na Llydaweg = is the Welsh language more difficult than Breton?
⇨**caled**, ⇨**hawdd**, ⇨**anhawster**

anrheg (*plural* **-ion**) *noun, feminine*
= present; gift
dych chi wedi prynu'ch anrhegion Nadolig? = have you bought your Christmas presents?

ansawdd *noun, masculine or feminine*
= quality
mi °fydd ansawdd eu bywyd yn sicr yn parhau'n °bwnc llosg = the quality of their life is certain to remain a burning issue

ansicr *adjective*
= uncertain
mae dyfodol y °ganolfan yn edrych yn °fwy ansicr fyth ar ôl y penderfyniad

heddiw = the centre's future looks even more uncertain after today's decision
⇨**sicr**

anterth *noun, masculine*
= zenith, peak
yn ei anterth (*masculine*), **yn ei hanterth** (*feminine*) = at its peak, at its height:
pan oedd y gwaith 'ma yn ei anterth = when this work was at its height

anwybyddu *verbnoun*
= ignore
anwybyddwch nhw! = ignore them!
rhaid inni °beidio ag anwybyddu teuluoedd y dynion 'ma = we mustn't ignore these men's families

apwyntiad (*plural* **-au**) *noun, masculine*
= appointment
awgrymir i chi °wneud apwyntiad ar adeg arall = you are advised to make an appointment at another time

ar° *preposition*
personal forms: **arna i, arnat ti, arno fe, arni hi, arnon ni, arnoch chi, arnyn nhw**
• = on
dw i wedi gadael popeth ar y bwrdd i chi = I've left everything on the table for you
dyn ni eisiau i chi °ganolbwyntio ar eich gwaith am y tro = we want you to concentrate on your work for now
llong °ryfel nerthol ac arni naw hwyl = a powerful warship with nine sails
• (*with verbnoun*) = about to...
brysiwch, mae'r trên ar °fynd! = hurry up, the train's about to go!
⇨**ar °fin**
• (*with temporary physical and mental states*)
mae annwyd arna i = I've got a cold
oes ofn arnat ti? = are you afraid?
mae hiraeth ar Gwilym am °Gymru = Gwilym misses Wales

! *Similarly with* **(y) °ddannoedd** toothache, **y °frech °goch** measles, **y ffliw** 'flu, **hiraeth** longing/yearning, **peswch** cough, *and diseases generally. But ailments involving* **tost**, e.g. **pen tost** headache, **stumog °dost** stomach ache, *usually take* **gyda** *rather than* **ar°**.

- *expressions of state using* **ar:**
⇨**ar agor** = open
⇨**ar °ben** = finished, done with
⇨**ar °ddihun** = awake
⇨**ar °dân** = on fire, ablaze
⇨**ar °fai** = at fault, to blame
⇨**ar °frys** = in a hurry
⇨**ar °gadw** = away (*in proper place*)
⇨**ar °gael** = available
⇨**ar °gau** = closed
⇨**ar °glo** = locked
⇨**ar °goll** = lost
⇨**ar ôl** = left, remaining
⇨**ar °wahân** = apart, separate
⇨**ar °werth** = for sale
- (*expressing possession of a quality or characteristic*)
mae arogl arbennig ar y bwyd 'ma, on'd oes? = this food has a distinctive smell, doesn't it?
blas ar °Gymru = a taste of Wales

> **!** *common verbs governing* **ar°**
> **blino ar°** = get tired of
> **cael gwared ar°** = get rid of
> **diflasu ar°** = get bored with
> **edrych ar°** = look at
> **gweiddi ar°** = shout at
> **gwenu ar°** = smile at
> **gwrando ar°** = listen to
> **manteisio ar°** = take advantage of
> **sylwi ar°** = notice, take notice of
> **syllu ar°** = stare at
> **ymosod ar°** = attack

- (*other common idiomatic usages*)
faint sy arna i i chi? = how much do I owe you?
ar y cyfan, mae'r sefyllfa °gyffredinol yn °well heddiw na ddoe = on the whole, the general situation is better today than yesterday
tydy o °ddim yn gweithio ar hyn o °bryd = he's not working at the moment
dw i eisau bod ar 'y ⁿmhen 'n hun = I want to be on my own

ar°
look up phrases consisting of **ar°** + *noun/verbnoun alphabetically*

ara(f) *adjective*
= slow

mae ei °long yn rhy araf = his ship is too slow
bydd y tywydd diflas a niwlog yn symud yn ara °deg tua'r dwyrain = the dull and misty weather will move gradually eastwards
siaradwch yn arafach os gwelwch yn °dda = speak more slowly please

arafu *verbnoun*
= slow down
arafwch nawr! = reduce speed now!
⇨**ara(f)**

ar agor
= open (*adjective*)
tan pryd mae'r llyfrgell ar agor heddiw? = till when is the library open today?
⇨**agor**, ⇨**agored**

arall (*plural* **eraill**) *adjective*
- = another; other
°gymera i'r crys arall hefyd = I'll take the other shirt as well
mae'r ceir eraill i gyd yn rhy °ddrud = all the other cars are too expensive
- = ...else
dych chi eisiau unrhywbeth arall? = do you want anything else?
pwy arall sy'n dod heno? = who else is coming tonight?

> **!** *This is one of the few adjectives in modern Welsh that has a plural form which must be used with plural nouns. This form is pronounced as if spelt* **erill**. *Arall/eraill is a true adjective, and needs a noun to be attached to. A different pronominal form is used for* another one, the other one, the others.

⇨**(y) llall**, ⇨**(y) lleill**

arbed *verbnoun*
= save (*time, money, etc*)
er mwyn arbed arian = in order to save money
bydd hyn yn arbed ychydig o amser, on' bydd? = this will save a bit of time, won't it?
⇨**achub**, ⇨**cynilo**

ar °ben *adverb*
= finished; done with; at an end
mae hi ar °ben 'da ni nawr! = now we're done for!
⇨**pen**

arbennig *adjective*
- = special
  mae heddiw yn °ddiwrnod arbennig iawn inni i gyd = today is a very special day for us all
- = particular
  oes gynnoch chi °rywbeth arbennig mewn golwg? = have you got something particular in mind?
- **(arbennig o° + *adjective*)** = especially..., particularly...
  rhaid cyfadde °fod y °gân 'ma'n arbennig o °dda = it must be admitted that this song is particularly good

ar °bwys *preposition (South)*
- = near
  personal forms: **ar ⁿmhwys (i), ar dy °bwys (di), ar ei °bwys (e), ar ei ʰphwys (hi), ar ein pwys (ni), ar eich pwys (chi), ar eu pwys (nhw):**
  wi'n byw ar °bwys y parc bellach = I live near the park now
  der i eistedd ar ⁿmhwys i! = come and sit by me!

archeb (*plural* **-ion**) *noun, feminine*
- = order
  diolch am eich archeb = thank you for your order

archebu *verbnoun*
- = order
  archebwch nawr cyn i'n stoc i gyd °ddiflannu! = order now before all our stock disappears!

archfarchnad (*plural* **-oedd**) *noun, feminine*
- = supermarket
  fe agorir archfarchnad newydd ar ymylon y °dre °fis Tachwedd = a new supermarket will be opened on the outskirts of town in November

ardal (*plural* **-oedd**) *noun, feminine*
- = area, region
  chwiliwch am °ddosbarthiadau yn eich ardal chi = look for classes in your area
  mae'n amlwg mai'r ardaloedd gwledig, fel arfer, sy'n diodde = it's clear that it is the rural areas, as usual, that are suffering
  ⇒**bro**

ar °dân
- = on fire

roedd yr adeiladau i gyd ar °dân erbyn i'r °frigâd °dân °gyrraedd = all the buildings were on fire by the time the fire brigade arrived
⇒**tân**

ar °draws *preposition*
- = across
  personal forms: **ar ⁿnhraws (i), ar dy °draws (di), ar ei °draws (e), ar ei ʰthraws (hi), ar ein traws (ni), ar eich traws (chi), ar eu traws (nhw)**
  bydd effeithiau'r newid 'ma i'w gweld ar °draws y cwriciwlwm = the effects of this change will be visible across the curriculum
  peidiwch torri ar ⁿnhraws i! = don't interrupt me!

arddegau *plural noun*
- = teens
  llyfr a °fydd yn apelio'n °bennaf at °bobol yn eu harddegau = a book that will appeal mainly to teenagers

ardderchog *adjective*
- = excellent
  diolch am eich gwaith ardderchog yn ystod yr °ŵyl = thanks for your excellent work during the festival

ar °ddihun
- = awake
  wyt ti ar °ddihun? = are you awake?
  ⇒**dihuno**, ⇒**effro**

arddwrn (*plural* **arddyrnau**) *noun, masculine (sometimes also* **garddwrn** (*plural* **garddyrnau**) *noun, masculine*
- = wrist

arestio *verbnoun*
- = arrest
  fe °gafodd dyn ei arestio yn y °dre neithiwr = a man was arrested in town last night
  arestiwyd tri o °bobol tu allan i'r Llew Du Nos °Wener °ddiwetha = three people were arrested outside the Black Lion last Friday night

arf (*plural* **-au**) *noun, masculine or feminine*
- = weapon
  cedwir yr holl arfau yn °barod i'w defnyddio = all the weapons are kept ready for use

ar °fai
= at fault, to blame
ti sy ar °fai am hyn oll! = this is all your fault!
⇒**bai**

arfer
1 (*plural* **-ion**) *noun, feminine*
= custom; habit
o'n i am °gael gair â rhywun am hen arferion yr ardal 'ma = I wanted to have a chat with someone about the old customs of this area
2 (*with verbnoun*)
= usually..., used to...
maen nhw'n arfer gadael y bin sbwriel tu allan = they usually leave the dustbin outside
o'n i'n arfer dod adre ar y bws = I used to come home on the bus

ar °fin
= about to
roedd hi ar °fin llyncu'r caws pan °glywodd hi sŵn = she was about to swallow the cheese when she heard a noise
oedd y rhaglen ar °fin dechrau pan °gaethon ni °doriad trydan = the programme was just about to start when we had a power cut

arfog *adjective*
= armed

arfordir *noun, masculine*
= coast
mae'r pentre wedi'i °leoli ar arfordir deheuol Llydaw = the village is situated on the south coast of Brittany

ar °frys
= in a hurry; quickly
°alla i °ddim aros—dw i ar °frys = I can't hang around—I'm in a hurry
⇒**brysio**

ar °fyrder
• = at short notice
• = urgently
ymholiad annibynnol sy eisiau, a hynny ar °fyrder = what is needed, and urgently, is an independent enquiry
⇒**byr**

ar °gadw
= (tidied) away
teganau ar °gadw, °blantos! = toys away, children!
⇒**cadw**

ar °gael
= available
brechdanau ffres ar °gael fan hyn °bob bore = fresh sandwiches available here every morning
⇒**cael**

ar °gau
= closed, shut
bydd yr amgueddfa ar °gau °Ddydd Llun nesa = the museum will be closed next Monday
⇒**cau**

ar °glo
= locked
mae'r drws 'ma ar °glo = this door is locked
⇒**clo**

ar °goll
= lost
dw i'n meddwl bod ni ar °goll = I think we're lost
dw i °ddim eisiau i'r nodiadau 'ma °fynd ar °goll = I don't want these notes lost
⇒**colli**

ar °gyfartaledd
= on average
faint o °weithiau dych chi'n mynd i'r °dre °bob wythnos ar °gyfartal? = how many times do you go to town each week on average?
⇒**cyfartal**

ar °gyfer *preposition*
= for (*all general senses*); for the benefit of
personal forms: **ar ⁿnghyfer (i), ar dy °gyfer (di), ar ei °gyfer (e), ar ei ʰchyfer (hi), ar ein cyfer (ni), ar eich cyfer (chi), ar eu cyfer (nhw):**
yn addas ar °gyfer grwpiau a gwyliau teulu = suitable for groups and family holidays
darparwyd amrywiaeth o °weithgareddau ar eu cyfer = a variety of activies was provided for them

! ar °gyfer *is the usual expression corresponding to* 'for' *in its most general senses;* →**i °** *is an alternative when there is a definite sense of something received:* **Mae 'na °lythyr i ti ar y bwrdd** There's a letter for you on the table; ⇒**dros°** *means* 'for' *where the sense is* 'on behalf of'; *and*

⇨**am°** *means* 'for' *in the sense of* 'in exchange for' *and* 'for a period of time'. *Although, being a two-word expression,* **ar °gyfer** *looks as though it might be the most specialised of the four, in fact it is really the most neutral, and is rarely inappropriate in cases of doubt.*

argyfwng (*plural* **argyfyngau**) *noun, masculine*
= crisis, emergency
wrth i'r argyfwng yn Bosnia °ddyfnhau, beth °fydd ymateb y Cenhedloedd Unedig? = as the crisis in Bosnia deepens, what will be the United Nations' response?

argyhoeddi *verbnoun*
= convince
bydd eisiau eu hargyhoeddi nhw rhyw ffordd neu'i gilydd, on' bydd? = they'll have to be convinced one way or another, won't they?

arhosfa *noun, feminine*
= waiting room

ar hyd *preposition*
• = along
maen nhw'n rhedeg ar hyd pen y wal = they're running along the top of the wall
• = all through (*in expressions of time*)
ar hyd y nos = all through the night
• **ar hyd a lled** = the length and breadth of:
mae'r prif °bleidiau wrthi'n canfasio ar hyd a lled Cymru = the main parties are hard at work canvassing the length and breadth of Wales
⇨**hyd**, ⇨**o hyd**

ar hyn o °bryd
= at the moment
does neb ar °gael i'ch helpu chi ar hyn o °bryd = there is no-one available to help you at the moment
⇨**pryd**

arian *noun, masculine*
• = money
mae'r llywodraeth wedi neilltuo arian = the government has set money aside
• = silver
⇨**pres**

ariannol *adjective*
= financial

ariannu *verbnoun*
= finance

arllwys *verbnoun* (*South*)
= pour
⇨**tywallt**

(ar)oglau (*plural* **arogleuon**) *noun, masculine*
= smell
'na'r oglau °glywon ni ddoe! = there's that smell we smelt yesterday!

> **!** *Despite appearances,* **aroglau** (**oglau** *in many parts of Wales) is a singular. Nevertheless, a new singular* **arogl** *has been formed by wrongly analysing the* **-au** *as a plural ending (like English* 'pea' *from original singular* 'pease'), *and* **arogl** *and* **oglau** *now co-exist happily enough. Notice in the example that* ⇨**clywed** (*usually* 'hear') *is used in native speech for* 'smell', *and also, for that matter, sometimes for* 'taste' *and* 'feel', *depending on context.*

ar ôl

1 *preposition*
= after
personal forms: **ar 'yn ôl (i)** *or* **ar f' ôl (i), ar dy ôl (di), ar ei ôl (e), ar ei hôl (hi), ar ein hôl (ni), ar eich ôl (chi), ar eu hôl (nhw):**
mi °ddaeth Wiliam yn ôl i °Gymru ar ôl y rhyfel = Wiliam came back to Wales after the war
pam na °ddoi di draw ar ôl saith? = why don't you come round after seven?

> **!** *In more formal language* ⇨**wedi** *is frequently used as a synonym for the preposition* **ar ôl**, *but in normal registers the two words have distinct usages, with* **wedi** *largely confined to use with verbnouns.*

2 *conjunction*
= after
mi °ganodd y ffôn °ddwy °funud ar ôl i chi °fynd = the phone rang two minutes after you'd gone
°ga i °air â Bethan ar ôl i chi °fynd = I'll have a word with Bethan after you go

> **!** *This is one of a number of time conjunctions in Welsh that are used*

with the construction **i +** [person] +
°verbnoun. *The tense of the
corresponding verb in English is clear
from the main verb in the Welsh—note
the differing translations for* **ar ôl i chi
°fynd** *in the two examples above.*

arolwg barn (*plural* **arolygon barn**)
noun, masculine
= opinion poll

aros (*stem* **arhos-**) *verbnoun*
• = wait
　na i aros amdanoch chi fan hyn = I'll
　wait for you here
• = stay, remain
　**aros lle wyt ti eiliad!, arhoswch lle
　dych chi eiliad!** = stay where you are a
　moment!

ar °ran
= on behalf of
personal forms: **ar 'yn rhan (i), ar dy
°ran (di), ar ei °ran (e), ar ei rhan (hi),
ar ein rhan (ni), ar eich rhan (chi), ar
eu rhan (nhw)**
**mae'n °bleser gen i °gael diolch i chi
ar °ran rhieni ac athrawon Ysgol
Llaneglwys** = it's a pleasure for me to
be able to thank you on behalf of the
parents and teachers of Llaneglwys
School
fe °fu Ieuan Williams yno ar ein rhan ni
= Ieuan Williams has been there on
our behalf
⇨**rhan,** ⇨**o °ran**

ar unwaith
= at once, immediately
dere 'ma ar unwaith! = come here at
once!
⇨**unwaith**

aruthrol *adjective*
= huge, immense
**fe °gafodd Cymru ei ʰchydnabod gan
°gwango aruthrol o °bwerus** = Wales
was recognised by an immensely
powerful quango

ar °wahân
= apart (**i°** from);
**cadwch y °ddau 'na ar °wahân nes i mi
°ddod yn ôl** = keep those two apart till
I get back
⇨**gwahanol,** ⇨**ac eithrio,** ⇨**heblaw**

arwain (*stem* **arweini-**) *verbnoun*
= lead

**mae'n °debyg y byddai'r °fath
°weithred yn arwain at sefyllfa °fwy
cymhleth fyth** = such a course of
action would probably lead to an even
more complicated situation

arweinydd (*plural* **arweinwyr**) *noun,
masculine*
= leader

ar °werth
= for sale
**mae nifer o °dai ar °werth yn yr ardal
'ma** = there are a number of houses for
sale in this area
⇨**gwerthu**

arwerthiant *noun, masculine*
= sale
**bydd arwerthiant fan hyn yn syth ar ôl
Nadolig** = there'll be a sale here
straight after Christmas

arwydd (*plural* **-ion**) *noun, masculine*
= sign
**mae'r ffigurau'n arwydd o
ansefydlogrwydd yn yr economi** =
the figures are a sign of instability in
the economy
**°welwch chi'r arwydd 'na uwchben y
siop?** = do you see that sign over the
shop?

arwyddo *verbnoun*
= sign
**arwyddwch fan hyn os gwelwch yn
°dda** = sign here please
⇨**llofnodi**

arwyddocaol *adjective*
= significant

ar y gweill
⇨**gweill**

asgell (*plural* **esgyll**) *noun, feminine*
= wing (*figurative senses*)
**mae asgell °dde'r °blaid yn dal i
achosi problemau i'r arweinydd** = the
right wing of the party is still causing
the leader problems
**mae asgell °wleidyddol y mudiad yn
cadw'n °dawel iawn ar y pwnc** = the
political wing of the movement is
keeping very quiet on the subject

asgellwr (*plural* **asgellwyr**) *noun,
masculine*
= wing, winger (*in rugby etc*)

asgwrn (plural **esgyrn**) noun,
masculine
= bone
oedd e wedi torri asgwrn yn ei °fraich
= he had broken a bone in his arm

astud
yn astud = attentively
gwrandewch yn astud! = listen .
attentively!

astudio verbnoun
= study
**beth wyt ti'n astudio yn y °brifysgol,
'te?** = what are you studying at
university, then?

at° preposition
personal forms: **ata i, atat ti, ato fe, ati
hi, aton ni, atoch chi, atyn nhw**
• = to (motion towards)
dewch ata i = come to me
• = up to, as far as (motion towards but
stopping short of going in)
ewch at (or **hyd at**) **y goleuadau, yna
trowch i'r °dde** = go up to the lights,
then turn right

> **!** The two senses above show the
> primary meaning of **at°**, namely
> motion towards or up to a person or
> object, but not into. For this reason we
> must use **at°** when talking of writing 'to'
> people or sending things 'to' people,
> but ⇒**i°** when writing or sending
> things to places (where obviously
> there is a sense of 'entering' a place):
> so **ysgrifennu at y Prif °Weinidog**
> (to) write to the Prime Minister, but
> **ysgrifennu i °Lundain** (to) write to
> London. Similarly **mynd i'r °feddygfa**
> (to) go to the surgery, but **mynd at y
> meddyg** (to) go to the doctor('s)

• = towards—often **tuag at°** in this sense
**does gynno fo °ddim drwg °deimlad
tuag ati** = he bears her no ill will
['...has no bad feeling towards her']
**mae'n °bwysig bod ninnau'n cyfrannu
°rywsut tuag at °ddatrys y °broblem
'ma** = it's important that we also
contribute in some way towards
solving this problem

> **!** In older and more formal styles of
> the language, towards is usually
> ⇒**tua(g)** on its own, but this is used
> now for about (approximation).

• (expressing purpose) = for
at beth mae'r peth 'ma? = what is this
thing for?

> **!** ommon verbs governing **at°**:
> **anelu at°** = aim at/towards
> **anfon at°** = send to (person)
> **cofio at°** = remember (someone) to
> (someone)
> **cyfeirio at°** = refer to
> **cyfrannu at°** = contribute to/towards
> **danfon at°** = send to (person)
> **edrych ymlaen at°** = look forward to
> **hala at°** = send to (person)
> **nesáu at°** = approach
> **paratoi at°** = prepare for
> **synnu at°** = be surprised at
> **tynnu at°** = draw closer to (a time)
> **ychwanegu at°** = add to
> **ysgrifennu at°** = write to (person)

• (other common idiomatic usages):
mynd ati i° + verbnoun = go about ...ing
**sut dyn ni'n mynd ati i °roi gwybod i
°bawb?** = how do we go about letting
everyone know?
ewch ati! = get on with it!
ac ati = and so on
te, coffi, brechdanau, rholion ac ati =
tea, coffee, sandwiches, rolls and so on

atal verbnoun
= stop; prevent (**rhag** from)
**bydd yr heddlu yn ceisio atal y
protestwyr rhag dod i mewn** = the
police will be trying to stop the
protesters getting in
⇒**rhwystro**, ⇒**stopio**

atalfa cyflymder (plural **atalfeydd
cyflymder**) noun, feminine
= speed-check
= sleeping policeman

atal-genhedlu verbnoun
• = contraception.
• = contraceptive

ateb 1 (plural **-ion**) noun, masculine
= answer, reply
oeddech chi'n disgwyl ateb? = were
you expecting a reply?
**mi °ddywedwyd nad nifer yr atebion
cywir oedd yn °bwysig** = it was said
that it wasn't the number of correct
answers that was important
2 verbnoun
= answer, reply

na i °drio ateb eich cwestiwn = I'll try
and answer your question

os na atebith e, triwch eto ar ôl cinio =
if he doesn't answer, try again after
lunch

atgoffa *verbnoun*
= remind (**am°** about)
°ga i'ch atgoffa chi i gyd °fod y tâl
cofrestru bellach yn °ddyledus? =
can I remind you all that the
registration fee is now due?

atgyweirio *verbnoun*
= repair
**mae eisiau i ti °gael atgyweirio'r
oriawr 'na, on'd oes?** = you need to
get that watch repaired, don't you?
⇨**trwsio**

athrawes (*plural* -au) *noun, feminine*
= (female) teacher
**a gadewch inni °ddiolch i'r tair
athrawes hefyd** = and let's thank the
three teachers as well

athrawon *plural of*
⇨**athro**

athro (*plural* **athrawon**) *noun,
masculine*
= (male) teacher

> **!** *The plural is used also of mixed
> male and female teachers.*

**athro mewn ysgol uwchradd o'n i
°bryd hynny** = I was a teacher in
secondary school at that time
**faint o athrawon rhan-amser sy'n
gweithio fan hyn?** = how many part-
time teachers work here?

aur *noun, masculine*
= gold
nid aur popeth melyn (*proverb*) = all
that glisters is not gold

awdurdod (*plural* -au) *noun,
masculine*
= authority
**cynyddu mae pwysau ar yr awdurdod
lleol i °wella'r sefyllfa** = pressure is
increasing on the local authority to
improve the situation

awgrymu *verbnoun*
= suggest
°fyddai neb yn awgrymu mynd yn ôl i'r
hen °ddyddiau, na °fydden nhw? = no-

one would suggest going back to the
old days, would they?
**awgrymir i chi °wneud apwyntiad ar
adeg arall** = you are advised to make
an appointment at another time

awr (*plural* **oriau**) *noun, feminine*
= hour
o'n i 'na am awr a hanner = I was there
for an hour and a half
**dyw e °ddim yn dweud dim byd yn yr
hysbyseb am oriau gwaith** = it doesn't
say anything in the advert about
working hours

Awst *noun, masculine*
= August (*also* **mis Awst**)
**dw i'n cael ⁿmhenblwydd ar °ddiwedd
mis Awst** = I have my birthday at the
end of August
**mi °fyddwn ni yn ôl erbyn yr ugeinfed
o °fis Awst** = we'll be back by the
twentieth of August
⇨**Ionawr**

awyddus *adjective*
= keen; eager
dyn ni i gyd yn awyddus i °ddechrau =
we're all keen to get started
⇨**brwd**

awyr *noun, feminine*
• = air
mae'r awyr yn °denau fan'ma = the air
is thin here
• = sky
**mae awyr °las uwchben y
mynyddoedd o'n blaen ni** = there is
blue sky over the mountains ahead

awyren (*plural* -nau) *noun, feminine*
= aeroplane

awyrgylch *noun, masculine or
feminine*
= atmosphere
**rhaid sicrhau awyrgylch dymunol os
ydy unrhyw °ddosbarth i °lwyddo** = a
pleasant atmosphere must be ensured
if any class is to succeed

baban (*plural* **-od**) *noun, masculine*
= baby
**ewch i °weld ydy'r baban yn dal i
°gysgu** = go and see if the baby is still
asleep

bach *adjective, comparative* ⇒**llai**,
superlative ⇒**lleia(f)**
• = little; small
mae'r bocs yn rhy °fach = the box is
too small
⇒**bychan**
• (*as adjective modifier*) = a bit
**oedd e bach yn siomedig, dw i'n
credu** = he was a bit disappointed, I
think
• (*as term of endearment*) = dear
paid poeni, bach = don't worry, dear

bachgen (*plural* **bechgyn**) *noun,
masculine*
= boy
dau °fachgen sy gynnyn nhw = they've
got two boys
tybed lle bydd y bechgyn yn cysgu? =
I wonder where the boys will be
sleeping?

bai *noun, masculine*
• = blame; fault
ti sy ar °fai! = you are to blame!
• = trouble
**y bai yw °fod neb eisiau cymryd y
cyfrifoldeb** = the trouble is that no-one
wants to take the responsibility

baich (*plural* **beichiau**) *noun,
masculine*
= burden; load
**ar ysgwyddau rhywun arall bydd y
baich o hyn ymlaen** = someone else
will be shouldering the burden from
now on

balch *adjective*
= pleased, happy, glad (**o°** to)
**dyn ni'n °falch iawn o °gael eich
cwmni heno** = we are very glad to have
your company tonight

banc (*plural* **-iau**) *noun, masculine*
= bank

galwa i yn y banc ar y ffordd yn ôl = I'll
call at the bank on the way back

bant *adverb* (*South*)
= off; away
bant â ni! = off we go!
bydd y teulu bant dros y Sul = the
family will be away over the weekend
⇒**i ffwrdd**

bara *noun, masculine*
= bread
torth o °fara = a loaf of bread
tafell o °fara = a slice of bread
bara menyn = bread and butter

bardd (*plural* **beirdd**) *noun, masculine*
= poet, bard
gwlad beirdd a ʰchantorion = a land of
poets and singers

barn (*plural* **-au**) *noun, feminine*
= opinion
**beth yw'ch barn am y cynllun gwaith
newydd?** = what do you think about
the new work plan?

bath *noun, masculine*
• = bath
• ⇒**math**

bathodyn *noun, masculine*
= badge
**mi °gewch chi °fathodyn a ʰcherdyn
aelodaeth am °ddim** = you'll get a
badge and membership card free

baw *noun, masculine*
= muck; mud
Jac-codi-baw = JCB (*mechanical
excavator*)

bawd (*plural* **bodiau**) *noun, feminine*
= thumb
dw i wedi agor 'y ⁿmawd = I've cut my
thumb

be' *pronoun*
⇒**beth**

becso *verbnoun*
= worry; care
paid â becso! = don't worry!
**does neb yn becso dim am °bethau
felly dyddiau 'ma** = nobody cares a
damn about such things these days
⇒**poeni**

bechan
⇒**bychan**

bechgyn *plural of*
⇒**bachgen**

bedd (*plural* -**au**) *noun, masculine*
= grave
mae bedd un o'n gwleidyddion enwoca i'w weld rhywle yn y °fynwent 'ma = somewhere in this cemetery you can see the grave of one of our most famous politicians

beic (*plural* -**iau**) *noun, masculine*
= bicycle, bike
beic mynydd = mountain bike

beicio *verbnoun*
= ride a bike, cycle

beichiog *adjective*
= pregnant
°glywes i °fod dy chwaer yn °feichiog eto = I heard that your sister was pregnant again

beichiogrwydd *noun, masculine*
= pregnancy

beio *verbnoun*
= blame

beirdd *plural of*
⇒**bardd**

beirniadaeth *noun, feminine*
• = criticism
beirniadaeth °ddigon hallt a °ddaeth o °du'r bwrdd llywodraethol = quite harsh criticism came from the board of governors
• = adjudication
fe °gafwyd beirniadaeth °deg a ʰthrylwyr = we had a fair and thorough adjudication

beirniadu *verbnoun*
• = criticise
fe °gawson ni'n beirniadu am °fethu marchnata'r digwyddiadau'n °ddigonol = we were criticised for failing to market the events sufficiently
• = judge (*competition*)

bellach *adverb*
= now
bellach mae'n gweithio fel cynhyrchydd gyda ʰchwmni teledu annibynnol = now he works as a producer with an independent television company

gyrrwr lori o'n i am °bymtheng ⁿmlynedd, ond myfyriwr hŷn dw i **bellach** = I was a lorry driver for fifteen years, but now I'm a mature student
dw i °ddim yn byw yno bellach = I don't live there any more

> ❗ *This word is used for 'now' when there is some idea of a change in circumstances from what was previously the case—the first two examples above show this clearly, and while* ⇒**nawr**/⇒**rwan** *is not exactly wrong in these cases, the natural choice with native speakers is* **bellach**. *With negatives it means* '(not) any more', *as in the third example.*

bennu *verbnoun* (*South*)
= finish
wyt ti wedi bennu 'to? = have you finished yet?

> ❗ *This word is the general term for 'finish' in many Southern areas, while the standard language usually insists on* ⇒**gorffen**.

⇒**gorffen**, ⇒**cwpla**

benthyca *verbnoun*
= borrow; lend

benthyg *noun, masculine*
= loan
°ga i °fenthyg...? = can I borrow...?:
°ga i °fenthyg dy °feic am awr neu °ddwy? = can I borrow your bike for an hour or two?

ber
⇒**byr**

berwi *verbnoun*
• = boil
mae'r tegell yn berwi = the kettle is boiling
• (*figuratively*) = heave (*with people*)
oedd y lle 'ma'n berwi neithiwr = this place was heaving (with people) last night

beth? (*often* **be'?** *in normal speech*) *pronoun*
= what?
beth °ddigwyddodd? = what happened?
be' sy 'da ti fan'na? = what have you got there?

beth sy'n bod? = what's the matter?, what's up?

hidiwch be' fo! = never mind!

> ! *This question word is followed in the present tense (and **wedi-** perfect tense) by **ydy** in identification sentences, and otherwise **sy** when it is the subject and **mae** when the object of the sentence. Compare the following:*
>
> **beth ydy hwn?** = what is this? (*identification sentence*)
>
> **beth sy'n digwydd?** = what is happening? (**beth** *is subject*)
>
> **beth mae'ch brawd yn °wneud dyddiau 'ma?** = what is your brother doing these days? (**beth** *is the object,* **'ch brawd** *the subject*)

⇒**yr hyn**

beth bynnag *pronoun*

• = whatever

beth bynnag dych chi eisiau, ewch ag e nawr = whatever you want, take it now

• = in any case, anyway

bydd hi'n rhy hwyr erbyn hyn, beth bynnag = it'll be too late by now, anyway

⇒**bynnag**

beunyddiol *adjective*

= daily; everyday, day-to-day

rhaglen am °fywyd beunyddiol yn Sarajevo = a programme about day-to-day life in Sarajevo

byth a beunydd = forever and a day; all the time

biau *defective verb*

= own

pwy (sy) biau'r car coch 'na? = whose is that red car?

nhw (sy) biau fe = it's theirs ['They own it']

ⁿnhad oedd biau'r siop 'ma adeg hynny = my father owned this shop at that time

pwy °fydd biau'r hawliau cyhoeddi? = who will own the publishing rights?

> ! *This defective verb is used only in conjunction with the verb **bod**, and does not use the particle **yn** to link to **bod** as would be the case with normal verbnouns. See examples above. It is also unusual in that its subject always precedes it—because its function is to identify the possessor of something, it requires identification sentence structure instead of neutral verb-first order. The verb **sy** in the above examples is optional, since **biau** these days has acquired its own verbal force. So, for example, both **Pwy biau...?** and **Pwy sy biau...?** are heard, with no difference in meaning. In the other tenses (last two examples) the **oedd** and °**fydd** must be retained.*

bil (*plural* -iau) *noun, masculine*

= bill

mae'ch bil trydan yn dal heb ei °dalu = your electricity bill is still unpaid

blaen (*plural* -au) *noun, masculine*

• = front; fore

ar y blaen o hyd! = still at the forefront!

• (*as adjective*) = front

eisteddwch i gyd yn y rhes °flaen = all of you sit in the front row

⇒**o °flaen**, ⇒**o'r blaen**, ⇒**ymlaen**

blaendal (*plural* -iadau) *noun, masculine*

= (*monetary*) deposit

blaenoriaeth (*plural* -au) *noun, feminine*

= priority

rhaid inni °gael ein blaenoriaethau'n iawn = we must get our priorities right

blaenorol *adjective*

= previous; former

mae'r adroddiad ma'n °fwy beirniadol o °lawer na'r un blaenorol = this report is far more critical than the previous one

⇒**o'r blaen**, ⇒**cyn-°**

blaenwr (*plural* blaenwyr) *noun, masculine*

= forward (*in football, rugby*)

blaidd (*plural* bleiddiau *or* bleiddiaid) *noun, masculine*

= wolf

blas (*plural* -au) *noun, masculine*

= taste, flavour (**ar°** of)

dim ond rhyw °flas °ges i arno = I only got a little taste of it

blas ar °Gymru = a taste of Wales

blasus *adjective*

= tasty

ble? *adverb*
= where?
ble buoch chi trwy'r prynhawn? =
where have you been all afternoon?
**dyn ni eisiau gwybod ble a ʰphryd
°gaethoch chi'ch geni** = we want to
know where and when you were born

> **!** *This question word varies from
> region to region—**lle?** and °**le?** are
> widely used alternatives in many
> areas.* **Ble** *is regarded as standard,
> and is the norm in writing.* **Pa °le?** *is
> confined to formal writing.*

⇒**lle?**

bleiddiaid, bleiddiau *plural of*
⇒**blaidd**

blin *adjective*
= tiresome
mae'n °flin 'da fi (*South*) = I'm sorry

blinedig *adjective*
= tired
dw i'n teimlo braidd yn °flinedig = I'm
feeling rather tired
mae golwg blinedig iawn arnat ti = you
look very tired
⇒**blino**

blino *verbnoun*
= tire
wedi blino = tired
°**alla i °ddim dod nawr, dw i wedi blino**
= I can't come now, I'm tired

> **!** *Being a verbal phrase (particle* **wedi**
> *+ verbnoun) rather than a true
> adjective,* **wedi blino** *cannot be used
> when an adjective modifier (e.g.
> 'very', 'rather', 'too') is used with
> 'tired'—in these cases, the true
> adjective* ⇒**blinedig** *must be used
> instead.*

blodeuo *verbnoun*
= bloom, flower

blodyn (*plural* **blodau**) *noun, masculine*
= flower
on'd ydy'r blodau 'na'n °bert? = aren't
those flowers pretty?

blwch (*plural* **blychau**) *noun, masculine*
= box
**gofynnir i chi °roi tic yn y blwch
priodol** = you are requested to put a
tick in the appropriate box

**mae blwch pleidleisio ar y ffordd i
fyny i chi** = there's a ballot box on the
way up to you

blwydd
⇒**blwyddyn**

blwyddyn (*plural* **blynyddoedd,
blynyddau; blynedd, blwydd**)
noun, feminine
= year
⇒**blynyddol,** ⇒**eleni,** ⇒**llynedd**
See English-Welsh entry for examples

blynedd
⇒**blwyddyn**

blynyddol *adjective*
= annual
**mae disgwyl mai siomedig iawn °fydd
adroddiad blynyddol y cwmni eleni** =
the company's annual report is
expected to be a very disappointing
one this year

°**bob...**
⇒**pob**

bod 1 *verbnoun*
= be

> **!** ⇒**Bod** *box*

2 (*verbnoun functioning as conjunction*)
= that ... (is/are) etc.

> **!** *This special use of the verbnoun
> **bod** is required when the original
> sentence from which the subordinate
> clause has been derived begins, or
> began, with the present tense of
> **bod**— a common occurrence in
> Welsh. Note that, unlike a true
> conjunction, the **bod** forms combine
> the conjunction 'that' and the verb 'to
> be' in the one word. The personal
> pronoun variants are:* ʰ**mod i,** °**fod ti,**
> °**fod e, bod hi, bod ni, bod chi, bod
> nhw;** *a noun instead of a pronoun
> can take either **bod** or* °**fod:**
> **mae'n amlwg °fod rhywbeth o'i °le** =
> it's clear that something is wrong
> **cofia ʰmod i'n dod yfory** = remember
> that I am coming tomorrow
> **wyt ti'n meddwl bod hi'n iawn?** = do
> you think that she is right?
> **mae Ieuan yn honni °fod y
> cyfrifiadur °ddim yn gweithio'n
> iawn** = Ieuan claims that the
> computer is not working properly

Bod—'To Be'

Present and imperfect are anomalous and do not follow mutation principles for differentiation of affirmative, interrogative and negative:

PRESENT

present affirmative **dw i** (or **rwy**, or **wi**), **(r)wyt ti, mae e/hi, dyn ni** (South also **yn ni**, North **dan ni**), **dych chi** (North **dach chi**), **maen nhw**; present interrogative **ydw i?, wyt ti?, ydy e/hi?** (South also **yw e/hi?**), **ydyn ni?** (North **ydan ni?**), **(y)dych chi?** (North **(y)dach chi?**), **ydyn nhw?** (North **ydan nhw?**); negative **dw i ddim, (d)wyt ti ddim, dydy e/hi ddim** (South also **dyw e/hi ddim**, North also **tydy o/hi ddim**), **(dy)dyn ni ddim** (South also **yn ni ddim**, North also **(dy)dan ni ddim, (ty)dan ni ddim**), **dych chi ddim** (North also **dach chi ddim**), **(dy)dyn nhw ddim** (North also **(dy)dan nhw ddim, (ty)dan nhw ddim**).
ydw i'n hwyr? = *am I late?*
dydyn nhw °ddim fan hyn = *they are not here*
wyt ti o °ddifri? = *are you serious?*
mae e'n mynd = *he is going/he goes*
ydych chi'n dod neu °beidio? = *are you coming or not?*
(Literary Welsh forms of the present tense, sometimes encountered in more formal writing:
yr wyf, yr wyt, y mae, yr ydym, yr ydych, y maent)

present existential—three forms only (note no difference between singular and plural): affirmative **mae**, interrogative **oes**, negative **does dim**.
mae caws yn yr oergell = *there is cheese in the fridge*
mae anifeiliaid gwyllt fan hyn = *there are wild animals here*
oes caws yn yr oergell? = *is there cheese in the fridge?*
oes anifeiliaid gwyllt fan hyn? = *are there any wild animals here?*

does dim caws yn yr oergell = *there isn't any cheese in the fridge*
does dim anifeiliaid gwyllt fan hyn = *there are no wild animals here*

Some Southern areas have a special set of forms for the present negative of **bod**:
sa i, so ti, so fe, so hi, so ni, so chi, so nhw
or: **smo fi, smo ti, smo fe, smo hi, smo ni, smo chi, smo nhw**:
sa i'n gwybod = *I don't know* (= **dw i °ddim yn gwybod**)
smo fe'n siarad Cymraeg = *he doesn't speak Welsh* (= **dydy e °ddim yn siarad Cymraeg**)

Present + **wedi** (instead of **yn**):
mae e wedi mynd = *he has gone*
ydy e wedi mynd? = *has he gone?*
dydy e °ddim wedi mynd = *he hasn't gone*

In identification sentences, 3 singular present **mae** is replaced by **ydy/yw**, and 3 plural **maen** by **ydyn**:
cyfreithwyr yw'r °ddau = *they are both lawyers*
pwy ydyn nhw? = *who are they?*
In sentences where **mae** would be preceded by its own subject, a special form **sy** (or **sydd**) is used instead:
fe sy'n °gyfrifol am hyn = *he is responsible for this*
This form also serves as a relative, meaning 'who is/are...':
dyma'r °bobol sy'n helpu ni = *these are the people who are helping us*

IMPERFECT

(standard and written):
affirmative **roeddwn i, roeddet ti, roedd e/hi, roedden ni, roeddech chi, roedden nhw**; interrogative **oeddwn i?, oeddet ti?, oedd e/hi?, oedden ni?, oeddech chi?, oedden nhw?**; negative **doeddwn i ddim, doeddet ti ddim**,

continued overleaf

Bod—'To be' continued

---

doedd e/hi ddim, doedden ni ddim, doeddech chi ddim, doedden nhw ddim

(colloquial):
affirmative and interrogative **o'n i, o't ti, oedd e/hi, o'n ni, o'ch chi, o'n nhw;** negative **o'n i ddim, o't ti ddim** etc, or **do'n i ddim, do't ti ddim** etc
o'n nhw gartre? = were they at home?
o'n i ddim gartre ar y pryd = I wasn't at home at the time

Imperfect + **wedi** gives pluperfect:
o'n nhw wedi cytuno'n °barod = they had already agreed
o'n nhw wedi cytuno? = had they agreed?
do'n nhw °ddim wedi cytuno = they hadn't agreed

PRETERITE

The preterite is slightly anomalous:
preterite **bues i, buest ti** or **buost ti, buodd e/hi** or **bu e/hi, buon ni, buoch chi, buon nhw**
ble buoch chi trwy'r prynhawn? = where have you been all afternoon?
°fuest ti yng ⁿNghanada erioed? = have you ever been to Canada?

Other tenses behave as ordinary inflected verbs:

FUTURE AND PRESENT HABITUAL

bydda i, byddi di, bydd e/hi, byddwn ni, byddwch chi, byddan nhw
bydda i yn ôl ymhen awr = I'll be back in an hour
°fyddi di yno? = will you be there?
°fydda i byth yn sâl = I'm never ill
weithiau bydda i'n mynd am °dro cyn swper = sometimes I go for a walk before supper

CONDITIONAL

byddwn i, byddet ti, byddai fe/hi, bydden ni, byddech chi, bydden nhw or: **(ba)swn i, (ba)set ti, (ba)sai fe/hi, (ba)sen ni, (ba)sech chi, (ba)sen nhw**
mi °fyddai dealltwriaeth o'r iaith °Gymraeg yn °fanteisiol = an understanding of the Welsh language would be advantageous
sai lot mwy o °bobol wedi cael eu lladd tasen ni °ddim wedi bod yma = a lot more people would have been killed if we had not been here
bydd safon ei gwaith °bob tro yn uchel iawn = the standard of her work is always very high
sai hynny'n neis iawn, on' basai? = that would be very nice, wouldn't it?

---

mae'n ymddangos bod nhw °ddim yn °barod = it appears that they are not ready
°glywes i fod Eleri'n sâl = I heard that Eleri was ill
In the last example above, the sequence of tenses in English obscures the fact that what the speaker actually heard at the time was: **mae Eleri'n sâl** 'Eleri is ill'.
➡**y** conjunction, **mai, taw, na**ʰ/°

bodio verbnoun
= hitchhike

bodlon adjective
= willing; satisfied, happy (**â**ʰ with)

dych chi'n °fodlon dod yn ôl nes ymlaen? = are you willing to come back later on?
o'n nhw ddim yn °fodlon â'r trefniadau am °ryw °reswm = they weren't happy with the arrangements for some reason

bodloni verbnoun
= make do (**ar**° with)

bodd noun
wrth 'y ⁿmodd = in my element
wrth ei °fodd = in his element
wrth ei bodd = in her element
dw i wrth 'y ⁿmodd fan hyn = I'm in my element here

mae hi wrth ei bodd yn trefnu popeth
= she's in her element [when she's]
organizing everything

boddhaol *adjective*
= satisfactory
**dyw'r adroddiad 'ma °ddim yn
°foddhaol o °bell ffordd** = this report
is by no means satisfactory

boddi *verbnoun*
= drown; immerse
**mae eisiau boddi'ch hunan yn yr iaith
a'i diwylliant** = you need to immerse
yourself in the language and its
culture

bol (*plural* **-iau**), **bola** (*plural* **boliau**)
noun, masculine
= belly, stomach, tummy
ydy dy °fola'n rhoi dolur o °gwbwl? =
does your tummy hurt at all?
**dw i wedi cael llond bol(a) o'r dadlau
dibaid 'ma** = I've had it up to here with
this constant arguing

bôn *noun, masculine*
= base
yn y bôn = basically
**yn y bôn mae hyn yn °broblem
meddalwedd** = basically this is a
software problem

bord *noun, feminine* (*South*)
= table
⇒**bwrdd**

bore (*plural* **-au**) *noun, masculine*
= morning
bore da! = good morning!
bore fory = tomorrow morning

braf *adjective, comparative often*
brafiach
= fine, nice (*weather*)
mae'n braf bore 'ma, on'd ydy? = it's
fine this morning, isn't it?
**mae'n brafiach heddiw nag y bu hi
trwy'r wythnos** = it's nicer today than
it's been all week

> **!** *Usually this word is not susceptible
> to soft mutation—so* **mae'n braf**
> *rather than* **mae'n °fraf**, *although the
> latter is heard in some regions.*

braich (*plural* **breichiau**) *noun,*
feminine
= arm

mi °dorrodd ei braich = she broke her
arm
**mi aeth y °ddwy °fraich ym ⁿmraich i
lawr y stryd** = the two of them went
arm in arm down the street
⇒**cesail**

braidd *adverb*
= rather
ti'n edrych braidd yn °flinedig = you're
looking rather tired
**a dweud y gwir, oedd y prisiau'n uchel
braidd** = actually, the prices were
rather high

> **!** *This qualifier can come either before
> or after the adjective; if before, it must
> also precede a predicative* **yn°**—
> *compare for example* ⇒**tra,** ⇒**mor°,**
> ⇒**rhy°**

brain *plural of*
⇒**brân**

brân (*plural* **brain**) *noun, feminine*
= crow
mor ddu â'r °frân = as black as a crow
gwyn y gwêl y °frân ei ʰchyw (*proverb*)
= all mothers see the best in their
children (*literally:* the crow sees her
chicks as white)

bras *adjective*
• = rough, approximate
**°ellwch chi °ddweud yn °fras faint
°fydd angen?** = can you say roughly
how much will be needed?
llythyren bras = capital letter
**cofiwch °ddefnyddio llythrennau bras
wrth °gwblhau'r ffurflen hon** =
remember to use capital letters in
completing this form

braslun (*plural* **-iau**) *noun, masculine*
= outline; sketch

brathu *verbnoun* (*North*)
= bite (*usually of animals*)
ydy'r ci 'na'n brathu? = does that dog
bite?
⇒**cnoi**

brawd (*plural* **brodyr**) *noun, masculine*
= brother
dych chi'n nabod ⁿmrawd i? = do you
know my brother?
**faint o °frodyr a chwiorydd sy gynno
fo?** = how many brothers and sisters
has he got?

brawddeg (*plural* **-au**) *noun, feminine*
= sentence
**ailysgrifennwch y brawddegau
anghywir** = rewrite the incorrect
sentences

brecwast *noun, masculine*
= breakfast
**be' °gaethoch chi i °frecwast bore
'ma?** = what did you have for breakfast
this morning?

brech *noun, feminine*
= pox
y °frech °goch = measles
brech yr ieir or **y °frech ieir** =
chickenpox
y °frech Almaenig or **y °frech °goch
°fach** = German measles
y °frech °wen = smallpox
**mae'r °frech °goch arni ers dydd
Llun** = she's had measles since Monday

> **!** *These terms, since they denote
> temporary physical states, use* **ar°**
> *'on' with the person affected;* ⇒**ar°**

brechdan (*plural* **-au**) *noun, feminine*
= sandwich
**brechdanau ffres ar °gael fan hyn
°bob bore** = fresh sandwiches
available here every morning

brechiad (*plural* **-au**) *noun, masculine*
= inoculation, vaccination

brechu *verbnoun*
= inoculate, vaccinate

brenhines (*plural* **breninesau**) *noun,
feminine*
= queen
brenhinoedd a breninesau Lloegr =
the kings and queens of England

brenhinoedd *plural of*
⇒**brenin**

brenhinol *adjective*
= royal

brenin (*plural* **brenhinoedd**) *noun,
masculine*
= king
etholwyd Harold yn °frenin Lloegr =
Harold was elected king of England

breninesau *plural of*
⇒**brenhines**

brest *noun, feminine*
= chest
**fe °gafodd y trydydd dyn anafiadau i'w
°frest** = the third man received
injuries to his chest

breuddwyd (*plural* **-ion**) *noun,
masculine or feminine*
= dream
**fe °fu'n °freuddwyd ganddi ers tair
blynedd** = it has been a dream of hers
for three years

breuddwydio *verbnoun*
= dream
mae'n °debyg mai breuddwydio o'n i =
I must have been dreaming

brifo *verbnoun*
= hurt; wound
lle mae'n brifo? = where does it hurt?
mae ei ʰtheimladau wedi'u brifo = her
feelings have been hurt
⇒**dolur**

bro (*plural* **-ydd**) *noun, feminine*
= region

> **!** *The phrase* **y °Fro °Gymraeg**, *or
> often simply* **y °Fro**, *is used to mean
> 'Welsh-speaking Wales', ie the
> heartlands of the country where the
> language maintains a strong
> presence as the main medium of
> communication in everyday life.*

⇒**ardal**

brodor (*plural* **-ion**) *noun, masculine*
= native (**o°** of)
brodor o °Lanelli yw awdur y llyfr hwn
= the author of this book is a native of
Llanelli

brodyr *plural of*
⇒**brawd**

broga (*plural* **-od**) *noun, masculine*
= frog
⇒**llyffant**

bron
1 *adverb*
= almost; nearly
mae hi bron yn wyth o'r °gloch = it's
almost eight o'clock
**nawr bod ein taith gyda'n gilydd bron
ar °ben, mae'n amser ffarwelio** = now
that our journey together is almost
over, it's time to say goodbye

oedd bron iawn inni °dynnu'r cynnig yn ôl = we very nearly withdrew the offer

roedd e bron â ʰchrio = he was almost crying

> **!** Like ⇒**braidd**, the qualifier **bron** precedes predicative **yn°**. Notice in the last but one example that, when used of a past action, **bron** requires **i** + [person] + °verbnoun.

2 (plural **-nau**) noun, feminine
= breast

brwd adjective
= keen; enthusiastic
mae'r gwaith dysgu'n °galed, ond o °leia mae'r myfyrwyr yn °frwd = the learning is hard, but at least the students are keen
⇒**awyddus**

brwdfrydedd noun, masculine
= enthusiasm

brwdfrydig adjective
= enthusiastic

brwnt adjective (South)
= dirty
⇒**bud(u)r**

brwydr (plural **-au**) noun, feminine
= battle
trechwyd y Sacsoniaid mewn brwydr °waedlyd yn Hastings = the Saxons were defeated in a bloody battle at Hastings

brwydro verbnoun
= fight; struggle

bryn (plural **-iau**) noun, masculine
= hill
mae'r adran wedi symud lan y bryn yn °ddiweddar = the department has recently moved up the hill
⇒**mynydd, rhiw**

brys
gwasanaethau brys plural noun = emergency services
⇒**ar °frys**

brysio verbnoun
= hurry
brysiwch, neu mi °fyddwn ni'n colli'r trên! = hurry, or we'll miss the train!
bydd rhaid iddyn nhw °frysio, on' bydd? = they'll have to hurry, won't they?

buan adjective
gwella'n °fuan! = get well soon!
tair drama arbennig yn dod yn °fuan i °Ddyfed a ʰPhowys = three special plays coming soon to Dyfed and Powys

buchod plural of
⇒**buwch**

bud(u)r adjective (North)
= dirty
⇒**brwnt**

budd noun, masculine
= benefit; profit
tybed a °fydd y trefniadau newydd o °fudd inni yng ⁿNghymru? = I wonder if the new arrangements will be of benefit to us in Wales?
budd-dâl diweithdra = unemployment benefit
⇒**lles**

buddsoddi verbnoun
= invest
mae eisiau i'r llywodraeth °fuddsoddi yn ein rheilffyrdd = the government needs to invest in our railways

buddsoddiad (plural **-au**) noun, masculine
= investment

buddugol adjective
= victorious

buddugoliaeth (plural **-au**) noun, feminine
= victory
mae'r holl °gonsesiynau yn dilyn buddugoliaethau ym maes darlledu = all the concessions follow on from victories in the field of broadcasting

busnes (plural **-au**) noun, masculine
= business
busnesau lleol °fydd yn diodde °gynta = it is local businesses that will suffer first

busnesa verbnoun
= interfere; stick one's nose in
paid busnesa! = mind your own business!

buwch (plural **buchod**) noun, feminine
= cow
faint o °fuchod sy gynnoch chi erbyn hyn? = how many cows have you got now?
⇒**gwartheg**

bwlch (*plural* **bylchau**) *noun, masculine*
= gap
chwilio am °fwlch yn y °farchnad dw i
= I'm looking for a gap in the market
**llenwch y bylchau yn y brawddegau
canlynol** = fill in the gaps in the
following sentences

bwrdd (*plural* **byrddau**) *noun,
masculine*
= table
rhowch y papurau ar y bwrdd = put
the papers on the table
⇒**bord**

bwriad (*plural* **-au**) *noun, masculine*
= intention; purpose; aim
**beth yn union oedd ei bwriad wrth
°fynd yn °gyhoeddus fel hyn?** = what
exactly was her intention in going
public like this?
o °fwriad = on purpose, intentionally
fe °lunies i'r cwestiwn felly o °fwriad =
I intentionally phrased the question
so
⇒**nod**

bwriadol *adjective*
= deliberate; purposeful
nest ti hynny'n °fwriadol! = you did
that on purpose!
⇒**pwrpasol,** ⇒**anfwriadol**

bwriadu *verbnoun*
= intend
**beth dych chi'n bwriadu °wneud
nawr?** = what do you intend to do
now?

bwrw *verbnoun*
• = strike; beat
lloches i °fenywod sy'n cael eu bwrw =
a shelter for battered women
• (*precipitation*)
mae'n bwrw eira = it's snowing
mae'n bwrw glaw = it's raining

bws (*plural* **bysiau**) *noun, masculine*
= bus
pryd mae'r bws nesa'n dod? = when
does the next bus come?
safle bysiau = bus stop

bwthyn (*plural* **bythynnod**) *noun,
masculine*
= cottage
**mae gynnyn nhw °fwthyn bach yng
ⁿNgorllewin Iwerddon** = they've got a
little cottage in the West of Ireland

bwyd (*plural* **-ydd**) *noun, masculine*
= food
**heb °olau a gwres byddai'r °gadwyn
°fwyd yn torri** = without light and heat
the food chain would break
bwydydd wedi'u rhewi = frozen foods

> **!** *The phrase* **eisiau bwyd** (*'need of
> food'*) *is used for hunger; being a
> temporary physical state, it requires*
> **ar°** *with the person* (⇒**ar°**):
> **oes eisiau bwyd arnoch chi?** = are
> you hungry?

bwydlen (*plural* **-ni**) *noun, feminine*
= menu
°gawn ni °weld y °fwydlen? = can we
see the menu?

bwydo *verbnoun*
= feed
dw i heb °fwydo'r anifeiliaid = I haven't
fed the animals

bwyta *verbnoun*
= eat
mi °fwytodd e °bopeth = he ate
everything
mae e heb °fwyta dim ers bore ddoe =
he hasn't eaten anything since
yesterday morning

> **!** *This verb is usually pronounced* **bita**
> (*etc*) *in normal speech* (*so, for
> example,* **°fitodd, °fita** *above*).

bwyty (*plural* **bwytai**) *noun, masculine*
= restaurant; café

bychan *adjective* (*feminine* **bechan,**
plural **bychain**)
= small, little; slight
datblygiad ar °raddfa °fechan = a
small-scale development
bu cynnydd bychan dros yr Haf =
there has been a slight increase over
the summer

> **!** *This word is preferred in certain
> instances where its more common
> part-synonym* **bach** *has an idiomatic
> use, notably* **tŷ bychan** *small house
> vs* **tŷ bach** (*euphemism for*) *toilet.*

⇒**bach,** ⇒**mân**

bychanu *verbnoun*
= belittle

byd *noun, masculine*
= world; earth
y byd o'n cwmpas = the world about us
mae nifer o asiantaethau dros y byd yn chwilio am °beryglon tebyg o'r gofod = a number of agencies across the world are looking for similar dangers from space
beth yn y byd sy'n digwydd fan hyn? = what on earth is going on here?
⇨**daear**, ⇨**dim byd**

byd-enwog *adjective*
= world-famous

bydd, bydd-
⇨**bod**

byddar *adjective*
• = deaf
roedd ei ʰthad wedi bod yn °fyddar iawn ers blynyddoedd = her father had been very deaf for years
• (*as plural noun* **byddariaid**) = deaf people

byddin (*plural* **-oedd**) *noun, feminine*
= army
eu rhoi nhw yn y °fyddin sy eisiau = they need putting in the army

bygwth (*stem* **bygyth-**) *verbnoun*
= threaten, menace
mae'r awdurdod lleol yn bygwth mynd â'r mater ymhellach = the local authority is threatening to take the matter further

bygythiad (*plural* **-au**) *noun, masculine*
= threat

bygythiol *adjective*
= threatening, menacing

bynnag *particle*
= -ever

> **!** *This word exists as a particle in the modern language, and is attached to question words—it alters their meaning from interrogative to indefinite, characterised in English by the addition of '-ever'. So, for example,* **pwy?** *who?,* **pwy bynnag** whoever.
> **beth bynnag dych chi eisiau, ewch ag e nawr** = whatever you want, take it now

pwy bynnag ydyn nhw, dw i ddim eisiau gweld nhw = whoever they are, I don't want to see them
faint bynnag sy'n dod, rhaid edrych yn °ofalus ar °bob tocyn = however many are coming, every ticket must be carefully checked
byddwn ni'n ffeindio chi, lle bynnag byddwch chi wedi'ch cuddio = we'll find you, wherever you're hidden.
na i °drio ateb pa °gwestiynau bynnag sy gyda chi = I'll try and answer whatever questions you have
⇨**beth bynnag**, ⇨**pwy bynnag**
⇨**beth?**, ⇨**faint?**, ⇨**lle?**, ⇨**pa°?**, ⇨**pwy?**

byr *adjective*
(*feminine* **ber**, *plural* (*rare*) **byrion**)
= short
gwobr am stori °fer yn y °Gymraeg = a prize for a short story in Welsh
rhaid edrych yn °fanwl ar yr effeithiau cyfnod byr hefyd = the short-term effects must also be closely looked at

byrder
⇨**ar °fyrder**

byrhau *verbnoun*
= shorten

bys (*plural* **-edd**) *noun, masculine*
= finger
dw i wedi agor 'y ⁿmys = I've cut my finger
dangos dy °fysedd! = show (me) your fingers!
bys troed (*plural* **bysedd traed**) = toe

bysiau *plural of*
⇨**bws**

byth *adverb*
• = never
dw i byth yn gweld nhw dyddiau 'ma = I never see them these days
o'n i byth yn gweld nhw °bryd hynny = I never used to see them then
anghofia i byth! = I'll never forget!
• = ever
Cymru am byth! = Wales forever!

> **!** *This word means 'never' or 'ever' according to context. However, it is restricted in use to* **yn** *tenses and the future.*

⇨**erioed**, ⇨**fyth**

bythynnod *plural of*
⇨**bwthyn**

byw*
1 *verbnoun*
= live
pwy oedd yn byw drws nesa ar y pryd, 'te? = who lived next door at the time, then?
mae'r tai yn dal i'w gweld, ond does neb yn byw ynddyn nhw ers blynyddau = the houses are still to be seen, but no-one has lived in them for years
2 *adjective*
= live (*broadcast etc*)
yn °fyw o °Faes yr Eisteddfod = live from the Eisteddfod field

bywiog *adjective*
= lively

bywiogi *verbnoun*
= enliven, liven up

bywoliaeth *noun, feminine*
= living, livelihood
sut mae e'n ennill ei °fywoliaeth? = how does he earn his living?

Cc

cacen (*plural* **-nau**) *noun, feminine*
= cake
siop °gacennau = cake shop
⇨**teisen**

cadair (*plural* **cadeiriau**) *noun, feminine*
= chair
mae eisiau symud y cadeiriau 'ma i gyd = all these chairs need moving

cadarn *adjective*
= firm, fast
mae'n °bryd inni sefyll yn °gadarn = it is time for us to stand firm

cadarnhau (*stem* **cadarnha-**) *verbnoun*
= make firm; confirm
fe °gadarnhaodd y cwmni nad oedden nhw wedi meddwl am syniad o'r °fath = the company confirmed that they had not thought about such an idea

cadeirydd (*plural* **-ion**) *noun, masculine*
= chairman/chairwoman

cadno (*plural* **-id**) *noun, masculine* (*South*)
= fox
⇨**llwynog**

cadoediad (*plural* **-au**) *noun, masculine*
= ceasefire
mae ofn na °all y cadoediad °bara'n hir = there is a fear that the ceasefire cannot last long

cadw (*stem* **cadw-**) *verbnoun*
• = keep
°gadwn ni'r rhain i ti, 'te = we'll keep these for you, then
neith mêl °ddim cadw = honey will not keep
dw i °ddim eisiau'ch cadw chi = I don't want to keep you
cadwch draw! = keep away!
• = preserve
byddai system fel hyn yn cadw'r elfen °ddemocrataidd = a system like this

would preserve the democratic element

⇒**ar °gadw**

cadwyn (*plural* **-i, -au**) *noun, feminine*
= chain (*also figurative*)
heb °olau a gwres byddai'r °gadwyn °fwyd yn torri = without light and heat the food chain would break

cae (*plural* **-au**) *noun, masculine*
= field
fe °werthon ni'r cae 'na °flwyddyn yn ôl = we sold that field a year ago

cael *verbnoun* (*irregular*)
preterite **ces i, cest ti, cafodd e/hi, cawson ni, cawsoch chi, cawson nhw**
common variants: 3singular **caeth, cas,** *1plural* **caethon, cafon,** *2plural* **caethoch, cafoch,** *3plural* **caethon, cafon**
future **ca i, cei di, ceith e/hi, cawn ni, cewch chi, cân nhw**
common variants: 3singular **caiff,** *1plural* **cewn**
conditional (*of restricted use in the modern language*) **celwn i, celet ti, celai fe/hi, celen ni, celech chi, celen nhw**
or **cawn i, caet ti, câi fe/hi, caen ni, caech chi, caen nhw**
autonomous/impersonal forms: present/future **ceir,** *past* **cafwyd**
• = get, receive; have (*where this means 'get', 'receive'*)
dw i'n cael grawnffrwyth i °frecwast °bob bore = I have grapefruit for breakfast every morning
be' °gest ti i Nadolig? = what did you get for Christmas?
°ga i °bwys o °gaws? = can I have a pound of cheese?
cafodd y plant °ganiatâd i °fynd = the children got permission to go
ceir sesiwn hyfforddi tiwtoriaid prynhawn dydd Sadwrn = there will be a tutor training session on Saturday afternoon
cafwyd ymateb da = a good response was had
• = be allowed to
ond °ga i °ddeud un peth? = but can I say one thing?
cafodd y plant °fynd = the children were allowed to go

ydyn ni'n cael gweld y ffilm heno? = are we allowed to see the film tonight?
arhoswch i mi °gael meddwl = let me think
dere i mi °gael gweld = come here so I can see
°gawn ni °weld = we'll see
• = get (someone to do something)
mae'n anodd cael iddi °ddeall = it's difficult to get her to understand
• = have/get (something done)
mae Dafydd wedi cael torri ei °wallt = Dafydd has had his hair cut
mae eisiau i ti °gael atgyweirio'r oriawr 'na, on'd oes? = you need to get that watch repaired, don't you?
• (*forming the passive—in this use it is followed by a possessive adjective + verbnoun of the action involved*)
= be
°gest ti dy °dalu? = were you paid?
cafodd tri o °bobol eu hanafu = three people were injured
lle a ʰphryd °gawsoch chi'ch geni? = where and when were you born?
basai fo wedi cael ei °ddiswyddo = he would have been sacked
oedd y tŷ 'ma'n cael ei °godi ar y pryd = this house was being built at the time
mi °geith y siop ei ʰchau am y tro ola yfory = the shop will be closed for the last time tomorrow

cael hyd i°
= find
nes i °fethu cael hyd iddo = I couldn't find it
⇒**dod o hyd i°, ffeindio**

cangen (*plural* **canghennau**) *noun, feminine*
= branch (*also figurative*)
mae peiriannau hefyd ar °gael yn y canghennau canlynol = machines are also available at the following branches

cais (*plural* **ceisiadau**) *noun, masculine*
• = attempt; = try
tri ʰchais i °Gymro = three tries for a Welshman
• = application
anfonwch am ffurflen °gais nawr! = send for an application form now!

roedden nhw wedi gwneud cais am
°gymorth ariannol = they had made
an application for financial help
⇒ymgais

caled *adjective*
comparative **caletach** *superlative*
caleta(f)
= hard (*also figurative*)
**mae'r gwaith yn rhy °galed i °rywun o
dy oedran di** = the work is too hard for
someone of your age

calon (*plural* **-nau**) *noun, feminine*
= heart
mi °gafodd e °drawiad ar y °galon = he
had a heart attack
diolch o °galon! = heartfelt thanks!

call *adjective*
= wise (*usually in the sense of
possessing knowledge*)
dyn ni °fawr callach = we're none the
wiser

cam (*plural* **-au**) *noun, masculine*
= step
ymuno â dosbarth yw'r cam cynta =
joining a class is the first step

cam- *verb prefix*
= mis-; wrongly

camarwain (*stem* **camarweini-**)
verbnoun
= mislead
⇒arwain

camarweiniol *adjective*
= misleading
**mae'r adroddiad 'na'n °gamarweiniol
braidd** = that report is rather
misleading

camdreiglo *verbnoun*
= wrongly apply (grammatical)
mutation, apply wrong mutation.
⇒treiglo

camdrin (*stem* **camdrini-**) *verbnoun*
= mistreat
**mae ffermwr o °Bonteglwys wedi'i
°gyhuddo o °gamdrin anifeiliaid** = a
farmer from Ponteglwys has been
accused of mistreating animals
⇒trin

camddeall *verbnoun*
= misunderstand
dych chi wedi ⁿnghamddeall, dw i'n

meddwl = you have misunderstood
me, I think
⇒deall

camera (*plural* **camerâu**) *noun,
masculine*
= camera
**rho ffilm newydd yn 'y ⁿnghamera i mi,
nei di?** = put a new film in my camera
for me, will you?

camgymeriad (*plural* **-au**) *noun,
masculine*
= mistake
**rhaid inni °gyfadde °fod
camgymeriadau wedi'u gwneud** = we
have to admit that mistakes have been
made
⇒gwall

camp (*plural* **-au**) *noun, feminine*
= feat, achievement
oedd hynny'n °dipyn o °gamp! = that
was quite an achievement!

campus *adjective*
= excellent, splendid (*also as
interjection*)

camymddwyn *verbnoun*
= misbehave; (*as noun*) misbehaviour
**mae gormod o °gamymddwyn wedi
bod yn °ddiweddar** = there's been too
much misbehaviour lately
⇒ymddwyn

can *numeral*
⇒can(t)

cân (*plural* **caneuon**) *noun, feminine*
= song
**roedd hi'n canu caneuon pop pan
oedd hi'n °fis oed** = she was singing
pop songs when she was a month old
maen nhw wedi newid eu cân = they've
changed their tune

caniad (*plural* **-au**) *noun, masculine*
= phone call, ring
rho °ganiad inni wythnos nesa = give
us a ring next week

caniatâd *noun, masculine*
= permission
**mae modd apelio yn erbyn caniatâd
cynllunio** = one can appeal against
planning permission

caniataol *adjective*
cymryd yn °ganiataol = take for
granted, assume

bydda i'n cymryd yn °ganiataol na °fydd y dosbarth yn parhau am °dymor arall = I will assume that the class will not be continuing for another term

caniatáu *verbnoun*
= permit, allow
°allwn ni °ddim caniatáu i hyn °ddigwydd eto = we cannot allow this to happen again

canlyniad (*plural* **-au**) *noun, masculine*
= result
oes unrhywun fan hyn yn gwybod y canlyniad? = does anyone here know the result?
o °ganlyniad = as a result, consequently

canlynol *adjective*
= following; ...which follows/follow
cyfieithwch y brawddegau canlynol = translate the following sentences

canllaw (*plural* **-iau**) *noun, masculine or feminine*
= handrail; (*figurative*) guideline
dyma'r canllawiau y dylid eu dilyn wrth °baratoi erthygl = these are the guidelines that should be followed in preparing an article

canmlwyddiant *noun, masculine*
= centenary
mae'n braf cael eich croesawu fan hyn i °ddathlu canmlwyddiant ein mudiad = it's nice to be able to welcome you here to celebrate our movement's centenary

canmol *verbnoun*
= praise
rhaid canmol y plant am eu gwaith eleni = the children are to be praised for their work this year

cannoedd *plural of*
⇒**cant**

canol (*plural* **-au**) *noun, masculine*
• = centre
maen nhw'n byw mewn fflat yng °nghanol y °dre = they live in a flat in the town centre
• = middle
rhowch y lleill yn y canol = put the others in the middle

canolbarth *noun, masculine*
= central region

o °ganolbarth Lloegr mae °nheulu'n dod yn °wreiddiol = my family come from the Midlands (of England) originally

canolbwyntio *verbnoun*
= concentrate (*attention, etc*) (**ar°** on)
dw i eisiau i chi °ganolbwyntio ar y °broblem = I want you to concentrate on the problem
roedd y rhaglen °deledu wedi canolbwyntio ar achos gwraig o'i etholaeth = the television programme had concentrated on the case of a woman from his constituency

canolfan (*plural* **-nau**) *noun, feminine*
= centre (*building*)
cofiwch °alw yn ein canolfannau croeso = remember to call at our reception centres

canolig *adjective*
= medium, middling
maint oedolion: Canolig/Mawr/Mawr lawn = adult sizes: Medium/Large/Extra Large

canolog *adjective*
= central
dyw'r gwres canolog °ddim yn gweithio'n iawn = the central heating isn't working properly

canolwr (*plural* **canolwyr**) *noun, masculine*
= referee; arbitrator
dw i wedi rhoi'ch enw i lawr fel canolwr = I've put your name down as a referee *or* for a reference

canrif (*plural* **-oedd**) *noun, feminine*
= century
°dair canrif yn °ddiweddarach, mae dramâu Molière yn dal i °lwyddo = three centuries on, Molière's plays are still a success
gwahanol iawn oedd y sefyllfa yn y °ganrif °ddiwetha = the situation was very different in the last century

can(t) (*plural* **cannoedd**) *numeral (masculine)*
= a hundred

! *The shorter form* **can** *is used with a directly following singular noun, cf* ⇒**chwe(ch)**, ⇒**pum(p)**. *However, this usage is confined these days to set* *phrases, while the usual construction with this numeral is* **cant o°** + *plural noun.* **...y cant** *corresponds to* '...percent'. **Hanner can(t)** *is the normal term for 'fifty'.*

mae can punt/cant o °bunnoedd ar ôl = there's a hundred pounds left
mae'n amlwg °fod cannoedd o °filoedd o °bunnoedd wedi mynd ar °goll = it is obvious that hundreds of thousands of pounds have gone missing
roedd diweithdra wedi cyrraedd pedwardeg y cant mewn ardaloedd gwledig = unemployment had reached forty percent in rural areas
bydd e'n dathlu ei hanner cant wythnos nesa = he'll be celebrating his fiftieth next week
...mewn wythnos lle gwelwyd dros °gant a hanner o enillwyr = ...in a week which saw over a hundred and fifty winners

canu *verbnoun*
• = sing
noson o hwyl a ʰchanu = an evening of fun and singing
• (*of bell, phone*) = ring
dw i'n moyn gorffen y gwaith copïo 'ma cyn i'r °gloch °ganu = I want to finish this copying before the bell goes/rings

car (*plural* **ceir**) *noun, masculine*
= car
Dwyn Ceir yn Arafu = Car Thefts Drop
⇨**modur**

carchar *noun, masculine*
= prison
carchar i'r °wraig °gipiodd °faban o ysbyty = prison for the woman who snatched a baby from a hospital

carcharu *verbnoun*
= imprison

caredig *adjective*
= kind
'na °garedig! = how kind!
a °fyddai'n cwsmeriaid mor °garedig â dod â'u platiau'n ôl = would our customers be so kind as to bring their plates back?

cariad *noun, masculine*
• = love

dw i'n teimlo cymysgedd o °gariad ac atgasedd tuag ato = I feel a mixture of love and hate towards it
• (*plural* **-on**) = boyfriend/girlfriend
ydy Medi'n dod â'i ʰchariad newydd heno? = is Medi bringing her new boyfriend tonight?
• (*term of endearment*) = dear
beth sy'n bod, cariad? = what's the matter, dear?

cario *verbnoun*
= carry
mi °garia i'r rhain i ti = I'll carry these for you

carreg (*plural* **cerrig**) *noun, feminine*
= stone; rock
mae agor y °ganolfan newydd 'ma'n °garreg °filltir yn hanes ein cymuned = the opening of this new centre is a milestone in the history of our community
⇨**maen**

cartre(f) (*plural* **cartrefi**) *noun, masculine*
= home
mae'r adran wedi symud i'w ʰchartref newydd gyferbyn Neuadd y °Dre = the department has moved to its new home opposite the Town Hall
⇨**gartre(f)**, ⇨**ymgartrefu**, ⇨**aelwyd**

caru *verbnoun*
= love
wi'n dy °garu di = I love you

> **!** *This verb is also used in Southern areas with unreality endings to mean* would like, *and in this sense only is a synonym for* **hoffwn i** *and* **leiciwn i**:
> **be' °garet tithau °weud ar y pwnc 'ma, 'te?** = what would you like to say on this subject, then?

cas *adjective*
• = nasty (**wrth°** to)
oedd e'n °gas wrthat ti, 'te? = was he nasty to you, then?
• = °**gas gen i...** I hate... (*etc*)
°**gas gen i °fresych** = I hate cabbage

casáu *verbnoun*
= hate
mae'r °ddau'n casáu ei gilydd = they hate each other

casgliad (*plural* **-au**) *noun, masculine*
• = collection

mae gynno fo °gasgliad enfawr o
stampiau = he's got a huge stamp
collection
• = conclusion
   dw i wedi dod i'r casgliad °fod... = I've
   come to the conclusion that...

casglu *verbnoun*
• = collect; gather
   **o'n nhw'n casglu newyddion o °bob
   cwr o'r byd** = they collected/were
   collecting news from all over the
   world
• (*figurative*) = gather, conclude
   **dw i'n casglu o hyn, felly, bod chi'n
   bwriadu ymddiswyddo wedi'r cwbwl**
   = I gather from this, then, that you
   intend to resign after all

castell (*plural* **cestyll**) *noun, masculine*
• = castle
• (*chess*) = rook

cath (*plural* **-od**) *noun, feminine*
= cat

cau (*stem* **cae-**) *verbnoun*
= close, shut
   bydd y llyfrgell yn cau am °bump heno
   = the library will close at five this
   evening
   **fe °gaewyd y ffatri °ddechrau'r
   °flwyddyn** = the factory was closed at
   the beginning of the year
⇒**ar °gau**

cawl *noun, masculine*
= soup
(*figurative*) = a mess
   **maen nhw wedi gwneud cawl o'r peth
   'ma** = they've made a mess of this

cawod (*plural* **-ydd**) *noun, feminine*
= shower
   **...gydag ysbeidiau heulog a
   ʰchawodydd yma ac acw** = ...with
   sunny periods and scattered showers
   dw i eisiau cael cawod °gynta = I want
   to have a shower first
   °elli di °drwsio'r °gawod inni? = can
   you fix the shower for us?

caws *noun, masculine*
= cheese
   mae peth caws ar ôl yn yr oergell =
   there's a bit of cheese left in the fridge

cefn *noun, masculine*
= back

mae ⁿnghefn i'n rhoi dolur = my back is
hurting
rhowch eich bagiau yn y cefn = put
your bags in the back

cefnder (*plural* **cefndyr**) *noun,
masculine*
= (male) cousin
   mae'r dyn 'na'n °gefnder i mi = that
   man is my cousin
⇒**cyfnither**

cefndir (*plural* **-oedd**) *noun,
masculine*
= background
   **i °ddechrau, °allwch chi °ddweud
   rhywbeth wrthon ni am eich cefndir?**
   = to begin with, can you tell us
   something about your background?

cefn gwlad *noun, masculine*
= countryside, country (*as opposed to
town*)
   **theatr a °allai °deithio ar hyd
   ardaloedd diarffordd cefn gwlad
   Cymru** = a theatre that could travel all
   over the inaccessible areas of the
   Welsh countryside

cefnogaeth *noun, feminine*
= support

cefnogi *verbnoun*
= support
   dewch i'n cefnogi ni! = come and
   support us!

cefnogol *adjective*
= supportive

cefnu *verbnoun*
= turn one's back (**ar°** on)

ceffyl (*plural* **-au**) *noun, masculine*
= horse
   **beiciau mynydd a ʰcheffylau i'w llogi
   yn yr ardal** = mountain bikes and
   horses (available) to be hired in the
   area

ceg (*plural* **-au**) *noun, feminine*
= mouth
   ac fe agorodd y llew mwya ei °geg =
   and the biggest lion opened his mouth
   cau dy °geg! = shut your mouth!, shut
   up!

cegin (*plural* **-au**) *noun, feminine*
= kitchen

cer i eistedd yn y °gegin eiliad, nei di?
= go and sit in the kitchen for a
moment, will you?

ceidwadol *adjective*
= conservative
y °Blaid °Geidwadol = the Conservative
Party

Ceidwadwr (*plural* **Ceidwadwyr**)
noun, masculine
= Conservative
noson erchyll arall i'r Ceidwadwyr =
another horrible night for the
Conservatives

ceiniog (*plural* **-au**) *noun, feminine*
= penny; pence
dwy °bunt a hanner can ceiniog = two
pounds and fifty pence

ceir *plural of*
⇨**car**

ceisio *verbnoun*
= try
**fe °geisiwn ni °ddod yn ôl yr un adeg
wythnos i heddiw** = we'll try and come
back the same time a week today
**rhaid ceisio derbyn person fel ag y
mae** = one must try and accept a
person as they are

celf (*plural* **-au**) *noun, feminine*
= art; craft
gweithdy celf a ʰchrefft = arts and
crafts workshop

celfi *plural noun* (*South*)
= furniture
⇨**dodrefn**

celfyddyd (*plural* **-au**) *noun, feminine*
= art
Canolfan y Celfyddydau = the Arts
Centre

Celt (*plural* **-iaid**) *noun, masculine*
= Celt
**does neb yn sicr pryd daeth y Celtiaid
i °Brydain** = nobody is certain when
the Celts came to Britain

Celtaidd *adjective*
= Celtic

celwydd (*plural* **-au**) *noun, masculine*
(*plural often* **clwyddau** *in North*)
= lie
dweud clwyddau mae o = he's telling
lies

celwyddgi (*plural* **celwyddgwn**)
noun, masculine
= liar

cenedl (*plural* **cenhedloedd**) *noun,
feminine*
= nation
**a gobeithio nad ydyn nhw °ddim yn
ystyried ein bod yn °ddwy °genedl** =
and I hope they don't consider that we
are two nations
y Cenhedloedd Unedig = The United
Nations

cenedlaethol *adjective*
= national
Llyfrgell °Genedlaethol Cymru = the
National Library of Wales

cenedlaetholdeb *noun, masculine*
= nationalism

cenedlaetholwr (*plural*
cenedlaetholwyr) *noun, masculine*
= nationalist

cenhedlaeth (*plural* **cenedlaethau**)
noun, feminine
= generation

cenhedloedd *plural of*
⇨**cenedl**

cenhinen (*plural* **cennin**) *noun,
feminine*
= leek

cenllysg *plural noun* (*North*)
= hail
mae'n bwrw cenllysg = it's hailing
⇨**cesair**

cer
⇨**mynd**

cerbyd (*plural* **-au**) *noun, masculine*
= vehicle
anaddas i °gerbydau nwyddau trwm
= unsuitable for heavy goods vehicles

cerdyn (*plural* **cardiau**) *noun, masculine*
= card
**yn ni °ddim yn danfon cardiau Nadolig
eleni** = we're not sending Christmas
cards this year
ydy'ch cerdyn siec gyda chi? = have
you got your cheque card?
cerdyn aelodaeth = membership card
cerdyn datgelu = scratchcard
cerdyn post = postcard

cerdd (*plural* **-i**) *noun, feminine*
= poem

cyfrol o °gerddi = a volume of poems

cerdded (*stem* **cerdd-**) *verbnoun*
= walk
faint o °filltiroedd naethon nhw °gerdded? = how many miles did they walk?
dyw'r banc °ddim yn °bell–pum munud o °waith cerdded = the bank isn't far–five minutes' walk

Cernyweg *noun, feminine*
= Cornish language

cerrig *plural of*
⇒**carreg**

cesail *noun, feminine*
dan 'y ⁿnghesail = under my arm
dan ei °gesail = under his arm
dan ei ʰchesail = under her arm
a bant ag e, a'r mochyn dan ei °gesail = and off he went with the pig under his arm
⇒**braich**

cesair *plural noun (South)*
= hail
mae'n bwrw cesair = it's hailing
⇒**cenllysg**

cestyll *plural of*
⇒**castell**

cewyn (*plural* **-nau**) *noun, masculine (South)*
= nappy, diaper
nei di nôl cewyn i mi o'r stafell molchi, cariad? = will you fetch me a nappy from the bathroom, dear?

ci (*plural* **cŵn**) *noun, masculine*
= dog

cicio *verbnoun*
= kick
cafodd y °bêl ei ʰchicio dros yr ystlys = the ball was kicked into touch

ci defaid *noun, masculine (plural* **cŵn defaid**)
= sheepdog

cig *noun, masculine*
= meat
dan ni °ddim yn bwyta cig = we don't eat meat
cig eidion = beef
cig moch = bacon

cigydd (*plural* **-ion**) *noun, masculine*
= butcher

cinio *noun, masculine*
= lunch, dinner
mae cinio'n °barod = lunch is ready
ffoniwch fi eto amser cinio = phone me again at lunchtime
⇒**swper**

cipio *verbnoun*
• = seize, snatch
carchar i'r wraig °gipiodd faban o ysbyty = prison for the woman who snatched a baby from a hospital
• = capture
cipiwyd Lloegr gan y Normaniaid = England was captured by the Normans

cipolwg *noun, masculine*
= (quick) look; glance
°ga i °gipolwg? = can I have a look?

claddu *verbnoun*
= bury
mae'r hen °gi wedi'i °gladdu yn yr °ardd = the old dog's buried in the garden
⇒**palu**

claf (*plural* **cleifion**) *noun, masculine*
= patient
roedd rhaid i'r cleifion i gyd °gael eu symud = all the patients had to be moved

clasurol *adjective*
= classical
mi °dderbyniodd ei °dad addysg °glasurol = his father (had) received a classical education

clawr (*plural* **cloriau**) *noun, masculine*
= (book) cover
gweler hefyd llun y clawr blaen = see also front cover picture
mae'r llyfr hefyd ar °gael mewn cloriau meddal = the book is also available in paperback
clawr/cloriau caled = hardback
clawr/cloriau meddal = paperback

clefyd (*plural* **-au, -on**) *noun, masculine*
= disease
y Pla Du oedd y clefyd cyffwrdd gwaetha yn Ewrop erioed = the Black Death was the worst contagious disease ever in Europe

cleifion *plural of*
⇒**claf**

clem *noun, feminine*
= notion
does dim clem 'da fi = I've no idea, I haven't got a clue

clirio *verbnoun*
= clear
cliriwch y stafell 'ma cyn i chi °fynd! = clear this room before you go!

clo *noun, masculine*
= lock
mostly in phrases involving
rhoi (*stem* **rhoi-, rhodd-**) **... dan °glo** = put ... under lock
or **rhoi clo ar° ...** = put a lock on...
°ddylen ni °roi'r cwpwrdd dan °glo? = should we lock the cupboard?
cofiwch ei ʰchadw hi dan °glo °bob amser = remember to keep it locked at all times
⇒**ar °glo,** ⇒**cloi**

cloc (*plural* **-iau**) *noun, masculine*
= clock
mae'r cloc newydd °daro deuddeg = the clock has just struck twelve
mae'r cloc wedi sefyll = the clock has stopped
mae'r cloc ar ei hôl hi = the clock is slow
mae'r cloc yn ennill / mae'r cloc yn °fuan = the clock is fast
cloc larwm = alarm clock

cloch (*plural* **clychau**) *noun, feminine*
= bell
canwch y clychau! = ring the bells!
⇒**o'r °gloch**

cloi *verbnoun*
= lock
dach chi wedi cloi? = have you locked (up)?
⇒**ar °glo,** ⇒**clo**

clorian *noun, feminine*
= balance; scales

cloriannu *verbnoun*
= appraise; assess
ydy hi'n iawn inni °gloriannu'r gwaith 'ma cyn i'r ail °gyfrol ymddangos? = is it right for us to assess this work before the second volume has appeared?

clou *adjective* (*South*)
= quick

o'n i'n moyn gair bach clou 'da chi = I wanted a quick word with you
dewch yma, °glou! = come here, quick!

cludiant *noun, masculine*
• = transport
cludiant am °ddim = free transport
• = delivery
gan °gynnwys cludiant = including delivery

cludo *verbnoun*
= carry; transport
mae'r darnau'n llai, ac felly'n rhatach ac yn haws eu cludo = the pieces are smaller, and so cheaper and easier to transport

clust (*plural* **-iau**) *noun, feminine or masculine*
= ear
oedd clust °dost 'da fi trwy'r dydd ddoe = I had earache all day yesterday
dw i at 'y ⁿnghlustiau mewn papur = I'm up to my ears in paper

clustnodi *verbnoun*
= earmark
mae arian wedi'i °glustnodi'n °barod ar °gyfer y cynllun = money has already been earmarked for the scheme

clwt *noun, masculine*
ar y clwt = on the dole
ers pryd mae e ar y clwt bellach? = how long has he been on the dole now?

clwyddau *plural noun*
⇒**celwydd**

clymblaid (*plural* **clymbleidiau**) *noun, feminine*
= (political) coalition

clymu *verbnoun*
= tie, attach (**wrth°** to)
mae rhyw elfen °gyfrin sy'n °gryfach nag iaith yn eich clymu wrth °wlad = some mystic element which is stronger than language ties you to a country
⇒**ynghlwm**

clywed (*stem* **clyw-**) *verbnoun*
• = hear
°glywest ti'r newyddion? = did you hear/have you heard the news?

braf oedd clywed am eich llwyddiant!
= it was good to hear about your
success!
- • = smell
'na'r oglau °glywon ni ddoe! = there's
that smell we smelt yesterday!
- • = listen (*generally imperative only*)
clywch!–mae rhywun yn dod!
= listen!–someone's coming!
trwm ei °glyw = hard of hearing
(*masculine*)
trwm ei ʰchlyw = hard of hearing
(*feminine*)

cnoi *verbnoun*
= bite; chew
paid cnoi yn y dosbarth! = don't chew
in class!
⇒**brathu**

'co *adverb* (*South*)
= there; over there
'co fe! = there it is!

> **!** *This is the standard* ⇒**dacw°**, *and is
> widely used in Southern areas both
> for this and for* ⇒**dyna°** (*itself often
> shortened to* ⇒**'na°**)

coblyn *intensifier*
mae'n °goblyn o °beth = it's a hell of a
thing
mae o'n °goblyn o hen = he's awfully
old

coch *adjective* (*plural* (*rare, now mostly
in set phrases*) **cochion**)
= red
arhoswch fan hyn tra bod golau coch
= wait here when light is red
cyn °goched â gwaed = as red as blood

codi *verbnoun*
- • = rise
**mae prisiau tai wedi codi'n sylweddol
yn °ddiweddar** = house prices have
risen appreciably/substantially of late
- • = raise
maen nhw wedi codi'u prisiau = they
have raised their prices
- • = arise
mae dau °fater yn codi o hyn oll = two
matters arise from all this
- • = get up
pryd nest ti °godi bore 'ma? = when
did you get up this morning?
- • = charge

faint maen nhw'n °godi fan hyn? =
how much do they charge here?
- • = build
**wrth °gwrs °fod codi tai a ʰphontydd
°gryn °dipyn yn haws na ʰchodi
pontydd gwleidyddol** = of course,
building houses and bridges is quite a
bit easier than building political
bridges
⇒**adeiladu**

coed *plural noun*
- • = trees
°welwch chi'r coed fan acw? = do you
see the trees over there?
**er bod coed yn hanfodol i iechyd y
°Ddaear** = although trees are essential
to the well-being of the Earth
- • (*group of trees*) = wood
- • (*material*) = wood
... wedl'l °wneud o °goed = ... made of
wood
⇒**pren**

coeden (*plural* **coed**) *noun, feminine*
= tree

coel *noun, feminine*
- • = belief
**mae 'na hen °goel y byddai'r mwg yn
eich gwneud yn °ddall** = there is an
old belief that the smoke would make
you blind
- • = credence
**does neb yn rhoi °fawr o °goel ar
hynny** = no-one gives that much
credence

coelio *verbnoun*
= believe
coeliwch neu °beidio = believe it or not
⇒**credu**

coes (*plural* **-au**) *noun, feminine*
= leg
**mae'r °goes 'ma'n °wanach ers y
°ddamwain** = this leg is weaker since
the accident
dim ond tynnu dy °goes o'n i = I was
just pulling your leg

co(f) (*plural* **cofion**) *noun, masculine*
- • = memory
mae gynni hi °go da = she's got a good
memory
- • = mind
**enwau sy'n dwyn Cymru a'i
mynyddoedd i °gof** = names which

bring to mind Wales and its mountains

mi °fasai fo'n mynd o'i °go! = he'd go crazy!

• (plural only) = wishes (in greetings)

cofion cynnes oddiwrth °bawb yn y swyddfa = best wishes from everyone in the office

cofio verbnoun
= remember

wi'n cofio dy °dad = I remember your father

wyt ti'n cofio dod fan hyn pan oedden ni'n °fyfyrwyr? = do you remember coming here when we were students?

cofiwch ni at °weddill y teulu, 'te = remember us to the rest of the family, then

---

! The imperatives **cofia, cofiwch** are used as tags in the spoken language, corresponding to '..., mind (you)'

dim byd yn ei herbyn, cofiwch = nothing against her, mind

---

cofrestr (plural **-au, -i**) noun, feminine
= register

cofrestru verbnoun
= register

rhaid i °bob defnyddiwr °gofrestru ar y peiriant hwnnw = every user must register on that machine

coginio verbnoun
= cook; do the cooking

ti sy'n coginio heno = you're doing the cooking this evening

bydda i'n edrych ar °bob agwedd o °goginio ar °gyfer y Nadolig = I'll be looking at every aspect of cooking for Christmas

cogydd (plural **-ion**) noun, masculine
= cook

cogyddes (plural **-au**) noun, feminine
= cook

colled (plural **-ion**) noun, feminine
= loss

colli verbnoun
• = lose

paid colli dy °fenig tro 'ma = don't lose your gloves this time

• = miss

fe °gollon ni'r bws = we missed the bus

bydd un °fargen na °ellir mo'i ʰcholli °bob wythnos = there will be one unmissable bargain every week

wi'n dy °golli di = I miss you

⇒**ar °goll**

copa (plural **-on, copâu**) noun, masculine
= summit (also figurative); top

er bod y copaon yn codi rhwng 4000' a 6000' uwchlaw'r môr... = although the summits rise between 4000' and 6000' above the sea ...

... gan edrych ar draws y dyffryn tuag at °gopa Mynydd Washington = ... looking across the valley towards the summit of Mount Washington

copïo verbnoun
= copy

corff (plural **cyrff**) noun, masculine
= body

daethpwyd o hyd i °gorff ar y traeth bore 'ma = a body has been found on the beach this morning

bydd nifer o °gyrff swyddogol yn ystyried y °broblem yn °fanwl = a number of official bodies will be giving the problem close consideration

cornel (plural **-i**) noun, feminine or masculine
= corner

cer i eistedd yn y °gornel = go and sit in the corner

cosb noun, feminine
• = punishment
• = penalty

cosbi verbnoun
= punish; penalize

roedd y llys wedi methu â rhoi ystyriaeth °lawn i °ddulliau eraill o'i °gosbi = the court had failed to give full consideration to other methods of punishing him

fe °allen nhw °gael eu cosbi'n ariannol am yr oedi = they could be penalized financially for the delay

cosi verbnoun
= itch

costus adjective
= expensive, dear

mae disgwyl y bydd gwyliau tramor yn llai costus fyth eleni = holidays abroad are expected to be even less expensive this year
⇒**drud**

côt (*plural* **cotiau**) *noun, feminine*
= coat
gostyngiadau anhygoel ar siwmperi a ʰchotiau! = amazing reductions on jumpers and coats!

côt °law (*plural* **cotiau glaw**)
= raincoat

crac *adjective*
= angry, cross
paid mynd yn °grac = don't get cross

credu *verbnoun*
• = think
sa i'n credu °fod hynny'n iawn = I don't think that's right
• = believe (**ynⁿ, mewn** in)
maen nhw'n credu yng ⁿghyfiawnder ein hachos = they believe in the justice of our cause
dw i °ddim yn credu mewn pethau felly = I don't believe in things like that
⇒**meddwl**, ⇒**coelio**

cref
⇒**cryf**

creision *plural noun*
= crisps
°ga i °becyn o °greision hefyd? = can I have a packet of crisps as well?
creision ŷd = cornflakes

creu *verbnoun*
= create; make
fe °fu ymddygiad od Menna'n creu cryn °benbleth i Derek = Menna's odd behaviour has been creating quite a bit of confusion for Derek
gobeithio bod nhw °ddim yn bwriadu creu helynt heno = I hope they're not out to make trouble tonight

creulon *adjective*
= cruel

creulondeb *noun, masculine*
= cruelty

crio *verbnoun*
= cry, weep
paid â ʰchrio, cariad = don't cry, dear
⇒**llefain**, ⇒**wylo**

croen *noun, masculine*
• = skin
yn aml iawn bydd effeithiau'r cyffuriau 'ma i'w gweld ar y croen hefyd = very often the effects of these drugs are seen on the skin as well
• (*of fruit*) = peel
wedyn mae rhaid tynnu croen yr afal = then (you) have to peel the apple

croes (*plural* **-au**) *noun, feminine*
= cross
yn °groes i° = contrary to; (go) against
mae'n amlwg y bydd unrhyw °benderfyniad o'r °fath yn °groes i °ddymuniadau'r °gymuned = it's clear that any such decision will be contrary to the wishes of the community
mae'r dull ymarferol yma o °ddysgu'n °groes i'r ffasiwn °bresennol = this practical method of teaching goes against the present fashion

croesawu *verbnoun*
= welcome
dyma °ddatblygiad i'w °groesawu gan °bawb = this is a development to be welcomed by everyone

croesawydd (*plural* **-ion**) *noun, masculine*
= receptionist (*male or female*)

croesffordd *noun, feminine*
= crossroads
ewch hyd at y °groesffordd, yna trowch i'r °dde = go as far as the crossroads, then turn right

croesi *verbnoun*
= cross
edrychwch yn °ofalus cyn croesi'r stryd = look carefully before crossing the street
mae yna ffin na ʰchaiff milwyr y Cenhedloedd Unedig ei ʰchroesi = there is a boundary that the United Nations soldiers cannot cross

croeso *noun, masculine*
= welcome
croeso i °Gymru = welcome to Wales
croeso i °bawb = all welcome
estynnwyd croeso cynnes i aelodau newydd = a warm welcome was extended to new members
dw i'n amau °dawel °fach °fod yna °groeso iddyn nhw = I suspect deep down that they are welcome

cron
⇨**crwn**

crwn *adjective* (*feminine* **cron**)
= round
chwiliwch am arwydd crwn = look for a round sign
rhodd gan °Ford °Gron Llaneglwys = a gift from Llaneglwys Round Table

crwydro *verbnoun*
= wander
mae'n treulio ei amser yn crwydro strydoedd Aberystwyth = he spends his time wandering the streets of Aberystwyth

cryf *adjective* (*feminine* **cref**, *plural (rare)* **cryfion**)
= strong
mae gwrthwynebiad cryf wedi bod yn °ddiweddar = there has been strong opposition lately
bydd gwyntoedd cryfion ledled y °wlad trwy'r dydd yfory = there will be strong winds all over the country all day tomorrow

cryn°
cryn °dipyn = quite a bit
cryn nifer = quite a few, quite a number:
mae cryn °dipyn o °drafod wedi bod yn °barod = there has already been quite a bit of discussion
mi oedd 'na °gryn nifer hefyd yn siarad yn ei herbyn = there were also quite a number speaking against her

crynoddisg (*plural* -**iau**) *noun, masculine*
= compact disc, CD
detholiad eang o °dapiau a ʰchryno-ddisgiau i fyny'r grisiau = a wide selection of tapes and CDs upstairs

crynu *verbnoun*
= tremble, shake
o'n i'n clywed y llawr yn crynu = I felt the floor tremble

crys (*plural* -**au**) *noun, masculine*
= shirt

cudd *adjective*
• = hidden
gofal—mynedfa °gudd = caution—hidden entrance
• = secret

profion cudd ar esgyrn = secret tests on bones

cuddio *verbnoun*
= hide
mae'r anrhegion i gyd wedi'u cuddio dan y °goeden Nadolig = all the presents are hidden under the Christmas tree

cul *adjective*
= narrow
mae'r ffordd yn rhy °gul fan hyn = the road is too narrow here
mi °ddylai fo °geisio bod yn llai cul ei °feddwl, wedwn i = he ought to try and be less narrow-minded, I would say

curo *verbnoun*
• = strike; hit; beat
curwch yr wyau a'r hufen gyda'i gilydd = beat the eggs and cream together
• (*defeat*) = beat
fe °gurodd Llanilar °glwb Llanrhystud = Llanilar beat Llanrhystud club
⇨**taro**, ⇨**trechu**

cusan *noun, masculine or feminine*
= kiss
naeth hi chwythu cusan ata i = she blew me a kiss
⇨**sws**

cusanu *verbnoun*
= kiss

cwbl, cwbwl *noun, masculine*
= (the) lot, all
°gymera i'r cwbl = I'll take the lot
dyna'r cwbwl am heno = that's all for this evening
y cwbl sy eisiau nawr ydy llofnod ar y gwaelod = all that's needed now is a signature at the bottom
nhw sy'n °gyfrifol, wedi'r cwbwl = it is they who are responsible, after all
⇨**cyfan**

cwbl°, cwbwl° *adverb*
= quite, completely
mae hynny'n °gwbwl °ddiangen = that is completely unnecessary
mae newid yn rhywbeth °gwbl naturiol ym ⁿmyd natur = change is something quite natural in the world of nature
⇨**hollol°**

cwblhau *verbnoun*
= complete

mae gofyn i chi °gwblhau'r °dasg 'ma erbyn hanner dydd = you are required to complete this task by midday

cwch (*plural* **cychod**) *noun, masculine*
= boat
yn ni i gyd yn yr un cwch bellach = we're all in the same boat now
⇒**llong**

cwestiwn (*plural* **cwestiynau**) *noun, masculine*
= question

cwm (*plural* **cymoedd**) *noun, masculine*
= valley
...tra bod diweithdra yng ⁿNghymoedd y De'n dal i °gynyddu = ...while unemployment in the Valleys (of the South) is still rising
⇒**dyffryn,** ⇒**glyn**

cwmni (*plural* **cwmnïau**) *noun, masculine*
= company (*all senses*)
...er na °fyddai'r cwmnïau awyrennau'n cyfadde hynny = ...although the aeroplane companies would not admit that
o °ddelio â ʰchwmni teuluol dych chi'n sicr o °dderbyn gwasanaeth da = dealing with a family company ensures you good service
taith °gerdded yng ⁿnghwmni Dafydd Parry = a walk in the company of Dafydd Parry

cwmpas
⇒**o °gwmpas**

cwmwl (*plural* **cymylau**) *noun, masculine*
= cloud

cŵn *plural of*
⇒**ci**

cwpan (*plural* **-au**) *noun, masculine*
= cup
Gêm °Derfynol Cwpan y Byd = the World Cup Final

> **!** *This word denotes the object itself, while an extension* **cwpanaid** *(nearly always* ⇒**panaid** *in normal speech) is used for* 'cupful', *and is therefore required in expressions like* 'a cup of tea'.

cwpla *verbnoun* (*South*)
= finish

ti wedi cwpla dy °waith cartre? = have you finished your homework?
⇒**gorffen,** ⇒**bennu**

cwpwrdd (*plural* **cypyrddau**) *noun, masculine*
= cupboard

cwr (*plural* **cyrion**) *noun, masculine*
= edge; corner
byddwn ni'n cyhoeddi erthyglau gan arbenigwyr o °bob cwr o °Gymru = we will be publishing articles by experts from every corner of Wales
lleolir y coleg ar °gyrion Parc Cenedlaethol Eryri = the college is situated on the edges of Snowdonia National Park

cwrdd (âʰ) *verbnoun*
= meet
mae'n °dda gen i °gwrdd â chi! = I'm pleased to meet you!
nawn ni °gwrdd fan hyn yfory, 'te = we'll meet here tomorrow, then

cwrs (*plural* **cyrsiau**) *noun, masculine*
= course
treuliodd hi °flwyddyn yn Ffrainc fel rhan o'i ʰchwrs Ffrangeg = she spent a year in France as part of her French course

cwrtais *adjective*
= polite
cofia bod yn °gwrtais heno = remember to be polite this evening

cwrw *noun, masculine*
= beer

cwympo *verbnoun* (*South*)
• = fall
°fyddi di'n cwympo a ʰchael dolur = you will fall and hurt yourself
• = drop
ti wedi cwympo dy °fenig = you've dropped your gloves
⇒**syrthio**

cwyn (*plural* **-ion**) *noun, masculine*
= complaint
yn sgîl cwynion °fod y bws ysgol wedi gadael chwe munud yn °gynnar... = following complaints that the school bus left six minutes early...

cwyno *verbnoun*
= complain (**arᵒ, amᵒ** about)

maen nhw'n cwyno o hyd = they're
always complaining
⇒**achwyn**

cychwyn (stem **cychwynn-**)
verbnoun
= start; start out (*on journey, etc*)
neith y car °ddim cychwyn = the car
won't start
mi °ddylen ni °gychwyn cyn iddi nosi =
we ought to start out before nightfall
cychwyn ar °daith = to start out on a
journey
**ymateb siomedig a °gafwyd o'r
cychwyn cynta** = the response right
from the start has been disappointing
⇒**dechrau**

cyd
ar y cyd = jointly
**fe °fydd y °ddau °gwmni'n gweithio ar
y cyd o hyn ymlaen** = the two
companies will be working jointly
from now on
⇒**ynghyd**

cyd°- *verb prefix*
= with; co-
cyd-ddigwydd = coincide
cydweithio âʰ rhywun = work with
someone, collaborate with someone
cydweithredu = co-operate

cydfynd *verbnoun*
• = go along (**âʰ** with)
**°alla i °ddim cydfynd â'r penderfyniad
'ma** = I can't go along with this
decision
• = agree
**mae'n amlwg °fod y °ddau adroddiad
'ma'n cydfynd** = these two reports
clearly agree

cydnabod (stem **cydnabydd-**)
verbnoun
= acknowledge, recognise (*fact*)
**mae eisiau cydnabod yr angen i
°fynegi teimladau negyddol** = the
need to express negative feelings must
be acknowledged

cydnabyddiaeth *noun, feminine*
= acknowledgement, recognition

cydweithio *verbnoun*
• = collaborate
• (*as noun*) = collaboration
**mae llwyddiant y °fenter 'ma'n
dibynnu ar °gydweithio** = the success

of this venture depends on
collaboration

cydwladol *adjective*
= international
less common alternative for
⇒**rhyngwladol**

cydymdeimlad *noun, masculine*
= sympathy (**âʰ** with)
**mae'n amlwg °fod gan yr awdur °gryn
°gydymdeimlad â'i °brif °gymeriad** =
the author obviously has quite a bit of
sympathy with his main character

cydymdeimlo *verbnoun*
= sympathize, have sympathy (**âʰ** with)

cyfaddawdu *verbnoun*
= compromise
**fe °ddwedwyd wedyn °fod 'na °le i
°gyfaddawdu wedi'r cwbwl** = it was
later said that there was room for
compromise after all

cyfadde(f) *verbnoun*
= admit
**rhaid i mi a ʰphawb arall °gyfadde fod
camgymeriadau wedi'u gwneud** = I
and everyone else must admit that
mistakes have been made

cyfaill (*plural* **cyfeillion**) *noun,
masculine*
= friend
Annwyl °gyfeillion = Dear friends
Cyfeillion y °Ddaear = Friends of the
Earth
⇒**ffrind**

cyfalafiaeth *noun, feminine*
= capitalism

cyfamser *noun, masculine*
= meantime
yn y cyfamser = in the meantime,
meanwhile
**yn y cyfamser, dylid sgrifennu at
Aelodau Seneddol** = in the meantime,
one should write to MPs

cyfan
1 *noun, masculine*
= (the) lot, (the) whole, all; the whole
thing
**yn achos Lloegr mi °gymerodd y
cyfan °fwy o amser** = in the case of
England the whole thing took more
time

ar y cyfan, maen nhw'n hollol °gywir = on the whole, they are quite correct
ydy Theatr Genedlaethol Lloegr yn cynrychioli'r °genedl honno yn °gyfan? = does the English National Theatre represent that nation in its entirety?
mae'r cyfan i gyd wedi'i °ddifetha! = the whole thing is spoilt!
ti sy biau'r car, wedi'r cyfan = it's your car, after all
2 *as adjective*
= whole
drwy °Gymru °gyfan = through the whole of Wales
⇒**cwbwl**

cyfarchiad (*plural* **-au, cyfarchion**) *noun, masculine*
= greeting
Cyfarchion y Tymor = Season's Greetings
⇒**llongyfarch**

cyfarfod (*plural* **-ydd**) *noun, masculine*
= meeting
cynhaliwyd Cyfarfod Blynyddol Agored y Cyngor ar y 6ed o °Fehefin = the Open Annual Meeting of the Council was held on June 6th

cyfartal *adjective*
= equal
mae'r cwmni'n rhwym i °gyfleoedd cyfartal = the company is committed to equal opportunities
⇒**ar °gyfartaledd**

cyfarwydd *adjective*
= familiar
o'n i'n meddwl ar y pryd °fod yr enw 'na'n swnio'n °gyfarwydd °rywsut = I thought at the time that that name sounded somehow familiar
⇒**anghyfarwydd**

cyfarwyddiadau *plural noun*
= directions, instructions
mae'r pecyn yn cynnwys cyfarwyddiadau llawn = the pack includes full instructions

cyfarwyddwr (*plural* **cyfarwyddwyr**) *noun, masculine*
= director
unwaith eto mae'r cwmni dawns yn chwilio am °gyfarwyddwr newydd = once again the dance company is looking for a new director

cyfateb *verbnoun*
• = match
byddwch hefyd yn ennill gwobr os bydd pump allan o'r chwech yn cyfateb = you will also win a prize if five out of the six match
• = correspond
i beth mae hwn yn cyfateb yn Saesneg? = what does this correspond to in English?

cyfatebol *adjective*
= corresponding, matching

cyfathrebol *adjective*
= communicative

cyfathrebu *verbnoun*
= communicate
gall y fforwm °ddatblygu i °fod yn °gyfrwng cyfathrebu effeithiol = the forum may develop into an effective medium of communication

cyfeillgar *adjective*
= friendly

cyfeillgarwch *noun, masculine*
= friendship

cyfeiriad (*plural* **-au**) *noun, masculine*
• = address
beth yw'ch cyfeiriad? = what is your address?
• = direction
y deng awr o °deledu sy'n dod o °gyfeiriad BBC Cymru = the ten hours of television that comes from BBC Cymru
• = reference
naeth e °gyfeiriad at y rhyfel o °gwbwl? = did he make any reference to the war at all?

cyfeirio *verbnoun*
= refer (**at°** to)
Cyfeiriaf at eich llythyr dyddiedig y pumed o °Fai (*formal*) = I refer to your letter of the 5th May

cyfenw (*plural* **-au**) *noun, masculine*
= surname
beth yw'ch cyfenw? = what is your surname?
⇒**enw**

....

cyff-
words beginning **cyff-** *are listed according to Welsh alphabetical order following* **cyfy-**

....

cyfieithiad (*plural* **-au**) *noun, masculine*
= translation
ydy'r cyfieithiad yn °barod? = is the translation ready?

cyfieithu *verbnoun*
= translate; interpret
mae'r °ddogfen 'ma heb ei ʰchyfieithu = this document hasn't been translated
bydd y gallu i °gyfieithu ar y pryd yn °fantais = the ability to interpret will be an advantage
⇒**dehongli**

cyfieithydd (*plural* **cyfieithwyr**) *noun, masculine*
= translator (*male or female*)

cyflawni *verbnoun*
• = fulfil
rhaid cyflawni'n dyletswyddau = we must fulfil our responsibilities
• = accomplish
llongyfarchiadau iddo ar °gyflawni'r °gamp yma = congratulations to him on accomplishing this feat

cyfle (*plural* **-oedd**) *noun, masculine*
= chance; opportunity
°gawn ni °gyfle i ffonio adre? = will we have a chance to phone home?
mae'r llyfr yn °gyfle i °gofio am °ddyn na ʰchafodd ei haeddiant cyn hyn = the book is an opportunity to remember a man who has not so far had his due
⇒**siawns**

cyflenwad (*plural* **-au**) *noun, masculine*
= supply
mae cyflenwadau tanwydd yn isel iawn = fuel supplies are very low

cyflenwi *verbnoun*
= supply
fe °ddaw'r llong °gyflenwi'n ôl ymhen tri mis = the supply ship will come back in three months' time

cyfleus *adjective*
= convenient
gallwn ni °drafod y manylion ar adeg °gyfleus i chi = we can discuss the details at a time convenient to you
dewch yn ôl ata i pan °fo'n °gyfleus = get back to me when convenient

cyflog (*plural* **-au**) *noun, masculine*
= salary; wages; pay

cyflogedig (*plural* **-ion**) *adjective*
functioning as noun, masculine
= employee (*male or female*)

cyflogi *verbnoun*
= employ
mae angen cyflogi rhywun i °dreulio blwyddyn yn Abergwaun = we need to employ someone to spend a year in Fishguard

cyflogwr (*plural* **cyflogwyr**) *noun, masculine*
= employer

cyflwr (*plural* **cyflyrau**) *noun, masculine*
= (physical) condition, state
fel y gwelwch, mae'r beic mewn cyflwr arbennig o °dda erbyn hyn = as you (can) see, the bike is now in a particularly good condition
⇒**amod**

cyflwyno *verbnoun*
• = present
cyflwynwyd basgedaid o °flodau iddi gan °ddau o'r plant lleiaf = she was presented with a basket of flowers by two of the smallest children
• = introduce
°ga i °gyflwyno Mr Jones? = may I introduce Mr Jones?

cyflym *adjective*
= fast, quick
mae e'n hoff o °geir cyflym = he likes fast cars
mae gwerslyfrau yn ymddangos yn °weddol °gyflym yn Lloegr = textbooks appear fairly quickly in England

cyflymder *noun, masculine*
= speed

cyflymu *verbnoun*
= speed up

cyfnewid (*stem* **cyfnewidi-**) *verbnoun*
= exchange (**am°** for)
gadewch inni °gyfnewid rhifau ffôn, 'te = let's exchange phone numbers, then
graddfa °gyfnewid = exchange rate

cyfnewidfa (*plural* **cyfnewidfeydd**) *noun, feminine*
= [telephone] exchange

cyfnither (*plural* **-oedd**) *noun, feminine*
= (female) cousin
mae hi'n °gyfnither i mi = she's my cousin
⇒**cefnder**

cyfnod *noun, masculine*
• = time (*period*)
bydd e yno am °gyfnod = he'll be there for a time
• = period
gwahoddir ceisiadau am y swydd newydd hon am °gyfnod o °dair blynedd = applications are invited for this new job for a period of three years
Cyfnod y Dadeni = the Renaissance period
• = era
mae'n °ddechrau cyfnod newydd yng ⁿngwleidyddiaeth y °wlad = it's the start of a new era in the politics of the country
• (*in a few set phrases*) = term
cyfnod byr = short term
cyfnod hir = long term
rhaid edrych yn °fanwl ar yr effeithiau cyfnod byr hefyd = the short-term effects must also be closely looked at
⇒**adeg**, ⇒**oes** *noun*

cyfoes *adjective*
= modern, contemporary; current
drama °gyfoes a °fydd yn apelio'n arbennig at °bobol ifanc = a modern drama that will be of particular appeal to young people
materion cyfoes = current affairs
⇒**modern**

cyfoeth *noun, masculine*
= wealth, riches (*also figurative*)

cyfoethog *adjective, comparative* **cyfoethocach**, *superlative* **cyfoethoca(f)**
• = rich, wealthy
dyw'r °bobol 'ma °ddim yn °gyfoethog o °bell ffordd = these people are not rich by any means
yr Unol °Daleithiau yw'r °wlad °gyfoethoca yn y byd = the United States is the richest country in the world
• *plural* **cyfoethogion** used as *noun* = the rich
y cyfoethogion segur = the idle rich

cyfraith (*plural* **cyfreithiau**) *noun, feminine*
= law
yng ⁿngolwg y °gyfraith mae'r madarch hudol yn °beryglus iawn = in the eyes of the law the magic mushrooms are very dangerous
⇒**deddf**, ⇒**anghyfreithlon**

cyfraniad (*plural* **-au**) *noun, masculine*
= contribution

cyfrannu *verbnoun*
= contribute (**at°** to)
fe °allech chi °gyfrannu at °lu o achosion da = you could contribute to a host of good causes

cyfreithiwr (*plural* **cyfreithwyr**) *noun, masculine*
= lawyer

cyfres (*plural* **-i, -au**) *noun, feminine*
= series
bydd cyfres o eitemau arbennig ar °gyfer y Nadolig = there will be a series of special items for Christmas

cyfri(f)
1 *verbnoun*
= count
nei di °gyfri'r rheina i mi? = will you count those for me?
⇒**rhifo**
2 *noun, masculine*
= account
mae angen rhifau'ch cyfrif cadw a'ch cyfrif cyfredol = we need the numbers of your savings account and your current account

cyfrifiadur (*plural* **-on**) *noun, masculine*
= computer
mae cyfrifiaduron wedi newid ein bywydau i gyd = computers have changed all our lives

cyfrifiannell (*plural* **cyfrifiannellau**) *noun, feminine*
= calculator
bydd rhaid gadael eich cyfrifiannellau tu allan i'r stafell, mae arna i ofn = you'll have to leave your calculators outside the room, I'm afraid

cyfrifol *adjective*
= responsible

y cwestiwn sy'n codi yw pa °gorff °ddylai °fod yn °gyfrifol? = the question that arises is which body should be responsible?
ti sy'n °gyfrifol! = <u>you</u> are responsible!, this is <u>your</u> responsibility!

cyfrifoldeb (*plural* **-au**) *noun, masculine*
= responsibility
cyfrifoldeb y llywodraeth °fyddai ariannu'r system = it would be the government's responsibility to finance the system

cyfrinachol *adjective*
= secret; confidential; in confidence
adroddiad cyfrinachol = a secret report
pob ymholiad yn °gyfrinachol = every enquiry is in confidence

cyfrwng (*plural* **cyfryngau**) *noun, masculine*
= medium; (*plural*) media
dysgir yn °bennaf drwy °gyfrwng y °Gymraeg = teaching is mainly done through the medium of Welsh
y cyfryngau torfol = the mass media

cyfweld (*stem* **cyfwel-**) (**â**[h]) *verbnoun*
= interview
bydd Elinor yn cyfweld ag un o'n hactorion enwoca ar ôl yr egwyl = Elinor will be interviewing one of our most famous actors after the break

cyfweliad (*plural* **-au**) *noun, masculine*
= interview

cyfyngedig *adjective*
= limited
ond brysiwch—dim ond nifer cyfyngedig sydd ar °gael! = but hurry—there are only a limited number available!
Cyfrifiaduron Cymru Cyf. = Wales Computers Ltd.

cyfystyr *adjective*
= synonymous (**â**[h] with), tantamount (**â**[h] to)
mi °fyddai'r °fath °gyfaddawdu'n °gyfystyr ag ildio = such a compromise would be tantamount to capitulation
⇨**ystyr**

cyffredin *adjective*
• = common
camenw sydd mor °gyffredin erbyn hyn fel na °ellir ei osgoi = a misnomer which is so common now that it cannot be avoided
Tŷ'r Cyffredin = the House of Commons
• = ordinary
ysgol °gyffredin oedd hi = it was an ordinary school
⇨**anghyffredin**

cyffredinol *adjective*
= general
fel sy'n digwydd gyda pob rheol °gyffredinol, mae 'na eithriadau = as with every general rule, there are exceptions
beth yn °gyffredinol yw'r ffordd °orau i °fynd ati? = what generally is the best way to go about it?

cyffrous *adjective*
= exciting
rhaglen °gyffrous i °bobol yn eu harddegau = an exciting programme for teenagers
on'd yw hyn yn °gyffrous? = isn't this exciting?

cyffur (*plural* **-iau**) *noun, masculine*
= drug
gall yr effaith hon hefyd °gael ei [h]thrin â [h]chyffuriau = this effect can also be treated with drugs
bu °farw 14 o °bobol ifainc ar ôl cymryd cyffuriau eleni = 14 young people died after taking drugs this year
⇨**moddion**

cyffwrdd (*stem* **cyffyrdd-**) (**â**[h]) *verbnoun*
= touch
gofynnir i chi °beidio â gadael i'ch plant °gyffwrdd â'r arddangosion = you are asked not to let your children touch the exhibits

cyngerdd (*plural* **cyngherddau**) *noun, masculine*
= concert

cynghori *verbnoun*
= advise; give advice
bydd rhywun ar °gael i'ch cynghori chi = someone will be on hand to advise you

cyngor *noun, masculine*
- (*plural* **cynghorau**) = council
  eisoes mae'r cyngor yn ymchwilio i'r sefyllfa = the council is already investigating the situation
- (*plural* **cynghorion**) = counsel, advice
  mae angen rhoi gwybodaeth a ᶰchyngor i °rieni = we need to give information and advice to parents

cyhoeddi *verbnoun*
- = publish
  peryglir y grant os na ᶰchyhoeddir yn °brydlon = delayed publication will jeopardize the grant [*lit: 'The grant will be jeopardized if publishing is not done on time'*]
- = as noun (act of) publication
  aeth deugain ᶰmlynedd heibio ers cyhoeddi'r °gyfrol °gynta = forty years have gone by since the publication of the first volume

cyhoeddus *adjective*
= public
llwybr cyhoeddus = public footpath

cyhuddiad (*plural* **-au**) *noun, masculine*
= charge, accusation

cyhuddo *verbnoun*
= accuse (**o°** of); charge (**o°** with)
mae tri dyn bellach wedi'u cyhuddo o °lofruddiaeth = three men are now charged with murder

cylch (*plural* **-oedd**) *noun, masculine*
- = circle
  tynnwch °gylch â llinell drwy'i °ganol = draw a circle with a line through the middle
- = (surrounding) district
  Sioe Amaethyddol Llaneglwys a'r cylch = Llaneglwys and district Agricultural Show

cylchgrawn (*plural* **cylchgronau**) *noun, masculine*
= magazine
'Sothach' yw'r unig cylchgrawn a anelir at °bobl ifanc = 'Sothach' is the only magazine aimed at young people

cyllell (*plural* **cyllyll**) *noun, feminine*
= knife
cyllell °fara = breadknife

cyllid *noun, masculine*
= finance
diffyg cyllid yw gwraidd y °broblem = lack of finance is the root of the problem

cyllideb *noun, masculine*
= budget

cymaint *adverb*
- = so much/many
  mae cymaint ar eich meddwl chi, nes bod chi'n anghofio'r cyfan = there's so much on your mind that you forget the whole lot
- = as much/many (**âʰ** as)
  °ges i °ddwywaith °gymaint â ddoe = I got twice as much/many as yesterday
- = such
  pam yr oedd y digwyddiad yma o °gymaint o °ddiddordeb i seryddion? = why was this event of such interest to astronomers?

! *As a quantity expression, **cymaint** requires a following **o°** when a noun is specified, as in the example above.*

dyw'r busnes 'ma °ddim yn 'y ᶰmhoeni fi °gymaint â hynny = this business doesn't bother me all that much
rhyw °gymaint = a certain amount
mae rhyw °gymaint ar ôl = there is a certain amount left
⇒**cynifer**

cymdeithas (*plural* **-au**) *noun, feminine*
= society
ffoniwch am °ragor o °fanylion am °weithgareddau eraill y °gymdeithas = phone for more details about the society's other activities

cymdeithasol *adjective*
= social

cymdeithasu *verbnoun*
= socialize

cymdogion *plural of*
⇒**cymydog**

cymeradwyo *verbnoun*
= recommend
llyfr i'w °gymeradwyo i °bawb = a book to be recommended to everyone

cymharu *verbnoun*
= compare (**âʰ** with)

bydd eisiau cymharu'r °ddwy stori =
the two stories will have to be
compared

**sut mae'r sefyllfa fan'na'n cymharu
â'r un fan hyn?** = how does the
situation there compare with the one
here?

> **!** 'compared with...' *is phrased as
> 'from its comparing with...,' with
> mutation difference depending on the
> subject:* **o'i °gymharu â**[h] *(masculine)*,
> **o'i** [h]**chymharu â**[h] *(feminine)*, **o'u
> cymharu â**[h] *(plural)*
> **mae'r °farchnad yn edrych yn °well
> o'i** [h]**chymharu â llynedd** = the
> market is looking better compared
> with last year

cymhleth *adjective*
= complicated, complex
**mae'r sefyllfa'n un °gymhleth dros
°ben** = the situation is an extremely
complicated one

cymhwyster *(plural* **cymwysterau**)
noun, masculine
= qualification
**pa °gymwysterau'n union sy gynnoch
chi?** = exactly what qualifications have
you got?

cymorth *noun, masculine*
= help, aid, assistance
**bydd y dosbarth derbyn yn elwa'n
°fawr o'i** [h]**chymorth °bob bore** = the
reception class will benefit greatly
from her help every morning

Cymraeg *noun, feminine*
• = Welsh language
**siaradwch °Gymraeg os gwelwch yn
°dda** = speak Welsh please
**mae'r °ddogfen hon hefyd ar °gael yn
y °Gymraeg** = this document is also
available in Welsh
**beth dych chi'n galw'r pethau 'ma yn
°Gymraeg?** = what do you call these
things in Welsh?
ydyn nhw'n medru Cymraeg? = do
they speak Welsh?
**byddai'r gallu i °gyfathrebu drwy
°gyfrwng y °Gymraeg yn °fantais** =
the ability to communicate through
the medium of Welsh would be an
advantage
• *(as adjective)* = Welsh-speaking
ond yn y °Gymru °Gymraeg mae'r

patrwm yn °bur °wahanol = but in
Welsh-speaking Wales the pattern is
quite different
y °Fro °Gymraeg = *name for the Welsh-
speaking heartlands of Wales*

> **!** *Note that* 'in Welsh' *is not* *yng
> Nghymraeg *as you might expect, but*
> **yn °Gymraeg**, *probably a contraction
> of* **yn y °Gymraeg**, *which is itself also
> used. And although* **Cymraeg** *is a
> feminine noun, it does not mutate
> following adjectives:* **Cymraeg da**
> good Welsh, **Cymraeg gwael**
> bad/poor Welsh.

Cymraes *(plural* **-au**) *noun, feminine*
= Welshwoman
Cymraes yw ei °wraig, 'te? = is his wife
Welsh, then?

Cymreig *adjective*
= Welsh *(pertaining to Wales)*
**roedd e'n °falch o'i °gysylltiadau
Cymreig** = he was proud of his Welsh
connections
**fo oedd y Prif °Weinidog a sefydlodd y
Swyddfa °Gymreig** = he was the Prime
Minister who established the Welsh
Office

Cymro *(plural* **Cymry**) *noun, masculine*
= Welshman
Cymro oedd dy °dad? = was your
father Welsh *or* a Welshman?
**mae'r Cymry ar y blaen o'r diwedd
gyda pum munud o'r gêm ar ôl** = the
Welsh are in the lead at last with five
minutes left of the game

Cymru *noun, feminine*
= Wales
croeso i °Gymru = welcome to Wales
ar °gael ledled Cymru = available
throughout Wales
**°ga i °ofyn i chi ers pryd dych chi'n
byw yng** [n]**Nghymru bellach?** = can I
ask how long you have lived in Wales
now?
**mae'r cysylltiadau rhwng Llydaw a
** [h]**Chymru'n agosach fyth** = the
links between Brittany and Wales are even
closer
Cymru am byth! = Wales forever!

Cymry
⇒**Cymro**

cymryd (*stem* **cymer-**) *verbnoun*
- = take (*most senses*)
  mi °fyddwn ni'n cymryd ein hamser = we will take our time
  faint °gymerith y °daith? = how long will the trip take?
  mae hi heb °gymryd ei moddion = she hasn't taken her medicine
- = have
  °gymerwch chi °banaid o °de? = will you have a cup of tea?
  °gymera i °ddwsin o'r rheina = I'll have a dozen of those

> **!** *Where* 'take' *means* 'accompany', ⇒**mynd â**[h] *is the preferred translation, though many speakers use* **cymryd** *here as well.*

cymuned (*plural* **-au**) *noun, feminine*
= community
mae darn ohono o °fewn ffiniau'r °gymuned = part of it is within the boundaries of the community

cymwysterau *plural of* ⇒**cymhwyster**

cymydog (*plural* **cymdogion**) *noun, masculine*
= neighbour
...neu efallai bod eich cymdogion yn cadw sŵn dan °berfeddion = ...or perhaps your neighbours make a noise until all hours

cymylog *adjective*
= cloudy
mi °fydd hi'n °gymylog iawn trwy'r dydd yfory = it will be very cloudy all day tomorrow

cymysg *adjective*
= mixed
mae gen i °deimladau cymysg = I have mixed feelings

cymysgu *verbnoun*
- = mix
  fe °wŷr pawb nad yw dŵr ac olew yn cymysgu = everyone knows that water and oil don't mix
  peidiwch â'u cymysgu nhw 'to = don't mix them yet
- = mix up, confuse
  dych chi wedi cymysgu'r °ddau °beth 'na = you've got those two things mixed up

cyn
1 *preposition*
= before
ffonia i chi eto cyn Nadolig = I'll phone you again before Christmas
y gobaith yw y bydd y sefyllfa'n °fwy eglur cyn bo hir = the hope is that the situation will be clearer before long
cyn pen dim roedd aroglau powdwr yn llenwi'r awyr = in no time at all the smell of powder filled the air

> **!** **cyn** *is used when reference is made to time, but not where* 'before' *has the spatial meaning of* 'in front of'— 'before your very eyes'—*which requires* ⇒**o °flaen**. *As a time word,* **cyn** *also has a function as a conjunction—see below.*

⇒**gerbron**, ⇒**o'r blaen**
2 *conjunction*
= before (**i** + *subject* + °*verbnoun*)
°well inni °glirio'r llanast 'ma cyn i Elwyn °gyrraedd = we'd better clear (up) this mess before Elwyn arrives
ond brysiwch cyn iddyn nhw °fynd i gyd! = but hurry before they all go!

> **!** *Notice that no* **i** *construction is necessary when the subject on either side of the* 'before' *is the same person or persons:*
> **°ga i °air â hi cyn gadael** = I'll have a word with her before I leave/before leaving
> *Notice also that the verbnoun after* **cyn** *is neutral as to tense, with the verb in the first part of the sentence setting the context and indicating the right sequence of tenses in English. This principle is true for all time conjunctions in Welsh.*
> **°ga i °air â hi cyn iddi (hi) °adael** = I'll have a word with her before she leaves
> **°ges i °air â hi cyn iddi (hi) °adael** = I had a word with her before she left
> *In the normal speech of many areas, a* 'that...' *construction using* **bod** *(etc) coexists happily enough with the* **i** *construction that the standard language insists on:*
> **°dria i °orffen fan hyn cyn bod nhw'n dod** = I'll try and finish here before they come (*cf standard:* **...cyn iddyn nhw °ddod**)

...ond cyn bo' chi'n dechrau, dewch i °gwrdd â rhai o'r staff = ...but before you start, come and meet some of the staff (cf standard: ...cyn i chi °ddechrau, ...)

And some regions even allow inflected verb forms after cyn:
cuddia fe cyn daw e = hide it before he comes

cyn°... (âʰ...) adverb
= as... (as...)
a ʰchyn °belled â'ch bod chi'n parhau i °ddod yma... = and as long as you continue to come here...
cyn °gynted â ʰphosib, cyn °gynted ag y bo modd = as soon as possible

❗ *This alternative way of saying 'as...as...' is restricted in use these days largely to set phrases as in the examples given. Notice that, unlike the more common ⇒mor°... (âʰ...), cyn° also adds the ending -ed to the adjective—so mor °goch but cyn °goched 'as red'. This word does not mutate words beginning ll- and rh-.*

⇒morº

cynddrwg adjective
= as bad
dyw hi °ddim cynddrwg â hynny = it's not as bad as (all) that

❗ *This word, like all equative adjectives, does not use the linking particle ynº with a preceding verb bod 'to be'—so while we say, for example, dyw hi °ddim yn °ddrwg it's not bad, we don't say *dyw hi °ddim yn °gynddrwg.*

cynhesu verbnoun
= warm up

cynhyrchu verbnoun
= produce
roedden ni am °gynhyrchu llyfryn deniadol = we wanted to produce an attractive booklet

cynifer adverb
• = so many
mae 'na °gynifer ar ôl! = there are so many left!
• = as many (âʰ as)
does dim cynifer o °bobol fan hyn â ddoe = there aren't as many people here as yesterday

tair damwain mewn cynifer o °ddyddiau = three accidents in as many days

❗ *As a quantity expression, cynifer requires a following oº when a noun is specified. Notice also that while ⇒cymaint can be used to mean either so much/as much or so many/as many, cynifer can only refer to plurals. So we can say cymaint o °bobol or cynifer o °bobol so many people, but only cymaint o °fwyd so much food.*

⇒nifer

cynilo verbnoun
= save (money)
mae cynilo arian mor hawdd ag ABC = saving money is as easy as ABC
⇒arbed

cynlleied adverb
• = so few
mae cynlleied o °rieni fan hyn! = there are so few parents here!
• = so little
mae cynlleied o amser ar ôl! = there's so little time left!
• = as few (âʰ as)
mae rhaid gorffen y gêm gyda ʰchynlleied o °gardiau ag sy'n °bosib = you have to finish the game with as few cards as possible
• = as little (âʰ as)
enilles i ugain punt—cynlleied â hynny? = I won twenty pounds—as little as that?
• = so small
fe °gafodd yr actorion eu siomi, cynlleied oedd y °gynulleidfa = the actors were disappointed, so small was the audience

❗ *As a quantity expression, cynlleied requires a following oº when a noun is specified. It can refer to singulars and plurals, hence the various translations possible.*

cynllun (plural -iau) noun, masculine
• = plan
dyma ⁿghynllun mewn un gair: 'swyddi' = here's my plan in one word: 'jobs'
• = scheme
cynllun cyffuriau yn helpu teuluoedd = drug scheme helps families

• = design
mae cynllun yr adeilad yn °drawiadol = the design of the building is striking

cynllunio *verbnoun*
• = plan
mae angen cynllunio i °ddod â mwy o adnoddau hamdden i'r ardal = we need to plan to bring more leisure resources to the area
• = design

cynnal (*stem* **cynhali-**) *verbnoun*
• = hold (*function etc*)
bydd gwrandawiadau'n cael eu cynnal ymhob cwr o °Gymru ym mis Chwefror = auditions will be held all over Wales in February
cynhelir disgo i °godi arian tuag at °Gymdeithas Rhieni Ysgol Llaneglwys = a disco will be held to raise money for Llaneglwys School Parents' Association
• = carry out (*test etc*)
roedd y profion wedi'u cynnal yn sgîl y tân difrifol yn Sellafield llynedd = the tests had been carried out following the serious fire at Sellafield last year
• = support, maintain

cynnar *adjective*
comparative **cynharach**, *superlative* **cynhara(f)**
= early
mae'n rhy °gynnar i °bobol °greadigol fel fi = it's too early for creative people like me
fe °fydda i'n mynd i'r gwely'n °gynharach na Rowena fel arfer = I go to bed earlier than Rowena usually

cynnau *verbnoun*
= light; ignite
ydy rhywun yn mynd i °gynnau tân? = is someone going to light a fire?

cynnes *adjective*
comparative **cynhesach**, *superlative* **cynhesa(f)**
= warm
cadwch yn °gynnes! = keep warm!
mae'n °gynhesach fan hyn nawr nag oedd hi bore 'ma = it's warmer (in) here now than it was this morning
⇒**twym**

cynnig
1 (*plural* **cynigion**) *noun, masculine*
• = offer; proposal
dewiswch o amrywiaeth o °gynigion cyffrous i'r teulu = choose from a range of exciting family offers
• = motion (*in meeting, etc*)
siaradodd neb yn erbyn yn cynnig = nobody spoke against the motion
2 (*stem* **cynigi-**) *verbnoun*
= offer
mae'r bwrdd yn cynnig ystod o °gymorth i °gwmnïau newydd = the board offers a range of help to new companies

cynnwys (*stem* **cynhwys-**)
1 *verbnoun*
• = include
mae cost y °daith yn cynnwys yswiriant personol = the cost of the trip includes personal insurance
• = contain
mae'r bocs 'ma'n cynnwys y dogfenni i gyd = this box contains all the documents
⇒**gan °gynnwys**
2 *noun, masculine*
= contents (*of book etc*)

cynnydd *noun, masculine*
• = increase; growth
yn y degawdau diwethaf bu cynnydd mawr yn y °farchnad = in the last decades there has been a great increase in the market
mae chwyddiant ar °gynnydd = inflation is on the increase
• = progress
mae'r dosbarth dechreuwyr yn gwneud cynnydd = the beginners' class is making (good) progress
⇒**twf**

cynnyrch (*plural* **cynhyrchion**) *noun, masculine*
• = produce
• = product
cynnyrch o °Gymru = produce of Wales

cynradd *adjective*
(*of school*) = primary
mae hyn oll yn rhan o °fywyd ysgol °gynradd mewn ardal °wledig = all this is part of primary school life in a rural area
daeth 21 o °blant ysgolion cynradd Cylch Ystwyth ynghyd = 21 children

from Ystwyth district primary schools came together
⇒**uwchradd**

cynrychioli *verbnoun*
= represent
y °broblem yw bod nhw'n cynrychioli seddi o'r tu allan i °Gymru = the problem is that they represent seats outside Wales

cynrychiolydd (*plural* **cynrychiolwyr**) *noun, masculine*
= representative

cynta(f) *adjective*
= first
dyma'r tro cynta i mi ymweld â'r °dre 'ma = this is the first time I've visited this town
cymerwch y stryd °gynta ar y chwith = take the first street on the left

> **!** *This ordinal numeral is the only one in Welsh to follow its noun—cf* ⇒**ail°**, ⇒**trydydd**. *In compound numerals* (eleventh, twenty-first *etc.*) **unfed** *is used instead:* **yr unfed ar hugain** *the twenty-first. There is a permanently mutated variant* ⇒**°gynta** *which is used as an adverb.*

cynulleidfa (*plural* **-oedd**) *noun, feminine*
= audience
ydyn nhw'n ymwybodol o beth ydy angen eu cynulleidfa? = are they aware of what the needs of their audience are?
oedd y digwyddiad yn denu cynulleidfaoedd pitw = the event attracted meagre audiences

cynulliad (*plural* **-au**) *noun, masculine*
= assembly
y Cynulliad = the (Welsh) Assembly

cynyddol *adjective*
= increasing

cynyddu *verbnoun*
= increase
cynyddu mae'r galwadau am i'r Gweinidog ymddiswyddo = calls for the Minister to resign are increasing

cyrff *plural of*
⇒**corff**

cyrraedd (*stem* **cyrhaedd-**) *verbnoun*
• = arrive
pryd mae'r trên yn cyrraedd? = when does the train arrive?
• = reach
mae cyrraedd pobol yn elfen °bwysig = reaching people is an important element
mi na i °bopeth sy o °fewn 'y nghyrraedd = I'll do everything in my power

cysgod (*plural* **-ion**) *noun, masculine*
= shade; shadow
o'n nhw'n gorwedd dan °gysgod y °goeden = they were lying in the shade of the tree

cysgu *verbnoun*
= sleep
cysga'n °dawel = sleep tight

cyson *adjective*
• = regular
eir yno'n °gyson = people go there regularly
• = consistent
mi °fyddai'n syniad da iddo °geisio bod yn °gyson am unwaith = it would be a good idea for him to try and be consistent for once
⇒**rheolaidd**

cystadleuaeth (*plural* **cystadlaethau**) *noun, feminine*
= competition

cystadlu *verbnoun*
= compete; enter (*competition*)
pwy sy am °gystadlu? = who wants to compete?
does gan neb o'r staff na'u perthnasau hawl i °gystadlu = no member of staff or their relations is allowed to enter the competition

cystal *adjective*
= so good; as good (**â**[h] as)
mae e cystal â neb yn y dosbarth = he's as good as anyone in the class

> **!** *This word, like all equative adjectives, does not use the linking particle* **yn°** *with a preceding verb* **bod** *to be—so while we say, for example,* **mae e'n °dda** *he's good, and* **mae e'n °well** *he's better, we don't say* *mae e'n °gystal.

cysylltiad (*plural* **-au**) *noun, masculine*
= connection, link

cysylltu *verbnoun*
= contact; get in touch (**â**[h] with)
ffurflenni ar °**gael drwy** °**gysylltu â'n swyddfa** = forms available by contacting our office
cysylltwch â ni yn °**ddi-oed!** = get in touch with us at once!

cytsain (*plural* **cytseiniaid**) *noun, feminine*
= consonant
⇒**llafariad**

cytundeb (*plural* **-au**) *noun, masculine*
• = agreement
bydd rhaid iddyn nhw °**ddod i** °**gytundeb** °**ryw ffordd neu'i gilydd** = they'll have to come to an agreement one way or another
• = contract
pryd °**gawn ni arwyddo cytundeb?** = when can we sign a contract?

cytuno *verbnoun*
= agree (**â**[h] with)
ydy pawb yn cytuno â fi? = does everyone agree with me?
cytuno'n llwyr! = I quite agree!
⇒**anghytuno**

cythraul *noun, masculine*
• = devil
cer i °**gythraul!** = go to hell!
• (*as intensifier*)
be' °**gythraul wyt ti'n** °**wneud?** = what the hell are you doing?
⇒**diawl**, ⇒**uffern**

cyw (*plural* **-ion**) *noun, masculine*
= chick
peidiwch cyfri'r cywion cyn iddyn nhw °**ddeor** (*proverb*) = don't count your chickens before they're hatched

cyweirio *verbnoun*
= repair
bydd rhaid cael ei °**gyweirio, on' bydd?** = it'll have to be repaired, won't it?

cyw iâr (*plural* **cywion ieir**) *noun, masculine*
= chicken
does dim cyw iâr ar y °**fwydlen heno** = there's no chicken on the menu tonight

cywilydd *noun, masculine*
= shame
cywilydd arnat ti! = shame on you!
does dim eisiau bod â [h]**chywilydd, nag oes?** = there's no need to feel ashamed, is there?
mae cywilydd arna i = I am ashamed

> **!** *Like many nouns denoting temporary physical and emotional states,* **cywilydd** *is used with* **ar**° + *person where the sentence structure allows, as in the last example.*

cywir *adjective*
• = correct
£2 o °**wobr i'r ymgais cywir cyntaf allan o'r het** = A prize of £2 for the first correct entry out of the hat
• (*in letters*) = sincere, true
Yr eiddoch yn °**gywir** = Yours truly
Yn °**gywir iawn** = Yours very truly
⇒**anghywir**

cywiro *verbnoun*
= correct
newch chi °**gywiro** [n]**ngwallau iaith i mi?** = will you correct my language errors for me?

CHch

ch-

Many words you may encounter beginning ch- will in fact be aspirate mutations of c-, and should therefore be looked up under this separate letter. A good indicator of ch- root words in Welsh is that they nearly all begin chw-.

'ch *adjective*

= your

> ! *This is a contracted form, used after vowels, of the possessive adjective* ⇒**eich.**

lle mae'ch bagiau? = where are your bags?

ydy'ch rhif ffôn yn y llyfr? = is your phone number in the book?

ewch â'ch sbwriel chi adre = take your rubbish home

dylai'ch gwaith cwrs °fod i mewn erbyn diwedd y mis = your course work should be in by the end of the month

chadal *particle*

= according to; so...say(s)

> ! *This is a Northern colloquial contraction of* ⇒**chwedl** *which has taken on its own particularized meaning. It is mainly used with names or extended pronouns.*

fo oedd y gorau, chadal nhwthau = he was the best, so they say

chdi *pronoun*

= you

> ! *This is a widespread colloquial Northern variant of* ⇒**ti,** *but has certain restrictions on use, notably that it cannot be used as the subject with preterite verbs—so not* *°welest chdi *'you saw' but* °**welest ti** *as standard.*

mi °ddo i hefo chdi rwan = I'll come with you now

mi °weles i chdi yn y °dre neithiwr = I saw you in town last night

chi *pronoun*

= you

sut dych chi? = how are you?

lle °fuoch chi trwy'r dydd? = where have you been all day?

mae pawb yn aros amdanoch chi = everyone's waiting for you

dim ond chi sy ar ôl = you are the only ones left

°welwch chi'r siop 'na gyferbyn y banc? = do you see that shop opposite the bank?

chi sy ar °fai! = you are to blame!

bydda i eisiau gweld chi'ch dwy ar ôl cinio, iawn? = I'll want to see you two after lunch, OK?

mae'n gwneud i chi °feddwl, on'd ydy? = it makes you think, doesn't it?

> ! ⇒**you** *on the English-Welsh side*

chimod *contraction of* dych chi'n gwybod

= you know, y'know

> ! *This is very colloquial, but very common, and is used in Southern areas as a parenthetical expression in the same way as its English counterpart. It cannot start a sentence, and instead nearly always appears in the form of a 'tag' at the end, or as a pause-filler. The* **ti** *equivalent is* ⇒**timod.** *Northern areas use inflected forms of* ⇒**gwybod** *instead.*

'sdim llawer i °gael erbyn hyn, chimod = there's not many around these days, you know

wel...chimod...dw i °ddim yn siwr = well...you know...I'm not sure

⇒**gwybod,** ⇒**timod**

chithau *pronoun*

= you

> ! **chithau** *is one of the special set of expanded pronouns that are used— though not that frequently—to convey emphasis or some idea of contrast with, or echoing of, what has gone before. With the possessive* ⇒**eich, chithau** *can replace following* **chi** *to give special emphasis or contrast.*

Nadolig Llawen i chi!—A chithau! = a Happy Christmas to you!—And (to) you too!

ewch chithau i ofyn = <u>you</u> go and ask
beth am eich car chithau? = what
  about <u>your</u> car?
⇒**chi**

chwaer (*plural* **chwiorydd**) *noun,*
  feminine
  = sister
  dyma 'n chwaer i = this is my sister
  faint o chwiorydd sy 'da ti? = how
    many sisters have you got?

chwaith *adverb.*
  = (not)...either
  na finnau chwaith = me neither
  **dw i °ddim yn nabod e, ac dw i °ddim
    eisiau nabod e chwaith** = I don't
    known him, and I don't want to know
    him either
  **°fydd y Rhyddfrydwyr °ddim yn hapus
    chwaith** = the Liberals won't be happy
    either

> **!** *This adverb is used with negative*
> *verbs and other words with negative*
> *connotations. A different adverb*
> ⇒**naill ai** *is needed for the positive*
> *sense either...(or...).*

chwalu *verbnoun*
  • = scatter
  • = destroy
    chwalwyd tŷ gan °daflegryn = the
      house was destroyed by a missile
  • = demolish
    **chwalwyd dros °ddau °ddwsin o
      ffermdai** = over two dozen farmhouses
      were demolished
  • = blow up
    **fe °gafodd y tractor ei chwalu'n
      yfflon gan °fom mortar** = the tractor
      was blown to pieces by a mortar bomb

chwaneg, chwanag *adverb*
  (*North*)
  = more
  ⇒**rhagor**

chwarae (*stem* **chwarae-**) *verbnoun*
  = play
  pwy chwaraeodd ddoe? = who played
    yesterday?
  **mae Cymru'n chwarae yn erbyn
    Lloegr yfory** = Wales are playing
    (against) England tomorrow

> **!** **chwarae** *is also used for playing*
> *musical instruments, except for*

canu'r °delyn play the harp, *and
  other stringed instruments where both*
  canu *and* **chwarae** *are used. The
  phrase* **chwarae teg (i°)** *fair play is
  widely used in a concessionary
  sense, rather like* 'admittedly', *or* 'you
  have to admit', *or* 'you've got to hand it
  to him/her/them'.
  **ond, chwarae teg, mae e wedi
    gwneud ei °orau** = but you've got to
    admit he's done his best
  **oedd hynny'n °dipyn o °gamp,
    chwarae teg iddi** = you've got to
    hand it to her, that was quite an
    achievement

maes chwarae = playing field

chwaraeon *plural noun*
  = sport(s), games
  **o'n i °ddim yn rhy hoff o chwaraeon
    yn yr ysgol** = I wasn't too keen on
    games/sport at school

chwarddu *verbnoun*
  = laugh
  chwarddodd pawb = everyone laughed
⇒**chwerthin**

chwarter (*plural* **-i, -au**) *noun,*
  masculine
  = quarter
  mae'n chwarter i wyth = it's a quarter
    to eight
  mae'n tynnu at chwarter wedi pump =
    it's getting on for a quarter past five

chwe^h, chwech *numeral*
  = six

> **!** *As with* ⇒**pum(p),** *the shorter form
> of this numeral is used with a directly
> following singular noun (though some
> areas do not follow this rule), while the
> longer form is used in other instances,
> for example with a following* **o°** +
> *plural noun, or on its own. As is
> generally the case in the modern
> spoken language, the aspirate
> mutation after* **chwe** *is by no means
> rigidly adhered to, and certainly
> instances of aspiration of* **p-** *and* **t-**
> *are very much confined to set
> phrases like* **chwe ^hphunt** £6.

mae chwech wedi mynd yn °barod =
  six have gone already
**dwy °bunt a chwe ^hcheiniog, os
  gwelwch yn °dda** = two pounds and
  six pence, please.

chwe afal, chwech o afalau = six apples
faint sy ar ôl?—chwech = how many
are left?–six
lle chwech (*Northern euphemism*) =
toilet
dw i'n gorfod mynd i'r lle chwech = I've
got to go to the loo

chweched *adjective*
= sixth
bydd aelodau o'r chweched dosbarth
ar °gael i'ch tywys o °gwmpas yr
ysgol = members of the sixth form
will be on hand to take you round the
school

! *Ordinal numerals are adjectives, but
behave in a special way. All other than
*⇒cynta *precede the noun. With
feminine singular nouns, the noun
itself undergoes soft mutation, as
does the ordinal after the article—so:*
y chweched dyn *the sixth man, but* y
chweched °ferch *the sixth girl;* y
trydydd car *the third car, but* y
°drydedd °goeden *the third tree.*

chwedl (*plural* -au) *noun. feminine*
= fable, fairytale, tale
chwedlau'r hen °Lychlynwyr = tales of
the old Norsemen

chwedlonol *adjective*
= fabulous (*also figurative*)

chwedyn *adverbial phrase*
(*contraction of* ac wedyn)
= and then
aethon ni allan, chwedyn °ddaethon
ni'n ôl = we went out, and then we
came back
⇒wedyn

Chwefror *noun, masculine*
= February
does dim stafelloedd rhydd 'da ni tan
°ganol mis Chwefror = we haven't got
any rooms free till the middle of
February
⇒Ionawr

ch'wel
contraction of dych chi'n gweld
= you see
rhaid gwneud e ffordd hyn, ch'wel =
you have to do it like this, you see
⇒gweld, ⇒t'wel

chwerthin (*stem* chwerth-)
verbnoun
= laugh
mi chwerthes i nes o'n i'n °wan = I
laughed till I was weak
peidiwch â chwerthin am ei °ben o! =
stop laughing/don't laugh at him!
⇒chwarddu

chwerthinllyd *adjective*
= laughable, ludicrous

chwerw *adjective*
= bitter
mi °fydd hi'n °bwysig i chi °beidio
gadael iddo °fynd yn chwerw = it'll be
important for you not to let him get
bitter

chweugain *numeral*
= a hundred and twenty

! *This unusual throwback to pre-
decimal coinage is still used
colloquially for 'fifty pence' (the old
'ten shillings', i.e. half of a pound,
which used to comprise 240 pence).*

dim ond pisin chweugain sy gynna i =
I've only got a fifty-pence piece

chwibanu *verbnoun*
= whistle
pwy sy'n chwibanu yn y cefn 'na? =
who's whistling at the back there?

chwilio *verbnoun*
= look (am° for); seek
oeddech chi'n chwilio amdana i? =
were you looking for me?

chwiorydd *plural of*
⇒chwaer

chwith *adverb, adjective*
= left
cymerwch yr ail stryd ar y chwith =
take the second street on the left
trowch i'r chwith = turn left
dangos dy °law chwith = show (me)
your left hand
mynd yn chwith *or* mynd o'r chwith =
go wrong
mi aeth popeth yn chwith bore 'ma =
everything went wrong this morning

chwydu *verbnoun*
= throw up, vomit

! *In colloquial speech* chwdu *is the
usual pronunciation of this word.*

chwyddiant *noun, masculine*
= inflation
mae chwyddiant yn dal i °fod yn °broblem = inflation is still a problem

chwyldro (*plural* **-adau**) *noun, masculine*
= revolution (*usually figurative*)
draw yn y gorllewin, mae yna chwyldro iaith tawel yn digwydd = over in the west, there is a quiet linguistic revolution happening
...ymhell cyn y Chwyldro Ffrengig = ...long before the French Revolution

chwyldroadol *adjective*
= revolutionary

chwys *noun, masculine*
= sweat
roedd o mewn chwys = he was in a sweat

chwysu *verbnoun*
= sweat, perspire

chwythu *verbnoun*
= blow
bydd y gwyntoedd yn chwythu'n ysgafn o'r gorllewin = the winds will be blowing gently from the west
neith o chwythu'r tŷ i lawr = it will blow the house down

Dd

da *adjective*
= good
comparative ⇨**gwell** better, *equative* ⇨**cystal** as/so good, *superlative* ⇨**gorau** best
bore da! = good morning!
noswaith °dda! = good evening!
nos da! = good night!
mae'r °ddrama wedi'i hysgrifennu'n °dda = the play has been well written
mae'n °dda gen i °gwrdd â chi = I'm pleased to meet you
da oedd clywed °fod popeth yn iawn = it was good to hear that everything is OK

'da *preposition* (*South*)
= with
⇨**gyda**

dacw° *adverb*
= over there
edrychwch! dacw °rai nawr, yng ⁿghefn yr harbwr = look! there are some over there now, at the far end of the harbour
⇨**acw**, ⇨**'co**

dadansoddi *verbnoun*
= analyse
mi °fydd hi'n cymryd tipyn o amser i °ddadansoddi'r ffigurau i gyd = it'll take a bit of time to analyse all the figures

dadl (*plural* **-euon**) *noun, feminine*
= argument; debate
ar yr un pryd bu dadl ffyrnig ymysg gwyddonwyr = at the same time there has been a fierce debate among scientists

dadlau *verbnoun*
= argue, contend
mae llyfr newydd yn dadlau °fod y °frwydr dros yr iaith wedi'i ʰcholli'n °barod = a new book argues that the fight for the language has already been lost

dadleuol *adjective*
= controversial

fe °fydd ffilm °ddadleuol yn cael ei
dangos ar y sianel wedi'r cyfan = a
controversial film will be shown on
the channel after all

dadlwytho *verbnoun*
= unload
°gawn ni °banaid °gynta, wedyn
dadlwytho'r lori = we'll have a cup of
tea first, then (we'll) unload the lorry

daear *noun, feminine*
= earth
does mo'i °debyg ar wyneb y °ddaear
= there's nothing (else) like it on the
face of the earth
uffern ar y °ddaear = hell on earth
⇒byd, ⇒pridd

daeargryn *noun, masculine or
feminine*
= earthquake

dafad (*plural* **defaid**) *noun, feminine*
= sheep

dagrau *plural noun*
⇒deigryn

dangos *verbnoun*
= show (i° to)
°ellwch chi °ddangos i mi ar y map lle
mae'r °orsaf? = can you show me on
the map where the station is?
dangoswch i'r lleill, newch chi? =
show it to the others, will you?
rhaid diolch iddyn nhw am °ddangos
cymaint o hyder yn y cylchgrawn =
they must be thanked for showing
such confidence in the magazine

dail *plural noun*
= leaves; foliage
bydd y °goeden 'ma wedi colli'i dail
erbyn hynny = this tree will have lost
its leaves by then
⇒deilen

dal (*stem* **dali-**) *verbnoun*
• = catch
os na °ddaw e cyn hir, bydd rhaid inni
°ddal y bws = if he doesn't come soon,
we'll have to catch the bus.
• (*with* **ati**) = persevere, stick at
(*something*)
daliwch ati! = stick at it!
rheswm arall i mi °ddal ati oedd siarad
â pobol lleol = another reason for me
to keep at it was talking to local people
• (*expressing continuation*)

! ⇒still 2 *on the English-Welsh side.*

• = rely, depend
does dim dal ar y bysiau fan hyn = you
can't rely on the buses here

dall *adjective*
• = blind
mae hi'n mynd yn °ddall = she's going
blind
• *plural* **deillion** used as noun:
y deillion = the blind
dim cŵn ac eithrio cŵn y deillion = no
dogs except guide dogs

damwain (*plural* **damweiniau**) *noun,
feminine*
= accident
mi °gafodd hi °ddamwain ar y ffordd
i'w gwaith = she had an accident on
the way to (her) work
mae 'na ofnau y bydd yr uned
°ddamweiniau'n gorfod cau = there
are fears that the accident unit will
have to close
ar °ddamwain, drwy °ddamwain = by
accident
°ges i'r ateb cywir ar °ddamwain = I
got the right answer by accident
mi °ddigwyddodd y cyfan drwy
°ddamwain = the whole thing
happened by accident

dan° (*also* **o dan°**) *preposition*
= under
personal forms **dana i, danat ti, dano
fe, dani hi, danon ni, danoch chi,
danyn nhw** (*or* **o dana i, o danat ti** *etc*)
mae'r llyfrau dan y bwrdd = the books
are under the table
rhaid cyflwyno gwaith o dan ffugenw
= work must be submitted under a
pseudonym
mae popeth dan °reolaeth =
everything's under control
dim yn addas i °blant dan °dair blwydd
oed = not suitable for children under
three years old
gweithgareddau dan °do = indoor
activities (*literally*: 'under roof')

! *Occasionally used (with certain
verbnouns) to indicate simultaneous
action (for which the more usual
preposition is* ⇒wrth°):
crwydro'r strydoedd dan °ganu =
wandering the streets singing

danfon *verbnoun*
= send (**i**° to (*place*); **at**° to (*person*))
°allech chi °ddanfon rhagor o °fanylion ata i? = could you send me more details?
danfonwch eich ffurflen °gais i'r cyfeiriad isod = send your application form to the address below
⇨**anfon,** ⇨**hala**

dannoedd *noun, feminine*
= toothache
mae'r °ddannoedd arna i = I've got toothache

> **!** *This word, denoting as it does a temporary physical state, uses* **ar**° *with the person affected;* ⇨**ar**°

dant (*plural* **dannedd**) *noun, masculine*
= tooth
wyt ti'n gofalu am dy °ddannedd °bob dydd, 'te? = do you look after your teeth every day, then?

darganfod (*stem* **darganfydd-**)
verbnoun
= discover
°allwch chi °ddarganfod y trysor sy wedi'i °guddio rhywle ar y tudalen yma? = can you discover the treasure that is hidden somewhere on this page?

darlledu *verbnoun*
= broadcast
mae'r holl °gonsesiynau yn dilyn buddugoliaethau ym maes darlledu = all the concessions follow on from victories in the field of broadcasting

darllen *verbnoun*
= read
darllenwch y cyfarwyddiadau'n °ofalus = read the instructions carefully
es i i °gysgu wrth °ddarllen = I fell asleep while (I was) reading
ymarferion darllen-a-deall = reading comprehension exercises

darn (*plural* **-au**) *noun, masculine*
= piece
bydd eisiau arnoch chi i gyd °ddarn o °bapur = you'll all need a piece of paper

darpar° *adjective*
= prospective (*precedes noun*)

darpar-ymgeisydd = prospective candidate

darparu *verbnoun*
= provide
ein nod yw darparu'r gwasanaeth gorau posibl i'n cwsmeriaid = our aim is to provide the best possible service to our customers
darperir lluniaeth ysgafn = light refreshments will be provided

datblygu *verbnoun*
= develop
°gawn ni °weld sut mae pethau'n datblygu = we'll see how things develop
fe °ddatblygwyd y syniad o °bont °grog = the idea of a suspension bridge was developed

datgan *verbnoun*
• = declare
• = announce
mae'r llywodraeth wedi datgan na °fydd y cytundeb yn cael ei adnewyddu = the government has announced that the contract will not be renewed

datganiad (*plural* **-au**) *noun, masculine*
= announcement
datganiad i'r °wasg = press release

datgloi *verbnoun*
= unlock

datrys *verbnoun*
= solve
mae un °broblem yn dal heb ei datrys = there is one problem still unsolved

dathlu *verbnoun*
i °ddathlu'r dengmlwyddiant mae llyfr wedi'i lansio = to celebrate the tenth anniversary a book has been launched

dau° (*feminine* **dwy**°) *numeral*
= two
dewch draw tua dau o'r °gloch = come round about two o'clock
mae 'na °ddwy stafell arall lan llofft = there are two other rooms upstairs
°gwrddes i ag e °ddwy °flynedd yn ôl = I met him two years ago
mae eu merch yn °ddwy °flwydd oed = their daughter is two years old

> **!** *Both forms of this numeral not only cause soft mutation of a following noun, but also themselves undergo soft mutation when preceded by the definite article:* **y °ddau, y °ddwy** 'the two . . .', 'both . . .':
> **y °ddau °lyfr** = both books
> **y °ddwy °gadair 'na** = both (of) those chairs
> *Where the numeral is used on its own with reference to people or animals, the feminine form is reserved for instances where both are female; the masculine form is used not only for two males, but also for one male and one female. So* **y °ddwy ohonoch chi** both of you *refers unambiguously to two females, while* **y °ddau ohonoch chi** *could be two males, or a male and a female.* Similarly **chi'ch dwy** versus **chi'ch dau** you two; **ni'n dwy** versus **ni'n dau** we two; *and* **ill dwy** versus **ill dau** they two.
> **dim ond ni'n dwy sy ar ôl** = there's only us two *(feminine)* left
> **mi °gaethon nhw eu gwlychu ill dau ar y ffordd adre** = The two of them *(masculine, or masculine + feminine)* got soaked on the way home
> **. . . a'r °ddau o °fewn milltir i'w gilydd** = . . . each within a mile of the other

dawnsio *verbnoun*
= dance
cyfle i °ddawnsio ac ymarfer eich Cymraeg ar yr un pryd = a chance to dance and practise your Welsh at the same time
ymhlith yr atyniadau bydd dawnsio gwerin = attractions will include folk-dancing

de
1 *noun, masculine*
= south
⇒**gogledd** *for phrasings involving points of the compass*
2 *noun, feminine*
= right
ewch yn syth ymlaen fan hyn, yna trowch i'r °dde = go straight on here, then turn right

> **!** *The two senses are differentiated by gender, which becomes apparent when there is a definite article present*: **y de** the south, **y °dde** the right

deall* *verbnoun*
= understand
mae'n °ddrwg gen i, dw i °ddim yn deall = I'm sorry, I don't understand
o'n i °ddim yn deall beth oedd o'n °feddwl = I didn't understand what he meant

dechrau *(stem* **dechreu-***) verbnoun*
• = begin, start
°gawn ni °ddechrau? = can we start?
• *(as noun)* = beginning, start
mae'n °ddechrau cyfnod newydd yn hanes ein hiaith = it's the beginning of a new era in the history of our language
⇒**cychwyn**

deddf *(plural* **-au***) noun, feminine*
= law, statute
mae Cymry Cymraeg yn galw am °ddeddf iaith newydd = Welsh speaking people are calling for a new language law

> **!** *This word is usually pronounced* **deddw** *in speech.*

⇒**cyfraith**

defaid *plural of*
⇒**dafad**

defnydd *(plural* **-iau***) noun, masculine*
• = material
canllawiau ar gyfer cludo defnyddiau hylosg = guidelines for the transport of flammable materials
• = use
°driwn ni °wneud defnydd da o'r °wybodaeth 'ma = we'll try and make good use of this information
⇒**deunydd**

defnyddio *verbnoun*
= use
defnyddiwch y côd post °bob amser = use the post code every time

defnyddiol *adjective*
= useful

deffro *verbnoun (North)*
= wake, wake up

pryd dych chi'n deffro fel arfer? =
when do you usually wake up
bydd rhaid deffro'r plant = the
children will have to be woken

deg *numeral*
= ten
mae'n hanner awr wedi deg = it's half
past ten
bydd deg o siaradwyr yn y rali yfory =
there will be ten speakers at the rally
tomorrow

> **!** *An alternative form* **deng** *is usual
> before* **mil** thousand, **milltir** mile(s),
> **mis** month(s), ⁿ**mlynedd** year(s),
> **munud** minute(s), ⁿ**niwrnod** day(s)
> *and often before* **awr** hour(s) *and*
> **wythnos** week(s).
> **mae'n °ddeng munud i wyth** = it's
> ten (minutes) to eight

⇒**pum(p)**

degfed *adjective*
= tenth
**mae'n °debyg i'r llyfr °gael ei
ysgrifennu yn y °ddegfed °ganrif** =
the book was probably written in the
tenth century

> **!** *Ordinal numerals are adjectives, but
> behave in a special way. All other
> than* ⇒**cynta** *precede the noun.
> With feminine singular nouns, the
> noun itself undergoes soft
> mutation, as does the ordinal after
> the article—so:* **y degfed dyn** the
> tenth man *but* **y °ddegfed °ferch** the
> tenth girl; **y trydydd car** the third car
> *but* **y °drydedd °goeden** the third
> tree.

deheuol *adjective*
= southern; southerly
gair deheuol ydy hwnna = that's a
southern word
**bydd y gwyntoedd deheuol yn para'n
°gryf trwy'r dydd yfory** = the
southerly winds will stay strong all
day tomorrow

> **!** *The paraphrase* **o'r de** *from the
> south is often used as an alternative
> in many cases—***gair o'r de ydy
> hwnna**

dehongli *verbnoun*
= interpret (*not in the sense of
'translate'*)
**ond sut y gellir mynd ati i °ddehongli'r
olion ar y safle?** = but how can we go
about interpreting the remains on the
site?
⇒**cyfieithu**

deigryn (*plural* **dagrau**) *noun,
masculine*
= tear(drop)
aeth i °gysgu yn ei dagrau = she cried
herself to sleep

deilen (*plural* **dail**) *noun, feminine*
= leaf
**oedd o'n crynu fel deilen erbyn y
diwedd** = he was shaking like a leaf by
the end
⇒**dail**

deintydd (*plural* **-ion**) *noun, masculine*
= dentist
**dw i'n gorfod mynd at y deintydd
pnawn 'ma** = I've got to go to the
dentist('s) this afternoon

delfrydol *adjective*
• = ideal, perfect
**ac o sôn am Nadolig, dyma anrheg
°ddelfrydol i'r plant** = and talking of
Christmas, here's an ideal present for
the children
dyma °le delfrydol am stiwdio = this is
a perfect place for a studio
• = idealistic
rhaid peidio bod yn rhy °ddelfrydol =
one mustn't be too idealistic

delio *verbnoun*
= deal (**â**ʰ with)
**o °ddelio â ʰchwmni teuluol dych chi'n
sicr o °dderbyn gwasanaeth da** =
dealing with a family company
ensures you good service

deniadol *adjective*
= attractive
**roedden ni am °gynhyrchu llyfryn
deniadol** = we wanted to produce an
attractive booklet

denu *verbnoun*
= attract
**denu ymwelwyr sy eisiau yn hytrach
na'u troi i ffwrdd** = we need to attract
visitors rather than turn them away

derbyn (*stem* **derbyni-**) *verbnoun*
• = accept
  fe °gafodd ei °dderbyn ar °gwrs = he
  was accepted on a course
  **er iddyn nhw °dderbyn y prif
  argymhellion...** = although they
  accepted the main
  recommendations...
• = receive
  **derbyniwyd dros °ddwsin o
  °geisiadau** = over a dozen applications
  have been received

derbynfa *noun, feminine*
= reception (*room*)
  **mae rhywun yn aros amdanoch chi yn
  y °dderbynfa** = someone is waiting for
  you in reception

derbyniol *adjective*
= acceptable

derbynnydd (*plural* **derbynyddion**)
noun, masculine
• = receptionist
• (*of telephone*) = receiver

derbynyddes (*plural* **-au** *noun,
feminine*
= receptionist

dere
⇒**dod**

deud
⇒**dweud**

deuddeg *numeral*
= twelve
  pan o'n i °ryw °ddeuddeg oed... =
  when I was about twelve...
  **°wela i di am hanner awr wedi
  deuddeg** = I'll see you at half past
  twelve

> **!** *This is the native term for 12, while a
> 'decimalized' form* **undeg dau** *is
> promoted in schools. Even so, there is
> no alternative to* **deuddeg** *for telling
> the time, and native speakers use*
> **deuddeg** *anyway. An alternative form*
> **deuddeng** *is used in the same
> circumstances as is* **deng** *for* ⇒**deg**.

deuddegfed *adjective*
= twelfth
  **fe °fyddwn ni yma tan y deuddegfed o
  °fis Medi** = we'll be here till the twelfth
  of September
⇒**pumed**

deuddydd *adverb*
= two days
  **mi °fydd y °gynhadledd yn para am
  °ddeuddydd** = the conference will last
  two days
⇒**diwrnod**, ⇒**dydd**

deufis *adverb*
= two months
  **disgwylir i'r ymchwiliad cyhoeddus
  °bara am °ddeufis** = the public inquiry
  is expected to last for two months

deugain *numeral*
= forty
  **aeth deugain ⁿmlynedd heibio ers
  cyhoeddi'r °gyfrol °gynta** = forty years
  have gone by since the publication of
  the first volume
  mae deugain punt arnyn nhw inni =
  they owe us forty pounds

> **!** **deugain**, *the original numeral for*
> forty, *appears these days more
> restricted in use than* ⇒**ugain**
> twenty, *and is mostly used with
> 'years'* (*note nasal mutation of*
> **blynedd** *in the example above*) *and*
> 'pounds'. *But* 'forty pence' *is usually*
> **pedwardeg ceiniog**, *using the new
> decimal form.*

deunydd (*plural* **-iau**) *noun, masculine*
= material
  **dyma i chi ychydig o °ddeunydd
  darllen yn y cyfamser** = meanwhile
  here's some reading material for you
⇒**defnydd**

dewis
1 *noun, masculine*
• = choice
  ti sy â'r dewis = the choice is yours
• = selection
  dewis eang o °lyfrau = a wide selection
  of books
2 *verbnoun*
= choose
  dewiswch eich rhifau = choose your
  numbers
  **°allwn i °ddim °fod wedi dewis amser
  gwell** = I couldn't have chosen a better
  time

di *pronoun*
= you
⇒**dy°**, ⇒**ti**

di-° *prefix (prefixed mainly to nouns)*
= -less, without...
  **mae'r car yn cychwyn yn °ddi-ffwdan
yn y bore** = the car starts without any
fuss in the morning
  **does neb eisiau'r °fath °ddiweithdra
fan hyn yng ⁿNghymru** = no-one wants
that kind of unemployment here in
Wales
  **teulu di-Gymraeg oedd yn byw fan'na
°bryd 'ny** = a non-Welsh-speaking
family used to live there then
  mi aeth yr holl °daith yn °ddidrafferth
= the whole trip went without a
hitch
  **mae'r cwestiwn 'na'n °gwbwl
°ddiystyr** = that question is quite
meaningless
  maes parcio di-dâl = free car park (*lit:
'car park without payment'*)

> **!** *Sometimes verbs are formed from
> di°- + noun, e.g.* ⇒**diswyddo** *dismiss,
> sack from* ⇒**swydd** *job;* ⇒**digalonni**
> *lose heart, from* ⇒**calon** *heart.*

dianc (*stem* **dihang-**) *verbnoun*
= escape (**rhag** from)
  **roedd yn rhan o'r ymgais i °ddianc
rhag cysgod 1979** = it was part of the
attempt to escape from the shadow of
1979

diawl *noun, masculine*
• = devil
  i'r diawl ag e! = to hell with him!
• *as intensifier*
  be' °ddiawl wyt ti'n °wneud? = what
the hell are you doing?
⇒**cythraul,** ⇒**uffern**

diawledig *adjective*
= bloody (*intensifier*)

dibaid *adjective*
= ceaseless; endless; constant
  **dw i wedi cael llond bol(a) o'r dadlau
dibaid 'ma** = I've had it up to here with
this constant arguing
  **os bydd lorïau trymion yn gyrru'n ôl
a blaen yn °ddibaid...** = if heavy
lorries drive ceaselessly back and
forth...
⇒**peidio**

di-ben-draw *adjective*
= endless; ceaseless

**bydden nhw'n crwydro'r moroedd yn
°ddi-ben-draw** = they would endlessly
wander the seas

dibynnu *verbnoun*
• = depend (**ar°** on)
  **mae llawer iawn yn dibynnu ar y
pleidlais 'ma** = a great deal depends/is
depending on this vote
  mae'n dibynnu (ar) faint sy'n dod = it
depends how many come
• = rely (**ar°** on)
  gallwch chi °ddibynnu arnon ni = you
can rely on us

didrafferth *adjective*
= without a hitch, without problems;
smoothly
  os eith popeth yn °ddidrafferth... = if
everything goes smoothly...

diddefnydd *adjective*
= useless

diddordeb (*plural* **-au**) *noun,
masculine*
= interest
  **oes diddordeb gennych chi mewn
dysgu Cymraeg fel ail iaith?** = are you
interested in teaching Welsh as a
second language?
  **pam yr oedd y digwyddiad yma o
°gymaint o °ddiddordeb i seryddion?**
= why was this event of such interest to
astronomers?

diddorol *adjective*
= interesting
  **mae'n °ddiddorol gweld mor ffyrnig
°fu'r dadlau rhwng y °ddwy °blaid** =
it's interesting to see how fierce the
quarreling has been between the two
parties
  **ceir erthyglau diddorol °bob mis ar
°wahanol °bynciau** = there are
interesting articles on various subjects
every month

diferyn (*plural* **diferion**) *noun,
masculine*
= drop (*of liquid*)
  chwe wythnos heb °ddiferyn o °law =
six weeks without a drop of rain
  °gymeri di °ddiferyn? = will you have a
drink?

diflannu *verbnoun*
= disappear, vanish

mae'r amseroedd wedi newid, ac mae diwydiant trwm wedi diflannu °fwy na lai = times have changed, and heavy industry has more or less disappeared

diflas *adjective*
- = miserable; dull
  byddai byd di-liw yn °ddiflas dros °ben = a world without colour would be extremely dull
- = boring
  'na °ddiflas! = how boring!

difri(f)
in: **o °ddifri** = serious (*intent*)
wyt ti o °ddifri? = are you serious?
rhaid cymryd y gwrthwynebiadau o °ddifri = the objections must be taken seriously

difrifol *adjective*
= serious (*not trivial*)
mae'r sefyllfa'n un °ddifrifol = the situation is (a) serious (one)
mae dyn arall yn °ddifrifol °wael yn yr ysbyty = another man is seriously ill in hospital

difrod *noun, masculine*
= damage
achoswyd gwerth pum mil o °bunnoedd o °ddifrod = five thousand pounds' worth of damage was caused
⇒**niwed**

difyr *adjective*
- = entertaining
  dyma °gyfrol °ddifyr a darllenadwy = this is an entertaining and readable volume
- = pleasant
⇒**annifyr**

diffodd *verbnoun*
- = extinguish, put out
- = switch off (*appliances*)
  diffoddwch y goleuadau wrth °adael = switch off the lights as you leave

diffyg (*plural* **-ion**) *noun, masculine*
- = lack, want
  diffyg cyllid yw gwraidd y °broblem = lack of finance is the root of the problem
  mae'r cwynion yn ymwneud â diffyg gwybodaeth = the complaints are to do with lack of information

...yn ⁿniffyg gwell gair... = ...for want of a better word...
- = defect
  mae diffyg yn y ffigurau = there is a defect in the figures

digalonni *verbnoun*
- = lose heart
  peidiwch digalonni! = don't lose heart!
- = discourage
  mae'n °bwysig bod myfyrwyr °ddim yn cael eu digalonni = it's important that students not be discouraged

digon *adverb*
= enough
oes digon o °le fan hyn? = is there enough room here?
mae digon o seddi i °bawb yn y stafell arall = there are enough seats for everybody in the other room
mae gynni hi °ddigon fel y mae = she's got enough as it is
ydy pum punt yn °ddigon? = is five pounds enough?
...os nad yw'r °derminoleg yn °ddigon hyblyg = ...if the terminology is not flexible enough
mi naeth yn °ddigon da hebdda i = he/she did well enough without me
gallech chi °feddwl y byddai awr yn hen °ddigon o amser = you might think that an hour would be more than enough time
digon yw digon = enough is enough
'na °ddigon am heddiw = that's enough for today

> ! *As a quantity expression,* **digon** *requires a following* **o°** *when a noun is specified; but not when it qualifies an adjective.*

digonol *adjective*
= sufficient, adequate
°gawn ni °weld a °fydd y grant yn °ddigonol eleni = we shall see whether the grant will be sufficient this year

digwydd *verbnoun*
= happen, occur
beth sy wedi digwydd? = what has happened?
beth °ddigwyddodd? = what happened?
beth sy'n digwydd? = what's happening/going on?

ac os digwydd i chi °fod yn yr ardal °rywdro, beth am °ddod i'n gweld? = and if you happen to be in the area anytime, what about coming to see us?
petai hyn yn digwydd, byddai rhaid ystyried dau °berygl = if this were to happen, two dangers would have to be considered

digwyddiad (plural **-au**) noun, masculine
= event; happening

dihangfa noun, feminine
= emergency exit
sicrhewch eich bod chi'n gwybod ble mae'r °ddihangfa agosaf = make sure you know where the nearest emergency exit is

dihuno verbnoun (South)
= wake (up)
pryd nest ti °ddihuno? = when did you wake up
dihuna! = wake up!
bydd rhaid dihuno fe = we'll have to wake him up
⇒**ar °ddihun**, ⇒**deffro**

dileu verbnoun
• = delete, cross out/off
dw i am °ddileu 'n enw o'r rhestr = I want to cross my name off the list
• = get rid of
mae peryg y byddai'n rhaid dileu cwmnïau bach = there is a danger that small companies would have to be got rid of

dilyn verbnoun
= follow (also figurative)
dilynwch fi! = follow me!
mae ambell i °ddarn yn anodd ei °ddilyn = the occasional piece is hard to follow

dillad plural noun
= clothes
dych chi eisiau i mi °dynnu ⁿnillad? = do you want me to take my clothes off?

dilledyn noun, masculine
= garment

dim
1 pronoun
• = nothing
wi'n gwybod dim am y peth = I know nothing about it

bydd yn costio'r peth nesa i °ddim = it'll cost next to nothing
• = anything (mainly in negative senses)
mi aeth allan heb °ddweud dim = he/she went out without saying anything
• (as adjective) = no
does dim lle yma = there is no space here
°fydd dim cyfle i chi ailfeddwl wedyn = you'll have no chance to rethink later
pob dim = every single thing
erbyn inni °gyrraedd roedd pob dim wedi mynd = by the time we arrived every last thing had gone
⇒**dim byd**, ⇒**dim ots**, ⇒**i'r dim**
2 particle
= not

> **!** This particle, which negates all verbs in modern Welsh, follows the subject, and is therefore always seen with soft mutation—**°ddim**—except in abbreviated style where the verb is understood but not expressed. The literary equivalent ⇒**ni** (particle) precedes the verb with a variety of mutation patterns, and is entirely restricted to formal written Welsh.
> **°fydda i °ddim yn hir** = I won't be long
> **dw i °ddim eisiau mynd** = I don't want to go
> **dw i'n mynd, ond dyw'r lleill °ddim** = I'm going, but the others are not
> **°ddylech chi °ddim gweiddi fel 'ny** = you shouldn't shout like that
> **aethon ni °ddim yn y diwedd** = we didn't go in the end
> **dim yn addas i °gerbydau nwyddau trwm** = not suitable for heavy goods vehicles
> [abbreviated form of: **dydy'r ffordd 'ma °ddim yn addas...** = this road is not suitable...]
> In focused sentences:
> **dim Iwan °dorrodd y ffenest** = it wasn't Iwan that broke the window

⇒**mo**, ⇒**ni** particle

dim byd pronoun
= nothing
does dim byd ar ôl = there's nothing left
does gen i °ddim byd yn ei erbyn o'n °bersonol, cofia = I have nothing against him personally, mind

beth yw can punt dyddiau 'ma? dim
byd! = what's a hundred pounds these
days? nothing!

! *This phrase is really just a reinforced
version of* ⇒**dim** *(pronoun), and the
single word can usually be
substituted with no difference in
sense or emphasis. All the same,* **dim
byd** *is probably the commoner usage
in the spoken language.*

dim ond *adverb*
= only
dim ond pum punt sy gen i = I've only
got five pounds

! *This colloquial expression
corresponds to the more standard
⇒***yn unig***, but precedes the term
qualified instead of following it (cf.
Pum punt yn unig sy gen i).*

dim ots (gyda/gan°)
= ...don't mind; doesn't matter, never
mind
dw i wedi anghofio'r llaeth.—dim ots =
I've forgotten the milk.—never mind
dim ots gen i aros = I don't mind
waiting
⇒**malio**

dinas (*plural* **-oedd**) *noun, feminine*
= city
**mae trosedd yn ein dinasoedd ar ei
ʰchynnydd** = crime in our cities is on
the increase

dinesydd (*plural* **dinasyddion**) *noun,
masculine*
= citizen

dinistrio *verbnoun*
= destroy

diniwed *adjective*
= harmless; innocent
golwg cwbl °ddiniwed sy arni = she
looks quite harmless

diod (*plural* **-ydd**) *noun, feminine*
= drink
pwy sy am °ddiod arall? = who wants
another drink?

! *The action of drinking, however, is
the unrelated word ⇒***yfed: yfest ti'r
°ddiod 'na?** *did you drink that drink?*

diodde(f) *verbnoun*
• = suffer

y plant sy'n diodde, fel arfer = it's the
children who suffer, as usual
• = stand, bear
**yr unig aelod o'r teulu sy'n gallu
dioddef dŵr croyw** = the only
member of the family that can stand
fresh water
°alla i °ddim diodde nhw = I can't stand
them
⇒**annioddefol**

di-oed *adjective*
= immediate
yr hyn sy eisiau ydy ymateb di-oed =
what is needed is an immediate
response
yn °ddi-oed = without delay, at once
cysylltwch â ni yn °ddi-oed! = get in
touch with us at once!
⇒**ar unwaith**, ⇒**oedi**

diog *adjective*
= lazy

diogel *adjective*
= safe (**rhag** from)
ydyn ni'n °ddiogel fan hyn? = are we
safe here?

diogelu *verbnoun*
= safeguard
**agwedd arall o °waith y Fforwm yw
diogelu'r °dafodiaith °leol** = another
aspect of the Forum's work is
safeguarding the local dialect

diogelwch *noun, masculine*
• = safety
**gwrthodwyd caniatâd am °resymau
diogelwch** = permission was refused
for safety reasons
• = security
**mae'r lluoedd diogelwch yn dal yn yr
ardal** = the security forces are still in
the area

diogi *noun, masculine*
= laziness

diolch *verbnoun*
• = thank
**mae'n braf cael diolch iddyn nhw i
gyd heno** = it's nice to be able to thank
them all this evening
• = thanks (**i°** to)
**mae'n °bosibl ein bod ni yma diolch i
°gomed** = it may be that we are here
thanks to a comet

• = thank you
diolch yn °fawr, llawer o °ddiolch = thanks a lot

diolchgar *adjective*
= thankful, grateful
fe °fyddwn i'n °dra diolchgar pe gallech chi... = I should be very grateful if you could...

di-os
in: **yn °ddi-os** = without a doubt
yn °ddi-os, dyma'r car gorau o'i °fath sy ar y °farchnad ar hyn o °bryd = this is without a doubt the best car of its type on the market at present

diri(f), di-ri(f) *adjective*
= innumerable, countless
collwyd llywbrau a ffyrdd cyhoeddus di-ri = countless paths and public ways have been lost

dirprwy (*plural* **-on**) *noun, masculine*
= deputy

dirwy (*plural* **-on**) *noun, feminine*
= fine
mae mwy nag un llysgenhadaeth heb °dalu ei dirwyon parcio = several embassies have yet to pay their parking fines

dirybudd *adjective*
= without warning
mi °ddaeth y newyddion 'ma'n °gwbwl °ddirybudd = this news came completely without warning

disglair *adjective*
comparative **disgleiriach,** *superlative* **disgleiria(f)**
= bright (*also figurative*)
dyfodol disglair i °gyfansoddwr ifanc o °Bonteglwys = a bright future for a young composer from Ponteglwys
⇒**llachar**

disgrifio *verbnoun*
= describe

disgwyl* *verbnoun*
• = expect
oeddech chi'n disgwyl ateb? = were you expecting a reply?
• = expectation
mae disgwyl y bydd y Rhyddfrydwyr yn pleidleisio yn erbyn = the Liberals are expected to vote against

• = wait
mae'r grŵp wedi blino disgwyl am °gyfleoedd = the group has got tired of waiting for opportunities

disgybl (*plural* **-ion**) *noun, masculine*
= pupil
faint o °ddisgyblion sy gynnoch chi yn yr ysgol 'ma? = how many pupils have you got in this school?

diswyddo *verbnoun*
= dismiss, sack
mae galwadau am i'r gweinidog °gael ei °ddiswyddo = there are calls for the minister to be sacked
⇒**swydd**, ⇒**ymddiswyddo**

dithau
⇒**tithau**

di-waith *adjective*
= unemployed
pa °ganran o °drigolion y °dre sy bellach yn °ddiwaith, 'te? = what percentage of the townspeople are now unemployed, then?
ond dydyn nhw'n °fawr o °gysur i'r di-waith ym ⁿMlaenau Ffestiniog = but they're not much comfort to the unemployed in Blaenau Ffestiniog

diwedd *noun, masculine*
= end
ac mi °fyddwn ni'n rhoi'r rhif ffôn 'na eto ar °ddiwedd y rhaglen = and we'll be giving that phone number again at the end of the programme
yn y diwedd, y °farchnad sy'n penderfynu = in the end, it's the market that decides
⇒**o'r diwedd**

diweddar *adjective*
comparative **diweddarach,** *superlative* **diweddara(f)**
• = recent, late
awn ni drosodd nawr i'r stiwdio newyddion am y penawdau diweddara = now we go over to the news studio for the latest headlines
dw i heb °weld e'n °ddiweddar = I haven't seen him recently
°flynyddoedd yn °ddiweddarach = years later
• (*precedes noun*) = late (*deceased*)
y diweddar Dr Pryce = the late Dr Pryce

diweithdra *noun, masculine*
= unemployment

diwetha(f) *adjective*
= last
ar y trên aethon ni tro diwetha = we
went by train last time

> **!** **diwetha(f)** *means* 'last' *in the sense
> of* 'most recent', *while* 'last' *in the
> sense of* 'last in a series' *is* ⇒**ola(f)**.
> *Compare:*
> °**weles i fe mis diwetha** = I saw him
> last month
> **Rhagfyr yw mis ola'r** °**flwyddyn** =
> December is the last month of the
> year

⇒**llynedd, neithiwr**

diwrnod (*plural* **-au**) *noun, masculine*
= day
pan °**ddaw'r diwrnod gwaith i** °**ben** = at
the end of the working day
fe °**fyddan nhw'n ôl** °**ryw** °**ddiwrnod** =
they'll be back some day
mi °**geith pawb** °**ddiwrnod rhydd**
°**ddydd Gwener nesa** = everyone will
have a day off next Friday
**ond, y diwrnod wedyn, dyma fe'n dod
yn ôl** = but, the next day, back he came

> **!** *The distinction between this word
> and* ⇒**dydd** *is not always easy to
> identify. But* **diwrnod** *really denotes a
> period of 24 hours, or* 'day' *as a set
> period of time rather than, for
> example, the opposite of night, and is
> therefore generally used with
> numbers (with* **pum, saith, naw** *and*
> **deng** *causing nasal mutation, e.g.*
> **pum** ⁿ**niwrnod** *five days). But see*
> ⇒**deuddydd** *and* ⇒**tridiau**.

diwydiannol *adjective*
= industrial

diwydiant (*plural* **diwydiannau**) *noun,
masculine*
= industry
**mae dyfodol diwydiant trwm yr ardal
bellach yn y** °**fantol** = the future of the
area's heavy industry is now in the
balance

diwylliannol *adjective*
= cultural

diwylliant (*plural* **diwylliannau**) *noun,
masculine*
= culture

blas ar hanes a diwylliant yr hen
°**Geltiaid** = a taste of the history and
culture of the ancient Celts

do *particle*
= yes

> **!** ⇒*Yes and No box on the English-
> Welsh side*

⇒**naddo**

doctor (*plural* **-iaid**) *noun, masculine*
= doctor
**mae rhai doctoriaid yn gwrthod gweld
cleifion ar ôl hanner nos** = some
doctors refuse to see patients after
midnight
⇒**meddyg**

dod (*North often* **dŵad**) *verbnoun
(irregular)*
imperative singular **der** *or* **dere**, (*North*)
tyrd, ty'd; *plural* **dewch**
preterite **des i, dest ti, daeth e/hi,
daethon ni, daethoch chi, daethon
nhw**
common variants: 3sg **dôth**
future **do i, doi di, daw e/hi, down ni,
dewch chi, dôn nhw**
common variants: 1sg **da**, *2sg* **dei**, *3sg*
deith, *1pl* **dewn**, *2pl* **dowch**, *3pl* **dân**
*conditional (of restricted use in the
modern language)* **delwn i, delet ti,
delai fe/hi, delen ni, delech chi, delen
nhw**
or **down i, doet ti, dôi fe/hi, doen ni,
doech chi, doen nhw**
*autonomous/impersonal forms:
present/future not in general use, past*
daethpwyd
• = come
ty'd o 'na, nei di? = come (down/away)
from there, will you?
dere 'mlaen! = come on!
dewch i'n gweld ni yn y °**flwyddyn
newydd** = come and see us in the new
year
°**ddaethoch chi ar y trên?** = did you
come by train?
mi °**ddo i efo chdi rwan** (*North*) = I'll
come (along) with you now
. . .pan °**ddaw'r bws** = . . .when the bus
comes
pam na °**ddewch chi draw ar ôl cinio?**
= why don't you come round after
lunch?

• = become
°wyddoch chi am °rywun o'ch cyfnod chi a °ddaeth yn enw cyfarwydd? = do you know of anyone from your period who became a familiar name?
mi °ddaw'n amlwg cyn bo hir = it will soon become clear
⇒**dod â^h**, ⇒**dod o hyd i°**

dod â^h *verbnoun*
= bring
mae angen cynllunio i °ddod â mwy o adnoddau hamdden i'r ardal = (we) need to plan to bring more leisure resources to the area
dewch â'ch arian poced = bring your pocket money

dod o hyd i°
= find, come across
°ddest ti o hyd i 'r allweddi yn y diwedd? = did you find the keys in the end?
daethpwyd o hyd i'w °gorff y bore wedyn = his body was found the following morning
⇒**cael hyd i°**, ⇒**ffeindio**

dodrefn *plural noun*
= furniture
⇒**celfi**

dodwy *verbnoun*
= lay (*eggs*)
ŵy newydd °ddodwy = a newly laid egg

doedd *etc*
⇒**bod**

dogfen (*plural* **-ni, -nau**) *noun, feminine*
• = document
mae 'na °ddogfenni'n bod sy'n dweud fel arall = documents exist which say otherwise
• (*as adjective*) = documentary
°well gen i'r rhaglenni dogfen = I prefer the documentary programmes

Dolig
⇒**Nadolig**

dolur *noun, masculine*
= pain
cael dolur = get hurt, hurt oneself
rhoi dolur = hurt
°fyddi di'n cwympo a cael dolur = you'll fall and hurt yourself
ydy dy °fraich yn dal i °roi dolur? = is your arm still hurting?

°gest ti °ddolur? = did you hurt yourself?
⇒**brifo**

doniol *adjective*
comparative **doniolach** *or* **mwy doniol**, *superlative* **doniola(f)** *or* **mwya doniol**
= funny
⇒**rhyfedd**

dos
⇒**mynd**

dosbarth (*plural* **-iadau**) *noun, masculine*
= class
ymuno â dosbarth yw'r cam cynta = joining a class is the first step
dau stamp dosbarth cynta, os gwelwch yn °dda = two first class stamps, please

dosbarthu *verbnoun*
• = distribute, give out
°elli di helpu fi i °ddosbarthu'r papurau 'ma? = can you help me give out these papers?
• = deliver

draig (*plural* **dreigiau**) *noun, feminine*
= dragon
y Ddraig Goch = the Red Dragon

draw *adverb*
= over
draw yn y gorllewin, mae yna chwyldro iaith tawel yn digwydd = over in the west, there is a quiet linguistic revolution happening
°weles i hi draw fan'na °ddeng munud yn ôl = I saw her over there ten minutes ago
• (*with certain verbs*) = round
fe °allwn ni °alw draw yfory = we can call round tomorrow
pam na °ddoi di draw wedyn? = why don't you come round later?
• (*with* **cadw**) = away
cadwch draw! = keep away!
⇒**tu draw**

drewi *verbnoun*
= stink, smell
mae rhywbeth yn drewi'n ofnadwy fan hyn! = there's a terrible smell here!

drewllyd *adjective*
= stinking

dringo *verbnoun*
= climb

hi oedd y °gynta i °ddringo i °gopa'r mynydd heb ocsigen = she was the first woman to climb to the summit of the mountain without oxygen
dringo coeden = to climb a tree

droeon adverb
= time and again; several times
tre sy wedi cipio'r penawdau droeon = a town which has seized the headlines time and again

> **!** This adverb is a fixed mutation of the plural of ⇒**tro** time

dros° (often **drost** before vowels) preposition
personal forms: **drosta i, drostat ti, drosto fe, drosti hi, droston ni, drostoch chi, drostyn nhw**
• = over
maen nhw wedi mynd drost y °bont = they've gone over the bridge
mi oedd teganau dros y lle i gyd = there were toys all over the place
°fedret ti edrych dros y rheina i mi? = could you look over these for me?
mae dros °fil o °bobol fan hyn yn °barod = there are over a thousand people here already
mae e wedi bod allan ers dros °ddwy awr = he's been out for over two hours
• = for (on behalf of, in favour of)
newch chi °fynd i'r siop drosti? = will you go to the shop for her?
°fydda i byth yn pleidleisio drostyn nhw 'to = I'll never vote for them again

> **!** This preposition is in origin a mutated form of **tros**—the base form is hardly ever encountered in the modern spoken language. The variant **drost** before vowels is common in speech, but never seen in writing.

⇒**drosodd**

dros ben adverbial phrase
= extremely, exceedingly

> **!** This qualifier follows the adjective it qualifies:
> **mae'r canlyniad yn un diddorol dros ben** = the result is an extremely interesting one.

⇒**tu hwnt**

dros dro adjectival phrase
= temporary
swydd dros dro = a temporary job

> **!** This phrase functions as an adjective, but does not undergo soft mutation after feminine singular nouns—see example above.

drosodd adverb
• = over, across
mae'n holl °bwysig bod ni'n llwyddo i °gael y neges 'ma drosodd = it's vital that we succeed in getting this message across
wedyn, aeth nifer o awyrennau drosodd eto tua diwedd y prynhawn = then, a number of aircraft went over again towards the end of the afternoon
bellach mae'r dyddiau 'na drosodd = now those days are over
oedd e'n dweud yr un peth drosodd a drosodd = he was saying the same thing again and again
• = overleaf
Cymraeg drosodd = Welsh overleaf
⇒**dros°**

°druan adjective
= poor

> **!** This mutated form of **truan** is used mainly with names and pronouns to say 'Poor ...' With a name you can either say **°druan o Dafydd!** or **Dafydd °druan!** poor Dafydd (similarly **°druan o Eleri** or **Eleri °druan!**—the sex of the individual has no bearing on the fixed mutation), while pronouns can only use the longer construction with **o°** **°druan ohoni!** poor her!, **°druan ohonyn nhw!** poor them!

drud adjective
comparative **drutach**, superlative **druta(f)**
= expensive, dear
mae'r rhain yn rhy °ddrud = these are too expensive
°glywes i °fod bwyd a pethau felly'n °ddrutach draw fan 'na = I heard that food and suchlike is more expensive over there
⇒**costus**

drwg *adjective*
comparative ⇒**gwaeth** worse, *equative*
⇒**cynddrwg** as/so bad, *superlative*
⇒**gwaetha(f)**
• = bad
sut dach chi heddiw?—dim yn °ddrwg
= how are you today?—not bad
mae pethau'n mynd o °ddrwg i °waeth
= things are going from bad to worse
• = naughty
plant drwg = naughty children
• (*as noun, masculine*) = trouble (=*'bad thing', 'problem'*)
y drwg yw bod hi bron yn amhosib profi'r peth = the trouble is that it's almost impossible to prove it
mae'n °ddrwg gen i (*North*) | **mae'n °ddrwg 'da fi** (*South*) = I'm sorry
dywedwyd ar ei rhan ei bod hi'n °wirioneddol °ddrwg ganddi = it was said on her behalf that she was really sorry
⇒**gwael**

drwodd *adverb*
= through
mi °gerddon nhw drwodd = they walked through
daliwch eiliad—na i °roi chi drwodd = hold on a moment—I'll put you through
ond pryd eith y penderfyniadau 'ma drwodd, tybed? = but I wonder when these decisions will go through?
⇒**drwy°**

drws (*plural* **drysau**) *noun, masculine*
= door
mae rhywun wrth y drws = someone's at the door

drwy° (*less frequently* ⇒**trwy°**; *often* **drw°** *in speech*) *preposition*
personal forms: **drwydda i, drwyddat ti, drwyddo fe, drwyddi hi, drwyddon ni, drwyddoch chi, drwyddyn nhw**
• = through
mae'r gwynt 'ma'n mynd yn syth drwyddat ti, on'd ydy? = this wind goes right through you, doesn't it?
a i drwy'r atebion gyda chi mewn munud = I'll go through the answers with you in a minute
• = by
ffurflenni ar °gael drwy °gysylltu â'n swyddfa = forms available by contacting our office

• = throughout, all (through)
mae'r lle 'ma dan ei sang drwy'r Haf = this place is packed out all summer
bydda i yno drwy'r wythnos = I'll be there all week

> **!** *In this last sense, the unmutated form* ⇒**trwy°** *is also very common. Notice the difference between* **drwy'r wythnos** *all week and* °**bob wythnos** *every week.*

⇒**drwodd**, ⇒**drwy °gydol**, ⇒**trwy°**

drwy °gydol *adverb*
= throughout, all through
perfformiadau drwy °gydol y °flwyddyn = performances all year round

> **!** *This phrase is a common alternative to the preposition* ⇒**drwy°** *in this sense.*

drych (*plural* **-au**) *noun, masculine*
= mirror

drysau *plural of*
⇒**drws**

du *adjective, plural (mostly in set phrases these days)* **duon**
= black
mae gynni hi °wallt du, on'd oes? = she's got black hair, hasn't she?
dal i ffynnu mae'r °farchnad °ddu = the black market still thrives
teledu du-a-gwyn = a black-and-white television

dull (*plural* **-iau**) *noun, masculine*
= method
mae'r dull ymarferol yma o °ddysgu'n °groes i'r ffasiwn °bresennol = this practical method of teaching goes against the present fashion

duw (*plural* **-iau**) *noun, masculine*
= god
cadwyd enwau dros °bedair mil o °dduwiau Celtaidd = the names of over four thousand Celtic gods have been preserved

duwies (*plural* **-au**) *noun, feminine*
= goddess

dŵad (*North*)
⇒**dod**

dweud (*also* **deud, gweud**) (*stem* **wed-, dwed-, dywed-**) *verbnoun*
= say; tell (**wrth°** to)

> **!** *This very common verb has a number of forms of the verbnoun —* **dweud** *is the standard, while* **deud** *is very common in the North, and* **gweud** *equally so in the South. For all practical purposes in the spoken language, the stem is* **wed-**, *while* **dwed-** *and* **dywed-** *represent increasing degrees of formality. Notice that this verb uses* ⇒**wrth°** *with the person talked to—see examples.*

be' wedest ti? = what did you say?
be' wedson nhw wrthat ti? = what did they say to you?
pwy wedith wrtho fe? = who'll tell him?
mae'n rhy °gynnar i °ddweud = it's too early to tell *or* say
dywedwyd bod y °drefn °gynllunio °bresennol yn °foddhaol = it was said that the present planning system was satisfactory
mi °geith pob un ohonoch ei °ddweud, peidiwch poeni = every one of you will have his say, don't worry
a dweud y gwir = actually, as a matter of fact
a dweud y gwir, oedd y prisiau'n uchel braidd = actually, the prices were rather high
dw i °ddim yn siwr, a dweud y gwir = I'm not sure, actually
⇒**siarad**

dwfn *adjective*
comparative **dyfnach**, *superlative* **dyfna(f)**
= deep (*also figurative*)
mae'r dŵr yn rhy °ddwfn fan hyn = the water's too deep here

dŵr (*plural* **dyfroedd**) *noun, masculine*
= water
er bod dŵr yn hanfodol i °fywyd pob anifail... = although water is essential to the life of every animal...
mae dyfroedd Afon Dyfrdwy yn fy ⁿngwaed bellach = the waters of the River Dee are in my blood now

dwsin (*plural* **-au**) *noun, masculine*
= dozen
...ymhlith y dwsinau o argymhellion a

°restrwyd = ...among the dozens of recommendations listed

dwy° *numeral*
⇒**dau°**

dwyieithog *adjective*
= bilingual
y bwriad yw sicrhau addysg °ddwyieithog i °bob plentyn yn y sir = the intention is to ensure a bilingual education for every child in the county

dwyieithrwydd *noun, masculine*
= bilingualism

dwylo *plural noun*
= hands
mae safon y cynhyrchu yn °ddiogel yn eu dwylo = the quality of production is safe in their hands
tasai fo'n syrthio i °ddwylo'r heddlu cudd... = if he fell into the hands of the secret police...
yn ⁿnwylo'r gelyn = in the hands of the enemy
⇒**llaw**

dwyn (*stem* **dyg-**) *verbnoun*
= steal
mae rhywun wedi dwyn ein tocynnau = someone's stolen our tickets
Dwyn Ceir yn Arafu = Car Thefts Drop

dwyrain *noun, masculine*
= east
⇒**gogledd** *for phrasings involving points of the compass*

dwyreiniol *adjective*
• = eastern, easterly
gwyntoedd dwyreiniol = easterly winds

> **!** *The paraphrase* **o'r dwyrain** *from the east is often used as an alternative in many cases:*
> **gwyntoedd o'r dwyrain** = easterly winds

• = oriental
mae hi'n astudio ieithoedd dwyreiniol yng ⁿNghaergrawnt = she's studying oriental languages at Cambridge

dwywaith *adverb*
= twice
bydd y Tywysog yn ymweld â ni °ddwywaith °bob tro = the prince visits us twice every time

dyn ni'n disgwyl dwywaith °gymaint o
°bobol heddiw = we're expecting twice
as many people today

dy° (often **d'** before vowels) *possessive
adjective*

• = your

> ! *This possessive adjective
> corresponds to the informal singular
> pronoun ⇒ti, while the equivalent for
> plural and formal singular ⇒chi is
> ⇒eich. As with all the possessive
> adjectives in the modern language,
> an 'echoing' or 'reinforcing' pronoun
> (in this case di) can optionally follow
> the noun.*

dy °gar di ydy hwn, 'te? = this is your
car, then?
beth yw d' enw di? = what's your
name?
mae dy °waith cartre heb ei °orffen =
your homework hasn't been finished
mi ffoniodd dy °fam = your mother
phoned

> ! *Notice that dy° is one of a small
> number of words in Welsh that are
> resistant to soft mutation—i.e. it never
> changes to *ddy, even when
> circumstances (here a preceding
> am°) would otherwise require a
> mutation*
> beth am dy °rieni? = what about your
> parents

• = you

> ! *When used in conjunction with a
> verbnoun, the possessive adjectives
> correspond to object pronouns in
> English. So dy° + verbnoun = '...ing
> you', or '... you'. The echoing pronoun
> is normally used in this construction*

wi'n dy °garu di = I love you
beth sy'n dy °boeni di? = what's
bothering you?

dychmygu *verbnoun*
= imagine
mi °ellwch chi °ddychmygu mor °falch
o'n i = you can imagine how pleased I
was

dychryn *verbnoun*
• = frighten, scare
...neu mi °fyddi di'n dychryn yr
anifeiliaid = ...or you'll frighten the
animals

• = have a fright
dychrynodd Hugan Fach Goch = Little
Red Riding Hood had a fright

dychrynllyd *adjective*
= frightful, fearful

dychwelyd (*stem* **dychwel-**) *verbnoun*
= return
dychweler y ffurflen erbyn y pumed o
Awst = please return the form by the
fifth of August

dydy, dydyn
⇒bod

dydd (*plural* **-iau**) *noun, masculine*
= day
beth wyt ti'n °wneud fan hyn amser
'ma o'r dydd? = what are you doing
here at this time of the day?
beth wyt ti'n °wneud dyddiau 'ma? =
what are you doing these days?
roedd pethau'n °well yn yr hen
°ddyddiau = things were better in the
old days
dan ni'n dod fan hyn °bob dydd = we
come here every day
bydda i gartre trwy'r dydd heddiw = I'll
be at home all day today
ers dyddiau dw i'n aros = I've been
waiting for days
°welwn ni chi °Ddydd Nadolig, 'te =
we'll see you on Christmas Day, then
fel arfer, bydd cathod yn cysgu yn
ystod y dydd = cats usually sleep by day

> ! *While ⇒diwrnod essentially means
> 'period of 24 hours', dydd essentially
> means 'day (as opposed to night)',
> though the distinction is far from
> clear-cut. It is true that the two words
> are hardly ever interchangeable, and
> certain idioms simply have to be
> learnt—those involving the plural
> 'days' virtually always require
> dyddiau.*

⇒deuddydd, ⇒diwrnod, ⇒Llun,
⇒tridiau

dyddiad (*plural* **-au**) *noun, masculine*
= date
beth yw'r dyddiad heddiw? = what's
the date today?
beth yw'ch dyddiad geni? = what is
your date of birth?

dyddiadur *noun, masculine*
= diary

nodyn i'w °roddi yn y dyddiadur = a note to put in the diary

dyfodol adjective, usually functioning as noun, masculine
= future
oes dyfodol i'r cynllun 'ma? = has this plan got a future?
adeg yma o'r °flwyddyn, edrych at y dyfodol sydd rhaid = this is the time of year for looking to the future

> **!** Although **dyfodol** is an adjective, when 'future' has an adjectival sense in English, Welsh generally uses a paraphrase—**i °ddod** to come, **a °ddaw** which will come, or **yn y dyfodol** in the future.
> **mae rhaid ystyried cenedlaethau i °ddod** = we must consider future generations

dyfroedd plural of
⇒**dŵr**

dyffryn (plural **-noedd**) noun, masculine
= (wide, flat) valley
beth nawr am °gyflwr yr amgylchedd ar hyd y dyffryn? = what now about the state of the environment along the valley?
⇒**cwm**, ⇒**glyn**

dylwn i etc verb
(verbnoun not in use)
personal forms: **dylwn i, dylet ti, dylai fe/hi, dylen ni, dylech chi, dylen nhw**
common variants: **dylswn i, dylset ti** etc; **dyliwn i, dyliet ti** etc
autonomous/impersonal form **dylid**
= ought to, should

> **!** This modal verb is used with unreality endings only, and followed by a soft-mutated verbnoun (except negative).
> **dylwn i °fynd** = I ought to go
> **fe °ddylech chi °gwyno, on' dylech?** = you should complain, shouldn't you?
> **°ddylen ni °ddweud wrtho?** = should we tell him?
> **°ddylset ti °ddim gwneud pethau felly** = you shouldn't do such things
> **cyfrol a °ddylai °fod ar silff °lyfrau pob un o'n darllenwyr** = a volume

that ought to be on the bookshelf of every one of our readers
To convey 'should have. . .', 'ought to have. . .', we need **dylwn i** (etc) + **°fod wedi** + verbnoun:
mi °ddylai John °fod wedi gweld Mair neithiwr = John should have seen Mair last night
°ddylwn i °fod wedi rhoi gwybod iddi? = should I have let her know?
°ddylwn i °ddim °fod wedi dod fan hyn = I shouldn't have come here
The impersonal form **dylid** is commonly used in more formal and/or official styles to express obligation; similarly the interrogative **a °ddylid?**, and the negative **ni °ddylid** for prohibition. As with all impersonal forms, none of these cause soft mutation:
dylid osgoi agwedd °feirniadol = a critical attitude should be avoided
a °ddylid dibynnu ar °gyfrifiaduron? = should computers be relied on?
ni °ddylid ysgrifennu o dan y llinell hon = do not write below this line

dyma° adverb
= here

> **!** This extended form of ⇒**yma** is used primarily to point things out from the view of the speaker. Spatially it refers to persons or objects close at hand, while ⇒**dyna°** and ⇒**dacw°** are further away. In translation it can correspond to 'Here is. . .', 'Here are. . .', 'This is. . .', 'These are. . .' wherever these involve pointing out things or people to someone else. The contracted form **'ma°** is common in speech.

dyma ⁿmrawd Dafydd = this is my brother Dafydd
'ma nhw = here they are
dyma i ti °bunt = here's a pound for you
dyma'r dogfenni o'ch chi eisiau gweld = here are the documents you wanted to see
dyma'ch stafelloedd = these are your rooms
ai dyma yw achos y camddeall? = is this the cause of the misunderstanding?

> **!** Sometimes **dyma°** is used in conjunction with a verbnoun to lend

vividness to a narrative sequence:
dyma agor y llyfr ar hap = so I
opened the book at random

dymchwel *verbnoun*
• = overthrow
  rhaid dymchwel y llywodraeth 'ma
  = this government must be
  overthrown
• = demolish
  bydd yn rhaid, os gwireddir y cynllun,
  °ddymchwel stryd °gyfan o °dai = it
  will be necessary, if the plan is
  realized, to demolish a whole street of
  houses

dymuno *verbnoun*
  = wish
  formal present 3sg **dymuna,** *1pl*
  dymunwn
  dymuna Hywel a Nerys °ddiolch yn
  °gynnes am y llu anrhegion = Hywel
  and Nerys wish to give warm thanks
  for the huge number of presents
  dymunwn yn °dda i Ann Williams a
  °fydd yn priodi yfory = we send good
  wishes to Ann Williams who is getting
  married tomorrow

dymunol *adjective*
  = pleasant
  doedd hynny °ddim yn °brofiad
  dymunol iawn, rhaid dweud = that
  wasn't a very pleasant experience, I
  must say

dyn (*plural* **-ion**) *noun, masculine*
  = man
  tri dyn mewn cwch = three men in a
  boat

> ❗ *This noun sometimes corresponds*
> *to the indefinite pronoun* 'one',
> *although* ⇒**rhywun** *is also common,*
> *if not commoner, in this sense.*
> **beth mae dyn i °fod i °wneud?** =
> what is one supposed to do?
>   *The distinction between this word*
> *and* ⇒**gŵr** *is not always easy to*
> *identify, as in some cases they appear*
> *interchangeable. But* **dyn** *is probably*
> *the more neutral or 'unmarked' word;*
> *furthermore, one of the main senses*
> *of* **gŵr**—'husband' *or* 'married man'—
> *is not shared with* **dyn.**

dyna°, 'na° *adverb*
  = there

> ❗ *This extended form of* ⇒**yna** *is used*
> *primarily to point things out form the*
> *view of the speaker. Spatially it refers*
> *to persons or objects further away*
> *than with* ⇒**dyma°**, *but closer than*
> *with* ⇒**dacw°**, *although it can refer to*
> *things quite close to the speaker, as in*
> *the third example below. In translation*
> *it can correspond to* 'There is. . .',
> 'There are. . .', 'That is. . .', 'Those are.
> . .' *wherever these involve pointing out*
> *things or people to someone else.*
> *The contracted form* **'na°** *is very*
> *widespread in natural speech.*
> *Usually the present tense of the verb*
> **bod** 'to be' *is not expressed with*
> **dyna°**—*though certain idiomatic*
> *phrasings have it, as in the sixth*
> *example below; otherwise it can be*
> *used with verbs as required.*
> **dyna'r dyn °alwodd bore 'ma** = that's
> the man who called this morning
> **dyna ei °wraig, draw fan'na** = there's
> his wife, over there
> **'na'r cwbwl sy gen i** = that's all I've
> got
> **dyna ⁿmagiau** = those are my bags
> **ai dyna'ch car chi?** = is that your car?
> **dyna yw arholiadau!** = that's exams
> (for you)!
> **dyna oedd ei °fwriad o'r cychwyn**
> **cynta** = that was his intention all
> along
> **'na (be') wedes i** = that's what I said
> **dyna (be') wedan nhw, siwr iawn i**
> **chi** = that's what they'll say, you can
> be sure
> **'na ni!** = there we are!
> **'na fe!** = that's it!
>   **dyna** + *verbnoun, with 1st person*
> *understood (or* **dyna** + *[subject]* + **yn**
> *verbnoun when talking of a third*
> *party) is used as a kind of historic*
> *present construction to give vividness*
> *to a narrated event:*
> **a dyna ffonio fe yn ôl** = and so I/we
> phone(d) him back
> **a dyna nhw'n ailfeddwl ar y °funud**
> **ola!** = and (suddenly) they change
> their minds at the last minute!
>   *The contracted form* **'na°** *is*
> *common with a following adjective as*
> *an exclamation—*'How . . .!':
> **'na neis!** = how nice!
> **'na °bert!** = how pretty!
> **'na °ryfedd!** = how funny!

dynes *noun, feminine (North)*
= woman

> **!** **merched** or **gwragedd** usually serve as the plural of this noun.

⇒**menyw**

dynol *adjective*
= human

dysgu *verbnoun*
• = learn
  mae dulliau dysgu wedi newid yn aruthrol = there have been huge changes in teaching methods
• = learn
  ers pryd dych chi'n dysgu Cymraeg? = how long have you been learning Welsh?

dysgwr *(plural* **dysgwyr***) noun, masculine*
= learner *(male) (almost always these days in the narrower sense of someone who is learning, or has learnt, Welsh)*
  a ʰpha °fath o °ddysgwr ydych chi, 'te? = and what kind of learner are you, then?
  dysgwr o °Wyddel = an Irishman who is learning/has learnt Welsh

dysgwraig *(plural* **dysgwragedd***) noun, feminine*
= learner *(female)*
  dysgwraig o °Lanelli sy wedi cipio'r °wobr eleni = a (woman) learner from Llanelli has taken the prize this year

dyw
⇒**bod**

ddaru *auxiliary*

> **!** *The auxiliary* **ddaru** *is used in speech in Northern areas to form the preterite. The construction is a simple one:* **ddaru** + *[subject]* + °*verbnoun. So, for example, from* **mynd** *'go', we get* **ddaru mi °fynd** *I went,* **ddaru ti °fynd** *you went,* **ddaru o °fynd** *he went,* **ddaru Sioned °fynd** *Sioned went. The interrogative is the same but for intonation—* **ddaru ti °fynd?** *did you go?, while the negative uses* °**ddim** *and demutates the verbnoun in the usual way—* **ddaru Sioned °ddim mynd** *Sioned didn't go. Note that the first person singular pronoun is always* **mi** *(not* **fi** *or* **i***) with* **ddaru**.

The affirmative marker ⇒**mi°** *can be used in the normal way with* **ddaru**.
  ddaru chi °weld nhw? = did you see them?
  ddaru nhw °weld ni? = did they see us?
  mi ddaru nhw °wneud hynny yn y °Drenewydd = they did that in Newtown
  ddaru ni °ddim dechrau tan ar ôl cinio = we didn't start till after lunch
  ddaru nhw °dalu?—do = did they pay?—yes

ddoe *adverb*
= yesterday
  est ti i'r cyfarfod ddoe? = did you go to the meeting yesterday?
  fe °gyrhaeddodd y papurau bore ddoe = the papers arrived yesterday morning

> **!** *The unmutated form of this word,* **doe**, *though still listed even in modern dictionaries, is obsolete, although it can be seen in* ⇒**echdoe***. While* ⇒**bore** *and* ⇒**prynhawn** *can be combined with* **ddoe***, 'yesterday evening' is not* *****nos ddoe, but* ⇒**neithiwr**.

Ee

e *pronoun*
- = he
  bydd e'n mynd yfory = he will come
  tomorrow
- = him
  does dim arian 'dag e = he hasn't got
  any money
  dw i heb °weld e ers dyddiau = I
  haven't seen him for days
- = it (*referring to masculine nouns*)
  dw i heb °weld e = I haven't seen it
- (*as 'echoing' pronoun with* ⇒**ei°**) = his:
  ei °gar e = his car

> **!** *Like all pronouns in Welsh,* **e** *serves
> as both subject and object pronoun—
> that is, 'he' and 'him'. The longer
> variant* ⇒**fe** (*pronoun*) *also means 'he'
> and 'him', but the two are not usually
> interchangeable. Generally,* **e** *is
> preferred when the preceding sound
> is a consonant, so that we have, for
> example,* **bydd e** *he will be, but*
> **byddai fe** = *he would be. An
> exception is the present tense of* **bod**,
> *where* **mae e** *is common—though
> even here many regions, particularly
> in the South, prefer* **ma' fe** (= **mae fe**).
> *After the plural imperative in* **-wch**
> *both* **e** *and* **fe** *are usual as object
> pronouns—so* **anwybyddwch e** *or*
> **anwybyddwch fe** *ignore him. The
> distinction between* ⇒**o** *and* ⇒**fo**
> *in the North more or less mirrors*
> **e/fe**, *but see under separate
> headwords.*
>   *The literary language has only one
> form* **ef** *which covers all spoken
> variants for 'he'/'him' and which,
> incidentally, is itself never found in
> unaffected speech.*
>   *Note that the affirmative particle*
> ⇒**fe°**, *though clearly the same word
> in origin, is now a word in its own
> right.*

⇒**fo**, ⇒**o**, ⇒**yntau**

eang *adjective*
  comparative **ehangach**, *superlative*
  ehanga(f)
  = wide, broad

bu beirniadaeth ehangach = there has
  been wider criticism
⇒**ehangu**

Ebrill *noun, masculine*
  = April
⇒**Ionawr**

economaidd *adjective*
  = economic
  **mae'n amlwg mai ffactorau
  economaidd °fydd yn penderfynu** =
  economic factors will clearly be
  decisive

echdoe *adverb*
  = the day before yesterday

echnos *adverb*
  = the night before last

edifaru *verbnoun*
  = regret

edmygu *verbnoun*
  = admire
  mae rhaid edmygu ei °dalent = you
  have to admire his talent

edrych *verbnoun*
  imperatives often (*singular*) **drycha!**
  (*plural*) **drychwch!** *in speech*
  = look (**ar°** at)
  ar beth wyt ti'n edrych? = what are you
  looking at?
  **edrychaf ymlaen at °glywed gennych
  cyn bo hir** (*formal*) = I look forward to
  hearing from you before long/in due
  course
  drychwch fan 'na! = look (over) there!

efallai *adverb*
  = perhaps, maybe

> **!** *When used with a following clause,
> this word requires a 'that . . .'
> construction.*

  **efallai bod hi'n °bryd ailgloriannu ei
  °yrfa** = perhaps it is time to reassess his
  career
  **efallai mai hynny sy'n egluro ei
  absenoldeb** = perhaps that is what
  explains his absence
  **efallai nad oes dadl economaidd dros
  ei °warchod** = perhaps there is no
  economic argument for conserving it
  bydd y lleill yn dod wedyn, efallai =
  perhaps the others will be along later
⇒**ella**, ⇒**hwyrach** *adverb*

efeilliaid
➡gefell

efelychu *verbnoun*
= imitate
mae hi'n naturiol °fod plant yn efelychu eu harwyr = children naturally imitate their heroes

efo (*also sometimes* **hefo**) *preposition* (*North*)
= with

> **!** *This quintessentially Northern word corresponds to* ➡**gyda,** ➡**'da** *in the South. The one area where they do not correspond is in expressions denoting possession, for which Northern areas use not* **efo** *but* ➡**gan°.** *Note that* **gyda** *is the form encountered in practically all registers of writing, with* **efo** *a purely spoken form.*

°ges i °drafferthion efo'r car bore 'ma = I had problems with the car this morning
mi °fydda i hefo chdi mewn munud = I'll be with you in a minute

effaith (*plural* **effeithiau**) *noun, feminine*
= effect
gall yr effaith hon hefyd °gael ei ʰthrin â ʰchyffuriau = this effect can also be treated with drugs

effeithio *verbnoun*
= affect, have an effect (**ar°** on)
gallai 1°C o °gynhesu effeithio ar °faint a natur y cymylau = 1°C of warming could affect the size and nature of the clouds

effeithiol *adjective*
= effective
mae angen datblygu dulliau mwy effeithiol o °ddysgu = more effective methods of teaching need to be developed

effro *adjective* (*North*)
= awake
mae o'n effro = he's awake
➡**ar °ddihun,** ➡**deffro**

eglur *adjective*
= clear
yn °gynta, °ga i °wneud un peth yn °gwbwl eglur? = first, can I make one thing perfectly clear?

egluro *verbnoun*
• = explain
prin y byddai yna amser i egluro = there would scarcely be time to explain
• = make clear
gadewch i mi egluro un peth = let me make one thing clear
➡**esbonio**

eglwys (*plural* **-i**) *noun, feminine*
= church

egni *noun, masculine*
= energy

egwyddor (*plural* **-ion**) *noun, feminine*
= principle
mae hyn yn °fater o egwyddor, wedi'r cwbwl = this is a matter of principle, after all

egwyl *noun, feminine*
= interval, break (*also between school lessons*)
bydd lluniaeth ar °gael yn ystod yr egwyl = refreshments will be available during the interval

enghraifft (*plural* **enghreifftiau**) *noun, feminine*
= example
°ellwch chi °roi enghraifft arall inni? = can you give us another example?
os edrychwn ni, er enghraifft, ar y sefyllfa yn Llydaw = if we look, for example, at the situation in Brittany
➡**esiampl**

ehangu *verbnoun*
• = broaden, widen
cynllun i ehangu'r ffordd rhwng Llanilar a Lledrod = a plan to widen the road between Llanilar and Lledrod
• = expand (**ar°** on) (*also figurative*)
°allwch chi ehangu ychydig ar eich rhesymau dros °fynd? = can you expand a bit on your reasons for going?
mae eisiau ehangu'n gorwelion, on'd oes? = we need to expand our horizons, don't we?
➡**eang**

ei° (*often* **'i** *after vowels*) *possessive adjective*

! *In all its uses, ei° sounds in normal speech (and always has) as if spelt* **i**—*the spelling is an artificial one based on mistaken etymology. Pronouncing it as written sounds affected to most native speakers.*

• = his
mae ei °ddylanwad yn amlwg, a'i °gyfraniad yn anferth = his influence is obvious, and his contribution huge
beth oedd ei swydd °gynta? = what was his first job?

• (*referring to masculine nouns*) = its
rhowch fe ar ei ochor = put it on its side

! *In very careful phrasing, interrogative pronouns used as the object of the sentence require a 'back-referring'* **ei°** *before a verbnoun. In normal speech this is not heard, though the mutation is.*

beth dych chi'n ei °feddwl?
beth dych chi'n °feddwl? (*spoken*) = what do you think?

• (*referring to masculine object of verbnoun*) = him
does neb yn ei °ddeall e = no-one understands him
ac mae'n °bleser i mi °gael ei °groesawu heno = and it's my pleasure to be able to welcome him this evening

• (*referring to masculine object of verbnoun*) = it
llenwch yr holiadur a'i °ddychwelyd erbyn diwedd yr wythnos = fill in the questionnaire and return it by the end of the week

! *Note that, in the above uses only, as with all the possessive adjectives,* **ei** *can be accompanied by an optional 'reinforcing' pronoun* (**e/fe**) *after the noun or verbnoun.*

• (*in passive constructions using* ⇒**cael**)
mi °gafodd y tŷ ei °ddinistrio = the house was destroyed
mae dyn wedi cael ei arestio = a man has been arrested
⇒**i'w**

ei^h (*often* '**i** *after vowels*) *possessive adjective*

! *In all its uses, ei^h sounds in normal speech (and always has) as if spelt* **i**—*the spelling is an artificial one based on mistaken etymology. Pronouncing it as written sounds affected to most native speakers.*
! *As well as causing aspirate mutation (though only consistently of* **c-** *in the spoken language),* **ei^h** *also prefixes* **h-** *to a following vowel—again this usage is variable through the regions, though it is the norm in the standard language.*

• = her
mae ei ^hchar oddiar y ffordd ar hyn o °bryd = her car is off the road at the moment
sut mae Meleri'n dod ymlaen yn ei hysgol newydd? = how is Meleri getting on in her new school?

• (*referring to feminine nouns*) = its
ond o ble daeth y °gomed, a beth yw ei hanes? = but where did the comet come from, and what is its history?

• (*referring to feminine object of verbnoun*) = her
bydd eisiau ei holi hi wedyn = she'll have to be asked (about it) later (*lit: 'There will be need to ask her...'*)

• (*referring to feminine object of verbnoun*) = it
darllenwch y °ddogfen amgaeedig a'i llofnodi = read the enclosed document and sign it

! *Note that, in the above uses only, as with all the possessive adjectives,* **ei^h** *can be accompanied by an optional 'reinforcing' pronoun* (**hi**) *after the noun or verbnoun.*

• (*in passive constructions using* ⇒**cael**)
mae dynes wedi cael ei harestio = a woman has been arrested
fe °allai'r ysgol °gael ei gorfodi i eithrio = the school could be forced to opt out
⇒**i'w**

eich (*usually* '**ch** *after vowels*) *possessive adjective*

! *This word is always pronounced with the indistinct 'uh' sound normally associated with* **y** *in Welsh. Pronouncing it as written sounds affected to most native speakers.*

! *This word corresponds to the pronoun* ⇒**chi**, *and is used in all cases where* **chi** *would be the appropriate term of reference.*

• = your
  °**fydd eich rhieni °ddim yn rhy hapus** = your parents won't be too pleased
  mae'ch ffrindiau chi wedi mynd yn °barod = your friends have already gone
• (*as object of verbnoun*) = you
  mi °ddaw rhywun i'ch gweld cyn hir = someone will be along to see you before long
  °**alla i'ch helpu chi?** = can I help you?

! *Note that, in the above uses only, as with all the possessive adjectives,* **eich** *can be accompanied by an optional 'reinforcing' pronoun* (**chi**) *after the noun or verbnoun.*

• (*in passive constructions using* ⇒**cael**)
  °**gawsoch chi'ch siomi, 'te?** = you were disappointed, then?
  ydych chi wedi cael eich camdrin fel hyn o'r blaen? = have you been mistreated like this before?
⇒**dy°**

eich gilydd *pronoun*
⇒**gilydd**

eiddo *noun, masculine*
• = property
  eiddo fi ydy hwnna = that's my property
• = that/those of... (*referring back to previously stated noun*)
  mae'n dadleuon ninnau'n °gryfach nag eiddo'r °Wrthblaid = our arguments are stronger than those of the Opposition
• **yr eiddoch yn °gywir** (*at end of letter*) = yours truly

ei °gilydd *pronoun*
⇒**gilydd**

eiliad (*plural* **-au**) *noun, feminine*
  = second
  ugain eiliad = twenty seconds
  daliwch eiliad! = hold on a second!

ein (**'n** *after vowels*) *possessive adjective*

! *This word is generally pronounced* **yn** (*i.e. to rhyme roughly with English 'sun'*) *in normal speech.*

• = our
  archebwch nawr cyn i'n stoc i gyd °ddiflannu! = order now before all our stock disappears!
  beth am ein plant ni? = what about our children?
• = us
  bydd yr arian yn ein galluogi i °wella'r sefyllfa'n sylweddol = the money will enable us to improve the situation considerably
  unwaith eto mae'r llywodraeth wedi'n twyllo ni i gyd = once again the government has deceived us all

! *Note that, in the above uses only, as with all the possessive adjectives,* **ein** *can be accompanied by an optional 'reinforcing' pronoun* (**ni**) *after the noun or verbnoun.*

• (*in passive constructions using* ⇒**cael**)
  os cawn ni'n stopio gan yr heddlu = if we get stopped by the police
  dw i °ddim eisiau inni °gael ein beirniadu am hyn = I don't want us to be criticised for this
  mae'n ein galw'n °gelwyddgwn = he calls us liars

ein gilydd *pronoun*
⇒**gilydd**

eira *noun, masculine*
  = snow
  disgwylir eira trwm yn y Gogledd heno = heavy snow is expected in the North tonight
  mae'n bwrw eira = it's snowing

eisiau *noun, masculine, functioning as verbnoun*

! *This word is variously pronounced* **isie, isio, ise,** *but never as spelt.*
! *Though usually functioning as a verbnoun, this word is a noun and does not use a linking* **yn** *with the verb* **bod**—*so* **dw i eisiau** = I want (*not:* *dw i'n eisiau*). *Not being a verbnoun, it has no stem, and therefore cannot take endings of any kind. Past reference is done with the imperfect:* **o'n i eisiau** = I wanted,

roedd y °ferch eisiau... = the girl
wanted...

• (functioning as verbnoun) = want
dych chi eisiau dod? = do you want to
come?
pwy sy eisiau rhagor o °goffi? = who
wants some more coffee?
o'n i eisiau cael gair â chi = I wanted to
have a word with you
'swn i °ddim eisiau'ch rhwystro chi = I
wouldn't want to disturb you
⇨**moyn**, ⇨**am°**
• (functioning as noun) = want; need
mae eisiau cynnal cyfarfod = a
meeting needs to be held
**mae eisiau dweud wrthyn nhw be' ydy
be', on'd oes?** = they need telling
what's what, don't they?
oes eisiau dweud wrthi? = does she
need to be told?
oes eisiau bwyd arnat ti? = are you
hungry?
byddwn ni'n gweld eich eisiau = we'll
miss you
⇨**angen**, ⇨**rhaid**

eisoes adverb
= already
**mae'r cwmni eisoes wedi ennill enw
iddyn nhw eu hunain** = the company
have already earned a name for
themselves
⇨**yn °barod**

eistedd verbnoun
= sit, sit down
eisteddwch fan hyn = sit (down) here
**fe °gododd ar ei heistedd pan oedd
hi'n °bythefnos oed** = she sat up when
she was a fortnight old

! **eistedd i lawr** = sit down, is
generally regarded as an anglicism.

eisteddfod (plural -**au**) noun, feminine
= eisteddfod

eitha(f) adverb
= quite, fairly
maen nhw'n edrych yn eitha hyderus
= they're looking fairly confident
**sut wyt ti'n teimlo erbyn hyn?—eitha
da** = how are you feeling now?—quite
good
i'r eitha(f) = extremely (a less common
alternative to ⇨**tu hwnt** and ⇨ **dros
°ben**)

eithrio
⇨**ac eithrio**

eleni adverb
= this year
**mae mwy fyth o °ddosbarthiadau'n
cael eu cynnal eleni** = even more
classes are being held this year
lle dach chi'n mynd eleni? = where are
you going this year?

! The phrase (**y**) °**flwyddyn yma** is
also heard in some areas, but **eleni** is
regarded as correct.

⇨**blwyddyn**, ⇨**llynedd**

elfen (plural -**nau**) noun, feminine
= element
**byddai system fel hyn yn cadw'r elfen
°ddemocrataidd** = a system like this
would preserve the democratic
element

elw noun, masculine
= profit
**mae'r diwydiant yn gwneud elw dros
°gyfnod byr yn unig** = the industry
makes a profit only over the short term

elwa verbnoun
• = profit (**o°** from)
• = benefit (**o°** from)
**yn ôl Mr Williams, bydd elusennau'n
elwa mwy o'r loteri yn y pendraw** =
according to Mr Williams, charities
will benefit more from the lottery
eventually

ella adverb (North)
= perhaps, maybe

! When used with a following clause,
this word requires a 'that ...'
construction.

ella °fod o wedi colli'r bws = perhaps
he's missed the bus
ddaru o °ddim gweld nhw, ella =
perhaps he didn't see them
⇨**efallai**, ⇨**hwyrach** adverb

enfawr adjective
= huge, enormous
**y cwbwl sydd i'w °weld erbyn hyn yw
twll enfawr yng ⁿghanol y stryd** = all
that can be seen now is a huge hole in
the middle of the road

enfys (plural -**au**) noun, feminine
= rainbow

ennill (*stem* **enill-**) *verbnoun*
- = win
  pwy enillodd neithiwr? = who won last night?
  dw i wedi ennill gwobr! = I've won a prize!
- = gain
  dych chi wedi ennill pwysau, wi'n credu = you've gained weight, I think
- = earn
  faint mae o'n ennill dyddiau 'ma? = what does he earn these days?

enw (*plural* **-au**) *noun, masculine*
- = name
  enwau Cymraeg ar °blanhigion = Welsh names for plants
- = reputation (*often with* **da** good)
  mae gynnyn nhw enw da am °brydlondeb = they've got a reputation for punctuality
⇒**cyfenw**

enwedig *adjective*
  = special
  yn enwedig = especially
  ond bydd hi'n teimlo'n oerach, yn enwedig yn y Gogledd = but it will feel colder, especially in the North
⇒**arbennig**

enwog *adjective*
  comparative **enwocach,** *superlative* **enwoca(f)**
  = famous, renowned
  fe °fydd perfformwyr enwog yn cymryd rhan = famous performers will be taking part
  bydd Elinor yn cyfweld ag un o'n hactorion enwoca ar ôl yr egwyl = Elinor will be interviewing one of our most famous actors after the break

er
1 *preposition*
  = for

> ! *This rather literary preposition is mostly encountered these days in the phrase* **er cof am°** *in memory of. In formal writing it can mean 'for the sake of' or 'in order to', for which the modern language uses* ⇒**er mwyn**; *also 'since', for which the modern language uses* ⇒**ers.**

  er glendid ni ʰchanaiteir cŵn yn yr adeilad hon = for reasons of

hygiene dogs are not allowed in this building
⇒**er gwaetha,** ⇒**er mwyn**
2 *conjunction*
- = although

> ! *This conjunction is used with a following 'that ...' clause. The construction* **er i°** + *subject* + °*verbnoun is usual with reference to the past (see second example below).*

  er °fod y bechgyn wedi pysgota'n °dda ... = although the boys fished well ...
  er iddo honni °fod dim byd o'i °le = although he claimed that nothing was wrong
  er na °fyddai'r cwmnïau awyrennau'n cyfadde hynny = although the aeroplane companies would not admit that
- = however ... (+ *equative adjective*)
  er mor anodd yw hi, does dim dewis 'da ni = however difficult it is, we haven't got any choice
  ansawdd ydy'r peth pwysica, er mor uchel ydy'r prisiau = quality is the most important thing, however high the prices are
  er cymaint dych chi'n °wario, °fydd hi °ddim yn °ddigon = however much you spend, it won't be enough
⇒**er hynny**

eraill *adjective*
⇒**arall**

erbyn
1 *preposition*
  = by (*in time expressions*)
  mi °fydd yr adeilad newydd yn °barod erbyn diwedd y mis = the new building will be ready by the end of the month
  rhaid cofrestru erbyn y degfed o °fis Awst = you must register by the tenth of August
  oedd pawb wedi mynd adre erbyn hynny = everyone had gone home by then

> ! *The phrase* **erbyn hyn** by now *is also frequently used for 'now' where there is an implication of change of situation or circumstance (like* ⇒**bellach***):*

sut wyt ti'n teimlo erbyn hyn? = how are you feeling now?

2 *conjunction*
= by the time (that)
rhaid i'r stafell °fod yn °daclus erbyn i mi °ddod yn ôl = the room has got to be tidy by the time I get back
roedd y cyfarfod wedi dod i °ben erbyn inni °gyrraedd = the meeting had finished by the time we arrived

> **!** *Note that, as a conjunction,* **erbyn** *is followed by* **i** *+ subject +* °*verbnoun.*

⇒**yn erbyn**

erchyll *adjective*
= horrible
rhaid atal peth mor erchyll rhag digwydd eto = such a horrible thing must be prevented from happening again

er gwaetha(f) *preposition*
= despite, in spite of
mae disgwyl i'r gêm °fynd yn ei blaen er gwaetha'r tywydd oer = the game is expected to go ahead despite the cold weather

er hynny *adverb*
= however, all the same, despite that
er hynny, mae tystiolaeth yn dangos nad oes gwahaniaeth mawr = all the same, evidence shows that there isn't much difference
⇒**fodd bynnag,** ⇒**serch hynny**

erioed *adverb*

> **!** *This word means both 'ever' and 'never' according to context; also 'never' as a one-word answer. In all these senses it is the equivalent of* ⇒**byth,** *but the two are not interchangeable—***erioed** *is required where past time in relation to the speaker is indicated. In practical terms this means that you should use it with the preterite and with all* **wedi-** *tenses. Occasionally* **erioed** *corresponds to 'always', where this refers to the past.*

• = ever
°**glywest ti erioed y °fath rwtsh?** = did you ever hear such nonsense?
°**fuoch chi erioed yn yr Eidal?** = have you ever been to Italy?

• = never
°**fues i erioed yn yr Eidal** = I've never been to Italy
dw i erioed wedi gweld y ffilm 'na = I've never seen that film
°**faset ti wedi cytuno?—erioed!** = would you have agreed?—never!
• = always
o'n i eisiau mynd i °ddysgu erioed = I always wanted to go into teaching
⇒**byth**

er mwyn
1 *preposition*
= for the sake of
mi arhoson nhw efo'i gilydd er mwyn y plant = they stayed together for the sake of the children
er dy °fwyn di naethon ni hyn! = we did this for your sake!
2 *conjunction*
• = in order to
er mwyn rhoi cyfle i °ddysgwyr ymarfer eu Cymraeg = in order to give learners a chance to practise their Welsh
• = so that
er mwyn i mi °gael gwneud y trefniadau priodol = so that I can make the appropriate arrangements

> **!** *In this sense* **er mwyn** *is followed by* **i** *+ subject +* °*verbnoun.*

ers
1 *preposition*
• = since
mae'r °frech °goch arni ers dydd Llun = she's had measles since Monday
• = for
gyrfa ym ⁿmyd teledu °fu uchelgais Carys ers blynyddoedd = a career in the world of television has been Carys's ambition for years
dan ni heb °weld chi ers tro = we haven't seen you for a long time

> **!** *The present tense is more natural in Welsh with* **ers** *when the time period referred to extends to the present for the speaker—so, not '*ers pryd wyt ti wedi bod yn aros fan hyn?' mirroring the English construction, but:*
> **ers pryd wyt ti'n aros fan hyn?** = how long have you been waiting here?

because the person addressed is still waiting when spoken to. Similarly with the vaguer **ers faint?***:*
ers faint dych chi'n dysgu Cymraeg? = how long have you been learning Welsh?

2 *conjunction*
= since
mae'r sefyllfa wedi newid yn °gyfangwbwl ers i chi °fod yno = the situation has completely changed since you were there

! *Note that, as a conjunction,* **ers** *is followed by* **i** *+ subject +* °*verbnoun.*

erthygl (*plural* **-au**) *noun, feminine*
= article

esbonio *verbnoun*
= explain
ond °allech chi esbonio rhywbeth inni ...? = but could you explain something to us ...?
⇒**egluro**

esgeuluso *verbnoun*
= neglect

esgid (*plural* **-iau**; *usually* **sgidiau** *in speech*) *noun, feminine*
= shoe
mae eisiau trwsio'r esgid chwith 'ma = this left shoe needs repairing
tynnwch eich sgidiau! = take your shoes off!
gwisga dy sgidiau! = put your shoes on!

esgob (*plural* **-ion**) *noun, masculine*
= bishop (*also chess piece*)

esgus (*plural* **-ion**) *noun, masculine*
= excuse

esgusodi *verbnoun*
= excuse
esgusodwch fi = excuse me

esgyll *plural of*
⇒**asgell**

esgyrn *plural of*
⇒**asgwrn**

esiampl (*plural* **-au**) *noun, feminine*
= example
fe °ddylai fe °fod wedi gosod esiampl i'r lleill = he should have set an example to the others
⇒**enghraifft**

estron *adjective*
= foreign
bydd cyfle i °bob disgybl °ddysgu ail iaith estron = every pupil will have the opportunity to learn a second foreign language
⇒**tramor**

estyn (*stem* **estynn-**) *verbnoun*
= extend, stretch
estynnir croeso cynnes i °bawb = a warm welcome is extended to all

estyniad (*plural* **-au**) *noun, masculine*
= extension

etifeddiaeth *noun, feminine*
= inheritance, heritage

etifeddu *verbnoun*
= inherit

eto (*often* **'to** *in speech*) *adverb*
• = again
dw i am eich gweld chi eto ymhen tair wythnos = I want to see you again in three weeks time
mae'r un peth wedi digwydd eto = the same thing has happened again
eto i gyd, efallai y gallen ni °gyfaddawdu °rywsut = then again, we might be able to come to some sort of compromise
dim eto! = not again!
• = yet
ydyn nhw wedi cyrraedd 'to? = have they arrived yet?
wyt ti wedi gwneud dy °waith cartre eto? = have you done your homework yet?

ethol *verbnoun*
= elect
etholwyd Harold yn °frenin Lloegr = Harold was elected king of England

etholiad (*plural* **-au**) *noun, masculine*
= election

etholwr (*plural* **etholwyr**) *noun, masculine*
= elector

eu (*often* **'u** *after vowels*) *possessive adjective*

! *In all its uses,* **eu** *sounds in normal speech (and always has) as if spelt* **i**, *Pronouncing it as written sounds affected to most native speakers.*
! *Although causing no consonant mutation,* **eu** *does prefix* **h-** *to a*

Ff

following vowel—this usage is variable through the regions, though it is the norm in the standard language.

• = their

ac, yn naturiol iawn, mae pobol yn poeni am eu diogelwch = and, very naturally, people worry about their safety

sut mae'r plant yn dod ymlaen yn eu hysgol newydd? = how are the children getting on in their new school?

mae eu hymchwiliadau nhw'n dangos nad oes dim o'i °le = their investigations show that there is nothing wrong

• (*as object of verbnoun*) = them

dw i wedi'u gadael nhw yn rhywle, mae arna i ofn = I've left them somewhere, I'm afraid

casglwch y papurau at ei gilydd a'u rhoi ar y bwrdd = collect up the papers and put them on the table

! *Note that, in the above uses only, as with all the possessive adjectives,* **eu** *can be accompanied by an optional 'reinforcing' pronoun (***nhw***) after the noun or verbnoun.*

• (*in passive constructions using* ⇒**cael**)

ac fe °fydd rhagor o °dai yn cael eu codi fan hyn = and more houses will be built here

⇒**i'w**

euog *adjective*

= guilty

cafwyd dyn ugain oed yn euog o °lofruddiaeth ddoe = a twenty-year-old man was found guilty of murder yesterday

ewin (*plural* **-edd**) *noun, masculine*

= nail (*of finger, toe*)

Ewrop *noun, feminine*

= Europe

mae gan °Gymru °ddyfodol gwell fel rhan o Ewrop, meddai = Wales has a better future as part of Europe, he said

Ewropeaidd *adjective*

= European

ewythr (*plural* **-edd, -od**) *noun, masculine*

= uncle

mae'n ewythr i mi = he's my uncle

faint *adverb*

= how much; how many

faint sy'n dod? = how many are coming?

faint mae dy °frawd yn gwahodd? = how many is your brother inviting?

faint ydy'r afalau fan hyn? = how much are the apples here?

faint oedd yn °bresennol? = how many were present?

faint sy wedi cofrestru? = how many have registered?

faint mae'r cwmni wedi'i °fuddsoddi? = how much has the company invested?

faint °ddaeth yn y diwedd? = how many came in the end?

does dim ots faint o °wrthwynebiad sydd i'r datblygiad = it doesn't matter how much opposition there is to the development

! *This question-word (a permanently mutated variant of* ⇒**maint**) *takes different forms of the present tense of* **bod** *depending on its function in the sentence:* **sy** *when it is the subject (example 1 above),* **mae** *when it is the object (example 2 above), and* **ydy/yw** *in identification sentences (example 3 above). The first two also apply with the perfect (examples 4 and 5), which in Welsh is identical to the present except for the use of* **wedi** *before the verbnoun instead of* **yn**. *But the distinction is not made in other tenses, or with other verbs, except that soft mutation will appear after the subject as usual. As a quantity expression,* **faint?** *requires* **o°** *before the noun quantified.*

fan'cw *adverb*

= over there (*medium to long distance*)

fan'cw mae'r teulu'n byw bellach = the family live over there now

! **fan'cw** *is a widely used alternative in speech and informal writing for* ⇒**acw**.

fan hyn *adverb*
= here
dere fan hyn! = come here!
fan hyn mae'r °broblem = this is where
the problem is

> ! **fan hyn** *is a widely used alternative
> in speech and informal writing for the
> more standard* ⇒**yma**

fan'ma (*also* **fam'ma**) *adverb*
= here
beth am °osod y °babell fam'ma? =
how about putting the tent here?

> ! **fan'ma** *is a spoken alternative in
> some areas for* ⇒**fan hyn** *and* ⇒**yma**

fan'na *adverb*
= there
**rhowch nhw lawr draw fan'na os
gwelwch yn °dda** = put them down
over there, please

> ! **fan'na** *is a widely used spoken
> alternative for* ⇒**yna**

fath â[h]**, fatha**[h] *adverb*
= as, like (*in comparisons*)
mi oedd o'n °wan fath a [h]**chath °fach** =
he was as weak as a kitten

> ! *This is a colloquial alternative to the
> standard* ⇒**mor°** ... **â**[h]—**roedd e mor
> °wan â** [h]**chath °fach**

°fawr *adverb with negative verb*
= (not) much
**does 'na °fawr o °obaith i unrhywun
°gael gwaith yma** = there's not much
hope of anybody getting work here
**ond does neb yn rhoi °fawr o °goel ar
hynny** = but no-one gives that much
credence
[h]**chafodd °fawr ei °ddweud** = not much
was said
**ond dydyn nhw'n °fawr o °gysur i'r di-
waith ym** [n]**Mlaenau Ffestiniog** = but
they're not much comfort to
the unemployed in Blaenau
Ffestiniog

> ! *This is a fixed mutation of* ⇒**mawr**,
> *and is used exclusively with this
> specialised meaning.*

fe *pronoun*
= he, him; it (*generally not abstract*)

> ! *This variant of* ⇒**e** *is used*:
> a) *generally as the object* ('him'/'it') *of
> a verb with endings*
> **fe °weles i fe yn y °dre** = I saw him in
> town
> b) *generally after words ending in a
> vowel, particularly as the object of
> such verbnouns*
> **mi naeth yr heddlu (ei) stopio fe** =
> the police stopped him
> c) *with the 'conjugated' prepositions*;
> **beth amdano fe?** = what about him?
> d) *after other prepositions ending in a
> vowel*
> **oes car 'da fe?** = has he got a car?
> e) *with the only 3rd person singular
> verb form (other than* **mae**) *that ends
> in a vowel, the
> conditional/hypothetical ending* -**ai**
> **basai fe wrth ei °fodd, on' basai?** =
> he'd be in his element, wouldn't he?
> **fe °ddylai fe °fod wedi dweud** = he
> should have said
> f) *as the focused form of the pronoun*
> **fe sy'n °gyfrifol** = (it is) he who is
> responsible
> In Northern dialects ⇒**fo** *appears
> instead of* ⇒**o** *under the same
> criteria.*
> Note, however, that in the standard
> language **mae** *is followed by* **e**,
> *though many Southern dialects use* **fe**
> *here as well*—**mae fe wedi mynd** *for*
> **mae e wedi mynd**.

fe° *particle*

> ! *This particle is used optionally
> before verb forms with endings in
> main clauses to indicate that a
> statement (and not a question or a
> negative) is being made. It is not used
> with the present or imperfect forms of
> **bod**, and it is not used in subordinate
> clauses. Its use is more common in
> Southern parts of Wales, though it is
> not unknown in the North. Some
> areas, however, seem not to use
> affirmative particles at all, and the
> literary language prefers to do without
> them.*
> **fe °gollon ni o °bedair gôl i °dair** =
> we lost by four goals to three
> **fe °ddylech chi ymddiheuro** = you
> ought to apologise
> *but in a subordinate clause:*

**dw i'n meddwl y dylech chi
ymddiheuro** = I think that you ought
to apologise
[not: * Dw i'n meddwl y fe °ddylech
chi ymddiheuro]
fe °fyddai hynny'n iawn = That would
be OK
fe agora i'r drws i chi = I'll open the
door for you

⇨**mi°**

fel conjunction
• = as
**rhaid ceisio derbyn person fel ag y
mae** = one must try and accept a
person as they are
**o'n i'n gweithio fel ysgrifenyddes ar y
pryd** = I was working as a secretary at
the time
**fel mae'n digwydd, mae copi 'da fi fan
hyn** = as it happens, I've got a copy
here
**roedd y lle'n llawn °dop, fel sy'n
digwydd °bob dydd Iau** = the place
was full up, as happens every
Thursday
• = like
rhaid gwneud e fel hyn = you have to
do it like this
paid siarad â hi fel 'ny! = don't talk to
her like that!
**rhyfedd fel mae'r pethau 'ma'n
digwydd** = funny how these things
happen
⇨**megis**

fel arall adverb
= otherwise
**er bod nhw'n dweud °fod popeth yn
iawn, mae hyn yn awgrymu fel
arall** = although they say that
everything is alright, this suggests
otherwise
fel arall bydd rhaid inni aros =
otherwise we'll have to wait

fel arfer adverb
• = as usual
**dyma nhw'n dod i mewn yn hwyr, fel
arfer** = here they are coming in late, as
usual
• = usually
**fel arfer yr heddlu lleol sy'n delio â
hyn** = usually it's the local police that
deal with this

fel ei gilydd adverb
= alike (when comparing two things)
**bydd y llyfr 'ma'n apelio at °fechgyn a
merched fel ei gilydd** = this book will
appeal to boys and girls alike

felly adverb
• = therefore
felly mae rhaid inni °wneud safiad =
therefore we have to make a stand
• = so, then
felly, lle °gest ti dy °fagu? = so, where
were you brought up?
**newyddion da i °bawb felly ar
°ddechrau'r °flwyddyn** = good news
for everyone, then, at the beginning of
the year
• (as adjective) = such
dw i °ddim yn poeni am °bethau felly =
I don't worry about such things

fersiwn (plural **fersiynau**) noun,
masculine
= version
**mae fersiwn Saesneg o'r ffurflen
hefyd ar °gael** = an English-language
version of this form is also available

fesul adverb
fesul un = one by one
fesul dau = two by two, in twos
**fyth ers i'r straeon °ddechrau
ymddangos fesul un...** = ever since
the stories started to appear one by
one...

fi pronoun
= I, me

! This version of the first person
pronoun is used:
a) always as the object of the
imperative
dilynwch fi! = follow me!
ffonia fi = phone me
b) generally as the object of
verbnouns ending in a vowel
nest ti anghofio fi? = did you forget
me?
c) optionally (alongside ⇨**i** pronoun)
as the object of other verbnouns
paid gadael fi fan hyn! = don't leave
me here!
d) after non-conjugated prepositions
oedd pawb yn gwybod heblaw fi =
everyone knew except me
e) optionally (alongside ⇨**mi**) after
the preposition ⇨**i**

cyn i fi °fynd = before I go
f) as the focused form of the pronoun
fi °fydd yn °gyfrifol am hynny = (it is)
I (who) will be responsible for that

➡**i,** ➡**mi** *pronoun*

finnau *pronoun*
= I, me

> ❗ **finnau** *is one of the special set of
> expanded pronouns that are used—
> though not that frequently—to convey
> emphasis or some idea of contrast
> with, or echoing of, what has gone
> before.*
> **a finnau!** = me too!
> **na finnau chwaith!** = me neither!
> **..., ond rhaid i finnau aros fan hyn** =
> ..., but *I've* got to wait here

➡**fi**

fintau *pronoun*
= he, him
➡**yntau**

fo *pronoun* (*North*)
= he, him; it

> ❗ *This pronoun is used in many
> Northern areas in place of* ➡**fe**
> (*pronoun*), *just as* ➡**o** (*pronoun*) *is
> used in place of* ➡**e**
> **beth amdano fo?** = what about
> him/it?
> **does gynno fo °ddim amynedd** = he
> hasn't got any patience
> **paid gwylltio fo!** = don't get him
> angry!
> **fo oedd yn cwyno** = *he* was (the one)
> complaining

°fod *conjunction*
= that ... (is/are...)
➡**bod 2** *verbnoun functioning as
conjunction*

fodd bynnag *adverb*
= however
rhaid bod yn °ofalus, fodd bynnag =
one must be careful, however
➡**er hynny, serch hynny**

fothau *pronoun* (*North*)
= he, him

> ❗ *This is one of the special set of
> expanded pronouns that are used—
> though not that frequently—to convey
> emphasis or some idea of contrast*

*with, or echoing of, what has gone
before.*

°fu
➡**bod**

fy[n] *possessive adjective*

> ❗ *When the word following is
> susceptible to nasal mutation,* **fy** *is
> usually not pronounced, or at most
> sounds like* **y': (y')** [n]**mhlant** *my
> children,* **(y')** [n]**nillad** *my clothes, with
> words not susceptible to nasal
> mutation it is pronounced* **yn** *or* **'n,**
> *less frequently as* **fy** *or* **f': yn sgidiau**
> *or* **fy sgidiau** *my shoes,* **yn arian** *or* **f'
> arian** *my money. You should follow
> local practice on this point.*

• = my
lle mae [n]**magiau (fi)?** = where are my
bags?
oedd [n]**mrawd i'n sâl ddoe** = my brother
was ill yesterday
'n llyfrau i ydy'r rheina = those are my
books
• (*as object of verbnoun*) = me
°ellwch chi [n]**nghlywed i?** = can you
hear me?
doedd neb yn °barod i [n]**nghefnogi fi** =
no-one was prepared to support me

> ❗ *Note that in the above uses, as with
> all the possessive adjectives,* **fy/'n**
> *can be accompanied by an optional
> 'reinforcing' pronoun (***i** *or* **fi***) after the
> noun or verbnoun.*

• (*in passive construction with* ➡**cael**)
fe °ges i 'n siomi = I was disappointed
pryd °ga i [n]**nhalu?** = when will I be
paid?

°fydda, °fyddi, °fydd *etc*
➡**bod**

fyny
➡**i fyny**

fyth *adverb*
= even (*with comparative adjectives*)
**mae'r lolfa'n °fach, ond mae'r °gegin
yn llai fyth** = the sitting room is small,
but the kitchen is even smaller
mae'r afon yn ehangach fyth fan hyn =
the river is even wider here
**bellach mae'r sefyllfa'n °fwy peryglus
fyth** = now the situation is even more
dangerous

mae mwy fyth o °gwynion wedi bod eleni = there have been even more complaints this year

mae llai fyth o °gyfleoedd i °bobol ifanc dyddiau 'ma = there are even fewer opportunities for young people these days

---

! *fyth is a permanently mutated form of* ⇒**byth** *which has taken on a meaning and use of its own with comparative forms of adjectives and derived adverbs. Note that* **fyth** *even ... is always mutated, while* **byth** *ever/never is always in radical form. Do not confuse* **fyth**, *which is used only where 'even' is linked to a comparative, with* ⇒**hyd yn oed**.

FF, ff

ffa *plural noun*
= beans

ffactor (*plural* **-au**) *noun, masculine*
= factor
..., ond mae ffactorau eraill i'w hystyried, on'd oes? = ..., but there are other factors to be considered, aren't there?

ffa dringo *plural noun*
= runner beans

ffaelu
⇒**ffili**

ffafriol *adjective*
= favourable
mae'r rhagolygon yn ffafriol ar gyfer y gêm °fawr yfory = the forecast is favourable for the big game tomorrow

ffair (*plural* **ffeiriau**) *noun, feminine*
= fair
dewch i Ffair Gwanwyn yr ysgol = come to the school Spring Fair

ffaith (*plural* **ffeithiau**) *noun, feminine*
= fact
ydy'r ffaith °fod pawb yn eich erbyn yn eich poeni chi o °gwbwl? = does the fact that everyone is against you bother you at all?

ffa pob *plural noun*
= baked beans

ffarwelio *verbnoun*
= say goodbye
mae'n amser ffarwelio = it's time to say goodbye

ffasiwn° *adjective* (*precedes noun*)
= such
°well i mi °beidio deud ffasiwn °bethau! = I'd better not say such things!

ffasiynol *adjective*
= fashionable

ffatri (*plural* **ffatrïoedd**) *noun, feminine*
= factory
mi °gafodd ffatri °ddillad arall ei ʰchau yn y De wythnos 'ma = another

clothes factory was closed in the South this week

ffeindio *verbnoun*
= find
os na ffeindiwch chi nhw, dewch yn ôl
= if you don't find them, come back
⇒**cael hyd i°**, ⇒**dod o hyd i°**

ffenest (*plural* **-ri**) *noun, feminine*
= window
oedd hi'n edrych drwy'r ffenest ar y pryd = she was looking out of the window at the time

fferm (*plural* **-ydd**) *noun, feminine*
= farm

ffermdy (*plural* **ffermdai**) *noun, masculine*
= farmhouse
chwalwyd dros °ddau °ddwsin o ffermdai = over two dozen farmhouses were demolished

ffermwr (*plural* **ffermwyr**) *noun, masculine*
= farmer

ffïaidd *adjective*
= foul, horrid

ffili (*also* **ffaelu**) *verbnoun*
= not be able, be unable
wi'n ffili deall beth sy'n bod arno fe = I can't understand what's the matter with him
o'n nhw'n ffili dod o hyd iddi = they couldn't find it
yn ni'n ffili gweld y teledu = we can't see the TV
dw i wedi ffili cael gafael arno = I haven't managed to get hold of him

> ! **ffili** *is used colloquially in many, particularly Southern, areas as a synonym for* °**ddim yn gallu** *cannot, with* ⇒**methu** *performing the same function more generally in Wales.*

ffilm (*plural* **-iau**) *noun, feminine*
= film

ffin (*plural* **-iau**) *noun, feminine*
= border; boundary (*also figurative*)
ydyn ni dros y ffin 'to? = are we over the border yet?
mae yna ffin na ʰ**chaiff milwyr y Cenhedloedd Unedig ei** ʰ**chroesi** =

there is a boundary that the United Nations soldiers cannot cross

ffitrwydd *noun, masculine*
= fitness
stafell ffitrwydd = fitness room
ffitrwydd corfforol = physical fitness
⇒**heini**

fflat (*plural* **-iau**) *noun, feminine*
= flat, apartment

ffliw *noun, masculine*
= flu

> ! *This term indicating a temporary state of health is used with* ⇒**ar°** *when a person is stated*:
> **mae'r ffliw arna i ers wythnos bellach** = I've had the flu for a week now

ffoadur (*plural* **-iaid**) *noun, masculine*
= refugee

ffoi *verbnoun*
= flee

ffôl *adjective*
= foolish, stupid
'sdim eisiau gwneud sylwadau ffôl, nag oes e? = there's no need to make stupid remarks, is there?

ffolineb *noun, masculine*
= foolishness

ffon (*plural* **ffyn**) *noun, feminine*
= stick
mae'n bwrw hen °wragedd a ffyn = it's raining cats and dogs

ffôn (*plural* **ffonau**) *noun, masculine*
= phone
ffôn symudol = mobile phone

ffonio *verbnoun*
= phone
ffonia i chi heno! = I'll phone you this evening!

fforc (*plural* **ffyrc**) *noun, feminine*
= fork

ffordd
1 *noun, feminine* (*plural* **ffyrdd**)
• = road
y ffordd o'ch blaen ar °gau = road ahead closed

• = way
mae 'na ffordd haws o °wneud hyn =
there is an easier way of doing this
2 *adverb*
= how? (*very colloquial for* ⇒**sut** *adverb*)
ffordd ych chi'n gwybod? = how do
you know

ffordio *verbnoun*
= afford
°alla i °ddim ffordio'r un yna = I can't
afford that one

fforest (*plural* **-ydd**) *noun, feminine*
= forest

ffotograffydd (*plural* **ffotograffwyr**)
noun, masculine
= photographer

Ffrainc *noun, feminine*
= France
aethon ni i Ffrainc llynedd = we went
to France last year

fframwaith (*plural* **fframweithiau**)
noun, masculine
= framework
**bydd rhaid gweithio o fewn fframwaith
ehangach o hyn ymlaen** = we will
have to work within a wider
framework from now on

Ffrances (*plural* **-au**) *noun, feminine*
= Frenchwoman

Ffrancwr (*plural* **Ffrancwyr**) *noun,
masculine*
= Frenchman
**pum munud ar ôl, ac mae'r Ffrancwyr
ar y blaen** = five minutes left, and the
French are in the lead

ffres *adjective*
= fresh
**brechdanau ffres ar °gael yma °bob
bore** = fresh sandwiches available here
every morning

ffreutur (*plural* **-au**) *noun, feminine*
= canteen, refectory

ffrind (*plural* **-iau**) *noun, masculine*
= friend
yn ni i gyd yn ffrindiau fan hyn = we're
all friends here
mae e'n hen ffrind i mi = he's an old
friend of mine

ers pryd wyt ti'n ffrindiau ag e? = how
long have you been friends with him?
⇒**cyfaill**

ffrog (*plural* **-iau**) *noun, feminine*
= dress; frock

ffrwd (*plural* **ffrydiau**) *noun, feminine*
= stream

ffrwydriad (*plural* **-au**) *noun,
masculine*
= explosion

ffrwydro *verbnoun*
= explode
**mi ffrwydrodd bom yng ⁿghanol y
°ddinas ddoe** = a bomb exploded in
the city centre yesterday

ffrwydrol *adjective*
= explosive

ffrwydryn (*plural* **ffrwydron**) *noun,
masculine*
= explosive

ffrwyth (*plural* **-au**) *noun, masculine*
= fruit

ffurf (*plural* **-iau**) *noun, feminine*
= form; shape
**mae'r °blaned yn derbyn egni gan yr
haul ar ffurf gwres** = the planet
receives energy from the sun in the
form of heat

ffurfio *verbnoun*
= form

ffurfiol *adjective*
= formal
mae 'na °le i iaith °fwy ffurfiol hefyd =
there is a place for more formal
language as well

ffurflen (*plural* **-ni**) *noun, feminine*
= form
anfonwch am ffurflen °gais nawr! =
send for an application form now!
**llenwch y ffurflen isod a'i dychwelyd
aton ni** = fill in the form below and
return it to us

ffwdan *noun, feminine*
= fuss; trouble
**mae'r car yn cychwyn yn °ddi-ffwdan
yn y bore** = the car starts without any
fuss in the morning

ffwdanu *verbnoun*
= fuss, make a fuss

ffynhonell (*plural* **ffynonellau**) *noun, feminine*
= source
bydd gweddill yr arian yn dod o ffynonellau preifat = the rest of the money will come from private sources

ffyrdd *plural of*
⇒**ffordd**

gadael (*stem* **gadaw-**) *verbnoun*
imperative singular **gad,** *imperative plural* **gadewch**
• = leave
pryd dych chi'n bwriadu gadael? = when are you thinking of leaving?
gad dy °fagiau lle maen nhw = leave your bags where they are
lle °adawest ti fe, 'te? = where did you leave it, then?
• = let

> ! *In the sense of* let, *this word takes the construction* **i°** + [*person/thing*] + °*verbnoun*:
> **gadewch i mi °fod!** = leave me alone!
> **mae'n °werth gadael i'r CD °droi tan y diwedd** = it's worth letting the CD (keep on) turn(ing) to the end
> **gadewch inni °fynd** = let's go

gaea(f) *noun, masculine*
= winter
yn y gaeaf = in (the) winter
yn y gaeaf diwetha = last winter
yn y gaeaf nesa *or* **yn y gaeaf sy'n dod** = next winter
yng ⁿngaeaf 1991 = in the winter of 1991
trwy'r gaeaf = all through the winter
°bob gaeaf = every winter

Gaeleg yr Alban *noun, feminine*
= Scottish Gaelic language

gafael *verbnoun*
• = grasp, take hold (**ynⁿ** of)
paid gafael yna i fel 'ny! = don't grab hold of me like that!
• *functioning as noun, feminine*
= grasp, grip, hold
wi'n ffili cael gafael arno = I can't get hold of it

gafr (*plural* **geifr**) *noun, feminine*
= goat

gair (*plural* **geiriau**) *noun, masculine*
= word
°ges i °air â hi neithiwr = I had a word with her last night

galw (*stem* **galw-**) *verbnoun*
= call

beth dych chi'n galw'r peth 'ma yn °Gymraeg? = what do you call this thing in Welsh?

pam na °alwch chi heibio wedyn? = why don't you call round later on?

pryd nest ti °alw? = when did you call?

mae galw ar y gweinidog i ymddiswyddo = there are calls for the minister to resign

galwad (*plural* **-au**) *noun, masculine* = call

°ges i °alwad ffôn bore 'ma = I got a phone call this morning

galwedigaeth (*plural* **-au**) *noun, feminine*
• = occupation
• = vocation

galwedigaethol *adjective*
 − vocational, occupational

gallu *verbnoun*
 present: **galla i, gelli di, gall e/hi, gallwn ni, gellwch chi, gallan nhw**
 common variants: **galli di, gallwch chi**
 imperfect/conditional: **gallwn i, gallet ti, gallai fe/hi, gallen ni, gallech chi, gallen nhw**
 impersonal/autonomous present/future: **gellir**
 impersonal/autonomous unreality: **gellid**
1 (*functioning as verb*)
• = can, be able

os ydach chi'n °ddigon dewr, gallwch °fentro i'r môr = if you're brave enough, you can venture into the sea

°allwn i ddim °fod wedi dewis amser gwell = I couldn't have chosen a better time

fe °allai mai fan hyn y stopion nhw = it could (be) that they stopped here

bydd un °fargen na °ellir mo'i ᵇcholli °bob wythnos = there will be one unmissable bargain every week

enghraifft °dda o'r hyn y gellid ei °alw'n °gomedi °ddu = a good example of what could be called black comedy

°alla i °fynd nawr? = can I go now?

> **!** *In its primary meaning of* 'can', **gallu** *can be (and generally is in the North) replaced by* ⇒**medru**, *except where the sense is permission (last example above); in this case the alternative would be* ⇒**cael** (**°ga i °fynd nawr?**).

• = may, might; (*with* **°fod wedi** may/might have)

fe °alli di °fod yn iawn, ond... = you may be right, but...

gallech chi °feddwl y byddai awr yn hen °ddigon o amser = you might think that an hour would be more than enough time

mi °all e °fod wedi gadael yn °barod = he may have left already

gallet ti °fod wedi syrthio! = you might have fallen!

2 (*functioning as noun*)
= ability/abilities

mae'r °dasg tu hwnt i °allu ffotograffydd = the task is beyond the abilities of a photographer

galluog *adjective*
= able, capable

myfyrwraig °alluog iawn = a very able student

galluogi *verbnoun*
= enable

gan° *preposition*
 personal forms: **gen i, gen ti, ganddo fe, ganddi hi, ganddon ni, gennych chi, ganddyn nhw**
 or (*especially North*): **gynna i, gyn ti, gynno fo, gynni hi, gynnon ni, gynnoch chi, gynnyn nhw**
• (*in Northern possession construction*)
= with

mae gynno fo °ddigon = he's got enough

oes gynnoch chi °gar? = have you got a car?

does gynna i °ddim pres = I haven't got any money

faint sy gynnyn nhw? = how many/much have they got?

°fydd gynnon ni °ddigon o amser? = will we have enough time?

mae gan 'n chwaer i °gariad newydd = my sister's got a new boyfriend

dim ond mis sy gan y llywodraeth ar ôl = the government has only got a month left

• = from (*where something is handed over*)

faint °gest ti gynno fo? = how much did you get from him?

• = by (*authorship*)

'1984' gan George Orwell = '1984' by George Orwell

• = by (*agent in passive sentences*)
cafodd ei holi gan yr heddlu = he/she was questioned by the police
chwalwyd y tŷ gan °daflegryn = the house was destroyed by a missile

• (*idiomatic usages involving subjective feeling*)
mae'n °ddrwg gen i = I'm sorry
°well gan y plant °wylio'r teledu = the children prefer watching TV
(*cf.* **°well i'r plant °wylio'r teledu** = the children had better watch TV)
mae'n °dda gen i °gwrdd â chi = I'm pleased to meet you
(does) dim ots gen i = I don't mind/care

> **!** *In the possession construction, where it corresponds to Southern* ⇨**gyda, 'da, gan°** *is an indicator of Northern speech, and this is also broadly true of the idiomatic usages listed above. Otherwise,* ⇨**efo** *is used in the North for* 'with'. *All other uses for* **gan°** *above are standard for the whole country, though* ⇨**oddiwrth°** *is a common alternative for* 'from'.

gan amla *adverb*
= mostly; most often
ymwelwyr o °Loegr sy'n gofyn hynny gan amla = it's mostly visitors from England that ask that

gan °fod *conjunction*
= since
gan ei bod yn °ddiwedd tymor... = since it is the end of term...
⇨**am (°fod)**

gan °fwya *adverb*
= mostly, for the most part

gan °gynnwys *adverb*
= including
..., gan °gynnwys cludiant = ..., including delivery
⇨**cynnwys**

gardd (*plural* **gerddi**) *noun, feminine*
= garden

garddio *verbnoun*
= garden, do the gardening

garddwrn
⇨**arddwrn**

garej (*plural* **-ys**) *noun, masculine*
= garage

gartre(f) *adverb*
= (at) home
ydy Sioned gartre? = is Sioned home?
dw i eisiau i ti °fod gartre erbyn naw = I want you home by nine

> **!** *Officially there is a distinction between* **gartre(f)** *indicating location at home and* ⇨**adre(f)** *indicating motion towards home, but in practice either is heard in both senses depending on region.*

garw *adjective*
= harsh; rough
tywydd garw = rough weather
piti garw! = what a (great) shame!

gefell (*plural* **gefeilliaid**) *noun, masculine and feminine*
= twin

> **!** *Unusually, this word generally undergoes soft mutation in the plural after the article:* **yr °efeilliaid** the twins

geifr *plural of*
⇨**gafr**

geirfa (*plural* **-oedd**) *noun, feminine*
= vocabulary

geiriadur (*plural* **-on**) *noun, masculine*
= dictionary

gelyn (*plural* **-ion**) *noun, masculine*
= enemy
ennill ffrindiau i'r iaith sy eisiau yn hytrach na gwneud gelynion = what's needed is to win friends for the language rather than make enemies

gelyniaethus *adjective*
= hostile

gêm (*plural* **-au**) *noun, feminine*
= game

> **!** *Although feminine, this word, like many loanwords beginning* **g-**, *is resistant to soft mutation:*
> **°welest ti'r gêm °fawr neithiwr?** = did you see the big game last night?

gên *noun, feminine*
= jaw; chin

genedigaeth *noun, feminine*
= birth

llongyfarchiadau ar °enedigaeth eich merch °fach = congratulations on the birth of your little daughter

geneth (*plural* **-od**) *noun, feminine* (*North*)
= girl
yr °eneth °gaeth ei gwrthod = the girl who was rejected (*title of a traditional song*)

geni *verbnoun*
  past impersonal: **ganwyd** *or* **ganed** (*no other forms used*)
• = give birth to
  lle °gawsoch chi'ch geni? = where were you born?
  °ges i °ngeni yng °Nghaerdydd = I was born in Cardiff
  ganed Alun Rhys ym °Mhorthmadog = Alun Rhys was born in Porthmadog
• (*functioning as noun, masculine*)
  = birth
  dyddiad geni = date of birth
  man geni = place of birth
⇨**genedigaeth**

ger *preposition*
= near (*with geographical location only*)
  maen nhw'n byw yng °Nghapel Bangor ger Aberystwyth = they live in Capel Bangor near Aberystwyth

gerbron *preposition*
= before (*court, tribunal, etc*)
  ymddangosodd tri o °ddynion gerbron Llys Ynadon Llaneglwys y bore 'ma = three men appeared before Llaneglwys Magistrates Court this morning
⇨**cyn**, ⇨**o °flaen**, ⇨**o'r blaen**

gerddi *plural of*
⇨**gardd**

gerllaw
1 *preposition*
  = near
  o'n i'n aros mewn gwesty gerllaw'r afon ar y pryd = I was staying in a hotel near the river at the time
2 *adverb*
  = nearby
  ceir cyfoeth o atyniadau gerllaw = there is a wealth of attractions nearby

gilydd *pronoun*
= (each) other, (one) another

! *This word is used only in conjunction with the possessive adjectives* **ei**, **ein** *and* **eich:**
ei gilydd = each other (*talking of 'them'*)
ein gilydd = each other (*talking of 'us'*)
eich gilydd = each other (*talking of 'you'*)
  In addition, these expressions are used with ⇨**gyda** (*South*) *or* ⇨**efo** (*North*) *'with' to mean 'together', which Welsh phrases as 'with each other':*
gyda'i gilydd, efo'i gilydd = together (*talking of 'them'*)
gyda'n gilydd, efo'n gilydd = together (*talking of 'us'*)
gyda'ch gilydd, efo'ch gilydd = together (*talking of 'you'*)
mae'r °ddau'n casáu ei gilydd = they (two) hate each other
fe °fuon nhw'n siarad â'i gilydd = they've been talking to each other
siaradwch â'ch gilydd = talk to one another
dan ni isio bod efo'n gilydd (*North*) = we want to be together
°allwch chi °ddim eistedd gyda'ch gilydd heddiw (*South*) = you can't sit together today
dw i'n gorfod casglu popeth at ei °gilydd °gynta = I have to get everything together first

glan (*plural* **-nau**) *noun, feminine*
• = bank, shore
  ar °lan yr afon = on the bank of the river
  ar °lan y môr = by the sea
• (*in plural*) = coast
  bydd y cymylau isel yn styfnig mewn mannau ger y glannau = the low clouds will be reluctant to move in places near the coast

glân
1 *adjective*
  = clean
  ydy'ch sgidiau chi'n °lân? = are your shoes clean?
2 (*usually as derived adverb* **yn °lân**)
  = completely, utterly
  oedd e'n methu'n °lân â gwneud y gwaith = he was quite unable to do the work

wedi blino'n °lân = dog-tired;
completely tired out
Cymro glân = a pure Welshman, a
Welshman through and through

glanhau (North also **llnau**) verbnoun
= clean
hen °bryd inni °lanhau'r ffenestri = it's
high time we cleaned the windows
⇒**golchi**

glanio verbnoun
= land (aircraft)
mi °laniodd yr awyren yn °ddidrafferth
= the aeroplane landed without
trouble

glas adjective (plural (very rare)
gleision)
= blue
mae'r awyr yn °las = the sky is blue
°well gen i'r un glas tywyll = I prefer
the dark blue one
y bore glas = dawn, daybreak
yn oriau glas y bore = in the early
hours of the morning

> **!** **glas** is also used to refer to the
> green of vegetation; in this use it is
> much more restricted, though of
> common occurrence in place names.

glaswellt noun, masculine
= grass
peidiwch â ʰcherdded ar y glaswellt =
do not walk on the grass
⇒**gwair**

glaw noun, masculine
= rain
mae'n bwrw glaw = it's raining
mae golwg glaw arni = it looks like rain
(on the way)
glaw mân = drizzle

glawio verbnoun
= rain
mae'n glawio = it's raining (= **mae'n
bwrw glaw**)

glo noun, masculine
= coal
rhaid cludo'r glo ar y rheilffyrdd = the
coal must be transported on the
railways
**cynlluniau diwygiedig oddi wrth °Lo
Prydain** = revised plans from British
Coal

glöwr (plural **glowyr**) noun, masculine
= (coal)miner

glud noun, masculine
= glue

gludo verbnoun
= glue, stick

glyn (plural **-noedd**) noun, masculine
= valley, glen
⇒**cwm**, ⇒**dyffryn**

glynu verbnoun
= stick, adhere (**wrth°**, **at°** to)
glynwch wrth eich gilydd! = stick
together!
bydd rhaid glynu at ein stori = we will
have to stick to our story

go° adverb (precedes adjective)
= pretty, fairly, rather
sut dach chi bore 'ma?—go lew = how
are you this morning?—pretty well
faint sy ar ôl?—go ychydig = how
much is left?—not much at all
go aml y bydden ni'n mynd yno = we
used to go there pretty often

> **!** **go°** is very close in meaning to
> ⇒**eitha**, but is less common, perhaps
> because it often has an additional
> connotation of subjective judgment.

gobaith (plural **gobeithion**) noun,
masculine
= hope
**°fyddi di'n cael dy arian yn ôl?—dim
gobaith!** = will you get your money
back?—some hope!

gobeithio verbnoun
• = hope
**does ond gobeithio na °fydd angen y
°fath ymateb** = one can only hope that
such a response will not be needed
• (as adverb) = I/we hope, hopefully
gobeithio na °ddaw hi = I hope she
doesn't come
byddwn ni'n ôl erbyn deg, gobeithio =
we'll be back by ten, hopefully

gofal noun, masculine
= care; caution
**mae'r °ddau bellach dan °ofal yr
awdurdod lleol** = both are now under
the care of the local authority
gofal—mynedfa °gudd = caution—
hidden entrance
gofal! = watch out!

gofalu verbnoun
• = look after, take care (**am°** of)

pwy °fydd yn gofalu am y plant? = who will look after the children?

> ❗ *The phrasings* **edrych ar ôl** *and* **cymryd gofal***, though anglicisms, have wide currency in some areas.*

• = watch out; take care

gofalwch bod chi °ddim yn niweidio'r peth 'ma = watch out that you don't damage this

gofalus *adjective*

= careful

ond byddwch yn °ofalus serch hynny = but be careful all the same

os na °fydd y llywodraeth yn °ofalus iawn... = if the government is not very careful....

gofidio *verbnoun*

= worry

paid gofidio! = don't worry!

⇒**poeni**, ⇒**pryderu**

gofod *noun, masculine*

= space

mae hi'n anodd dychmygu mor °fawr yw'r gofod = it's hard to imagine how big space is

cafodd Harry siwt °ofod yn anrheg Nadolig = Harry got a spacesuit as a Christmas present

gofyn (*stem* **gofynn-**)

1 *verbnoun*

= ask

fe °ofynnoch chi beth °fyddwn i'n ei °wneud gyda'r arian = you asked what I would do with the money

naeth e °ofyn i mi am °beidio dod = he asked me not to come

gofynnwch am °fanylion y Rhaglen Teithiau Tywys = ask for details of the Guided Tour Programme

2 (*plural* **-ion**) *noun, masculine*

= requirement

bydd gofyn i chi asesu'ch myfyrwyr = you will be required to assess your students

gogledd *noun, masculine*

= north

yn y gogledd = in the north

yng ⁿNgogledd Cymru = in North Wales

yng ⁿNgogledd yr Eidal = in the North of Italy

tua'r gogledd = towards the north

o'r gogledd = from the north

o °Ogledd Cymru = from North Wales

o °Ogledd yr Eidal = from the North of Italy

i'r gogledd o °Gaerdydd = to the north of Cardiff

gogleddol *adjective*

= northern, northerly

mae acen °ogleddol iawn 'da hi = she's got a very northern accent

---

> ❗ *This adjective is not generally used in geographical names*—'Northern Italy' *is usually phrased as* **Gogledd yr Eidal**—'the North of Italy' *The paraphrase* **o'r gogledd** 'from the north' *is often used as an alternative in many cases*:
> **gwyntoedd o'r gogledd** = northerly winds

---

gohirio *verbnoun*

= postpone

dyma'r °ddarlith a °ohiriwyd o °dymor y Pasg = this is the lecture that was postponed from the Easter term

go iawn *adverb functioning as adjective*

= real; proper; genuine

dydy'r ffaith 'ma'n °ddim ond tanlinellu'r °broblem go iawn = this fact only underlines the real problem

bellach mae hi wedi mynd yn sefyllfa 'ni a nhw' go iawn = now it has become a real 'us and them' situation

golau

1 *noun* (*plural* **goleuadau**)

= light

yn sydyn, dyma °olau llachar o'u blaen = suddenly they saw a bright light in front of them

maen nhw'n °fwy amlwg mewn golau uwch fioled = they are more apparent in ultra-violet light

2 *adjective*

= light

dyw hi °ddim yn °olau iawn fan hyn, nag ydy? = it's not very light in here, is it?

golchi *verbnoun*

= wash

nei di °olchi'r llestri i mi? = will you wash the dishes for me?

⇒**ymolchi**

goleuo *verbnoun*

= light, shine light on

go lew *adverb*
= OK
**sut dach chi heddiw?—go lew/ yn °o
lew** = how are you today?—OK

> **!** *This expression is mostly used as
> above, as a response to 'How are
> you?'. It can also modify* ⇒**tipyn**, *so
> that* **tipyn go lew** *is equivalent to* **cryn
> °dipyn** *quite a bit/quite a few:*
> **faint sy ar ôl 'da chi?—tipyn go lew**
> = how many have you got left?—quite
> a few; how much have you got left?—
> quite a bit

golwg *noun, feminine*
• = look
golwg ar y prif stori i °gau = a look at
the main story to close
mae golwg glaw arni, on'd oes? = it
looks like rain, doesn't it?
• = view
**un o'r pechodau mwyaf yn ei golwg
oedd diogi** = one of the greatest sins in
her view was laziness
• = appearance
**yn ôl pob golwg maen nhw'n °ddigon
iach** = to all appearances they are
healthy enough

golygu *verbnoun*
= mean
**gall hyn °olygu ymuno â grŵp
cadwraethol lleol** = this can mean
joining a local conservation group
⇒**meddwl**, ⇒**ystyr**

golygus *adjective*
= goodlooking, handsome

gollwng (*stem* gollyng-) *verbnoun*
= let go, release
paid gollwng 'n llaw o hyd = stop
letting go of my hand all the time

gor°- *prefix*
= over-; too...
*This prefix generally attaches to
verbnouns and adjectives. Examples:*
gorboblogi = overpopulate
gorddrafft = overdraft
gorfwyta = overeat, eat too much
(⇒**bwyta**)
gorhoff = too fond (**o°** of)
(⇒**hoff**)
gorlawn = too full, over full;
overcrowded
(⇒**llawn**)

goroleuo = overexpose (*photograph*)
(⇒**golau**)
gorweithio = overwork
(⇒**gweithio**)
gorwneud = overdo
(⇒**gwneud**)
goryfed = overdrink, drink too much
(⇒**yfed**)
mae'r stafell 'ma'n °orlawn = this room
is overcrowded
**dw i °ddim yn °orhoff o °foron, rhaid i
mi °ddweud** = I'm not too fond of
carrots, I must say
nest ti °oryfed neithiwr, on' do? = you
drank too much last night, didn't you?
paid gorwneud pethau, na nei di? =
don't overdo things, will you?

> **!** *With adjectives, the use of* **gor°**- *is
> restricted, and if in doubt it is safer to
> use* ⇒**rhy°**

gorau *adjective*
= best
hon ydy'r ffordd °orau = this is the best
way
p'un sy °orau 'da ti? = which one do
you like best?
gorau po gynta = the sooner the
better
mi naethon ni'n gorau glas = we did
our level best
hwn yw'r gorau ohonyn nhw i gyd =
this one is the best of all of them
rhoi'r gorau i° *or* **rhoi gorau i°** = give up:
mi °roddodd hi'r gorau i'w swydd = she
gave up her job
bydd rhaid i mi °roi'r gorau iddi = I'll
have to give it up
⇒**da**, ⇒**o'r gorau**

gorchymyn (*plural* **gorchmynion**)
noun, masculine
= order
dilyn gorchmynion oedden nhw = they
were following orders

gorfod* *verbnoun*
= have to, must
pryd dych chi'n gorfod mynd? = when
do you have to go?
ydyn nhw'n gorfod aros? = do they
have to stay?
**mae'r pwyllgor wedi gorfod
ailhysbysebu'r swydd** = the
committee has had to readvertise the
position

! **gorfod** *is equivalent to* ⇒**rhaid** *in its primary meaning only of obligation. Unlike* **rhaid,** *however, it is a verbnoun and is used accordingly, while* **rhaid** *requires a special construction—compare the second example above with its* **rhaid** *equivalent:* **oes rhaid iddyn nhw aros?.** *Note also that the other main meaning of* **rhaid,** *supposition, is not shared by* **gorfod,** *so, for example* you must be mad! *can only be rendered by* **rhaid.** *But for obligation senses, the two are broadly interchangeable (though* **rhaid** *is statistically more common);* **gorfod,** *however, is preferred in examples such as the third above, where the required* **wedi** *(for* 'have/has had to', *etc) is difficult to accommodate in the* **rhaid** *construction.*

gorfodi *verbnoun*
= force, compel
fe °allai'r ysgol °gael ei gorfodi i eithrio = the school could be forced to opt out

gorffen (*stem* **gorffenn-**) *verbnoun*
= finish
dylwn i °orffen y gwaith 'ma °gynta = I ought to finish this work first
pryd mae'r rhaglen 'ma'n gorffen? = when does this programme finish?
mae'r gwaith 'ma heb ei °orffen = this work is not finished
⇒**bennu,** ⇒**cwpla**

Gorffennaf *noun, masculine*
= July
⇒**Ionawr**

gorffennol *adjective, usually functioning as noun, masculine*
= (the) past
mae'n gorffennol ni'n °bwysig inni = our past is important to us

gorffwys
1 *verbnoun*
= rest
rhaid i chi °orffwys = you must rest
2 *noun, masculine*
= rest
cyfnod o °orffwys sy eisiau nawr = what is needed now is a period of rest

gorlwytho *verbnoun*
= overload

gorllewin *noun, masculine*
= west
⇒**gogledd** *for phrasings involving points of the compass*

gorllewinol *adjective*
= western; westerly
bydd gwyntoedd gorllewinol yn chwythu'n°gryfach yfory = westerly winds will be blowing more strongly tomorrow

! *The paraphrase* **o'r gorllewin** *from the west is often used as an alternative in many cases:*
gwyntoedd o'r gorllewin = westerly winds

gormod *adverb*
= too much; too many
mae hyn yn °ormod! = this is too much!
mi aeth popeth yn °ormod iddi yn y diwedd = everything got to be too much for her in the end
roedd gormod o °bobol, a dim digon o °le = there were too many people, and not enough room
roedd gormod o °ddadlau rhyngddon ni = there was too much arguing between us
dych chi'n cwyno gormod (/°ormod) = you're complaining too much
mae gormod o °waith 'da fi,
mae gen i °ormod o °waith = I've got too much work
mae rhai o'r rheina wedi cael gormod, dw i'n meddwl = some of those have had too much, I think
mae 'na °ormod o °gwestiynau'n dal heb eu penderfynu = there are too many questions still undecided

! *As a quantity expression,* **gormod** *requires a following* **o°** *when a noun is specified*

gorsaf (*plural* **-oedd**) *noun, feminine*
= station
na i °gasglu chi o'r °orsaf = I'll collect you from the station
fe °fyddai hynny'n golygu rhwydwaith o °orsafoedd radio lleol = that would mean a network of local radio stations

gorwedd *verbnoun*
= lie; lie down

°dreulies i wythnos °gyfan yn
gorwedd ar y traeth = I spent a whole
week lying on the beach

gorwel (plural **-ion**) noun, masculine
= horizon
mae eisiau ehangu'n gorwelion, on'd
oes? = we need to expand our
horizons, don't we?

gorwneud verbnoun
= overdo
mae'n °bwysig i chi °beidio gorwneud
pethau = it's important that you don't
overdo things

gosod verbnoun
• = set
mi °gei di °osod y bwrdd = you can set
the table
fe °fethodd pob cynnig i °osod cwotâu
= every motion to set quotas failed
• = put
fe °gewch chi °osod y pethau fan hyn =
you can put the things here
• = let (property)
ar °osod—tŷ gwyliau yn y
Lot/Dordogne, Ffrainc = to let—
holiday home in the Lot/Dordogne,
France
⇒**rhoi**

gostwng (stem **gostyng-**) verbnoun
= lower, reduce

gostyngiad (plural **-au**) noun,
masculine
= reduction, price cut
gostyngiadau anhygoel ar siwmperi a
ʰchotiau! = amazing reductions on
jumpers and coats!

gradd (plural **au**) noun, feminine
= degree
..., gyda'r tymheredd yn disgyn i
°bedair gradd Celsius = ..., with the
temperature dropping to four degrees
Celsius
mae gynni hi °radd mewn Astroffiseg
= she's got a degree in astrophysics
⇒**i °raddau**

graddfa (plural **graddfâu** or
graddfeydd) noun, feminine
• = scale
datblygiad ar °raddfa °fechan = a
small-scale development
• = rate

beth °fydd effaith hyn ar y °raddfa
°gyfnewid, 'te? = how will this affect
the exchange rate, then?

grisiau plural noun
= stairs
ewch i fyny'r (/ewch lan y) grisiau = go
upstairs
mae'r stafell °wely arall lawr y grisiau
= the other bedroom is downstairs
⇒**staer**

grŵp (plural **grwpiau**) noun, masculine
= group

grym noun, masculine
= power, force
(bod) mewn grym = (be) in force
(dod) i °rym = (come) into force:
mae'r cyfarwyddyd yn dal i °fod
mewn grym = the directive is still in
force
dyn ni'n clywed bod yr egwyddor o
'sybsidiaredd' i °ddod i °rym = we
hear that the principle of
'subsidiarity' is to come into force

grymus adjective
= powerful

gwadu verbnoun
= deny
ydych chi'n gwadu iddyn nhw °alw
arnoch chi neithiwr, 'te? = are you
denying that they called on you last
night, then?
bellach mae rhai'n gwadu unrhyw
°wybodaeth o'r iaith = some now deny
any knowledge of the language

gwaed noun, masculine
= blood
mae dyfroedd afon Dyfrdwy yn fy
ⁿngwaed bellach = the waters of the
River Dee are in my blood now

gwaedlyd adjective
= bloody

gwaedu verbnoun
= bleed

gwael adjective
• = bad, poor
os yw'r tywydd yn °wael, gallwch chi
eistedd ger y tân = if the weather is
bad, you can sit by the fire
°gaethon ni ambell i adolygiad gwael =
we got the odd bad review
Cymraeg gwael sy gynno fo = his
Welsh is poor

• = ill
wyt ti'n teimlo'n °wael? = are you feeling ill?

> ! *In the sense of* 'bad' **gwael** *often seems to have a more subjective or judgmental sense than the multipurpose* ⇒**drwg**

⇒**drwg**, ⇒**sâl**

gwaeledd *noun, masculine*
= illness
ar °gau am °weddill yr wythnos oherwydd gwaeledd = closed for the rest of the week because of illness
⇒**salwch**

gwaelod *noun, masculine*
= bottom
rhowch eich enw llawn ar °waelod y tudalen ola = put your full name at the bottom of the last page
⇒**pen ôl**

gwaeth *adjective*
= worse
mae pethau'n mynd o °ddrwg i °waeth = things are going from bad to worse
mae hyn yn °waeth fyth nag o'n i'n °ddisgwyl! = this is even worse than I expected!
⇒**drwg**

gwaetha(f) *adjective*
= worst
hon ydy'r rhaglen °deledu °waetha erioed = this is the worst television programme ever
bydd y gwaetha drosodd ymhen ychydig = the worst will soon be over
⇒**drwg**

gwaetha'r modd *adverb*
= unfortunately
siomedig °fu'r ymateb hyd yn hyn, gwaetha'r modd = the response has been disappointing so far, unfortunately
⇒**anffodus**

gwaethygu *verbnoun*
= worsen, get worse
gwaethygu mae'r sefyllfa yng ⁿGogledd y °wlad = the situation in the North of the country is getting worse

gwag *adjective*
comparative **gwacach**, *superlative* **gwaca(f)**

• = empty
mae'r °ddau °fwthyn yn °wag bellach = both cottages are empty now
• = vacant
rhagor o swyddi gwag tu fewn = more vacant positions inside

gwahaniaeth (*plural* **-au**) *noun, masculine*
= difference
beth yw'r gwahaniaeth rhwng ...? = what's the difference between...?
pa °wahaniaeth mae'n °wneud o °gwbwl? = what difference does it make at all?

gwahanol *adjective*
• = different
mae agweddau pobol yn °wahanol dyddiau 'ma, wrth °gwrs = people's attitudes are different these days, of course
• (**gwahanol°**, *preceding the noun*)
= various
dŵr yn ei °wahanol ffurfiau sy'n chwarae'r rhan °bwysicaf = it is water in its various forms that plays the most important part

gwahanu *verbnoun*
= separate (**â**ʰ from)
mae Elen a Rhodri wedi gwahanu = Elen and Rhodri have separated
⇒**priodi**, ⇒**ysgaru**

gwahardd *verbnoun*
= forbid; prohibit; ban
mae'r heddlu wedi gwahardd i °bobol °fynd i mewn,
mae'r heddlu wedi gwahardd pobol rhag mynd i mewn = the police have forbidden people to go in
gwaherddir copïo'r fideogram hwn = copying of this videogram is prohibited
°ges i ⁿngwahardd o'r °dafarn 'ma llynedd = I was banned from this pub last year

gwahodd *verbnoun*
= invite (**i°** to)
gwahoddir ceisiadau am y swydd newydd hon am °gyfnod o °dair blynedd = applications are invited for this new job for a period of three years

gwahoddiad (*plural* **-au**) *noun, masculine*
= invitation

gwair *noun, masculine*
• = hay
buon nhw wrthi trwy'r dydd yn lladd y gwair = they've been at it all day cutting the hay
• = grass

> ! *Although the usual dictionary definition of this word is 'hay', it is commonly used in both North and South for 'grass', while* ⇒**glaswellt** *is a more literary term.*

gwaith
1 *noun, masculine*
= work
beth ydy'ch gwaith chi? = what is your job?
gwaith caled iawn oedd hi = it was very hard work

> ! *This noun is also used in conjunction with verbnouns to 'reinforce' a noun function:*
> **dw i'n moyn gorffen y gwaith copio 'ma cyn i'r °gloch °ganu** = I want to finish this copying before the bell goes

2 (*plural* **gweithiau**) *noun, feminine*
= time
faint o °weithiau ydyn ni wedi gweld y ffilm 'ma?—°dairgwaith o leia = how many times have we seen this film?—three times at least
dw i wedi dweud wrthat ti cant o °weithiau! = I've told you a hundred times!

> ! *This word for time is used when the sense is of* 'how many times?'—*therefore it is used with (feminine!) cardinal numbers to mean 'once', 'twice', 'three' times, etc:* ⇒**unwaith, dwywaith, tairgwaith** *etc. In sentences these are normally subject to soft mutation (see example) because they are adverbs of time. Note also the mutated plural* °**weithiau** 'sometimes', *and* **sawlgwaith?** *which is equivalent to* **faint o °weithiau?** 'how many times?'. *For* 'first time', 'second time', *etc* ⇒**tro.**

⇒**adeg,** ⇒**amser,** ⇒**weithiau**

gwall (*plural* **-au**) *noun, masculine*
= mistake, error

newch chi °gywiro ⁿngwallau iaith i mi? = will you correct my language errors for me?
⇒**camgymeriad**

gwallgo(f) *adjective*
= mad, crazy
⇒**gwyllt**

gwallt *noun, masculine*
= hair
ti wedi cael torri dy °wallt! = you've had your hair cut!

gwallus *adjective*
= full of mistakes; defective

gwan *adjective*
= weak
dw i'n dal i °deimlo'n °wan braidd = I'm still feeling rather weak
mae'r te 'ma'n edrych yn sobor o °wan = this tea looks awfully weak

gwanwyn *noun, masculine*
= spring
yn y gwanwyn = in (the) spring
yn y gwanwyn diwetha = last spring
yn y gwanwyn nesa *or* **yn y gwanwyn sy'n dod** = next spring
yng ⁿngwanwyn 1991 = in the spring of 1991
trwy'r gwanwyn = all through the spring
°**bob gwanwyn** = every spring

gwared *in:*
cael gwared = get rid (**âʰ**/**arᵒ** of)
oedd rhaid cael gwared ag e = it had to be got rid of

gwaredu *verbnoun*
= get rid of
ar ôl gwaredu tensiwn, gall yn aml °weld y sefyllfa'n °fwy clir = after getting rid of tension, one can often see the situation more clearly

gwario *verbnoun*
= spend (*money*)
paid ti â'i °wario fo i gyd! = don't you spend it all!
faint °wariest ti arni? = how much did you spend on it/her?
⇒**treulio**

gwarth *noun, masculine*
= disgrace; scandal

gwartheg *plural noun*
= cattle
⇒**buwch**

gwarthus *adjective*
= disgraceful
mae hynny'n °warthus! = that's disgraceful!

gwasanaeth (*plural* **-au**) *noun, masculine*
= service

gwasg *noun, feminine*
= press
dw i'n cytuno °fod y °wasg yn gallu mynd dros °ben llestri weithiau = I agree that the press can go over the top sometimes

gwastad *adjective*
= flat, level
mae eisiau lle gwastad i °wneud hyn yn iawn = we need a flat place to do this properly
⇒**wastad**

gwastraff *noun, masculine*
= waste (**o°** of)
mi oedd hynny'n °wastraff llwyr o amser = that was a complete waste of time

gwawr *noun, feminine*
= dawn, daybreak
mi °gododd gyda'r °wawr = he/she got up at dawn

gwddf (*plural* **gyddfau**) *noun, masculine*
• = neck
oedd e hyd at ei °wddf yn y dŵr = he was up to his neck in the water
• = throat
mae gwddf tost 'da fi = I've got a sore throat

! *The singular of this word is usually pronounced* **gwddw** *in speech. A variant word* **gwddwg** (*plural* **gyddygau**) *is heard in many Southern areas.*

gwdihŵ (*plural* **gwdihwiaid**) *noun, feminine* (*South*)
= owl
⇒**tylluan**

gwedd *noun, feminine*
= look; form; appearance
ar ei newydd °wedd = in its new look:
y Fiesta ar ei newydd °wedd = the new-look Fiesta

gweddill (*plural* **-ion**) *noun, masculine*
• = rest; remainder
...ac mae'r gweddill yn hanes = ...and the rest is history
bydd y gweddill yn dod cyn hir = the rest will be along shortly
• (**yn**) °**weddill** = left over
...gyda saith punt yn °weddill = ...with seven pounds left over

gweddol° *adverb*
= fairly
mae gwerslyfrau yn ymddangos yn °weddol °gyflym yn Lloegr = textbooks appear fairly quickly in England
sut dych chi bore 'ma?—gweddol = how are you this morning?—OK

gweddu (i°) *verbnoun*
= suit
maen nhw'n gweddu i'w gilydd = they suit each other

gweddw
1 (*plural* **-on**) *noun, feminine*
= widow
fe °adawyd hi'n °weddw = she was widowed
2 *adjective*
= widowed
gŵr gweddw = widower

gweiddi *verbnoun*
= shout (**ar°** at)
°**ddylet ti °ddim °fod wedi gweiddi fel 'ny** = you shouldn't have shouted like that

gweill *plural noun*
ar y gweill = planned; in the pipeline
oes rhywbeth 'da ti ar y gweill heno? = have you got anything planned tonight?
mae geiriadur newydd ar y gweill = a new dictionary is planned

gweithdy (*plural* **gweithdai**) *noun, masculine*
= workshop

gweithgylch (*plural* **-oedd**) *noun, masculine*
= (*medical, dental, legal etc*) practice

gweithio *verbnoun*
= work
lle mae'ch gŵr yn gweithio? = where does your husband work?

dyw'r peth 'ma °ddim yn gweithio = this thing isn't working/doesn't work

gweithredol *adjective*
= active
mae'n tueddu i °gyfrannu mewn ffordd °weithredol = he tends to make an active contribution

gweithredu *verbnoun*
= act; operate
maen nhw'n gweithredu'n °groes i °bolisïau'r llywodraeth = they are acting contrary to the government's policies
gweithredir system oriau hyblyg = a system of flexible hours is in operation

gweld (*stem* **gwel-**) *verbnoun*
• = see
common variants: preterite plural forms can take **-s-** *after the stem, so* **gwelson ni, gwelsoch chi, gwelson nhw**
doedd dim byd i'w °weld = there was nothing to be seen
ble °welsoch chi'r aderyn 'ma? (or ...°weloch chi...) = where did you see this bird?
fe °weles i nhw yn y °dre neithiwr = I saw them in town last night
°wela i chi! = I'll see you! (*colloquial leave taking formula*)
°welwn ni chi wythnos nesa! = we'll see you next week!
°gawn ni °weld = we'll see
gadewch inni °weld nawr... = let's see now...
2singular **gweli (di)**, *2plural* **gwelwch (chi)** *are frequently used as presents:*
fel y gwelwch, mae'r beic mewn cyflwr arbennig o °dda = as you (can) see, the bike is in a particularly good condition (*alternative to:* **fel dych chi'n gweld, ...**)
mae popeth yn ⁿnwylo'r cyfreithwyr.— gwela i = everything is in the hands of the lawyers.—I see

! *The parenthetical expressions* °**weli di**, °**welwch chi** *or* (*South*) **t'wel, ch'wel** *are in common use for* 'you see':
..., ond, °welwch chi, oedd hi'n °wahanol iawn °bryd hynny = ..., but, you see, it was very different then
doedd hi °ddim yn °gyfleus, t'wel = it wasn't convenient, you see

Note the official phrase for 'please'— **os gwelwch yn °dda**—*which, however, coexists with the widespread loanword* **plîs**.
A special literary autonomous/impersonal form **gweler** *is used in writing by way of an imperative:*
gweler uchod = see above
gweler hefyd llun y clawr blaen = see also front cover picture

gwely (*plural* **-au**) *noun, masculine*
= bed

gwell
1 *adjective*
• = better
wyt ti'n teimlo'n °well erbyn hyn? = are you feeling better now?
mae'r un yma'n °well o °lawer na'r un yna = this one is much better than that one
efallai y dylwn i °ddod gyda chi?— gwell fyth! = perhaps I should come with you?—even better!
• (*as modal, with* **i°**)

! *In this sense,* **gwell** *usually appears with soft mutation, and is followed by* **i°** + [*subject*] + °*verbnoun*:
°**well inni °fynd** = we'd better go
°**well iddyn nhw aros fan hyn** = they'd better wait here
°**well i mi °beidio deud ffasiwn bethau!** = I'd better not say such things!
°**well i'r plant °dacluso'u stafelloedd** = the children had better tidy their rooms

2 (*with* **gan°/gyda**) = prefer; would rather

! *In this sense* **gwell** *again usually appears with soft mutation, and is followed by* ⇒**gyda** (*I'**da**) (*South*) *or* ⇒**gan°** (*North*) + [*subject*] + °*verbnoun or* °*noun*; 'prefer x to y' *in this construction requires* ⇒**naʰ**
p'un sy'n °well 'da chi? = which (one) do you prefer?
°well 'da fi °goffi na te = I prefer coffee to tea
°well gynna i °de na ʰchoffi = I prefer tea to coffee
°well 'da fi °gerdded na dal y bws = I'd rather walk than catch the bus

⇒**da**

gwella *verbnoun*
- = improve, get better
  °fydd y sefyllfa °ddim yn gwella yn y dyfodol agos = the situation won't improve in the near future
- = recover, get better
  gwella'n °fuan! = get better soon!
  dych chi'n siwr bod chi wedi llwyr °wella? = are you sure you've completely recovered?

gwelliant (*plural* **gwelliannau**) *noun, masculine*
= improvement
'na °welliant! = that's better!

gwendid (*plural* **-au**) *noun, masculine*
= weakness
⇒**gwan**

Gwener *in:*
Dydd Gwener = Friday
Nos °Wener = Friday night
⇒**Llun** *for phrases involving days of the week*

gwenu *verbnoun*
= smile (**ar°** at)
gwenwch i gyd! = everybody smile!
daeth i mewn dan °wenu = he/she came in smiling

gwerdd
⇒**gwyrdd**

gwerinwr (*plural* **gwerinwyr**) *noun, masculine*
(*chess*) = pawn

gwers (*plural* **-i**) *noun, feminine*
= lesson (*also figurative*)
oes 'na °wersi i °Gymru? = are there lessons for Wales?
⇒**dosbarth**

gwersyll (*plural* **-oedd**) *noun, masculine*
= camp

gwersyllu *verbnoun*
= camp, go camping

gwerth (*plural* **-oedd**) *noun, masculine*
= worth; value
achoswyd difrod gwerth dros °ddeng mil o °bunnoedd = over ten thousand pounds worth of damage was caused
mi °fyddai'n °werth gofyn iddo rhag ofn = it would be worth asking him just in case

gwerthfawr *adjective*
= valuable

gwerthfawrogi *verbnoun*
= appreciate
mae pawb yma'n gwerthfawrogi'ch cyfraniad dros y blynyddoedd = everyone here appreciates your contribution over the years

gwerthu *verbnoun*
= sell
yn ni'n gorfod gwerthu'r ail °gar = we've got to sell the second car
°werthes i'r cwbwl am ugain punt = I sold the whole lot for twenty pounds
⇒**ar °werth**

gwestai
- (*plural* **gwesteion**) *noun, masculine*
  = guest
  aed â nifer o °westeion i'r ysbyty gydag anawsterau anadlu = a number of guests were taken to hospital with breathing difficulties
- *plural of*
⇒**gwesty**

gwesty (*plural* **gwestai**) *noun, masculine*
= hotel
arhoson ni yng ⁿngwesty'r Savoy = we stayed in the Savoy hotel

gweud (*South*)
⇒**dweud**

gwibdaith (*plural* **gwibdeithiau**) *noun, feminine*
= trip, excursion
dyn ni'n mynd ar °wibdaith o amgylch Bae Ceredigion = we're going on a trip round Cardigan Bay

gwin (*plural* **-oedd**) *noun, masculine*
= wine

gwir
1 *noun, masculine*
= truth
y gwir amdani yw. . . = the truth of it is. . .

! *Note the expression* **a dweud y gwir**, *literally* 'to tell the truth', *but corresponding to the much more common English expression* 'actually'.
a dweud y gwir, dwi'n teimlo cymysgedd o °gariad ac atgasedd

tuag ati = actually, I feel a mixture of love and hate towards her

2 *adjective* (**gwir°**—*precedes noun*)
= real
mae gwir angen eich cefnogaeth = we really need your support
mae'n °wir °ddrwg gen i am hyn = I'm really sorry about this
mae Sioned yn mynd i'r Unol °Daleithiau.—°wir? = Sioned's going to the United States.—really?

gwirfoddol *adjective*
= voluntary

gwirfoddolwr (*plural* **gwirfoddolwyr**) *noun, masculine*
= volunteer

gwirfoddolwraig *noun, feminine*
= volunteer

gwirion *adjective*
= silly
dadl °wirion iawn = a very silly argument

gwirionedd *noun, masculine*
= truth
mewn gwirionedd = in truth, really
tydw i °ddim mewn gwirionedd yn erbyn, ond tydw i °ddim o °blaid chwaith = I'm not really against, but I'm not in favour either

gwirioneddol° *adverb*
= really (+ *adjective*)
mae'n °wirioneddol °bwysig = it's really important
dywedwyd ar ei rhan ei bod hi'n °wirioneddol °ddrwg ganddi = it was said on her behalf that she was really sorry

gwisg *noun, feminine*
= dress, costume

gwisgo *verbnoun*
• = wear, be dressed in
beth wyt ti'n °wisgo heno? = what are you wearing tonight?
• = put on (*clothes*)
gwisga dy sgidiau, nei di? = put on your shoes, will you

gwlad (*plural* **gwledydd**) *noun, feminine*
= country
hyd yn oed mewn gwlad °fechan fel Cymru. . . = even in a small country like Wales. . .

gwledig *adjective*
= rural
mae'r sefyllfa'n °waeth fyth yn yr ardaloedd gwledig = the situation is even worse in the rural areas
Cymru °wledig = rural Wales

gwleidydd (*plural* **-ion**) *noun, masculine*
= politician

gwleidyddiaeth *noun, feminine*
= politics

gwleidyddol *adjective*
= political
dyw hi °ddim yn ffasiynol i °wneud jôcs gwleidyddol anghywir = it's not fashionable to make politically incorrect jokes

gwlyb *adjective*
feminine (*rare*) **gwleb**, *comparative* **gwlypach**, *superlative* **gwlypa(f)**
= wet
mi °fydd hi'n °wlyb trwy'r dydd yfory = it will be wet all day tomorrow
bydd hi'n °wlypach o °lawer yn y De nag yn y Gogledd = it will be a lot wetter in the South than in the North

gwlychu *verbnoun*
= soak, drench
°ges i ⁿgwlychu ar y ffordd adre = I got soaked on the way home

gwneud
1 *verbnoun* (*irregular*)
generally pronounced **gneud,** *or even* **neud,** *in speech.*
preterite: **nes i, nest ti, naeth e/hi, naethon ni, naethoch chi, naethon nhw**
future: **na i, nei di, neith e/hi, nawn ni, newch chi, nân nhw**
common variants: **naiff e/hi, newn ni**
conditional (of restricted use in the modern language):
nawn i, naet ti, nâi fe/hi, naen ni, naech chi, naen nhw *or (South):* **nelwn i, nelet ti, nelai fe/hi, nelen ni, nelech chi, nelen nhw**
autonomous/impersonal forms: non-past **gwneir,** *past* **gwnaed** *or* **gwnaethpwyd**

> **!** *More formal language insists on fuller forms with* **gw-** *prefixed, so* **gwnes i, gwnaethon ni, gwnân nhw,** *etc, but this is very unusual in unaffected speech apart from the verbnoun, the response-word* **Gwna** *(Yes,) I will (do), and the imperatives* **gwna** *(singular) and* **gwnewch** *(plural)*

- = do
  - **dw i'n gorfod gwneud ⁿngwaith cartre °gynta?** = I've got to do my homework first
  - **be' nest ti wedyn?** = what did you do then?
  - **be' nawn ni, 'te?** = what shall we do, then?
  - **naen nhw mo hynny heddiw** = they would not do that today
- = make
  - **pwy sy wedi gwneud y llanast 'ma?** = who has made this mess?
  - **rhaid gwneud ymdrech arbennig** = we must make a special effort
  - **gwnaed yng ⁿNghymru**
  - **gwnaethpwyd yng ⁿNghymru** = made in Wales
- (*used with* **i°**—*verbnoun only*)
  - **bydd sawl ffordd o °wneud i'ch arian °fynd ymhellach** = there will be a number of ways of making your money go further
  - **dw i am °wneud iddyn nhw °ddeall** = I want to make them understand
- **2** *as auxiliary*

> **!** *The affirmative markers* ⇒**fe°** *and* ⇒**mi°** *are generally less used when* **gwneud** *is an auxiliary than when it is a verb in its own right.*

- *preterite*
  - **pryd nest ti °weld nhw?** = when did you see them?
  - **naeth Aled °ddim mynd** = Aled didn't go
  - **naethon nhw °alw draw wythnos diwetha** = they called round last week
  - **naethoch chi °brynu'r pethau eraill, on'do?** = you bought the other things, didn't you?
- *future*
  - **os neith pawb aros wedyn, bydd y bwyd yn dod** = if everyone will wait then, the food will come

- **ond mynd o Sir Aberteifi nân nhw wedyn, yndefê?** = but they'll go from Cardiganshire then, won't they?
- **mi neith cig °gadw mewn rhewgell** = meat will keep in a freezer

> **!** *Note that the 1st person future forms are commonly used to express intention:*
> **na i °ofyn iddo** = I'll ask him
> **nawn ni ffonio yfory** = we'll phone tomorrow
> *and in this use, as with the future of* **gwneud** *generally as an auxiliary, the inflected future of the main verb is always an alternative—so* **na i °ofyn** = **gofynna i** *I'll ask,* **nawn ni ffonio** = **ffoniwn ni** *we'll phone; and indeed* **os neith pawb aros** = **os arhosith pawb** *if everyone will wait.*
> *In addition, the 2nd person future forms* **nei di** *and* **newch chi** *have an important special function as the polite request formula* Will you. . .?
> **nei di °fwrw golwg dros hyn i mi?** = will you take a look at this for me?
> **newch chi °gau'r ffenest os gwelwch yn °dda?—gwna** = will you shut the window please?—(Yes,) I will (do)
> *and as tags after* **paid/peidiwch. . .** (⇒**peidio**):
> **peidiwch anghofio, na newch chi?** = don't forget, will you?
> **. . .ond paid ti â dweud dim, na nei di?** = . . .but don't you say anything, will you?

- *with focused verbnoun*
  - **ond gwrthod naethon nhw!** = but they <u>refused</u>!
  - (*focused variant of* **naethon nhw °wrthod** *or* **gwrthodon nhw**)
  - **colli nân nhw yn y diwedd ta beth** = they will lose in the end anyway
  - (*focused variant of* **nân nhw golli** *or* **collan nhw**)

gwneuthuriad *noun, masculine*
= manufacture
  - **mae'r peiriannau i gyd o °wneuthuriad tramor** = the machines are all of foreign manufacture

gwobr (*plural* **-au**) *noun, feminine*
= prize
  - **Rhiannon enillodd y °wobr °gynta** = (it was) Rhiannon (who) won the first prize

gwobrwyo *verbnoun*
= give *or* award a prize to

gŵr (*plural* **gwŷr**) *noun, masculine*
= husband

> **!** *This word can also mean* 'man'
> (*though generally in the sense of a
> married man, the opposite of* **llanc**
> bachelor); *the general term for* 'man',
> *however, is* ⇒**dyn**.

gwraidd (*plural* **gwreiddiau**) *noun,
masculine*
= root (*also figurative*)
**y ffaith yma sy wrth °wraidd y
°broblem** = it's this fact that's at the
root of the problem

> **!** *An alternative singular* **gwreiddyn** *is
> used in many transferred senses.*

gwraig (*plural* **gwragedd**) *noun,
feminine*
= wife; woman
dyma ⁿngwraig Bethan = this is my
wife Bethan
**hen °wraig ar ei ʰphen ei hun ydy hi
nawr** = she's an old woman on her own
now
⇒**dynes**, ⇒**menyw**

gwraig tŷ (*plural* **gwragedd tŷ**)
= housewife

gwraig °weddw (*plural* **gwragedd
gweddw**)
= widow

gwrandawiad (*plural* **-au**) *noun,
masculine*
= audition

gwrando (*stem* **gwrandaw-**) *verbnoun*
= listen (**ar°** to)
imperative singular **gwranda**, *plural*
gwrandewch
dw i'n hoff o °wrando ar y radio = I like
listening to the radio
gwrandewch ar hyn! = listen to this!

gwregys (*plural* **-au**) *noun, masculine*
= belt

gwregys diogelwch
= safety belt

gwreiddiol *adjective*
= original
**maen nhw'n gweithredu'n hollol
°groes i'r amcan gwreiddiol** = they are

acting completely contrary to the
original purpose
o °Lanelli wi'n dod yn °wreiddiol = I
come from Llanelli originally

gwres *noun, masculine*
• = heat
dewch yn nes i chi °gael gwres y tân =
come closer so you can get the heat of
the fire
gwres canolog = central heating
• (*fever*) = temperature
mae gwres arni = she's got a
temperature

gwrth°- *prefix*
= anti-, counter-
Examples:
gwrthchwyldroadol *adjective* =
counterrevolutionary
(⇒**chwyldro**)
gwrth-ddweud *verbnoun* = contradict
(⇒**dweud**)
gwrthgynhyrchol *adjective* =
counterproductive
(⇒**cynhyrchu**)
gwrth-hiliol *adjective* = antiracist
(⇒**hiliol**)
gwrthrewydd *noun, masculine* =
antifreeze
(⇒**rhewi**)
gwrth-Seisnig *adjective* = anti-
English
(⇒**Seisnig**)
gwrthweithio *verbnoun* = counteract
(⇒**gweithio**)
gwrthymosodiad (*plural* **-au**) *noun,
masculine* = counterattack
(⇒**ymosod**)

gwrthdaro *verbnoun*
= collide; clash
**naeth y °ddau °gar °wrthdaro o °flaen
neuadd y °dre** = the two cars collided
in front of the town hall
**. . .yn y gwrthdaro diweddar gyda
Sbaen** = . . .in the recent clashes with
Spain

gwrthod *verbnoun*
= refuse
**maen nhw'n gwrthod ymweld â'r ardal
ar eu pennau eu hunain** = they are
refusing to visit the area on their own

gwrthwynebiad (*plural* **-au**) *noun,
masculine*
= opposition; objection; resistance

gwrthwynebu *verbnoun*
- = oppose, object to
  mae'r °gymuned °leol yn gwrthwynebu'r cynllun = the local community opposes the plan
- = resist
  rhaid inni °wrthwynebu'r ymosodiadau 'ma = we must resist these attacks

gwybod* *verbnoun (irregular)*
= know (*facts*)

> **!** ⇒Gwybod box

⇒chimod, ⇒timod, ⇒nabod

gwybodaeth *noun, feminine*
- = knowledge
  mae gynno fo °wybodaeth eang o'i °bwnc = he's got a wide knowledge of his subject
- = information
  am °ragor o °wybodaeth, ffoniwch ni yn y prif swyddfa = for more information, phone us at the main office

gwych *adjective*
= fine, great, marvellous
  mi °fasai hynny'n °wych! = that would be great!
  sut oedd y cyngerdd?—gwych! = how was the concert?—great!
  perfformiad gwych = a marvellous performance

gwydr (*plural* **-au**) *noun, masculine*
= glass (*material and vessel*)

gwydraid *noun, masculine*
= glass(ful)
  °gymerwch chi °wydraid o °win? = will you have a glass of wine?

gwyddbwyll *noun, feminine*
= chess

Gwyddel (*plural* **-od**) *noun, masculine*
= Irishman

Gwyddeleg *noun, feminine*
= Irish language

Gwyddeles (*plural* **-au**) *noun, feminine*
= Irishwoman

gwyddoniaeth *noun, feminine*
= science

gwyddonol *adjective*
= scientific

gwyddonydd (*plural* **gwyddonwyr**) *noun, masculine*
= scientist

gŵyl (*plural* **gwyliau**) *noun, feminine*
= festival
  noddir yr °gŵyl gan °Fwrdd yr Iaith °Gymraeg = the Festival is sponsored by the Welsh Language Board

gwyliau *plural noun*
= holiday; holidays
  o'n i'n arfer mynd yno adeg gwyliau'r Haf = I used to go there during the summer holidays

gwylio *verbnoun*
= watch
  y cwbwl dych chi'n °wneud yw gwylio'r teledu = all you do is watch television
  mae'r gaeaf cystal ag unrhyw °dymor i °wylio adar = winter is as good a season as any for birdwatching
⇒edrych

gwyllt *adjective*
- = wild
- (*figurative*) = mad, angry

gwyn *adjective*
feminine **gwen**,
comparative **gwynnach**, *superlative* **gwynna(f)**
= white

gwynt (*plural* **-oedd**) *noun, masculine*
= wind
  bydd y gwyntoedd yn chwythu'n ysgafn o'r gorllewin = the winds will be blowing lightly from the west

gwyntog *adjective*
= windy
  mi °fydd hi'n °wyntog iawn trwy'r dydd yfory = it will be very windy all day tomorrow

gwŷr *plural of*
⇒gŵr

gwyrdd *adjective* (*feminine* **gwerdd**)
= green

gwystl (*plural* **-on**) *noun, masculine*
= hostage

gyda^h (*before vowels* **gydag**) *preposition*

> **!** *This word is often in speech contracted to* **'da^h**, **'dag**, *especially in possession constructions.*

Gwybod—'To Know'

present: **gwn i, gwyddost ti, gŵyr e/hi, gwyddon ni, gwyddoch chi, gwyddon nhw**

common variants: **gwyddan nhw**

imperfect: **gwyddwn i, gwyddet ti, gwyddai fe/hi, gwydden ni, gwyddech chi, gwydden nhw**

The present and imperfect inflected forms are by and large interchangeable with the ordinary constructions using verb 'to be' + **gwybod**. So, for example, **gwn i** is equivalent to **dw i'n gwybod** 'I know', and **gwyddwn i** to **o'n i'n gwybod** 'I knew'.

gwn i am °rywun °allai'ch helpu chi
dw i'n gwybod am °rywun °allai'ch helpu chi = *I know of someone who could help you*

fe °wydden ni °fod rhywbeth o'i °le
o'n ni'n gwybod °fod rhywbeth o'i °le = *we knew that something was wrong*

But in some set phrases the inflected forms are more common:

am °wn i	*for all I know; I suppose*
hyd y gwn i	*as far as I know*
..., mi °wn	*..., I suppose, I dare say*
⇒**'sgwn i**	*I wonder* (North; ⇒**tybed**)
pwy a °ŵyr?	*who knows?*
Duw a °ŵyr	*God knows*
°wyddost ti	*y'know* (North)
wsti	(contraction of above)
°wyddoch chi	*y'know* (North)

The common and useful phrase 'I don't know' is heard variously as:

dw i °ddim yn gwybod (standard, and heard everywhere)
dwn i °ddim *(North)*
dwn 'im (contraction of above)
°wn i °ddim (supposedly standard, but rarely heard in unaffected native speech, and considered 'learner-Welsh' by some)

sa i'n gwybod (South; ⇒**bod**)
smo fi'n gwybod (South; ⇒**bod**)

It is important to remember that **gwybod** does not denote an action and therefore cannot form a preterite—where English has 'he knew', Welsh says **(r)oedd e'n gwybod** or **gwyddai fe**, and not *gwybododd e or *gwybuodd e, which are not Welsh. Similarly, 'did you know?' is **oeddech chi'n gwybod?** or **°wyddech chi?** and not *wybodoch chi? or *wybuoch chi? For the same reason, the preterite auxiliaries ⇒**gwneud** and ⇒**ddaru** cannot be used with **gwybod**.

°wyddoch chi am °rywun o'ch cyfnod chi a °ddaeth yn enw cyfarwydd? = *do you know of anyone from your period who became a familiar name?*

fe °ŵyr pawb nad yw dŵr ac olew yn cymysgu = *everyone knows that water and oil don't mix*

a does °wybod beth °ddaw o hyn oll = *and there's no knowing what will come of all this*

The expression **rhoi gwybod i°** means 'inform', 'let...know':

rhowch °wybod i mi erbyn yfory = *let me know by tomorrow*

°allet ti °roi gwybod inni y naill ffordd neu'r llall? = *could you let us know one way or the other?*

The expression **heb yn °wybod (i°)** means 'unbeknownst (to)': **mi aethon nhw ar y llong i Iwerddon heb yn °wybod i'w teuluoedd** = *they went on the ship to Ireland, unbeknownst to their families*

---

gydag/'dag, *are not used before the following words*: **y** *the*, **ei°** *his*, **ei**[h] *her*, **ein** *our*, **eich** *your*, **eu** *their*, *which instead themselves contract to give*

gyda'r *with the*, **gyda'i°** *with his*, **gyda'i**[h] *with her*, **gyda'n** *with our*, **gyda'ch** *with your*, **gyda'u** *with their*.

> As with all words causing aspirate mutation, the practice is not followed consistently, especially with words beginning **p-** and **t-**.

• = with
es i gyda ffrind = I went with a friend
dw i °ddim yn rhy °dda gydag arian, chimod = I'm not too good with money, you know
fe °ddaw'n amlwg gydag amser = it'll become clear in time
agores i y' ⁿmys i gyda ʰchyllell °fara = I cut my finger with a breadknife
ydych chi'n cymryd siwgwr gyda'ch te? = do you take sugar with your tea?
• (*indicating possession*) (*South*)
mae dau o °blant 'da nhw = they've got two children
oes car 'da chi? = have you got a car?
does dim anifeiliaid anwes 'da Sarah = Sarah hasn't got any pets
°fydd dim amser 'dag e, dw i °ddim yn credu = he won't have time, I don't think
• (*in idiomatic phrases*)
gyda llaw = by the way, incidentally
gyda'r nos = in the evening
gyda'i gilydd *etc.* = together (⇒ **gilydd**)
⇒**âʰ**, ⇒**efo**, ⇒**gan°**

gyferbyn
1 *preposition* (*optionally followed by* **âʰ**)
= opposite
mi °welwch chi fe gyferbyn y banc (*or*: . . .**gyferbyn â'r banc**) = you'll see it opposite the bank
2 *adverb*
= opposite
maen nhw'n byw gyferbyn = they live opposite

gynnau *adverb*
= just (now); just (then)
be' wedodd hi gynnau? = what did she just say?

°gynt *adverb*
• = formerly
bu °farw H., °gynt o °Fethesda = H., formerly of Bethesda, has died
• = previously, before
oedd e wedi cwrdd â hi y °flwyddyn °gynt yn Llundain = he had met her the year before in London
• = earlier; early

°ddaethon nhw °ddeng munud yn °gynt = they came ten minutes early
• = quicker, more quickly
mae'r amser yn mynd yn °gynt pan dych chi'n cael hwyl, on'd ydy? = time goes quicker when you're having fun, doesn't it?

°gynta *adverb*
= first
fi °welodd e °gynta! = I saw it first!
°well inni °ddarllen drwyddo °gynta = we'd better read through it first
⇒**cynta(f)**

gyrfa (*plural* **-oedd**) *noun, feminine*
= career

gyrru *verbnoun*
= drive
gyrrwch yn °ofalus drwy'r pentref = drive carefully through the village

gyrrwr (*plural* **gyrwyr**) *noun, masculine*
= driver

gyrrwr bws (*plural* **gyrwyr bysiau**)
noun, masculine
= bus driver

gyrrwr lori (*plural* **gyrwyr lorïau**)
noun, masculine
= lorry driver

Hh

ha(f) *noun, masculine*
= summer
⇒**haf**

haeddu *verbnoun*
= deserve
os ydy unrhywun yn haeddu swydd, Mrs Roberts yw honno = if anyone deserves a job, it's Mrs Roberts
dw i °ddim yn haeddu hyn ar °ben popeth arall = I don't deserve this on top of everything else

haerllug *adjective*
= cheeky

haf *noun, masculine*
= summer
yn yr haf = in (the) summer
yn yr haf diwetha = last summer
yn yr haf nesa *or* **yn y haf sy'n dod** = next summer
yn haf 1991 = in the summer of 1991
trwy'r haf = all through the summer
°bob haf = every summer

hafaidd *adjective*
= summery

haint *noun, feminine*
= disease; infection

hala *verbnoun*
= send
na i hala'r manylion atat ti ar °ddiwedd yr wythnos = I'll send you the details at the end of the week
⇒**anfon**, ⇒**danfon**, ⇒ **hela**

halen *noun, masculine*
= salt
°allech chi estyn yr halen os gwelwch yn °dda? = could you pass the salt please?

hallt *adjective*
• = severe, sharp
mi °gafodd nofel °ddiwetha'r awdur 'ma ei beirniadu'n hallt = this author's last novel was sharply criticised
• = salty
wrth °gwrs, am °fod y bwyd mor hallt, byddan nhw °bob amser yn sychedig

iawn = of course, since the food is so salty, they are always very thirsty

hamdden *noun, feminine*
= leisure
beth dych chi'n hoffi ei °wneud yn eich oriau hamdden? = what do you like doing in your free time?

hanes (*plural* **-ion**) *noun, masculine*
• = history
llyfr i °bob un sy'n ymddiddori yn ein hanes = a book for everyone who is interested in our history
• = story
oes gennych chi hanesion neu atgofion sy'n °werth eu cofnodi? = have you got any stories or recollections that are worth recording?
mae fersiwn diwygiedig ar y gweill, yn ôl pob hanes = a revised version is said to be planned

hanesyddol *adjective*
= historic(al)

hanfod
in: **yn ei hanfod** = essentially

hanfodol *adjective*
= essential
mae coed yn hanfodol i iechyd y °Ddaear = trees are essential to the well-being of the Earth

hanner (*plural* **hanerau, haneri**) *noun, masculine*
= half
bydd tua hanner y goleuni'n cyrraedd wyneb y °Ddaear = about half the light reaches the face of the Earth
gallech °dorri'ch bil siopa yn ei hanner = you could cut your shopping bill in half

hanner cant
= fifty

hapus *adjective*
= happy
penblwydd hapus! = happy birthday!
byddan nhw'n hapusach lle maen nhw = they'll be happier where they are

hardd *adjective*
= beautiful
i mi mae'r mynydd-dir yn y gorllewin yn harddach fyth = for me the

mountainous country in the west is
even more beautiful

haul *noun, masculine*
= sun

hawdd *adjective*
comparative **haws** *or* **hawddach,**
superlative **hawsa(f)** *or* **hawdda(f)**
= easy
  wrth °gwrs °fod codi tai a ʰphontydd
  °gryn °dipyn yn haws na ʰchodi
  pontydd gwleidyddol = of course,
  building houses and bridges is quite a
  bit easier than building political
  bridges
⇨**rhwydd**

hawl (*plural* **-iau**) *noun, feminine*
= right (**ar°** + *noun,* **i°** + *verbnoun* to)
  does gan neb o staff na'u perthnasau
  hawl i °gystadlu – no member of staff
  or their relations is allowed to enter
  the competition
  hawliau dynol = human rights

hawlio *verbnoun*
= claim (= *lay claim to*), demand

haws
⇨**hawdd**

heb° *preposition*
• = without
  cenedl heb iaith, cenedl heb °galon = a
  nation without a language (is) a nation
  without a heart
  es i'n syth heibio heb sylwi = I went
  straight past without noticing
• (= **ddim wedi** *where recent action is*
  referred to)
  dw i'n meddwl °fod e heb °ddod yn ôl
  o °ginio = I don't think he's come back
  from dinner
  dw i heb °fwydo'r anifeiliaid = I haven't
  fed the animals
  mae un °broblem yn dal heb ei datrys
  = there is one problem still unsolved

heblaw (*often* **'blaw** *in speech*)
preposition
= apart from, except
  cafodd pob un ohonon ni °fynd 'blaw
  fi = every one of us was able to go
  except me
⇨**ac eithrio,** ⇨**ar wahân i°**

hedfan *verbnoun*
= fly

y ffordd °gyflyma °fyddai hedfan i
°Gaeredin = the quickest way would be
to fly to Edinburgh
oedd hi'n hedfan awyren yn °ddeunaw
oed = she was flying a plane at
eighteen

heddiw (*often* **heddi** *in speech*)
adverb
= today
  'na °ddigon am heddi, 'te = that's
  enough for today, then
  fan hyn mae hi wedi aros hyd heddiw
  = here it has remained to this day
  °ddo i'n ôl wythnos i heddiw = I'll
  come back a week today

heddlu *noun, masculine*
= police
  roedd y lladron wedi mynd erbyn i'r
  heddlu °gyrraedd = the thieves had
  gone by the time the police arrived
  mae Heddlu Dyfed-Powys yn
  ymchwilio i'r digwyddiad = Dyfed-
  Powys Police are investigating the
  incident

heddwas (*plural* **heddweision**) *noun,*
masculine
= policeman

hefo
⇨**efo**

hefyd *adverb*
= also; as well
  mae'r ffurflen yma hefyd ar °gael yn
  Saesneg = this form is also available
  in English
  fe °fydda i'n dod hefyd = I'll come as
  well
  hefyd, bydd eisiau dod â ʰchôt °law =
  also, you will need to bring a raincoat

heibio (*usually* **+ i°**) *adverb*
= past, by
  ewch heibio i'r banc, ac mi °welwch
  chi fe ar y chwith = go past the bank,
  and you'll see it on the left
  °weles i nhw wrth i'r bws °fynd heibio
  = I saw them as the bus went by

heini *adjective*
= fit; active
  cadw'n heini = keep fit
  dosbarthiadau cadw'n heini = keep fit
  classes
⇨**ffitrwydd**

heintus *adjective*
= diseased; infected

hela *verbnoun*
- • = hunt
- • = send
⇨**anfon,** ⇨**danfon,** ⇨**hala**

helaeth *adjective*
= extensive, wide
**mae dewis helaeth o °gyrsiau ar °gael
trwy'r °flwyddyn** = a wide choice of
courses is available all year round
i °raddau helaeth = to a great degree,
largely

helynt (*plural* **-ion**) *noun, masculine*
= trouble, bother
**gobeithio bod nhw °ddim yn bwriadu
creu helynt heno** = I hope they're not
out to make trouble tonight

hen° *adjective*
comparative **henach** *or* (*especially in
the sense elder or senior*) **hŷn,**
superlative **hena(f)** *or* **hyna(f)**
- • = old
hen °bethau yw'r rhain i gyd = these
are all old things
pethau hen iawn = very old things
dych chi'n llawer henach na fi = you're
much older than me

> ! **hen°** *precedes the noun, unless it is
itself qualified, as in the second
example above*

- • (**wedi hen°** + *verbnoun*) = long since...;
...long ago
**mi °fyddai rhywun wedi hen °gamu i
mewn** = someone would have stepped
in long ago
- • (*endearing and derogatory*)
yr hen °blentyn bach! = (you) poor little
child!
cadw draw, yr hen °fochyn! = keep
away, you pig!

heno *adverb*
= tonight; this evening
**mae'n noson °brysur tu hwnt ar y
meysydd pêl-droed heno** = it's an
extremely busy evening on the
football fields tonight

> ! *In the spoken language an
extended variant* **heno 'ma** *is used in
an emphatic sense—'this very night',*

or often simply as an alternative to
heno.

heol (*plural* **-ydd**) *noun, feminine*
= road; street

her (*plural* **-iau**) *noun, feminine*
= challenge

herio *verbnoun*
= challenge
**bydd y cwmni'n herio'r penderfyniad
yn y llys yn y °flwyddyn newydd** = the
company will challenge the decision
in court in the new year

het (*plural* **-iau**) *noun, feminine*
= hat

heulog *adjective*
= sunny
mi °fydd hi'n heulog trwy'r dydd yfory
= it'll be sunny all day tomorrow

hi *pronoun*
- • = she
wedodd hi °ddim byd wrtha i = she
didn't say anything to me
hi yw'r °brifathrawes = she is the
headteacher
- • = her
°gest ti °air â hi ddoe? = did you have a
word with her yesterday?
ffonia i hi nawr = I'll phone her now
- • = it (*including abstract senses*)
ydy hi'n oer heddiw? = is it cold today?

> ! *As with the other pronouns,* **hi** *is
optionally (though widely) used after
a noun with the possessive adjective*
⇨**ei**[h]:
beth yw ei gwaith hi? = what is her
job?
be' wedodd ei gŵr hi wrthi? = what
did her husband say to her?
*When 'it' is used in an abstract
sense (i.e. not referring to a particular
object), then* **hi** *is always used in
Welsh:*
mae hi'n oer (*contracted in speech
to* **mae'n oer**) = it is cold
**°fydd hi'n °gyfleus i mi °alw bore
'fory?** = will it be convenient for me to
call tomorrow morning?
siapa hi! = get a move on! (*literally
shape it!*)
But if 'it' refers to an object, then **hi**
*is used only if the word for that object
is feminine in Welsh:*

lle mae'r ffurflen 'na?—dw i wedi gadael hi ar y bwrdd i ti = where's that form?—I've left it on the table for you

⇨**hithau**

hiliol *adjective*
= racist

hinsawdd *noun, feminine*
= climate (*also figurative*)

hir *adjective*
comparative **hirach** *or* (*archaic*) **hwy,** *superlative* **hira(f)** *or* (*archaic*) **hwya(f);** *equative* **cyhyd**
= long
pa mor hir oedd e? = how long was it?
mae'r un yma'n hirach na'r lleill = this one's longer than the others
°**fydda i °ddim yn hir** = I won't be long
yn ni °ddim yn moyn aros yn rhy hir, 'twel = we don't want to stay too long, you see
bydd y swyddfa'n cysylltu â chi eto cyn bo hir = the office will contact you again before long

hiraeth *noun, masculine*
= longing (*for home etc*) (**am°** for)
hiraeth am °Gymru = a longing for Wales

hithau *pronoun*
= she; it; her

> **!** **hithau** *is one of the special set of expanded pronouns that are used— though not that frequently—to convey emphasis or some idea of contrast with, or echoing of, what has gone before.*
> **cer i °ofyn i hithau, 'te** = go and ask her, then
> **a hithau'n tynnu at saith o'r °gloch, dyma'r penawdau** = with it coming up to seven o'clock, here are the headlines
> *With the possessive* ⇨**ei**ʰ, *hithau can replace following* **hi** *as echoing pronoun to give special emphasis or contrast:*
> **beth am ei** ʰ**char hithau?** = what about her car?

⇨**hi**

hofrennydd (*plural* **hofrenyddion**)
noun, masculine
= helicopter

hoff *adjective*
• = fond (**o°** of)
ydy hi'n hoff ohono? = is she fond of him?
dydy'r capten °ddim yn hoff o °weld ei °griw yn segura fel hyn = the captain doesn't like seeing his crew loafing around like this
• = keen (**o°** on)
dw i °ddim yn hoff o °ddringo = I'm not keen on climbing
• **hoff°** (*precedes noun*) = favourite
p'un ydy'ch hoff °raglen ar y teledu ar hyn o °bryd? = what is your favourite programme on the television at the moment?

hoffi* *verbnoun*
= like
wyt ti'n hoffi afalau? = do you like apples?
dw i °ddim yn hoffi teithio ar y bws = I don't like travelling on the bus

> **!** *With unreality endings,* **hoffi** *means 'would like...', either with nouns or verbnouns:*
> **hoffet ti afal?** = would you like an apple?
> **hoffech chi °ddod eto wythnos nesa?** = would you like to come again next week?
> **pwy ohonoch chi hoffai °gyfrannu?** = who among you would like to make a contribution?

⇨**leicio,** ⇨**caru**

holi *verbnoun*
= ask; make enquiries
mae'r °wers nesa'n delio â holi'r ffordd = the next lesson deals with asking the way
holi cwestiwn = to ask a question
sesiwn holi ac ateb = a question-and-answer session

holl° *adjective* (*precedes noun*)
= whole; all
mae'r holl °fater bellach yn ⁿ**nwylo'r cyfreithwyr** = the whole matter is now is the hands of the lawyers
be' ydy'r holl sŵn 'ma? = what's all this noise?

mae'r holl °blant yn gwylio'r teledu = all the children are watching television

> ! When used with plural nouns, **holl** is an alternative to the more common ⇨**i gyd** which, however, follows its noun—**mae'r plant i gyd yn gwylio'r teledu.**

⇨**drwy°**, ⇨**pob**

hollol° adverb
- = quite, completely
  ar y cyfan, maen nhw'n hollol °gywir = on the whole, they are quite correct
- = perfectly
  mae'n °ddull hollol °gyfreithlon o ymddwyn = it is a perfectly legal way of behaving

⇨**cwbl°**, **cwbwl°**

hon
1 pronoun
= this (one/person/thing) (feminine)
pwy yw hon? = who is this? (girl, woman etc)
2 adjective (mainly literary and formal)
= this (feminine)
dychweler y ffurflen hon erbyn y degfed o °fis Mehefin = this form should be returned by the tenth of June

⇨**y... 'ma**

honna pronoun
= that (one/person/thing) (feminine)
Spoken variant of ⇨**honno 1**

honni verbnoun
= claim
... er iddo honni °fod dim byd o'i °le = ... although he claimed that nothing was wrong
honnir °fod tystiolaeth °berthnasol wedi'i ʰchuddio = it is claimed that material evidence has been withheld

honno
1 pronoun
= that (one/person/thing) (feminine)
os ydy unrhywun yn haeddu swydd, Mrs Roberts yw honno = if anyone deserves a job, it's Mrs Roberts
2 adjective (mainly formal and literary)
= that (feminine)
ei dychwelyd i'r swyddfa honno ar unwaith = return it to that office at once

⇨**y ... 'na**

hosan (plural usually **sanau**) noun, feminine
= sock

hufen noun, masculine
= cream
hufen iâ = ice cream

hun pronoun (with possessive adjectives) (North)
- = self
  bydd rhaid trefnu'n hun yn °well y tro nesa = we'll have to organize ourselves better next time
  yr unig °wendid ydy ei °fod yn bychanu ei hun = the only weakness is that he belittles himself
- (emphasizing possessor)
  eich car eich hun ydy hwn, 'te? = is this your own car, then?

> ! Welsh expresses, for example, 'my own house' as 'my house myself'

hunan (plural **hunain**) pronoun (with possessive adjectives) (South)
- = self
  mae'r cwmni eisoes wedi ennill enw iddyn nhw eu hunain = the company have already earned a name for themselves
  mae ein gallu i °dwyllo'n hunain yn anhygoel = our ability to deceive ourselves is incredible
  na i °fynd 'n hunan = I'll go myself
- (emphasizing possessor)
  ⁿghar 'n hunan yw hwn = this is my own car
  rhaid i'ch plant °ddod â'u harian eu hunain = your children must bring their own money

> ! Welsh expresses, for example, 'my own house' as 'my house myself'

hunan°- prefix
= self-
hunangyflogedig adjective = self-employed
(⇨**cyflog**)
hunanbarch noun, masculine = self-respect
(⇨**parch**)
hunanddinistriol adjective = self-destructive, suicidal
(⇨**dinistrio**)

hunanymwybodol *adjective* = self-aware
(⇒**ymwybodol**)
hunanwasanaeth *noun, masculine* =
self-service
(⇒**gwasanaeth**)

hurt *adjective*
= silly, foolish

hwb *noun, masculine*
= boost
afraid yw dweud y bu'r ymateb hwn yn hwb mawr i'r diwydiant = needless to say, this reponse has been a great boost to the industry
⇒**hybu**

hwn
1 *pronoun*
= this (one) (*masculine*)
beth ydy hwn yn °Gymraeg? = what is this in Welsh?
2 *adjective* (*mainly literary and formal*)
= this (*masculine*)
rhowch °wybod i'r prif swyddfa os collir y llyfryn hwn = inform the main office if this booklet is lost
⇒**y ... 'ma**

hwnna *pronoun*
= that (one/person/thing) (*masculine*)
spoken variant of ⇒**hwnnw (1)**

hwnnw
1 *pronoun*
= that (one/person/thing) (*masculine*)
pwy ydy hwnnw, 'te? = who is that (man), then?
rho hwnnw ar y bwrdd °gynta, nei di? = put that on the table first, will you?
2 *adjective* (*mainly formal and literary*)
= that (*masculine*)
fe °fydd pawb ond Brychan Llyr yn parhau gyda'r gwaith hwnnw = everyone but Brychan Llyr will continue with that work
⇒**y ... 'na**

hwnt
⇒**tu hwnt**

hwrdd (*plural* **hyrddod**) *noun, masculine*
= ram
⇒**maharen**

hwyad, hwyaden (*plural* **hwyaid**)
noun, feminine
= duck

cynhelir ras hwyaid heno am chwech o'r °gloch = a duck race will be held this evening at six o'clock

hwyl *noun, feminine*
• = fun
noson o hwyl = an evening of fun/a convivial evening
• = (good *or* convivial) atmosphere
'sdim llawer o hwyl fan hyn heno, nag oes? = there's not much atmosphere here this evening, is there?
• (*as exclamation*) = goodbye
hwyl (nawr)! = goodbye!

hwylio *verbnoun*
= sail, go sailing

hwyr *adjective*
comparative **hwyrach**
= late
gwell hwyr na hwyrach = better late than never
°flynyddoedd yn hwyrach ... = years later...
yn yr hwyr = in the evening:
cafwyd dawns ysgubor yn yr hwyr = there was a barn dance in the evening

hwyrach *adverb* (*North*)
= perhaps, maybe
hwyrach °fod o wedi mynd, 'ta? = perhaps he's gone, then?
⇒**efallai**, ⇒**ella**

hyblyg *adjective*
= flexible
gweithredir system oriau hyblyg = a system of flexible hours is in operation
dyw'r °derminoleg °ddim yn °ddigon hyblyg = the terminology is not flexible enough

hybu *verbnoun*
= promote; boost
cynllun newydd i hybu'r iaith = a new scheme to promote the language
⇒**hwb**

hyd
1 *noun, masculine*
= length
ar hyd a lled = the length and breadth (of)
tywydd garw ar hyd a lled Cymru = bad weather the length and breadth of Wales
⇒**ar hyd**, ⇒**o hyd**
2 *conjunction*
= till, until

ewch yn syth ymlaen hyd y gwelwch
chi'r goleuadau = go straight on until
you see the lights

hyd° *preposition*
• = up to, up till, until
   **bydd y llinellau ar agor hyd °ddiwedd
   yr wythnos** = the lines will be open till
   the end of the week
   **ond hyd yn °ddiweddar doedd neb yn
   byw fan'na** = but until recently
   nobody lived there
• = as far as, up to (*distance*)
   **ond mae cerdded hyd °gopa'r bryn yn
   °waith dymunol iawn** = but walking
   up to the top of the hill is very
   pleasant work

> **!** *This preposition, particularly in its
> 'distance' sense, is often used in
> conjunction with* **at°** *in the spoken
> language:*
> **ewch yn syth ymlaen hyd at y
> goleuadau, yna trowch i'r chwith** =
> go straight ahead as far as the lights,
> then turn left

hyder *noun, masculine*
= confidence
   mae hyder newydd yn y °dre = there is
   a new confidence in the town
   **diffyg hyder, fel arfer, yw'r °broblem
   °fwya** = a lack of confidence, as usual,
   is the biggest problem

hydre(f) *noun, masculine*
= autumn
   yn yr hydre = in (the) autumn
   yn yr hydre diwetha = last autumn
   yn yr hydre nesa *or* **yn yr hydre sy'n
   dod** = next autumn
   yn hydre 1991 = in the autumn of 1991
   trwy'r hydre = all through the autumn
   °bob hydre = every autumn

Hydre(f) *noun, masculine*
= October
⇒**Ionawr**

hyd yma, hyd yn hyn *adverbs*
= so far, up till now
   un o'i °lwyddiannau mwya hyd yma =
   one of his greatest successes so far

hyd yn oed *adverb*
= even
   **mi °fedrech chi hyd yn oed °ddadlau
   °fod...** = you could even argue that...

°**allai hyd yn oed y rheolwyr presennol**
°**ddim gwarantu ei °ddyfodol** = even
the present managers could not
guarantee its future
⇒**fyth**

hyfryd *adjective*
= nice, pleasant
   °**ddwedwn i °ddim °fod o'n lle hyfryd
   iawn** = I wouldn't say it was a very nice
   place

hyfforddi *verbnoun*
• = train
   bydd rhaid eu hyfforddi nhw = they'll
   need to be trained
• (*functioning as noun and adjective*) =
   training
   **ceir sesiwn hyfforddi tiwtoriaid
   prynhawn dydd Sadwrn** = there will
   be a tutors' training session on
   Saturday afternoon

hyfforddiant *noun, masculine*
= training
   dan hyfforddiant = trainee, apprentice:
   mecanydd dan hyfforddiant = trainee
   mechanic

hyll *adjective*
= ugly

hyn
1 *pronoun*
= this (thing/matter/situation *etc.*)
   rhaid gwneud e fel hyn = (you) have to
   do it like this
2 *adjective*
• = this (*used by some speakers for* ⇒**hwn**
   and ⇒**hon**)
   dewch ffordd hyn! = come this way
• (*mainly formal and literary*) = these
   rhaid cadw'r drysau hyn ynghau =
   these doors must be kept closed

> **!** *In the spoken language, the
> pronouns* **hyn** *this and* **hynny** *that are
> the abstract counterparts of* **hwn/hon**
> *and* **hwnna/honna**. *So, for example,
> we say of a concrete object* **beth ydy
> hwn?** *what is* this?, *but of a situation*
> **mae hyn yn °warthus** this *is
> disgraceful. Similarly* **pwy ydy
> honna?** *who is* that *(woman)? but*
> **beth mae hynny'n °feddwl?** *what
> does* that *mean? The adjectival uses
> of these words are generally
> restricted to formal and literary style,*

and here **hyn** *means* these *while* **hynny** *means* those: **y geiriau hyn** these words, **y geiriau hynny** those words—*for which the spoken language would have* **y geiriau 'ma, y geiriau 'na** *respectively*.

⇨**yr hyn**, ⇨**hyn oll**

hŷn
⇨**hen**

hyna
⇨**hen**

hynny

> **!** *This word is very often pronounced* **'ny** *in speech*

1 *pronoun*
= that
peth tra gwahanol yw hynny = that is quite a different thing/matter
efallai mai hynny sy'n egluro ei absenoldeb = perhaps that is what explains his absence
paid siarad â hi fel 'ny! = don't talk to her like that!
2 *adjective*
(*mainly formal and literary*) = those
ni ʰchadwyd yr addewidion hynny = those promises were not kept
⇨**hyn**

hynod *adjective*
= remarkable
peth hynod yw lliw = colour is a remarkable thing
⇨**hynod o°**

hynod o° *adverb*
= extraordinarily, remarkably, amazingly
mae'r °ddau wedi bod yn hynod o °gefnogol i'r ysgol = both have been extraordinarily supportive of the school
⇨**hynod**, ⇨**andros**

hyn oll *pronoun*
= all this
a does °wybod beth °ddaw o hyn oll = and there's no knowing what will come of all this

hysbyseb (*plural* -ion) *noun, feminine*
= advertisement
gweler ein hysbyseb yn yr atodiad wythnosol = see our advertisement in the weekly supplement

hysbysebu *verbnoun*
= advertise

hysbysfwrdd (*plural* hysbysfyrddau) *noun, masculine*
= noticeboard

hytrach
in: **yn hytrach (naʰ)** = rather (than)
mi °ddylen ni anelu at °gyfaddawdu yn hytrach na gwrthdaro = we ought to aim for compromise rather than confrontation

I i

i *pronoun*
= I, me

> ! *This pronoun has variants* ⇒**fi** *and*
> ⇒**mi**. *The short form is used:*
> *a) as the subject of verbs—e.g.* **dw i** I
> am, **o'n i** I was, **bydda i** I will be,
> **dylwn i** I ought to, **fe °godes i** I got
> up, **arhosa i fan hyn** I'll stay here *etc.*
> *b) generally with the 'conjugated' or*
> *amalgamated prepositions—***arna i**
> on me, **hebdda i** without me, *and*
> *similarly* **wrtha i, gynna i** *or* **gen i,**
> **amdana i, ata i** *etc. Many Southern*
> *dialects, however, prefer* **fi** *in all these*
> *cases—***arna fi, wrtha fi** *etc. Note that*
> *the preposition* **i** *uses either* **fi** *or* **mi: i**
> **mi/fi** *to me.*
> *c) as the (mainly optional) 'echoing' or*
> *reinforcing pronoun with the*
> *possessive adjective* ⇒**fy**ⁿ *(/f', 'yn,*
> *'n, ⁿ) my—so for example* ⁿ**mhlant i**
> my children, **'n ffenest i** my window.
> *Similarly as the object of*
> *verbnouns—*°**Ellwch chi** ⁿ**ghlywed**
> **i?** Can you hear me? *Again, Southern*
> *dialects often prefer* **fi** *for these*
> *related uses.*
> *d) with compound prepositions: for*
> *example* **o** ⁿ**mlaen i** in front of me, **yn**
> **'n erbyn i** against me, **ar 'n ôl i** after
> me *etc. This is really a possessive as*
> *in use c) above. Note that free-*
> *standing prepositions require* **fi:** *for*
> *example* **gyda fi** with me, **heblaw fi**
> apart from me.

Dafydd Jones dw i = I'm Dafydd Jones
o'n i °ddim yn gwybod yn iawn lle o'n i
= I didn't really know where I was
ffonies i nhw neithiwr = I phoned them
last night
mi °rodda i'r rhain fan'ma i chi = I'll
put these here for you
°**ddylwn i °ddweud wrtho?** = should I
tell him?
peidiwch poeni amdana i = don't
worry about me
mae'n °ddrwg gen i = I'm sorry
does gynna i °ddim newid = I haven't
got any change
sgrifenna ata i! = write to me!

rhowch nhw ar 'y ⁿ**nesg i** = put them
on my desk
der i eistedd wrth 'n ochor i = come
and sit beside me
⇒**innau**

i° *preposition*
personal forms: **i mi/fi, i ti, iddo fe, iddi**
hi, inni/i ni, i chi, iddyn nhw
• = to
dw i'n mynd i sgrifennu ato fo = I'm
going to write to him
dych chi'n mynd i Ffrainc eto eleni? =
are you going to France again this
year?
• = for
mae gen i anrheg °fach i ti = I've got a
little present for you
mae llythyr i chi ar eich desg = there's
a letter for you on your desk
ond beth ydy ystyr y penderfyniad
'ma i'r gweddill ohonon ni? = but
what does this decision mean for the
rest of us?
• (*indicating possession of intrinsic*
characteristic)
mae i'r °gyfrol °dair rhan = the volume
has three parts
mae'r dyn 'na'n °gefnder i mi = that
man is my cousin
mae i Eglwys Sain Cynog
°**bensaernïaeth hynod** = Sain Cynog
Church has a remarkable
architecture
• (*linking certain conjunctions to their*
subjects)
°**ga i °air â hi cyn iddi (hi) °fynd** = I'll
have a word with her before she goes
°**ges i °air â hi cyn iddi (hi) °fynd** = I
had a word with her before she went
bydd popeth wedi mynd erbyn inni
°**gyrraedd** = everything will have gone
by the time we arrive
...wrth i'r llywodraeth °gyhoeddi'r
ffigurau diweithdra diweddara = ...as
the government publishes/published
the latest unemployment figures
• = that (*with past sense or reference in*
reported speech)
dw i'n siwr i mi ei ʰ**chlywed hi'n canu** =
I'm sure (that) I heard her singing
ydych chi'n gwadu iddyn nhw °alw
arnoch chi neithiwr, 'te? = are you
denying that they called on you last
night, then?

'i
⇒**ei°**, ⇒**ei**ʰ

iâ *noun, masculine*
= ice
⇒**rhew**

iach *adjective*
= healthy
mae pobol yn iachach yn °gyffredinol y dyddiau 'ma nag o'r blaen = people are generally healthier these days than before
⇒**iechyd**

iaith (*plural* **ieithoedd**) *noun, feminine*
= language; (*as adjective*) linguistic
oes diddordeb gennych chi mewn dysgu Cymraeg fel ail iaith? = are you interested in teaching Welsh as a second language?
draw yn y gorllewin, mae yna chwyldro iaith tawel yn digwydd = over in the west, there is a quiet linguistic revolution happening

iasoer *adjective*
= chilly; chilling

Iau
in:
Dydd Iau = Thursday
Nos Iau = Thursday night
⇒**Llun**

iau
⇒**ifanc**

iawn
1 *adverb* (*follows adjective*)
= very
mae'n oer iawn tu allan = it's very cold outside
2 *adjective*
= right; proper; all right; OK
dych chi'n iawn = you're right
er bod nhw'n dweud °fod popeth yn iawn, mae hyn yn awgrymu fel arall = although they say that everything is all right, this suggests otherwise
°alla i °ddim anadlu 'n iawn = I can't breathe properly
3 *interjection*
= OK
aros fan'na!—iawn! = stay there!—OK!

ie *particle*
= yes

> **!** ⇒**Yes and No** *box on the English-Welsh side*

iechyd *noun, masculine*
= health
gofalu am iechyd y °gymuned = looking after the health of the community
iechyd da! = cheers!
⇒**iach**

ieithoedd *plural of*
⇒**iaith**

ieua(f)
⇒**ifanc**

ieuenctid *noun, masculine*
= youth (*period of life, not person*)
cynhelir disgo yng ⁿNghlwb Ieuenctid Bontfach = a disco will be held in Bontfach Youth Club
mae'r °bobol 'ma wedi colli'u hieuenctid = these people have lost their youth

ifanc *adjective*
plural **ifainc**; *comparative* **iau** *or* (*spoken*) **ifancach** *or* **fengach**, *superlative* **ieua** *or* (*spoken*) **ifanca** *or* **fenga**
= young
mae'n edrych yn rhy ifanc, on'd ydy? = he/she looks too young, doesn't he/she?
mae'r grŵp yn cael ei °redeg gan °bobol ifainc i °bobol ifainc = the group is run by young people for young people
mae ⁿmrawd i'n iau na fi = my brother is younger than me
hwn ydy'r anifail fenga sy gynnon ni = this is the youngest animal we've got

> **!** *In the second example the singular* **ifanc** *is also heard—although* **ifanc** *is one of the few adjectives in modern Welsh to have a regularly used plural form, many speakers treat it as invariable for singular and plural; so* **pobol ifanc** *beside* **pobol ifainc**.

ifê *particle*

> **!** *This colloquial particle performs the same function as the more standard* ⇒**ai**, *introducing a focused question (i.e. question that does not begin with a verb).*
> **ifê Ffrangeg mae'r bobol 'na'n siarad, 'te?** = is it French those people are speaking, then?

i °fod i°

= supposed to (be), meant to (be)

dach chi i °fod i aros nes bod rhywun yn dod = you're supposed to wait until someone comes

beth mae hynny i °fod i °feddwl, 'te? = what is that supposed to mean, then?

> **!** *The final* **i°** *is dropped in abbreviated responses, corresponding to* 'supposedly' *or even* 'apparently':
> **fan hyn mae rhaid inni °balu?—i °fod** = is this where we have to dig?—supposedly
> **felly mae'r car yn °barod?—i °fod** = so the car's ready?—apparently

i fyny *adverb (also* **fyny** *in speech)*

= up

eith ⁿnghar °ddim i fyny'r allt = my car won't go up the hill

i fyny ar y bryn maen nhw'n byw = they live up on the hill

mae'r stafelloedd gwely fyny'r grisiau = the bedrooms are upstairs

⇨**lan**

i ffwrdd *(often simply* **ffwrdd** *in speech) adverb*

= off; away

ffwrdd â ni! = off we go!

°allet ti °droi'r teledu i ffwrdd? = could you turn the television off?

byddwn ni i ffwrdd tan °ddydd Mercher = we'll be away till Wednesday

⇨**bant**

i gyd *pronoun*

= all

mi oedd hi'n °gyd-ddigwyddiad anffodus, 'na i gyd = it was an unfortunate coincidence, that's all

mae'r myfyrwyr i gyd yn aros = all the students are waiting, the students are all waiting

wi'n trio anghofio amdanyn nhw i gyd = I'm trying to forget about them all

> **!** **i gyd** *follows the noun or pronoun it refers to, while* ⇨**holl°** *precedes;* **i gyd** *is probably more common generally in speech. Without a noun or pronoun to attach to,* **i gyd** *is not*

usually possible *(but note first example above)—in this case* ⇨**popeth** *can be used instead. Note also* **y cyfan i gyd** *the whole lot*

i °lawr, °lawr *adverb*

= down

fe °gafodd ei saethu i °lawr wythnos union yn ôl = he was shot down exactly a week ago

ewch lawr y stryd fan hyn, yna trowch i'r °dde = go down the street here, then turn right

dewch lawr! = come down!

tro'r teledu lawr ychydig, nei di? = turn the TV down a bit, will you?

ill *pronoun*

= they

in: **ill dau, ill dwy** the two of them, they both

ill tri, ill tair the three of them, they three

fe °gaethon nhw eu gwlychu ill dwy = they both *(feminine)* got soaked

⇨**dau°**, ⇨**tri**, ⇨**nhw**

i mewn *adverb*

= in

dewch i mewn! = come in!

ydy Dafydd i mewn heddiw? = is Dafydd in today?

i mewn â ni! = in we go!

gwasgwch hwn i mewn = press this in

> **!** *This adverb is used where there is a sense of motion to the English* 'in', *and also (second example above) where no location is specified, i.e. when* 'in' *stands on its own.*

⇨**mewn**, ⇨**ynⁿ** *preposition*

innau *pronoun*

= I; me

> **!** **innau** *is one of the special set of expanded pronouns that are used— though not that frequently—to convey emphasis or some idea of balance or contrast with, or echoing of, what has gone before.*
> **cerwch chi °gynta, mi °ddo innau toc** = you go first, I'll come in a minute

⇨**i**

Ionawr *noun, masculine*
= January

> **!** **ym mis Ionawr** or **yn Ionawr** = in
> January (*names of months*
> *susceptible to nasal mutation will take*
> *it after* **yn**ⁿ**: yng** ⁿ**Ngorffennaf** = in
> July)
> °**bob mis Ionawr** = *every January*
> **ar y degfed o** (°**fis**) **Ionawr** = *on the*
> *tenth of January*
> **erbyn y degfed o** (°**fis**) **Ionawr** = *by*
> *the tenth of January*
> (*names of months susceptible to soft*
> *mutation will take it after* **o**°**: y degfed**
> **o** °**Fehefin** = *the tenth of June*)
> **erbyn (mis) Ionawr** = *by January*
> **mis Ionawr nesa/diwetha** = *next/last*
> *January*
> **yn hwyr ym mis Ionawr** = (in) late
> January
> **yn** °**gynnar ym mis Ionawr** = *(in)*
> *early January*
> °**ddechrau mis Ionawr** = *at the*
> *beginning of January*
> °**ddiwedd mis Ionawr** = *at the end of*
> *January*
> **am** °**weddill mis Ionawr** = *for the*
> *remainder of January*
> **tan (**°**fis) Ionawr** = *till January*
> **trwy gydol mis Ionawr** = *throughout*
> *January*
> °**welwn ni chi** °**fis Ionawr** = *we'll see*
> *you in January*

i °**raddau** *adverbial phrase*
= to a certain extent, to an extent
⇒**helaeth**

i'r dim *adverbial phrase*
= exactly; perfect
dw i wedi trefnu'r cyfarfod ar gyfer
saith o'r gloch.—i'r dim! = I have
arranged the meeting for seven
o'clock.—perfect!
⇒**union**

i'r eitha *adverb*
= extremely

is
⇒**isel**

isa(f)
⇒**isel**

ise
⇒**eisiau**

isel *adjective*
comparative **is,** *superlative* **isa(f)**
= low
mae'r nifer sy wedi pleidleisio yn
erbyn yn isel iawn iawn = the number
that have voted against is very very low
mae hi'n edrych braidd yn isel ei
hysbryd = she looks rather depressed
bydd y galw am °**dai newydd yn is**
eleni = the demand for new houses
will be lower this year
mae eisiau mynd °**dipyn yn is** = you/we
need to go a bit lower/further down
dyma'r ffigurau isa ers blynyddoedd =
these are the lowest figures for years

is-etholiad (*plural* **-au**) *noun,*
masculine
= by-election

isio
⇒**eisiau**

isod *adjective, adverb*
= below (*on document etc*)
gweler isod = see below
llenwch y ffurflen isod a'i dychwelyd
aton ni = fill in the form below and
return it to us
⇒**uchod**

i'w *contracted form*
= to his; to her; to its; to their
wedi hynny, roedd popeth arall yn
cwympo i'w °**le** = after that,
everything else fell into (its) place
mae'r °**ddynes arall yn dioddef o**
anafiadau difrifol i'w ʰ**choesau** = the
other woman is suffering from serious
injuries to her legs
mi aethon nhw ar y llong i Iwerddon
heb yn °**wybod i'w teuluoedd** = they
went on the ship to Ireland,
unbeknownst to their families

> **!** *This represents* **i** + **ei**°, **i** + **ei**ʰ *and* **i**
> + **eu**—*all these combinations appear*
> *as* **i'w** *in both spoken and written*
> *forms of the language. Note that the*
> *mutations after* **ei**° *and* **ei**ʰ *remain in*
> *force.*

Iwerddon *noun, feminine*
= Ireland
⇒**Gwyddel,** ⇒**Gwyddeles**

L l

label (*plural* **-i**) *noun, feminine*
= label

labelu *verbnoun*
= label

lamp (*plural* **-au**) *noun, feminine*
= lamp

lan *adverb* (*South*)
= up
**maen nhw'n byw lan y bryn, wi'n
  credu** = they live up the hill, I think
**mae'n haws mynd lan na dod lawr,
  chimod** = it's easier going up than
  coming down, you know
awn ni lan staer = let's go upstairs
⇒**i fyny**

lansio *verbnoun*
= launch
**fe °geith prosiect newydd ei lansio yn
  y °dre wythnos nesa** = a new project
  will be launched in the town next
  week

lapio *verbnoun*
= wrap
lapiwch eich parseli'n °ofalus = wrap
  your parcels carefully

larwm *noun, masculine*
= alarm
canwch y larwm drwy °dorri'r gwydr =
  sound the alarm by breaking the glass
⇒**rhybudd**

°lawn mor° (+ *adjective*)
= just as . . .
**mae'r medrau hyn °lawn mor
  °werthfawr** = these skills are just as
  valuable
wi °lawn mor euog â ti = I'm just as
  guilty as you

lawnt (*plural* **-iau, -ydd**) *noun, feminine
or masculine*
= lawn
**peidiwch cerdded ar y lawntydd os
  gwelwch yn °dda** = please do not walk
  on the lawns

lawr
⇒**i lawr**

ledled *adverb*
= throughout; all over . . .; the length
  and breadth of . . .
ar °gael ledled Cymru = available
  throughout Wales
**bydd y gwyntoedd cryfion yn
  cynyddu ledled y °wlad heno** = the
  strong winds will increase all over the
  country tonight

lefel (*plural* **-au**) *noun, feminine*
= level
cyrsiau ar °gael ar °bob lefel = courses
  available at all levels
⇒**safon**

leicio* *verbnoun*
= like
wyt ti'n leicio afalau? = do you like
  apples?
dw i °ddim yn leicio teithio ar y bws = I
  don't like travelling on the bus

> **!** *With unreality endings* **leicio** *means
> 'would like . . .', either with nouns or
> verbnouns:*
> **leiciet ti afal?** = would you like an
> apple?
> **leiciech chi °ddod eto wythnos
> nesa?** = would you like to come
> again next week?
> *In many areas the stem for this verb
> (used with unreality endings) is not*
> **leici-** *but* **leics-** (*cf.* ⇒**dylwn**)
> **leicswn i °fynd yna** = I'd like to go
> there
> **leicsech chi ymaelodi?** = would you
> like to join?
> **leicswn i °ddim deud ar y °foment** =
> I wouldn't like to say at the moment

⇒**hoffi**, ⇒**caru**

lein (*plural* **-iau**) *noun, feminine*
= line

> **!** *This word is of much more
> restricted use than the general word*
> ⇒**llinell**; *its main meaning is a railway
> line—***lein °fach** *narrow gauge
> railway—though even here* **llinell** *is
> also used:* **prif °linell** *or* **prif lein** *main
> line railway.*

letysen (*plural* **letys**) *noun, feminine*
= lettuce

litr (*plural* **-au**) *noun, masculine*
= litre

> ! *As a quantity expression,* **litr** *requires a following* **o°** *when a noun is specified:*
> **cymerwch °dri litr o °ddŵr** = take three litres of water

liwt (*plural* **-iau**) *noun, feminine*
- • = lute
- • (*idiomatic use*)
  mae e'n gweithio ar ei liwt ei hun(an) = he's working for himself
  gweithîo ar 'n liwt 'n hun(an) dw i bellach = I'm working for myself now

loes (*plural* **-au**) *noun, feminine*
= ache; pain

lol *noun, masculine*
= nonsense
twt lol! = (stuff and) nonsense!
hen lol! = what nonsense!
paid ti â °chymryd unrhyw lol gynnyn nhw = don't you take any nonsense from them

lôn (*plural* **lonydd**) *noun, feminine*
= lane
ewch i'ch lôn (*on motorway*) = get in lane

lori (*plural* **lorïau**) *noun, feminine*
= lorry; truck
lori °lo (*plural* **lorïau glo**) = coal lorry
lori °gymalog (*plural* **lorïau cymalog**) = articulated lorry

lot *noun, feminine*
= a lot; much; many
mae 'na lot °fawr o'r pethau 'na fan'ma = there are a (great) lot of those things here
beth wyt ti'n °feddwl am hyn?—dim lot = what do you think of this?—not much

> ! *This quantity word borrowed from English is very commonly used in the spoken language instead of* ⇒**llawer**; *but while* **llawer** *has* **iawn** *as its intensifier* (**llawer iawn** very much, very many), **lot** *uses* °**fawr**.

lwc *noun, feminine*
= luck
pob lwc! = good luck!
wrth lwc, dyw'r rhan °fwya ohonyn nhw °ddim yn °wenwynig = luckily, most of them are not poisonous

lwcus *adjective*
= lucky
o'ch chi'n lwcus fan'na, on'd oeddech chi? = you were lucky there, weren't you?

lwfans (*plural* **-au**) *noun, masculine*
= allowance
maen nhw'n cael lwfans °bob mis gan eu rhieni = they get an allowance every month from their parents

LL11

llachar *adjective*
= bright
byddai'r dilledyn 'ma'n rhy °lachar, on' byddai? = this garment would be too bright, wouldn't it
⇒**disglair**

Lladin *noun, feminine*
= Latin

lladrata *verbnoun*
= thieve, rob
mae hyd yn oed plant ysgol °gynradd yn cael eu cyhuddo o °ladrata yn y °dre = even primary school children are being accused of thieving in the town
⇒**dwyn**

lladron *plural of*
⇒**lleidr**

lladd *verbnoun*
= kill
'sai lot mwy o °bobol wedi cael eu lladd tasen ni °ddim wedi bod yma = a lot more people would have been killed if we hadn't been here
lladdwyd dyn mewn damwain ar yr un ffordd ddoe = a man was killed in an accident on the same road yesterday

llaeth *noun, masculine*
= milk
⇒**llefrith**

llaethdy (*plural* **llaethdai**) *noun, masculine*
= dairy

llafar *noun, masculine, functioning as adjective*
in: **iaith °lafar** spoken language (*as opposed to* **iaith ysgrifenedig** written language *or* **iaith °lenyddol** literary language)
mae'r gair 'na'n perthyn i'r iaith °lafar yn unig = that word belongs solely to the spoken language

llafariad (*plural* **llafariad**) *noun, masculine*
= vowel
⇒**cytsain**

llafur *noun, masculine*
= labour; toil
y °blaid °Lafur = the Labour Party

llafurio *verbnoun*
= labour; toil

llai
1 *adjective*
• = smaller
rhywbeth llai sy eisiau fan hyn, dw i'n meddwl = we need something smaller here, I think
mae'r tŷ newydd yn llai na'r un oedd gynnon ni o'r blaen = the new house is smaller than the one we had before
• = lesser
byddai dyn llai wedi rhoi'r gorau iddi = a lesser man would have given up
2 *adverb*
= less; fewer
mae llai o °gyfle i °gael swyddi lleol dyddiau 'ma = there is less chance of getting local jobs these days
mi oedd llai nag ugain o °bobol yn y cyfarfod = there were fewer than twenty people in the meeting
bydd y rhain yn costio llai yn y siopau mawr = these will cost less in the big shops
llai o'r clebran 'na! = less of that chatter!
⇒**bach**, ⇒**llawer**, ⇒**lleia(f)**

llais (*plural* **lleisiau**) *noun, masculine*
= voice
mae hi'n °bwysig °fod llais Cymru'n cael ei °glywed yn Ewrop = it's important that Wales's voice be heard in Europe

llaith *adjective*
= damp

(y) llall *pronoun* (*plural* **(y) lleill**)
= (the) other (one)
mae un 'da fi fan hyn, ond °le mae'r llall? = I've got one here, but where's the other?
mae'r llall yn cael ei °gadw tu °fewn = the other one is kept inside
nawn ni °boeni am y lleill wedyn = we'll worry about the others later
mi °ddaw'r lleill ar y bws nesa, mae'n °debyg = the others will probably be along on the next bus

! *These are the pronoun equivalents of the adjectives* ➪**arall** (*plural* **eraill**) *other; so* **y llall** *means the same as* **yr un arall** *the other one, and* **y lleill** *means the same as* **y rhai eraill** *the other ones*

llamu *verbnoun*
= leap; bound

llan (*plural* **-nau**) *noun, feminine*
= church

! *Generally in place names, where it causes soft mutation of a following name or other element*—**Llanfair** Mary's (**Mair**) *church. Similarly* **Llangeitho, Llanafan, Llanfihangel**. *This word indicates the site of a church, or the area immediately round it, rather than the building itself, which is usually* ➪**eglwys**.

llanc (*plural* **-iau**) *noun, masculine*
= lad
hen °lanc (*North*) = bachelor

llances (*plural* **-au**) *noun, feminine*
= lass

llannerch (*plural* **llennyrch, llanerchau**) *noun, feminine*
= glade, clearing

llanw (*plural* **-au**) *noun, masculine*
= tide; tidal flow

! **penllanw** (*noun, masculine*) *is used for* 'high tide', *and* **trai** (*noun, masculine*) *for* 'low tide'

llath *noun, feminine*
= yard
mae mwy nag wyth can llath o'r twnel wedi'i °ddinistrio gan y tân = more than eight hundred yards of the tunnel has been destroyed by the fire

llau *plural of*
➪**lleuen**

llaw (*plural* **dwylo**) *noun, feminine*
= hand
dangos dy °law, 'te = show (me) your hand, then
mae popeth yn ⁿnwylo'r cyfreithwyr erbyn hyn = everything is in the hands of the lawyers now

gyda llaw = by the way, incidentally
➪**dwylo**, ➪**maes o °law**

llawen *adjective*
= merry; cheerful
Nadolig Llawen! = Merry Christmas!
Noson °Lawen = *evening gathering for entertainment, like Fest Noz in Brittany*

llawenydd *noun, masculine*
= joy, happiness

llawer *adverb*
= much; many; a lot
does dim llawer ar ôl = there is not much left/there are not many left
mae llawer o °bethau'n dal heb eu dweud = many things have still not been said
dw i heb °ddysgu llawer, rhaid i mi °ddweud = I haven't learnt much, I must say
mae 'na °lawer iawn o ieithoedd yn yr un sefyllfa = there are very many languages in the same situation
ti'n llawer rhy °fach i °wneud 'ny! = you're much too small to do that!
mae'r beic 'na'n rhy swnllyd o °lawer = that bike is much too noisy
llawer o °ddiolch! = many thanks!

! *As a quantity expression,* **llawer** *requires a following* **o°** *when a noun is specified.*

➪**lot**, ➪**faint**, ➪**o °lawer**

llawes (*plural* **llewys**) *noun, feminine*
= sleeve

llawfeddyg (*plural* **-on**) *noun, masculine*
= surgeon

llawfeddygaeth *noun, feminine*
= surgery

llawfeddygol *adjective*
= surgical

llaw-°fer *noun, feminine*
= shorthand

llawlyfr (*plural* **-au**) *noun, masculine*
= handbook

llawn *adjective*
= full
mae'r cwpwrdd yn llawn anrhegion = the cupboard is full of presents

llawr (*plural* **lloriau**) *noun, masculine*
= floor; storey
dewch i'n swyddfa ni ar yr ail °lawr =
come to our office on the second floor

llawysgrif (*plural* **-au**) *noun, feminine*
= manuscript

llawysgrifen *noun, feminine*
= handwriting

lle
1 *noun, masculine* (*plural* **-fydd, -oedd**)
• = place
cofiwch eu rhoi nhw'n ôl yn y lle iawn
= remember to put them back in the
right place
**does 'na °ddim llefydd parcio fan'ma
amser 'ma o'r dydd** = there are no
parking places here at this time of day
**mae'n °gwbwl amlwg °fod rhywbeth
o'i °le fan hyn** = it's quite obvious that
something is wrong here
• = space
**mi °fydd digon o °le i °bawb, swn i'n
meddwl** = there'll be enough space for
everyone, I should think
• = room
**...ond fe °ddwedwyd wedyn °fod 'na
°le i °gyfaddawdu wedi'r cwbwl** =
...but it was later said that there was
room for compromise after all
2 *adverb*
= where
lle mae'r lleill? = where are the others?
cer i °ofyn lle dylen ni °roi'r rhain = go
and ask where we should put these

> **!** *In its use as an adverb 'where',* **lle** *is
> a very common (probably more
> common) alternative for the 'official'*
> ⇒**ble***. A mutated form* °**le** *is heard in
> many Southern areas.*

llecyn (*plural* **-nau**) *noun, masculine*
= spot, place
llecyn hyfryd am °bicnic = a nice spot
for a picnic

llechen (*plural* **llechi**) *noun, feminine*
= slate

lled° *adverb*
= fairly
cadw fo'n lled °wastad = keep him
fairly flat

lledaenu *verbnoun*
= spread

**mae storïau Arthur wedi lledaenu trwy
Ewrop ers y Canol Oesoedd** = the
stories of Arthur have spread through
Europe since the Middle Ages
**mae'r anifeiliaid 'ma'n lledaenu
clefydau** = these animals spread
diseases

lledr *noun, masculine*
= leather

llefain *verbnoun* (*South*)
= cry; weep
paid llefain, bach = don't cry, dear
⇒**crio**, ⇒**wylo**

llefaru *verbnoun*
= utter, speak

llefarydd (*plural* **-ion**) *noun, masculine*
= spokesman, spokeswoman
**dwedodd llefarydd ar °ran y cwmni
°fod cyfreithwyr wedi'u galw i mewn** =
a spokesman/woman on behalf of the
company said lawyers had been called
in

llefrith *noun, masculine* (*North*)
= milk
⇒**llaeth**

llefydd *plural of*
⇒**lle**

lleia(f)
1 *adjective*
• = smallest
**cyflwynwyd basgedaid o °flodau iddi
gan °ddau o'r plant lleiaf** = she was
presented with a basket of flowers by
two of the smallest children
• = least
bydd hi'n anodd, a dweud y lleia = it'll
be difficult, to say the least
2 *adverb*
= least
p'un ydy'r eitem °leia costus? = which
is the least expensive item?
°gymera i'r tri lleia trwm = I'll take the
three least heavy (ones)
⇒**bach**, ⇒**llai**, ⇒**o °leia**

lleiafrif (*plural* **-oedd**) *noun, masculine*
= minority
**dim ond lleiafrif bychan sy'n meddwl
felly** = only a small minority think
that way

lleidr (*plural* **lladron**) *noun, masculine*
= thief; robber

elynir lladron = thieves will be prosecuted

lleihau *verbnoun*
- = lessen
  bydd y glaw wedi lleihau erbyn y nos = the rain will have lessened by evening
- = decrease
  mae galw am y rhain yn lleihau = demand for these is decreasing.
- = reduce
  mae'r llywodraeth yn bwriadu lleihau budd-dâl diweithdra = the government intends to reduce unemployment benefit
⇒**llai**

(y) lleill
⇒**(y) llall**

lleisio *verbnoun*
= voice, give voice to
mi °geith pob un ohonoch chi °leisio'i °farn = every one of you will be allowed to voice his opinion

llen (*plural* **-ni**) *noun, feminine*
= curtain

llên *noun, feminine*
= literature (*in its broadest sense including literary tradition, lore etc.*)
⇒**llenyddiaeth**

llenwi *verbnoun*
- = fill
  mae'r lle'n llenwi, on'd yw e? = the place is filling up, isn't it?
  llenwch y gwydrau cyn dechrau = fill the glasses before you start
- = fill in
  llenwch y bylchau yn y brawddegau canlynol = fill in the gaps in the following sentences

llenyddiaeth (*plural* **-au**) *noun, feminine*
= literature
llyfr am °Gymru, ei hanes a'i llenyddiaeth = a book about Wales, its history and its literature

llenyddol *adjective*
= literary
bydd y cwrs byr 'ma'n canolbwyntio ar yr iaith °lenyddol = this short course will be concentrating on the literary language

lleoedd *plural of*
⇒**lle**

lleol *adjective*
= local
mae'n °debyg mai busnesau lleol °fydd yn diodde fel arfer = as usual, it is local businesses that will probably suffer
ewch lawr i'r siop °leol = go down to the local shop

lleoli *verbnoun*
= locate
wedi'i °leoli (*masculine*), **wedi'i lleoli** (*feminine*), **wedi'u lleoli** (*plural*) = located
mae'r °ganolfan newydd wedi'i lleoli ar ymylon y °dre = the new centre is located on the outskirts of town

lleoliad (*plural* **-au**) *noun, masculine*
= location

lles *noun, masculine*
= benefit, good
o °les = of benefit
er lles = for the benefit of
i °bwy mae hyn o °les? = who is this of any benefit to?
mae'r cyfan er lles plant mewn angen = the whole thing is for the benefit of children in need
⇒**budd**

llesteiriant (*plural* **llesteiriannau**) *noun, masculine*
= hindrance; frustration

llesteirio *verbnoun*
= hinder; frustrate

llestri *noun, plural*
= dishes, crockery
nei di °olchi'r llestri i mi? = will you wash the dishes for me?
dros °ben llestri = over the top
does dim eisiau mynd dros °ben llestri, nag oes? = there's no need to go over the top, is there?

lletchwith *adjective*
= awkward
o'n i'n teimlo braidd yn lletchwith, a dweud y gwir = I felt a bit awkward actually

llety (*plural* **-au**) *noun, masculine*
= accommodation
cysylltwch â'r swyddfa °lety am °ragor o °fanylion = contact the accommodation office for more details

llethol *adjective*
= overwhelming
mwyafrif llethol = overwhelming majority
mae'r mwyafrif llethol wedi pleidleisio yn erbyn = the overwhelming majority has voted against

lleuad (*plural* **-au**) *noun, feminine*
= moon

> ! *Phases of the moon are* **lleuad °lawn** full moon, **lleuad newydd** new moon, **lleuad °gilgant** crescent moon

lleuen (*plural* **llau**) *noun, feminine*
= louse

llew (*plural* **-od**) *noun, masculine*
= lion

llewes (*plural* **-au**) *noun, feminine*
= lioness

llewys *plural of*
⇒**llawes**

llewygu *verbnoun*
= faint
oedd bron iawn iddo °lewygu yn y °fan a'r lle = he very nearly fainted on the spot

llewyrchus *adjective*
= shining, glowing (*often figurative*)
mae gyrfa °lewyrchus bellach o'i blaen = a shining career now lies before her

llidiart (*plural* **llidiardau**) *noun, masculine*
= gate

llif
• (*plural* **-iau**) *noun, feminine*
= saw
mae llifiau cadwyn trydanol hefyd ar °gael i'w llogi = electric chain saws are also available for hire
• (*plural* **-ogydd**) *noun, masculine*
= flood
mae llifogydd yn dal i effeithio'n °ddifrifol ar ardaloedd gogleddol yr Eidal = floods are still seriously affecting northern areas of Italy

llifeiriant (*plural* **llifeiriannau**) *noun, masculine*
= flood (*usually figurative*)

llifo *verbnoun*
= flow

mae'r afonydd yn llifo i'r môr = the rivers flow into the sea

llifogydd *plural of*
⇒**llif**

llinell (*plural* **-au**) *noun, feminine*
= line
tynnwch °linell ar draws y tudalen = draw a line across the page
mae rhai llinellau ffôn bellach yn rhatach nag o'r blaen = some phone lines are now cheaper than before
⇒**lein**, ⇒**llinyn**

llinyn (*plural* **-nau**) *noun, masculine*
• = line
fe °lwyddwyd i °ddod â llinyn ar y llong = (they) succeeded in bringing a line aboard the ship
• = string
clymu rhywbeth â llinyn = to tie something with string

llipa *adjective*
= limp

llithren *noun, feminine*
= slide (*in playground*)

llithrig *adjective*
= slippery

llithro *verbnoun*
= slip, slide

lliw (*plural* **-iau**) *noun, masculine*
= colour
...gyda holl °liwiau'r enfys = ...with all the colours of the rainbow
cynigir pum set teledu lliw = five colour TV sets are on offer

lliwgar *adjective*
= colourful

lliwio *verbnoun*
= colour, colour in

lliwiog *adjective*
= coloured

llnau
⇒**glanhau**

llo (*plural* **-i**, **-eau**) *noun, masculine*
= calf

lloches (*plural* **-au**) *noun, feminine*
= shelter, refuge
fe °gawson ni °loches o dan °goeden = we found shelter under a tree

Lloegr *noun, feminine*
= England

o °**Loegr** mae ei °**deulu'n dod yn**
°**wreiddiol** = his family come from
England originally
fe °**gaeth ei geni a'i magu yn Lloegr** =
she was born and bred in England
⇒**Saesneg**, ⇒**Sais**

lloeren (*plural* **-nau, -ni**)
= satellite
fe °**fydd y cwmni yn gwerthu soseri**
lloeren = the company will sell
satellite dishes

llofnod (*plural* **-au, -ion**) *noun,*
masculine
= signature

llofnodi *verbnoun*
= sign
llofnodwch fan hyn ar y gwaelod os
gwelwch yn °**dda** = sign here at the
bottom please
⇒**arwyddo**

llofrudd (*plural* **-ion**) *noun, masculine*
= murderer

llofruddiaeth (*plural* **-au**) *noun,*
feminine
= murder

llofruddio *verbnoun*
= murder
mae dyn ugain oed wedi'i °**gyhuddo o**
°**lofruddio dyn arall yng** ⁿ**nghanol y**
°**dre** = a twenty-year-old man has been
accused of murdering another man in
the town centre

llofft *noun, feminine*
= top storey
lan llofft (*South*) = upstairs

llogi *verbnoun*
= hire
gallen ni hedfan yno, a llogi car wedyn
= we could fly there, and then hire a
car
ar °**log** = on hire
i'w °**logi** (*masculine*), **i'w llogi** (*feminine*
and plural) = for hire

llong (*plural* **-au**) *noun, feminine*
= ship
⇒**cwch**

llong °**ofod** (*plural* **llongau gofod**)
noun, feminine
= spacecraft

llongwr (*plural* **llongwyr**) *noun,*
masculine
= sailor

llond *noun, feminine* (*precedes noun*)
= -ful
tair llond llwy o siwgwr = three
spoonfuls of sugar
mi oedd 'na °**lond stafell o** °**bobol** =
there was a roomful of people
dw i wedi cael llond bol(a) o'r dadlau
dibaid 'ma = I've had it up to here with
this constant arguing

llongyfarch *verbnoun*
= congratulate
mae'n °**bleser i mi** °**gael eich**
llongyfarch heno ar eich llwyddiant =
it's a pleasure for me to be able to
congratulate you this evening on your
success

llongyfarchiadau *noun, plural*
= congratulations
llongyfarchiadau ar dy °**ddyrchafiad!** =
congratulations on your promotion!

llonydd
1 *noun, masculine*
= peace, quiet,
...cyn belled â'u bod yn cael llonydd i
°**fwrw ymlaen â'u gwaith** = ...as long as
they get peace and quiet to carry on
with their work
gad/gadewch °**lonydd iddo!** = leave
him in peace!
2 *adjective*
= tranquil

lloriau *plural of*
⇒**llawr**

llosgi *verbnoun*
= burn
mae'r pentre wedi'i °**losgi'n ulw** = the
village has been burnt to the ground

llu (*plural* **-oedd**) *noun, masculine*
• = host; huge number
ers hynny mae llu o erthyglau wedi
ymddangos = since then a host of
articles has appeared
dewch yn llu! = come in (your) droves!
• = force
mae'r lluoedd diogelwch yn dal yn yr
ardal = the security forces are still in
the area

llun (*plural* **-iau**) *noun, masculine*
= picture

tynnwch °lun o'r hyn °welsoch chi = draw a picture of what you saw

Llun

in: **dydd Llun** = Monday
°Ddydd Llun = on Monday
Nos °Lun = on Monday night
ar °ddydd Llun = on Mondays
°bob dydd Llun = every Monday
bore (dydd) Llun = Monday morning
°fore (dydd) Llun = on Monday morning
pnawn (dydd) Llun = Monday afternoon
dydd Llun diwetha = last Monday
dydd Llun nesa = next Monday
dydd Llun sy'n dod = next Monday
o °ddydd Llun tan/hyd °ddydd Mercher = from Monday till Wednesday
erbyn dydd Llun = by Monday
wythnos i °ddydd Llun = a week Monday

lluniaeth *noun, feminine*
= refreshments
darperir lluniaeth ysgafn = light refreshments will be provided

llunio *verbnoun*
= form; fashion; shape

lluosi *verbnoun*
= multiply

lluosog *adjective, often functioning as noun, masculine*
= plural
beth ydy lluosog y gair 'na? = what is the plural of that word?

lluosogi *verbnoun*
= multiply

llusgo *verbnoun*
= drag
mae'n °debyg i'r meini anferth 'ma °gael eu llusgo fan hyn = these huge stones were probably dragged here

lluwch (*plural* **-feydd**) *noun, feminine*
= snowdrift

lluwchwynt (*plural* **-oedd**) *noun, masculine*
= blizzard

llw *noun, masculine*
= oath; word of honour

ar 'yn llw = on my word of honour, you can take my word for it
tyngu llw = swear an oath

llwch *noun, masculine*
= dust
gad i mi °gael gwared o'r llwch 'ma ymhobman = let me get rid of this dust everywhere

llwgu *verbnoun* (*North*)
= starve; be starving
dw i ar °lwgu!, dw i bron â llwgu! = I'm starving!
⇒**newynu**

llwnc (*plural* **llynciau**) *noun, masculine*
= swallow, gulp

llwy (*plural* **-au**) *noun, feminine*
= spoon
llond llwy = spoonful

llwyaid *noun, feminine*
= spoonful

llwybr (*plural* **-au**) *noun, masculine*
= path (*also figurative*)
byddan nhw'n troedio llwybr peryglus iawn = they will be treading a very dangerous path
llwybr ceffyl = bridleway
llwybr cyhoeddus = public footpath

llwyd *adjective*
= grey
papur llwyd = brown paper

llwyddiannus *adjective*
= successful

llwyddiant (*plural* **llwyddiannau**) *noun, masculine*
= success
mae llwyddiant y cynllun 'ma dros y blynyddoedd yn amlwg i °bawb = the success of this scheme over the years is obvious to everyone
pob llwyddiant! = good luck! (*in exams, tests, etc*)

llwyddo *verbnoun*
= succeed, be successful; be a success
mae'r °gorfforaeth wedi llwyddo i °gyfiawnhau codi'r °drwydded °deledu = the corporation has succeeded in justifying raising the television licence
naethoch chi °lwyddo, 'te? = were you successful, then?
°dair canrif yn °ddiweddarach, mae dramâu Molière yn dal i °lwyddo =

three centuries on, Molière's plays are still a success

llwyfan (*plural* **-nau**) *noun, feminine*
= stage
daeth yr amser iddi ymddangos ar °lwyfan ehangach = the time has come for her to appear on a wider stage

llwyfannu *verbnoun*
= stage

llwyn (*plural* **-i**) *noun, masculine*
• = grove
• = bush

llwynog (*plural* **-od**) *noun, masculine* (*North*)
= fox
⇒**cadno**

llwyr *adjective*
• = complete
dych chi'n siwr bod chi wedi llwyr °wella? = are you sure you've completely recovered?
dechreuwyr llwyr yw'r myfyrwyr i gyd fan hyn eleni = the students here this year are all complete beginners
• = quite
cytuno'n llwyr! = (I) quite agree!

llwyth *noun, masculine*
• (*plural* **-au**) = tribe
• (*plural* **-i**) = load

llwytho *verbnoun*
= load

llychlyd *adjective*
= dusty

llydan *adjective*
= broad; wide
bydd eisiau agor y ffenest 'ma'n llydan = this window will have to be opened wide

Llydaweg *noun, feminine*
= Breton language

llyfn *adjective* (*feminine* **llefn**)
= smooth
llyncu'n llyfn = swallow rapidly, wolf down

llyfr (*plural* **-au**) *noun, masculine*
= book
dychwelwch y llyfr canlynol cyn °gynted ag y bo modd os gwelwch yn °dda = please return the following book as soon as possible

llyfrgell (*plural* **-oedd**) *noun, feminine*
= library
bydd y llyfrgell yn cau am °bump o'r °gloch heno = the library will close at five o'clock tonight

llyfrgellydd (*plural* **llyfrgellwyr**) *noun, masculine*
= librarian (*male or female*)

llyfryn (*plural* **-nau**) *noun, masculine*
= booklet, small book
°ga i °ddau °lyfryn o stampiau dosbarth cynta? = can I have two books of first class stamps?

llyfu *verbnoun*
= lick

llyffant (*plural* **-od**, **llyffaint**) *noun, masculine*
• = toad
• = frog

> **!** *In the North, this word is used for both 'toad' and 'frog', with* **llyffant du** *for 'toad' and* **llyffant melyn** *for 'frog' if a distinction needs to be made. In the South it means 'toad', while* ⇒**broga** *is 'frog'.*
> **'llyffaint' ydyn nhw i gyd inni** = they're all 'llyffaint' to us (*i.e. frogs and toads*)

llygad (*plural* **llygaid**; *North also* **llygadau**) *noun, masculine*
= eye
cadw dy °lygaid ar °gau am eiliad, nei di? = keep your eyes shut for a moment, will you

llygoden (*plural* **llygod**) *noun, feminine*
= mouse

llygoden °fawr (*plural* **llygod mawr**)
= rat

llygredd *noun, masculine*
= pollution; contamination
golwg ar °lygredd metelau trymion yn yr amgylchedd = a look at heavy metal pollution in the environment

llygru *verbnoun*
= pollute; contaminate

llynges *noun, feminine*
= navy; fleet

llym *adjective* (*feminine* **llem**)
= harsh, severe

yr allwedd i hyn oll yw bod yn °gadarn heb °fod yn llym = the key to all this is being firm without being harsh

llyn (*plural* **-noedd**) *noun, masculine*
• = lake
   mynyddoedd a llynnoedd Gogledd Cymru = the mountains and lakes of North Wales
   Ardal y Llynnoedd = The (English) Lake District
• = pond

llyncu *verbnoun*
   = swallow

(y) llynedd *adverb*
   = last year
   ...ond gwahanol iawn oedd y rhagolygon llynedd = ...but the outlook was very different last year
   oedd o'n byw fan'ma tan llynedd = he lived here till last year

> ! *The* **y** *element is usually omitted in speech, but its underlying presence still blocks soft mutation, as in the second example above after* **tan°**.
> *In some areas the non-standard* **(y)** **°flwyddyn °ddiwetha** *is heard instead, probably by analogy with English.*

⇒**blwyddyn**, ⇒**eleni**, ⇒**diwetha(f)**

llys (*plural* **-oedd**) *noun, masculine*
   = court
   ymddangosodd pump o °bobol gerbron y llys bore 'ma = five people appeared before court this morning
   Llys y °Goron = Crown Court
   Llys Ynadon = Magistrates' Court

llys°- *prefix*
   = step-
   llysfam = stepmother
   llysfrawd = stepbrother
   llyschwiorydd = stepsisters

llysiau *noun plural*
   = vegetables

llysfwytawr (*plural* **llysfwytawyr**)
⇒**llysieuwr**

llysfwytawraig (*plural* **llysfwytawragedd**)
⇒**llysieuwraig**

llysieuwr (*plural* **llysieuwyr**) *noun, masculine*
   = vegetarian

llysieuwraig (*plural* **llysieuwragedd**) *noun, feminine*
   = vegetarian

llythrennol *adjective*
   = literal
   °fedrech chi esbonio beth mae hyn yn °feddwl yn llythrennol? = could you explain what this means literally?

llythyr (*plural* **-au, -on**) *noun, masculine*
   = letter
   daeth llu o °lythyron ar yr un pwnc i'n swyddfa wythnos diwetha = a load of letters on the same subject came to our office last week

llythyren (*plural* **llythrennau**) *noun, feminine*
   = letter (*of alphabet etc*)
   llythyren °flaen (*plural* **llythrennau blaen**) = initial letter
   llythyren °fras (*plural* **llythrennau bras**) = capital letter

llyw *noun*
   in: **wrth y llyw** = at the helm:
   bydd arweinydd gwahanol wrth y llyw erbyn diwedd y °flwyddyn = a different leader will be at the helm by the end of the year

llywodraeth (*plural* **-au**) *noun, feminine*
   = government
   y llywodraeth °fyddai â'r cyfrifoldeb i °wneud hyn = it is the government that would be responsible for doing this

llywodraethol *adjective*
   = governing

llywodraethu *verbnoun*
   = govern

llywodraethwr (*plural* **llywodraethwyr**) *noun, masculine*
   = governor

llywodraethwraig (*plural* **llywodraethwragedd**) *noun, feminine*
   = governor

llywydd (*plural* **-ion**) *noun, masculine*
   = president (*of organisation, company etc*)

llywyddiaeth *noun, feminine*
   = presidency

Mm

'ma
⇨**dyma°**, ⇨**y ... 'ma**

mab (*plural* **meibion**) *noun, masculine*
= son
mae'r bachgen 'ma'n °fab iddo = this boy is his son

mabolgampau *plural noun*
= games, athletics

mabwysiadu *verbnoun*
= adopt (*all senses*)
byddai'n °well inni °fabwysiadu system °fwy hyblyg = it would be better for us to adopt a more flexible system

machlud *verbnoun*
= set (*of the sun*)
...erbyn i'r haul °fachlud = ...by the time the sun sets/set

madarchen (*plural* **madarch**) *noun, feminine*
= mushroom

maddau (*stem* **maddeu-**) (**i°**) *verbnoun*
= forgive; pardon
maddeuwch i mi am °fod mor hwyr = forgive me for being so late

mae
⇨**bod**

maen (*plural* **meini**) *noun, feminine*
= stone
mae'n °debyg i'r meini anferth 'ma °gael eu llusgo fan hyn = these huge stones were probably dragged here

> **!** *Usually denotes monumental or prehistoric stones, while the general term is* ⇨**carreg**

maer (*plural* **meiri**) *noun, masculine*
= mayor
agorir y °ganolfan gan °Faer y °dre = the centre will be opened by the Mayor of the town

maeres (*plural* **-au**) *noun, feminine*
= mayoress

maes (*plural* **meysydd**) *noun, masculine*
= field (*also figurative*)

mae'n noson °brysur tu hwnt ar y meysydd pêl-droed heno = it's an extremely busy evening on the football fields tonight
erthyglau difyr gan arbenigwyr yn eu maes = entertaining articles by experts in their field

maes awyr (*plural* **meysydd awyr**) *noun, masculine*
= airport

maes chwarae (*plural* **meysydd chwarae**) *noun, masculine*
= playing field

maes o °law *adverb*
= presently, soon
°ddo i yn ôl atat ti maes o °law = I'll get back to you presently

maes parcio (*plural* **meysydd parcio**) *noun, masculine*
= car park

maestref (*plural* **-i**) *noun, feminine*
= suburb

mafonen (*plural* **mafon**) *noun, feminine*
= raspberry

magor
⇨**ymagor**

magu *verbnoun*
• = bring up, rear
fe °gaeth ei geni a'i magu yn Lloegr = she was born and bred in England
• = gain
mae'n °bwysig bod nhw'n gallu magu hyder yn yr iaith = it's important that they can gain confidence in the language

maharen (*plural* **meheryn**) *noun, masculine*
= ram
⇨**hwrdd**

mai *conjunction*
= that (*in reported speech—focused clauses*)
wedodd e mai Ioan °dorrodd y ffenest = he said that (it was) Ioan (that) broke the window
mae ofnau mai dyfnhau mae'r argyfwng yn Bosnia = there are fears that the crisis in Bosnia is deepening

rhaid i mi'ch atgoffa chi mai chi'n sy'n °gyfrifol am hyn = I must remind you that (it is) you (who) are responsible for this

efallai mai chi °fydd hi! = it could be you!

> **!** see **Focus** and **Reported speech** in the Grammar reference section.
>
> In some Southern areas ⇨**taw** is used instead of **mai**, and in some Northern areas ⇨**na** (conjunction) is used instead of **mai**; **mai** is preferred in the written language. Neither **mai** nor **taw** is susceptible to mutation under any circumstances.

⇨**y** conjunction

Mai noun, masculine
= May
⇨**Ionawr**

main adjective
= thin; slender

> **!** Note the term **yr iaith °fain** used for referring obliquely to the English language

maint noun, masculine
= size
gallai 1°C o °gynhesu effeithio ar °faint a natur y cymylau = 1°C of warming could affect the size and nature of the clouds

maith adjective
(in set expressions involving time)
amser maith yn ôl = a long time ago
°flynyddoedd maith yn ôl = many years ago
cytundeb a °fydd yn sicrhau swyddi am °flynyddoedd maith = a contract which will secure jobs for years to come

malio verbnoun (South)
= mind, care about
°fyddwn i °ddim yn malio mynd = I wouldn't mind going
⇨**dim ots**

malu verbnoun
= grind
malu awyr (figurative) = talk nonsense

malwoden (plural **malwod**) noun, feminine
= snail; slug

mam (plural **-au**) noun, feminine
= mother; mum, mummy
o Iwerddon mae ei mam yn dod, wi'n credu = her mother comes from Ireland, I think
°ga i °air efo dy °fam? = can I have a word with your mummy?

mamgu (plural **-od**) noun, feminine (South)
= grandmother; granny
⇨**nain**

mamiaith noun, feminine
= mother tongue, native language
ydy'r °Gymraeg yn °famiaith i chi? = is Welsh your native language?

mân adjective
• = small; tiny; fine
cerrig mân = small stones
rhaid torri'r nionod yn °fân = the onions must be cut up fine
arian mân = small change
glaw mân = drizzle
• = minor (in this sense often precedes the noun, in which case **mân°**)
mae 'na °rai mân °wallau, ond 'na i gyd = there are some minor errors, but that's all

man a man adverb
= might as well

> **!** This modal expression takes the construction **i** + subject + °verbnoun:
> **man a man i mi agor y rhain tra bo fi 'ma** = I might as well open these while I'm here

⇨**waeth**

Manaweg noun, feminine
= Manx language

maneg (plural **menig**) noun, feminine
= glove

mantais (plural **manteision**) noun, feminine
= advantage
byddai'r gallu i siarad Cymraeg yn °fantais yn y swyddi hyn = the ability to speak Welsh would be an advantage in these jobs

manteisio verbnoun
= take advantage (**ar°** of)
sut gallwn ni °fanteisio ar y cyfle 'ma? = how can we take advantage of this opportunity?

manteisiol *adjective*
- = advantageous
- = profitable

mantol *noun, feminine*
in: **yn y °fantol** in the balance
ydy, mae dyfodol y cwmni bellach yn y °fantol = yes, the company's future is now in the balance
dal yn y °fantol mae tynged y chwarel = the quarry's fate is still in the balance
⇒**clorian**

manwl *adjective*
- = exact
mae eisiau bod yn °fanwl fan hyn = one needs to be exact here
- = close; detailed
bydd rhaid edrych yn °fanwl ar y cynlluniau 'ma = these plans will have to be looked at closely
rhoddir sylw manwl i °gymwysterau pob ymgeisydd = close attention will be given to every applicant's qualifications

manylion *plural noun*
= details
cofiwch °ofyn am °fanylion ein cyrsiau dysgu pell = remember to ask for details of our distance learning courses
na i hala'r manylion atat ti ar °ddiwedd yr wythnos = I'll send you the details at the end of the week

manylu *verbnoun*
= go into detail (**ar°** on)

map (*plural* **-iau**) *noun, masculine*
= map

marchnad (*plural* **-oedd**) *noun, feminine*
= market

marchog (*plural* **-ion**) *noun, masculine*
- = rider
= horseman
= knight
- (*chess*) = knight

marchogaeth *verbnoun*
= ride (*horse*)

marw
1 *verbnoun*
- = die

! *This verb is defective in that it does not normally take inflections, though* **marwodd** *he/she died at least is heard in some areas. The normal way to say 'died' or 'has died' is* **bu °farw**, *with* **buon nhw °farw** *possible for 'they died':*
bu °farw ei chwaer ym 1977 = his sister died in 1977
buon nhw °farw °flynyddoedd yn ôl = they died years ago
As a true verbnoun, **marw** *can be used with* **yn** *where a general ongoing process is indicated:*
mae cannoedd yn marw °bob dydd yn Ethiopia = hundreds are dying every day in Ethiopia
while **wedi marw** *is the stative term for* '*dead*'
mae e wedi marw ers blynyddoedd = he's been dead for years

- (*functioning as noun*) = death
cyn ei °farw yn °ddyn ifanc union ugain ⁿmlynedd yn ôl = before his death as a young man exactly twenty years ago
2 *adjective* (*plural* **meirw**) *functioning as plural noun*
= the dead
hen iawn yw'r ywen sy'n cysgodi'r meirw = the yew tree which gives shade to the dead is very old

marwol *adjective*
= deadly; mortal; fatal
mi °gafodd e ergyd °farwol = he received a fatal blow

marwolaeth (*plural* **-au**) *noun, feminine*
= death

mas *adverb* (*South*)
= out
⇒**allan**

masnach *noun, feminine*
- = commerce
- = trade
- = business

masnachol *adjective*
= commercial; business-

mater (*plural* **-ion**) *noun, masculine*
- = matter; issue
mae dau °fater yn codi o hyn oll = two matters arise from all this
- **materion cyfoes** = current affairs

rhaglen newydd o adran materion cyfoes BBC Cymru = a new programme from the BBC Cymru current affairs department

math (*plural* **-au**) *noun, masculine or feminine*
= type, kind
= species
fe °gollir rhai mathau o °blanhigion = some types/species of plants will be lost
does dim byd o'i °fath yn bod dyddiau 'ma = nothing of its kind exists these days

> **!** *Note that* **y °fath°** (*with* **math** *as a feminine*) *is used adjectivally to mean* such..., such a...:
> **does neb yn gallu deall y °fath °weithred** = nobody can understand such an action
> **dw i °ddim eisiau clywed y °fath °bethau** = I don't want to hear such things

mathemateg *noun, feminine*
= mathematics

mathemategwr, mathemategydd (*plural* **mathemategwyr**) *noun, masculine*
= mathematician

mawr *adjective*
= big; large; great
comparative ⇒**mwy**, *superlative* ⇒**mwya(f)**
man a man i mi °gymryd yr un mawr, 'te = I might as well take the big one, then
mae'r storm wedi gadael twll mawr yn y to = the storm has left a big hole in the roof
un o °ddynion mawr ein cenhedlaeth = one of the great men of our generation
diolch yn °fawr = thanks a lot
⇒**°fawr**

Mawrth:
• *in*: **dydd Mawrth** = Tuesday
Nos °Fawrth = Tuesday night
• **mis Mawrth** = March
⇒**Llun** *for phrases involving days of the week*
⇒**Ionawr**

mecanwaith (*plural* **mecanweithiau**) *noun, masculine*
= mechanism

mecanydd (*plural* **-ion**) *noun, masculine*
= mechanic

mecanyddol *adjective*
= mechanical

Medi *noun, masculine*
= September
⇒**Ionawr**

medru *verbnoun*
present: **medra i, medri di, medr e/hi, medrwn ni, medrwch chi, medran nhw**
imperfect/conditional: **medrwn i, medret ti, medrai fe/hi, medren ni, medrech chi, medren nhw**
autonomous/impersonal non-past: **medrir**
• = can; be able
°fedri di °ddarllen hwn? = can you read this?
mi °fedrech chi hyd yn oed °ddadlau °fod... = you could even argue that...
°fedra i °ddim deall beth mae'n trio °ddweud = I can't understand what he's trying to say
°fedrech chi °ddangos inni lle mae'r amgueddfa? = could you show us where the museum is?
pwy °fedr ateb y cwestiwn 'ma? = who can answer this question?
• = be competent in; know how to
mae'n medru ei °gyfraith = he knows his law
mae'n medru darllen = he knows how to read

> **!** **medru** *and* ⇒**gallu** *are interchangeable in most senses of* 'can', *but* **gallu** *has additional uses not shared by* **medru**, *notably with expressions of the type* 'could have', 'might have'—**gallu** (*etc.*) **°fod wedi**. *Conversely, the second sense above is not shared with* **gallu**.

medd
⇒**meddai**

meddai *verb*
= says; say; said

! *This verb is used in conjunction with quoted speech:*
"Dos yn ôl a gofyn iddo, 'te," **meddai fi** = "Go back and ask him, then," I said
It is most frequently used with the third persons singular and plural—the **nhw** *form can alternatively be spelt* **medden nhw,** *and* **medd** *is sometimes encountered with nouns, but generally the form is invariable for person in the modern spoken language.*
The expression **meddai nhw** *is used for the doubtful* 'So they say' *in response to a statement:*
Mae eira ar y ffordd.—Meddai nhw = There's snow on the way.—So they say

meddal *adjective*
= soft
mae'r un yma'n rhy °feddal = this one is too soft

meddiannu *verbnoun*
= occupy
mae swyddfeydd y °brifysgol wedi'u meddiannu gan °brotestwyr = the university offices have been occupied by protestors

meddiant (*plural* **meddiannau**) *noun, masculine*
= possession
mae nifer °fawr o arfau bellach ym meddiant yr heddlu = a large number of weapons are now in the possession of the police

meddw *adjective*
• = drunk
oedd e'n °feddw erbyn hanner dydd = he was drunk by midday
meddw °gaib = blind drunk
• = *plural* **meddwon** *used as noun:* drunks, drunkards
dacw'r meddwon yn dod = here come the drunks

meddwl
1 (*stem* **meddyli-**) *verbnoun*
• = think (**am°** about, of)
'Mae'n rhy hwyr', meddyliodd Aled = 'It's too late.' thought Aled
roedd e'n meddwl mai Cymru enillodd ddoe = he thought that Wales won yesterday

dw i °ddim yn meddwl °fod hynny'n iawn = I don't think that's right
nawr yw'r amser, felly, i °feddwl am °feddwl am °brosiect arbennig = now is the time, then, to think about a special project
⇒**credu**
• = mean
beth mae'r gair 'ma'n °feddwl? = what does this word mean?
⇒**golygu**, ⇒**ystyr**
2 *noun, masculine* (*plural* **meddyliau**) = mind
mae cymaint ar eich meddwl chi, nes bod chi'n anghofio'r cyfan = there's so much on your mind that you forget the whole lot

meddyg (*plural* **-on**) *noun, masculine*
= doctor
⇒**doctor**

meddylgar *adjective*
= thoughtful

meddyliol *adjective*
= mental

mefusen (*plural* **mefus**) *noun, feminine*
= strawberry

megis *conjunction*
= such as
cyfres o °lyfrau ar °destunau megis enwau lleoedd, tafodieithoedd ac ati = a series of books on subjects such as place names, dialects and so on

! *This is a formal and literary synonym for* ⇒**fel,** *and does not occur in unaffected speech.*

Mehefin *noun, masculine*
= June
⇒**Ionawr**

meibion *plural of*
⇒**mab**

meiddio *verbnoun*
= dare
paid ti â meiddio! = don't you dare!
°feiddiech chi °ddim! = you wouldn't dare!

meini *plural of*
⇒**maen**

meitin
in: **ers meitin** a long time since, a good while ago

dw i heb °weld ti ers meitin = I haven't seen you for a while

meithrin *verbnoun*
• = nurture
• **ysgol °feithrin** (*plural* **ysgolion meithrin**) = (Welsh language) nursery school

mêl *noun, masculine*
= honey

melyn *adjective* (*feminine* **melen**)
= yellow
golau melyn = yellow light
cafodd e °ddirwy am °barcio ar °linell °felen = he got a fine for parking on a yellow line

melys *adjective*
• = sweet
• *plural* **melysion** *used as noun*
= sweets
ʰ**chewch chi °ddim melysion tan wythnos nesa** = you won't get any sweets till next week

mellt *collective*
= lightning
mellt a taranau (*or* **mellt a ʰtharanau**) = thunder and lightning

mellten *noun, feminine*
= flash/bolt of lightning;
cafodd ei °daro gan °fellten = he was struck by lightning

melltigedig *adjective*
= accursed

melltith (*plural* **-ion**) *noun, feminine*
= curse

menig *plural of*
⇒**maneg**

menter (*plural* **mentrau**) *noun, feminine*
= venture; enterprise
mi naeth nifer o °fentrau newydd ymsefydlu yn y °dre eleni a llynedd = a number of new enterprises set up in the town this year and last

mentro *verbnoun*
= venture

menyn *noun, masculine*
= butter
bara menyn = bread and butter

menyw (*plural* **-od**) *noun, feminine*
= woman
⇒**dynes**

merch (*plural* **-ed**) *noun, feminine*
• = girl
roedd y °ddwy °ferch yn °wahanol iawn = the two girls were very different
• = daughter
mae gynnyn nhw °ferch naw oed = they've got a nine-year-old daughter

Mercher
in: **dydd Mercher** Wednesday
Nos °Fercher = Wednesday night
⇒**Llun**

merlota *verbnoun*
• = pony-trekking
• = go pony-trekking

merlyn (*plural* **-nod, merlod**) *noun, masculine*
= pony

mesur
1 (*plural* **-au**) *noun, masculine*
= measure
2 (*also* **mesuro**) *verbnoun*
= measure

methiant *noun, masculine*
= failure
ond methiant, hyd yn hyn, °fu pob ymdrech i °gael theatr = but so far every effort to get a theatre has been a failure

methu *verbnoun*
= fail (*with following verbnoun, optionally followed by* **âʰ**)
roedd y llys wedi methu â rhoi ystyriaeth °lawn i °ddulliau eraill o'i °gosbi = the court had failed to give full consideration to other methods of punishing him
fe °fethodd pob cynnig i °osod cwotâu = every motion to set quotas failed

---

! methu *is used colloquially as a synonym for* **ddim yn gallu/medru** cannot
dw i'n methu gweld = I can't see
(= **dw i °ddim yn gallu/medru gweld** *or* °**alla/°fedra i °ddim gweld**)

---

mewn *preposition*
= in
oes diddordeb gennych chi mewn dysgu Cymraeg fel ail iaith? = are you interested in teaching Welsh as a second language?

! *This preposition is used where the noun following is non-specific, while a different word* ⇒**ynⁿ** *(preposition) is used with specific nouns. For details of what constitutes a specific noun in this context, see discussion under* **ynⁿ** *(preposition), but compare for example:*

arhoson ni mewn gwesty = we stayed in a hotel

arhoson ni yng ⁿngwesty'r Savoy = we stayed in the Savoy hotel *and*

oedd hi'n dysgu mewn ysgolion lleol = she was working in local schools

oedd hi'n gweithio yn yr ysgolion lleol = she was working in the local schools

Note, however, that **mewn** *does not necessarily correspond to 'in a...' (though it often does)—with plural nouns it corresponds to 'in' just as* **yn** *does. Conversely, note that 'in' without a following 'the' in English is not necessarily* **mewn***; for example* **yn Llundain** *in London (***yn** *used here because a place name is clearly specific), and that the absence of the definite article in Welsh does not automatically indicate using* **mewn***:* **yng ⁿnghanol y ^odre** *in the middle of the town (***yn** *used here because, although the genitive construction requires removal of the first definite article in Welsh—***canol y ^odre** *the middle of the town—the noun is still specific, and this is the deciding factor as always.*

⇒**i mewn,** ⇒**ynⁿ** *preposition*

mewnfudiad (*plural* **-au**) *noun, masculine*
= immigration (*particularly used of immigration into Wales of non-Welsh-speaking people*)

mewnfudwr (*plural* **mewnfudwyr**) *noun, masculine*
= immigrant

mewnlifiad (*plural* **-au**) *noun, masculine*
= influx (*particularly in the sense of outsiders moving into Welsh-speaking areas, and with negative connotations*)

mewnol *adjective*
= internal

meysydd *plural of*
⇒**maes**

mi° *particle*

! *This particle, like its counterpart* ⇒**fe°***, is used optionally before verb forms with endings* <u>in main clauses</u> *to indicate that a statement (and not a question or a negative) is being made. It is* <u>not</u> *normally used with the present forms of* **bod***; with the imperfect of* **bod** *(where, unlike* **fe°***, it can be used) the preferred literary standard affirmative forms must have their initial* **r-** *removed—***mi oedd** *'was' rather than* ***mi roedd***. It is not used in subordinate clauses. Its use is more common in Northern parts of Wales, though it is not unknown in the South. Some areas, however, seem not to use affirmative particles at all, and the literary language prefers to do without them.*

mi oedden nhw i gyd yno = they were all there

mi °gollodd o'r cyfan = he lost the lot

mi °fyddwn i'n °falch o'u helpu nhw = I'd be glad to help them

brysiwch, neu mi °fyddwn ni'n colli'r trên! = hurry, or we'll miss the train!

Notice in the last example that **mi°***, while causing soft mutation, is impervious to this mutation itself—so the preceding* **neu°** *has no effect on it.*

mi *pronoun*
= I; me

! *In the modern language the use of this variant of* ⇒**i** *(pronoun) and* ⇒**fi** *is restricted to two main circumstances: after the preposition* **i** *(so* **i mi** *to/for me, but* **i fi** *is very common as well); and with the Northern preterite auxiliary* ⇒**ddaru***:*

well i mi °fynd = I'd better go

rhowch y gweddill i mi = give the rest to me

ddaru mi °weld nhw neithiwr = I saw them last night

ddaru mi °ddim gweld nhw = I didn't see them

The extension of **mi** *to other circumstances—a not uncommon example in writing is* ***gyda mi** *(for* gyda fi)—*is an affectation and does not reflect the facts of the living language.*

microdon (*plural* **-nau**) *noun, feminine*
= microwave

migwrn (*plural* **migyrnau**) *noun, masculine*
= ankle

mil (*plural* **-oedd**) *noun, feminine*
= thousand
mi oedd dros °dair mil o °bobol yn y neuadd = there were over three thousand people in the hall
mae miloedd o adar wedi diflannu efo'r coed a'r gwrychoedd = thousands of birds have disappeared with the trees and hedges

miliwn (*plural* **miliynau**) *noun, feminine*
= million
mae dros °filiwn o °bunnoedd wedi mynd ar °goll, meddai = over a million pounds has gone missing, he/she said

miliwnydd (*plural* **-ion**) *noun, masculine*
= millionaire

milwr (*plural* **milwyr**) *noun, masculine*
= soldier (*plural also used for* troops)
disgwylir i'r Cenhedloedd Unedig °ddanfon rhagor o °filwyr i'r ardal = the UN is expected to send more troops to the region

milwrol *adjective*
= military

milltir (*plural* **-oedd**) *noun, feminine*
= mile
mi °fyddan nhw °filltiroedd i ffwrdd erbyn hyn = they'll be miles away by now
byddwn ni'n cerdded deng milltir °bob dydd = we'll be walking ten miles a day

min (*plural* **-ion**) *noun, masculine*
= edge
⇒**ar °fin**

miniog, minog *adjective*
= sharp (*knife*)

minnau *pronoun*
= I; me

! **minnau** *is one of the special set of expanded pronouns that are used— though not that frequently—to convey emphasis or some idea of contrast with, or echoing of, what has gone before. It corresponds to* ⇒**mi** *pronoun, and is thus of very restricted use in the modern language.*

mis (*plural* **-oedd**) *noun, masculine*
= month
ym ⁿmha °fis dych chi'n cael eich penblwydd? = what month is your birthday?
dan ni fan'ma am °dri mis o °leia = we're here for three months at least
symudon ni yn ôl i °Gymru ym mis Medi llynedd = we moved back to Wales in September last year
⇒**Ionawr,** ⇒**deufis**

misol *adjective*
= monthly

misolyn (*plural* **misolion**) *noun, masculine*
= monthly magazine

mitsio *verbnoun*
= skive, bunk off school

mo *particle*
personal forms: **mohona i, mohonot ti, mohono fe, mohoni hi, mohonon ni, mohonoch chi, mohonyn nhw**

! ⇒**Mo** *box*

⇒**dim** *particle*

mochyn (*plural* **moch**) *noun, masculine*
= pig (*also figurative*)
yr hen °fochyn (du)! = you pig!

mochyn daear (*plural* **moch daear**) *noun, masculine*
= badger

modern *adjective*
= modern
mae'n °bosibl bellach astudio iaith °fodern hefyd = it's also possible now to study a modern language
ieithoedd modern = modern languages
⇒**cyfoes**

modfedd (*plural* **-i**) *noun, feminine*
= inch
deng modfedd o hyd = ten inches long

Mo

This particle is a contraction of the negative particle **ddim** with the preposition ⇒**o°**. In Welsh the negative particle cannot be directly followed by a specific element—specific in this context covers the following:

1. words preceded by the definite article
2. pronouns
3. words preceded by possessive adjectives ('my', 'your', etc)
4. proper names

All of the above by definition specify a particular example of the thing being talked about—for example, we say 'a car' when we are not referring to any particular one, but 'the car' when we have a specific one in mind; we use pronouns when we already know who it is we're talking about 'Where is Fred?' 'I haven't seen him'; when we say 'my car' we obviously have a specific car in mind; and clearly a proper name like 'Fred' or 'London' indicates a specific person or place. The practicalities of this are that, where **ddim** would be followed immediately by a specific element, this **ddim** has to be changed to **mo**. This will happen when we have an negative inflected verb (i.e. preterite or inflected future) with a following object. So, for example, 'I did not see' is °**weles i** °**ddim**, and if we add the object 'the car' we would expect *Weles i ddim y car—but this leaves us with **ddim** next to **y car** (a specific phrase by 1 above), and so we change **ddim** to **mo**, giving °**weles i**

mo'r car (the **y** changes to **'r** simply because **mo** ends in a vowel). Similarly, °**weles i mo'ch ffrindiau** 'I didn't see your friends', and °**weles i mo Fred** 'I didn't see Fred'. Note from this last example that °**weles i ddim Fred** strictly speaking means 'I didn't see any(one called) Fred'. Because **mo** includes the preposition ⇒**o°**, it has the same personal endings. So 'I didn't see them' will be not *weles i ddim nhw but °**weles i mohonyn nhw**.

°**welwn ni mohoni hi 'to** = *we won't see her again*

°**dales i mo'r** °**ddirwy** = *I didn't pay the fine*

lliwiau na °**welsoch chi mo'u tebyg erioed o'r blaen** = *colours the like of which you have not ever seen before*
Notice that tenses of the verb using auxiliaries (including not only **bod** but also the **nes i** and **ddaru** preterites) never need **mo**, because the object of the negative verb is never next to the **ddim**—there is always an intervening verbnoun. Compare:

agores i mo'r ffenest
but **nes i** °**ddim agor y ffenest**,
ddaru mi °**ddim agor y ffenest**
= *I didn't open the window*
Similarly
agora i mo'r ffenest
but °**fydda i** °**ddim yn agor y ffenest**
= *I won't open the window*
Some speakers in some areas use **ddim** regardless, however, though this usage is generally considered substandard.

---

modrwy (*plural* **-au**) *noun, feminine*
= ring

modryb (*plural* **-edd**) *noun, feminine*
= aunt
oedd hi'n °**fodryb i** ⁿ**ngŵr i** = she was my husband's aunt

modur (*plural* **-on**) *noun, masculine* (*especially North*)
= car

oes gen ti °**fodur newydd?** = have you got a new car?
⇒**car**

modurwr (*plural* **modurwyr**) *noun, masculine*
= motorist

modd *noun, masculine*
= way, manner
yn yr un modd ag y mae hi'n amhosibl

disgrifio lliw... = in the same way as it is impossible to describe colour...

> **!** *The construction* **oes modd i°** + *subject* + *°verbnoun is used to ask if something is possible—a polite request:*
> **oes modd i mi siarad â Mr Williams?** = is it possible for me to speak to Mr Williams?
> (*equivalent to* **°ga i siarad..., °alla i siarad..., ydy hi'n °bosib i mi siarad...**)

moddion *plural noun*
- = medicine
  cymerwch y moddion 'ma °ddwywaith yr wythnos = take this medicine twice a week
- = cure
  does dim moddion yn erbyn twpdra = there's no cure for stupidity
⇒**cyffur**

moes (*plural* **-au**) *noun, feminine*
- = morality
- *plural* **moesau** morals

moesol *adjective*
= moral

moethus *adjective*
= luxurious

mofyn *verbnoun* (*South*)
- = want
  wyt ti'n mofyn rhagor? = do you want some more?
- = fetch
  cer i mofyn y llaeth i mi, nei di? = go and fetch the milk for me, will you?

> **!** *Note that, as in the second example above,* **mofyn** *is not susceptible to mutation.*

⇒**eisiau,** ⇒**moyn,** ⇒**nôl**

mogfa *noun, feminine*
= asthma
mae'r °fogfa arni = she's got asthma

moment (*plural* **-au**) *noun, feminine*
= moment
ar y °foment = at the moment
⇒**ar hyn o °bryd**

mor° *adverb*
- = so
  mae'r stafell 'ma mor °fawr! = this room is so big!

dyn ni mor hwyr! = we're so late!
- **mor°...âʰ/ag...** = as...as...
  mor °ddu â'r °frân = as black as a crow
  ewch mor °bell ag y medrwch chi ar y ffordd 'ma = go as far as you can on this road
- = how
  mi °ellwch chi °ddychmygu mor °falch o'n i = you can imagine how pleased I was

> **!** *This word is unusual in that in replaces the linking* **yn°** *in sentences where we would expect it. Compare:*
> **mae'r awyren yn °gyflym** = the plane is fast
> *but* **mae'r awyren mor °gyflym** (*not* **mae'r awyren yn mor gyflym*) = the plane is so fast
> *Note also that, although it causes soft mutation (though not of* **ll-** *or* **rh-**)*, it never takes soft mutation itself.*

⇒**yr un mor°**

môr (*plural* **moroedd**) *noun, masculine*
= sea; ocean
ar °lan y môr = by the sea
Môr Iwerydd = the Atlantic Ocean
Y Môr Canoldir or **Môr y Canoldir** = the Mediterranean
Y Môr Tawel = the Pacific Ocean
Y Môr Tawch, Môr y Gogledd = the North Sea

morgrugyn (*plural* **morgrug**) *noun, masculine*
= ant

môr-leidr (*plural* **môr-ladron**) *noun, masculine*
= pirate

moronen (*plural* **moron**) *noun, feminine*
= carrot

morthwyl (*plural* **-ion**) *noun, masculine*
= hammer

morwr (*plural* **morwyr**) *noun, masculine*
= sailor

moyn *verbnoun* (*South*)
- = want
  ydyn nhw'n moyn dod? = do they want to come?
- = fetch

cer i moyn y llaeth = go and fetch the milk

> **!** Note that, as in the second example above, **mofyn** is not susceptible to mutation.

⇨**eisiau,** ⇨**mofyn,** ⇨**nôl**

mud adjective
= dumb; mute

mudiad (plural **-au**) noun, masculine
= (political etc) movement
⇨**symudiad**

munud noun, masculine or feminine
= minute
°**ddo i mewn munud!** = I'll be there in a minute!

> **!** **munud** is always feminine in the phrase **ar y °funud ola(f)** at the last minute:
> **a dyna nhw'n ailfeddwl ar y °funud ola!** = and (suddenly) they change their minds at the last minute!

mur (plural **-iau**) noun, masculine
= wall (usually external)
mae'r archeolegwyr wrthi'n chwilio am hen °furiau'r °dre = the archaeologists are busy looking for the old town walls
⇨**wal**

mwg noun, masculine
= smoke
achosir y rhan °fwya o °farwolaethau gan °fwg = most deaths are caused by smoke
⇨**ysmygu**

mwgwd (plural **mygydau**) noun, masculine
= mask
pwy oedd y dyn 'na mewn mwgwd? = who was that masked man?

mwll adjective
= muggy, close, sultry, stuffy
mae'n °fwll iawn heddiw, on'd ydy? = it's very muggy today, isn't it?
⇨**trymaidd**

mwy
1 adverb
• = more
roedd mwy o °bobol yn °bresennol y tro 'ma = more people were present this time

> **!** This quantity sense of **mwy**—with **o°**—is the only one for which ⇨**rhagor** is a close synonym (though **rhagor** strictly speaking has the connotation of 'in addition', 'extra' etc.)

mae'n °fwy na ʰ**pharod i ymddeol oherwydd y newid yn natur ei swydd** = he's more than ready to retire because of the change in the nature of his job
• = more (in comparative of adjectives)
dw i'n teimlo'n °fwy hyderus erbyn hyn = I'm feeling more confident now

> **!** **mwy** coexists side by side with the ending **-ach** as a way of forming comparative adjectives—generally the longer the adjective, the more likely it is to use **mwy** rather than **-ach**, so **hardd** beautiful, **harddach** more beautiful, but **cyfforddus** comfortable, **mwy cyfforddus** more comfortable. Two-syllable adjectives often appear with either: **hapus** happy, **hapusach** or **mwy hapus** happier.

2 adjective
= bigger
mae eisiau stafell °fwy = a bigger room is needed
⇨**mawr,** ⇨**llawer,** ⇨**rhagor**

mwya(f)
1 adverb
= most (mainly in superlative of adjectives)
hwn yw'r un mwya costus ohonyn nhw i gyd = this is the most expensive of them all
p'un o'r trefi 'ma ydy'r un °fwya poblogaidd gyda twristiaid? = which of these towns is the most popular with tourists?

> **!** **mwya** coexists side by side with the ending **-a(f)** as a way of forming superlative adjectives—generally the longer the adjective, the more likely it is to use **mwya** rather than **-a(f)**, so **hardd** beautiful, **hardda** most beautiful, but **cyfforddus** comfortable, **mwya cyfforddus** most comfortable. Two-syllable adjectives often appear with either: **hapus** happy, **hapusa** or **mwya hapus** happiest.

2 *adjective*
= biggest
maen nhw wedi ennill gyda'r °bleidlais °fwya erioed = they've won with the biggest vote ever
⇨**mawr**

mwyach *adverb*
= ...any more (*with negatives*)
dan ni °ddim yn gweld nhw mwyach = we don't see them any more
does neb yn mynd yno mwyach = no-one goes there any more

mwyafrif *noun, masculine*
= majority; most
mae'r mwyafrif llethol wedi pleidleisio yn erbyn = the overwhelming majority has voted against
mae'r mwyafrif wedi arwyddo = most have signed
plannwyd cymysgfa o °goed, ond deri oedd y mwyafrif ohonyn nhw = a range/mixture of trees was planted, but most of them were oak

mwyar duon *plural noun*
= blackberries

mwyn
⇨**er mwyn**

mwynglawdd (*plural* **mwyngloddiau**) *noun, masculine*
= (gold, lead etc) mine

mwyngloddio *verbnoun*
= mine

mwyngloddiwr (*plural* **mwyngloddwyr**) *noun, masculine*
= miner (other than coal miner)

mwynhad *noun, masculine*
= enjoyment

mwynhau (*stem* **mwynheu-**) *verbnoun*
= enjoy
naethoch chi °fwynhau, 'te? = did you enjoy (it), then?
galwch am °gyngor ynglŷn â sut i °fwynhau Eryri = call for advice on how to enjoy Snowdonia

mya (*abbreviation of* **milltir yr awr**)
= mph

myfyriwr (*plural* **myfyrwyr**) *noun, masculine*
= student

pan o'n i'n °fyfyriwr fan hyn ugain ⁿmlynedd yn ôl... = when I was a student here twenty years ago...

myfyrwraig (*plural* **myfyrwragedd**) *noun, feminine*
= (female) student

mymryn *noun, masculine*
= bit, iota, jot
mi °alla i'ch sicrhau nad oes 'na °ddim mymryn o °wir yn y stori 'ma = I can assure you that there is not one iota of truth in this story

myglyd *adjective*
= smoky

mynd *verbnoun*
imperative: **cer, cerwch** (*South*), **dos, ewch** (*North*)
preterite: **es i, est ti, aeth e/hi, aethon ni, aethoch chi, aethon nhw**
future: **a i, ei di, eith e/hi, awn ni, ewch chi, ân nhw**
   common variants: 3 singular: **aiff**, *1 plural* **ewn**
conditional (*of restricted use in the modern language*): **elwn i, elet ti, elai fe/hi, elen ni, elech chi, elen nhw**
   or **awn i, aet ti, âi fe/hi, aen ni, aech chi, aen nhw**
autonomous/impersonal forms: non-past **eir**, *past* **aethpwyd** *or* **aed**
• = go
'swn i °ddim yn mynd yno ar °ben 'n hun = I wouldn't go there on my own
hoffet ti °fynd i'r sinema heno? = would you like to go to the cinema tonight?
cer i °ofyn ydyn nhw'n °barod = go and ask if they're ready
dos yn ôl i °weithio = get back to work
pan es i adre... = when I went home...
fe aethon ni i Iwerddon llynedd = we went to Ireland last year
a i i °weld nhw wedyn = I will go and see them later on
eith ⁿnghar °ddim i fyny'r allt = my car will not go up the hill
ân nhw °ddim hebdda i, °wyddoch chi = they will not go without me, you know
os eith popeth yn °ddidrafferth... = if everything goes smoothly...
eir yno'n °gyson = people go there regularly

• = become; get
**bellach mae hi wedi mynd yn sefyllfa
'ni a nhw' go iawn** = now it has
become a real 'us and them' situation
**wrth °fynd yn hŷn, mae rhywun yn
sylweddoli mwy** = as one gets old, one
realises more

mynd â^h *verbnoun*
= take (*where this means* accompany)
inflected forms ⇒**mynd**
**beth bynnag dych chi eisiau, ewch ag
e nawr** = whatever you want, take it
now
a i â nhw i'r stafell arall = I'll take them
into the other room
aethpwyd/aed â tri o °bobol i'r ysbyty
= three people were taken to hospital
⇒**cymryd**

mynedfa (*plural* **mynedfeydd**) *noun,
feminine*
= entrance (*of building etc*)
gofal—mynedfa °gudd = warning—
concealed entrance
⇒**allanfa**

mynediad *noun, masculine*
= entrance (= *permission to enter*),
admission
mynediad am °ddim = entrance free

mynegai (*plural* **mynegeion**) *noun,
masculine*
= index

mynegi *verbnoun*
= express
**mi °geith pob un ohonoch chi °fynegi
ei °farn** = every one of you will be
allowed to express his opinion
⇒**ymadrodd**

mynnu *verbnoun*
• = insist (on)
**dw i'n mynnu aros fan hyn nes bod
rhywun yn dod i ⁿngweld i** = I insist on
staying here till someone comes to see
me
mynnwch eich hawliau! = insist on
your rights!
mi °fynnodd °fod hynny'n iawn =
he/she insisted that that was right
• = will; please
gwnewch fel y mynnoch (chi) = do as
you will, do as you please
cymer faint °fynni di = take as much as
you please

! *The special inflected forms*
mynnoch *and* **mynni** (*or* **mynnot**)
*are only encountered in this type of
set phrase corresponding to* 'please'.

mynwent (*plural* **-ydd**) *noun, feminine*
= cemetery
**mae bedd un o'n gwleidyddion
enwoca i'w weld rhywle yn y
°fynwent 'ma** = somewhere in this
cemetery you can see the grave of one
of our most famous politicians

mynych *adjective*
yn °fynych = frequently
⇒**aml**

mynychu *verbnoun*
• = attend (*school etc*)
**mae'r plant yn mynychu ysgol
°gynradd °leol** = the children attend a
local primary school
• = frequent
**mae e'n mynychu gwahanol °lefydd
yn y °dre** = he frequents various places
in town

mynydd (*plural* **-oedd**) *noun,
masculine*
= mountain
mae aur yn y mynyddoedd acw = there
is gold in those mountains
**beiciau mynydd a ^hcheffylau i'w llogi
yn yr ardal** = mountain bikes and
horses available for hire locally
gwneud môr a mynydd o°... = make a
mountain out of a molehill about...
⇒**bryn**, ⇒**rhiw**

mynydda *verbnoun*
= mountaineer, go mountaineering

mynydd-dir (*plural* **-oedd**) *noun,
masculine*
= mountainous country

mynyddig *adjective*
= mountainous

Nn

'n

> **!** *This contracted form, used after vowels, corresponds to any of the following:*
>
> *1* ⇒**yn** *particle*
> **dw i'n mynd adre yfory** = I'm going home tomorrow
>
> *2* ⇒**yn°** *particle*
> **bydd y trên 'ma'n °gynnar** = this train will be early
>
> *3* ⇒**fyⁿ**
> **dw i wedi colli 'n sgidiau** = I've lost my shoes
>
> *4* ⇒**ein**
> **cysylltwch â'n swyddfeydd** = contact our offices
> *Note that (strictly speaking at least)* **ynⁿ** *(preposition)* 'in' *cannot be abbreviated to* '**n** *in any circumstances. Compare*:
> **maen nhw'n gweithio'n °galed** = they are working hard
> **maen nhw'n gweithio yn Aberystwyth** = they work in Aberystwyth

na *conjunction*

= that (*in reported speech—focused clauses*)
dw i'n siwr na fo sy'n iawn = I'm sure that *he* is right
mae'n °debyg na Bae Colwyn °fydd yn ennill = Colwyn Bay will probably win

> **!** *This is a regional (mainly Northwestern) variant of* ⇒**mai**; *it is not accepted in the written language, but is the normal word in its area.*

naʰ

1 (*before vowels* **nag**) *conjunction*
= than
gwell hwyr na hwyrach = better late than never
°**well gen i °de na ʰchoffi** = I prefer tea to coffee
mae aur yn °fwy gwerthfawr nag arian = gold is more valuable than silver

naʰ

2 *conjunction*

= nor, and not; (*with negatives*) or, or...either
dw i °ddim yn deall y jôc 'na—na finnau (chwaith) = I don't understand that joke—neither do I
°**fedr o °ddim rhedeg, na ʰcherdded yn iawn hyd yn oed** = he can't run, nor even walk properly
°**alla i °ddim diodde te na ʰchoffi** = I can't stand tea or coffee

naʰ

3 (*before vowels* **nag**) *prefix*
= no

> **!** *Generally a 'no' response in Welsh has to be modelled on the phrasing of the question, in the same way as 'yes' responses—the verb of the question is repeated (with changes to person where appropriate) and prefixed by the negative marker* **na** (**nag** *before vowels). So, for example, a question beginning* **Ydy...?** *will have* **Nag ydy** *for the answer; similarly* **Oes...?** *Is/are there...?* **Nag oes; Oedd...?** *Was...?* **Nag oedd;** °**Fyddwch chi...?** *Will you (be)...?* **Na °fydda/°fyddwn;** °**Ga i...?** *Can I (have)...?* **Na ʰchewch;** °**Allan nhw...?** *Can I...?* **Na °allan.** *Notice in the last example that* **nag** *is not used before vowels resulting from mutation of original* **g-;** **na°** *is used with* **gallan**, *and then mutates it.*
>
> *Questions phrased in the preterite, however, have an invariable* ⇒**naddo** *for 'no', and this is also true with some speakers for questions phrased with* ⇒**wedi**. *This prefix is also used in the spoken language to phrase negative questions where there is some implication or expectation that the person addressed might disagree:*
> **nag ych chi nawr yn wynebu rhwygiadau yn y °blaid?** = aren't you now facing splits in the party?
> (*meaning: surely you are, aren't you?—even though the person addressed is almost certainly going to say 'No, we're not')*

⇒**on'd**

na°/ʰ *conjunction*

= that... not...
• (*in relative clauses*)
bydd 'na un °fargen °bob wythnos na °ellir mo'i ʰcholli = there will be one

unmissable bargain each week (*literally: 'one bargain that one cannot miss it...'*)

lliwiau na °welsoch chi mo'u tebyg erioed o'r blaen = colours the like of which you have never seen before (*literally: '...that you have not seen their like...'*)

• (*in subordinate clauses*)

efallai na °fydda i yn ôl mewn pryd = I might not be back in time (*literally: 'perhaps that I will not be back in time'*)

mae hi'n °wir na °ddylen ni °wrthwynebu'r penderfyniad 'ma = it's true that we should not oppose this decision

pam na °ddoi di draw pnawn heno? = why don't you come round this evening? (*literally: 'why that you will not come...'*)

os na °fydd digon o °bobol... = if there aren't enough people... (*literally: 'if that there will not be enough people'*)

> ! With the present and imperfect of **bod**, this word takes the form **nad**:
> **gwnewch yn siwr nad ydyn nhw'n camymddwyn** = make sure that they're not misbehaving
> **dw i'n siwr nad oes llawer ar ôl** = I'm sure that there is not much left
> In this use the **nad** construction is an alternative to the **bod** (*etc.*) ... °**ddim** phrasing more popular in teaching manuals:
> **gwnewch yn siwr bod nhw °ddim yn camymddwyn** = make sure that they're not misbehaving
> Both constructions are admissible in the spoken language, with no obvious distinction, except after words like ⇒**pam** and ⇒**os**, where **na(d)** is the norm.

'na° *adverb*

= there is/are; that is; those are

> ! This is a very commonly used abbreviated form of ⇒**dyna°**:
> **mi oedd hi'n °gyd-ddigwyddiad anffodus, 'na i gyd** = it was an unfortunate coincidence, that's all
> **'na °ddigon am heddi, 'te** = that's enough for today, then
> It is used in exclamations with a following adjective, corresponding to

English 'How...!', *or with a following noun, corresponding to English* 'What a...!':

> **'na °bert!** = how pretty!
> **'na °fargen!** = what a bargain!

⇒**'co**, ⇒**yna**, ⇒**y ... 'na**

nabod* *verbnoun*

= know (*person*)

dych chi'n nabod ⁿmrawd? = do you know my brother?

o'n i °ddim yn nabod nhw ar y pryd = I didn't know them at the time

wyt ti'n nabod ei °rieni? = do you know his parents?

fe °ddaethon ni i ('w) nabod nhw drwy'n gwaith = we got to know them through our work

> ! Notice that **nabod**, by its meaning, is a stative verb and cannot form a preterite in the living language—I knew him is **o'n i'n nabod e**, *literally* 'I was knowing him' *because this is a continuous and unchanging state of affairs at the time.*

⇒**gwybod**

nacáu (*often* **'cau** *in speech*) *verbnoun*

= refuse

mae'r car 'ma'n 'cau mynd = this car refuses to go *or* won't go

⇒**pallu**

nad

⇒**na°/ʰ** *conjunction* (*note*)

nad *conjunction*

= that... not... (*in focused clauses*)

> ! This is a rather more formal equivalent of **mai dim** used in focused reported speech clauses but where the focused element is itself negated. Compare:
> **ond efallai mai nhw sy'n °gyfrifol wedi'r cwbwl** = but perhaps they are responsible after all
> **ond efallai nad nhw sy'n °gyfrifol wedi'r cwbwl,**
> **ond efallai mai dim nhw sy'n °gyfrifol wedi'r cwbwl** = but perhaps they are not responsible after all
> Its use is less frequent in the spoken language than **mai dim**.

⇒**mai**

Nadolig, Dolig *noun, masculine*
(*often with definite article*)
= Christmas
Nadolig Llawen! = Merry Christmas!
gwledd o °lyfrau ar °gyfer y Nadolig = a
feast of books for Christmas

nadredd, nadroedd *plural of*
⇒**neidr**

naddo *adverb*
= no

> **!** *This response word is used to*
> *answer to questions phrased in the*
> *preterite. It is invariable for person.*
> **°Welest ti'r ffilm neithiwr?—Naddo**
> = Did you see the film last night?—No
> **Ddaru chi °dalu?—Naddo** = Did you
> pay?—No
> *In the spoken language it is often*
> *used also with questions involving*
> **wedi**:
> **Ydyn nhw wedi mynd 'to?—Naddo**
> (*instead of* **Nag ydyn**) = Have they
> gone yet?—No
> *This is frowned upon by purists, who*
> *argue that grammatically the above*
> *sentence begins with a present tense*
> *verb, albeit then modified by* **wedi**,
> *and that a present tense negation is*
> *required. But it can just as easily be*
> *argued that the choice of* **naddo** *is*
> *determined by meaning rather than*
> *grammar—in other words that* **naddo**
> *is associated in the minds of*
> *speakers with past time rather than*
> *the abstraction of preterite*
> *grammatical form. This must be so in*
> *any case, otherwise no-one would*
> *use* **naddo** *in these circumstances,*
> *and many do.*

⇒**do**

nag
⇒**na**[h] *conjunction,* ⇒**na**[h] *prefix*

nage *particle*
= no

> **!** *This word is of much more*
> *restricted use in Welsh than 'no' in*
> *English—it is used as an negative*
> *response only to questions which*
> *begin with an element that is not the*
> *verb, generally focused questions*
> *Compare:*
> **Dych chi'n mynd i °Lanelli**
> **heddiw?—Nag ydw** = Are you going
> to Llanelli today—No
> **I °Lanelli dych chi'n mynd**
> **heddiw?—Nage** = Are you going to
> Llanelli today?, Is it to Llanelli that
> you're going...?—No
> **Heddiw dych chi'n mynd i**
> **°Lanelli?—Nage** = Are you going to
> Llanelli today?, Is it today that you're
> going to Llanelli?—No
> *For further details* ⇒**Yes and No**
> *box on the English-Welsh side*
> *There is also an emphatic extended*
> *form* **nage ddim**, *used to contradict*
> *statements of all kinds, whether*
> *focused or not:*
> **Mae'n edrych arna i!—Nage °ddim,**
> **mae'n edrych arna i!** = He's looking
> at me!—No he's not, he's looking at
> me!

nai (*plural* **neiaint**) *noun, masculine*
= nephew
mae'n nai i mi = he's my nephew

naid
in: **blwyddyn naid** = leap year
⇒**neidio**

naill ai... (neu°...) *conjunction*
= either... (or...)
naill ai dan ni'n mynd yn syth, neu dan
ni'n gorfod aros fan hyn = either we
go straight away, or we have to wait
here
⇒**chwaith**

(y) naill°... y llall...
= (the) one...the other
mae'n amlwg nad yw'r naill
°ddamcaniaeth neu'r llall yn egluro'r
sefyllfa'n iawn = clearly neither the
one theory nor the other explains the
situation properly
°weles i nhw'n mynd i mewn, y naill ar
ôl y llall = I saw them going in, one
after the other

nain (*plural* **neiniau**) *noun, feminine*
(*North*)
= grandmother, granny
dos i °weld ydy Nain eisiau dŵad hefo
ni = go and see if Granny wants to
come with us
⇒**mamgu**

nam (*plural* **-au**) *noun, masculine*
= fault; defect

os oes nam ar y cryno-°ddisg hwn,
rhowch °wybod i'r llyfrgell = if this
compact disc has a fault, inform the
library

nant (plural **nentydd**) noun, feminine
= stream; brook
**gwelwyd nentydd a ʰthiroedd gwlyb
yn diflannu** = streams and wetlands
have been seen to disappear

natur noun, feminine
= nature
**cipolwg arall ar y byd natur o'n
cwmpas** = another look at the world
of nature around us
**mae'n °fwy na ʰpharod i ymddeol
oherwydd y newid yn natur ei swydd**
= he's more than ready to retire
because of the change in the nature of
his job

naturiol adjective
= natural

naw numeral
= nine

nawdeg numeral
= ninety

nawdd noun, masculine
= protection, patronage
Nawdd Cymdeithasol = Social Security
dan nawdd = under the auspices of

nawddoglyd adjective
= patronising

nawfed adjective
= ninth

> **!** Ordinal numerals are adjectives, but
> behave in a special way. All other than
> ⇒**cynta** precede the noun. With
> feminine singular nouns, the noun
> itself undergoes soft mutation, as
> does the ordinal after the article—so:
> **y nawfed dyn** the ninth man but **y
> nawfed °ferch** the ninth girl; **y
> trydydd car** the third car but **y
> °drydedd °goeden** the third tree.

nawr adverb
= now
dw i eisiau i chi °wneud y gwaith nawr
= I want you to do the work now
nawr yw'r amser i wynebu'n gelynion
= now is the time to face our enemies

nawr 'te, pwy sy am helpu fan hyn? =
now then, who wants to help here?

> **!** The literary language often writes
> this word **yn awr**, but this is an
> affectation.

⇒**bellach**, ⇒**rwan**, ⇒**tro**

neb pronoun
= no-one, nobody
does neb yma = there's no-one here
°gwrddes i â neb = I didn't meet
anybody
does neb yn gwybod dim fan'ma =
nobody knows anything here
Pwy °welest ti yno?—Neb o °bwys =
Whom did you see there?—No-one
important
⇒**anad**, ⇒**fawr**

nef (plural **-oedd**) noun, feminine
= heaven

> **!** Mostly in the phrases **iaith yr
> nefoedd** the language of heaven
> (affirmed to be Welsh); and **nefoedd!**
> or **nefoedd wen!** Heavens (above)!
> These last two are often toned down
> to **nefi blw!** in colloquial speech.

neges (plural **-au**, **-euon**) noun,
feminine
= message
hoffech chi °adael neges iddo? =
would you like to leave him a message?

negyddol adjective
= negative
agwedd negyddol iawn sy gynni hi =
she's got a very negative attitude

neidio verbnoun
= jump, leap
neidia di ar y bwrdd, 'te = you jump
(up) on the table, then
wedi neidio, rhy hwyr peidio (proverb)
= look before you leap
⇒**naid**

neidr (plural **nadredd**, **nadroedd**) noun,
feminine
= snake

neilltuo verbnoun
= set aside
mae'r llywodraeth wedi neilltuo arian
= the government has set money aside
⇒**o'r neilltu**

neilltuol *adjective*
= particular, special

neis *adjective, comparative* **neisiach**
= nice
'na neis! = how nice!
mae'n °fenyw neis iawn = she's a very
nice woman
**mae'n neisiach heddiw nag oedd hi
ddoe, on'd ydy?** = it's nicer today than
it was yesterday, isn't it?

neithiwr *adverb*
= last night
**oedd unrhywbeth diddorol ar y teledu
neithiwr?** = was there anything
interesting on the television last
night?
oedd neithiwr yn °waeth fyth = last
night was even worse
⇒**diwetha(f)**, ⇒**ddoe**, ⇒**heno**, ⇒**nos**

nenfwd (*plural* **nenfydau**) *noun,
masculine*
= ceiling

nentydd *plural of*
⇒**nant**

nepell
only in the literary phrase:
nid nepell not far
⇒**pell**

nerf (*plural* **-au**) *noun, feminine*
= nerve
mae hi'n mynd ar y' nerfau o hyd =
she's always getting on my nerves

nerfus *adjective*
= nervous

nerfusrwydd *noun, masculine*
= nervousness

nerth (*plural* **-oedd**) *noun, masculine*
= strength, power
**mae'r clwb pêl-droed lleol yn mynd o
nerth i nerth** = the local football club
is going from strength to strength
ac i ffwrdd ag e nerth ei °draed = and
off he went as fast as his legs would
carry him

! *There are a number of words for
'power' in Welsh—***nerth** *tends to be
used for physical strength, while*
⇒**egni** *means 'energy',* ⇒**pŵer**
usually political power, and ⇒**ynni**
very similar to **egni**, *and meaning
power as a commodity.*

nes
1 *conjunction*
= until, till
**bydd rhaid aros nes iddyn nhw
°gyrraedd** = we'll have to wait until
they arrive
**naethon ni aros nes iddyn nhw
°gyrraedd** = we waited until they
arrived

! *Generally this conjunction is used
with the construction* **i°** *+ [subject] +
°verbnoun, as in the examples
above—and notice above also that,
since the verbnoun in Welsh is neutral
or 'empty' with regard to time, the
translation in English, which always
requires time reference to be
explicitly stated, may vary according
to context.*
*Unlike some other conjunctions,
however,* **nes** *can be used with a
reported speech construction where*
bod/°fod *(etc.) would be possible (i.e.
not in cases where* ⇒**y** *conjunction
would be needed):*
**arhoswch yma nes bod lle'n dod yn
rhydd** = wait here until a place
becomes free.
**dw i'n dweud dim nes bod y
gweddill wedi dod** = I'm saying
nothing till the others have come
*In the colloquial speech of some
areas,* **nes bod hi'n...** *is used for*
⇒**tan°** *until with clock-time:*
**bydd y °wers °gynta yn mynd nes
bod hi'n ddeg o'r °gloch** = the first
lesson will go on until ten o'clock
(*instead of:* **...mynd tan °ddeg...**)

2 *adjective*
= closer, nearer
**dewch yn nes er mwyn i mi °glywed yn
iawn** = come closer so I can hear
properly

nesa(f) *adjective*
= next
pwy sy nesa, 'te? = who's next, then?
be' nesa? = what next?
°wela i di wythnos nesa = I'll see you
next week
bydd yn costio'r peth nesa i °ddim = it
will cost next to nothing

nesáu *verbnoun*
= approach, get near (**at**° to)
ond nawr, gyda'r amser yn nesáu at saith o'r °gloch... = but now, with the time approaching seven o'clock...

nes ymlaen *adverb*
= later on
⇒**wedyn**

neu° *conjunction*
= or
te neu °goffi? = tea or coffee?

> **!** *This conjunction causes soft mutation of both nouns and verbnouns, but not of inflected verb forms, which may also follow it, though less frequently. Compare the next two examples:*
> **cewch °fwyta yng Nghaffi Meinir neu °baratoi bwyd eich hunain** = you can eat in Meinir's Café or prepare your own food
> **cewch aros mewn tŷ teras cyfforddus neu dewch â'ch pabell!** = you can stay in a comfortable terraced house, or bring your tent! *Although not immediately apparent from the English, where the imperative form is the base form anyway, the structure of the second Welsh example above is different in that* 'bring' *is not dependent on* 'can' *as* 'prepare' *is in the first example*
> **neu gellir rhodio'r llwybr troed** = or one can walk the footpath

neuadd (*plural* **-au**) *noun, feminine*
= hall
gofynnir i °bawb ymgynnull yn y neuadd = everyone is asked to assemble in the hall
neuadd °breswyl (*plural* **neuaddau preswyl**) = hall of residence

neu'i gilydd *pronoun*
= (some...) or other
mae pawb yn cofio rhyw °lun neu'i gilydd mae o wedi'i °weld = everyone remembers some picture or other that they've seen
fe °gawn ni'r arian °rywsut neu'i gilydd = we'll get the money somehow or other
nawn ni °ddatrys y °broblem °ryw ffordd neu'i gilydd = we'll solve the problem some way or other

newid
1 (*stem* **newidi-**) *verbnoun*
= change
byddan nhw'n gorfod newid yr holl °gloeon yn y tŷ = they will have to change all the locks in the house
mi newidiodd y sefyllfa'n °gyfangwbl o fewn pythefnos = the situation changed completely within a fortnight
2 (*plural* **-iadau**) *noun, masculine*
= change
mae llawer o newidiadau wedi bod = there have been a lot of changes
mae newid yn rhywbeth °gwbl naturiol ym ⁿmyd natur = change is something quite natural in the world of nature
daeth yr amser am newid = the time has come for a change
3 (*no plural*) *noun, masculine*
= change (*money*)
oes gen ti newid am °bapur deg punt? = have you got change for a tenner?

newidiol *adjective*
= changeable

newydd
1 *adjective*
= new
dan ni angen car newydd = we need a new car
fel dych chi'n gweld, mae athrawes newydd 'da ni heddiw = as you see, we have a new teacher today
Blwyddyn Newydd °Dda! = Happy New Year!
newydd sbon = brand new
⇒**newyddion**
2 (**newydd°**) *adverb*

> **!** *This word is used with a following verbnoun in place of* ⇒**wedi** *to indicate that an action has just happened. Compare:*
> **maen nhw wedi mynd** = they have gone
> **maen nhw newydd °fynd** = they have just gone
> **mae hi newydd °droi hanner awr wedi saith** = it's just turned half past seven
> *Notice that* **newydd°** *incorporates the meaning of* **wedi**, *and that* *newydd wedi is therefore wrong.*

Remember that **newydd**º *in this sense causes soft mutation, while* **wedi** *does not.*

newydd-ºddyfodiad (*plural* **newydd-ºddyfodiaid**) *noun, masculine*
= newcomer

newyddiadur (*plural* **-on**) *noun, masculine*
= newspaper
less common term for ⇒**papur newydd**

newyddiadurwr (*plural* **newyddiadurwyr**) *noun, masculine*
= journalist

newyddion *plural noun*
= news
bydd rhagor o newyddion am saith = there'll be more news at seven
byddwn ni'n dod â'r holl newyddion atoch chi = we will bring you all the news

newyn *noun, masculine*
= famine; hunger

newynu *verbnoun*
= starve
⇒**llwgu**

nhw *pronoun*
= they; them

> ! *This word is always pronounced* **nw** *in unaffected speech, despite the spelling.*

be' wedson nhw? = what did they say?
º**welon ni nhw yn y ºdre neithiwr** = we saw them in town last night
maen nhw wedi ymddeol erbyn hyn = they have retired now
rhowch ºwybod iddyn nhw cyn ºgynted ag y bo modd = let them know as soon as possible
nhw sy ar ºfai = (it is) they (who) are to blame
nhw biau nhw = they are theirs

> ! *third person plural verb forms are used exclusively with this pronoun in Welsh—compare the following pairs,*
> **maen nhw'n byw yn Llaneglwys** = they live in Llaneglwys
> **mae Alun a Sara'n byw yn Llaneglwys** = Alun and Sara live in Llaneglwys

mi ºddylen nhw ºddweud rhywbeth = they ought to say something
mi ºddylai'r rhieni ºddweud rhywbeth = the parents ought to say something.
> *Unless the word* **nhw** *is specifically mentioned, plural subjects in Welsh are treated as singulars.*

nhwthau *pronoun*
= they; them

> ! *This is one of the special set of expanded pronouns that are used—though not that frequently—to convey emphasis or some idea of contrast with, or echoing of, what has gone before.*
> **eu car nhwthau ydy hwnna** = that's <u>their</u> car
> **...,ond does 'na ºddim galw amdani bellach, chadal nhwthau** = ..., but there's no call for it any more, so <u>they</u> say

ni *pronoun*
= we; us
fe ºfyddwn ni yn y cyfarfod = we will be at the meeting
dyn ni'n moyn aros = we want to stay
'sgwn i ºfasen nhw'n ºbarod i'n helpu ni? = I wonder if they would be prepared to help us?
ysgrifennwch aton ni = write to us
ni sy'n ºgyfrifol am yr hyn ºddigwyddodd = (it is) <u>we</u> (who) are responsible for what happened
ni ydy'r rhai mwya dibynadwy = <u>we</u> are the most reliable

> ! 'We two' *or* 'the both/two of us' *is* **ni'n dau/dwy:**
> **dim ond ni'n dau sy ar ôl bellach** = it's only the two of us left/it's just you and me now
> *As with the other pronouns,* **ni** *is optionally (though widely) used after a noun with the possessive adjective* ⇒**ein:**
> **edrychwch ar ein prisiau ni!** = look at our prices!
> **mae'n chwaraewyr ni i gyd yn ffit ac yn ºbarod i ºfynd heno** = our players are all fit and ready to go this evening
> **mae'n hysgol newydd ni'n llai** = our new school is smaller

ni^{h/o} (*before original vowels* **nid**) *particle* (*Literary Welsh*)
= not
ni ^h**chaniateir cŵn** (*Literary Welsh*) = dogs are not allowed
nid ydynt yn °dda yn y tymor byr (*Literary Welsh*)
for: **dydyn nhw °ddim yn °dda yn y tymor byr** = they are not good in the short term
ni °wyddwn y'i gwelasech (*Literary Welsh*)
for: **o'n i °ddim yn gwybod bod chi wedi'i °weld e** = I didn't know you'd seen him
nid euthum (*Literary Welsh*)
for: **es i °ddim** = I didn't go

! *This negative particle simply does not exist in the living language, which always uses °***ddim** *following the verb for negation in main clauses.* **Ni**, *on the other hand, precedes the verb, and causes aspirate mutation where possible, or failing that soft mutation. So, for example, where the living language has* °**glywes i °ddim** *or* ^h**chlywes i °ddim** *I didn't hear, the literary language insists on* **ni** ^h**chlywais**; *where the living language has* °**fydda i °ddim** *I won't be, the literary language insists on* **ni °fyddaf.** *The persistence of this particle in all kinds of formal writing is all the more extraordinary for the fact that no native speaker would dream of using it in speech, and its presence is a sure sign of writing aiming at a perceived 'elevated' style.*

⇒**dim** *particle*

nid *particle* (*Literary Welsh*)
= not

! *This word is used to negate a focused word or phrase, i.e. one that has been placed at the start of the sentence for emphasis or contrast. Compare the following pairs:*
Iwan °dorrodd y ffenest = (it was) Iwan (who) broke the window
nid Iwan °dorrodd y ffenest = it wasn't Iwan who broke the window
heddiw aethon nhw = they went today
nid heddiw aethon nhw, ond ddoe =

it wasn't today that they went, but yesterday
In the spoken language **nid** *has a rather formal feel to it, and* ⇒**dim** *is widely used instead:* **dim Iwan °dorrodd y ffenest, dim heddiw aethon nhw**

⇒**ni**^{h/o} *particle*

nifer (*plural* **-oedd**) *noun, masculine or feminine*
= number
mae nifer o °broblemau wedi codi = a number of problems have arisen
roedd nifer °fawr o °bobol yn °bresennol = a large number of people were present
...ond mi oedd 'na °gryn nifer hefyd yn siarad yn ei herbyn = ...but there were also quite a number speaking against her

---

! *This word signifies 'number' in the sense of items in a group, while* ⇒**rhif** *means number in a series, or the figures themselves.*

⇒**cynifer**

niferus *adjective*
= numerous

ninnau *pronoun*
= we; us

! *This is one of the special set of expanded pronouns that are used—though not that frequently—to convey emphasis or some idea of contrast with, or echoing of, what has gone before.*
mae gwledydd eraill yn rhuthro ymlaen, a ninnau wedi'n hanwybyddu = other countries are rushing on, while <u>we</u> have been ignored
mae'n dadleuon ninnau'n °gryfach nag eiddo'r °Wrthblaid = our arguments are stronger than those of the Opposition
dan ni °ddim yn danfon cardiau Nadolig—na ninnau (chwaith) = we don't send Christmas cards—neither do we

---

nionyn (*plural* **nionod**) *noun, masculine*
= (*North*) onion
⇒**wynwyn**

nith (*plural* **-oedd**) *noun, feminine*
= niece
mae hi'n nith i mi = she's my niece
faint o nithoedd sy gen ti, 'te? = how
many nieces have you got, then?

niwcliar *adjective*
= nuclear

niwed (*plural* **niweidiau**) *noun,*
masculine
= damage; harm
mae'r diwydiant yn gwneud niwed
mawr i °gymunedau lleol = the
industry does great damage to local
communities
⇒**difrod**

niweidio *verbnoun*
= damage; harm
gofalwch bod chi °ddim yn niweidio'r
peth 'ma = watch out that you don't
damage this

niweidiol *adjective*
= harmful

niwl *noun, masculine*
= fog; mist
mae niwl dros °lawer iawn o
ardaloedd y De bore 'ma = there is fog
across very many areas of the South
this morning

niwlog *adjective*
= foggy; misty

niwtral *adjective*
= neutral

niwtraleiddio *verbnoun*
= neutralize

nod (*plural* **-au**, **-ion**) *noun, masculine or*
feminine
= aim
beth yn union ydy nod yr ymchwil
'ma? = what exactly is the aim of this
research?

nodi *verbnoun*
= note; mark; note down
gellwch chi nodi fe yn eich llyfrau =
you can mark it in your books
dyddiad i'w nodi = a date to be noted

nodiad (*plural* **-au**) *noun, masculine*
= note (*for one's own use*)
cofia °wneud nodiadau manwl =
remember to make detailed notes
⇒**nodyn**, ⇒**papur**

nodiadur (*plural* **-on**) *noun, masculine*
= notebook

nodwedd (*plural* **-ion**) *noun, feminine*
= feature; characteristic

nodweddiadol *adjective*
= typical

nodwydd (*plural* **-au**) *noun, feminine*
= needle

nodyn (*plural* **nodau**) *noun, masculine*
= note
dyma nodyn byr i'ch atgoffa chi °fod...
= here is a short note to remind you
that...
⇒**nodiad**, ⇒**papur**

noddi *verbnoun*
= sponsor
noddir yr °Ŵyl gan °Fwrdd yr Iaith
°Gymraeg = the Festival is sponsored
by the Welsh Language Board

noeth *adjective*
= naked (*also figurative*); nude
dych chi erioed wedi mynd yn noeth
ar °gyfer ffilm neu °ddrama? = have
you ever gone naked for a film or play?

noethlymun *adjective*
= stark naked

nofel (*plural* **-au**) *noun, feminine*
= novel

nofelwr/nofelydd (*plural* **nofelwyr**)
noun, masculine
= novelist

nofio *verbnoun*
= swim
°fedra i °ddim nofio = I can't swim
dim nofio os ydy'r °faner °goch i'w
gweld = no swimming if the red flag is
visible

nofiwr (*plural* **nofwyr**) *noun, masculine*
= swimmer (*male*)

nofwraig (*plural* **nofwragedd**) *noun,*
feminine
= swimmer (*female*)

nôl *verbnoun*
= fetch
cer i nôl y llaeth, nei di? = go and fetch
the milk, will you?
nest ti nôl y llyfrau? = did you fetch the
books?

! *This verb is only used in the verbnoun form, and cannot take preterite, future or imperative personal endings.*

normal *adjective*
= normal

normaleiddio *verbnoun*
= normalize

normalrwydd *noun, masculine*
= normality

nos (*plural* **noseithiau**, *rarely* **-au**) *noun, feminine*
= night (*opposite of day*); evening
nos da! = good night!

! *Note that the expected mutation of* **da** *after the feminine* **nos** *does not occur because the combination* **s+dd** *generally assimilates to* **sd** *in the spoken language.*

nos dawch! (*North*) = good night!
Nos °Fawrth = Tuesday night/evening
nos yfory = tomorrow night/evening
byddwn ni'n aros yno dros nos = we'll be staying there overnight
mae hi wedi mynd yn nos = night has fallen
⇒**noson**, ⇒**neithiwr**

nosi *verbnoun*
= become night
bydd y glaw 'ma wedi cyrraedd y Gorllewin erbyn iddi nosi = this rain will have reached the West by nightfall

noson (*plural* **noseithiau**) *noun, feminine*
• = evening (*as a period of the day spent doing something*);
cafwyd noson °ddiddorol iawn = a very interesting evening was had
Noson °Lawen = *evening gathering for entertainment, like Fest Noz in Brittany*
• = night (*especially with numbers or adjectives*)
bydd e i ffwrdd am °dair noson = he'll be away for three nights
mae'n anodd ar ôl noson hwyr fel neithiwr, timod = it's difficult after a late night like last night, you know
⇒**nos**

noswaith (*plural* **noseithiau**) *noun, feminine*

= evening (*as opposed to day or night*)
noswaith °dda! = good evening!

! *This word is less used than its English equivalent, since* ⇒**nos** *often means either 'night' or 'evening' depending on context.*

nunlle, nunman *adverbs*
= nowhere; not anywhere
°weles i nhw nunlle, °weles i nhw nunman = I didn't see them anywhere

nwy (*plural* **-on, -au**) *noun, masculine*
= gas

nwyddau *plural noun*
= goods
anaddas i °gerbydau nwyddau trwm = unsuitable for heavy goods vehicles

nyddu *verbnoun*
= spin (*wool etc*)

nyrs (*plural* **-ys**) *noun, masculine or feminine*
= nurse
mae hi'n gweithio fel nyrs yng ⁿNghaerdydd = she's working as a nurse in Cardiff
nyrs o'n i °bryd hynny = I was a nurse at that time

nyrsio *verbnoun*
= nurse; do nursing

nyth (*plural* **-od**) *noun, feminine*
= nest

Oo

➪also many other set expressions beginning with **o°**, listed as separate entries.

o° *preposition*
personal forms: **ohona i, ohonat ti, ohono fe, ohoni hi, ohonon ni, ohonoch chi, ohonyn nhw**
common variants: **ohono i, ohonot ti**

• = of (*with quantity expressions*)
°**ga i °ddau °bwys o °gaws?** = can I have two pounds of cheese?
llawer o °ddiolch = many thanks

• = of (*singling out*)
°**gymera i'r un mwya o'r tri 'na** = I'll take the biggest of those three
pwy ohonoch chi sy wedi talu'n °barod? = who of you has paid already?

• (*generally with numbers over ten*)
ugain o °ddynion = twenty men (*but* **dau °ddyn** = two men)

> **!** It is difficult to give hard-and-fast rules about this, however—'twenty pounds', *for example, is more likely to be* **ugain punt** *than* **ugain o °bunnoedd.**

• = of (*specifying material*)
ac mae'r pethau 'na wedi'u gwneud o °bren, 'te? = and those things are made of wood, then?
tafarnwr o Sais = a landlord who is an Englishman

• = from
cyfarchion o °Bwllheli = greetings from Pwllheli
dw i'n dod o °Fangor yn °wreiddiol = I come from Bangor originally
bydd y gwyntoedd yn chwythu'n ysgafn o'r gorllewin = the winds will be blowing lightly from the west
mae pethau'n mynd o °ddrwg i °waeth = things are going from bad to worse
bydda i'n mynd am °dro o °bryd i'w gilydd = I go for a walk from time to time

• (*in comparisons*) = by
mae hwn yn °ddrutach o'r hanner = this is dearer by half
dych chi'n edrych yn °well o °lawer = you're looking much better

➪**gan°**, ➪ **oddiwrth°**, ➪**mo**

o *pronoun* (*North*)
= he; him

> **!** This pronoun is used in many Northern areas in place of ➪**e** just as ➪**fo** is used in place of ➪**fe**
> **mae o tu allan rhywle** = he's outside somewhere
> **oedd o'n gwybod yn iawn** = he knew very well
> **pryd ddaru o °fynd?** = when did he go?
> **nest ti °weld o, 'ta** = did you see him, then?
> **rhowch °rwymyn am ei ben o** = put a bandage round his head

➪**e**, ➪**fo**

o achos *preposition*
= because of
mae'r ffatri ar °gau wythnos 'ma o achos y streic = the factory is closed this week because of the strike
➪**achos**, ➪**oherwydd**

o amgylch *preposition*
= around; round; about
personal forms: **o 'n amgylch (i), o dy amgylch (di), o'i amgylch (e), o'i hamgylch (hi), o'n hamgylch (ni), o'ch amgylch (chi), o'u hamgylch (nhw)**
beth am °dro o amgylch y °dre? = what about a walk around the town?
bydd myfyrwyr y chweched dosbarth ar gael i'ch tywys o amgylch yr ysgol = sixth-form students will be on hand to guide you round the school

> **!** This word is very similar to, if not synonymous with, ➪**o °gwmpas**

o °blaid *adverb*
= in favour (of)
personal forms: **o ᶰmhlaid (i), o dy °blaid (di), o'i °blaid (e), o'i ʰphlaid (hi), o'n plaid (ni), o'ch plaid (chi), o'u plaid (nhw)**
ond does yr un o'r °ddau o °blaid tynnu'r milwyr allan = but neither of them is in favour of pulling the soldiers out

mae'r ffaith iddi °fod ar °restr °fer wedi
bod o'i ʰphlaid = the fact that she is on
a shortlist has been in her favour
⇒**plaid**

oblegid conjunction (Literary Welsh)
= because; because of
⇒**achos**, ⇒**o achos**, ⇒ **oherwydd**

o °blith preposition
= from among(st)
personal forms: **o'n plith** from among
us, **o'ch plith** from among you, **o'u
plith** from among them
fe aeth nifer °fawr o'u plith dros y môr
i'r Unol °Daleithiau = a great number
from among them went over the sea to
the United States

ochneidio verbnoun
= sigh

ochor, ochr (plural **ochrau**) noun,
feminine
= side
o'n nhw'n byw ochor draw i'r afon =
they lived on the other side of the river
mae 'na °ddadleuon cryf ar y °ddwy
ochor = there are strong arguments on
both sides
...ochr yn ochr â ʰpholisi o °lwyfannu
gwaith o'r gorffennol = ... side by side
with a policy of staging work from the
past

od adjective
= odd, strange
⇒**rhyfedd**

o dan°
⇒**dan°**

odliadur (plural **-on**) noun, masculine
= rhyming dictionary

odrif (plural **-au**) noun, masculine
= odd number

oddeutu preposition (Literary Welsh)
= about
⇒**o amgylch**, ⇒**o °gwmpas**, ⇒**tua**

oddiar° (also **oddi ar°**) preposition
= off, from
personal forms as ⇒**ar°**
fe syrthiodd oddiar ei °geffyl = he fell
from or off his horse

oddiwrth° (also **oddi wrth°**)
preposition
personal forms: as ⇒**wrth**

= from (used almost exclusively of
things or sentiments sent to someone)
Penblwydd hapus oddiwrth Eleri =
Happy Birthday from Eleri
llongyfarchiadau oddiwrthon ni i gyd
= congratulations from us all
⇒**gan°**

oed noun, masculine
• = age
faint ydy dy oed di? = how old are you?
(literally: how much is your age?)
pobol mewn oed = elderly people
• = (years) old
mae gynnyn nhw °fab saith oed =
they've got a seven-year-old son

> ! Although **oed** on its own means
> 'years old', a special word for 'year'
> blwydd (⇒**blwyddyn**) can optionally
> be used with it:
> mae hi'n ugain ⁿmlwydd oed or mae
> hi'n ugain oed = she is twenty years
> old

oedi verbnoun
= delay
peidiwch ag oedi—tanysgrifiwch
nawr! = don't delay—subscribe now!
ymddiheurwn am unrhyw oedi (formal)
= we apologize for any delay

oedran (plural **-nau**) noun, masculine
= age
beth ydy'ch oedran? = what is your
age?
..., ond o ystyried oedrannau'r plant ...
= ..., but considering the ages of the
children ...

oedrannus adjective
= elderly, aged

**oedd, oeddech, oedden,
oeddet, oeddwn**
⇒**bod**

oen (plural **ŵyn**) noun, masculine
= lamb

oer adjective
comparative **oerach**, superlative **oera(f)**
= cold
oedd hi'n oer iawn bore 'ma, on'd
oedd? = it was very cold this morning,
wasn't it?
mae'n oerach heddiw na ddoe = it's
colder today than yesterday
mae'r bwyd 'ma wedi mynd yn oer =
this food has gone cold

oerfel *noun, masculine*
= cold
oherwydd yr oerfel = because of the cold

oergell (*plural* **-oedd**) *noun, feminine*
= refrigerator, fridge
⇒**rhewgell**

oeri *verbnoun*
= grow *or* get cold
mae hi wedi oeri = it's got cold(er)

oes...?
⇒**bod**

oes (*plural* **-oedd, -au**) *noun, feminine*
• = age
y Canol Oesoedd = the Middle Ages
Oes yr Iâ = the Ice Age
yn oes oesoedd = for ever and ever.
• = life
carchar am oes = prison for life
ac ym ⁿMhorthmadog naeth hi aros am °weddill ei hoes = and in Porthmadog she stayed for the rest of her life

ofer *adjective*
= (in) vain; futile
ond ofer, hyd yma, °fu pob ymdrech i °wella'r sefyllfa = but every attempt to improve the situation so far has been in vain

o °fewn *preposition*
= within
bydd y gwaith wedi'i °orffen o °fewn wythnos, gobeithio = the work will be finished within a week, I hope
mi na i °bopeth sy o °fewn 'y ⁿnghyrraedd = I'll do everything in my power

o °flaen *preposition*
= in front of; ahead of
personal forms: **o ⁿmlaen (i), o dy °flaen (di), o'i °flaen (e), o'i blaen (hi), o'n blaen (ni), o'ch blaen (chi), o'u blaen (nhw)**
roedd y car wedi'i °barcio o °flaen yr °orsaf = the car was parked in front of the station
y ffordd o'ch blaen ar °gau = road ahead (of you) closed
sefwch o ⁿmlaen i os dach chi eisiau = stand in front of me if you want
⇒**cyn**, ⇒**gerbron**, ⇒ **o'r blaen**

ofn (*plural* **-au**) *noun, masculine*
= fear
dyn ni i gyd yn gorfod wynebu'n hofnau = we all have to face our fears

! *To express* 'afraid', *a temporary state of mind,* ⇒**ar°** *is used when the person is stated*:
mae ofn arna i = I'm afraid
oes ofn arnat ti? = are you afraid?
roedd ofn arnyn nhw = they were afraid
dych chi'n rhy hwyr, mae ofn arna i = you're too late, I'm afraid
In some areas **ofn** *is treated as a sort of verbnoun (but, like* ⇒**eisiau**, *without any linking* **yn**)
dach chi ofn cŵn? (*instead of* **oes arnoch chi ofn cŵn?**) = are you afraid of dogs?

ofnadwy (*often pronounced* **ofnadw** *in Southern speech*) *adjective*
• = awful, terrible
pwy awgrymodd inni °ddod i °weld y ffilm ofnadwy 'ma? = whose idea was it for us to come and see this awful film?
mae hi wedi troi'n °flwyddyn ofnadwy i'r llywodraeth = it has turned into an awful year for the government
Sut oedd y °daith, 'te?—Ofnadwy! = How was the trip, then?—Awful!
• (*as modifier*) = awfully

! *Two constructions are possible when* **ofnadwy** *is used with another adjective to mean* 'awfully...'—*either adjective +* **ofnadwy**, *or* **ofnadwy o +** °*adjective*:
mae'r pethau 'ma'n °gostus ofnadwy *or* **mae'r pethau 'ma'n ofnadwy o °gostus** = these things are awfully expensive
bydd y rheina'n °drwm ofnadwy, °wyddoch chi *or* **bydd y rheina'n ofnadwy o °drwm, °wyddoch chi** = those will be awfully heavy, you know

ofni *verbnoun*
= fear; be afraid
dw i'n ofni y bydd 'na °ragor o °broblemau cyn diwedd y mis = I'm afraid there will be more problems before the end of the month
mae hi'n ofni cŵn = she's afraid of dogs

offeryn *noun, masculine*
- (*plural* **offerynnau**)
 = (*musical*) instrument
 dych chi'n chwarae offeryn? = do you play an instrument?
- (*plural* **offer**) = tool; (*plural*) equipment
 roedd rhaid i'r °frigad °dân °ddefnyddio offer torri i'w rhyddhau = the fire brigade had to use cutting equipment to release them
 bydd offer cyfieithu ar °gael = translation equipment will be available

oglau
⇒**(ar)oglau**

ogof (*plural* **-au, -eydd**) *noun, feminine*
 = cave

o °gwmpas *preposition*
 = around; round; about
 personal forms: **o °nghwmpas (i), o dy °gwmpas (di), o'i °gwmpas (e), o'i ⁿchwmpas (hi), o'n cwmpas (ni), o'ch cwmpas (chi), o'u cwmpas (nhw):**
 y byd o'n cwmpas = the world about us
 aethon ni am °dro o °gwmpas y °dre cyn cinio = we went for a walk round town before lunch

ogystal
⇒**yn ogystal**

oherwydd
1 *conjunction*
 = because
 bydd y siop ar °gau heddiw oherwydd °fod nifer o'r staff yn sâl = the shop will be closed today because a number of the staff are ill

> **!** *The conjunction* **oherwydd**, *like its more common counterpart* ⇒**achos**, *is generally followed by a 'that ...' clause in Welsh.*

2 *preposition*
 = because of
 mae'n °fwy na ⁿpharod i ymddeol oherwydd y newid yn natur ei swydd = he's more than ready to retire because of the change in the nature of his job

o hyd *adverb*
- = still
 ar y blaen o hyd! = still at the forefront!
 mae'r °Gymraeg yn °bwysig iddo o hyd = the Welsh language is still important to him
- = always
 mae'n tynnu coes o hyd = he's always pulling people's legs
- = the whole time
 cerwch mas i chwarae—dych chi dan °draed o hyd! = go out and play—you're under (my) feet the whole time!

ôl (*plural* **olion**) *noun, masculine*
 = trace; mark
 roedd olion o'r °drosedd yn dal i'w gweld bore 'ma = traces of the crime were still visible this morning
⇒**ar ôl,** ⇒**yn ôl**

ola(f) *adjective*
 = last
 Rhagfyr yw mis ola'r °flwyddyn = December is the last month of the year

> **!** *This word means* 'last in a series', *while* ⇒**diwetha(f)** *means* 'most recent'. *Compare:*
> **roedd ei °lyfr diwetha'n °well na'r un newydd 'ma** = his last book was better than this new one
> **cyhoeddwyd ei °lyfr ola °ddeufis cyn ei °farw** = his last book was published two months before he died

o °lawer *adverb*
 = much (+ *comparative adjective*)

> **!** *This qualifier follows a comparative adjective.*
> **roedd eu cychod nhw'n °fasach o °lawer** = their boats were much shallower
> **mae'r un yma'n °fwy diddorol o °lawer** = this one is much more interesting
> *Also used with* ⇒**rhy°:**
> **maen nhw'n rhy swnllyd o °lawer** = they're far too noisy

⇒**llawer**

o °leia(f) *adverb*
 = at least
 dan ni fan'ma am °dri mis o °leia = we're here for three months at least
 mi °allet ti wedi dweud wrtha i yn °gynharach, o °leia = you could at least have told me earlier

olew *noun, masculine*
= oil

olion
⇒**ôl**

olrhain *verbnoun*
= trace; track
bydd llawer iawn yn dod draw er mwyn ceisio olrhain eu hachau = a great many come over to try and trace their ancestry

olwyn (*plural* **-ion**) *noun, feminine*
= wheel

oll *adjective*
= all; whole

> **!** *This word is not widely used in the modern language, except in a few set expressions:*
> **yn °gyntaf oll, gadewch inni °weld beth yn union sy gynnon ni** = first of all, let's see exactly what we've got
> **ddaru nhw °werthu'r cwbwl oll** = they sold the whole lot

⇒**holl°**, ⇒**i gyd**, ⇒**hyn oll**

on'
⇒**on'd**

ond *conjunction*
= but
wi'n nabod y °bobol 'ma, ond pwy yw'r rheina? = I know these people, but who are those?
. . ., ond mae rhaglen °gyntaf y °gyfres yn llwyddo = . . ., but the first programme in the series succeeds
aeth pawb ond fi = everyone went but me
mi °fedrai ysbrydoli ac arwain, ond iddo °gael y cyfle = he was able to inspire and lead, if only he was given the chance
⇒**dim ond**

on'd (*often* **on'** *before consonants*) *particle*

> **!** *This particle is used with verbs to form a negative interrogative 'tag' that anticipates an affirmative answer—in Welsh the answer 'yes' will be the verb with the* **on'(d)** *removed (and changes made for person as appropriate). Present and imperfect of* **bod** *use interrogative forms with*

this particle, other verbs (including other tenses of **bod***) use the unmutated affirmative forms.*
On'd ydyn nhw'n °bert?—Ydyn = Aren't they pretty?—Yes (they are)
Mae'n oer bore 'ma, on'd ydy?— Ydy = It's cold this morning, isn't it?— Yes (it is)
Mae bara ar ôl, on'd oes?—Oes = There is bread left, isn't there?—Yes (there is)
Roedd y °ddrama'n °dda, on'd oedd?—Oedd = The play was good, wasn't it?—Yes (it was)
Fe °fyddi di'n iawn, on' byddi?— Bydda = You'll be OK, won't you?— Yes (I will)
'Sai hynny'n neis iawn, on' basai?—Basai = That would be very nice, wouldn't it?—Yes (it would)
On' byddai hynny'n °well?—Byddai = Wouldn't that be better?—Yes (it would)
With the preterite, an invariable form **on' do?** *is used as the tag:*
Wedest ti wrthyn nhw, on' do?—Do = You told them, didn't you?—Yes
Mi °brynodd Aled y tocynnau, on' do?—Do = Aled bought the tickets, didn't he?—Yes

⇒**nag**

onest *adjective*
= honest
a bod yn onest, does dim amser 'da fi = to be honest, I haven't got time

oni (*before vowels* **onid**) *particle*

> **!** **oni** *belongs much more to the written than the spoken language, which generally prefers* ⇒**on'd**.

oni °fyddai'n °bosibl i awdurdod cynllunio °benodi panel dros dro? = wouldn't it be possible for a planning authority to appoint a temporary panel?

opera (*plural* **operâu**) *noun, feminine*
= opera

optimist (*plural* **-iaid**) *noun, masculine*
= optimist

optimistaidd *adjective*
= optimistic

optimistiaeth *noun, feminine*
= optimism

o °ran *adverb*
= as regards; concerning
mae hyn yn allweddol o °ran y maes darlledu yn y blynyddoedd nesa = this is crucial as regards the field of broadcasting in coming years
o °ran hynny = for that matter:
dw i °ddim yn nabod hi ac, o °ran hynny, dw i °ddim eisiau nabod hi = I don't know her and, for that matter, I don't want to know her
⇨**ar °ran**

o'r blaen *adverb*
= before
mae'r sefyllfa'n °well nag y bu hi erioed o'r blaen = the situation is better than it has ever been before
°fuoch chi fan hyn o'r blaen? = have you been here before?
⇨**cyn**, ⇨**gerbron**, ⇨ **o °flaen**

o'r diwedd *adverb*
= at last; finally (*with similar sense of 'overdue'*)
dyma'r bws yn dod—o'r diwedd! = Here comes the bus—At last!
dan ni i gyd yn °falch °fod ymateb swyddogol wedi dod o'r diwedd = we are all pleased that an official response has finally come

---

! *Note that this adverb does not mean 'in the end', which is* **yn y diwedd**.

⇨**diwedd**

oren
1 (*plural* **-nau**) *noun, masculine or feminine*
= orange
2 *adjective*
= orange

o'r °gloch *adverb*
= o'clock
beth am inni °gwrdd am saith o'r °gloch? = how about if we met at seven o'clock?
faint o'r °gloch ydy/yw hi? = what time is it?
am °bedwar o'r °gloch = at four o'clock
tua naw o'r °gloch = at about nine o'clock
mae'n °ddeg o'r °gloch = it's ten o'clock
mae hi tua deg o'r °gloch = it's about ten o'clock
⇨**cloch**

o'r gorau *adverb*
= all right (*signifying consent*)
⇨**iawn**

oriau
⇨**awr**

oriawr (*plural* **oriorau**) *noun, feminine*
= watch
mae'r oriawr 'ma wedi sefyll = this watch has stopped
mae'r oriawr 'ma °ddau °funud yn °fuan = this watch is two minutes fast
mae'r oriawr 'ma °ddau °funud ar ei hôl hi = this watch is two minutes slow

oriel (*plural* **-au**) *noun, feminine*
= gallery

o'r neilltu *adverb*
= to one side:
nawn ni °gadw'r cwestiynau 'ma o'r neilltu am y tro = let's keep these questions to one side for now
awn ni o'r neilltu am eiliad = let's go to one side for a moment
⇨**neilltuo**

ornest (*plural* **-au**) *noun, feminine*
= contest; battle

os *conjunction*
= if (*open conditions*)

! ⇨**If** *box on the English-Welsh side*

---

osgoi *verbnoun*
• = avoid
mae'n °bwysig ceisio osgoi'r °fath °wrthdaro yn y dyfodol = it's important to try and avoid such confrontation in future
• (*as adjective*)
ffordd (*plural* **ffyrdd**) **osgoi** = by-pass
traffig osgoi = diverted traffic

ots *noun, plural*
does dim ots = it doesn't matter
°fydd dim ots = it won't matter
does dim ots faint o °wrthwynebiad sydd i'r datblygiad = it doesn't matter how much opposition there is to the development
os nad oes ots gynnoch chi = if you don't mind

Pp

pa° *adjective*
= which...?; what...?
pa °flas hoffech chi? = what flavour
would you like?
**ym ⁿmha °ran o °Gymru °gaethoch
chi'ch geni?** = in which part of Wales
were you born?
pa un leiciet ti? = which one would you
like?
pa °rai o't ti'n defnyddio? = which ones
were you using?

! *This word corresponds to 'what'
only where this means 'which',
otherwise* ⇒**beth**. *In many Southern
regions,* ⇒**pwy°** *is always used
instead of* **pa°**.

---

pabell (*plural* **pebyll**) *noun, feminine*
= tent

paced (*plural* **-i**) *noun, masculine*
= pack; packet
°gymera i °ddau °baced o'r bisgedi 'na
= I'll have two packets of those biscuits
⇒**pecyn**

pacio *verbnoun*
= pack

padell (*plural* **-au**) *noun, feminine*
= bowl; pan
oedd gynno fo °lond °badell o °datws
= he had a panful of potatoes

paent *noun, masculine*
= paint

paentio *verbnoun*
= paint

paham
⇒**pam**

palmant (*plural* **palmentydd**) *noun,
masculine*
= pavement

palu *verbnoun*
= dig
dw i wedi bod wrthi'n palu'r °ardd =
I've been at work digging the garden
'na lle buon nhw'n palu trwy'r bore =
that's where they've been digging all
morning
⇒**claddu**

pallu *verbnoun* (*South*)
= refuse; fail
mae ⁿnghar i'n pallu mynd = my car
won't go
⇒**ffili,** ⇒**methu,** ⇒ **nacáu**

pam *adverb*
= why
**pam yr oedd y digwyddiad yma o
°gymaint o °ddiddordeb i seryddion?**
= why was this event of such interest to
astronomers?
**does neb yn gwybod pam °fod hyn yn
°bwysig iddyn nhw** = nobody knows
why this is important to them

! *Notice in the above example that*
pam *is generally followed by a 'that...'
clause (like* ⇒**achos** *and*
⇒**oherwydd** *because)—'...why that
this is important...'. The construction*
pam na° (*or* **naʰ**) (**pam nad** *before
original vowels*) + *inflected future is
used to make suggestions for actions
'Why don't you...?':*
pam na °ddoi di draw heno? = why
don't you come round this
evening?
pam na °werthi di nhw? = why don't
you sell them?
The literary variant of this word,
paham, *gives the impression of
affectation in speech and should be
avoided.*

---

pa mor°...?
= how...? (+ *adjective*)
**pa mor °bwysig yw'r iaith i ti'n
°bersonol?** = how important is the
language to you personally?
**mae'n dibynnu pa mor agos oedden
nhw yn y diwedd** = it depends how
close they were at the end
**pa mor uchel ydy'r mynydd 'na,
wedech chi?** = how high is that
mountain, would you say?
⇒**sut**

pan° (*often* **pen°** *in speech in Northern
areas*) *conjunction*
= when

! *This word is used with statements,
but not questions, for which* ⇒**pryd** *is
needed instead.*

---

pan o'n i'n °blentyn... = when I was a
child...

o'n i yn y °dafarn pan °glywes i'r **newyddion** = I was in the pub when I heard the news

mae'n anodd codi yn y bore pan mae'n oer fel hyn, on'd ydy? = it's hard getting up in the morning when it's cold like this, isn't it?

ffonia i chi pan °ddôn nhw, iawn? = I'll phone you when they come, OK?

⇒**pryd**

panaid *noun, masculine*
= cup (of tea)
°gymeri di °banaid? = will you have a cup of tea?

> **!** *This word, which is an abbreviated (but universally used) form of* **cwpanaid** *cupful, is used for the cup with the liquid inside it, while the basic word* ⇒**cwpan** *is the container only.*

pant (*plural* -**iau**) *noun, masculine*
= hollow

papur (*plural* -**au**) *noun, masculine*
• = paper
oes gen ti °ddarn o °bapur rhywle fan hyn? = have you got a piece of paper somewhere here?
dw i eisiau casglu'r papurau 'ma at ei gilydd °gynta = I want to gather these papers together first
• = note
dim ond papur deg punt sy gen i = I've only got a ten-pound note

papur newydd (*plural* **papurau newydd**) *noun, masculine*
= newspaper
⇒**newyddiadur**

pâr (*plural* **parau**) *noun, masculine*
= pair
gwnewch yr ymarfer 'ma mewn parau = do this exercise in pairs

para *verbnoun*
• = continue
...am °fod glo'r °fro'n para'n °ddeniadol fel tanwydd cartref = ...since the region's coal continues to be attractive as house fuel
• = last; = go on (**am°** for)
bydd y cyfarfod 'ma'n para am oriau = this meeting will last for hours

> **!** *This word is a widely used spoken equivalent of written* ⇒**parhau**.

paratoad (*plural* -**au**) *noun, masculine*
= preparation

paratoi *verbnoun*
= prepare
...tra bod y gweddill yn paratoi'r bwyd = ...while the rest are preparing the food

parc (*plural* -**iau**) *noun, masculine*
= park

parcio *verbnoun*
= park (*car etc*)
°allwn ni °barcio fan hyn, ti'n meddwl? = can we park here, do you think?
°ges i °ddirwy am °barcio'n anghyfreithlon = I got a fine for parking illegally

parch *noun, masculine*
= respect (**tuag at°** for)
mae eisiau mwy o °barch tuag at ein sefydliadau = more respect is needed for our institutions

parchedig *adjective*
= reverend

parchu *verbnoun*
= respect

parchus *adjective*
= respectable

parhad *noun, masculine*
= continuation

parhaol *adjective*
= permanent
o'n i'n gobeithio cael swydd °barhaol yn hytrach nag un dros °dro = I was hoping to get a permanent job rather than a temporary one

parhau *verbnoun*
= continue; last
fe °fydd pawb ond Brychan Llyr yn parhau gyda'r gwaith hwnnw = everyone but Brychan Llyr will continue with that work

> **!** *This more formal word corresponds to spoken* ⇒**para**

parod *adjective*
= ready; willing
ydych chi'n °barod? = are you ready?
hoffwn °ddiolch hefyd i Nia Williams am ei ʰchymorth parod = I would also

like to thank Nia Williams for her willing help
⇒**yn °barod**

parodrwydd noun, masculine
= readiness

parti noun, masculine
= party
faint sy'n dod i'r parti? = how many are coming to the party?
⇒**plaid**

partner (plural **-iaid**) noun, masculine
= partner
dyn ni i gyd yn °bartneriaid yn Ewrop bellach = we are all partners in Europe now

parthed preposition
= about, concerning

> **!** This is a literary equivalent of ⇒**ynglŷn â** and ⇒**ynghylch**

Pasg noun, masculine (often with the definite article)
= Easter
fe °fyddwn ni i gyd yn cael wyau Pasg, on' byddwn ni? = we'll all be getting Easter eggs, won't we?
°welwn ni chi ar ôl y Pasg = we'll see you after Easter
Sul y Pasg = Easter Sunday
(Dydd) Llun y Pasg = Easter Monday

pasio verbnoun
= pass
doedd 'na °ddim lle i °basio, ch'wel = there was no place to pass, you see

patrwm (plural **patrymau**) noun, masculine
= pattern
mae'r un patrwm i'w °weld yn yr ieithoedd Celtaidd eraill = the same pattern can be seen in the other Celtic languages

pawb pronoun
= everybody, everyone
dewch i mewn, °bawb! = come in, everybody!
mae pawb yn gwybod °fod hyn yn °wir = everyone knows that this is true
croeso i °bawb = all welcome

pe conjunction
= if (closed conditions)

> **!** ⇒**IF** box on English-Welsh side

pebyll plural of
⇒**pabell**

pecyn (plural **-nau**) noun, masculine
= pack; packet
°ga i °becyn o °greision os gwelwch yn °dda? = can I have a packet of crisps please?

pechod (plural **-au**) noun, masculine
= sin

pechu verbnoun
= sin

pedair
⇒**pedwar**

pedwar (feminine **pedair**) numeral
= four
mae'n ugain munud i °bedwar = it's twenty to four
pedwar bachgen yn erbyn pedair merch = four boys against four girls

> **!** Where the numeral is used on its own with reference to people or animals, the feminine form is reserved for instances where all four are female; the masculine form is used not only for four males, but also for any combination. So **y pedair ohonyn nhw** 'the four of them' refers unambiguously to four females, while **y pedwar ohonyn nhw** could be all males, or males and females

pedwaredd°
⇒**pedwerydd**

pedwerydd (masculine), **pedwaredd°** (feminine) adjective (precedes noun)
= fourth
dyma'r pedwerydd tro iddo °alw heddiw = this is the fourth time he's called today
gadewch inni edrych ar y °bedwaredd °frawddeg unwaith eto = let's look once again at the fourth sentence

> **!** Ordinal numerals are adjectives, but behave in a special way. All other than ⇒**cynta** precede the noun. With feminine singular nouns, the noun itself undergoes soft mutation, as does the ordinal after the article—so: **y pedwerydd dyn** 'the fourth man' but **y °bedwaredd °ferch** 'the fourth girl'

peidio *verbnoun*
   imperative singular **paid,** *plural*
   peidiwch
• = stop, cease
   ydy'r glaw wedi peidio? = has the rain
   stopped?
⇒**dibaid**
• (*used for negative commands*)

> **!** *To form negative commands,*
> **paid/peidiwch** (*corresponding to*
> *'Don't...') is used with the verbnoun—*
> *so, for example,* **arhoswch!** 'wait!'
> *becomes* **peidiwch aros!** 'don't
> wait!'; **agor y ffenest!** 'open the
> window!' *becomes* **paid agor y
> ffenest!** 'don't open the window!'. *In
> this use particularly,* **peidio** *is
> optionally linked to the following
> verbnoun by* **â^h/ag,** *especially when a
> reinforcing pronoun is present
> (second and third examples below)*
> **paid!** = don't!
> **paid ti â deud pethau felly!** = don't
>   you say such things!
> **peidiwch chi ag edrych nes bo fi'n
>   dweud!** = don't you look until I say!
> **peidiwch anghofio!** = don't forget!

• **peidio** *used in conjunction with* ⇒**rhaid**
   to mean 'must not...':
   rhaid inni °beidio siarad yn rhy uchel
   = we must not speak too loud
• *The set phrase* **...neu °beidio?** *is used
   as an all-purpose tag* '...or not?':
   dych chi'n dod neu °beidio? = are you
   coming or not?
   **...ond, yn °barod neu °beidio, mae'r
   sioe'n dechrau am saith** = ...but,
   ready or not, the show starts at seven

peilot (*plural* **-iaid**) *noun, masculine*
   = pilot

peint (*plural* **-iau**) *noun, masculine*
   = pint

peiriannydd (*plural* **peirianwyr**)
   noun, masculine
   = engineer

peiriant (*plural* **peiriannau**) *noun,
   masculine*
   = machine

peirianwaith *noun, masculine*
   = machinery

pêl (*plural* **peli**) *noun, feminine*
   = ball

pêl-droed *noun, masculine*
   = football
   **mae'n noson °brysur tu hwnt ar y
   meysydd pêl-droed heno** = it's an
   extremely busy evening on the
   football fields tonight

pelydr (*plural* **-au**) *noun, masculine*
   = ray
   mae hi wedi mynd i °gael pelydr-x =
   she's gone to get an x-ray
⇒**ymbelydredd**

pell *adjective*
   = far
   ydy hi'n °bell o fan hyn? = is it far from
   here?
   **mae'n anodd byw mewn byd sy mor
   °bell o °fod yn °berffaith** = it is hard to
   live in a world that is so far from
   (being) perfect
   o °bell ffordd (+ *adjective*) by a long
   way, far from:
   **dyw'r lle 'ma °ddim yn °ddelfrydol o
   °bell ffordd** = this place is far from
   ideal
⇒**nepell,** ⇒**ymhell,** ⇒ **ymhellach**

pellter *noun, masculine*
   = distance

pen (*plural* **-nau**) *noun, masculine*
• = head
   mae pen tost 'da fi = I've got a
   headache
   cau dy °ben, nei di? = shut up, will
   you?
• = top
   maen nhw'n byw ar °ben y bryn = they
   live on top of the hill
• = end
   a dyma ni wedi cyrraedd pen ein taith
   = and here we are at the end of our
   journey

> **!** *A number of common idioms and
> phrases use* **pen,** *notably the
> construction for* 'on my, your etc. own',
> *which in speech is* **ar °ben** +
> *possessive* + ⇒**hun** *or* **hunan**:
> **o'n i yno am awr ar °ben 'n hun** = I
>   was there for an hour on my own
> *Note* **yn y pen draw** 'eventually', 'in
> the long run' *and* **dod i °ben** 'come to
> an end':
> **yn y pen draw mae'r gwirionedd yn
>   sicr o °ddod i'r amlwg** = eventually
>   the truth is sure to come to light

mi °ddaeth y cyfan i °ben yn °fuan
iawn wedyn = the whole thing came
to an end very soon after
 The loanword **pen** *'pen' is generally
extended to* **pen sgrifennu** *or* **pen
sgwennu** *('writing pen') to avoid
ambiguity.*

⇨ar °ben, ⇨dros °ben, ⇨uwchben,
⇨ ymhen

pen°
⇨pan°

penbleth *noun, feminine*
= confusion; perplexity
mewn penbleth = confused
mynd i °benbleth = get confused

pencadlys (*plural* **-oedd**) *noun,
masculine*
= headquarters
**mae trafodaethau'n mynd yn eu blaen
ym "mhencadlys y cwmni** =
discussions are continuing at the
company headquarters

pencampwr (*plural* **pencampwyr**)
noun, masculine
= champion

pencampwraig (*plural*
pencampwragedd) *noun, feminine*
= champion

pencampwriaeth (*plural* **-au**) *noun,
feminine*
= championship

pendant *adjective*
= definite; firm
**mae eisiau penderfyniad pendant
erbyn yfory** = a definite decision is
needed by tomorrow
**yr hyn dan ni'n galw amdano ydy
ymateb pendant, 'na i gyd** = what we
are calling for is a firm response, that's
all
yn °bendant = definitely:
**°Fyddi di'n dod nos yfory?—Yn
°bendant!** = Will you be coming
tomorrow night?—Definitely!

penderfyniad (*plural* **-au**) *noun,
masculine*
= decision
**mae disgwyl y gallai'r penderfyniad
°ddod unrhyw °ddydd** = it is expected
that the decision could come any day
now

penderfynol *adjective*
= decisive; resolute

penderfynu *verbnoun*
= decide
**maen nhw wedi penderfynu aros am y
tro** = they've decided to stay for now
**does dim byd wedi'i °benderfynu hyd
yn hyn** = nothing has been decided so
far

pen draw
in: **yn y pen draw** = eventually
⇨pen

penelin (*plural* **-oedd**) *noun, masculine
or feminine*
= elbow

pen-glin (*plural* **pengliniau**) *noun,
masculine or feminine*
= knee
⇨pen-lin

penglog (*plural* **-au**) *noun, feminine*
= skull

penigamp *adjective*
= splended, marvellous

pen-lin (*plural* **-iau**) *noun, feminine*
= knee
⇨pen-glin

penlinio *verbnoun*
= kneel

pennaeth (*plural* **penaethiaid**) *noun,
masculine*
= chief; boss; head
**mi °fydd Pennaeth yr Adran
°Gynllunio yn °bresennol** = the Head
of the Planning Department will be
present

penna(f)
yn °benna(f) = mainly, chiefly:
**mae'r ffoaduriaid yn dod o'r Gogledd
yn °benna** = the refugees come mainly
from the North

pennawd (*plural* **penawdau**) *noun,
masculine*
= headline
dyma'r penawdau diweddara = here
are the latest headlines

penodi *verbnoun*
= appoint
**...erbyn i °reolwr newydd °gael ei
°benodi** = ...by the time a new
manager is appointed

penodol *adjective*
= particular; specific
nes i °ofyn am y rhain yn °benodol = I
specifically asked for these

pen-ôl (*plural* **penolau**) *noun,
masculine*
= bottom, buttocks
⇒**tin**

penrhyn (*plural* **-nau, -ion**) *noun,
masculine*
= peninsular

pensaer (*plural* **penseiri**) *noun,
masculine*
= architect

pensaernïaeth *noun, feminine*
= architecture

pensaernïol *adjective*
= architectural

pensil (*plural* **-iau**) *noun, masculine*
= pencil

pensiwn (*plural* **pensiynau**) *noun,
masculine*
= pension

pensiynwr (*plural* **pensiynwyr**) *noun,
masculine*
= pensioner

pensiynwraig (*plural*
pensiynwragedd) *noun, feminine*
= pensioner

pentre(f) (*plural* **pentrefi**) *noun,
masculine*
= village

pentwr (*plural* **pentyrrau**) *noun,
masculine*
= heap, pile (*also figurative*)
mae gynnyn nhw °bentwr o °waith =
they've got a pile of work

pentyrru *verbnoun*
= heap

perchennog (*plural* **perchnogion**)
noun, masculine
= owner, proprietor
**mae perchnogion siopau yn
Llaneglwys wedi dod at ei gilydd...** =
shop-owners in Llaneglwys have got
together...
⇒**biau,** ⇒**perthyn**

perchnogion *plural of*
⇒**perchennog**

pererin (*plural* **-ion**) *noun, masculine*
= pilgrim

pererindod *noun, feminine*
= pilgrimage

perfedd (*plural* **-ion**) *noun, masculine*
• = entrails, guts
• (*figurative*) = midst; middle
**ym ⁿmherfedd(ion) y °wlad maen
nhw'n byw** = they live in the heart of
the country
dan °berfeddion = until all hours
**cymdogion yn cadw sŵn dan
°berfeddion** = neighbours making a
noise until all hours

perffaith *adjective*
= perfect
on'd ydy'r lle 'ma'n °berffaith inni? =
isn't this place perfect for us?

perffeithio *verbnoun*
= perfect

perffeithrwydd *noun, masculine*
= perfection

perfformiad (*plural* **-au**) *noun,
masculine*
= performance

perfformio *verbnoun*
= perform
**mae'r actorion yn dal i °berfformio er
gwaetha popeth** = the actors are still
performing in spite of everything

perfformiwr (*plural* **perfformwyr**)
noun, masculine
= performer

perfformwraig (*plural*
perfformwragedd) *noun, feminine*
= performer

peri *verbnoun*
= cause
**bydd y gwaith yn peri anawsterau i
°yrwyr yn yr ardal dros yr Haf** = the
work will cause difficulties for drivers
in the area over the summer
⇒**achosi**

perllan (*plural* **-nau**) *noun, feminine*
= orchard

person (*plural* **-au**) *noun, masculine*
= person
ai dyna'r person iawn am y swydd? =
is that the right person for the job?

personol adjective
= personal
yn °gynta, °ga i °ofyn am ychydig o °fanylion personol? = first, can I ask for a few personal details?
siarad yn °bersonol, 'swn i °ddim eisiau = speaking personally, I wouldn't want to

personoliaeth (plural **-au**) noun, feminine
= personality

perswadio verbnoun
= persuade
bydd eisiau perswadio nhw i °ddod °rywsut, 'te, on' bydd? = they'll need to be persuaded somehow to come, then, won't they?

pert adjective
= pretty
sbia'r blodau 'na—on'd ydyn nhw'n °bert? = look at those flowers—aren't they pretty?

perthnasau plural noun
= relatives, relations
mae gynnon ni °berthnasau yn yr Alban = we've got relatives in Scotland
⇨**perthynas**

perthnasol adjective
= relevant
sut yn union mae hynny i °fod yn °berthnasol i'r °drafodaeth 'ma? = how exactly is that supposed to be relevant to this discussion?

perthyn* verbnoun
• = belong
ydy'r rhain yn perthyn i chi? = do these belong to you?
oedd y tŷ 'na'n perthyn i'r teulu °flynyddoedd yn ôl = that house belonged to the family years ago
• = be related
mae hi'n perthyn i mi = she's related to me

perthynas (plural **perthnasau**) noun, feminine
= relation, relationship
mae perthynas agos rhyngddyn nhw = there is a close relationship between them

peryg(l) (plural **peryglon**) noun, masculine
= danger

mae'n (or **mae 'na**) °**beryg i'r gweddill °fynd ar °goll** = there is a danger that the rest will be lost
mae asiantaethau dros y byd yn chwilio am °beryglon tebyg o'r gofod = agencies across the world are looking for similar dangers from space

peryglus adjective
= dangerous
yng ⁿngolwg y °gyfraith mae'r madarch hudol yn °beryglus iawn = in the eyes of the law the magic mushrooms are very dangerous

pesimist (plural **-iaid**) noun, masculine
= pessimist

pesimistaidd adjective
= pessimistic

pesimistiaeth noun, feminine
= pessimism

peswch noun, masculine
= cough

> **!** This word, denoting a temporary physical state, requires **ar°** with the person:
> **mae peswch arna i** = I've got a cough
> **oes peswch arni hi?** = has she got a cough?
> **ers pryd mae'r peswch 'na arnoch chi?** = how long have you had that cough?

pesychu verbnoun
= cough

pe tai, pe taswn,
= etc

> **!** ⇨**If** box on the English-Welsh side

petrol noun, masculine
= petrol
mae petrol yn mynd i °fod yn °ddrutach o chwech o'r °gloch heno = petrol is going to be more expensive from six o'clock tonight

petruso verbnoun
= hesitate
peidiwch petruso—cysylltwch â ni ar unwaith! = don't hesitate—contact us at once!

> **!** Note that **cyn** 'before' is generally used with a following verbnoun,

where English has simply 'hesitate to (do something)':
nes i °ddim petruso cyn llofnodi = I didn't hesitate to sign

petryal
1 *noun, masculine*
  = square
2 *adjective*
  = square

peth
1 (*plural* **-au**) *noun, masculine*
  = thing
  beth dych chi'n galw'r peth 'ma yn °Gymraeg? = what do you call this thing in Welsh?
  y peth mwya anodd ydy esbonio popeth wedyn, wrth °gwrs = the most difficult thing is explaining everything afterwards, of course
  paid ti â deud pethau felly! = don't you say such things!
  a phelly (*contracted form of* **a ʰphethau felly**) = and such things, and suchlike
  mae'n °beth od iawn, 'tydy? = it's very odd, isn't it?
  mae hynny'n meddwl yn union yr un peth = that means exactly the same thing
  Faint mae'n costio?—Y peth nesa i °ddim = How much does it cost?—Next to nothing
2 *adverb*
  = a bit (of), a little

> **!** *In this (colloquial) use,* **peth** *is the equivalent of* ⇒**ychydig**, *but unusually for a quantity word is not followed by* **o°** *before the noun—so, for example,* **ychydig o °gaws** *'a little cheese'* but **peth caws.**
> **roedden nhw wedi gwneud cais am °beth gwybodaeth ariannol** = they had made an application for a bit of financial information
> **°beth amser yn °ddiweddarach...** = a little while later...

piau
⇒**biau**

pibell** (*plural* **-au, -i**) *noun, feminine*
  = pipe
  lapiwch y pibellau'n °ofalus rhag ofn bod y dŵr yn rhewi = wrap the pipes carefully in case the water freezes

pigiad (*plural* **-au**) *noun, masculine*
  • = sting
  • = injection

pigion *plural noun*
  = excerpts; highlights
  rhai o °bigion yr wythnos yn y Neuadd °Ddawns = some of the week's highlights in the Dance Hall

pigo *verbnoun*
  • = sting; pierce
  ydy'r pryfed 'ma'n pigo? = do these insects sting?
  °ges i ⁿmhigo = I was/got stung
  • = pick
  paid pigo arna i! = stop picking on me!

pigog *adjective*
  = touchy, prickly
  ti'n °bigog iawn bore 'ma = you're very touchy/prickly this morning

pili-pala (*plural* **pili-palod**) *noun, masculine*
  = butterfly

> **!** *There are a wide variety of other terms in current use for* 'butterfly', *depending on region, including* **iâr °fach yr haf** (*plural* **ieir bach yr haf**), **colomen °fyw** (*plural* **colomennod byw**), **gloyn byw** (*plural* **gloynnod byw**)—*and numerous slight variations on this last term.*

pin (*plural* **-nau**) *noun, masculine*
  • = pin
  • = pen

pinc *adjective*
  = pink

piniwn
  in: **pôl piniwn** (*plural* **polau piniwn**) = opinion poll
⇒**arolwg barn**

piti *noun, masculine*
  = pity
  mae'n °biti! = it's a pity!
  piti garw! = what a (great) pity!
⇒**truan**

pitw *adjective*
  = meagre; sparse
  oedd y digwyddiad yn denu cynulleidfaoedd pitw = the event attracted meagre audiences

piws *adjective*
= purple

> **!** *This word is generally used in speech in place of the more literary term* **porffor**

pla (*plural* **plâu**) *noun, masculine*
= plague (*also figurative*)

plaen *adjective*
= plain
yn °blwmp ac yn °blaen:
bydd rhaid dweud wrtho fe 'n °blwmp ac yn °blaen = we'll have to tell him straight

plaid (*plural* **pleidiau**) *noun, feminine*
= (political) party
mae aelodaeth °gyffredin y °blaid yn erbyn y syniad = the ordinary membership of the party is against the idea.

> **!** *Names of political parties:*
> **y °Blaid °Geidwadol** = the Conservative Party
> **y °Blaid °Gomiwnyddol** = the Communist Party
> **y °Blaid °Lafur** = the Labour Party
> **y °Blaid °Ryddfrydol** = the Liberal Party
> (*but* **Y Democratiaid Rhyddfrydol** = the Liberal Democrats)
> **Plaid Cymru** (*Welsh Nationalist Party*)

⇒**o °blaid**, ⇒ **pleidleisio**

planed (*plural* **-au**) *noun, feminine*
= planet
fe °drawodd darnau o'r °gomed y °blaned lau eleni = pieces of the comet hit the planet Jupiter this year

planhigyn (*plural* **planhigion**) *noun, masculine*
= plant
creaduriaid a ʰphlanhigion a °fu °farw °filiynau o °flynyddoedd yn ôl = creatures and plants that died millions of years ago

plannu *verbnoun*
= plant
mae'r °ardd yn edrych yn °well ers inni °blannu'r holl °flodau 'ma = the garden looks better since we planted all these flowers

plant, plantos
⇒**plentyn**

plasty (*plural* **plastai**) *noun, masculine*
= mansion

plât (*plural* **platiau**) *noun, masculine*
= plate

pledio *verbnoun*
= plead
fe °blediodd y °ddau'n euog = they both pleaded guilty

pleidlais (*plural* **pleidleisiau**) *noun, feminine*
= vote

pleidleisio *verbnoun*
= vote (**dros°, i°** for)
pleidleisiwch droston ni °ddydd Iau nesa! = vote for us next Thursday!
roedd y rhan °fwya wedi pleidleisio â'u traed yn °barod = most had already voted with their feet

plentyn (*plural* **plant**) *noun, masculine*
= child
faint o °blant sy 'da chi erbyn hyn, 'te? = how many children have you got now, then?
mae dau o °blant 'da ni = we've got two children
y plant sy'n diodde, fel arfer = it's the children that suffer, as usual

> **!** *Note the diminutive plural form* **plantos** *often used with small children:*
> **dewch, °blantos!** = come (here), children!

pleser (*plural* **-au**) *noun, masculine*
= pleasure (someone)
mae'n °bleser i mi °gael eich croesawu heno = it's a pleasure for me to be able to welcome you tonight
gyda ʰphleser (*formal*) = with pleasure

plesio *verbnoun*
= please (someone)

plismon (*plural* **plismyn**) *noun, masculine*
= policeman
⇒**heddwas**

plith
in the compound preposition ⇒**ymhlith** *amongst and* ⇒**o °blith** *from among*

pluen (*plural* **plu**) *noun, feminine*
= feather

plwm *noun, masculine*
= lead (*metal*)

plwyf (*plural* **-i, -ydd**) *noun, masculine*
= parish

plwyfolyn (*plural* **plwyfolion**) *noun, masculine*
= parishioner

plygell (*plural* **-au**) *noun, masculine*
= folder

plygu *verbnoun*
= fold; bend
   ...a'i °**blygu** fo wedyn yn y canol fel hyn = ...and then fold it in the middle like this
   gwell plygu na ʰthorri (*proverb*) = better to bend than to break

plymer (*plural* **-iaid**) *noun, masculine*
= plumber

pnawn
⇒**prynhawn**

po *particle*

> **!** *This literary particle is found only in set expressions involving the superlative:*
> gorau po °**gynta** = the sooner the better
> gorau po °**fwya** = the more/bigger the better

pob *adjective*
= every
   rhaid i °**bob** defnyddiwr °**gofrestru** = every user must register
   bydd y rhaglen yn dod â'r newyddion diweddara °**bob mis** = the programme will bring (you) the latest news every month
   mae'n dod draw °**bob hyn a hyn**, timod = he comes round every now and then, you know
   mi °**geith pob un** ohonoch chi ei arian yn ôl = every one of you will get his money back
   y sglodyn pwysicaf ym ⁿ**mhob cyfrifiadur** yw'r prosesydd canolog = the most important chip in every computer is the central processor
   mi °**fydd hi** yma yfory, yn ôl pob tebyg = she'll be here tomorrow, in all likelihood

pob lwc! = good luck!
pob llwyddiant! = good luck (*in exams, tests, etc*)
°**bob yn ail** = alternate(ly), every other...
cynhelir cyfarfodydd °**bob yn ail wythnos** = meetings are held every other week

> **!** **pob** *means 'every' and is followed by a singular; 'all' is either* ⇒**i gyd** *or* ⇒**holl°**; *or, in the sense of 'everything',* ⇒**popeth,** ⇒**(y) cyfan** *or* ⇒**(y) cwbwl**

⇒**pawb,** ⇒**pob dim,** ⇒**popeth,** ⇒**ymhobman**

pob dim *pronoun*
= every (single) thing
   ...os ydy pob dim arall wedi methu = ...if everything else has failed

> **!** *This expression is more emphatic than the neutral* ⇒**popeth.**

pobi *verbnoun*
• = bake
• = roast

pobl, pobol (*plural* **pobloedd**) *noun, feminine*
= people
   faint o °**bobol** sy 'ma, ti'n meddwl? = how many people are here, do you think?
   wyth o °**bobol** yn unig ymgeisiodd = only eight people applied
   °**bobol bach!** = goodness me!

> **!** *This word is plural in sense, but behaves as a feminine singular, undergoing soft mutation after* **y** *and mutating a following adjective:* **y** °**bobol** °**garedig 'na** *those kind people. The plural* **pobloedd** *means 'peoples'.*

poblogaeth (*plural* **-au**) *noun, feminine*
= population

poblogaidd *adjective*
= popular
   p'un o'r trefi 'ma ydy'r un °**fwya poblogaidd** gyda twristiaid? = which of these towns is the most popular with tourists?

pobydd (*plural* **-ion**) *noun, masculine*
= baker

poced (*plural* **-i**) *noun, feminine*
= pocket
yn 'y ⁿmhoced oedd hi trwy'r amser =
it was in my pocket all the time
dewch â'ch arian poced! = bring your
pocket money!

poen (*plural* **-au**) *noun, masculine or
feminine*
= pain (*also figurative*)
on'd ydy bywyd yn °boen? = isn't life a
pain?

poeni *verbnoun*
= worry, bother
paid poeni! = don't worry!
**mae hyn wedi bod yn 'y ⁿmhoeni fi ers
amser** = this has been bothering me
for some time
⇒**gofidio**, ⇒**pryderu**, ⇒**becso**

poenus *adjective*
= painful
ydy'r °ben-glin yn °boenus? = is the
knee painful?

poeri *verbnoun*
= spit

poeth *adjective*
comparative **poethach**, *superlative*
poetha(f)
= hot
mi °fydd hi'n °boeth iawn heddiw = it
will be very hot today
pwylla, mae'r tegell yn °boeth! = watch
out, the kettle's hot!
⇒**twym**

polisi (*plural* **polisïau**) *noun, masculine*
= policy
**mae gan y Cyngor °bolisi cyfle
cyfartal** = the Council has an equal
opportunities policy

pont (*plural* **-ydd**) *noun, feminine*
= bridge
**ewch dros y °bont 'na, ac mi °welwch
chi hi ar y chwith** = go over that
bridge, and you'll see it on the left
**wrth °gwrs °fod codi tai a ʰphontydd
°gryn °dipyn yn haws na ʰchodi
pontydd gwleidyddol** = of course,
building houses and bridges is quite a
bit easier than building political
bridges
a °fo ben, bid °bont (*proverb*) = he who
would be a leader, let him be a bridge

popeth *pronoun*
= everything; all
popeth yn iawn? = everything OK?
**roedd popeth wedi'i °drefnu ymlaen
llaw** = everything had been arranged
in advance
ydy popeth yn °barod? = is everything
ready?
lle i °bopeth, a ʰphopeth yn ei °le = a
place for everything, and everything
in its place
⇒**(y) cwbwl**, ⇒**(y) cyfan**, ⇒**i gyd** ⇒**pob
dim**

popty (*plural* **poptai**) *noun, masculine*
= oven

porfa (*plural* **porfeydd**) *noun, feminine*
= pasture, grazing land

pori *verbnoun*
= graze

porthladd (*plural* **-oedd**) *noun,
masculine*
• = port
un o °borthladdoedd mwya Prydain =
one of Britain's biggest ports
• = harbour

porthor (*plural* **-ion**) *noun, masculine*
= porter

posib *adjective*
= possible
**fe °fydd hi'n °bosib darlledu rhaglenni
Saesneg hefyd** = it will be possible to
broadcast English (language)
programmes as well

posibilrwydd *noun, masculine*
= possibility
**fe °allan nhw wynebu'r posibilrwydd o
°golli'r hawl i °dderbyn llythyrau** =
they may face the possibility of losing
the right to receive letters

postio *verbnoun*
= post, put in the post

postmon, postman (*plural*
postmyn, postman) *noun, masculine*
= postman

potel (*plural* **-i**) *noun, feminine*
= bottle
°ga i °dair potel o °laeth? = can I have
three bottles of milk?

powdwr *noun, masculine*
= powder

powdwr golchi = washing powder

powlen (*plural* **-ni**) *noun, feminine*
= bowl, basin

prawf (*plural* **profion**) *noun, masculine*
• = test
 naeth o °fethu ei °brawf gyrru = he
 failed his driving test
• = trial
 **rhaid cofio °fod y moddion 'ma'n dal
 ar °brawf** = it must be remembered
 that this medicine is still on trial

pregeth (*plural* **-au**) *noun, feminine*
= sermon

pregethu *verbnoun*
 = preach
 pregethu i'r cadwedig ych chi fan'na =
 you're preaching to the converted
 there

pregethwr (*plural* **pregethwyr**) *noun,
masculine*
= preacher

preifat *adjective*
= private
 ffordd °breifat—dim troi na °pharcio =
 private road—no turning or parking

preifateiddio *verbnoun*
= privatize

preifatrwydd *noun, masculine*
= privacy

pren *noun, masculine*
• = wood, timber
 **ydy hwn wedi'i °wneud o °bren neu
 °beidio, 'te?** = is this made of wood or
 not, then?
• (*as adjective*) = wooden
 ceffyl pren Troea = the Trojan horse
⇒**coed**

pres *noun, masculine* (*North*)
= money
 oes gen ti °ddigon o °bres? = have you
 got enough money?

> **!** *This is the normal term for* 'money' *in
> Northern areas, while* ⇒**arian** *is
> found in the South, and always in the
> standard language.*

presennol *adjective*
• = present
 ydy pawb yn °bresennol? = is everyone
 present?

• (*as noun, masculine*) = (the) present
 **meddwl am y presennol sy eisiau yn
 hytrach na breuddwydio am y
 gorffennol** = thinking about the
 present is what's needed rather than
 dreaming about the past

presenoldeb *noun, masculine*
= presence

preswyl
⇒**neuadd**

preswylfa (*plural* **preswylfeydd**)
noun, feminine
= dwelling; abode

pridd *noun, masculine*
= earth, soil
⇒**daear**

prif° *adjective*
• = main, chief
• = primary
 beth yw prif °ddiddordebau'ch plant?
 = what are your children's main
 interests?
 **mae'r prif °reswm am hyn oll yn
 °gwbwl amlwg, wedyn i** = the main
 reason for all this is perfectly obvious,
 I would say

> **!** *This adjective precedes the noun
> and causes soft mutation.*

prifathrawes (*plural* **-au**) *noun,
feminine*
= (female) headteacher, headmistress
⇒**athrawes**

prifathro (*plural* **prifathrawon**) *noun,
masculine*
= (male) headteacher, headmaster
⇒**athro**

prifddinas (*plural* **-oedd**) *noun,
feminine*
= capital (city)
 Caerdydd ydy prifddinas Cymru =
 Cardiff is the capital of Wales
 wythnos o °ddathlu yn y °brifddinas
 = a week of celebrations in the
 capital
⇒**dinas**

priffordd (*plural* **priffyrdd**) *noun,
feminine*
• = highway
• = motorway
⇒**ffordd**

prifysgol (*plural* **-ion**) *noun, feminine*
= university
mae'r °ddau am °fynd i'r °Brifysgol wedyn = they both want to go to University afterwards
⇒**ysgol**

prin
1 *adjective*
= scarce; short
mae adnoddau'n °brin ofnadwy ar hyn o °bryd, 'chwel = resources are awfully short at the moment, you see
2 *adverb*
= scarcely, hardly

> **!** *Unlike English, this qualifying adverb is used with a following 'that' subordinate clause in Welsh*

prin y byddai yna amser i egluro = there would scarcely be time to explain
prin y gallwn i °gadw'n °dawel = I could hardly keep quiet
prin ⁿmod i'n cofio nhw nawr = I hardly remember them now
prin °fod angen dweud bod ni'n byw mewn cyfnod tyngedfennol = it scarcely needs to be said that we are living at a fateful time

prinder (*plural* **-au**) *noun, masculine*
= lack, shortage
prinder arian, wrth °gwrs, yw'r °broblem °fwya = lack of money, of course, is the biggest problem

prinhau *verbnoun*
= become scarce

priod *adjective*
= married (**â**ʰ/**ag** to)
dych chi'n °briod? = are you married?
roedd hi eisoes yn °briod â dyn arall = she was already married to another man

priodas (*plural* **-au**) *noun, feminine*
• = marriage
• = wedding

priodi *verbnoun*
= marry, get married (*takes either* **â**ʰ/**ag** *or direct object*)
priodi â rhywun *or* **priodi rhywun** = to get married to someone.
nest ti °briodi â'r °ferch drws nesa, 'te? = you married the girl next door, then?

naethon ni °briodi °ddeugain ⁿmlynedd yn ôl = we got married forty years ago

priodol *adjective*
• = proper
• = appropriate
gofynnir i chi °roi tic yn y blwch priodol = you are requested to put a tick in the appropriate box

pris (*plural* **-iau**) *noun, masculine*
= price
beth ydy pris y rheina? = what's the price of those?
edrychwch ar ein prisiau! = look at our prices!

problem (*plural* **-au**) *noun, feminine*
= problem
ydy hyn yn mynd i °fod yn °broblem i chi? = is this going to be a problem for you?
mae un °broblem yn dal heb ei datrys = there is one problem still unsolved

profedigaeth *noun, feminine*
= bereavement

profi *verbnoun*
• = prove
dyfarnwyd °fod y cyhuddiadau eraill heb eu profi = it was ruled that the other charges were not proved
• = try, sample
wyt ti'n moyn profi'r hyn sy 'da fi? = do you want to try what I've got?

profiad (*plural* **-au**) *noun, masculine*
= experience
siarad am 'y ⁿmhrofiadau 'n hunan ydw i nawr, cofiwch = I'm speaking about my own experiences now, mind

profiadol *adjective*
= experienced
mae'r cwrs wedi'i anelu at °ddysgwyr profiadol yn unig = the course is aimed at experienced learners only

proffwyd (*plural* **-i**) *noun, masculine*
= prophet

proffwydo *verbnoun*
= prophesy

proffwydoliaeth (*plural* **-au**) *noun, feminine*
= prophecy

proses (*plural* **-au**) *noun, masculine or feminine*
= process

prosesu *verbnoun*
= process

prosesydd geiriau (*plural* **prosesyddion geiriau**) *noun, masculine*
= word processor

prosiect, project (*plural* **-au**) *noun, masculine*
= project

protest (*plural* **-au**) *noun, masculine*
= protest
dywedodd llefarydd y byddai'r protest yn parhau = a spokesman said the protest would continue

protestio *verbnoun*
= protest
yn ni'n gorfod protestio yn erbyn y °dreth anghyfiawn 'ma = we have to protest against this unjust tax

protestiwr (*plural* **protestwyr**) *noun, masculine*
= protester

p'r un? *variant of*
pa un?
= which one?

pry copyn *noun, masculine*
⇒**pry(f)**

pryd?
1 *adverb*
= when?

! *This word is used for* 'when?' *in questions, while (in the standard language at least)* ⇒**pan°** *is required for statements. Compare:*
pryd maen nhw'n dod? = when are they coming?
oedd hi'n bwrw glaw pan °ddaethon nhw = it was raining when they came
But colloquial usage often allows **pryd** *in statements also:*
oedd hi'n bwrw glaw pryd daethon nhw
Note, however, that **pan°** *can never be used for the question* 'when?'.
Further examples:
pryd mae'r trên yn mynd? = when does the train go?
pryd byddet ti'n gwneud y gwaith? = when would you do the work?

ffonia a gofyn pryd mae'r cyngerdd yn dechrau = phone and ask when the concert starts
Note that after **pryd** *the third person singular and plural of* **bod** *is always* **mae, maen**, *and never* **ydy, ydyn**.

2 (*plural* **-iau**) *noun, masculine*
= time
ar hyn o °bryd = at the moment
ar °brydiau = at times
°bryd hynny = at that time, then
o °bryd i'w gilydd = from time to time
ar y pryd = at the time; simultaneous(ly)
mewn pryd = in time
mae'r marchnadoedd yn °dawel ar hyn o °bryd = the markets are quiet at the moment
mi °all y tirlun yma °drych yn °drist braidd ar °brydiau = this landscape can look rather sad at times
doedd dim llawer yn y siopau °bryd hynny, wrth °gwrs = there wasn't much in the shops then, of course
gobeithio y byddwn ni mewn pryd = I hope we'll be in time

3 (*plural* **-au**) *noun, masculine*
= meal

! *In the sense of* 'meal' (*note different plural*), **pryd** *usually appears as a longer phrase* **pryd o °fwyd**:
mae'n °bwysig bod nhw'n cael pryd o °fwyd °gynta = it's important that they have a meal first

Prydain *noun, masculine*
= Britain
Prydain °Fawr = Great Britain

Prydeinig *adjective*
= British

pryder (*plural* **-on**) *noun, masculine*
• = worry, fear
olew Cymreig—y gobeithion a'r pryderon = Welsh oil—the hopes and the fears
• = anxiety
mae cryn °dipyn o °bryder wedi bod = there has been quite a bit of anxiety

pryderu *verbnoun*
= worry
⇒**gofidio**, ⇒**poeni**, ⇒**becso**

prydferth *adjective*
= beautiful
mae rhannau o °Gymru'n °brydferth iawn = parts of Wales are very beautiful

prydferthwch *noun, masculine*
= beauty

prydlon *adjective*
= punctual; on time
dw i eisiau i chi i gyd °gyrraedd yn °brydlon = I want you all to arrive on time
peryglir y grant os na ʰchyhoeddir yn °brydlon = delayed publication will jeopardize the grant

prydlondeb *noun, masculine*
= punctuality

pry(f) (*plural* **pryfed**) *noun, masculine*
= insect

> ❗ *This is the general term in speech for small creatures, particularly insects and bugs. Note also* **pry copyn** *spider. A more specific technical term* **trychfilyn** (*plural* **trychfilod** *is used for* 'insect' *in more formal contexts.*

prynhawn (*often* **pnawn** *in speech*) (*plural* **-iau**) *noun, masculine*
= afternoon
°wela i di pnawn 'ma! = I'll see you this afternoon!
bydd y stondin ar agor prynhawn yfory = the stall will be open tomorrow afternoon
°gwrddes i ag e prynhawn (dydd) Llun = I met him on Monday afternoon

prynu *verbnoun*
= buy, purchase
°ga i °brynu diod i ti? = can I buy you a drink?
mi °brynodd e'r cyfan = he bought the lot

prysur *adjective*
= busy
lleolir yr Eisteddfod eleni wrth ochr ffordd °brysur yr A55 = this year the Eisteddfod is located beside the busy A55 road

pumed *adjective* (*precedes noun*)
= fifth

ymhellach i'ch llythyr dyddiedig y pumed o °Fai... = further to your letter dated the fifth of May...

> ❗ *Ordinal numerals are adjectives, but behave in a special way. All other than* ⇒**cynta** *precede the noun. With feminine singular nouns, the noun itself undergoes soft mutation, as does the ordinal after the article—so:* **y pumed dyn** *the fifth man but* **y °bumed °ferch** *the fifth girl.*

pum(p) *numeral*
= five
dim ond papur pum punt sy gen i = I've only got a five pound note
Faint o °lyfrau sy 'da chi fan'na?— Pump = How many books have you got there?—Five
mae pum llyfr ar y bwrdd *or* **mae pump o °lyfrau ar y bwrdd** = there are five books on the table

> ❗ *This numeral has the form* **pum** *when directly followed by the noun, otherwise it is* **pump**. *As with all low cardinal numerals there are two constructions: either [numeral + singular] or [numeral +* **o°** *+ plural] (see third example above). So, similarly, 'five men' is either* **pum dyn** *or* **pump o° ddynion**.

p'un? *variant of*
pa un?
= which one?

punnoedd, punnau *plural of*
⇒**punt**

punt (*plural* **punnoedd** *or* **punnau**) *noun, feminine*
= pound
mae arnat ti °ddeg punt i mi = you owe me ten pounds
dwy °bunt a hanner can ceiniog os gwelwch yn °dda = two pounds fifty pence please
achoswyd gwerth pum mil o °bunnoedd o °ddifrod = five thousand pounds' worth of damage was caused

> ❗ *Note these terms for amounts of money:* **punt a hanner** £1.50, **dwy °bunt a hanner** £2.50, **ugain punt** £20, **deugain punt** £40, **hanner can punt** £50, **can punt** *or* **cant o**

°**bunnoedd/°bunnau** £100, **dau °gan punt** or **dau °gant o °bunnoedd/°bunnau** £200, **mil o °bunnoedd/°bunnau** £1000, **miliwn o °bunnoedd/°bunnau** £1,000,000.

⇨**pwys**

pupur noun, masculine
= pepper

pur° adverb
= quite

pwdu verbnoun
= sulk
a does dim pwynt i ti °bwdu felly, nag oes? = and there's no point in you sulking like that, is there?

pŵer (plural **-au**) noun, masculine
= power

> **!** Used generally in the sense of 'wielded' power (like ⇨**grym**), but also sometimes for 'energy' in a very broad sense.

⇨**nerth**

pwerdy (plural **pwerdai**) noun, masculine
= power station

pwerus adjective
= powerful

pwll (plural **pyllau**) noun, masculine
= pool

pwll nofio (plural **pyllau nofio**) noun, masculine
= swimming pool

pwnc (plural **pynciau**) noun, masculine
= subject; topic
ceir darlithoedd ar °wahanol °bynciau = there will be lectures on various topics
pwnc llosg (plural **pynciau llosg**) = burning issue
pwnc trafod (plural **pynciau trafod**) = subject for discussion

⇨**testun**

pwnio verbnoun
= thump, hit
mi °bwnia i fe! = I'll thump him!

pwrpas (plural **-au**) noun, masculine
= purpose
beth yn union ydy pwrpas y °gynhadledd 'ma? = what exactly is the purpose of this convention?

o °bwrpas = deliberately, on purpose
⇨**pwrpasol**

pwrpasol adjective
= deliberate
yn °bwrpasol = deliberately, on purpose
nest ti hynny'n °bwrpasol, on'do? = you did that on purpose, didn't you?

⇨**bwriadol**

pwy?

1 pronoun
= who?; whom?
pwy aeth efo chi? = who went with you?
pwy oedd yn eistedd yma gynnau? = who was sitting here just now?
pwy °fydd yn ennill?, pwy enillith? = who will win?

> **!** When the subject of the sentence (as with the subject generally in Welsh), **pwy** is followed by soft mutation:
> **pwy °dorrodd y ffenest 'ma?** = who broke this window?
> In more formal style this word is followed by ⇨**(a)°** particle: **pwy a °dorrodd...?**
> **lle maen nhw bellach?—pwy a °ŵyr?** = Where are they now?—Who knows?
> This question word (like ⇨**beth?,** ⇨**faint?, pa un?** and **pa °rai?**) is followed in the present tense (and **wedi**-perfect tense) by **ydy** in identification sentences, and otherwise **sy** when the subject and **mae** when the object of the sentence. Compare the following:
> **pwy ydy'r dyn 'na?** = who is that man? (identification)
> **pwy sy'n dod i'r parti?** = who is coming to the party? ('Who' is the subject of the sentence)
> **pwy mae Alun yn helpu?** = who(m) is Alun helping? ('Who' is the object of the sentence, 'Alun' the subject)
> The erroneous 'rule' about not ending a sentence with a preposition in English is nonetheless valid for Welsh, which does not allow free-standing prepositions:
> **i °bwy mae'r llythyr 'ma?** = who is this letter for?
> **es i allan neithiwr—gyda pwy?** = I went out last night—who with?

at °bwy mae'r rhaglen 'ma wedi'i hanelu'n °benna? = who is this programme mainly aimed at?

It is important to remember that **pwy?** *is a question word, and so cannot be used for the other (relative) meaning of* 'who' *in English*—⇒**(a)°** *particle,* ⇒**sy(dd):**

pwy °daflodd y °bêl? = who threw the ball?

dyna'r °ferch (a) °daflodd y °bêl = there's the girl who threw the ball
Not: *Dyna'r °ferch pwy °daflodd y °bêl

pwy sy'n mynd heno? = who is going tonight?

dyna'r dyn sy'n mynd heno = there's the man who is going tonight
Not: *Dyna'r dyn pwy sy'n mynd heno
Not: *Dyna'r dyn pwy yn mynd heno

2 (pwy°) *adjective (South)*
= which?; what...?

> **!** *This word is used colloquially in the South for* ⇒**pa°:**
> **pwy °lyfr dych chi'n moyn?** = which book do you want?

pwy bynnag *pronoun*
= whoever
pwy bynnag ydyn nhw, dw i ddim eisiau gweld nhw = whoever they are, I don't want to see them

pwyll *noun, masculine*
• = sense
• = judgment
• **gan °bwyll**
  = carefully does it
  = hang on a minute
  gan °bwyll...paid ti â ʰchwympo = carefully does it...don't you fall
  gan °bwyll nawr, mae'n debyg o °fod dan y papurau 'ma = hang on a minute now, it's probably under these papers

pwyllgor (*plural* **-au**) *noun, masculine*
= committee
bydd y pwyllgor yn cwrdd eto °ddiwedd mis Mawrth = the committee will meet again at the end of March

pwyllo *verbnoun*
usually in the imperative **pwylla!,**

pwyllwch! look out!; be careful!
pwylla, neu mi °fyddi di'n cwympo! = be careful, or you'll fall!

pwynt (*plural* **-iau**) *noun, masculine*
= point
gêm °gyffrous, gydag Iwerddon yn ennill tri ʰphwynt = an exciting game, with Ireland winning three points
does dim pwynt cwyno, nag oes? = there's no point complaining, is there?
naw pwynt wyth miliwn o °bunnoedd oedd y °brif °wobr neithiwr = the jackpot was nine point eight million pounds last night

pwys (*plural* **-au**) *noun, masculine*
• = pound
  °ga i °ddau °bwys o °foron os gwelwch yn °dda? = can I have two pounds of carrots please?
  Faint yw'r caws 'na?—Punt a hanner y pwys = How much is that cheese?— One pound fifty per pound
⇒**punt**
• (*usually in plural*) = weight
  mae hi wedi dechrau ennill pwysau o'r diwedd = she's started putting on weight at last
  os dych chi am °golli pwysau... = if you want to lose weight...
• (*usually in plural*) = pressure
  bydd y llywodraeth yn dwyn pwysau arnyn nhw = the government will bring pressure on them
  o °bwys = important
  pobol o °bwys = important people, VIPs

pwysig *adjective*
comparative **pwysicach,** *superlative* **pwysica(f)**
= important
dych chi'n credu °fod hyn yn °bwysig, 'te? = do you think that this is important, then?
mae'n °bwysicach nag erioed i chi °ddefnyddio'r côd post cywir = it's more important than ever for you to use the correct post code

pwysigrwydd *noun, masculine*
= importance

pwyslais *noun, masculine*
= emphasis; stress

hoffwn i °fod wedi gweld tipyn mwy o
°bwyslais ar ei °flynyddoedd cynnar
= I would have liked to see a little more
emphasis on his early years

rhaid rhoi pwyslais ar y °ddau °air fel
ei gilydd = both words must be
stressed alike

pwysleisio *verbnoun*
= emphasize, stress

ond mi °bwysleisiodd mai ateb dros
°dro oedd hwn = but he emphasized
that this was (only) a temporary
solution

pwyso *verbnoun*
• = weigh

dylai eitemau ail °ddosbarth °beidio â
ʰphwyso mwy na **750g** = second class
items should not weigh more than
750g

na i °bwyso nhw i chi = I'll weigh them
for you

• = lean (**ar**° on; **yn erbyn** against)

bydd rhaid pwyso arno, on' bydd? =
he'll have to be leant on, won't he?

pwyth (*plural* **-au, -i**) *noun, masculine*
= stitch

talu'r pwyth (**yn ôl**) = retaliate, pay back

mi °dala i'r pwyth = I'll get my own back

pydredd *noun, masculine*
= rot; rottenness

pydru
• *verbnoun* = rot, go rotten

mae'r afalau 'ma wedi pydru = these
apples have gone rotten

• **wedi pydru** (*as adjective*) = rotten

afalau wedi pydru = rotten apples

pyllau *plural of*
⇨**pwll**

pymtheg *numeral*
= fifteen

> **!** *This is the native term for* 'fifteen',
> *while a 'decimalized' form* **undeg**
> **pump** *is promoted in schools. An*
> *alternative form* **pymtheng** *is used in*
> *the same circumstances as is* **deng**
> *for* ⇨**deg**.

pynciau *plural of*
⇨**pwnc**

pysgod *plural of*
⇨**pysgodyn**

pysgodyn (*plural* **pysgod**) *noun,*
masculine
= fish

mae pysgodyn diddorol arall yn dod
i'r cyffiniau hyn °bob haf = another
interesting fish comes to these parts
every summer

pa °fath o °bysgod sy gynnoch chi
heddiw? = what kind of fish have you
got today?

pysgod a sglodion = fish and chips

pysgota *verbnoun*
= fish

pysgotwr (*plural* **pysgotwyr**) *noun,*
masculine
= fisherman

pythefnos (*plural* **-au**) *noun,*
masculine or feminine
= fortnight

°fasai pythefnos i heddiw'n °gyfleus i
chi? = would a fortnight today be
convenient for you?

maen nhw wedi mynd i'r Eidal am
°bythefnos = they've gone to Italy for a
fortnight

'r
⇒**y** *definite article*

radicalaidd *adjective*
= radical
⇒**sylfaenol**

radio (*plural* **-s**) *noun, masculine or feminine*
= radio
°**allet ti °droi'r radio i lawr ychydig?** = could you turn the radio down a bit?
bydda i'n gwrando ar y radio bron °bob prynhawn = I listen to the radio almost every afternoon

ras (*plural* **-ys**) *noun, feminine*
= race

rasio *verbnoun*
= race
rasia i di'n ôl! = I'll race you back!

real *adjective*
= real

> **!** *This loanword is of restricted use in speech.*

⇒**go iawn,** ⇒ **gwirioneddol**

record (*plural* **-iau**) *noun, feminine*
= record (*sport, music*)
mae hi wedi torri record y byd = she's broken the world record
bydd eu record newydd yn y siopau erbyn y Dolig = their new record will be in the shops by Christmas

recordydd (*plural* **-ion**) *noun, masculine*
= recorder
recordydd fideo (*plural* **recordyddion fideo**) = video recorder
recordydd tâp (*plural* **recordyddion tâp**) = tape recorder

reit° *adverb*
= quite; really
mae hwnna'n edrych yn reit °dda, a dweud y gwir = that looks really good, actually

rinc (*plural* **-iau**) *noun, feminine*
= rink

rinc iâ (*plural* **rinciau iâ**) *noun, feminine*
= ice rink

roced (*plural* **-i**) *noun, feminine*
= rocket

roedd, roeddwn, roeddet, roeddech, roedden
⇒**bod**

rôl (*plural* **rolau**) *noun, feminine*
= rôle
efallai y bydd gynni hi rôl i'w chwarae hefyd = perhaps she will also have a rôle to play

rownd
1 (*plural* **-iau**) *noun, feminine*
= round (*in competition, etc*)
rownd °derfynol Cwpan y Byd = the final round of the World Cup
2 *adverb*
= round

> **!** *As an adverb, mostly in the phrase* **rownd y °gornel** *round the corner.* ⇒**o °gwmpas** *or* ⇒**o amgylch** *are the normal terms for* 'round'.

ruban (*plural* **-au**) *noun, masculine*
= ribbon

rwan, rŵan (*often* **wan** *in rapid speech*) *adverb* (*North*)
= now

> **!** *This word corresponds to Southern and standard* ⇒**nawr.**

rwan 'ta, be' sy'n digwydd fan'ma? = now then, what's happening here?
dw i eisiau fo, ac dw i eisiau fo rwan! = I want it, and I want it now!
rwan °fod o wedi dŵad, mi °gawn ni °ddechrau = now that he's here, we can start
dach chi'n bwriadu mynd rwan? = do you plan to go now?
⇒**bellach**

rwber (*plural* **-i**) *noun, masculine*
= rubber (*material, eraser*)

rysáit (*plural* **ryseitiau**) *noun, feminine*
= recipe

RHrh

rhad *adjective*
  comparative **rhatach**, *superlative*
    rhata(f)
  = cheap
  mae bron popeth yn rhatach fan hyn =
    almost everything is cheaper here
  yn rhad ac am °ddim = free, gratis
  **ffoniwch y cysylltydd yn rhad ac am
    °ddim ar 100** = phone the operator free
    on 100

rhaeadr (*plural* **-au**) *noun, feminine*
  = waterfall

rhaff (*plural* **-au**) *noun, feminine*
  = rope

rhag *preposition*
  = from; against (*mostly with verbs of
    stopping, preventing, hindering,
    sheltering, etc*)
  **rhaid atal peth mor erchyll rhag
    digwydd eto** = such a horrible thing
    must be stopped from happening
    again
  **byddwn ni'n rhwystro nhw rhag
    gwneud hynny** = we will prevent them
    from doing that
  lloches rhag y gwynt = shelter from
    the wind

rhag°- *prefix*
  = fore-; pre-
  rhagair *noun, masculine*
  = foreword
  (⇒**gair**)
  rhagddweud *verbnoun*
  = foretell
  (⇒**dweud**)
  rhagweld *verbnoun*
  = foresee
  (⇒**gweld**)
  rhagfarnllyd *adjective*
  = prejudiced
  (⇒**barn**)
  rhagflas *noun, masculine*
  = foretaste
  (⇒**blas**)
  rhagrybuddio *verbnoun*
  = forewarn
  (⇒**rhybudd**)

rhagymadrodd *noun, masculine*
  = preface
  (⇒**ymadrodd**)

rhagarweiniad (*plural* **-au**) *noun,
  masculine*
  = introduction

rhagarweiniol *adjective*
  = introductory; prefatory

rhagenw (*plural* **-au**) *noun, masculine*
  = pronoun

rhagfarn (*plural* **-au**) *noun, feminine*
  = prejudice

Rhagfyr *noun, masculine*
  = December
⇒**Ionawr**

rhaglen (*plural* **-ni**) *noun, feminine*
• = programme
  **hon yw'r rhaglen °deledu °waetha ym
    ⁿMhrydain erioed** = this is the worst
    television programme ever in Britain
  **mae rhaglen o °fesurau wedi'i llunio
    gan yr adran** = a programme of
    measures has been drawn up by the
    department
• = (computer) program
  **ond roedd y rhaglen 'na'n llawn
    gwallau, on'd oedd?** = but that
    program was full of bugs, wasn't it?

rhaglennu *verbnoun*
• = programme
• = (*computer*) program

rhagolwg (*plural* **rhagolygon**) *noun,
  masculine*
• = outlook; prospect
• (*often plural*) = forecast
  **dyma °ragolygon y tywydd am heno
    ac yfory** = here is the weather forecast
    for tonight and tomorrow

rhagor *adverb*
  = more
  leiciech chi °ragor? = would you like
    (some) more?
  mae rhagor ar y ffordd = more is on the
    way
  dw i °ddim eisiau clywed rhagor! = I
    don't want to hear (any) more!
  **unwaith yn rhagor os gwelwch yn
    °dda** = once more please

  ! *As a quantity expression,* **rhagor**
  requires a following **o°** *when a noun is
  specified:*

oes rhagor o °goffi ar °gael? = is there (any) more coffee available?

ceisiwch °feddwl am °ragor o enghreifftiau o °ragrith yn y nofel = try and think of more examples of hypocrisy in the novel

⇒chwaneg, chwanag, ⇒mwy *adverb*

rhagori *verbnoun*
= be better (**ar°** than), be superior (**ar°** to)

does dim caws ym ⁿMhrydain yn rhagori ar °gaws Caerffili = no cheese in Britain is better than Caerphilly cheese

rhagorol *adjective*
= excellent; preeminent

rhagrith *noun, masculine*
= hypocrisy

rhagrithiol *adjective*
= hypocritical

rhagrithiwr (*plural* **rhagrithwyr**) *noun, masculine*
= hypocrite

rhai

1 *pronoun*
= ones; some

> **!** *As a pronoun, **rhai** functions as the plural of ⇒**un***

°well gen i'r rhai coch = I prefer the red ones

pa °rai leiciet ti? = which ones would you like?

mae rhai yn meddwl felly, ond dim fi = some think so, but not me

mae rhai ar ôl, wi'n credu = there are some left, I think

2 *adjective*
= some

casgliad o storïau, rhai hen a rhai newydd, o °Gernyw = a collection of stories, some old (ones) and some new (ones), from Cornwall

oedd rhai pobol yn dal i °ddadlau mai buddugoliaeth oedd hi = some people were still arguing that it was a victory

⇒(y) rhain, ⇒(y) rheiny, (y) rheina, ⇒rhyw°

rhaid *noun, masculine*

> **!** *The most common use of **rhaid** is to express obligation in the construction*

rhaid + i° + [*subject*] + °[*verbnoun*]— *literally* '(There is) a necessity for [*subject*] to [*action*]'. *So, for example,* **rhaid i Alun °fynd** Alun must go, Alun has to go. **Mae** (*or even* **mae'n**) *is optional before* **rhaid**. *Notice that* **does dim rhaid** *means* '...need not...', *while* '... must not...' *is* **rhaid i** [*subject*] °**beidio** [*action*]

• (*expressing obligation*) = must; have to
(mae) rhaid i mi °fynd = I must go, I have to go

oes rhaid i mi °fynd? = must I go?, do I have to go?

does dim rhaid i mi °fynd = I need not go, I don't have to go

(mae) rhaid i mi °beidio mynd = I must not go

rhaid i mi a ʰphawb arall °gyfadde fod camgymeriadau wedi'u gwneud = I and everyone else must admit that mistakes have been made

rhaid i mi'ch atgoffa chi mai chi'n sy'n °gyfrifol am hyn = I must remind you that (it is) you (who) are responsible for this

> **!** *Other tenses are possible with* **rhaid**:
> **roedd rhaid iddyn nhw °fynd** = they had to go
> **oedd rhaid iddyn nhw °fynd?** = did they have to go?
> **doedd dim rhaid iddyn nhw °fynd** = they didn't have to go
> **bydd rhaid iddyn nhw °fynd** = they'll have to go
> °**fydd rhaid iddyn nhw °fynd?** = will they have to go?
> °**fydd dim rhaid iddyn nhw °fynd** = they won't have to go
> **byddai/basai rhaid iddyn nhw °fynd** = they would have to go
> °**fyddai/°fasai rhaid iddyn nhw °fynd?** = would they have to go?
> °**fyddai/°fasai dim rhaid iddyn nhw °fynd** = they would not have to go
> *In this primary sense of obligation,* ⇒**gorfod** *is a synonym for* **rhaid**, *but note that* **gorfod** *is a verbnoun not a noun like* **rhaid**, *and so has a different construction. Compare:*
> **rhaid iddyn nhw °fynd**
> **maen nhw'n gorfod mynd** = they have to go

• (*expressing supposition*) = **must**

> ❗ '*Must*' *can also imply supposition in English—'you must be mad!'* means *not* 'You are obliged to be mad,' *but rather* 'I suppose that you are mad'. *In Welsh,* **rhaid** *is used in these cases as well (note that* **gorfod** *is not), but with a different construction:* **rhaid** + '*that ...*' *clause. Compare:*
> **rhaid iddi °fod fan hyn** = she must *or* has to be here (*she is obliged to be*)
> **rhaid bod hi fan hyn** = she must be here (*I'm sure she is, because she can't be anywhere else*)

rhaid bod rhywbeth o'i °le = something must be wrong

rhaid bod nhw'n aros tan yfory = they must be waiting till tomorrow

rhaid mai Gwilym sy'n °gyfrifol wedi'r cwbwl = it must be that Gwilym is responsible after all

• (*as true noun*) = **need** (**wrth**° of)
mae'n rhaid wrth yr arian er mwyn sicrhau dyfodol y °Ganolfan = the money is needed in order to secure the Centre's future

angen, ⇒**eisiau**

(y) rhain *pronoun*
= **these (ones)**

> ❗ *This pronoun serves as the plural of* ⇒**hwn** *pronoun and* ⇒**hon** *pronoun*
> **faint yw'r rhain?** = how much are these?
> **°ddo i â'r rhain wedyn** = I'll bring these later
> *Note that 'these ...' used as an adjective with a following noun—for example 'these books'—is* ⇒**y ... 'ma.** *Compare:*
> **beth am y llyfrau 'ma?** = what about these books?
> **beth am y rhain?** = what about these?
>   *The pronoun* **y rhain** *is used on its own when no noun is stated. The word is a contraction of* **(y) rhai hyn** '*these ones*'.

⇒**y ... 'ma**

rhamantus *adjective*
= **romantic**

rhan (*plural* -nau) *noun, feminine*
= **part**

o °ba °ran o °Gymru dych chi'n dod? = what part of Wales do you come from?

mae'n rhan o'n hetifeddiaeth, on'd ydy? = it's part of our heritage, isn't it?

y rhan °fwya(f) = the majority, most:
mae'r rhan °fwya'n °debygol o °bleidleisio yn erbyn = most are likely to vote against

rhan amla = mostly:
dyn ni'n mynd i'r sinema rhan amla = mostly we go to the cinema

⇒**ar °ran**, ⇒**o °ran**

rhanbarth (*plural* -au) *noun, masculine*
= **region, district**

rhanbarthol *adjective*
= **regional, district**

rhandaliad (*plural* -au) *noun, masculine*
= **instalment**

rhaniad (*plural* -au) *noun, masculine*
= **division**

rhannol *adjective*
= **partial**
yn rhannol = partly, partially:
mae hyn wedi digwydd yn rhannol o °ganlyniad i °breifateiddio = this has happened partly as a result of privatisation

rhannu *verbnoun*
• = **share**
oedden ni'n rhannu fflat yn Abertawe ar y pryd = we were sharing a flat in Swansea at the time
• = **divide** (**yn**° into)
bydd eisiau ei °rannu'n °gyfartal = it will have to be divided equally

rhathu *verbnoun*
= **scrape**

rhaw (*plural* -iau, rhofiau) *noun, feminine*
= **spade, shovel**

rhechen, rhech (*plural* rhechod) *noun, feminine*
= **fart**

rhechu, rhechain *verbnoun*
= **fart**

rhedeg (*stem* rhed-) *verbnoun*
= **run**

rhedwch ar ei ôl e! = run after him!
peiriant sy'n rhedeg ar olew = a machine that runs on oil
pwy °fydd yn rhedeg y cwmni wedyn? = who will be running the company then?

rheg (*plural* **-feydd**) *noun, feminine*
= swearword

rhegi *verbnoun*
= swear; curse
mae e'n rhegi fel tincer/cath = he swears like a trooper
⇒**tyngu**

rheidrwydd *noun, masculine*
= necessity

rheiddiadur (*plural* **-on**) *noun, masculine*
= radiator

rheilffordd (*plural* **rheilffyrdd**) *noun, feminine*
= railway
beth sy eisiau nawr yw buddsoddi yn y rheilffordd 'ma = what's wanted now is investment in this railway
yr unig lein °fach a °redir gan °Reilffyrdd Prydeinig = the only narrow-gauge line run by British Rail

(y) rheiny, (y) rheina *pronoun*
= those (ones)

> **!** *This pronoun serves as the plural of*
> ⇒**hwnnw/hwnna** *pronoun and*
> ⇒**honno/honna** *pronoun:*
> **faint yw'r rheina?** = how much are those?
> **°ddo i â'r rheiny wedyn** = I'll bring those later
>   *Note that* 'these ...' *used as an adjective with a following noun—for example* those books—*is* ⇒**y ... 'na**. *Compare:*
> **beth am y llyfrau 'na?** = what about those books?
> **beth am y rheina?** = what about those?
>   *The pronoun* **y rheina/rheiny** *is used on its own when no noun is stated. The word is a contraction of* **(y) rhai hynny** 'those ones'.

⇒**y ... 'na**

rheithgor (*plural* **-au**) *noun, masculine*
= jury

rheithiwr (*plural* **rheithwyr**) *noun, masculine*
= juror (male)

rheithwraig (*plural* **rheithwragedd**) *noun, feminine*
= juror (female)

rheol (*plural* **-au**) *noun, feminine*
= rule
byddai hynny'n °groes i'r rheolau = that would be contrary to the rules
mae rheolau'r gêm yn °gymhleth braidd = the rules of the game are rather complicated
y cadeirydd sy'n penderfynu fel rheol = it's the chairman that decides as a rule
mae'n rheol 'da fi bo fi byth yn darllen adolygiadau = I make it a rule never to read reviews

rheolaeth (ar°) *noun, feminine*
= control
rhaid cadw rheolaeth ar ein hymateb emosiynol = we must keep control of our emotional response
mae popeth dan °reolaeth = everything's under control

rheolaidd *adjective*
= regular
mae'r rhan °fwya o'r berfau 'ma'n rheolaidd = most of these verbs are regular
maen nhw'n mynd yno'n rheolaidd = they go there regularly
⇒**cyson**

rheoli *verbnoun*
• = control
rheoli'ch teimladau = control one's feelings
• = manage
rheoli cwmni = manage a company

rheolwr (*plural* **rheolwyr**) *noun, masculine*
= manager
°ga i °wneud apwyntiad i °weld y rheolwr yfory? = can I make an appointment to see the manager tomorrow?

rhes (*plural* **-i, -au**) *noun, feminine*
= row
eisteddwch i gyd yn y rhes °flaen = all of you sit in the front row

rhes o °dai = a row of houses

rhestr (*plural* **-au, -i**) *noun, feminine*
= list
mae gen i °restr °fach fan hyn i'n helpu ni = I've got a little list here to help us
y cwbwl galla i °ddweud ydy'ch bod chi ar y rhestr °fer = all I can say is that you're on the short list

rhestru *verbnoun*
= list, make a list

rheswm (*plural* **rhesymau**) *noun, masculine*
= reason
beth yw'r rheswm am hyn? = what is the reason for this?
mae'n °bwysig am sawl rheswm = it's important for a number of reasons
wrth °reswm = of course

rhesymol *adjective*
= reasonable
mae rhaid inni °fod yn rhesymol = we must be reasonable
nwyddau o ansawdd am °brisiau rhesymol = quality goods at reasonable prices

rhew *noun, masculine*
= frost; ice
mae'r rhew dros °bopeth = the frost has covered everything
⇒**iâ**

rhewgell (*plural* **-oedd**) *noun, feminine*
= freezer
⇒**oergell**

rhewi *verbnoun*
= freeze
mae'n rhewi! = it's freezing!
mae'r dŵr 'ma wedi rhewi = this water has frozen

rhiant
⇒**rhieni**

rhieni *plural noun*
= parents
mae angen rhoi gwybodaeth a ʰchyngor i °rieni = we need to give information and advice to parents

> **!** *A singular form* **rhiant** *noun, masculine is confined largely to writing:*
> **Annwyl °Riant, ...** = Dear Parent, ...

rhif (*plural* **-au**) *noun, masculine*
= number
beth ydy'ch rhif ffôn chi? = what is your phone number?
dw i °ddim yn gwybod rhif eu tŷ nhw = I don't know the number of their house

> **!** *This word implies a written figure in numerals, while* ⇒**nifer** *is used in the broader sense of 'a number (of people, things, etc)'.*

rhifo *verbnoun*
= count
maen nhw'n dysgu rhifo = they're learning how to count
⇒**cyfri(f)** *verbnoun*

rhifyn (*plural* **-nau**) *noun, masculine*
= number (*of a magazine etc*), issue
mae rhifyn y Nadolig yn y siopau nawr! = the Christmas issue is in the shops now!

rhinwedd (*plural* **-au**) *noun, masculine or feminine*
= virtue

rhinweddol *adjective*
= virtuous

rhiw (*plural* **-iau**) *noun, feminine*
• = hill
mewn tŷ ar °droed y rhiw = in a house at the foot *or* bottom of the hill
• = slope
⇒**bryn**, ⇒**mynydd**

rhodfa (*plural* **rhodfeydd**) *noun, feminine*
• = avenue
• = parade

rhodio *verbnoun*
= stroll

rhodd (*plural* **-ion**) *noun, feminine*
= gift, donation
°ges i hwnna'n rhodd = I was given that
⇒**anrheg**

rhoi, rhoid (*stem* **rhoi-, rhodd-**) *verbnoun*
imperative singular **rho**, *plural* **rhowch** *or* **rhoddwch**
• = give

beth am °roi tanysgrifiad fel anrheg i
ffrind? = what about giving a
subscription as a present to a friend?
°roddes i °bum punt iddo = I gave him
five pounds
mi °rodda i fe yn ôl i ti yfory = I'll give it
back to you tomorrow
rho °ganiad inni wythnos nesa = give
us a ring next week
rhoddedig = donated
• = put
**°allet ti °roi'r pethau 'ma ar y bwrdd i
mi?** = could you put these things on
the table for me?
**rhowch y gweddill fan hyn, newch
chi?** = put the rest here, will you?
eu rhoi nhw yn y °fyddin sy eisiau =
they need putting in the army
⇒**gosod**

rholyn (plural **rholion**) noun,
masculine
= (bread) roll

rhonc adjective
= utter; rank; complete

> ! Particularly in the phrase **Saeson
> rhonc** English (people) through-and-
> through—but 'a Welshman through-
> and-through' is **Cymro glân**.

rhos (plural **-ydd**) noun, feminine
• = moor
• = heath

rhosyn (plural **-nau**) noun, masculine
= rose

Rhufain noun, feminine
= Rome

Rhufeinig adjective
= Roman
hen ffordd °Rufeinig yw hon = this is
an old Roman road

Rhufeiniwr (plural **Rhufeinwyr,
Rhufeiniaid**) noun, masculine
= Roman

rhugl adjective
= fluent
ydy hi'n rhugl yn y °Gymraeg? = is she
fluent in Welsh?
**anelir y cwrs at °ddysgwyr heb °fod yn
rhugl** = the course is aimed at learners
who are not fluent

rhuthro verbnoun
= rush
mi °ruthrodd e drwy'r °gegin = he
rushed through the kitchen
bydd rhaid rhuthro, on' bydd? = we'll
have to get a move on, won't we?

rhwng preposition
= between
personal forms: **rhyngdda i, rhyngddat
ti, rhyngddo fe, rhyngddi hi,
rhyngddon ni, rhyngddoch chi,
rhyngddyn nhw.**
Variants: **rhyngddo i, rhyngddot ti;** also
variants with **rhyng-** and **rhynth:**
**cyfle arall i °weld y gêm rhwng Cymru
a Lloegr** = another chance to see the
game between Wales and England
**fe °gafodd y ffordd rhwng Lledrod a
Llanilar ei hailagor prynhawn 'ma** =
the road between Lledrod and Llanilar
was reopened this afternoon
rhyngddat ti a fi... = between you and
me...
bydda i yno rhwng dau a tri, gobeithio
= I'll be there between two and three, I
hope

> ! **rhwng**, unlike most simple
> prepositions, does not cause
> mutation of the following noun.

rhwyd (plural **-au, -i**) noun, feminine
= net

rhwydo verbnoun
= net

rhwydwaith (plural **rhwydweithiau**)
noun, masculine
= network
bydd rhwydwaith o °orsafoedd llai =
there will be a network of smaller
stations

rhwydd adjective
comparative **rhwyddach**, superlative
rhwydda(f)
= easy
°allwch chi symud yn rhwydd? = can
you move easily?
**mae siarad yn °gyhoeddus yn dod yn
rhwydd iddo** = public speaking comes
easy to him
⇒**hawdd**

rhwyfo verbnoun
= row (boat)

rhwygiad (*plural* **-au**) *noun, masculine*
= tear, split (*also figurative*)
rhwygiadau yn y °blaid = splits in the party

rhwygo *verbnoun*
= tear, split

rhwym *adjective*
= bound (**o°** to)
mae hi'n rhwym o °fwrw glaw = it's bound to rain
dan ni'n rhwym o °fod yn hwyr = we are bound to be late

rhwymo *verbnoun*
= bind

rhwymyn *noun, masculine*
= bandage
rhowch °rwymyn am ei ben o = put a bandage round his head

rhwystr (*plural* **-au**) *noun, masculine*
= hindrance, obstacle

rhwystro *verbnoun*
= hinder; prevent (**rhag** from)
mae'r protestwyr yn °benderfynol o'u rhwystro nhw °gymaint ag sy'n °bosib = the protesters are determined to hinder them as much as possible
byddwn ni'n rhwystro nhw rhag gwneud hynny = we will prevent them from doing that

rhy° *adverb*
= too
mae hwn yn rhy °fach i mi = this is too small for me
mi °ddaeth yn rhy agos = he came too close
peidiwch bod yn rhy hir = don't be too long
wel, dw i °ddim yn rhy hapus efo'r sefyllfa = well, I'm not too happy with the situation
mae'r staff yn gweithio mewn lle °rhy °gyfyng = the staff are working in a place (that is) too confined
dych chi'n llawer rhy °bigog = you're much too touchy

! *Note that* 'too much/too many' *is* ⇒**gormod**, *although* **rhy °lawer** *is sometime encountered in speech. The prefix* ⇒**gor°** *can be used with certain adjectives in the sense of*

rhy°, *but this usage is restricted, and if* **in** *doubt it is safer to use* **rhy°**.

⇒**o °lawer**

rhybudd (*plural* **-ion**) *noun, masculine*
= warning; notice
ac mae 'na °rybudd o stormydd ger y glannau heno = and there is a storm warning on the coast tonight
rhaid diolch iddyn nhw am °ddod ar °fyr °rybudd fel hyn = they must be thanked for coming at short notice like this

⇒**larwm**

rhybuddio *verbnoun*
= warn
dw i wedi rhybuddio nhw °ddwywaith yn °barod = I've warned them twice already
fe °rybuddiodd e bod rhaid i °gyhoeddwyr symud gyda'r oes = he warned that publishers must move with the times

rhydd *adjective*
• = free
dros y byd mae pobol yn ysu am °fod yn rhydd = throughout the world people are yearning to be free
dych chi'n rhydd yfory? = are you free tomorrow?
ond mi °fydd 'na °bleidlais °rydd ar y diwedd heno = there will be a free vote at the end tonight
• = loose
ond mae'r gwydr yn rhydd fan hyn, °welwch chi? = but the glass is loose here, do you see?

⇒**rhad**, ⇒**rhyddhau**

Rhyddfrydol *adjective*
= Liberal

rhyddhau *verbnoun*
• = set free, release
mae'n °debyg y bydd y tri'n cael eu rhyddhau prynhawn 'ma = the three will probably be set free this afternoon
• = release (*all senses*)
yn °ddiweddar rhyddhawyd caset o'u caneuon mwya poblogaidd = a cassette of their most popular songs was released recently
yn ôl ffigurau a °ryddhawyd heddiw... = according to figures released today...

rhyddiaith *noun, feminine*
= prose

rhyddid *noun, masculine*
= freedom, liberty

rhyfedd

1 *noun, masculine*
= wonder
mae'n rhyfedd i mi °fod e wedi dod yn ôl = it's a wonder to me that he's come back
mi °gollon nhw, a ʰpha °ryfedd? = they lost, and small wonder
does °ryfedd = (+ *'that...' clause*) = it's no wonder
does °ryfedd na ʰchlywes i °ddim rhagor ganddo am hyn = it's no wonder I didn't hear anything more from him about this

2 *adjective*
= odd, funny, strange
'na °ryfedd! = how odd!
beth ydy'r peth bach rhyfedd 'ma, 'te? = what's this funny little thing, then?
rhyfedd fel mae'r pethau 'ma'n digwydd = funny how these things happen
⇒**doniol**, ⇒**od**

rhyfel (*plural* **-oedd**) *noun, masculine or feminine*
= war
mae'r rhyfel wedi bod yn ergyd °fawr i awdurdod Rwsia = the war has been a great blow to Russia's authority
mae'n stori ni'n dechrau yn ⁿnyddiau tywylla'r Ail °Ryfel Byd = our story begins in the darkest days of the Second World War

rhyfela *verbnoun*
= wage war

rhyngwladol *adjective*
= international
bydd llu ymosod rhyngwladol ar ei ffordd erbyn diwedd yr wythnos = an international taskforce will be on its way by the end of the week
mae'r °Groes °Goch °Ryngwladol wedi tynnu'i ʰphobol allan yn °barod = the International Red Cross have already pulled their people out

rhyw *noun, feminine*
= sex

wi'n credu bod gormod o °ryw ar y teledu dyddiau 'ma = I think there's too much sex on television these days

rhyw° *adjective*
= some (+ *singular*)
mae rhyw °ddyn tu allan = some man (or other) is outside
byddwn ni'n dweud rhyw stori wrthyn nhw, dw i'n siwr = we'll tell them some story (or other), I'm sure.
mi °ddôn nhw'n ôl °ryw °ddiwrnod = they'll come back some day
nawn ni °ddatrys y °broblem °ryw ffordd neu'i gilydd = we'll solve the problem some way or other

rhywbeth *pronoun*
= something
mae newid yn rhywbeth °gwbl naturiol = change is something quite natural
oes rhywbeth yn bod? = is there something the matter?

rhywfaint *pronoun*
= a certain amount
oedd rhywfaint o °Gymraeg 'da hi = she had a certain amount of Welsh

> **!** *A variant phrase* **rhyw °gymaint** *is also encountered.*

rhywiol *adjective*
= sexual

rhywle *adverb*
= somewhere

> **!** *This word usually appears in its soft mutated form* **°rywle**, *or with* **yn** *'in'* + *radical form*

°ga i °roi'r rhain i lawr °rywle? = can I put these down somewhere?
rhaid bod nhw yn rhywle = they must be somewhere

rhywrai
⇒**rhywun**

rhywsut *adverb*
= somehow, in some way

> **!** *This word usually appears in its soft mutated form* **°rywsut**

mi na i'r gwaith °rywsut = I'll do the work somehow
dyw'r syniad 'ma °ddim yn gweithio °rywsut = this idea isn't working somehow

fe °gawn ni'r arian °rywsut neu'i
gilydd = we'll get the money somehow
or other

rhywun *pronoun*
- = someone
  mae rhywun wrth y drws = there's
  someone at the door
  **sut °all rhywun yn Llundain °wybod
  unrhywbeth am °Ben Llyn?** = how can
  someone in London know anything
  about Pen Llyn?
  **byddai'n rhaid i °rywun °fynd i'r °afael
  â'r pwnc** = someone would have to get
  to grips with the subject
- *plural* **rhywrai** some people
  **mae 'na °rywrai sy °ddim yn meddwl
  felly** = there are some people who
  don't think that way

S s

sach (*plural* **-au**) *noun, feminine*
= sack; bag
cofiwch °ddod â sach °gysgu =
remember to bring a sleeping bag

Sadwrn
= *in:* **dydd Sadwrn** Saturday
⇨**Llun**

saer (*plural* **seiri**) *noun, masculine*
- = carpenter
- = mason

Saesneg *noun, feminine*
- = English language (*sometimes used
  with definite article* **y**)
  beth ydy ystyr hyn yn Saesneg? =
  what does this mean in English?
  **nofel wedi'i °chyfieithu o'r °Gymraeg
  i'r Saesneg** = a novel translated from
  Welsh into English
- (*as adjective*) = English-language
  **mae fersiwn Saesneg o'r ffurflen
  hefyd ar °gael** = an English-language
  version of this form is also available

> **!** **Saesneg** *is pronounced* '**Sisneg**' *in
> unaffected speech. The definite
> article is often used with the noun,
> though not after* **yn** '*in*'. *So* **o'r
> Saesneg** '*from English*' *but* **yn
> Saesneg** '*in English*' (*see examples
> above*).

⇨**Lloegr**, ⇨**main**

Saesnes (*plural* **-au**) *noun, feminine*
= Englishwoman

> **!** *This word is pronounced* '**Sisnes**' *in
> unaffected speech.*

Saeson *plural of*
⇨**Sais**

saeth (*plural* **-au**) *noun, feminine*
= arrow

saethu *verbnoun*
= shoot; fire
**mi °gafodd un o'r terfysgwyr ei
saethu'n °farw** = one of the terrorists
was shot dead
**maen nhw'n chwilio am °beilot
°gafodd ei saethu i lawr °ddydd Llun**

= they are looking for a pilot who was shot down on Monday

mi saethon nhw i'r awyr = they fired into the air

⇒**tanio**

saethydd (*plural* **-ion**) *noun, masculine*
= archer

saethyddiaeth *noun, feminine*
= archery

safbwynt (*plural* **-iau**) *noun, masculine*
= standpoint; point of view

mae angen mwy o °barch tuag at safbwyntiau pobol eraill = we need more respect for other people's points of view

safiad (*plural* **-au**) *noun, masculine*
= stand

gwneud safiad = make a stand:
mae'n °bwysig bod rhywun yn gwneud safiad ynghylch hyn = it's important that someone make a stand on this

safio *verbnoun*
= save (*all senses*)

> **!** This is a commonly used loanword covering the senses of both ⇒**achub** and ⇒**arbed**.

bydd hyn yn safio amser inni = this will save us time

safle *noun, masculine*
safle bysiau = bus stop

safon (*plural* **-au**) *noun, feminine*
• = level; standard

cwrs penwythnos ar °gyfer dysgwyr o °bob safon = a weekend course for learners at every level

... i sicrhau bod ein safonau ni'n aros yr un ag erioed = ...to ensure that our standards remain the same as ever
• = quality

mae safon y cynhyrchu yn °ddiogel yn eu dwylo = the quality of production is safe in their hands

defnyddiau adeiladu o safon = quality building materials

⇒**lefel**

safonol *adjective*
= standard

sang
in: **dan ei sang** (*of a room*) packed, full to the rafters:

roedd y lle dan ei sang = the place was packed

sa i *etc*
⇒**bod**

sai, 'sai
⇒**bod**

saib (*plural* **seibiau**) *noun, masculine*
= pause; break

⇒**seibiant**

sail (*plural* **seiliau**) *noun, feminine*
• = base; basis; foundation

y nod yw defnyddio'r ymchwil fel sail ar °gyfer gwaith ysgol = the aim is to use the research as a basis for schoolwork

roedd y pamffledi'n chwalu parch at seiliau'r °Deyrnas = the pamphlets were destroying respect for the foundations of the Kingdom
• = grounds

roedd y °weithred wedi'i gohirio ar sail pryderon am °ddiogelwch = the action had been put off on the grounds of fears about safety

⇒**seilio**

saim *noun, masculine*
= grease; fat

sain (*plural* **seiniau**) *noun, feminine*
= sound

seiniau'r iaith = the sounds of the language

⇒**sŵn**

Sais (*plural* **Saeson**) *noun, masculine*
= Englishman

Sais o swydd Efrog °fydd ein Hysgrifennydd Gwladol newydd = our new Secretary of State will be an Englishman from Yorkshire

bydd y tîm °fydd yn herio'r Saeson wedi ei °gyhoeddi erbyn hyn = the team that will challenge the English will have been announced by now

tafarnwr o Sais = a (pub) landlord who is an Englishman

..., fel mae'r Saeson yn ei °ddweud = ..., as the English say

⇒**Lloegr**

saith *numeral*
= seven

> **!** With 'years' and 'days', *this numeral is generally followed by nasal*

mutation: so **saith ⁿmlynedd** *is usual for* 'seven years', *though* **saith blynedd** *is not uncommon; similarly* **saith ⁿniwrnod** 'seven days', *with* **saith diwrnod** *often heard as well. Otherwise the radical is the norm, though soft mutation is also encountered sometimes, e.g.* **saith ceiniog** *or* **saith °geiniog** 'seven pence'.

⇒**pum(p)**

sâl *adjective*
= ill
ers pryd dych chi'n teimlo'n sâl? = how long have you been feeling ill?
⇒**gwael**

salwch *noun, masculine*
= illness
bydd y siop ar °gau heddiw oherwydd salwch = the shop will be closed today because of illness
⇒**gwaeledd**

sant (*plural* **saint** *or* **seintiau**) *noun, masculine*
= saint

santes (*plural* **-au**) *noun, feminine*
= (*female*) saint

sarhad (*plural* **-au**) *noun, masculine*
= insult
wi'n credu bod hi'n sarhad i'n cenedl = I think it is an insult to our nation

sarhau *verbnoun*
= insult

sarhaus *adjective*
= insulting

sathru *verbnoun*
= trample, tread (+ *direct object or* **ar°** on)
ti wedi sathru arno! = you've trodden all over it!
oedd y lle wedi'i sathru = the place was (all) trampled

sawdl (*plural* **sodlau**) *noun, masculine or feminine*
= heel
ar ein sodlau ni maen nhw = they're (right) on our heels

sawl
1 *adverb*
• = how many?

! *This word differs from* ⇒**faint?** *in that it is followed directly by a singular noun.*
sawl llyfr sy 'da ti fan 'na? = how many books have you got there?

sawlgwaith? = how many times? (= **faint o °weithiau?**)
sawl un? = how many?:
sawlgwaith est ti yno? = how many times did you go there?
mae Susan wedi dod â rhagor o °gwpanau—sawl un? = Susan has brought some more cups—how many?
• = a number of, several
mae'n °bwysig am sawl rheswm = it's important for a number of reasons
mae canlyniadau sawl prosiect ymchwil yn dal heb eu cyhoeddi eto = the results of a number of research projects have yet to be published

! *In this sense,* **sawl** *is the equivalent of* ⇒**nifer** (**o°**), *but again uses the singular noun without* **o°**.

2 *pronoun*

! *Occasionally* **y sawl** (*note definite article*) *is encountered in more elevated style for* **yr un** 'the one (who)' *or* **pwy bynnag** 'whoever'.
y sawl sy'n credu... = whoever believes...

sbectol *noun, feminine*
= glasses, spectacles
bydda i'n gorfod gwisgo sbectol, mae'n °debyg = I'll probably have to wear glasses

sbel
in: **am sbel** = for a little while, for a spell

sbio *verbnoun* (*North*)
= look, look at (*particularly in command forms*)
sbiwch hwnna! = look at him!
sbia faint sy gynnon ni = look how many we've got
⇒**edrych**

sbon
in: **newydd sbon** = brand new
agorir canolfan hamdden newydd sbon yno yfory = a brand new leisure centre will be opened there tomorrow

sboncen *noun, feminine*
= squash
beth am ymuno â'ch clwb sboncen lleol? = what about joining your local squash club?

sbort *noun, feminine*
= fun
o'n nhw'n gwneud sbort am ei °ben o trwy'r bore = they were making fun of him all morning
°gawn ni sbort fan hyn! = we'll have fun here!
am sbort! = what fun!

sbwriel *noun, masculine*
= rubbish
ewch â'ch sbwriel adre os gwelwch yn °dda = please take your rubbish home with you
⇒**sothach**

sebon *noun, masculine*
= soap

sech, 'sech, sen, 'sen, set, 'set
⇒**bod**

sedd (*plural* **-i, -au**) *noun, feminine*
= seat
mae digon o seddi i °bawb = there are plenty of seats for everyone
fe °fydd rhai o seddi Cymru'n gorfod newid eto ar ôl yr etholiad = some seats in Wales will have to change again after the election
sedd °ddiogel (*plural* **seddi/-au diogel**) = safe seat
sedd °flaen (*plural* **seddi/-au blaen**) = front seat
sedd °gefn (*plural* **seddi/-au cefn**) = back seat
sedd ymylol (*plural* **seddi/-au ymylol**) = marginal seat

sef *adverb*
= namely, that is to say
fe °fyddwn ni'n gwneud yr hyn gallwn ni, sef rhoi help lle bo angen = we will do what we can, namely give help where needed
... erbyn 6500 CC, sef °ddwy °fil o °flynyddoedd ynghynt = ... by 6500 BC, that is to say two thousand years earlier

sefydliad (*plural* **-au**) *noun, masculine*
= institution; institute

stori °gyfoes sydd yn edrych ar °gymdeithas a'n sefydliadau crefyddol = a contemporary story that looks at society and our religious institutions
Sefydliad y Merched = Women's Institute

sefydlog *adjective*
= stable; settled

sefydlogrwydd *noun, masculine*
= stability

sefydlu *verbnoun*
= establish, set up
fo oedd y Prif °Weinidog a sefydlodd y Swyddfa °Gymreig = he was the Prime Minister who established the Welsh Office
dim ond dau sy wedi sefydlu eu busnesau eu hunain = only two (of them) have set up their own businesses

sefyll (*stem* **saf-** *or* **sef-**) *verbnoun*
= stand
sefwch fan hyn, newch chi? = stand here, will you?
roedd rhywun yn sefyll tu allan = someone was standing outside
mae ymgeisydd newydd yn sefyll dros y Rhyddfrydwyr = a new candidate is standing for the Liberals

seibiant (*plural* **seibiannau**) *noun, masculine*
= rest; respite; breather
yn y cyfamser mi °gawn ni seibiant bach = in the meantime we'll have a little breather

seicoleg *noun, feminine*
= psychology

seicolegol *adjective*
= psychological

seicolegydd (*plural* **seicolegwyr**) *noun, masculine*
= psychologist

seiliedig *adjective*
= based (**ar°** on)
nofel seiliedig ar ei °brofiadau yn ystod yr Ail °Ryfel Byd = a novel based on his experiences during the Second World War

seilio *verbnoun*
= base (**ar°** on)

cyfres o °luniau wedi'u seilio ar chwedlau'r Celtiaid = a series of pictures based on the legends of the Celts
⇨**sail**

seimllyd *adjective*
= greasy; fatty

seiniau *plural of*
⇨**sain**

seiri *plural of*
⇨**saer**

Seisnig *adjective*
= English (*pertaining to England*)

seithfed *adjective*
= seventh

> **!** *Ordinal numerals are adjectives, but behave in a special way. All other than* ⇨**cynta** *precede the noun. With feminine singular nouns, the noun itself undergoes soft mutation, as does the ordinal after the article—so:* **y seithfed dyn** 'the seventh man' *but* **y seithfed °ferch** 'the seventh girl'

selsigen (*plural* **selsig**) *noun, feminine*
= sausage

senedd (*plural* **-au**) *noun, feminine*
= parliament
byddai'r ymgyrch dros Senedd i °Gymru'n parhau = the campaign for a Parliament for Wales would continue

serch hynny *adverb*
= however; all the same; nevertheless
serch hynny, fe °welwyd rhai fflachiadau o'r ffrwydradau mwyaf = all the same, some flashes from the biggest explosions were seen
⇨**er hynny,** ⇨**fodd bynnag**

seren (*plural* **sêr**) *noun, feminine*
= star (*also figurative*)
un o sêr disgleiria'r nefoedd yw Spica = Spica is one of the brightest stars in the heavens
seren °ddwbl (*plural* sêr dwbl) = binary star
seren °wib (*plural* sêr gwib) = shooting star
seren y gogledd = polestar
noson yng ⁿghwmni sêr y byd teledu Cymraeg = an evening in the company of the stars of Welsh television

seryddiaeth *noun, feminine*
= astronomy

seryddwr (*plural* **seryddwyr**) *noun, masculine*
= astronomer

serth *adjective*
= steep

set (*plural* **-iau**) *noun, feminine*
= set
ac mi °ellwch chi ennill set °gyfan o'i °lyfrau yn ein cystadleuaeth heno = and you can win a complete set of his books in our competition this evening

setlo *verbnoun*
= settle (down)
naeth hi erioed setlo yn yr ysgol = she never settled in school
bydd pethau wedi setlo ychydig erbyn 'ny, dw i'n siwr – I'm sure things will have settled down a bit by then

sgerbwd (*plural* **sgerbydau**) *noun, masculine*
= skeleton

sgi (*plural* **sgïau**) *noun, feminine*
= ski

sgidiau *plural noun*
= shoes
tynnwch eich sgidiau! = take your shoes off!
gwisga dy sgidiau! = put your shoes on

> **!** *This is the normal spoken plural form of* ⇨**esgid**.

sgil (*plural* **-iau**) *noun, masculine*
= skill
bydd cyfle hefyd i ymarfer eich sgiliau cyfathrebu = there will also be an opportunity to practise your communication skills

sgîl
⇨**yn sgîl**

sgîl-effaith (*plural* **sgîl-effeithiau**) *noun, masculine*
= side-effect
beth am sgîl-effeithiau'r moddion newydd 'ma? = what about the side-effects of these new drugs?

sgïo *verbnoun*
= ski
mae atyniadau'r °ganolfan yn cynnwys pwll nofio a llethr sgïo = the

centre's attractions include a swimming pool and a ski slope

sgleinio *verbnoun*
= polish, shine
mae eisiau golchi'r ceir 'ma i gyd a'u sgleinio wedyn = all these cars have got to be washed and then polished

sglodyn (*plural* **sglodion**) *noun, masculine*
= chip
faint ydy sglodion yn unig? = how much are chips on their own?
pysgod a sglodion = fish and chips

sglodyn silicon (*plural* **sglodion silicon**) *noun, masculine*
= silicon chip

sgôr (*plural* **sgoriau**) *noun, feminine*
= score

sgorio *verbnoun*
= score
a dyma'r Ffrancwyr wedi sgorio eto! = and the French have scored again!

sgrech (*plural* **-iadau**) *noun, masculine*
= shriek

sgrechian, sgrechu *verbnoun*
= shriek

sgrifennu *verbnoun*
= write
na i sgrifennu atyn nhw yfory = I'll write to them tomorrow

> **!** *This word, and its common variant* ⇒**sgwennu**, *are the norm for* 'write' *in the spoken language, while the written and formal language prefers* ⇒**ysgrifennu**. *Note that, as with verbs for* 'send', 'write to...' *is* **sgrifennu at°** *with people, and* **sgrifennu i°** *with places.*

sgrîn (*plural* **sgriniau**) *noun, feminine*
= screen

sgrîn °flaen (*plural* **sgriniau blaen**) *noun, feminine*
= windscreen

sgubo *verbnoun*
= sweep
mi °fyddai'n hawdd sgubo'r adroddiad o'r neilltu = it would be easy to sweep the report to one side

sgwâr (*plural* **sgwariau**) *noun, feminine*
• = square

byddwn ni'n ymgynnull ar Sgwâr y °Farchnad bore fory am naw = we will gather on Market Square tomorrow morning at nine
• (*as adjective*) = square

sgwennu *verbnoun*
= write
pwy sgwennodd y llythyr 'ma? = who wrote this letter?

> **!** *This word, and its common variant* ⇒**sgrifennu**, *are the norm for* 'write' *in the spoken language, while the written and formal language prefers* ⇒**ysgrifennu**. *Note that, as with verbs for* 'send', 'write to...' *is* **sgwennu at°** *with people, and* **sgwennu i°** *with places.*

'sgwn i *verb* (*North*)
= I wonder
'sgwn i be' °ddigwyddodd fan'ma? = I wonder what happened here?
'sgwn i ydyn nhw wedi cyrraedd? = I wonder if they've arrived?
ond ai dyna oedd ei °fwriad, 'sgwn i? = but is that what he meant to do, I wonder?
⇒**gwybod**, ⇒**tybed**

sgwrs (*plural* **sgyrsiau**) *noun, feminine*
= conversation; chat
gwrandewch unwaith eto ar y sgwrs, yna atebwch y cwestiynau = listen once again to the conversation, then answer the questions
°gawn ni sgwrs °fach ar ôl y °wers, iawn? = we'll have a little chat after the lesson, OK?

sgwrsio (*sometimes* **sgyrsio**) *verbnoun*
= chat

si (*plural* **sïon**) *noun, masculine*
= rumour; talk
mae 'na si bod nhw'n mynd i °gau'r ffatri = there is talk that they are going to close the factory

siaced (*plural* **-i**) *noun, feminine*
= jacket

sianel (*plural* **-i**) *noun, feminine*
= channel (*also TV/radio*)
mi °fydd sianel °deledu newydd ar yr awyr erbyn mis Ebrill = a new television channel will be on the air by April

...o °blith y cannoedd o sianeli teledu sy ar °gael yn yr Unol °Daleithiau = ...from among the hundreds of television channels available in the United States

siâp (*plural* **siapiau**) *noun, masculine*
= shape
siapa hi!/siapwch hi! = get a move on!

siarad *verbnoun*
• = speak (**â**[h] to; **am**° about)
dych chi'n siarad Cymraeg? = do you speak Welsh?
siaredir Cymraeg yma = Welsh spoken here
ydy e wedi siarad â hi am hyn oll, 'te? = has he spoken to her about all this, then?
• = talk (**â**[h] to; **am**° about)
siaradwch â'ch gilydd am °ddeng munud = talk to each other for ten minutes
maen nhw'n siarad lol, 'na i gyd = they're talking nonsense, that's all
mae gormod o siarad fan hyn = there's too much talk(ing) here
⇨**dweud**, ⇨**sôn**

siaradus *adjective*
= talkative

siaradwr (*plural* **siaradwyr**) *noun, masculine*
= speaker

siaradwraig (*plural* **siaradwragedd**) *noun, feminine*
= speaker

siawns (*plural* **-iau**) *noun, feminine or masculine*
= chance
gyda siawns o un mewn 54 o ennill deg punt... = with a chance of one in 54 of winning ten pounds
⇨**cyfle**

sibrwd (*stem* **sibryd-**) *verbnoun*
= whisper

sicr *adjective*
= sure, certain (**o**° to)
yn y pen draw mae'r gwirionedd yn sicr o °ddod i'r amlwg = eventually the truth is sure to come to light
yn sicr = certainly:
yn sicr mae newid o °ryw °fath ar y ffordd = certainly change of some sort is on the way

⇨**siwr**

sicrhau *verbnoun*
• = assure
galla i'ch sicrhau y byddwn ni'n gwneud yr hyn gallwn ni = I can assure you that we will do what we can
• = ensure
rhaid inni sicrhau cyfrinachedd = we have to ensure confidentiality
• = secure

sicrwydd *noun, masculine*
= certainty
does dim sicrwydd pendant mai fan hyn y cafodd ei °eni = there is no (definite) certainty that he was born here
i sicrwydd = for certain, for sure:
go °brin y cawn ni °wybod i sicrwydd pwy oedden nhw = we can hardly know for certain who they were

siec (*plural* **-iau**) *noun, feminine*
= cheque
°ga i °dalu â siec? = can I pay by cheque?
sieciau'n °daladwy i °Ysgol °Gynradd Llaneglwys = cheques payable to Llaneglwys Primary School

siglen (*plural* **-ni**) *noun, feminine*
= swing (*in playground*)

siglo *verbnoun*
= shake; swing

silff (*plural* **-oedd**) *noun, feminine*
= shelf

sillaf (*plural* **-au**) *noun, feminine*
= syllable

sillafu *verbnoun*
= spell
sut mae sillafu hynny, 'te? = how is that spelt, then?

sinema (*plural* **sinemâu**) *noun, feminine*
= cinema
beth am inni °fynd i'r sinema heno? = what about us going to the cinema this evening?

sioc (*plural* **-iau**) *noun, masculine*
= shock
°ges i sioc = I got a shock, I was shocked

siocled (*plural* **-i**) *noun, masculine*
= chocolate

sioe (*plural* **-au**) *noun, feminine*
= show
**dyma ni'n edrych ymlaen unwaith eto
at y sioeau amaethyddol** = here we
are once more looking forward to the
agricultural shows

siom (*plural* **-au**) *noun, feminine or
masculine*
= disappointment
**°ges i siom °fawr wrth °ddarllen y
nofel 'ma** = I was very disappointed
when I read this novel

siomedig *adjective*
• = disappointed
**dw i'n meddwl °fod y plant yn
siomedig braidd** = I think the
children are a bit disappointed
• = disappointing
**perfformiad siomedig iawn °welon ni
ddoe** = it was a very disappointing
performance that we saw yesterday

siomi *verbnoun*
= disappoint
fe °ges i'n siomi = I was disappointed.

siop (*plural* **-au**) *noun, feminine*
= shop
**mae siop °flodau newydd ei hagor yn
y °dre** = a flower shop has just been
opened in the town

siopa *verbnoun*
= shop, do the shopping

siopleidr (*plural* **siopladron**) *noun,
masculine*
= shoplifter

sir (*plural* **-oedd**) *noun, feminine*
= (Welsh) county
Cyngor Sir Gwynedd = Gwynedd
County Council
mae rhai o'r hen siroedd yn dal efo ni
= some of the old counties are still
with us

> ❗ *This word is used only for Welsh
> county names, while* ⇒**swydd** *is used
> for counties elsewhere in the British
> Isles.*

siswrn *noun, masculine*
= scissors

siwgwr, siwgr *noun, masculine*
= sugar

dach chi'n cymryd siwgwr? = do you
take sugar?

siwmper (*plural* **-i**) *noun, feminine*
= jumper (*clothing*)

siwr *adjective*
= sure, certain
wyt ti'n siwr am hynny? = are you sure
about that?
**dw i'n siwr na °fydd neb yn erbyn y
syniad fan hyn** = I'm sure there won't
be anyone against the idea here

> ❗ *Generally this word is
> interchangeable with* ⇒**sicr**, *except
> that* 'certainly' *is always* **yn sicr**. *Note
> also the set phrase* **siwr o °fod**:
> **fe °fyddan nhw yma cyn hir, siwr o
> °fod** = they'll surely be here soon
> **naethon nhw °lwyddo?—siwr o °fod**
> = did they manage it?—I expect so

sleisen (*plural* **sleisys**) *noun, feminine*
= slice (**o°** of)
°gymera i °ddwy sleisen o'r bara 'na =
I'll have two slices of that bread
⇒**tafell**

smotyn (*plural* **smotiau**) *noun,
masculine*
= spot
oedd ei hwyneb hi'n smotiau i gyd =
her face was covered in spots

smo *etc*
⇒**bod**

smwddio *verbnoun*
= iron, do the ironing

smygu *verbnoun*
= smoke
dw i °ddim yn smygu = I don't smoke
⇒**ysmygu**, ⇒**mwg**

snobyddiaeth *noun, feminine*
= snobbery

snobyddlyd *adjective*
= snobbish, snobby

so *etc*
⇒**bod**

sobor, sobr *adjective*
• = sober; serious
**mae ⁿngwaith i'n dibynnu ar °fod yn
°barchus a sobor** = my work depends
on me being respectable and sober

- (*as intensifier with* **o°** + *adjective*) = awfully
  mae'r te 'ma'n edrych yn sobor o °wan = this tea looks awfully weak

sodlau *plural of*
⇒**sawdl**

soffistigedig *adjective*
= sophisticated

sôn (*stem* **soni-**) *verbnoun*
- = talk (**am°** about)
  mae 'na un peth bach na sonies i amdano ddoe = there's one little thing I didn't talk about yesterday
  ac o sôn am °gychod, ... = and talking of boats, ...
  mae'r sôn am symiau enfawr o arian yn gwrthod diflannu = the talk about huge sums of money refuses to go away
  mae rhyw sôn am °ddatganiad nes ymlaen heddiw = there is talk of an annoucement later today
⇒**siarad**
- = mention
  heb sôn am° = not to mention:
  rhaid ystyried y goblygiadau, heb sôn am y costau = we have to consider the implications, not to mention the costs
  paid sôn! = get away (with you)!:
  es i ar °goll ar y ffordd rhwng y coleg a'r °dafarn—paid sôn! = I got lost on the way between the college and the pub—get away!/you never!

sosban (*plural* **-au**) *noun, feminine*
= saucepan

soser (*plural* **-i**) *noun, feminine*
- = saucer
- = (satellite) dish
  fe °fydd y cwmni wedi cyflymu'r °broses o °werthu soseri lloeren = the company will have speeded up the process of selling satellite dishes

sosialaeth *noun, feminine*
= socialism

sosialydd (*plural* **sosialwyr**) *noun, masculine*
= socialist

sothach *noun, masculine*
= nonsense; rubbish
pwy sgwennodd y sothach 'ma? = who wrote this rubbish?
⇒**sbwriel**

sownd *adjective*
= (*stuck*) fast *or* tight
wi'n sownd! = I'm stuck!

staer *noun, feminine*
= stairs
mae hi lan staer (/lawr staer) ar y °foment = she's upstairs (downstairs) at the moment
⇒**grisiau**

stafell (*plural* **-oedd**) *noun, feminine*
= room
faint o stafelloedd sy ar y llawr 'ma? = how many rooms are there on this floor?

> ❗ This is the normal form in the spoken language, while written and formal language prefers ⇒**ystafell**

stafell °fwyta (*plural* **stafelloedd bwyta**) = dining room
stafell °fyw (*plural* **stafelloedd byw**) = living room
stafell molchi (*plural* **stafelloedd molchi**) = bathroom
stafell °wely (*plural* **stafelloedd gwely**) = bedroom

stamp (*plural* **-iau**) *noun, masculine*
= stamp
°ga i °ddau stamp dosbarth cynta ac un ail °ddosbarth? = can I have two first class stamps and one second class?

staplydd (*plural* **-ion**) *noun, masculine*
= stapler

'sti *particle* (*North*)
= you know
tydi hi °ddim yn rhy hwyr, 'sti = it's not too late, you know

> ❗ This is a very colloquial, but very common, contraction of **°wyddost ti?**, and is used in Northern areas as a parenthetical expression in the same way as its English counterpart. It cannot start a sentence, and instead nearly always appears in the form of a 'tag' at the end, or as a pause-filler. The **chi** equivalent is **°wyddoch chi?** which is not so routinely contracted. Southern areas use contractions of non-inflected forms instead.

⇒**gwybod,** ⇒**chimod,** ⇒ **timod**

stiwdio (*plural* **-s**) *noun, feminine*
= studio

stondin (*plural* **-au**) *noun, masculine*
= stall

stordy (*plural* **stordai**) *noun, masculine*
= warehouse

stori (*plural* **storïau** or **straeon**) *noun, feminine*
= story
bydd y stori °fer 'ma'n °gyfarwydd i chi i gyd = this short story will be familiar to you all
fyth ers i straeon am °lygredd °ddechrau ymddangos... = ever since stories about corruption started to appear...

storm (*plural* **-ydd**) *noun, feminine*
= storm

stormus *adjective*
= stormy

straeon
⇨**stori**

streic (*plural* **-iau**) *noun, feminine*
= strike
mae'r nifer sy wedi pleidleisio dros streic yn isel iawn = the number who have voted for a strike is very low

stribed or **stribedyn** (*plural* **stribedi**) *noun, masculine*
= strip (*of material, land, etc*)

strwythur (*plural* **-au**) *noun, masculine*
= structure
mae eisiau meistroli strwythur yr iaith yn ogystal â'i geiriau = one must master the structure of the language as well as its words

stryd (*plural* **-oedd**) *noun, feminine*
= street
ewch i lawr y stryd °gynta ar y °dde 'ma = go down the first street on the right here

stumog (*plural* **-au**) *noun, feminine*
= stomach
mae stumog °dost 'da fi = I've got stomach ache

styfnig *adjective*
= stubborn

un styfnig iawn ydy hi, cofia = she's very stubborn, mind

sudd (*plural* **-ion**) *noun, masculine*
= juice
p'un leiciet ti, sudd afal neu sudd oren? = which would you like, apple juice or orange juice?

suddo *verbnoun*
= sink
mae 'na ofnau °fod y llong °danfor wedi suddo = there are fears that the submarine has sunk
. . . cyn i'r llong °ryfel 'ma °gael ei suddo ym 1942 = . . . before this battleship was sunk in 1942

sugno *verbnoun*
= suck

sugnwr llwch *noun, masculine*
= vacuum cleaner

Sul
in: **dydd Sul**
= Sunday

> **!** *Note that this word has a wider meaning in the expressions* **dros y Sul** 'over the weekend' *and* **bwrw'r Sul** 'spend the weekend':
> **°welwn ni chi dros y Sul °rywbryd** = we'll see you sometime over the weekend
> **lle dych chi'n bwriadu bwrw'r Sul, 'te?** = where are you planning to spend the weekend, then?

⇨**Llun**

sustem
⇨**system**

sut?

> **!** *This word is pronounced* **shwd** *or* **shwt** *in Southern areas*

1 *adverb*
= how
sut mae'r teulu? = how is the family?
sut oedd y °daith? = how was the journey?
sut aeth hi yn y diwedd, 'te? = how did it go in the end, then?
does neb yn gwybod sut bydd yr °olygfa 'ma'n edrych yfory = nobody knows what this scene will look like tomorrow

sut dach chi'n deud hynny yn °Gymraeg? = how do you say that in Welsh?

sut felly? *or* **sut hynny?** = how come?: **°fyddan nhw °ddim yn gorfod talu wedi'r cyfan—sut hynny?** = they won't have to pay after all—how come?

⇨**pa mor°**

2 (sut°) *adjective*
= what kind of...?

sut °dre, felly, yw Llaneglwys? = what kind of town, then, is Llaneglwys?

sut °dywydd °gaethoch chi yno? = what kind of weather did you have there?

> **!** *This adjectival use is a colloquial alternative for* **pa °fath o°**

sŵ (*plural* **-au**) *noun, masculine or feminine*
= zoo

swil *adjective*
= shy

'sdim eisiau bod yn swil = there's no need to be shy

swildod *noun, masculine*
= shyness

swllt (*plural* **sylltau**) *noun, masculine*
= shilling

swmpus *adjective*
= bulky, hefty

fel y gwelwch chi, mae'r adroddiad yn un digon swmpus = as you (can) see, the report is quite a hefty one

swn, 'swn
⇨**bod**

sŵn *noun, masculine*
= noise; sound

pwy sy'n gwneud yr holl sŵn 'na? = who's making all that noise?

°glywest ti'r sŵn 'na gynnau? = did you hear that sound/noise just then?

cadw sŵn = make a noise *or* racket

o'n nhw'n cadw sŵn trwy'r nos, wi'n gweud 'that ti = I'm telling you, they were making a noise all night

swnllyd *adjective*
= noisy

y bai yw °fod y peiriant ei hunan yn swnllyd braidd = the trouble is that the engine itself is rather noisy

swper *noun, masculine or feminine*
= supper; evening meal

beth am °gael swper nawr, a gorffen hyn wedyn? = why don't (we) have supper now, and finish this later?

⇨**cinio**

sws (*plural* **-us**) *noun, feminine or masculine*
= kiss

ty'd â sws i mi = give me a kiss

hwyl a sws = goodbye and a kiss (*affectionate ending to letter*)

⇨**cusan**

swydd (*plural* **-i**) *noun, feminine*
• = job

mae disgwyl y bydd eu penderfyniad yn dod â ʰchannoedd o swyddi i'r ardal = their decision is expected to bring hundreds of jobs into the area

o'n i'n gobeithio cael swydd °barhaol yn hytrach nag un dros °dro = I was hoping to get a permanent job rather than a temporary one

• = (*English, Scottish or Irish*) county

yn Swydd Stafford mae hi'n byw bellach = she lives in Staffordshire now

⇨**sir**

swyddfa (*plural* **swyddfeydd**) *noun, feminine*
= office

cysylltwch â'n swyddfa am °ragor o °fanylion = contact our office for more details

llefarydd ar °ran y Swyddfa °Gymreig = a spokesman for the Welsh Office

swyddog (*plural* **-ion**) *noun, masculine*
= officer, official

mae'n amlwg °fod swyddogion y cyngor wedi camddeall y sefyllfa = council officials have clearly misunderstood the situation

swyddogol *adjective*
= official

mae'r cwmni bellach yn ⁿnwylo'r Derbynnydd Swyddogol = the company is now in the hands of the Official Receiver

swyn (*plural* **-ion**) *noun, masculine*
= charm, spell

swyno *verbnoun*
= charm, enchant

swynol *adjective*
= charming, enchanting

sy (or **sydd**) *verb*

> **!** *This word is part of the verb* **bod** *'to be'—it is present tense third person singular/plural, and so corresponds to* **mae**, *with the basic meaning 'is/ are'. It coexists with* **mae**, *and is used in place of it in three circumstances.*

• = who/which is/are (*relative use*)
y dyn sy'n siarad = the man who is speaking
gofynnwch i'r dyn sy tu allan = ask the man who is outside
mae 'na °rai sy wedi colli popeth = there are some who have lost everything
llyfr sy'n esbonio'r prif egwyddorion = a book which explains the main principles
mae eisiau rhywun sy °ddim yn nabod yr ardal = we need someone who doesn't know the area

• = is/are

> **!** **sy** *is used instead of* **mae** *when the subject of the sentence has been placed at the start of the sentence. Compare the following neutral and focused sentences:*
> **mae Angharad yn darllen y newyddion heno** (*neutral—nothing emphasised*) = Angharad is reading the news tonight
> **Angharad sy'n darllen y newyddion heno** = Angharad is reading the news tonight (*i.e. not Bethan*)
> *Further examples:*
> **ti sy ar °fai!** = (it is) you (who) are to blame!
> **y plant sy'n diodde** = (it's) the children (that) suffer
> **dim ond dau sy ar ôl** = there are only two left (*literally: '(it is) only two (that) are left'*)
> **dyn enwog iawn sy gyda ni heno** = we have a very famous man with us tonight (*literally: (it is) a very famous man (that) is with us tonight'*)

• = is/are (*after question-words representing the subject of the sentence*)

> **!** **sy** *is used in place of* **mae** *after question words which are themselves*

the subject—this means that ⇒**pwy?**, ⇒**beth?**, ⇒**faint?**, **pa un?/p'un?** and **pa °rai** (*which can all refer to persons or things*) *are followed by* **sy** *in the present tense (and perfect, which uses present tense +* ⇒**wedi**) *when they are the subject:*
pwy sy'n dod heno? = who is coming this evening?
Contrast this with
pwy ydy honna? = who is that woman (*identification sentence*)
pwy mae Elwyn yn helpu? = who(m) is Elwyn helping? (**pwy** *represents object, not subject*)
Other question words such as ⇒**lle?** where?, ⇒**pryd?** when? *and* ⇒**sut?** how?, *cannot refer to people or things, and so cannot be the subject—they are always followed by* **mae** (*or* **maen** *with* **nhw**) *in the present.*

sych *adjective*
comparative **sychach,** *superlative* **sycha(f)**
= dry
mi °fydd hi'n parhau'n sych ac yn heulog yfory = it will continue dry and sunny tomorrow
mae eisiau rhywle sych iawn = we need somewhere very dry

sychdaflwr *noun, masculine*
= tumble-drier

syched *noun, masculine*
= thirst

> **!** *This term indicating a temporary physical condition is used with* ⇒**ar°** *when a person is stated:*
> **mae syched arna i** = I'm thirsty
> **oedd syched arnyn nhw?** = were they thirsty?
> **gobeithio na °fydd gormod o syched ar y plant** = I hope the children won't be too thirsty

sychu *verbnoun*
= dry

sychydd gwallt *noun, masculine*
= hairdryer

sydyn *adjective*
• = sudden

yna, yn sydyn iawn, dyma fe'n codi ar ei °draed = but, very suddenly, he got to his feet
• (*North*) = quick
  maen nhw'n mynd yn sydyn = they go quickly
⇒**cyflym**

sydd
⇒**sy**

syfrdanu *verbnoun*
= astound, amaze
mi °ges i 'n syfrdanu gan y ffilm 'ma = I was astounded by this film

sylfaen (*plural* **sylfeini**) *noun, feminine*
• = base
• = foundation
• (*in plural*) = the basics, basic principles
  sylfeini'r °Gymraeg = the basics of Welsh
⇒**bôn**

sylfaenol *adjective*
= basic, fundamental
byddan nhw wedi dysgu'r °eirfa sylfaenol erbyn diwedd y °flwyddyn = they will have learnt the basic vocabulary by the end of the year

sylfaenydd (*plural* **sylfaenwyr**) *noun, masculine*
= founder

sylfeini *plural of*
⇒**sylfaen**

sylw *noun, masculine*
= attention
rhoddir sylw manwl i °gymwysterau pob ymgeisydd = close attention will be given to every applicant's qualifications

sylwebaeth (*plural* **-au**) *noun, feminine*
= commentary

sylweddol *adjective*
= appreciable, substantial
mae prisiau tai wedi codi'n sylweddol yn °ddiweddar = house prices have risen appreciably *or* substantially of late

sylweddoli *verbnoun*
= realize
o'n i heb sylweddoli hynny, a dweud y gwir = I hadn't realized that, actually

sylwi *verbnoun*
= notice (**ar°** with object)
o'n i heb sylwi, a dweud y gwir = I hadn't noticed, actually
roedd aelodau wedi dechrau sylwi ar °gysondeb yr adroddiadau beirniadol = members had begun to notice the consistency of the critical reports

syllu *verbnoun*
= stare, gaze (**ar°** at)
paid syllu arna i felly! = stop staring at me like that!

symbylu *verbnoun*
= stimulate, spur

syml *adjective*
comparative **symlach,** *superlative* **symla(f)**
= simple
na i °drio gwneud pethau mor syml ag y galla i = I'll try and make things as simple as I can
mae'n symlach nag o'n i'n °feddwl = it's simpler than I thought

symledd *noun, masculine*
= simplicity

symleiddio *verbnoun*
= simplify

symud *verbnoun*
= move
pryd symudoch chi i °Gymru? = when did you move to Wales?
°elli di symud y °gadair 'ma draw fan'na i mi? = can you move this chair over there for me?
°welwch chi'r peth bach 'na'n symud ar °draws y sgrîn? = do you see that little thing moving across the screen?

symudiad (*plural* **-au**) *noun, masculine*
= move, movement
⇒**mudiad**

symudol *adjective*
= mobile, movable

syndod (*plural* **-au**) *noun, masculine*
= surprise
oedd hi'n syndod i mi faint oedd e'n yfed = it was a surprise to me how much he was drinking
⇒**synnu**

synhwyro *verbnoun*
= sense
⇨**synnwyr**

synhwyrol *adjective*
= sensible

syniad (*plural* **-au**) noun, masculine
= idea
**does gynna i °ddim syniad lle gallen
nhw °fod** = I've no idea where they
could be
syniad da! = good idea!
**'s gynna i °ddim syniad, mae ofn arna
i** = I've no idea, I'm afraid

synnu *verbnoun*
= be surprised; wonder
**ti'n meddwl dôn nhw'n hwyr?—
synnwn i °ddim** = do you think they'll
come late?—I shouldn't wonder
**mi °fasech chi'n synnu mor °debyg
ydy "ngwaith i a'ch gwaith chi** = you'd
be surprised how similar my work and
your work are
o'n i'n synnu gweld nhw = I was
surprised to see them
⇨**syndod**

synnwyr (*plural* **synhwyrau**) noun,
masculine
• = sense
y pum synnwyr = the five senses
• = reason
**mae hyn yn mynd y tu hwnt i °bob
synnwyr** = this goes beyond all reason
synnwyr cyffredin = common sense

syrffedu (**ar°**) *verbnoun*
= have enough (**ar°** of), be tired (**ar°** of)
dw i wedi syrffedu arni = I've had
enough of it

syrthio *verbnoun*
= fall
paid ti â syrthio! = don't you fall!
mi syrthiodd oddiar ei °feic = he fell off
his bike
⇨**cwympo**

system, sustem (*plural* **-au**) noun,
masculine
= system

syth *adjective*
= straight
dyw'r llinell 'ma °ddim yn syth = this
line isn't straight

ewch yn syth ymlaen lawr fan hyn = go
straight on down here
fe °redodd e'n syth drwy'r °gegin = he
ran straight through the kitchen
yn syth = straight away, directly:
**bydd rhaid i'r comisiwn ailedrych ar
°rai o'r etholaethau'n syth** = the
commission will have to look again at
some of the constituencies straight
away
fe aeth yn °blismon yn syth o'r ysgol =
he became a policeman straight from
school

Tt

ta *conjunction* (*North*)
= or

> ! *This word is used in Northern areas where choice between two things is involved*

heddiw ta fory dach chi am °fynd? = do you want to go today or tomorrow?
⇒**neu°**

'ta *particle* (*North*)
= then
rwan 'ta, beth sy gynnon ni? = now, then, what have we got?
iawn 'ta - ffwrdd â ni! = OK then - off we go!
⇒**'te**

ta beth

1 *pronoun*
= whatever
mae eisiau meddwl am °gyfiawnder, ta beth yw hwnna = we need to think about justice, whatever that is
2 *adverb*
= anyway
does neb yn cytuno â chi, ta beth = nobody agrees with you anyway

tabled (*plural* **-i**) *noun, feminine*
= tablet

taclus *adjective*
= tidy
bydd eisiau cadw'r pethau 'ma'n °daclus, on' bydd? = these things will have to be kept tidy, won't they?

tacluso *verbnoun*
= tidy (up)
tacluswch eich stafelloedd, newch chi? = tidy up your rooms, will you?

Tachwedd *noun, masculine*
= November
⇒**Ionawr**

tad (*plural* **-au**) *noun, masculine*
= father
roedd ⁿnhad yn nabod nhw °flynyddoedd yn ôl = my father knew them years ago
mae hi'n byw gyda'i ʰthad = she lives with her father

Hen °Wlad fy ⁿNhadau = (Old) Land of my Fathers

tad-cu (*plural* **tad-cuod**) *noun, masculine* (*South*)
= grandfather
⇒**taid**

taenu *verbnoun*
• = spread (out)
gad inni °daenu nhw ar y gwely = let's spread them out on the bed
• = scatter
⇒**lledaenu**

taer *adjective*
• = earnest; urgent
..., waeth pa mor °daer yw'r angen = ..., however urgent (is) the need
• = eager
taer yw'r gwir am y golau (*proverb*) = the truth will out (*literally*: the truth is eager for the light)

tafarn (*plural* **-au, tafarndai**) *noun, feminine or masculine*
= pub
pwy sy am °fynd i'r °dafarn heno? = who wants to go to the pub this evening?

tafarnwr (*plural* **tafarnwyr**) *noun, masculine*
= pub landlord

tafell (*plural* **-i, -au, tefyll**) *noun, feminine*
= slice (**o°** of)
°gymera i °dafell o'r un yna, os gwelwch yn °dda = I'll have a slice of that one, please
⇒**sleisen**

taflegryn (*plural* **taflegrau**) *noun, masculine*
= missile

taflen (*plural* **-ni**) *noun, feminine*
= leaflet; sheet
cymerwch °daflen yn y siop = take a leaflet in the shop
cysylltwch â'r swyddfa am °daflen °wybodaeth °gyflawn = contact the office for a full information sheet

taflu, taflyd (*stem* **tafl-**) *verbnoun*
• = throw
mae eisiau i °rywun stopio nhw rhag taflu cerrig fel 'ny = someone should stop them throwing stones like that

°gafodd e ei °daflu allan bron yn syth = he was thrown out almost at once
• = throw away
bydd rhaid taflu nhw = they'll have to be thrown away

taflunydd (*plural* **-ion**) *noun, masculine*
= projector

taflyd
⇒**taflu**

tafod (*plural* **-au**) *noun, masculine*
= tongue
dangos dy °dafod, nei di? = show (me) your tongue, will you?
pryd o °dafod = a telling-off:
°fyddi di'n cael pryd o °dafod = you'll get a telling-off

tafodiaith (*plural* **tafodieithoedd**) *noun, feminine*
= dialect
mae lle canolog i'n tafodieithoedd yn ein bywydau beunyddiol = our dialects have a central place in our everyday lives

tafodieithol *adjective*
= dialectal

tagfa *noun, feminine*
= strangulation; asphyxia

tagfa °geir (*plural* **tagfeydd ceir**) *noun, feminine*
= traffic jam

tagu *verbnoun*
= strangle, choke

tai *plural of*
⇒**tŷ**

taid (*plural* **teidiau**) *noun, masculine* (*North*)
= grandfather
⇒**tad-cu**

tair
⇒**tri**

taith (*plural* **teithiau**) *noun, feminine*
= journey; trip
sut oedd y °daith? = how was the journey?
teithiau o amgylch Bae Ceredigion = trips around Cardigan Bay
⇒**teithio**

tal *adjective*
comparative **talach**, *superlative* **tala(f)**
= tall

mae hi'n °dalach na fi = she's taller than me
pwy ydy'r tala fan hyn? = who is the tallest here?
⇒**taldra**

tâl (*plural* **talau**) *noun, masculine*
= payment; charge; fee
dim tâl ychwanegol = no extra charge
mae'ch tâl aelodaeth yn °ddyledus = your membership fee is due

taladwy *adjective*
= payable
sieciau'n °daladwy i °Gyngor y Sir = cheques payable to the County Council

talai (*plural* **taleion**) *noun, masculine*
= payee

talaith (*plural* **taleithiau**) *noun, feminine*
= state; province
pythefnos i °ddau yn ⁿnhalaith Arizona = a fortnight for two in the state of Arizona

talcen (*plural* **-nau**, **-ni**) *noun, masculine*
= forehead

taldra *noun, masculine*
= tallness; height
... o °daldra = ... in height:
gall yr anifeiliaid 'ma °gyrraedd deg troedfedd o °daldra = these animals can reach ten feet in height

talent (*plural* **-au**) *noun, feminine*
= talent

talentog *adjective*
= talented

talfyriad (*plural* **-au**) *noun, masculine*
• = abbreviation
• = abridgement

talfyrru *verbnoun*
• = abbreviate
• = abridge

taliad (*plural* **-au**) *noun, masculine*
= payment

talu *verbnoun*
= pay
talwch yma = pay here
telir eich cyflog yn °fisol = your salary will be paid monthly

ydych chi wedi talu ac arddangos? =
have you paid and displayed?
dw i heb °gael ⁿhalu = I haven't been
paid
mi °dala i iddo fo'r hyn sy arna i iddo =
I'll pay him what I owe him
faint °dalest ti am y rhain? = how
much did you pay for these?
bydd hi'n talu i chi °fynd yno = it'll pay
you to go there

talwr (*plural* **talwyr**) *noun, masculine*
= payer

tamaid (*plural* **tameidiau**) *noun,
masculine*
= piece; bit
mae tamaid o °gaws ar ôl yn yr oegell
= there's a piece of cheese left in the
fridge
°gest ti dy siomi?—tamaid bach =
were you disappointed?—a little bit
⇒**darn**, ⇒**tipyn**

tan° *preposition*
= until, till

! *This preposition is used primarily
with time-words, while the conjunction
'until (...something happens') is* ⇒**nes**
(*conjunction*). *Compare:*
na i aros yma tan wyth = I'll wait here
until eight
but: **na i aros yma nes iddyn nhw
°alw** (*or:* **... nes bod nhw'n galw**) = I'll
wait here until they call
**°fyddwn ni °ddim yn gweld nhw tan
Nadolig** = we won't see them till
Christmas
but: **°fyddwn ni °ddim yn gweld nhw
nes i'r tywydd °wella** (*or:* **... nes bod
y tywydd yn gwella**) = we won't see
them until the weather gets better
*But sometimes, especially in the
spoken language,* **tan** *is used as a
conjunction, where* ⇒**nes**
(*conjunction*) *would be expected in
the standard language:*
**nes i °ddim addysgu 'n hun go iawn
tan i mi symud i °Loegr** = I didn't
educate myself properly till I moved
to England
Note that in the literary language **tan°**
means 'under', *which in the living
language is* ⇒**dan°** *or* ⇒**o dan.**

⇒**hyd** *conjunction,* ⇒ **nes** *conjunction*

tân (*plural* **tanau**) *noun, masculine*
= fire
ydy rhywun yn mynd i °gynnau tân? =
is someone going to light a fire?
**roedd yr adeiladau i gyd ar °dân erbyn
i'r °frigâd °dân °gyrraedd** = all the
buildings were on fire by the time the
fire brigade arrived
⇒**ar °dân**, ⇒**tanio**

tanbaid *adjective*
= fervent; burning

tanddaear, tanddaearol
adjective
= underground
rheilffordd °danddaear = underground
railway

tanfor(ol) *adjective*
= undersea, submarine
llong °danfor = submarine

tanio *verbnoun*
• = set fire to, set alight
**gad inni °danio'r holl °bapurau 'ma
nawr, 'te** = let's set fire to all these
papers now, then
• = fire (*projectile*)
mae milwyr wedi tanio ar °brotestwyr
= soldiers have fired on protesters
⇒**tân**, ⇒ **saethu**

tanlinellu *verbnoun*
= underline (*also figurative*)
tanlinellwch y gwallau i gyd =
underline all the mistakes
**dydy'r ffaith 'ma'n °ddim ond
tanlinellu'r °broblem go iawn** = this
fact only underlines the real problem
⇒**llinell**

tanwydd (*plural* **-au**) *noun, masculine*
= fuel

tanysgrifiad (*plural* **-au**) *noun,
masculine*
= subscription

tanysgrifio *verbnoun*
= subscribe, take out a subscription (**i°**
to)
neu beth am °danysgrifio? = or what
about subscribing?
**naethon ni °danysgrifio i'r cylchgrawn
'ma llynedd, on'do?** = we took out a
subscription to this magazine last
year, didn't we?

tâp (plural **tapiau**) noun, masculine
= tape

tâp fideo (plural **tapiau fideo**) noun, masculine
= video tape

taran (plural **-au**) noun, feminine
• = thunder
• = clap of thunder
°**glywest ti'r °daran 'na?** = did you hear that thunder?

taranu verbnoun
= thunder

tarddiad (plural **-au**) noun, masculine
= derivation; source

tarddu verbnoun
= derive (**o°** from), come from
mae'n °debyg °fod y gair yn tarddu o'r Ffrangeg = the word probably derives from French
o °ba °wlad mae'r bwydydd 'ma'n tarddu? = what country do these foods come from?

tarian (plural **-nau**) noun, feminine
= shield

taro (stem also **traw-**) verbnoun
= hit; strike
°**gafodd ei °daro gan °gar** = he was hit by a car
mi °ges i ⁿnharo gan ei brwdfrydedd = I was struck by her enthusiasm
...pan °drawodd darnau o'r °gomed y °blaned Iau eleni = ...when pieces of the comet hit the planet Jupiter this year

> **!** This word has a broader range than the more literal ⇒**bwrw** and ⇒**curo**, being used also for most figurative or transferred senses of 'strike'—for example **taro bargen** strike a bargain, **taro ar olew** strike oil, **taro'r awr** strike the hour etc.

tarw (plural **teirw**) noun, masculine
= bull

tasg (plural **-au**) noun, feminine
= task
mae'n °bryd inni wynebu'r °dasg sydd o'n blaen ni = it's time for us to face the task which is before us

tatws plural noun
= potatoes
= potato

> **!** A single potato is usually **taten** noun, feminine

tatws pob = baked potatoes

taw conjunction (South)
= that (in reported speech - focused clauses)

> **!** For a detailed discussion of focused reported speech, see **Grammar reference** section.

o'n i'n meddwl taw fe °wedodd 'ny = I thought that it was he who said that
°**glywes i taw heno maen nhw'n dod** = I heard that it was tonight that they were coming
mae'n amlwg taw nhw sy'n °gyfrifol = it's obvious that they are responsible
efallai taw Sioned oedd yn iawn wedi'r cwbwl = perhaps it was Sioned who was right after all
⇒**y** conjunction, ⇒ **mai**, ⇒**na** conjunction

ta waeth adverb
= never mind
°**fydd hi byth yn cynnig panaid i mi - ond ta waeth am hynny** = she never offers me a cup of tea - but never mind about that

tawel adjective
comparative **tawelach**, superlative **tawela(f)**
= quiet; peaceful
byddwch yn °dawel! = be quiet!
oedd hi'n °dawelach nag arfer yn y siop heddiw = it was quieter than usual in the shop today
llecyn tawel ar °lan yr afon = a quiet/peaceful spot by the river

tawelwch noun, masculine
= quiet; quietness; silence

tawelu verbnoun
= go quiet; quieten down
mae'r adar wedi tawelu = the birds have gone quiet

te noun, masculine
= tea
hoffech chi °banaid o °de? = would you like a cup of tea?

'te particle
= then
nawr 'te—be' nawn ni? = now then— what shall we do?

beth ti'n moyn °wneud, 'te? = what do you want to do, then?

reit 'te—bant â ni! = right then—off we go!

⇒**'ta**

tebyg

1 *adjective*

• = likely

mae'n °bur °debyg mai Jones °fydd yn derbyn y swydd = it's very likely that Jones will get the job

> **!** *The expression* **mae'n °debyg**, *with a following* 'that...' *clause, corresponds to* 'probably' *or, sometimes* 'must' *in the 'supposition' sense* (⇒**rhaid**):
>
> **mae'n °debyg bod ni'n rhy hwyr** = we are probably too late
>
> **mae'n °debyg °fod rhywbeth o'i °le** = something must be wrong
>
> **mae'n °debyg mai breuddwydio o'n i** = I must have been dreaming

• = like; similar (**i°** to)

mae honna'n °debyg iawn i'r un °weles i = that one is very like the one I saw

2 *noun, masculine*

• = likelihood

mi °fydd hi yma yfory, yn ôl pob tebyg = she'll be here tomorrow, in all likelihood

• = like

lliwiau na °welsoch chi mo'u tebyg erioed o'r blaen = colours the like of which you have not ever seen before

tebygol *adjective*

= likely (**o°** to)

mae'r diffyg tebygol o £4 biliwn felly'n °gwbl °groes i'r disgwyl = the likely deficit of £4 billion is therefore completely against expectations

tebygolrwydd *noun, masculine*

= likelihood; probability

tebygrwydd *noun, masculine*

= similarity; likeness

teg *adjective*

comparative **tecach,** *superlative* **teca(f)**

= fair

teg yw gofyn a oes pwynt inni °fynd â hyn ymhellach = it is fair to ask whether there is any point in our taking this any further

> **!** *Note the common expression* **chwarae teg** fair play—*used in a concessive or admissive sense:*
>
> **maen nhw wedi gwneud yn °dda iawn, chwarae teg iddyn nhw** = they've done very well, fair play to them

yn ara(f) °deg = slowly

tegell (*plural* **-au**) *noun, masculine*

= kettle

mae'r tegell yn berwi = the kettle's boiling

wyt ti wedi rhoi'r tegell i °ferwi? = have you put the kettle on?

teilwng *adjective*

= worthy; deserving (*adjudication in eisteddfod competitions*)

neb yn °deilwng nobody deserving (*the prize*)

teimlad (*plural* **-au**) *noun, masculine*

= feeling

teimlo *verbnoun*

= feel

dw i'n teimlo'n °flinedig = I feel tired

sut mae'n teimlo? = how does it feel?

mi °fedra i °deimlo fo °rywle fan hyn = I can feel it somewhere here

mae'r gweithlu bellach yn teimlo nad yw eu swyddi'n °ddiogel = the workforce now feel that their jobs are not safe

⇒**cydymdeimlo**

teipiadur (*plural* **-on**) *noun, masculine*

= typewriter

teipio *verbnoun*

= type

teipydd (*plural* **-ion**) *noun, masculine*

= typist

teipyddes (*plural* **-au**) *noun, feminine*

= typist

teirw *plural of*

⇒**tarw**

teisen (*plural* **-nau**) *noun, feminine*

= cake

⇒**cacen**

teitl (*plural* **-au**) *noun, masculine*

= title

beth ydy teitl y llyfr? = what is the title of the book?

teithiau *plural of*
⇨**taith**

teithio *verbnoun*
  = travel; make a trip
  **ei °brif °ddiddordebau ydy teithio a
  darllen** = his main interests are
  travelling and reading
⇨**taith**

telediad (*plural* **-au**) *noun, masculine*
  = (*TV*) transmission

teledu *noun, masculine*
  = television, TV
  beth sy ar y teledu heno? = what's on
  television this evening?
  dw i eisiau gwylio'r teledu = I want to
  watch TV
  nei di °ddiffodd y teledu? = will you
  switch off the television?
  teledu lloeren = satellite TV

telyn (*plural* **-au**) *noun, feminine*
  = harp

telynor (*plural* **-ion**) *noun, masculine*
  = harpist

telynores (*plural* **-au**) *noun, feminine*
  = harpist

tenau *adjective*
  comparative **teneuach,** *superlative*
    teneua(f) (or *with* **mwy, mwya)**
  = thin
  ti'n edrych yn °denau ofnadwy! = you
  look awfully thin!
  **gofala °fod ti °ddim yn torri nhw'n rhy
  °denau** = watch you don't cut them
  too thin

terfyn (*plural* **-au**) *noun, masculine*
  = end
  rhoi terfyn ar° rywbeth = to put an end
  to something

terfynol *adjective*
  = final
  rownd °derfynol Cwpan y Byd = the
  final round of the World Cup

terfysgaeth *noun, feminine*
  = terrorism

terfysgwr (*plural* **terfysgwyr**) *noun,
  masculine*
  = terrorist

term (*plural* **-au**) *noun, masculine*
  = term

**yn ⁿnhermau pêl-droed o leiaf, trasiedi
  yw hi** = in terms of football at least, it
  is a tragedy
⇨**tymor**

testun (*plural* **-au**) *noun, masculine*
• = text
  **byddwn ni'n edrych yn °fanwl ar y
  testun** = we will be taking a detailed
  look at the text
• = subject
  beth ydy testun y °ddarlith? = what is
  the subject of the lecture?
⇨**pwnc**

teulu (*plural* **-oedd**) *noun, masculine*
  = family
  sut mae'r teulu dyddiau 'ma? = how's
  the family these days?
  dych chi wedi cwrdd â ⁿnheulu? = have
  you met my family?

teuluol *adjective*
  = family, familial

tew *adjective*
  comparative **tewach,** *superlative*
    tewa(f)
• = fat
  mae'r un yma'n °dewach na'r lleill =
  this one is fatter than the others
• = thick (*especially of liquids, etc*)
  **peidiwch gwneud y cymysgedd yn
  rhy °dew** = don't make the mixture too
  thick

teyrnas (*plural* **-oedd**) *noun, feminine*
  = kingdom
  y °Deyrnas Unedig = the United
  Kingdom

teyrnasu *verbnoun*
  = reign
....
th-
  look up **th-** after all the **t**'s
....

ti *pronoun*
  = you (*familiar singular*)
  °welest ti nhw? = did you see them?
  °weles i ti = I saw you
  beth sy'n bod arnat ti? = what's the
  matter with you?
  oes car 'da ti? = have you got a car?
  ti sy'n °gyfrifol am hyn = (it is) <u>you</u>
  (who) are responsible for this
  ti oedd yn iawn = <u>you</u> were right

  ! *This pronoun is used with single
  individuals on familiar terms with the*

speaker. In practice this means:
    a close friend; a close member of
    the family; a child; an animal; a god
    In all other instances, including all
cases where more than one individual
is addressed, ⇒**chi** *and related*
words must be used.

    There is a variant form **di**, *which is*
used instead of **ti** *in the following*
circumstances:
    a) in the inflected future
pam na °ddoi di hefo ni? = why don't
you come with us?
°gymeri di °ragor? = will you take
some more?
    b) generally as the 'echoing'
pronoun with the possessive
adjective **dy°**
beth yw dy °gyfeiriad di? = what is
your address?
mae dy °lyfrau di ar y bwrdd = your
books are on the table
    c) generally as a reinforcing pronoun
after a singular imperative
aros di fan hyn tra bo' fi'n ffonio =
you wait here while I phone
but not after **paid**:
paid ti â dweud pethau felly! = don't
you say such things!

⇒**chi**, ⇒**tithau**, ⇒ **chdi.**

ticed (*plural* **-i**) *noun, masculine*
    = ticket
⇒**tocyn**

tîm (*plural* **timau**) *noun, masculine*
    = team

timod *contraction of* **wyt ti'n gwybod**
    = you know, y'know
⇒**gwybod**, ⇒**chimod**

tin (*plural* **-au**) *noun, feminine*
    = arse; backside

tipyn *noun, masculine*
    = a bit; a little bit
**dych chi'n siarad Cymraeg?—tipyn
(bach)** = do you speak Welsh?—a (little)
bit
mae'n teimlo °dipyn yn °well heddiw =
he's feeling a bit better today
mae tipyn ar ôl = there's a bit left
**mae cryn °dipyn o °drafod wedi bod
yn °barod** = there has already been
quite a bit of discussion
bydd yn rhaid mynd °dipyn yn uwch =
(you) will have to go a bit higher

**hoffwn i °fod wedi gweld tipyn mwy o
°bwyslais ar ei °flynyddoedd cynnar**
    = I would have liked to see a little more
emphasis on his early years

tir (*plural* **-oedd**) *noun, masculine*
    = land
**mae'r tir yn rhy isel fan'ma, °welwch
chi** = the land is too low here, you see
oedd y rhan °fwya'n gweithio ar y tir =
most were working on the land

tirlun (*plural* **-iau**) *noun, masculine*
    = landscape
**mi °all y tirlun yma edrych yn °drist
braidd ar °brydiau** = this landscape
can look rather sad at times

tisian *verbnoun*
    = sneeze

tithau *pronoun*
    = you (*familiar singular*)

> **!** *This is one of the special set of
> expanded pronouns that are used—
> though not that frequently—to convey
> emphasis or some idea of contrast
> with, or echoing of, what has gone
> before. A variant* **dithau** *is used
> where* **di** *would replace* ⇒**ti**.

Nadolig Llawen i ti!—a tithau! = a
Happy Christmas to you!—and (to) you
too!
iawn—mi °gei dithau ffonio nhw! =
OK—<u>you</u> can phone them!
⇒**ti**

tiwtor (*plural* **-iaid**) *noun, masculine*
    = tutor

tiwtora *verbnoun*
    = act/work as a tutor

tlawd *adjective*
    comparative **tlotach,** *superlative*
    tlota(f), *plural* **tlodion**
    = poor
**oedd pobol yn °dlotach o °lawer °bryd
hynny** = people were much poorer
then
mor °dlawd â llygoden eglwys = as
poor as a church mouse

tlodi *noun, masculine*
    = poverty

tlws *adjective* (*feminine* **tlos**)
    = pretty
⇒**pert**

to (plural **-eau**, **-eon**) noun, masculine
= roof
rhoi'r ffidil yn y to = give up, abandon:
o'n i'n teimlo fel rhoi'r ffidil yn y to = I
felt like giving up
to bach = circumflex accent

toc adverb
= soon, shortly
°fydda i 'na toc = I'll be there in a
moment
toc ar ôl i'r Rhufeiniaid °adael = just
after the Romans left

tocyn (plural **-nau**) noun, masculine
= ticket
dw i heb °brynu'r tocynnau = I haven't
bought the tickets
⇒**ticed**

tocyn tymor (plural **tocynnau tymor**)
= season ticket

toddi verbnoun
= melt; thaw

toddydd (plural **-ion**) noun, masculine
= solvent

toiled (plural **-au**, **-i**) noun, masculine
= toilet

! **tŷ bach** or (North) **lle chwech** are
widely used as euphemisms.

tollti
⇒**tywallt**

ton (plural **-nau**) noun, feminine
= wave

tôn (plural **tonau**) noun, feminine.
• = tone
• = tune

tonfedd (plural **-i**) noun, feminine
= wavelength

top (plural **-iau**) noun, masculine
= top
ar °dop... = on the top of...
llawn °dop = full up:
dyn ni'n llawn °dop ers bore 'ma =
we've been full up since this morning
⇒**copa**, ⇒**pen**

torf (plural **-eydd**) noun, feminine
= crowd
**mae'r °dorf yn amlwg yn dechrau colli
amynedd nawr** = the crowd are clearly
beginning to lose patience now

torfol
in: **y cyfryngau torfol** = the mass media

torheulo verbnoun
= sunbathe

torri verbnoun
• = break
nes i °dorri ⁿghoes llynedd = I broke
my leg last year
canwch y larwm drwy °dorri'r gwydr =
sound the alarm by breaking the glass
mae'r rhain wedi'u torri = these are
broken
• = cut
**gallech °dorri'ch bil siopa yn ei
hanner** = you could cut your shopping
bill in half
torri ar °draws = interrupt
peidiwch torri ar ⁿnhraws i! = don't
interrupt me!
⇒**agor**
• = tear
torrwch y papur fel hyn = tear the
paper like this
⇒**rhwygo**

torth (plural **-au**) noun, feminine
= loaf
°ga i °dorth °wen os gwelwch yn °dda?
= can I have a white loaf please?

tost adjective
• = sore; aching; painful
oes pen tost 'da hi? = has she got a
headache?
mae stumog °dost 'da fi = I've got
stomach ache
• (South also:) = ill
wi'n teimlo'n °dost = I feel ill

tra
1 conjunction
= while

! As a conjunction, **tra** is followed by a
'that...' clause.

ac un peth arall, tra bo fi 'ma... = and
another thing, while I'm here...
2 adverb
= quite; entirely; very
peth tra gwahanol yw hynny = that's
quite a different thing/matter
sustem °dra effeithiol = a very effective
system

trachefn, **°drachefn** adverb
= again

> **!** *A rare alternative for* ⇨**eto**

traddodiad (*plural* **-au**) *noun,*
masculine
= tradition
pobl sy'n ymfalchïo yn eu hiaith a'u
traddodiadau = people who are proud
of their language and their traditions

traddodiadol *adjective*
= traditional

traean (*plural* **-au**) *noun, masculine*
= third (*fraction*)

traed *plural of*
⇨**troed**

traeth (*plural* **-au**) *noun, masculine*
= beach
yna aethon ni i'r traeth = then we went
to the beach

traethawd (*plural* **traethodau**) *noun,*
masculine
= essay; dissertation

trafnidiaeth *noun, feminine*
• = transport
bydd eisiau buddsoddi mewn addysg,
iechyd, trafnidiaeth ac ati = (we) will
need to invest in education, health,
transport and so on
• = traffic
⇨**traffig**

trafod *verbnoun*
= discuss
mae'n hen bryd inni °drafod hyn oll =
it's high time we discussed all this

trafodaeth (*plural* **-au**) *noun, feminine*
= discussion
dw i am ehangu'r °drafodaeth ychydig
= I want to broaden the discussion a bit

trafferth (*plural* **-ion**) *noun, feminine or*
masculine
• = trouble, bother
pam mynd i'r °drafferth o °ddefnyddio
dros °fil o °eiriau? = why go to the
trouble of using over a thousand
words?
• (*in plural*) = trouble, problems,
difficulties
°ges i °drafferthion ar y ffordd yn ôl = I
had problems on the way back
⇨**didrafferth**

trafferthu *verbnoun*
= go to trouble, bother

trafferthus *adjective*
= troublesome

traffig *noun, masculine*
= traffic
traffig osgoi = diverted traffic

tragwyddol *adjective*
= eternal

trais *noun, masculine*
= violence
mae 'na °lai o °drais a ʰphethau
dyddiau 'ma, ond... = there is less
violence and (such) things these days,
but...

tramgwydd *noun, masculine*
maen (*plural* **meini**) **tramgwydd** =
stumbling block

tramor
1 *adverb*
= abroad
dych chi'n mynd tramor eleni? = are
you going abroad this year?
2 *adjective*
= foreign
mae'r peiriannau i gyd o °wneuthuriad
tramor = the machines are all of
foreign manufacture
⇨**estron**

trannoeth *adverb*
= the next day

> **!** *Usually* °**drannoeth** *because of its*
adverbial use.

°**drannoeth, fe °gododd y °ddau fel**
arfer = the next day, the two of them
got up as usual

traul (*plural* **treuliau**) *noun, feminine*
= consumption
traul tanwydd = fuel consumption
ar °draul = at the expense of:
mi °gyflawnodd ei °waith arloesol ar
°**draul ei iechyd** = he completed his
pioneering work at the expense of his
health

trawiad (*plural* **-au**) *noun, masculine*
= stroke; blow
trawiad ar y °galon = heart attack

trawiadol *adjective*
= striking, impressive

traws
⇨**ar °draws**

trawsblannu *verbnoun*
= transplant (*also figurative*)

trawsnewid (*stem* **trawsnewidi-**)
verbnoun
= transform

tre(f) (*plural* **trefi, trefydd**) *noun,
feminine*
= town
**y °dre °fwya ar hyd yr arfordir
gorllewinol** = the biggest town along
the west coast

> **!** *Note that* 'in (to) town' *and* 'to town'
> *require the definite article in Welsh:*
> **awn ni i'r °dre, 'te** = let's go into town,
> then
> **mae'n byw °rywle yn y °dre bellach**
> = he/she lives somewhere in town
> now

trechu *verbnoun*
= defeat, beat
**trechwyd y Sacsoniaid mewn brwydr
°waedlyd yn Hastings** = the Saxons
were defeated in a bloody battle at
Hastings
⇒**curo**

tref
⇒**tre(f)**

trefn (*plural* **-au**) *noun, feminine*
• = order
rhowch nhw yn ⁿnhrefn yr °wyddor =
put them in alphabetical order
• = system
**mae'r rhan °fwya wedi addasu'n iawn
i'r °drefn newydd** = most have adapted
OK to the new system

trefniad (*plural* **-au**) *noun, masculine*
= arrangement

trefniadur (*plural* **-on**) *noun,
masculine*
= (personal) organizer (*book*)

trefniant (*plural* **trefniannau**) *noun,
masculine*
= arrangement

trefnu *verbnoun*
= arrange; organize
**dyn ni wedi trefnu cwrdd wythnos
nesa** = we've arranged to meet next
week
**fe °drefnwyd y cyfan gan ysgolion
lleol** = the whole thing was organized
by local schools

trefnus *adjective*
= orderly; in order

trefnydd (*plural* **-ion**) *noun, masculine*
= organizer
pwy °fydd trefnydd y cwrs 'ma? = who
will be the organizer of this course?

trefol *adjective*
= urban

treial (*plural* **-on**) *noun, masculine*
= trial
**cynhelir treialon cŵn defaid yma
°ddydd Sadwrn nesa** = sheepdog
trials will be held here next Saturday
**disgwylir iddyn nhw °fynd i °dreial yn
y °flwyddyn newydd** = they are
expected to go on trial in the new year
⇒**trio**

treiddgar *adjective*
= penetrating

treiddio *verbnoun*
= pierce, penetrate

treiglad (*plural* **-au**) *noun, masculine*
= (grammatical) mutation
treiglad meddal = soft mutation
treiglad llaes = aspirate mutation
treiglad trwynol = nasal mutation

treiglo *verbnoun*
= mutate (*initial letter*)

treisio *verbnoun*
= rape

treisiol *adjective*
= violent

trên (*plural* **trenau**) *noun, masculine*
= train
dw i'n meddwl awn ni ar y trên
or: **dw i'n meddwl awn ni gyda'r trên** =
I think we'll go by train

treth (*plural* **-i**) *noun, feminine*
= tax
**fe °fydd hynny'n gostwng lefel eich
trethi** = that will lower the level of your
taxes
treth ar °werth (T.A.W.) = value added
tax (V.A.T.)

trethdalwr (*plural* **trethdalwyr**) *noun,
masculine*
= taxpayer

treuliau teithio *plural noun*
= travelling expenses

treulio *verbnoun*
= spend (*time*)
°dreulies i wythnos °gyfan yn gorwedd ar y traeth = I spent a whole week lying on the beach
⇨**gwario**

tri[h] *numeral* (*feminine* **tair**)
= three
mae gynnon ni °dri o °blant = we've got three children
lleolir y dramâu eleni mewn tair prif °ganolfan = the plays this year will be located in three main centres
bydd y tri ohonon ni'n mynd gyda'n gilydd = the three of us will go together

> **!** *In the literary language,* **tri** (*but not* **tair**) *is followed by the aspirate mutation—so* **tri** [h]**cheffyl** *three horses but* **tair coeden** *three trees. In the spoken language* **tri ceffyl** *is just as common. As always, aspirate mutation of* **p-** *and* **t-** *is even less likely in speech.*
>   *When the numeral functions as a pronoun (i.e. without a following noun),* **tair** *is only used where all three individuals referred to are feminine—otherwise* **tri**.

⇨**trydydd**

trideg *numeral*
= thirty

tridiau *adverb*
= (period of) three days
bydd y °gynhadledd yn para am °dridiau = the conference will last for three days
⇨**diwrnod,** ⇨**dydd**

trigolion *plural noun*
= inhabitants; dwellers
pa °ganran o °drigolion y °dre sy bellach yn °ddiwaith, 'te? = what percentage of the townspeople are now unemployed, then?

trin (*stem* **trini-**) *verbnoun*
• = treat (*patient*)
lle dych chi'n cael eich trin ar hyn o °bryd? = where are you being treated at the moment?
• = deal with

dyn anodd ei °drin = a difficult man to deal with
⇨**delio**

triniaeth (*plural* **-au**) *noun, feminine*
= treatment
mae'r gweddill yn cael triniaeth mewn ysbytai lleol = the rest are receiving treatment in local hospitals

trio *verbnoun*
= try
beth dych chi'n trio °ddweud? = what are you trying to say?
°dries i °ddwywaith cyn rhoi'r gorau iddi = I tried twice before giving up

> **!** *A variant form* **treial** *is heard in some areas.*

⇨**ceisio**

trist *adjective*
= sad
on'd ydyn nhw'n edrych yn °drist? = don't they look sad?

tristwch *noun, masculine*
= sadness

tro (*plural* **-eon, -eau**) *noun, masculine*
• = time
dyma'r pedwerydd tro i mi °ofyn = this is the fourth time I've asked
dan ni heb °weld ti ers tro = we haven't seen you for a (long) time
'na °ddigon am y tro = that's enough for now
mae ymwelwyr yn dod yn ôl yma °dro ar ôl tro = visitors come back here time after time

> **!** *This word is used for* 'time' *when talking about* 'how many times'. *For* 'once', 'twice', 'three times' *etc.*
> ⇨**gwaith** *noun, feminine*
>   *A related adverb is* ⇨**droeon** *more than once, several times*

• = turn
dy °dro di nawr! = your turn now!
mynd am °dro = go for a walk:
aethon ni am °dro ar ôl cinio = we went for a walk after lunch

troad (*plural* **-au**) *noun, masculine*
= turn
ar °droad y °ganrif = at the turn of the century

trobwynt (*plural* **-iau**) *noun, masculine*
= turning point

troed (*plural* **traed**) *noun, masculine or feminine*
= foot
cerwch mas i chwarae—dych chi dan °draed o hyd! = go out and play—you're under my feet the whole time!
mae rhywbeth ar °droed = something is afoot
tŷ bychan ar °droed y rhiw = a little house at the foot of the hill

troedfedd (*plural* **-i**) *noun, feminine*
= foot

troedio *verbnoun*
= walk; tread
troedio llwybrau'r ardal = walking the region's paths

troi (*stem* **tro-, troi-** or **trodd-**) *verbnoun*
= turn
trowch i °dudalen 26 = turn to page 26
nei di °droi'r teledu i lawr ychydig? = will you turn the television down a bit?
mi °droddodd hi i fyny ar y diwedd = she turned up at the end
roedd hi newydd °droi i °fod yn ysgol °gyfun = it had just turned into (being) a comprehensive school
nes i °droi'r swydd i lawr = I turned the job down

tros
⇒**dros**

trosedd (*plural* **-au**) *noun, feminine*
= crime
trosedd a ʰchosb = crime and punishment
cyflawni trosedd = commit a crime

troseddol *adjective*
= criminal

troseddu *verbnoun*
= commit crime
cafwyd lleihad o °fwy na 25% mewn achosion o °droseddu = there has been a reduction of more than 25% in cases of crime/criminal behaviour

troseddwr (*plural* **troseddwyr**) *noun, masculine*
= criminal

trosglwyddo *verbnoun*
= transfer
dw i am °drosglwyddo cant o °bunnoedd i ʰnghyfrif cadw = I want to transfer a hundred pounds to my savings account

trosi *verbnoun*
= translate
bydd rhaid ei °drosi i'r Saesneg °gynta, on' bydd? = it'll have to be translated into English first, won't it?
⇒**cyfieithu**

trosiad (*plural* **-au**) *noun, masculine*
= translation
⇒**cyfieithiad**

trosodd
⇒**drosodd**

trothwy (*plural* **-au, -on**) *noun, masculine*
= threshold
a ninnau ar °drothwy canrif newydd, ... = with us (being) on the threshold of a new century, ...

trowsus *noun, masculine*
= trousers

truan *adjective*
= poor; wretched
beth am yr aderyn truan 'ma? = what about this poor bird?
⇒**°druan**

trueni *noun, masculine*
= pity
'na °drueni! = what a pity!

trugaredd *noun, masculine*
= mercy

trwbl or **trwbwl** *noun, masculine*
= trouble
⇒**bai**, ⇒**trafferth**

trwchus *adjective*
= thick
mae'r eira'n °drwchus fan hyn = the snow is thick here

trwm *adjective*
comparative **trymach,** *superlative* **tryma(f)** *occasional plural* **trymion**
= heavy
ydy hwnna'n rhy °drwm i ti? = is that too heavy for you?
mae'n °drymach nag o'n i'n °feddwl = it's heavier than I thought
bydd cyfarpar arbennig i °bobol trwm eu clyw = there will be special equipment for people who are hard of hearing

trwodd *adverb*
= through

> **!** *This adverb—often* °**drwodd** *in speech—corresponds to the preposition* ⇒**trwy°/**⇒**drwy°.** *Compare:*
> **fe aeth y bws drwy'r °dre** = the bus went through the town
> *but* **fe aeth y bws drwodd** = the bus went through
> > *The same distinction is made with* ⇒**dros°** */* ⇒**drosodd**

mi °rodda i chi °drwodd = I'll put you through

trwsio *verbnoun*
= mend, fix
°elli di °drwsio'r cawod inni? = can you fix the shower for us?

trwy°

> **!** ⇒**drwy°,** *but* **trwy°** *is normal for time expressions of the type* **trwy'r prynhawn** all afternoon

oedd e fan hyn trwy'r amser! = it was here all the time!
bydda i yn 'yn swyddfa trwy'r dydd yfory = I'll be in my office all day tomorrow
⇒**drwy °gydol**

trwyadl *adjective*
= thorough
rhaid aros nes ei °fod yn cael ei ymchwilio'n °drwyadl = we must wait until it has been thoroughly investigated
⇒**trylwyr**

trwydded (*plural* **-au**) *noun, feminine*
= licence
trwydded °yrru (*plural* **trwyddedau gyrru**) = driving licence

trwyddedu *verbnoun*
= license

trwyn (*plural* **-au**) *noun, masculine*
= nose
°alla i °ddim anadlu'n iawn drwy ⁿnhrwyn = I can't breathe properly through my nose

trychineb (*plural* **-au**) *noun, masculine or feminine*
= disaster
oedd hi'n °drychineb! = it was a disaster!

trychinebus *adjective*
= disastrous

trydan *noun, masculine*
= electricity
mae'ch bil trydan yn dal heb ei °dalu = your electricity bill is still unpaid

trydanol *adjective*
= electric

trydanwr (*plural* **trydanwyr**) *noun, masculine*
= electrician

trydydd *adjective* (*feminine* **trydedd°**)
= third

> **!** *Ordinal numerals are adjectives, but behave in a special way. All other than* ⇒**cynta** *precede the noun. With feminine singular nouns, the noun itself undergoes soft mutation, as does the ordinal after the article—so:*
> **y trydydd car** the third car *but* **y °drydedd °goeden** the third tree.

dyma'r trydydd tro i mi °geisio = this is the third time I've tried
y °drydedd °goeden o'r chwith = the third tree from the left
ac yn °drydydd, ... = and thirdly, ...
⇒**tri**

trylwyr *adjective*
= thorough
bydd yr ymgeisydd llwyddiannus â gwybodaeth °drylwyr o'i °bwnc/ᵐphwnc = the successful candidate will have a thorough knowledge of his/her subject
⇒**trwyadl**

trymaidd *adjective*
= close, sultry
mae wedi bod yn °drymaidd heddiw = it's been close today
⇒**mwll**

trysor (*plural* **-au**) *noun, masculine*
= treasure

trywanu *verbnoun*
= stab
mi °gafodd dyn ei °drywanu yn y °dre neithiwr = a man was stabbed in the town last night

tu *noun, masculine*
= side

! *This word is of much more restricted use than* ⇒**ochor**, *and is found mostly in the prepositions* ⇒**tu allan**, ⇒**tu cefn**, ⇒**tu draw**, ⇒**tu fewn**, ⇒**tu hwnt**, ⇒**tu mewn** *and* ⇒**tu ôl**.
Note also the phrase **o °du** *from, used particularly where different parties or differing viewpoints are involved*:
ond beirniadaeth hallt a °ddaeth o °du'r llywodraethwyr = but harsh criticism came from the governors

tuaʰ (*before vowels* **tuag**) *preposition*

! *As always in the spoken language, aspirate mutation is applied inconsistently if at all, and in any case rarely with* **p-** *and* **t-**.

• = about, approximately
°ddo i'n ôl tua chwech, 'te = I'll come back (at) about six, then
mae tua dwsin ohonyn nhw ar ôl, dw i'n meddwl = there are about a dozen of them left, I think
• = towards

! *In this sense,* **tua** *is less frequent than* ⇒**tuag at°**

mae pobloedd yr ardal yn dechrau edrych tua'r Dwyrain = the peoples of the region are beginning to look towards the East

tuag at° *preposition*
= towards; in the direction of
mae angen mwy o °barch tuag at safbwyntiau pobol eraill = we need more respect for other people's points of view

tu allan (*or* **y tu allan**) *adverb*
= outside
mae'r cŵn yn byw tu allan = the dogs live outside

! *This adverb appears with the definite article when a preposition precedes*:
y °broblem yw bod nhw'n cynrychioli seddi o'r tu allan i °Gymru = the problem is that they represent seats outside Wales

tu cefn (*or* **y tu cefn**) (**i°**) *preposition*
= behind

°elli di sefyll tu cefn iddo am eiliad? = can you stand behind him for a moment?

! *This adverb appears with the definite article when a preposition precedes*:
o'r tu cefn daeth e = he came from behind

⇒**tu ôl**

tudalen (*plural* **-nau**) *noun, masculine or feminine*
= page
rhowch eich enw llawn ar °waelod y tudalen ola = put your full name at the bottom of the last page
mae tudalen °wag ar y diwedd = there's an empty page at the end

tu draw (*or* **y tu draw**) (**i°**) *preposition*
= beyond
mi aeth y canlyniadau y tu draw i °bob disgwyl = the results went beyond all expectations
⇒**draw**, ⇒**tu hwnt**

tuedd (*plural* **-iadau**) *noun, feminine*
= tendency

tueddol *adjective*
= inclined, having a tendency (**o°** to)

tueddu *verbnoun*
= tend (**i°** to)
mae rhieni'n tueddu i °feio'u hunain = parents tend to blame themselves

tu fas *adverb*
⇒**tu allan**

tu fewn (*or* **y tu fewn**) (**i°**) *preposition*
= within; inside
°gawn ni °weld beth sy tu fewn = let's see what's inside
mae rhai'n dal tu fewn i'r adeilad = some are still inside the building

! *This adverb appears with the definite article when a preposition precedes*:
mae'n edrych yn °well o'r tu fewn = it looks better from the inside

⇒**o fewn**

tu hwnt (*or* **y tu hwnt**) (**i°**)
1 *preposition*
= beyond

mae hyn wedi mynd tu hwnt i °bob rheswm = this has gone beyond all reason

mae'r °dasg tu hwnt i °allu ffotograffydd = the task is beyond the abilities of a photographer

maen nhw wedi diddanu cynulleidfaoedd dros °Gymru a tu hwnt = they have entertained audiences all over Wales and beyond

⇒**tu draw**

2 adverb (follows adjective)
= extremely

oedd y °ddarlith heddiw'n °ddiflas tu hwnt = the lecture today was extremely boring

⇒**dros ben**

tu mas adverb
⇒**tu allan**

tu mewn (or y tu mewn)
variant of ⇒**tu fewn**

tun (plural **-iau**) noun, masculine
= tin, can

tunnell (plural **tunelli**) noun, feminine
= ton

tu ôl (or y tu ôl) (**i°**) preposition
= behind

mae e'n gweithio tu ôl i'r bar heddiw = he's working behind the bar today

hynny, nid lles y °wlad, sydd y tu ôl i amryw o'i °benderfyniadau = that, (and) not the good of the country, is what is behind some of his decisions

⇒**tu cefn**

t'wel contraction of **wyt ti'n gweld**
= you see

⇒**gweld,** ⇒**ch'wel**

twf noun, masculine
= growth

gyda twf economïau marchnad yn ⁿNwyrain Ewrop... = with the growth of market economies in Eastern Europe...

⇒**cynnydd**

twll (plural **tyllau**) noun, masculine
• = hole

mae twll yn dy °grys! = there's a hole in your shirt!

y twll yn yr haen osôn = the hole in the ozone layer

• (derogatory) = dump

mae'r °dre 'ma'n °dwll o °le = this town is a dump

twll tin
= arsehole (also figurative)

twnel (plural **-au, -i**) noun, masculine
= tunnel

twp adjective
= stupid

paid bod yn °dwp! = don't be stupid!

twpdra noun, masculine
= stupidity

twpsyn noun, masculine
= fool, idiot

twr (plural **tyrau**) noun, masculine
= tower

twrist (plural **-iaid**) noun, masculine
= tourist

twristiaeth noun, feminine
= tourism

twt adjective
= tidy, neat

twt lol! = nonsense!

twyllo verbnoun
= deceive; cheat

mae ein gallu i °dwyllo'n hunain yn anhygoel = our ability to deceive ourselves is incredible

dw i °ddim eisiau gweld neb yn twyllo = I don't want to see anyone cheating

twym adjective (South)
comparative **twymach, twyma(f)**
• = warm
• = hot

mae'n °dwym heddiw, on'd yw hi? = it's hot today, isn't it?

⇒**cynnes,** ⇒**poeth**

twymo verbnoun
= warm/heat up; get warm/hot

twymydd (plural **-ion**) noun, masculine
= heater

twymyn (plural **-au**) noun, feminine
= fever

twyn (plural **-i**) noun, masculine
• = dune
• = hillock

twyn tywod (plural **twyni tywod**)
noun, masculine
= sand dune

tŷ (*plural* **tai**) *noun, masculine*
= house
o'n nhw'n rhannu tŷ °rywle yn y Gogledd = they shared a house somewhere in the North
mae'r tai fan hyn i gyd wedi'u llosgi'n ulw = all the houses here have been burnt to ashes
°welwch chi'r rhes o °dai fan 'cw? = do you see that row of houses over there?
mae eu tŷ nhw'n rhy °fach iddyn nhw = their house is too small for them
yn tŷ = at home
yn tŷ ni = in our home

> **!** *Note that* **tŷ bach** *is the standard euphemism for* 'toilet', *while* 'a small house' *is* **tŷ bychan**.

⇒**adre(f)**, ⇒ **gartre(f)**

tyb (*plural* **-iau**) *noun, masculine or feminine*
= opinion (*in the sense of 'estimation', and therefore less common than* ⇒**barn**)

tybed *adverb*
= I wonder
tybed oes amser 'da ni? = I wonder if we've got time?
pwy °fyddai wedi dweud hynny, tybed? = who would have said that, I wonder?
tybed be' °ddaeth ohono fo? = I wonder what became of him?

> **!** *This is an invariable word (but* ⇒**tybio**) *that can either begin the sentence or be tagged on at the end.*

⇒**'sgwn i**

tybiedig *adjective*
= supposed
awdur tybiedig y gwaith hwn = the supposed author of this work

tybio, tybied (*stem* **tybi-**) *verbnoun*
= suppose, imagine
°dybiwn i = I should imagine *or* suppose:
byddan nhw yma erbyn chwech, °dybiwn i = they'll be here by six, I should imagine
⇒**tybed**

tyddyn (*plural* **-nau, -nod**) *noun, masculine*
= smallholding

tyfiant (*plural* **tyfiannau**) *noun, masculine*
= growth

tyfu *verbnoun*
= grow
mae storïau Arthur wedi tyfu a lledaenu trwy Ewrop = the Arthur stories have grown and spread through Europe
mae'r plant wedi tyfu, °fentra i = the children have grown, I bet
fe °dyfodd y galw am °bethau felly yn ystod y rhyfel = the demand for such things grew during the war
mae e'n tyfu tatws = he grows potatoes

tŷ gwydr (*plural* **tai gwydr**) *noun, masculine*
= greenhouse

tynged (*plural* **tynghedau**) *noun, feminine*
= fate; destiny
dal yn y °fantol mae tynged y chwarel = the fate of the quarry is still in the balance

tyngedfennol *adjective*
= fateful

tyngu *verbnoun*
= swear (*an oath*)
naeth e °dyngu na °fyddai fe'n dod yn ôl = he swore he would not come back
⇒**llw**, ⇒**rhegi**

tylwyth
in: **y tylwyth teg** = the fairy folk, the fairies

tyllau *plural of*
⇒**twll**

tyllu *verbnoun*
• = bore
• = perforate, make a hole/holes in

tylluan (*plural* **-od**) *noun, feminine*
= owl
⇒**gwdihŵ**

tymer (*plural* **tymherau**) *noun, feminine*
= temper
tymer °ddrwg iawn sy gynno fo = he's very bad-tempered

tymheredd (*plural* **tymereddau**) *noun, masculine*
= temperature

bydd y tymheredd yn cyrraedd deuddeg gradd erbyn y prynhawn = the temperature will reach twelve degrees by the afternoon

tymor (*plural* **tymhorau**) *noun, masculine*
• = season
  Cyfarchion y Tymor = Season's Greetings
  rhoddir tocyn tymor i °bob myfyriwr = a season ticket will be given to every student
• = term; semester
  pryd mae tymor y Gwanwyn yn dechrau? = when does the Spring term begin?
  tymor byr = short-term
  tymor hir = long-term
  ystyriaethau tymor hir ydy'r rhain i gyd = these are all long-term considerations

tyndra *noun, masculine*
  = tension
  cynyddu mae tyndra yn y Dwyrain Canol = tension is rising in the Middle East

tynnu *verbnoun*
• = pull; draw
  tynnwch i agor = pull to open
  tynnu dy °goes oedd e = he was pulling your leg
  tynna'r llenni, nei di? = draw the curtains, will you?
• = take off (*clothes*);
  tynnwch eich dillad = take your clothes off
• = draw (*picture*)
  °elli di °dynnu llun i mi, 'te? = can you draw me a picture, then?
• = take (*photograph*)
  pam na °ddewch chi draw i °gael tynnu'ch llun? = why don't you come over and have your picture taken?

tŷ sengl (*plural* **tai sengl**) *noun, masculine*
  = detached house

tystio *verbnoun*
• = testify
• (*on certificates*) = certify

tystiolaeth (*plural* **-au**) *noun, feminine*
  = evidence

tystysgrif (*plural* **-au**) *noun, feminine*
  = certificate

tŷ teras (*plural* **tai teras**) *noun, masculine*
  = terraced house

tywallt (*also* **tollti** *in some areas*) *verbnoun* (*North*)
  = pour
  ⇨**arllwys**

tywod *noun, masculine*
  = sand

tywydd *noun, masculine*
  = weather
  sut °dywydd °gest ti ar dy °wyliau? = what kind of weather did you have on your holiday?
  dyma °ragolygon y tywydd am heno ac yfory = here is the weather forecast for tonight and tomorrow

tywyll *adjective*
  comparative **tywyllach**, *superlative* **tywylla(f)**
  = dark
  mae'n rhy °dywyll i °weithio bellach = it's too dark to work now
  dyma'r lliw glas tywylla sy 'da ni = this is the darkest blue we've got

tywyllu *verbnoun*
  = darken; get dark
  gwnewch yn siwr bod chi gartre erbyn iddi °dywyllu = make sure you're home by the time it gets dark

tywyllwch *noun, masculine*
  = darkness

tywys *verbnoun*
  = lead; guide; show round
  bydd myfyrwyr y chweched dosbarth ar gael i'ch tywys o amgylch yr ysgol = sixth form students will be on hand to take you round the school

tywysog (*plural* **-ion**) *noun, masculine*
  = prince
  Tywysog Cymru = the Prince of Wales

tywysogaeth (*plural* **-au**) *noun, feminine*
  = principality

tywysoges (*plural* **-au**) *noun, feminine*
  = princess

TH

theatr (*plural* **-au**) *noun, feminine*
= theatre
theatr awyr agored = an open-air
theatre

thema (*plural* **themâu**) *noun, feminine*
= theme
⇒**pwnc**, ⇒**testun**

therapi (*plural* **therapïau**) *noun,*
masculine
= therapy
therapi gwaith = occupational therapy
therapi lleferydd = speech therapy

therapydd (*plural* **-ion**) *noun,*
masculine
= therapist
rhaid i mi °weld 'n therapydd = I must
see my therapist

thermomedr (*plural* **-au**) *noun,*
masculine
= thermometer

Uu

'u
stands for the possessive adjective ⇒**eu**
after vowels.

ucha(f)
⇒**uchel**

uchafbwynt (*plural* **-iau**) *noun,*
masculine
= high point, climax
daw'r cyfan i uchafbwynt ar y nos
Sadwrn olaf = the whole thing will
come to a high point on the last
Saturday night

uchder (*plural* **-au**) *noun, masculine*
= height

uchel *adjective*
comparative **uwch**, *superlative* **ucha(f)**
• = high
pa mor uchel y gall yr awyrennau 'ma
hedfan? = how high can these planes
fly?
bydd y tymereddau dros y °wlad
ychydig yn uwch heddiw na ddoe =
the temperatures across the country
will be a bit higher today than
yesterday
yr Wyddfa ydy'r mynydd ucha yng
ⁿNghymru = Snowdon is the highest
mountain in Wales

> **!** *The superlative* **ucha(f)** *also*
> *corresponds to* 'upper' *or* 'top' *(as an*
> *adjective)*:
> **y rhan ucha o'r corff** = the upper
> part of the body
> **well gen i eu rhoi nhw yn y**
> **dosbarth ucha'n syth** = I'd rather
> put them in the top class straight
> away

• (*voice*) = loud
paid siarad yn rhy uchel fan hyn =
don't speak too loud here
siaradwch yn uwch! = speak up!

ucheldir (*plural* **-oedd**) *noun,*
masculine
= highland

uchelgais (*plural* **uchelgeisiau**) *noun,*
masculine or feminine
= ambition

uchelgeisiol *adjective*
= ambitious
mae'r cwangos yn cael eu defnyddio gan °bersonoliaethau uchelgeisiol = the quangos are used by ambitious personalities

uchelwydd *noun, masculine*
= mistletoe

uchod
1 *adjective*
= above (*in documents etc*)
yr enwau uchod = the above names
2 *adverb*
..., fel y dywedwyd uchod = ..., as was said above
⇨**isod**

ufudd *adjective*
= obedient
roedd y ci'n dal i aros yn ufudd amdani = the dog was still waiting obediently for her

ufuddhau *verbnoun*
= obey

uffern *noun, feminine*
• = hell
uffern ar y °ddaear = hell on earth
• (*as intensifier*)
be' uffern dych chi'n °wneud? = what the hell are you doing
pwy uffern ydy hwnna? = who the hell is that?
⇨**diawl**, ⇨**cythraul**

uffernol *adjective*
• = hellish
• (*as intensifier*) = awfully, terribly
mae'n °ddrud uffernol, mae'n uffernol o °ddrud = it's awfully expensive

ugain (*plural* **ugeiniau**) *numeral*
• = twenty
ugain o °gystadleuwyr = twenty contestants
mae'n ugain munud i wyth = it's twenty to eight
dim ond papur ugain punt sy gen i = I've only got a twenty pound note
°gwrddes i ag e °gynta ugain °mlynedd yn ôl = I first met him twenty years ago
• (*plural often used to indicate indeterminate number, in the same way as 'scores' in English*):
°weloch chi'r ugeiniau o °bobol tu

allan i sinema Porthmadog neithiwr? = did you see the scores of people outside Porthmadog cinema last night?

! *This numeral, part of the original vigesimal system of counting in Welsh, is used throughout Wales by native speakers, while an alternative 'decimalized' version* **dau °ddeg** *is now promoted in the schools. However, another good reason for using this native form is that the artificial alternative sounds very like* ⇨**deuddeg** *12 (for which, in turn, a 'decimalized' alternative* **undeg dau** *has been produced for schools).*

ugeinfed *adjective*
= twentieth
⇨**pumed**

ulw *plural noun*
= cinders, ashes
llosgi'n ulw = burn to ashes, burn to the ground
mae'r pentre wedi'i °losgi'n ulw = the village has been burnt to the ground

un, un° *numeral*
= one
mae 'na un peth o'n i am °drafod â ti cyn mynd = there's one thing I wanted to discuss with you before going
mi °geith pob un ohonoch chi ei arian yn ôl = every one of you will get his money back
mae un °broblem yn dal heb ei datrys = there is one problem still unsolved
be' nawn ni efo'r un yma, 'ta? = what shall we do with this one, then?

! *This numeral causes soft mutation of a following feminine noun - so* **un ceffyl** *one horse but* **un °gath** *one cat*

⇨**cynta(f)**, ⇨**fesul**, ⇨ **(y) naill°**, ⇨**pa°**, ⇨**rhai** *pronoun*, ⇨**yr un**

undeb (*plural* **-au**) *noun, masculine*
= union
dych chi'n aelod o undeb? = are you a member of a union?
yr Undeb Sofietaidd = the Soviet Union

undonog *adjective*
= monotonous

undydd *adjective*
= one-day

cwrs undydd ar °gyfer dysgwyr **profiadol** = a one-day course for advanced learners

uned (*plural* **-au**) *noun, feminine*
= unit
unedau cegin o ansawdd ar °gael °bob amser = quality kitchen units always available
aed â hi i'r Uned Gofal Dwys = she was taken to the Intensive Care Unit

unedig *adjective*
= united
y °Deyrnas Unedig = the United Kingdom

unfan
in phrases of the type:
arhoswch yn eich unfan! = stay where you are!
naeth e aros yn ei unfan = he stayed where he was
naeth hi aros yn ei hunfan = she stayed where she was

uniaith *adjective*
= monolingual; monoglot
mae posteri uniaith °Gymraeg yn dal i'w gweld ymhobman = Welsh-only posters can still be seen everywhere
plant o °deuluoedd uniaith Saesneg = children from English-only families/monoglot English families

unig(°) *adjective*
• (*precedes noun and causes soft mutation*) = only
fe yw'r unig °ddyn sy'n °gymwys ar °gyfer swydd o'r °fath = he is the only man who is suitable for such a job
• (*follows noun*) = lonely
o'n nhw'n byw mewn bwthyn unig = they lived in a lonely cottage
⇨**yn unig**

unigol *adjective*
= singular; individual

unigolyn (*plural* **unigolion**) *noun, masculine*
= individual
mae hyn yn °fater i'r unigolyn = this is a matter for the individual

unigryw *adjective*
= unique
ond mae'r nodwedd 'ma'n °bell o °fod yn unigryw = but this characteristic is far from (being) unique

union *adjective*
= exact
fe °gafodd ei saethu i lawr wythnos union yn ôl = he was shot down exactly a week ago
yn union = exactly
byddwn ni yno am °dair wythnos (yn) union = we'll be there for three weeks exactly
beth yn union mae hyn yn °feddwl? = what exactly does this mean?
bydd y costau'n llawer uwch, felly? - yn union = so the costs will be much higher? - exactly
⇨**i'r dim**

uniongyrchol *adjective*
= direct
neu fe °allwch chi °gyfrannu'n uniongyrchol at eich hoff elusennau = or you can contribute directly to your favourite charities
debyd uniongyrchol = direct debit

unlle
in: **(dim) yn unlle** = (not) anywhere
⇨**nunlle**

unman
in: **(dim) yn unman** = (not) anywhere,
⇨**nunman**

uno *verbnoun*
• = join
beth am eu huno nhw? = what about joining them together?
• = merge
efallai y bydd eisiau eu huno nhw = perhaps they will have to be merged
yn Lloegr ceisiwyd uno rhai o'r ysgolion = in England an attempt was made to merge some of the schools
• = unite
⇨**ymuno**

unochrog *adjective*
= partisan, biased

unol *adjective*
= united
yn unol â[h] = in accordance with:
fe °redir y digwyddiad 'ma'n unol â rheolau'r clwb = this event will be run in accordance with club rules
yr Unol °Daleithiau = the United States

unrhyw° *adjective*
= any
bydden ni'n °ddiolchgar am unrhyw

°gymorth = we would be grateful for any help

ni °ellir atgynhyrchu unrhyw °ran o'r cyhoeddiad hwn... = no part of this publication can be reproduced...

> ! *Note that* **unrhyw°** *is only used when the sense of* 'any' *is* 'whatever kind/type'. *When, on the other hand,* 'any' *can be removed from the English sentence without altering the sense, then it is not translated in Welsh:*
> **oes afalau 'da chi heddiw?** = have you got any apples today?

unrhywbeth *pronoun*
= anything

byddai unrhywbeth yn °well na'r hyn sy gynnon ni ar hyn o °bryd = anything would be better than what we've got at the moment

unrhywbeth arall? = anything else?

> ! *Note however that* 'not...anything' *is normally* ⇒**dim byd**, *or* ⇒**dim**:
> **°alla i °weld dim** = I can't see anything
> **does dim byd ar ôl** = there isn't anything left

unrhywun *pronoun*
= anyone

mi °fasai unrhywun yn deall hynny = anyone would understand that

> ! *When anyone means* '(hypothetical) someone' *(as opposed to* 'no matter who' *in the example above),* ⇒**rhywun** *is possible as an alternative*
> **oes unrhywun eisiau rhagor o °fanylion, 'te?, oes rhywun eisiau rhagor o °fanylion, 'te?** = does anyone want more details, then?
> *Note that* 'not...anyone' *is normally* ⇒**neb**:
> **°weles i neb** = I didn't see anyone

unwaith
1 *adverb*
= once

dw i wedi dweud wrthat ti mwy nag unwaith heddiw! = I've told you more than once today!

unwaith yn rhagor os gwelwch yn °dda, unwaith eto os gwelwch yn °dda = once more please

2 *conjunction*
= once

unwaith bod y llong wedi mynd, bydd y lle 'ma'n tawelu = once the ship has gone, this place quietens down

unwaith y byddwn ni wedi arwyddo, °fydd 'na °ddim mynd yn ôl = once we have signed, there'll be no going back

> ! *As a conjunction,* **unwaith** *is generally followed by a* 'that...' *clause, but* **mae** *is sometimes found instead of* **bod/°fod**:
> **unwaith mae comed yn °gyfnodol, mae'r diwedd ar y ffordd** = once a comet is periodic, the end is on the way
> *In some Southern areas* **siwrnai** *or* **siwrne** *is used instead of* **unwaith**. **Unwaith** *also serves for* 'once upon a time' *(also* **un tro**):
> **unwaith, mewn gwlad °bell** = once upon a time, in a country far away

urdd *(plural* **-au***) noun, feminine*
= order *(movement)*

Urdd Gobaith Cymru *Welsh language youth movement, referred to as* **yr Urdd**

uwch
⇒**uchel**

uwchben *preposition*
= above; over

°welwch chi'r arwydd 'na uwchben y siop? = do you see that sign over the shop?

uwchfarchnad *(plural* **-oedd***) noun, feminine*
= supermarket
⇒**archfarchnad**

uwchlaw *preposition*
= above

mae'r copaon yn codi rhwng 4000' a 6000' uwchlaw'r môr = the summits rise between 4000' and 6000' above the sea

uwchradd *adjective*
= secondary *(school)*

yn yr ysgol uwchradd mae e yn °barod, 'te? = he's in secondary school already, then?

⇒**cynradd**

uwd *noun, masculine*
= porridge

waeth *adjective*

> **!** *This modal expression takes the construction* **i°** + *subject* + *°verbnoun*:
> **waeth inni °fynd** = we might as well go

⇒**man a man,** ⇒**well**

wal (*plural* **-iau**) *noun, feminine*
= wall (*usually internal*)
⇒**mur**

wastad *adverb*
= always
o'n i'n gweithio gyda merch a oedd wastad yn °grac iawn = I was working with a girl who was always very cross
dw i wastad yn dweud y gallai pethau °fod yn °waeth = I always say things could be worse
⇒**o hyd**

wats
⇒**oriawr**

wedi

> **!** ⇒**Wedi** box

wedyn *adverb*
• = then
trowch i'r °dde fan hyn, wedyn yn syth ymlaen am °filltir = turn right here, then straight on for a mile
wedyn bydd eisiau dod â nhw'n ôl = then (we) will have to bring them back
y ... wedyn the next ...:
ond, y diwrnod wedyn, dyma fe'n dod yn ôl = but, the next day, back he came

> **!** *In speech* **ac wedyn** 'and then' *is often* ⇒**chwedyn.**

• = later (on)
pam na °ddoi di draw wedyn? = why don't you come round later?
gad inni °adael y gweddill tan wedyn = let's leave the rest till later
⇒**yna,** ⇒**nes ymlaen**

weithiau *adverb*
= sometimes

mae pethau felly'n digwydd weithiau = such things happen sometimes
weithiau bydda i'n mynd am °dro cyn swper = sometimes I go for a walk before supper
⇒**gwaith** *noun, feminine*

wel *interjection*
= well
wel, lle °fuoch chi trwy'r dydd? = well, where have you been all day?
oes rhagor i °ddod?—wel, °gawn ni °weld = is there more to come?—well, we'll see

well *adverb*
• = (had) better

> **!** *This modal expression takes the construction* **i°** + *subject* + *°verbnoun*:
> **well inni °fynd** = we'd better go
> **well i'r rhieni °ofyn eu cwestiynau nhw °gynta, dw i'n meddwl** = the parents had better ask their questions first, I think
> **°ddylen ni °ddweud rhywbeth?— well inni °beidio** = should we say something?—we'd better not

• = prefer (+ *noun*), would rather (+ *verb*)

> **!** *In this sense* **well** *is used with* ⇒**gyda** (*I'***da**) (*South*) *or* ⇒**gan°** (*North*); *'to' or* 'than' *is* ⇒**na**ʰ
> **well 'da fi °goffi na te** = I prefer coffee to tea
> **well gynna i °de na ʰchoffi** = I prefer tea to coffee
> **well 'da fi °gerdded na dal y bws** = I'd rather walk than catch the bus

⇒**gwell**

wrth°
1 *preposition*
personal forms:: **wrtha i, wrthat ti, wrtho fe, wrthi hi, wrthon ni, wrthoch chi, wrthyn nhw**
common variants: **wrtho i, wrthot ti**

> **!** *In normal speech all these personal forms tend to lose the* **wr-**: **'tha i, 'that ti, 'tho fe** *etc.*

• (*proximity*)
= by; at
mae rhywun wrth y drws = someone is at the door
oedd o'n sefyll wrth y byrddau 'na trwy'r noson = he was standing by those tables all evening

Wedi

1 PARTICLE

This particle, which does not cause mutation, is used in place of ⇒**yn** *particle* to link a form of ⇒**bod** with a verbnoun when completed rather than ongoing action is indicated. Compare:

mae Gwenith yn darllen y papur = *Gwenith is reading the paper*

mae Gwenith wedi darllen y papur = *Gwenith has read the paper*

Note that there is a greater difference in form between the English sentences than between the Welsh ones, where the change of meaning from ongoing to completed action requires only the change of **yn** to **wedi**.

Further examples:

ydy'r lleill wedi mynd? = *have the others gone?*

mae'r byd wedi newid, a hynny er gwaeth, mae arna i ofn = *the world has changed, and for the worse, I'm afraid*

o'n nhw wedi cytuno'n °barod = *they had already agreed*

°fyddwn ni wedi gadael erbyn i chi °gyrraedd = *we will have left by the time you arrive*

pwy °fasai wedi meddwl? = *who would have thought (it)?*

ond wedi dweud hynny, efallai y dylen ni ailfeddwl = *but having said that, perhaps we should rethink*

Like ⇒**yn** *particle*, **wedi** is used to link a verbnoun to a preceding form of ⇒**bod** associated with it. Unlike **yn**, however, its sense of completed action also allows it to be used with modals like ⇒**dylwn** and ⇒**gallu**; in these cases **wedi** still requires a 'dummy' °**fod** for it to be attached to:

mi °ddylen ni °fod wedi esbonio'r sefyllfa °gynta = *we should have explained the situation first*

gallen nhw °fod wedi cael eu lladd = *they could have been killed*

The 'completed action' sense of **wedi** also leads it to be used in phrases denoting the result of an action. Compare:

°gafodd y ffenest ei ʰchau = *the window was closed* (action)

ffenest wedi'i ʰchau = *a closed window* (state)

In the first of these examples, we visualize the dynamic action of someone closing the window, for which ⇒**cael** + possessive adjective + verbnoun is used; while in the second we visualize a window that is closed (and may have been in that non-dynamic state for some time)—here **cael** (for dynamic action) is not appropriate, while **wedi** (completed action) is. Like **cael**, though, **wedi** here is followed by possessive adjective + verbnoun.

Further examples:

bwydydd wedi'u rhewi = *frozen foods*

dych chi wedi'ch trechu! = *you're beaten!*

nofel wedi'i sgrifennu yn Almaeneg = *a novel written in German*

2 PREPOSITION AFTER

As a preposition, **wedi** is a less common and more formal alternative to ⇒**ar ôl**:

daethon nhw'n ôl wedi'r rhyfel = *they came back after the war* (more usually ...**ar ôl y rhyfel**)

But it is obligatory in telling the time:

mae'n hanner awr wedi wyth = *it's half past eight*

and in the set phrases **wedi'r cwbwl** and **wedi'r cyfan** 'after all'

dim ond gyrrwr lori ydw i, wedi'r cwbwl = *I'm only a lorry-driver, after all*

and **wedi hynny** or **wedi 'ny** 'after that', 'then'

°glywes i °ddim byd mwy wedi 'ny = *I didn't hear anything else after that*

continued overleaf

Wedi continued

---

3 *CONJUNCTION* AFTER

As with its use as a preposition, **wedi** as a time conjunction (+ **i**° + subject + °verbnoun) is much less frequent and

more formal than **ar ôl**:
wedi iddyn nhw °fynd = *after they go/went* (more usually **ar ôl iddyn nhw °fynd**)

- (*with verbs of saying etc*)
  dw i wedi dweud wrthi'n °barod = I've already told her
  roedd e'n murmur yn °dawel wrtho'i hun = he was murmuring quietly to himself
  glynwch y peth 'ma wrth °waelod y silff = stick this thing to the bottom of the shelf
- (*with* ⇒**rhaid**)
  rhaid wrth °gefnogaeth °fwy ymarferol = there is a need for more practical support
- (*with adjectives indicating personal attitude or behaviour towards someone*)
  dig/crac wrth° = angry with
  caredig wrth° = kind to
  cas wrth° = nasty/mean to
  paid bod yn °ddig wrthyn nhw = don't be angry with them
  o'n i'n trio bod yn °garedig wrtho, 'na i gyd = I was trying to be kind to him, that's all
- (*with a verbnoun*)
  = *while ....ing, in ...ing:*
  o'n i'n teimlo'n annifyr °rywsut wrth siarad ag e = I felt awkward somehow while talking to him
- **wrthi**
  = *hard at it; busy*
  ti'n dal wrthi, 'te? = you're still hard at it, then?
  mae'r prif °bleidiau wrthi'n canfasio ar hyd a lled Cymru = the main parties are hard at work canvassing the length and breadth of Wales
  mae'r archeolegwyr wrthi'n chwilio am hen °furiau'r °dre = the archaeologists are busy looking for the old town walls
- (*in idiomatic phrases*)
  wrth °gwrs = of course
  wrth °reswm = of course, naturally

wrth lwc = luckily, as luck would have it:
peth gwahanol yw hynny, wrth °gwrs = that's different, of course
wrth lwc, roedd y trên yn hwyr iawn am unwaith = luckily, the train was very late for once

! *When* **wrth °gwrs** *stands at the front of the sentence, it is generally followed by a 'that...' clause:*
wrth °gwrs bod nhw'n dod gyda ni! = of course they're coming with us!

2 *conjunction*
= *as; while*

! *As a time conjunction* **wrth°** *is followed by the construction* **i**° + *subject +* °*verbnoun, with the tense of the English verb varying according to context.*

bydd llai o adar wrth iddyn nhw °golli eu cynefinoedd = there will be fewer birds as they lose their habitats
°gafodd e °air 'da pob un ohonyn nhw wrth iddyn nhw °fynd allan = he had a word with each of them as they went out
aros fan'na eiliad wrth i mi °orffen y gwaith 'ma = stay there a moment while I finish this work

! *Note that no* **i-** *construction is necessary when the subject on either side of the 'as/while' is the same person or persons:*
diffoddwch y goleuadau wrth °adael = switch off the lights as you leave

ŵy (*plural* **wyau**) *noun, masculine*
= egg

wyf
⇒**bod**

wylo *verbnoun*
   = weep; cry
   ⇒**crio**, ⇒**llefain**

ŵyn
   ⇒**oen**

wyneb (*plural* **-au**) *noun, masculine*
   = face
   dw i'n cofio fel byddai hi'n troi ei
   hwyneb tua'r ffenest = I remember
   how she would turn her face towards
   the window

wynebu *verbnoun*
   = face
   nag ych chi nawr yn wynebu
   rhwygiadau yn y °blaid? = aren't you
   now facing splits in the party?
   rhaid inni wynebu'r ffeithiau = we must
   face the facts

wynwyn, wynwns
   ⇒**nionyn**

ŵyr (*plural* **wyrion**) *noun, masculine*
   • = grandson
   • (*in plural*)
     = grandchildren

wyres (*plural* **-au**)
   = granddaughter

wysg
   in: **yn wysg ei °gefn** = backwards
     (*talking about 'him'* **e**)
   yn wysg eich cefn = backwards (*talking*
     about 'you' **chi**)
   yn wysg ei ʰchefn backwards (*talking*
     about 'her' **hi**)
   i lawr â James yn wysg ei °gefn =
     down (the hill) went James backwards

   > **!** *The possessive adjective in this*
   > *expression varies according to the*
   > *person or object referred to.*

wyt
   ⇒**bod**

wyth *numeral*
   = eight

   > **!** *Generally this numeral is followed*
   > *by an optional soft mutation of a*
   > *following noun. Another common*
   > *construction, however, is* **wyth + o°** +
   > *plural noun.*

   wyth punt *or* **wyth °bunt** = £8

wyth cant *or* **wyth °gant** = eight
   hundred
wyth ⁿmlynedd (*or* **wyth blynedd**) =
   eight years
wyth ⁿniwrnod (*or* **wyth diwrnod**) =
   eight days
wyth cath, wyth °gath *or* **wyth o**
   °gathod = eight cats.

wythfed *adjective*
   = eighth

   > **!** *Ordinal numerals are adjectives, but*
   > *behave in a special way. All other than*
   > ⇒**cynta** *precede the noun. With*
   > *feminine singular nouns, the noun*
   > *itself undergoes soft mutation, as*
   > *does the ordinal after the article—so:*
   > **yr wythfed dyn** *the eighth man but* **yr**
   > **wythfed °ferch** *the eighth girl*

wythnos (*plural* **-au**) *noun, feminine*
   = week
   °wela i chi wythnos i heddiw = I'll see
   you a week today
   mae hi wedi bod yn wythnos °brysur
   iawn = it's been a very busy week
   tan wythnos nesa, 'te! = till next week,
   then!
   bydd 'na un °fargen °bob wythnos na
   °ellir mo'i ʰcholli = there will be one
   unmissable bargain each week

   > **!** *Note in* **wythnos diwetha** *'last*
   > *week' that the expected mutation of*
   > **diwetha** *after the feminine* **wythnos**
   > *does not occur because the*
   > *combination* **s+dd** *generally*
   > *assimilates to* **sd** *in the spoken*
   > *language.*

wythnosol *adjective*
   = weekly

wythnosolyn (*plural* **wythnosolion**)
   noun, masculine
   = weekly magazine, weekly

y (*also* **yr, 'r**) *definite article*
= the

> ! ⇒**the** *on the English-Welsh side*

y (*before vowels* **yr**) *conjunction*
= that

> ! *This conjunction (often silent in normal speech) is used to introduce subordinate clauses (introduced by 'that...' in English) where the original statement began with an affirmative verb other than present tense of* **bod**.

dw i'n meddwl y bydd hi gartre = I think that she'll be at home
dw i'n meddwl y dylai hi °fod gartre = I think that she should be at home
mae disgwyl y bydd y ffatri'n cau = it is expected that the factory will close
dw i'n meddwl y byddai hynny'n °ormod = I think that that would be too much
mae'n °bosib y gall e °ddod = he may be able to come
In addition, many conjunctions use a 'that...' construction, as do qualifying expressions like 'perhaps' *and* 'probably':

...rhag ofn y byddan nhw'n hwyr = ...in case they are late
fel y dwedodd y gweinidog ddoe... = as the minister said yesterday
°debyg iawn y basen nhw'n cytuno = they would probably agree
efallai y dylech chi aros tan yfory = perhaps you ought to wait till tomorrow
prin y gallen ni °ganiatáu hynny = we could hardly allow that
Finally, **y** *is used in relative clauses to link a verb to its antecedent*:

rhywbeth y dylid meddwl amdano = something that should be thought about
oes gynnoch chi °lyfr y gallwn i °brynu (fe) i ⁿgwraig? = have you got a book that I could buy for my wife?
dyma'r union °broblem y sonies i amdani wythnos diwetha = this is

exactly the problem I talked about last week
y °bobol yr oedd eu merch fan hyn ddoe = the people whose daughter was here yesterday

⇒**(a)°**, ⇒**bod** *etc verbnoun functioning as conjunction*, ⇒ **mai**, ⇒**taw**, ⇒ **na**^h/°
See also **Reported Speech** *in the Grammar reference section*

y (*before vowels* **yr**) *particle*

> ! *These occur in literary and very formal spoken Welsh before present and imperfect tense forms of* **bod**— *for example* **y mae** 'is/are' *for* **mae, yr oedd** *for* **oedd** 'was/were' *for* **roedd, yr wyf** 'I am' *for* **dw i** *or* **wi**. *Using them in speech sounds affected.*

ychwaith
⇒**chwaith**

ychwaneg
⇒**chwaneg, chwanag**

ychwanegol *adjective*
= extra; in addition; additional
dim tâl ychwanegol = no extra charge
ai treth ychwanegol ar y tlawd yw'r loteri mewn gwirionedd? = is the lottery really an additional tax on the poor?

ychwanegu *verbnoun*
• = add (**at°** to)
°ga i ychwanegu rhywbeth fan hyn? = can I add something here?
• = increase
ydy hyn wedi ychwanegu at ein gwybodaeth o °gwbwl, tybed? = has this increased our knowledge at all, I wonder?

ychydig *adverb*
• = little
ychydig iawn o amser sy ar ôl 'da ni nawr = we've got very little time left now
faint o °Gymraeg sy gynno fo?—go ychydig = how much Welsh has he got?—not much at all
• = a little; a little bit
°alli di °roi ychydig rhagor i mi? = can you give me a little bit more?
bydda i'n ôl mewn ychydig = I'll be back in a bit
• = few

mae hi'n un o'r ychydig artistiaid
Cymreig go iawn = she is one of the
few genuinely Welsh artists
• = a few
dim ond ychydig °fisoedd cyn iddyn
nhw °golli'r etholiad cyffredinol =
only a few months before they lost the
general election
mae'r cyrff yn bod i °wasanaethu
ychydig o °bobol °bwerus = the
bodies exist to serve a few powerful
people

> **!** Unlike its more colloquial
> counterpart ⇒**peth** adverb, **ychydig**
> can be used with plural as well as
> singular nouns. It requires **o°** with a
> singular noun, but can appear without
> when a plural noun follows.

ŷd noun, masculine
= corn

ydi, ydw, ydy, ydych, ydyn
⇒**bod**

yfed (stem **yf-**) verbnoun
= drink
faint yfest ti neithiwr? = how much did
you drink last night?
beth am °rywbeth i yfed °gynta? =
what about something to drink first?

yfory (sometimes **fory** after a vowel)
adverb
= tomorrow
°wela i di yfory! = I'll see you tomorrow!
heddiw ta fory dach chi am °fynd? =
do you want to go today or tomorrow?
°fasai yfory'n °gyfleus? = would
tomorrow be convenient?

yng
⇒**yn**[n] preposition

ynganiad (plural **-au**) noun, masculine
= pronunciation

ynganu verbnoun
= pronounce
**gofalwch bod chi'n ynganu'r gair
'ma'n iawn** = make sure you
pronounce this word properly

ynghlwm adverb
= bound up (**wrth°** with)
⇒**clymu**

ynghyd preposition
= together (**â**[h] with)

daeth 21 o °blant ysgolion cynradd
Cylch Ystwyth ynghyd = 21 children
from Ystwyth district primary schools
came together
cafwyd cwestiynau ynghyd â barn a
sylwadau = questions were received
together with opinion(s) and
observations
⇒**cyd**

ynghylch preposition
= about, concerning
**mi °fu pryderon ynghylch dyfodol y
mudiad yn °ddiweddar** = there have
been worries lately concerning the
future of the movement
⇒**ynglŷn â**[h], ⇒**am**°

ynglŷn â[h] preposition
= about, concerning
**dyma °ofyn am °fwy o °fanylion
ynglŷn â'r holiadur** = so (we) asked for
more details about the questionnaire
⇒**ynghylch**, ⇒**am**°

ym
⇒**yn**[n] preposition

ym°- prefix

> **!** This is used to form verbs and
> derived nouns, and often, but by no
> means always, conveys the idea of
> 'self'.

• **ymbaratoi** verbnoun
= prepare oneself
(⇒**paratoi**)
• **ymddiswyddo**) verbnoun
= resign
(⇒**diswyddo**)
• **ymolchi** verbnoun
= wash oneself
(⇒**golchi**)
• **ymrywmo** verbnoun
= bind/commit oneself
(⇒**rhwymo**)
• **ymuno** verbnoun
= join (a club)
(⇒**uno**)

yma adverb
= here
oes rhywun yma? = is there anyone
here?
yma ym [n]**Mhentraeth maen nhw'n byw**
= here in Pentraeth (is where) they live
mi °fydd y tywydd yn oer, gyda
[h]**chawodydd yma ac acw** = the

weather will be cold, with showers
here and there

! *Sometimes* **yma** *is shortened to* **'ma**:
Aled sy 'ma = (it's) Aled here (*on
phone*)

⇒**dyma°**, ⇒**fan hyn**, ⇒**y .. 'ma**

y ... 'ma *adjective*
• = this
  **dyw'r stafell 'ma °ddim yn rhydd bore
  'ma** = this room is not free this
  morning
  faint °dalest ti am y car 'ma, 'te? = how
  much did you pay for this car, then?
  ydy'r bws 'ma'n mynd i Abergwaun? =
  does this bus go to Fishguard?
• = these
  dydy'r eitemau 'ma °ddim ar °werth =
  these items are not for sale
  ydy'r stafelloedd 'ma ar °gael? = are
  these rooms available?
  faint ydy'r planhigion 'ma? = how
  much are these plants?
  °brynes i'r sgidiau 'ma fan hyn ddoe =
  I bought these shoes here yesterday

! *In spoken Welsh 'this room' is
phrased 'the room here'* **y stafell 'ma**,
and 'these rooms' as 'the rooms here'
y stafelloedd 'ma. *Because of this
phrasing, there is no distinction
between 'this' and 'these' (+ noun) in
spoken Welsh. Gender of the noun is
immaterial (unlike in literary Welsh,
see below), except as regards the
definite article present in the
construction, which will cause soft
mutation of feminine singulars—see*
the *on the English-Welsh side for
details. The form of the definite article
will vary depending on circumstance
—see* **the** *on the English-Welsh side
for details of this as well.*
Sometimes **'ma** *is given its full form*
yma *in speech (e.g* **y stafell yma**) *but
the shortened form is far more
common in this use.*
*Note that literary Welsh uses the
true adjectives* ⇒**hwn** *(adjective),*
⇒**hon** *(adjective),* ⇒**hyn**
*(adjective)—usage not current in
unaffected speech but regularly
encountered in writing.*

---

ymadael (*stem* **ymadaw-**) *verbnoun*
• = leave (**â** with object)

**ymadawodd y brenin â'r ynys y
  diwrnod wedyn** = the king left the
  island the next day
• = depart
  trenau'n ymadael °bob awr = trains
  departing every hour

ymadawiad (*plural* **-au**) *noun,
masculine*
= departure

ymadrodd (*plural* **-ion**) *noun,
masculine*
= expression
  **mae'n hawdd cymysgu'r °ddau
  ymadrodd 'ma** = it's easy to confuse
  these two expressions
⇒**mynegi**

ymaelodi *verbnoun*
= become a member (**yn** of), join
  **ymaelodwch yn eich cangen °leol
  nawr!** = join your local branch now!
⇒**aelod**, ⇒**ymuno**

ymagor (*or* **magor**) *verbnoun*
= yawn (*also figurative*)

ymarfer
1 *verbnoun*
  = practise
  **bydd cyfle hefyd i ymarfer eich sgiliau
  cyfathrebu** = there will also be an
  opportunity to practise your
  communication skills
2 (*plural* **-ion**) *noun, masculine*
  = exercise; practice
  **mae'r llyfr yn cynnwys ymarferion,
  mynegai a geirfa °gyflawn** = the book
  includes exercises, index, and a
  complete vocabulary

ymarferol *adjective*
= practical
  **mae eisiau i'r gwersi °fod yn °fwy
  ymarferol** = the lessons need to be
  more practical

ymateb
1 *verbnoun*
  = respond (**i°** to)
  **sut ydan ni'n mynd i ymateb i'r
  datblygiad 'ma?** = how are we going to
  respond to this development?
2 (*plural* **-ion**) *noun, masculine*
  = response
  cafwyd ymateb da = a good response
  was had

rhaid cadw rheolaeth ar ein hymateb **emosiynol** = we must keep control of our emotional response

ymbarél (*plural* **-au, -i, -s**) *noun, masculine*
= umbrella

ymbelydredd *noun, masculine*
= radiation
⇒**pelydr**

ymchwil *noun, feminine*
= research

ymchwiliad (*plural* **-au**) *noun, masculine*
= investigation

ymchwilio *verbnoun*
= investigate, look (**i°** into)
eisoes mae'r cyngor yn ymchwilio i'r sefyllfa = the council is already investigating the situation

ymchwilydd (*plural* **ymchwilwyr**) *noun, masculine*
= researcher

ymdopi *verbnoun*
= cope (**âʰ** with)
y peth pwysig yn y' ⁿmarn i ydy—ydyn nhw'n ymdopi neu °beidio? = the important thing to my mind is—are they coping or not?

ymdrech (*plural* **-ion**) *noun, feminine*
• = effort
ond methiant, hyd yn hyn, °fu pob ymdrech i °gael theatr = but so far every effort to get a theatre has been a failure
• = struggle

ymdrechu *verbnoun*
• = make efforts
• = exert oneself
• = struggle

ymdrin (*stem* **ymdrini-**) (**âʰ**) *verbnoun*
= deal with, be concerning
doedd dim digon o °bobol ifanc i °fedru ymdrin â'r cychod = there were not enough young people to be able to deal with the boats
⇒**ymwneud**, ⇒**delio**

ymddangos *verbnoun*
• = appear
ymddangosodd pump o °bobol gerbron y llys bore 'ma = five people appeared before court this morning

does dim byd wedi ymddangos hyd yma = nothing has appeared so far
• = seem
mae'n ymddangos i mi bod nhw wedi camddeall °rywsut = it seems to me that they've misunderstood somehow

---

! *The phrase* **mae'n ymddangos** *(+ 'that...' clause, or tagged at the end of the sentence) is used for* 'apparently':
mae'n ymddangos °fod e'n sâl
or **mae'n sâl, mae'n ymddangos** = apparently he is ill
The written language (and to some extent the media) often uses the formal **ymddengys** *for* **mae'n ymddangos**:
ymddengys bod nhw wedi mynd yno gyda'i gilydd = it seems that they went there together
ymddengys er hynny y gall °fod pethau ychydig yn °wahanol yn yr Alban = it seems, however, that things may be rather different in Scotland

---

ymddeol *verbnoun*
= retire
athro o'n i, ond dw i wedi ymddeol bellach = I was a teacher, but I'm retired now

ymddeoliad (*plural* **-au**) *noun, masculine*
= retirement

ymddiddan *verbnoun*
• = converse
roedd y °ddau'n chwerthin ac yn ymddiddan yn llon â'i gilydd wrth °fynd = the two of them were laughing and conversing happily with each other as they went
• (*as noun, masculine*) = conversation
awr o ymddiddan = an hour of conversation

ymddiheuro *verbnoun*
= apologize (**am°** for)
rhaid i mi ymddiheuro am yr hyn wedes i ddoe = I must apologize for what I said yesterday
ymddiheurwn am unrhyw oedi (*formal*) = we apologize for any delay

ymddiried *verbnoun*
= trust (**ynⁿ** in)

°**alla i** °**ddim ymddiried ynddyn nhw** = I can't trust them

°**ga i ymddiried ynoch chi i** °**wneud hyn droston ni?** = can I trust you to do this for us?

ymddiriedaeth (*plural* -**au**) *noun, feminine*
= trust; confidence

ymddiriedolaeth (*plural* -**au**) *noun, feminine*
= trust
yr Ymddiriedolaeth °**Genedlaethol** = the National Trust

ymddiswyddo *verbnoun*
= resign
mae nifer o'r pleidiau llai'n galw am iddo ymddiswyddo = a number of the smaller parties are calling for him to resign
⇒**diswyddo**, ⇒**swydd**

ymddwyn *verbnoun*
= behave
°**bryd hynny roedd y** °**ddwy** °**wlad yn ymddwyn fel gweriniaethau de facto** = at that time both countries were behaving like de facto republics

ymddygiad *noun, masculine*
= behaviour
fe °**fu ymddygiad od Menna'n creu cryn** °**benbleth i Derek** = Menna's odd behaviour has been creating quite a bit of confusion for Derek

ymennydd (*plural* **ymenyddiau**) *noun, masculine*
= brain

ymenyn
⇒**menyn**

ymestyn *verbnoun*
• = stretch; extend
bryniau isel yn ymestyn i'r pellter = low hills stretching into the distance
• = be stretched out
roedd y °**gath yn ymestyn o** °**flaen y tân fel arfer** = the cat was stretched out in front of the fire as usual
⇒**estyn**

ymffrostio *verbnoun*
= boast

ymgais (*plural* **ymgeisiau**) *noun, masculine or feminine*
• = attempt

methiant oedd ei hymgais cynta = her first attempt was a failure
• = entry (*in competition*)
dwy °**bunt o** °**wobr i'r ymgais cywir cyntaf allan o'r het** = a prize of £2 for the first correct entry out of the hat
⇒**cais**

ymgartrefu *verbnoun*
= make a home; settle in
erbyn hyn mae teulu newydd o °**foch daear wedi ymgartrefu'n hapus** = a new family of badgers has now settled in happily
⇒**cartre(f)**

ymgeisio *verbnoun*
= apply (**am**° for)
gellwch ymgeisio drwy °**lenwi'r ffurflen isod** = you can apply by filling in the form below

ymgeisydd (*plural* **ymgeiswyr**) *noun, masculine*
= applicant; candidate
rhoddir sylw manwl i °**gymwysterau pob ymgeisydd** = close attention will be given to every applicant's qualifications

ymgynghori *verbnoun*
= take/seek advice (**â**[h] from)
rhowch amser inni i ymgynghori â nhw = give us some time to seek their advice

ymgynghorol *adjective*
= consultative; advisory

ymgymryd (**â**[h]) (*stem* **ymgymer-**) *verbnoun*
= undertake
ond, yn hwyr neu'n hwyrach, bydd rhywun yn gorfod ymgymryd â'r °**dasg** = but, sooner or later, someone will have to undertake the task

ymgynnull (*stem* **ymgynnull-**) *verbnoun*
= gather, assemble
pawb i ymgynnull yn y maes parcio os bydd y larwm yn canu = everyone to assemble in the carpark if the alarm sounds

ymgyrch (*plural* -**oedd**) *noun, masculine or feminine*
= campaign
datganoli'n tanio'r ymgyrch = devolution ignites the campaign

ymgyrchu *verbnoun*
= campaign
ar ôl pedair wythnos o ymgyrchu dibaid = after four weeks of non-stop campaigning
ond pwy sy'n ymgyrchu dros °ddiarfogi niwcliar dyddiau 'ma? = but who campaigns for nuclear disarmament these days?

ymhell *adverb*
• = far
y tro 'ma, dyma ni'n edrych ymhell i'r gorffennol = this time we are looking far into the past
• *(time)*
= long
ymhell cyn y Chwyldro Ffrengig = long before the French Revolution
⇒**pell**

ymhellach *adverb*
= further
bydd sawl ffordd o °wneud i'ch arian °fynd ymhellach = there will be a number of ways of making your money go further
mae'r awdurdod lleol yn bygwth mynd â'r mater ymhellach = the local authority is threatening to take the matter further
ymhellach i'ch llythyr dyddiedig y cynta o °fis Ionawr... = further to your letter dated the first of January ...
⇒**pell**

ymhen *adverb*
= in (*at the end of a period of time*)
°fydda i'n ôl ymhen awr = I'll be back in an hour
bydd popeth drosodd ymhen mis = it'll all be over in a month

ymhlith *preposition*
= among, amongst
personal forms: **yn ein plith** among us, **yn eich plith** among you, **yn eu plith** among them
ymhlith y dwsinau o argymhellion a °restrwyd = among the dozens of recommendations listed
ac roedd digon o °Gymry yn eu plith = and there were plenty of Welshmen among them
⇒**ymysg**

ymhlyg *adverb*
= implicit

ymhobman, ym "mhob man
adverb
= everywhere
mae'r pethau 'ma ar °gael ymhobman ar hyn o °bryd = these things are available everywhere at the moment
oedd 'na °ddŵr ymhobman pan °ddaethon ni i mewn = there was water everywhere when we got in

ymholi *verbnoun*
= enquire, make enquiries

ymholiad (*plural* **-au**) *noun, masculine*
= enquiry
ymholiadau at Swyddfa'r Eisteddfod = enquiries to the Eisteddfod Office

ymlacio *verbnoun*
= relax
mae hi'n °bwysig inni °allu ymlacio = it's important for us to be able to relax

ymladd *verbnoun*
= fight (**am°** for)
mae'r ymladd yno mor ffyrnig = the fighting there is so fierce
...wrth iddo °orfod ymladd am arian yn y dyfodol = ...as he has to fight for money in the future

ymlaen *adverb*
personal forms: **yn y' "mlaen (i), yn dy °flaen (di), yn ei °flaen (e), yn ei blaen (hi), yn ein blaen(au) (ni), yn eich blaen(au) (chi), yn eu blaen(au) (nhw)**
• = on
dewch ymlaen!, dere 'mlaen! = come on!
ymlaen â ni! = on we go!
tro'r teledu ymlaen, nei di? = turn the television on, will you?
• = ahead
bydd y cyfarfod yn mynd yn ei °flaen fel arfer = the meeting will go ahead as usual
• **yn ôl ac ymlaen** = back and forth, to and fro:
a dyna lle gadawodd e nhw, yn mynd yn ôl ac ymlaen trwy'r dydd = and that's where he left them, going back and forth all day long
• **edrych ymlaen at°** (*or sometimes* **i°** *with a noun*) = look forward to:
edrychaf ymlaen at °glywed gennych cyn bo hir (*formal*) = I look forward to hearing from you before long

Nia Williams sy'n edrych ymlaen i'r °ŵyl ar ei newydd °wedd = Nia Williams looks forward to the new-look festival
⇒o °flaen, ⇒o'r blaen

ymlaen llaw *adverb*
= in advance
byddai talu ymlaen llaw yn sicrhau'ch seddi = paying in advance would secure your seats

ymofyn
⇒mofyn, ⇒moyn

ymolchi (*or* **molchi**) *verbnoun*
= wash (oneself), have a wash
dw i'n mynd i molchi = I'm going to have a wash

! Note that the abbreviated (but common) form **molchi** does not mutate to *°folchi.

⇒golchi

ymosod (**ar°**) *verbnoun*
= attack
ar ôl i'r Almaen ymosod ar Rwsia'n °ddirybudd ym 1941 = after Germany's surprise attack on Russia in 1941
ymosodwyd ar y °ddau ar eu ffordd adre neithiwr = the two were attacked on their way home last night

ymosodiad (*plural* **-au**) *noun, masculine*
= attack

ymosodol *adjective*
= aggressive

ymrannu *verbnoun*
• = divide; separate
• (*as noun, masculine*) = division; separation
mae hyn yn creu teimlad o °rwystredigaeth ac o ymrannu = this creates a feeling of frustration and division

ymroddgar *adjective*
= diligent

ymroddi, ymroi (*stem* **ymrodd-**) *verbnoun*
= devote oneself; apply oneself

ymrwymiad (*plural* **-au**) *noun, masculine*
= commitment, agreement (*to do something*)

ymrwymo *verbnoun*
= commit oneself, bind oneself

ymuno *verbnoun*
• ymuno (**âʰ**) join (*an organisation, club etc*)
gall hyn °olygu ymuno â grŵp cadwraethol lleol = this can mean joining a local conservation group
• ymuno (**ynⁿ**) = join in with
gallwch chi ymuno yng ⁿngweithgarwch Blwyddyn yr Amgylchedd = you can join in with Year of the Environment activities
⇒ymaelodi

ymweld (**âʰ**) (*stem* **ymwel-**) *verbnoun*
= visit
gallen ni ymweld â'ch ysgol = we could visit your school
ymwelwch â'n siop anrhegion ar eich ffordd allan! = visit our gift shop on your way out!

ymweliad (*plural* **-au**) *noun, masculine*
= visit

ymwelydd (*plural* **ymwelwyr**) *noun, masculine*
= visitor

ymwneud (**âʰ**) *verbnoun*
= concern, be concerning, be about, be to do with, be related to
ffactorau'n ymwneud â diweithdra ymhlith pobol ifainc yr ardal = factors relating to unemployment among the young people of the area
mae'r cwynion yn ymwneud â diffyg gwybodaeth = the complaints are to do with lack of information

ymwybodol *adjective*
• = aware
ydyn nhw'n ymwybodol o beth ydy angen eu cynulleidfa? = are they aware of what the needs of their audience are?
• = conscious

ymwybyddiaeth *noun, feminine*
= consciousness

ymyl (*plural* **-on, -au**) *noun, masculine or feminine*
= border; edge
fe agorir archfarchnad newydd ar ymylon y °dre °fis Tachwedd = a new

supermarket will be opened on the outskirts of town in November
sefwch ar ymyl y palmant = stand at the edge of the pavement
yn ymyl = nearby
maen nhw'n byw yn ymyl = they live nearby

ymylol *adjective*
= marginal

ymylu *verbnoun*
= border (**ar°** on)
mae rhai o'r sylwadau 'na'n ymylu ar enllib = some of those remarks are bordering on libel

ymyrraeth *noun, feminine*
= interference

ymyrryd (*stem* **ymyrr-**) *verbnoun*
= interfere (**â[h]** with/in)
does neb eisiau ymyrryd â'u dull nhw o °fyw, nag oes? = nobody wants to interfere with their way of life, do they?

ymysg *preposition*
= among, amongst
personal forms: **yn ein mysg, yn eich mysg, yn eu mysg**
ar yr un pryd bu dadl ffyrnig ymysg gwyddonwyr = at the same time there has been a fierce debate among scientists
ychydig o °flynyddoedd yn ôl, cododd proffwyd yn eu mysg = a few years ago, a prophet arose among them
⇒**ymhlith**

yn ('**n** *after a vowel*) *particle*

> **!** *see* **Yn** *box*

⇒**yn[n]** *preposition*, ⇒**yn°** *particle*

yn° ('**n°** *after a vowel*) *particle*

> **!** *see* **Yn°** *box*

⇒**yn[n]** *preposition*, ⇒**yn** *particle*

yn[n] *preposition*
personal forms: **yna i, ynat ti, yno fe, yni hi, ynon ni, ynoch chi, ynyn nhw** *or:* **yndda i, ynddat ti, ynddo fe, ynddi hi, ynddon ni, ynddoch chi, ynddyn nhw**
Other common variants: **yno i, ynddo i, ynot ti, ynddot ti**
• = in

mi °fyddan nhw'n ôl yn yr Hydref = they'll be back in the autumn
mae e wedi rhoi radio newydd yn ei °gar = he's put a new radio in his car
dych chi'n byw yn Llundain? = do you live in London?
ddaru mi °gael gafael yno fo = I caught hold of him
• = at
mae peiriannau hefyd ar °gael yn y canghennau canlynol = machines are also available at the following branches
doedd neb o °bwys yn y parti = there was no-one important at the party

---

! *This preposition is used for* 'in/at' *where what follows is a specific word or phrase. Specific in this context covers the following:*
1 words preceded by the definite article
2 pronouns
3 words preceded by possessive adjectives ('my', 'your', etc)
4 proper names
When 'in' *is followed by a non-specific word, then* ⇒**mewn** *must be used instead, and the two words for* 'in' *are mutually exclusive. Among other things, this means that* 'in the ...' *will always use* **yn[n]**; *you cannot say* '*mewn yr °ardd' *for* 'in the garden'— *the choice is between* **yn yr °ardd** *in the garden (specific) or* **mewn gardd** *in a garden (non-specific).*
Before words beginning **b-, c-, g-** *and* **p-**, *the word* **yn** *itself changes as these letters undergo nasal mutation:*
yn[n] + **b-** *becomes* **ym [n]m-:**
ym [n]Mangor = in Bangor
yn[n] + **c-** *becomes* **yng [n]ngh-:**
yng [n]Nghaerdydd = in Cardiff
yn[n] + **g-** *becomes* **yng [n]ng-:**
yng [n]Ngwynedd = in Gwynedd
yn[n] + **p-** *becomes* **ym [n]mh-:**
ym [n]Mhwllheli = in Pwllheli
°weles i nhw yng [n]nghanol y °dre neithiwr = I saw them in the centre of town last night
ym [n]mha °ran o °Gymru °gaethoch chi'ch geni? = in which part of Wales were you born?
In many varieties of the spoken language the nasal mutation technically required after this

preposition is not applied, or is replaced by soft mutation; so **yn Dolgellau** *or* **yn °Ddolgellau** *(for standard* **yn ⁿNolgellau***)* in Dolgellau, **ym Bangor** *or* **yn °Fangor** *(for standard* **ym ⁿMangor***)* in Bangor, **yn Caerdydd** *or* **yn °Gaerdydd** *(for standard* **yng ⁿNghaerdydd***)* in Cardiff, **yn Tregaron** *or* **yn °Dregaron** *(for standard* **yn ⁿNhregaron***)* in Tregaron, **yn Pwllheli** *or* **yn °Bwllheli** *(for standard* **ym ⁿMhwllheli***)* in Pwllheli. *This is abhorred by 'purists' but is a fact nonetheless.*

⇒**i mewn,** ⇒**mewn,** ⇒ **yn** *particle,* ⇒**yn°** *particle*

yna *(often* **'na** *in speech) adverb*
• = there
  ydy Aled yna? = is Aled there?
  pwy sy 'na? = who is there?
  dw i eisiau'ch gweld chi i gyd yn eistedd yna'n °dawel = I want to see you all sitting there quietly
• = then
  ewch yn syth ymlaen fan hyn, yna trowch i'r °dde = go straight ahead here, then turn right
  yna aethon ni i'r traeth = then we went to the beach

> ❗ *In this use,* **yna** *is equivalent to* ⇒**wedyn**.

⇒**dyna°,** ⇒**fan'na,** ⇒**yno,** ⇒**y... 'na**

y ...'na *adjective*
• = that
  dyw'r stafell 'na °ddim yn rhydd bore 'ma = that room is not free this morning
  ydy'r bws 'na'n mynd i Aberteifi, tybed? = does that bus go to Cardigan, I wonder?
  dw i'n poeni am yr erthygl 'na o'n ni'n sôn amdani ddoe = I'm worried about that article we were talking about yesterday
• = those
  doedd y °bobol 'na °ddim yn ein grŵp ni = those people were not in our group
  ydy'r stafelloedd 'na ar °gael? = are those rooms available?
  faint ydy'r afalau 'na? = how much are those apples?

> ❗ *In spoken Welsh* 'that room' *is phrased* 'the room there' **y stafell 'na**, *and* 'those rooms' *as* 'the rooms there' **y stafelloedd 'na**. *Because of this phrasing, there is no distinction between* 'this' *and* 'these' *(+ noun) in spoken Welsh. Gender of the noun is immaterial (unlike in literary Welsh, see below), except as regards the definite article present in the construction, which will cause soft mutation of feminine singulars—see* ⇒**the** *on the English-Welsh side for details. The form of the definite article will vary depending on circumstance—see* ⇒**the** *on the English-Welsh side for details of this as well.*
>
> *Sometimes* **'na** *is given its full form* **yna** *in speech (e.g* **y stafell yna***) but the shortened form is far more common in this use.*
>
> *Note that Literary Welsh uses the true adjectives* ⇒**hwnnw** *(adjective),* ⇒**honno** *adjective,* ⇒**hynny** *adjective—usage not current in unaffected speech but regularly encountered in writing.*

ynad *(plural* **-on***) noun, masculine*
  = magistrate
  llys ynadon = magistrates' court

yn awr
⇒**nawr**

yn °barod *adverb*
  = already
  mae tri wedi mynd ar °goll yn °barod = three have been lost already
  mae'n wyth o'r °gloch yn °barod! = it's eight o'clock already!

> ❗ **yn °barod** *cannot be interposed in the way that English* 'already' *can— we can say* 'three have already been lost' *but not* ***mae tri wedi yn barod mynd ar goll**; **yn °barod** *follows the phrase it refers to.*

⇒**eisoes**

yn °bendant
⇒**pendant**

yndefê
⇒**yntefê**

Yn

This particle, which causes no mutation, is used before verbnouns. Its function is to link the verbnoun to a preceding form of the verb ⇒**bod** 'to be'. Verbnouns have no verbal force on their own (they merely convey the meaning of the verb) and therefore need some form of auxiliary verb if they are to be used as verbs in their own right. For example, **darllen** 'read' is the verbnoun, but if we want to say 'Sioned reads' we have to convey present time by using the present tense of **bod** (**mae**): **mae Sioned yn darllen**. In this example, which is typical, **darllen** conveys the action, while **mae** (the true verb grammatically) places that action in the present. The particle **yn** before **darllen** shows that it is associated with the preceding **mae** in an *auxiliary + verbnoun* relationship. Note that the **yn** must immediately precede the verbnoun, and that therefore the subject of the sentence will come before the **yn**:

roedd y plant yn chwarae yn yr °ardd
= *the children were playing in the garden*

ydy hi'n bwrw glaw? = *is it raining?*

bydd y gweddill yn dod nes ymlaen = *the rest will come later*

Since **yn** cannot be separated from its verbnoun by any other word, in negative sentences of this type the negative marker °**ddim** will come before **yn** as well:

doedd y plant °ddim yn chwarae yn yr °ardd = *the children weren't playing in the garden*

dyw hi °ddim yn bwrw glaw = *it isn't raining*

°**fydd y gweddill °ddim yn dod** = *the rest won't come*

Verbnouns only need this particle when associated with **bod**; other auxiliaries are available for more specific uses—notably ⇒**gwneud**, ⇒**gallu**, ⇒**medru**, ⇒**dylwn**, and **yn** must not be used to link these to the verbnoun. Compare:

a) **basai Elen yn mynd**
Elen would go

but: b) **dylai Elen °fynd**
Elen should go

In (a), **yn** is needed because the auxiliary **basai** is part of the verb **bod**; whereas in (b) **yn** must not be used because **dylai** is nothing to do with **bod**, but is an independent verb in its own right. Notice also that the absence of **yn** allows the soft mutation that always follows the subject in a Welsh sentence to take effect (°**fynd**), while the presence of **yn** blocks it (**mynd**).

A secondary function of **yn** is to indicate ongoing or uncompleted action. Look at the following examples:

mae'r bws yn mynd = *the bus is going*

roedd y bws yn mynd = *the bus was going*

bydd y bws yn mynd = *the bus will go*

In the first two, the image we have is of the bus in the process of going, either now or in the past; in the third example, the future by definition implies uncompleted action. To indicate completed action, **yn** can be replaced by ⇒**wedi**:

mae'r bws wedi mynd = *the bus has gone*

roedd y bws wedi mynd = *the bus had gone*

bydd y bws wedi mynd = *the bus will have gone*

In all these cases, the image we have, whether in the present, past or future, is of the bus having gone already. The particles **yn** and **wedi**, therefore, cannot be used with the same verbnoun together—for example *mae Dafydd yn wedi mynd—because they denote mutually exclusive ideas (incomplete v. completed action).

Note finally that, when the verbnoun in a [**bod**] + **yn** + [*verbnoun*] sentence is sent to the front of the sentence for focus (see FOCUS in the Grammar Reference section for discussion of this procedure),

continued overleaf

Yn continued

the **yn** is dropped because the structure of the sentence is disrupted. Compare:

(neutral) **mae'r sefyllfa'n gwaethygu** = *the situation is worsening*

(focused) **gwaethygu mae'r sefyllfa** = *the situation is worsening*

(neutral) **mae'r ffermwyr yn codi tatws** = *the farmers are digging potatoes*

(focused) **codi tatws mae'r ffermwyr** = *the farmers are digging potatoes*

Phrasings of the type **yn codi tatws mae'r ffermwyr* are affected hypercorrections.

Yn°

PREDICATIVE USE

This particle has a similar use to ⇒**yn** (particle)—but instead of a verbnoun it links an *adjective* or *noun* to a preceding form of the verb **bod** 'to be'. Most sentences (in both Welsh and English) involving the verb 'to be' either concern actions or descriptions, and the difference between them in Welsh is in the slightly differing particles used as links.

The constructions therefore are:

[**bod**] + [subject] + **yn** + [action]

[**bod**] + [subject] + **yn°** + [description]

Compare:

mae'r trên yn mynd [verbnoun **mynd**—action] = *the train is going*

but: **mae'r trên yn °fawr** [adjective **mawr**—description] = *the train is big*

Note that, as with ⇒**yn** (particle), the particle **yn°** always directly precedes the description-word, and therefore always follows the subject (and also the negative °**ddim** in negative sentences).

Further examples of descriptive sentences:

ydy hi'n oer tu allan? (adjective) = *is it cold outside?*

oedd e'n °beiriannydd gyda'r cwmni ar y pryd (noun) = *he was an engineer with the company at the time*

°**fydd y cynllun yn °barod erbyn hynny?** (adjective) = *will the plan be ready by then?*

°**fyddai hynny °ddim yn °dderbyniol, dw i °ddim yn meddwl** *(adjective)* = *that would not be acceptable, I don't think*

Compare also these two sentences:

mae'r trên yn hwyr = *the train is late*

mae'r trên hwyr yn °gynnar = *the late train is early*

Note that only nouns and adjectives can take this particle. If an adverb (for example an expression denoting place) is involved, no **yn°** is used, because giving the location of something is not the same as describing it. Compare:

mae'r llyfr yn °gostus = *the book is expensive*

mae'r llyfr fan hyn = *the book is here*

And even if an adverb in Welsh corresponds to an adjective in English, there will be no **yn°** in Welsh. For example, ⇒**ar °gael** 'available':

bydd ffurflenni ymaelodi ar °gael yfory = *membership forms will be available tomorrow*

The predicative use of **yn°** extends to use with verbs like 'feel', 'look', 'sound', 'proclaim', 'declare', 'reveal' and many others:

mae Sioned yn teimlo'n sâl = *Sioned is feeling ill*

Yn° continued

ti'n edrych yn iach iawn dyddiau 'ma
= *you're looking very healthy these days*

etholwyd Harold yn °frenin Lloegr =
Harold was elected king of England

and for the same reason **yn°** sometimes corresponds to as:

...cyn ei °farw yn °ddyn ifanc union
ugain ⁿmlynedd yn ôl = ...*before his death as a young man exactly twenty years ago*

ar ei wythfed penblwydd cafodd
Harry siwt °ofod yn anrheg = *on his eighth birthday Harry got a spacesuit as a present*

FORMING ADVERBS

The other main use of **yn°** is to form adverbs from adjectives, and in this it corresponds to the English ending '-ly'. So, for example, **tawel** 'quiet' gives **yn °dawel** 'quietly'. But you will also encounter **yn °dawel** meaning quiet, with **yn°** performing its primary function of

linking the adjective to the verb 'to be'. Compare:

mae'r plant 'ma'n °dawel, on'd ydyn
nhw? = *these children are quiet, aren't they?*

dw i eisiau i chi °weithio'n °dawel fan
hyn = *I want you to work quietly here*

Where two adverbs are used in conjunction, the second **yn°** can be dropped (and therefore the mutation with it):

...rhoi doctoriaid ar °flaen y °gad yn
°dechnegol a meddygol = ...*put(ting) doctors at the forefront of the battle technically and medically*

MUTATION

Note that **yn°** (like ⇒**mor°**) is unusual in that it does not cause soft mutation of **ll-** and **rh-**—so, for example:

roedd y bwyd yn °gostus = *the food was expensive*

but

roedd y stafell yn llawn = *the room was full*

---

yn erbyn *preposition*
personal forms: **yn 'yn erbyn (i), yn dy erbyn (di), yn ei erbyn (e), yn ei herbyn (hi), yn ein herbyn (ni), yn eich erbyn (chi), yn eu herbyn (nhw)**
= against

colli naeth Caerdydd o °dair gôl i
°ddwy yn erbyn Abertawe = Cardiff lost by three goals to two against Swansea

dim byd yn ei herbyn, cofiwch =
nothing against her, mind
⇒**erbyn**

ynni *noun, masculine*
= energy; power
ynni niwcliar—dim diolch! = nuclear power—no thanks!
⇒**nerth,** ⇒**egni**

yno *adverb*
= there (*out of sight of speaker*)
°fues i erioed yn Efrog Newydd, ond

mae gen i ffrindiau yno = I've never been to New York, but I've got friends there

gallai fe ffonio oddi yno, on' gallai? =
he could phone from there, couldn't he?

mi aeth hi i'r Eidal llynedd, ac mae'n
dal i °fod yno hyd y gwn i = she went to Italy last year and she's still there as far as I know

! *A variant* **fan'no** *is also found in speech.*

⇒**yna,** ⇒**acw**

yn ogystal *adverb*
= as well, in addition

yn ôl *adverb*
• = back
dewch yn ôl! = come back!
°fydda i'n ôl toc = I'll be back in a moment

a dyna lle gadawodd e nhw, yn mynd yn ôl ac ymlaen trwy'r dydd = and that's where he left them, going back and forth all day long

• = ago

mi °ddaethon ni fan hyn °ddeng ⁿmlynedd yn ôl = we came here ten years ago

amser maith yn ôl = a long time ago

• = according to

mae lefelau diweithdra'n codi, yn ôl ffigurau a °gyhoeddwyd heddiw = unemployment levels are rising, according to figures published today

bydd y cyfieithiad yn amrywio yn ôl y cyd-destun = the translation will vary according to (the) context

yn ôl pob golwg = by the looks of it

yn ôl pob tebyg = in all likelihood.

yn sgîl *preposition*
= in the wake of, following

yn sgîl y canlyniadau gwaetha erioed, beth yw dyfodol y °blaid yng ⁿNghymru? = following the worst results ever, what is the party's future in Wales?

roedd y profion wedi'u cynnal yn sgîl y tân difrifol yn Sellafield llynedd = the tests had been carried out following the serious fire at Sellafield last year

yntau *pronoun*
= he; him

> **!** This is one of the special set of expanded pronouns that are used—though not that frequently—to convey emphasis or some idea of contrast with, or echoing of, what has gone before.

wedi'r Ail °Ryfel Byd, ac yntau wedi morio'r byd... = after the Second World War, and he having sailed the world...

y °feistres yn marw, ac aderyn yn proffwydo °fod angau ar y ffordd i'w nôl yntau = the mistress dies, and a bird prophesies that death is on the way to take him as well

⇒**e**, ⇒**fe**

yntefê? *(or yndefê?) particle (South)*

> **!** This particle, rather like French 'n'est-ce pas?' or German 'nicht

wahr?', is an all-purpose tag to a statement, anticipating an affirmative response. It is generally used with focused (⇒mai) statements. The English equivalent will vary according to context because of the absence of such a tag in English.

caws o't ti am °brynu, yntefê? = it was cheese you wanted to buy, wasn't it?

ond mynd o Sir Aberteifi nân nhw wedyn, yndefê? = but they'll go from Cardiganshire then, won't they?

⇒**on'd**

ynteu *conjunction*
= or

> **!** This conjunction, usually ⇒ta in speech, is of more restricted scope than the English equivalent, being used between two mutually exclusive choices.

beth °gawson nhw, bachgen ynteu merch? = what did they have, a boy or a girl?

yn unig *adverb*
• = only

ceir a ʰcherbydau ysgafn yn unig = cars and light vehicles only

chwech yn unig sy ar ôl 'da fi = I've only got six left

• = solely

mae'r gair 'na'n perthyn i'r iaith °lafar yn unig = that word belongs solely to the spoken language

⇒**dim ond**, ⇒**unig**

ynys *(plural -oedd) noun, feminine*
= island

ynysedig *adjective*
= isolated; insulated

yn ystod *preposition*
= during

mi °ddigwyddodd y cyfan yn ystod y rhyfel = it all happened during the war

mae pethau wedi gwaethygu'n °raddol yn ystod y deng ⁿmlynedd diwetha = things have gradually got worse during the last ten years

⇒**cyfamser**

ynysu *verbnoun*
= isolate; insulate

yr
⇒**y** *definite article*, ⇒ **y** *conjunction*

yr hyn *pronoun*
= what
enghraifft °dda o'r hyn y gellid ei °alw'n °gomedi °ddu = a good example of what could be called black comedy
beth am yr hyn wedodd e ddoe, 'te? = what about what he said yesterday, then?
byddwn ni'n gwneud yr hyn dan ni'n gorfod °wneud, a dim mwy = we will do what we have to do, and no more
yr hyn sy eisiau fan hyn ydy ychydig o °gyfaddawdu = what's needed here is a bit of compromise

> **!** *At the start of a sentence* ⇒**beth** *is also possible, at least in the spoken language:*
> **beth sy eisiau fan hyn ydy ychydig o °gyfaddawdu**

yr un *pronoun*
• = not (a single) one
°glywes i'r un sylwad y gallwn i °gytuno ag e = I didn't hear a single comment that I could agree with
• (*of two*) = neither
ond does yr un o'r °ddau o °blaid tynnu'r milwyr allan = but neither of them is in favour of pulling the soldiers out

> **!** *In these first two senses, this pronoun is used with a negative verb, and generally replaces the normal negative marker* °**ddim**.

• = each
mae'r rhain yn costio ugain ceiniog yr un = these cost twenty pence each
⇒**un**

yr un mor° *adverb*
= just as...(**âʰ** as), every bit as ...(**âʰ** as)
ond stori arall ydy honna, er yr un mor °ddiddorol = but that is another story, though (one which is) just as interesting
⇒**mor°**

ysbaid (*plural* **ysbeidiau**) *noun, masculine or feminine*
= interval; spell
bydd yfory'n sych gydag ysbeidiau heulog yma ac acw = tomorrow will be dry with sunny intervals here and there

ysbïo *verbnoun*
= spy

ysbïwr (*plural* **ysbiwyr**) *noun, masculine*
= spy

ysbïwraig (*plural* **ysbiwragedd**) *noun, feminine*
= spy

ysbryd *noun, masculine*
• (*plural* **-oedd**)
= spirit
mae hi'n edrych braidd yn isel ei hysbryd = she looks rather depressed
• (*plural* **-ion**)
= ghost
...yn credu bod ysbryd Cati Wen yn hofran uwch y °fawnog = ...thinking that the ghost of Cati Wen hovered above the peat bog

ysbrydol *adjective*
= spiritual

ysbrydoli *verbnoun*
= inspire
wedi deng ⁿmlynedd mae'r llais yn dal i ysbrydoli = after ten years the voice still inspires

ysbrydoliaeth (*plural* **-au**) *noun, feminine*
= inspiration

ysbwriel
⇒**sbwriel**

ysbyty (*plural* **ysbytai**) *noun, masculine*
= hospital
mae hi yn yr ysbyty = she's in hospital
aethpwyd â tri o °ddynion i'r ysbyty neithiwr = three men were taken to hospital last night

ysgafn *adjective*
comparative **ysgafnach**, *superlative* **ysgafna(f)**
= light (*in weight*)
gofalwch bod hi °ddim yn rhy ysgafn, nawr = make sure it's not too light, now
ond i °ddod yn ôl at °faterion ysgafnach,... = but to come back to lighter matters,...

ysgafnhau *verbnoun*
= lighten (*in weight*)

ysgariad (*plural* **-au**) *noun, masculine*
= divorce

ysgaru *verbnoun*
= divorce (**â**[h] from); get a divorce, get
divorced
maen nhw wedi ysgaru = they've got
divorced/they're divorced
⇒**gwahanu**, ⇒**priodi**

ysgogi *verbnoun*
= impel, drive
beth yn union sy wedi'ch ysgogi i
°**wneud hyn?** = what exactly has
driven you to do this?

ysgogiad (*plural* **-au**) *noun, masculine*
= impulse

ysgol (*plural* **-ion**) *noun, feminine*
• = school
°**allet ti** °**fynd â'r plant i'r ysgol drosta i**
bore 'ma? = could you take the
children to school for me this
morning?
mae'r plant yn mynychu ysgol
°**gynradd** °**leol** = the children attend a
local primary school
ysgol °**gynradd** (*plural* **ysgolion**
cynradd) = primary school
ysgol uwchradd (*plural* **ysgolion**
uwchradd) = secondary school
• = ladder

ysgrifenedig *adjective*
= written

ysgrifenyddes (*plural* **-au**) *noun,*
feminine
= secretary

ysgrifennu *verbnoun*
= write
peidiwch ysgrifennu o dan y llinell
hon = do not write under this line
ysgrifennwch °**frawddeg yn** °**Gymraeg**
= write a sentence in Welsh
erthygl wedi'i hysgrifennu yn
Ffrangeg = an article written in
French

> **!** *As with verbs for* 'send', 'write to...' *is*
> **ysgrifennu at**° *with people, and*
> **ysgrifennu i**° *with places.*

⇒**sgrifennu**, ⇒ **sgwennu**

ysgrifennydd (*plural*
ysgrifenyddion) *noun, masculine*
= secretary

ysgwydd (*plural* **-au**) *noun, feminine*
= shoulder
ar ysgwyddau rhywun arall bydd y
baich o hyn ymlaen = someone else
will be shouldering the burden from
now on

ysgyfaint *plural noun*
= lungs

ysgytlaeth (*plural* **-au**) *noun,*
masculine
= milkshake

ysmygu *verbnoun*
= smoke
dim ysmygu yn y neuadd = no
smoking in the hall
gall ysmygu niweidio'ch iechyd =
smoking can damage your health

> **!** *This word is often* ⇒**smygu** *in*
> *speech.*

⇒**mwg**

ystad (*plural* **-au**) *noun, feminine*
= estate

ystad °**dai** (*plural* **ystadau tai**) *noun,*
feminine
= housing estate

ystad °**ddiwydiannol** (*plural*
ystadau diwydiannol) *noun, feminine*
= industrial estate

ystadegau *plural noun*
= statistics
yn ôl yr ystadegau diweddara a
°**ryddhawyd heddiw...** = according to
the latest statistics released today...

ystadegydd (*plural* **-ion**) *noun,*
masculine
= statistician

ystafell
⇒**stafell**

ystlum (*plural* **-od**) *noun, masculine*
= bat (*animal*)

ystod (*plural not commonly used*) *noun,*
feminine
= range
cyfle i °**fwynhau ystod** °**ddiddorol o**
°**ddramâu gan** °**wahanol** °**gwmnïau** =
a chance to enjoy an interesting range
of plays by various companies
⇒**yn ystod**

ystrydeb (*plural* **-au**) *noun, feminine*
= stereotype

ystrydebol *adjective*
= stereotyped, stereotypical

ystwyth *adjective*
= flexible; supple

ystyr (*plural* **-on**) *noun, feminine or
masculine*
= meaning, sense
beth ydy ystyr y gair 'ma? = what does
this word mean?
**roedd o'n arweinydd yng ⁿngwir ystyr
y gair** = he was a leader in the true
sense of the word
⇒**cyfystyr,** ⇒**golygu,** ⇒**meddwl**

ystyriaeth (*plural* **-au**) *noun, feminine*
= consideration

ystyried (*stem* **ystyri-**) *verbnoun*
= consider
**petai hyn yn digwydd, byddai rhaid
ystyried dau °berygl** = if this were to
happen, two dangers would have to be
considered

ysu (**am°**) *verbnoun*
= itch (*to do something*)
o'n i'n ysu am °fynd = I was itching to
go

yswiriant (*plural* **yswiriannau**) *noun,
masculine*
= insurance
yswiriant cynhwysfawr =
comprehensive insurance
yswiriant bywyd = life insurance
yswiriant trydydd person = third party
insurance

yswirio *verbnoun*
= insure, take out insurance on

ysywaeth *adverb*
= alas
⇒**gwaetha'r modd**

yw
⇒**bod**

a, an _indefinite article_

> **!** _There is no word for 'a' or 'an' in Welsh, and it is simply not translated. So_ **cath** _can mean 'cat' or 'a cat' depending on context;_ **damwain** _can mean 'accident' or 'an accident'. The only exception to this is when_ a/an _means 'per', in which case the definite article_ **y/yr** _is used in Welsh:_
> **sixty pence a pound** = chwedeg ceiniog y pwys
> **twenty miles an hour** = ugain milltir yr awr

abandon _verb_
- (_car, baby_)
  = gadael
- (_give up_)
  = rhoi'r ffidil yn y to

abbreviate _verb_
  = talfyrru

abbreviation _noun_
  = talfyriad (_plural_ -au) _masculine_

ability _noun_
  = gallu (_plural_ -oedd) _masculine_

able _adjective_
  = galluog
  to be able to do something = gallu/medru gwneud rhywbeth

aboard _preposition_
  = ar°; ar °fwrdd

about _preposition_
- (_approximately_)
  = tua^h
  about a hundred people = tua ʰchant o °bobol
- (_concerning_)
  = am°, ynglŷn â^h, ynghylch; parthed (_literary_)
  a novel about the war = nofel am y rhyfel
  what are you talking about? = am beth dych chi'n sôn?
  to be about something = ymwneud â rhywbeth
- (_around_)
  = o °gwmpas, o amgylch

- (_to be about to_)
  I'm about to go home = dw i ar °fin mynd adre
  the train's about to leave = mae'r trên ar °fynd

above _preposition_
  = uwchben, uwchlaw
  above the building = uwchben yr adeilad
  see above = gweler uchod
  the above remarks = y sylwadau uchod

abroad _adverb_
  = tramor

absence _noun_
  = absenoldeb _masculine_

absent _adjective_
  = absennol

accent _noun_
  = acen (_plural_ -nau, -ion) _feminine_

accept _verb_
  = derbyn (_stem_ derbyni-)
  to accept an offer = derbyn cynnig

acceptable _adjective_
  = derbyniol

accident _noun_
  = damwain (_plural_ damweiniau) _feminine_
  a car accident = damwain car
  I found it by accident = fe °ddes i o hyd iddo yn °ddamweiniol

accommodation _noun_
  = llety _masculine_

accompany _verb_
  = mynd â^h

accomplish _verb_
  = cyflawni

according to _preposition_
  = yn ôl; chadal (_colloquial_)

account _noun_
  = cyfri(f) (_plural_ cyfrifon) _masculine_

accountant _noun_
  = cyfrifydd (_plural_ cyfrifwyr) _masculine_

accusation *noun*
= cyhuddiad (*plural* -au) *masculine*

accuse *verb*
= cyhuddo

ache
1 *noun*
= tost
stomach ache = stumog °dost

> **!** *Ailments involving parts of the body + **tost** do not take **ar°**, but **'da/gan°**. So we say:*
> **mae annwyd arna i** = I've got a cold (*no body part mentioned*)
> *but* **mae pen tost 'da fi** = I've got a headache (*ailing part of the body*)

2 *verb*
my head is aching = mae pen tost 'da fi

achievement *noun*
= camp (*plural* -au) *feminine*

aching *adjective*
= tost

acknowledge *verb*
= cydnabod (*stem* cydnabydd-)

acknowledgement *noun*
= cydnabyddiaeth (*plural* -au) *feminine*

across *preposition*
= ar draws, dros°
across the road = dros y ffordd

act *verb*
• (*take action*)
= gweithredu
• (*in play*)
= chwarae (*stem* chwarae-) rôl

active *adjective*
• (*in operation*)
= gweithredol
• (*fit*)
= heini

activity *noun*
= gweithgaredd (*plural* -au) *masculine*

actor *noun*
= actor (*plural* -ion) *masculine*

actress *noun*
= actores (*plural* -au) *feminine*

actually *adverb*
= a dweud y gwir, mewn gwirionedd

> **!** *These phrases need to be placed either at the start or end of the phrase—they cannot be inserted in the middle as in English:*
> **I don't actually know** = dw i °ddim yn gwybod, a dweud y gwir
> = a dweud y gwir, dw i °ddim yn gwybod

adapt *verb*
= addasu

adaptation *noun*
= addasiad (*plural* -au) *masculine*

add *verb*
• (*increase, add to*)
= ychwanegu
• (*maths*)
= adio

addition *noun*
in addition = yn ychwanegol, ar °ben hynny

additional *adjective*
= ychwanegol

address *noun*
= cyfeiriad (*plural* -au) *masculine*
what's your address? = beth ydy'ch cyfeiriad (chi)?

adequate *adjective*
= digonol

adhere *verb*
= glynu
to adhere to something = glynu wrth °rywbeth

adjudication *noun*
= beirniadaeth (*plural* -au) *feminine*

admire *verb*
= edmygu

admission *noun*
(*entry*) = mynediad

admit *verb*
• (*confess*)
= cyfadde(f) (*stem* cyfaddef-)
it must be admitted that . . . = rhaid cyfadde...
• (*let in*)
= gadael (*stem* gadaw-) i mewn
I don't want to admit them = dw i °ddim am eu gadael nhw i mewn

adolescent *noun*
= llencyn (*plural* llanciau) *masculine*
= llances (*plural* -i) *feminine*

adopt *verb*
= mabwysiadu

adult *noun*
= oedolyn (*plural* oedolion) *masculine*

advance *noun*
in advance = ymlaen llaw

advantage *noun*
= mantais (*plural* manteision) *feminine*
to take advantage of something =
manteisio ar° rywbeth

advantageous *adjective*
= manteisiol

adventure *noun*
= anturiaeth (*plural* -au) *feminine*

advertise *verb*
= hysbysebu

advertisement *noun*
= hysbyseb (*plural* -ion) *masculine or*
feminine

advertising *noun*
= hysbysebu *verb noun*

advice *noun*
= cyngor
to take advice = ymgynghori
to give advice = cynghori, rhoi cyngor

advise *verb*
= cynghori

advisory *adjective*
= cynghorol, ymgynghorol

aerial *noun*
= erial (*plural* -au) *masculine or feminine*

aerobics *noun*
= aerobeg

aeroplane *noun*
= awyren (*plural* -nau) *feminine*

affair *noun*
= mater (*plural* -ion) *masculine*

affect *verb*
= effeithio ar°, cael effaith ar°

afford *verb*
= fforddio
I can't afford it = alla i °ddim fforddio fe

afraid *adjective*
to be afraid of something = ofni
rhywbeth
bod ag ofn rhywbeth

> **!** *But* to be afraid *in general terms, as*
> *a temporary mental state, is usually*
> *expressed using* **ofn ar°** + *person:*
> **I'm afraid** = mae ofn arna i
> **are you afraid?** = oes ofn arnat ti?

Africa *noun*
= Affrica *feminine*

African
1 *adjective*
= Affricanaidd
2 *noun*
= Affricanwr (*plural* Affricanwyr)
masculine
= Affricanes (*plural* -au) *feminine*
= Affricaniad (*plural* Affricaniaid)
masculine and feminine

after
1 *preposition*
• = ar ôl; = wedi (*more formal*)
after the war = ar ôl y rhyfel
wedi'r rhyfel (*more formal*)
• (*US: when telling the time*)
= wedi
five after four = pum munud wedi
pedwar
2 *conjunction*
= ar ôl; = wedi (*more formal*)
after they go = ar ôl iddyn nhw °fynd
after they went = ar ôl iddyn nhw °fynd
after the children sat/sit down = ar ôl
i'r plant eistedd
(wedi *used in all these cases in more*
formal style)

afternoon *noun*
= prynhawn (*colloquial*: pnawn) (*plural*
-iau) *masculine*
good afternoon! = prynhawn da!
tomorrow afternoon = prynhawn yfory
yesterday afternoon = prynhawn ddoe
this afternoon = prynhawn 'ma

afterwards *adverb*
= wedyn, wedi hynny

again *adverb*
= eto; (*literary*: = drachefn, trachefn)
once again = unwaith eto, unwaith yn
rhagor
again and again = °dro ar ôl tro

now and again = o °bryd i'w gilydd
never again = byth eto

against preposition
- (opposing)
= yn erbyn
against them = yn eu herbyn (nhw)
Wales against Ireland = Cymru yn erbyn Iwerddon
against me = yn 'y erbyn (i)
against you = yn dy erbyn (di)
= yn eich erbyn (chi)
against him = yn ei erbyn (e)
against her = yn ei herbyn (hi)
against us = yn ein herbyn (ni)
against them = yn eu herbyn (nhw)
against the others = yn erbyn y lleill
against Scotland = yn erbyn yr Alban
- (contrary to)
= yn °groes i°
this goes against our wishes = mae hyn yn mynd yn °groes i'n dymuniadau
- (next to)
= wrth°
against the wall = wrth y wal

age noun
- (years of life)
= oedran, oed
what is your age? = beth ydy'ch oedran (chi)?, faint ydy'ch oed (chi)?, faint oed dych chi?
three years of age = tair (blwydd) oed
at three years of age = yn °dair (blwydd) oed

> **!** The special word **blwydd** (feminine) is used with **oed** for years of age, though it can be omitted. It has special mutated forms after many of the common numerals:
> **two years of age** = dwy (°flwydd) oed
> **three years of age** = tair (blwydd) oed
> **four years of age** = pedair (blwydd) oed
> **five years of age** = pum ⁿmlwydd oed, pump oed
> **six years of age** = chwe blwydd oed, chwech oed
> **seven years of age** = saith (ⁿmlwydd) oed
> **eight years of age** = wyth (ⁿmlwydd/blwydd) oed
> **nine years of age** = naw (ⁿmlwydd) oed

ten years of age = deng ⁿmlwydd oed, deg oed
twenty years of age = ugain (ⁿmlwydd) oed
forty years of age = deugain (ⁿmlwydd) oed

- (period)
= oes; cyfnod
the Iron Age = yr Oes Haearn
the Age of the Renaissance = Cyfnod y Dadeni

> **!** **oes** is generally a long and relatively ill-defined period, while **cyfnod** tends to mean a period that dates can be assigned to.

aged adjective
a child aged three = plentyn tair oed

aggressive adjective
= ymosodol

ago preposition
= yn ôl

> **!** Expressions involving **ago** generally have soft mutation of the time word or phrase:
> **a minute ago** = °funud yn ôl
> **ten minutes ago** = °ddeng munud yn ôl
> **three years ago** = °dair blynedd yn ôl
> **years ago** = °flynyddoedd yn ôl

agree verb
- (with someone)
= cytuno â°, bod yn °gytun â°
I agree with you = dw i'n cytuno â chi dw i'n °gytun â chi
- (be consistent with)
= cydfynd â
this doesn't agree with what I heard = dyw hyn °ddim yn cydfynd â'r hyn °glywes i

agreement noun
- (contract; concurrence)
= cytundeb (plural -au) masculine
- (commitment)
= ymrwymiad (plural -au) masculine

agriculture noun
= amaethyddiaeth feminine

ahead
1 adverb
= ymlaen
go ahead = ewch ymlaen

2 *preposition*
= o °flaen
ahead of you = o'ch blaen

aid *noun*
= cymorth
first aid = cymorth cynta(f)

AIDS *noun*
= AID (*acronym for* Afiechyd Imiwnedd Diffygiol)

aim
1 *noun*
= bwriad (*plural* -au) *masculine*
= amcan (*plural* -ion) *masculine*
= nod (*plural* -au) *masculine or feminine*
to take aim at something = anelu at° rywbeth
2 *verb*
= anelu
to aim at something = anelu at° rywbeth

air *noun*
= awyr *feminine*

air force *noun*
= llu awyr *masculine*

air mail *noun*
= post awyr *masculine*
by air mail = drwy °bost awyr

airplane *noun*
= awyren (*plural* -nau) *feminine*

airport *noun*
= maes awyr (*plural* meysydd awyr) *masculine*

alarm *noun*
= larwm

alarm clock *noun*
= cloc larwm (*plural* clociau larwm) *masculine*

alas! *interjection*
= ysywaeth!

alight *adjective*
to set something alight = tanio rhywbeth

alike
1 *adjective*
they are very alike = maen nhw'n °debyg iawn i'w gilydd
2 *adverb*
boys and girls alike = bechgyn a merched fel ei gilydd

alive *adjective*
he's alive = mae'n byw

all
1 *adjective*
all the children = y plant i gyd *or* yr holl °blant
all this = hyn oll
2 *pronoun*
this is all I have = dyma'r cyfan/cwbwl sy gen i
is it all gone? = ydy popeth wedi mynd?
I'm not sure, that's all = dw i °ddim yn siwr, 'na i gyd
3 *adverb*
all the same = serch hynny
all day = trwy'r dydd
all week = trwy'r wythnos
all over the country = ledled y °wlad
= dros y °wlad i gyd

all right *adverb*
• (*signifying agreement*)
= o'r gorau
will you open the window?—all right = newch chi agor y ffenest?—o'r gorau
• (*OK, not bad*)
= go lew
how are you today?—all right = sut dych chi heddiw?—go lew

allow *verb*
= caniatáu
to allow someone to do something = caniatáu i° rywun °wneud rhywbeth

allowance *noun*
• (*state payment*)
= lwfans (*plural* -au) *masculine*
• (*US: pocket money*)
= arian poced *masculine*

almond *noun*
= almon (*plural* -au) *masculine or feminine*

almost *adverb*
= bron
it's almost ready = mae e bron yn °barod
= mae'n °barod, bron (â bod)
I almost fell = roedd bron i mi syrthio

alone *adverb*

> **!** *The spoken language uses* **ar °ben** [*possessive*] **hun** (*North*) / **hunan** (*South*). *For details of the difference*

between **hun** *and* **hunan**, *see Welsh-English side.*
I want to be alone = dw i eisiau bod ar °ben 'n hun(an), (*more formal:* ... ar 'y ⁿmhen 'yn hunan)
she wanted to be alone = oedd hi eisiau bod ar °ben ei hun(an), (*more formal:* ... ar ei ʰphen ei hunan)
they want to be alone = maen nhw eisiau bod ar °ben eu hun(ain), (*more formal:* ... ar eu pennau eu hunain)

leave him alone! = gad °lonydd iddo!

along *preposition*
= ar hyd
along the road = ar hyd y ffordd

aloud *adverb*
= yn uchel

already *adverb*
= yn °barod; eisoes (*formal*)

> **!** **yn °barod** *follows the phrase it refers to, and cannot be placed immediately after the main verb as in English:*
> **they've already gone** = maen nhw wedi mynd yn °barod
> **she's already here** = mae hi fan hyn yn °barod

also *adverb*
= hefyd

> **!** *With past tenses,* **hefyd** *generally has to come last in the sentence:*
> **I also saw a helicopter** = °weles i hofrennydd hefyd
> *With other tenses it usually comes last, but can appear after the subject:*
> **I'm also learning French** = dw i'n dysgu Ffrangeg hefyd
> = dw i hefyd yn dysgu Ffrangeg,

alternately *adverb*
= °bob yn ail

although *conjunction*
= er

> **!** **er** *is followed either by a* 'that...' *clause:*
> **although he is ill** = er °fod e'n sâl
> **although he'll be there** = er y bydd e yno

although he won't be there = er na °fydd e yno
or—in the past—by **i°** + *subject* + °*verbnoun:*
although I told him = er i mi °ddweud wrtho

always *adverb*
= wastad, o hyd, °bob amser, °bob tro; (*with past tenses*) = erioed
he always says that = mae e wastad yn dweud hynny
tickets always available = tocynnau °bob amser ar °gael

amaze *verb*
= syfrdanu

amazed *adjective*
I was amazed = fe °ges i 'n syfrdanu
he was amazed = fe °gafodd e ei syfrdanu
we were amazed = fe °gawson ni'n syfrdanu

amazing *adjective*
= syfrdanol, rhyfeddol

amazingly *adverb*
this thing is amazingly useful = mae'r peth 'ma'n hynod o °ddefnyddiol

ambition *noun*
= uchelgais (*plural* uchelgeisiau) *masculine or feminine*

ambitious *adjective*
= uchelgeisiol

ambulance *noun*
= ambiwlans (*plural* -ys) *masculine*

America *noun*
= America *feminine*

American
1 *adjective*
= Americanaidd
2 *noun*
= Americanwr (*plural* Americanwyr) *masculine*
= Americanes (*plural* Americanesau) *feminine*

among(st) *preposition*
= ymhlith; ymysg (*less common*)
among(st) them = yn eu plith (nhw)
= yn eu mysg (nhw)
among(st) us = yn ein plith (ni)
= yn ein mysg (ni)

among(st) you = yn eich plith (chi)
= yn eich mysg (chi)
among(st) the members = ymhlith yr
aelodau
= ymysg yr aelodau
from among(st) us = o'n plith (ni)

amount *noun*
a certain amount = rhywfaint, rhyw
°gymaint
a certain amount of food = rhywfaint o
°fwyd

amusement arcade *noun*
= arcêd °ddifyrion (*plural* arcedau
difyrion) *feminine*

amusing *adjective*
= difyr, doniol

an *indefinite article* ⇒**a**

analyze *verb*
= dadansoddi

analysis *noun*
= dadansoddiad (*plural* -au) *masculine*

ancestor *noun*
= hynafiad (*plural* hynafiaid) *masculine*
and feminine

and *conjunction*
= aʰ, (*before vowels and certain other
words*) ac
bread and cheese = bara a ʰchaws
ham and eggs = cig moch ac wyau
and so on = ac ati

> ! *The most common words that are
> preceded by* **ac** *rather than* **a** *even
> though they do not begin with vowels
> are:* **feᵒ** *and* **miᵒ** *(affirmative markers),*
> **mae, sy(dd), roedd, fel, felly, mai,
> morᵒ, mewn, wedyn**.
> *Conversely,* **a** *and not* **ac** *is used
> before* **ein, eich, ei** *and* **eu,** *giving*
> **a'n, a'ch, a'i** *and* **a'u.**

anger *noun*
= dicter *masculine*

angry *adjective*
= crac, dig
to get angry = mynd yn °grac
= gwylltio

animal *noun*
= anifail (*plural* anifeiliaid) *masculine*

ankle *noun*
= migwrn (*plural* migyrnau) *masculine*

announce *verb*
= datgan, cyhoeddi

announcement *noun*
= datganiad (*plural* -au) *masculine*
= cyhoeddiad (*plural* -au) *masculine*

annoy *verb*
= cythruddo

annoyed *adjective*
= dig, crac

annual *adjective*
= blynyddol

another
1 *adjective*
= arall
another book = llyfr arall
2 *pronoun*
= un arall
do you want another (one)? = dych chi
eisiau un arall?

> ! *There is a special phrase for* **one
> another** *which varies depending on
> who is being referred to:*
> ei gilydd (*referring to 'them'*)
> eich gilydd (*referring to 'you'*)
> ein gilydd (*referring to 'us'*)
> **they love one another** = maen nhw'n
> caru ei gilydd
> **do you know one another?** = dych
> chi'n nabod eich gilydd?
> **we will help one another** = byddwn
> ni'n helpu'n gilydd

answer
1 *noun*
= ateb (*plural* -ion) *masculine*
there was no answer = doedd dim ateb
2 *verb*
= ateb
to answer a question = ateb cwestiwn
to answer the phone = ateb y ffôn
answer back = ateb yn ôl

answering machine *noun*
= peiriant ateb (*plural* peiriannau ateb)
masculine

ant *noun*
= morgrugyn (*plural* morgrug)
masculine

anti-
= gwrth°-
anti-English = gwrth-Seisnig

antifreeze *noun*
= gwrthrewydd (*plural* -ion) *masculine*

antique
1 *adjective*
= hynafol
2 *noun*
= hynafolyn (*plural* hynafolion) *masculine*

antique shop *noun*
= siop hynafolion (*plural* siopau hynafolion) *feminine*, siop hen °bethau (*plural* siopau hen °bethau) *feminine*

anxiety *noun*
= pryder (*plural* -on) *masculine*

anxious *adjective*
= pryderus

any *adjective*
= unrhyw°
any car will do = neith unrhyw °gar y tro

> **!** *But* **any** *is not translated where it means* **some** *or in the combination* **not...any**:
> **have you got any cheese?** = oes caws 'da chi?
> **we haven't got any money** = does dim arian 'da ni

anybody ⇨anyone

anyone *pronoun*
• (*in questions*)
= unrhywun
do you know anyone who could help? = dych chi'n nabod unrhywun °allai helpu?
• (*in the negative*)
= neb
there isn't anyone here = does neb fan hyn
we didn't see anyone = °welon ni neb
• (*everyone*)
= unrhywun
anyone could do that = gallai unrhywun °wneud hynny

anything *pronoun*
• (*in questions*)
= unrhywbeth, rhywbeth
can I do anything? = °allai °wneud unrhywbeth/rhywbeth?

• (*in the negative*)
= dim byd, dim
there isn't anything here = does dim byd fan hyn
I didn't hear anything = ʰchlywes i °ddim byd
I don't know anything about them = dw i'n gwybod dim amdanyn nhw
• (*everything*)
= unrhywbeth
anything would be better than this = byddai unrhywbeth yn °well na hyn

anyway *adverb*
= beth bynnag, ta beth, ta waeth

anywhere *adverb*
= unrhywle
(not) anywhere = nunlle
= nunman
I didn't see them anywhere = °weles i nhw nunlle

apart 1 *adjective*
= ar wahân
keep them apart = cadwch nhw ar wahân
2 apart from *preposition*
= heblaw (*colloquial*: 'blaw); ar wahân i°; ac eithrio
no-one apart from me = neb heblaw fi

apartment *noun*
= fflat (*plural* -iau) *feminine*

apologize *verb*
= ymddiheuro
to apologize for something = ymddiheuro am° rywbeth
to apologize to someone for doing something = ymddiheuro i° rywun am °wneud rhywbeth

apology *noun*
= ymddiheuriad (*plural* -au) *masculine*

apparently *adverb*
= mae'n ymddangos
apparently he's away = mae'n ymddangos °fod e i ffwrdd
= mae e i ffwrdd, mae'n ymddangos

appear *verb*
= ymddangos

appearance *noun*
• (*look*)
= golwg, gwedd

• (act of appearing)
= ymddangosiad (plural -au) masculine

appetite noun
= chwant bwyd masculine, archwaeth masculine
lack of appetite = diffyg archwaeth

apple noun
= afal (plural -au) masculine

apple juice noun
= sudd afal masculine

appliance noun
= offeryn (plural offer) masculine, peiriant (plural peiriannau) masculine

applicant noun
= ymgeisydd (plural ymgeiswyr) masculine

application noun
= cais (plural ceisiadau) masculine

apply verb
= ymgeisio
to apply for something = ymgeisio am° rywbeth

appoint verb
= penodi
to appoint someone chairman = penodi rhywun yn °gadeirydd

appointment noun
= penodiad (plural -au) masculine

appraise verb
= cloriannu

appreciable adjective
= sylweddol

appreciate verb
= gwerthfawrogi

approach verb
= nesáu (at°)

appropriate adjective
= priodol

approve verb
= cymeradwyo

approximate adjective
= bras

approximately adverb
= tuaʰ
there are approximately forty people here = mae tua deugain o °bobol yma

! To say **at approximately** (a time) 'tuaʰ' alone, not 'am tuaʰ' is used:
they came at ten o'clock = fe °ddaethon nhw am °ddeg o'r gloch
they came at approximately ten o'clock = fe °ddaethon nhw tua deg o'r °gloch

apricot noun
= bricyllen (plural bricyll) feminine

April noun
= Ebrill, mis Ebrill masculine
see also **January**

Aquarius noun
= y Dyfrwr, y Cariwr Dŵr

archer noun
= saethydd (plural -ion) masculine

archery noun
= saethyddiaeth feminine

architect noun
= pensaer (plural penseiri) masculine

architectural adjective
= pensaernïol

architecture noun
= pensaernïaeth feminine

area noun
= ardal (plural -oedd) feminine, bro (plural -ydd) feminine

area code noun
= côd ardal (plural codau ardal) masculine

argue verb
= dadlau
to argue with someone = dadlau âʰ/gydaʰ rhywun
to argue about something = dadlau am °rywbeth
to argue against something = dadlau yn erbyn rhywbeth
to argue for something = dadlau dros° rywbeth
= dadlau o °blaid rhywbeth

argument noun
= dadl (plural -euon) feminine

Aries noun
= yr Hwrdd masculine

arise verb
= codi

arm *noun*
= braich (*plural* breichiau) *feminine*
arm in arm = °fraich ym ⁿmraich
under my arm = dan 'y ⁿnghesail

armchair *noun*
= cadair °freichiau (*plural* cadeiriau breichiau) *feminine*

armed *adjective*
= arfog
the armed forces = y lluoedd arfog

arms *plural noun*
= arfau *masculine plural*

army *noun*
= byddin (*plural* -oedd) *feminine*

around *preposition*
• (*location*)
= o amgylch, o °gwmpas
a trip around the town = taith o amgylch y °dre
the world around us = y byd o'n cwmpas (ni)
around me = o ⁿnghwmpas (i)
around you = o dy °gwmpas (di)
around him = o'i °gwmpas (e)
around her = o'i ʰchwmpas (hi)
around us = o'n cwmpas (ni)
around you = o'ch cwmpas (chi)
around them = o'u cwmpas (nhw)
• (*approximately*)
= tuaʰ
around a hundred people = tua ʰchant o °bobol
they came around seven = daethon nhw tua saith

arrange *verb*
= trefnu
to arrange a meeting = trefnu cyfarfod
to arrange to meet someone = trefnu cwrdd âʰ rhywun

arrangement *noun*
= trefniad *masculine*, trefniant (*plural* trefniannau) *masculine*

arrest *verb*
= arestio
three people were arrested = arestiwyd tri o °bobol

arrive *verb*
= cyrraedd (*stem* cyrhaedd-)
to arrive in Cardiff = cyrraedd Caerdydd

arrow *noun*
= saeth (*plural* -au) *feminine*

arse *noun*
= tin (*plural* -au) *masculine*

art *noun*
= celfyddyd (*plural* -au) *feminine*

art gallery *noun*
= oriel °gelfyddyd (*plural* orielau celfyddyd) *feminine*

article *noun*
= erthygl (*plural* -au) *feminine*

articulated lorry *noun*
= lori °gymalog (*plural* lorïau cymalog) *feminine*

artificial *adjective*
• = artiffisial
• (*false*)
= ffug

artist *noun*
= artist (*plural* -iaid) *masculine*

arts and crafts *plural noun*
= celf a ʰchrefft, celfyddyd a ʰchrefft

as
1 *conjunction*
• **as** = fel
as you know, . . . = fel dych chi'n gwybod . . .
• (*at the time when*)
= wrthº
as I went out = wrth i mi °fynd allan
• (*because, since*)
= gan °fod (*etc*)
as he isn't here, let's . . . = gan °fod e °ddim yma, gadewch inni . . .
2 *preposition*
she got the book as a present = fe °gafodd hi'r llyfr yn anrheg
he got a job as a teacher = fe °gafodd e swydd fel athro
I lived here as a child = o'n i'n byw fan hyn yn °blentyn
3 *adverb*
• (*in comparisons*)
= morº . . . âʰ . . ., cynº -ed . . . âʰ . . .
this one is as dear as that one = mae'r un yma mor °ddrud â'r un yna
as soon as possible = cyn °gynted ag y bo modd
we're just as angry as you = dyn ni °lawn mor °grac â chi
= dyn ni yr un mor °grac â chi

she sings as well as you (do) = mae hi'n canu cystal â ti
the same age as you = yr un oedran â chi

ashamed *adjective*
be ashamed (of) = teimlo cywilydd (o°/o achos)

> **!** *But* to be ashamed *in general terms, as a temporary mental state, is usually expressed using* **cywilydd ar°** + *person:*
> **I'm ashamed of what I did** = mae cywilydd arna i o achos yr hyn nes i
> **I'm very ashamed** = mae cywilydd mawr arna i
> **are you ashamed?** = oes cywilydd arnat ti?

ashes *noun*
= ulw *plural*
the house burnt to ashes = fe °losgodd y tŷ'n ulw

Asia *noun*
= Asia *feminine*

Asian
1 *adjective*
= Asiaidd
2 *noun*
= Asiad (*plural* Asiaid) *masculine and feminine*

aside *adverb*
= o'r neilltu
to set something aside = neilltuo rhywbeth

ask *verb*
• gofyn (*stem* gofynn-)
= holi
to ask a question = gofyn cwestiwn
to ask someone about something = holi rhywun am °rywbeth
to ask someone to phone = gofyn i °rywun am ffonio
• (*invite*)
= gwahodd
to ask someone to lunch = gwahodd rhywun i °ginio

asleep *adjective*
to be asleep = cysgu
to fall asleep = mynd i °gysgu

aspect *noun*
= agwedd (*plural* -au) *feminine*

assemble *verb*
• (*gather*)
= ymgynnull (*stem* ymgynull-
• (*put together*)
= cyfosod

assert *verb*
= honni

assess *verb*
= asesu

assignment *noun*
• (*task*)
= tasg (*plural* -iau) *feminine*
• (*essay*)
= traethawd (*plural* traethodau) *masculine*

assistance *noun*
= cymorth *masculine*

assistant *noun*
= cynorthwy-ydd (*plural* cynorthwywyr) *masculine*

assure *verb*
= sicrhau
to assure someone that . . . = sicrhau rhywun °fod . . .

asthma *noun*
= y °fogfa *feminine*
he's got asthma = mae'r °fogfa arno (fe)
has she got asthma? = ydy'r °fogfa arni (hi)?
does she get asthma? = ydy hi'n diodde o'r °fogfa?

astound *verb*
= syfrdanu

astronomer *noun*
= seryddwr (*plural* seryddwyr) *masculine*

astronomy *noun*
= seryddiaeth *feminine*

at *preposition*
• (*location*)
= ynⁿ
at the Town Hall = yn Neuadd y °Dre
at school = yn yr ysgol
at the meeting = yn y cyfarfod
at home = gartre(f)
• (*beside*)
= wrth°
at the desk = wrth y °ddesg
there's someone at the door = mae rhywun wrth y drws

- (*time*)
  at ten o'clock = am °ddeg o'r °gloch
  at about ten o'clock = tua deg o'r °gloch
  at four years of age = yn °bedair (blwydd) oed

athlete *noun*
= mabolgampwr (*plural* mabolgampwyr) *masculine*
= mabolgampwraig (*plural* mabolgampwragedd) *feminine*

athletics *noun*
= mabolgampau *plural*

Atlantic *noun*
= Môr Iwerydd

atmosphere *noun*
- (*most senses*)
  = awyrgylch (*plural* -oedd) *masculine*
- (*convivial mood*)
  = awyrgylch (*plural* -oedd) *masculine*; hwyl *feminine*

attach *verb*
= clymu
  to attach something to something = clymu rhywbeth wrth° rywbeth

attack
1 *noun*
= ymosodiad (*plural* -au) *masculine*
  an attack on someone = ymosodiad ar °rywun
  an attack on something = ymosodiad ar °rywbeth
  heart attack = trawiad (*plural* -au) ar y °galon
2 *verb*
= ymosod

> **!** **ymosod** *always uses* **ar°** *before the person or thing attacked:*
> **to attack someone** = ymosod ar° rywun
> **Germany attacked Russia** = ymosododd yr Almaen ar Rwsia

attempt
1 *noun*
= cais (*plural* ceisiadau) *masculine*, ymgais (*plural* ymgeisiadau) *masculine or feminine*
2 *verb*
= ceisio or trio
  to attempt to do something = ceisio/trio gwneud rhywbeth

attend *verb*
= mynychu
  to attend school = mynychu'r ysgol

attention *noun*
= sylw
  to draw someone's attention to something = tynnu sylw rhywun (tuag) at °rywbeth
  to pay attention = dal sylw
  to attract someone's attention = tynnu sylw rhywun

attentive *adjective*
= astud

attentively *adverb*
= yn astud

attic *noun*
= llofft (*plural* -ydd) *feminine*

attitude *noun*
= agwedd (*plural* -au) *feminine*

attract *verb*
= denu

attraction *noun*
= atyniad (*plural* -au) *masculine*

attractive *adjective*
= deniadol

audience *noun*
= cynulleidfa (*plural* -oedd) *feminine*

audition *noun*
= gwrandawiad (*plural* -au) *masculine*

August *noun*
= Awst, mis Awst *masculine*
see also **January**

aunt *noun*
= modryb (*plural* -edd) *feminine*
  she's my aunt = mae hi'n °fodryb i mi

Australia *noun*
= Awstralia *feminine*

Australian
1 *noun*
= Awstraliad (*plural* Awstraliaid) *masculine and feminine*
2 *adjective*
= Awstralaidd

author *noun*
= awdur (*plural* -on) *masculine*

authority *noun*
= awdurdod (*plural* -au) *masculine or feminine*

automatic *adjective*
= awtomatig

autumn *noun*
= hydre(f) *masculine*
in the autumn = yn yr hydre
all autumn = trwy gydol yr hydre

available *adjective*
• (*for purchase etc*)
= ar °gael, i °gael
tickets available here = tocynnau ar
°gael yma
there was nothing available = doedd
dim byd i °gael
• (*free*)
= rhydd
are you available tomorrow? = dych
chi'n rhydd yfory?

avenue *noun*
= rhodfa (*plural* rhodfeydd) *feminine*

average *adjective*
• (*medium*)
= cyfartalog
on average = ar °gyfartaledd
• (*ordinary*)
= cyffredin

avoid *verb*
= osgoi

awake *adjective*
= effro, ar °ddihun
are you awake? = wyt ti'n effro
= wyt ti ar °ddihun?
wide awake = hollol effro
= hollol ar °ddihun
to keep someone awake = cadw
rhywun ar °ddihun

award *noun*
= gwobr (*plural* -au) *feminine*

aware *adjective*
= ymwybodol
to be aware of the facts = bod yn
ymwybodol o'r ffeithiau

away *adverb*
• (*motion/location*)
= i ffwrdd, bant (*South*)
go away! = cer o 'ma!
miles away = milltiroedd i ffwrdd
• (*tidied away*)
= ar °gadw
toys away! = teganau ar °gadw!

awful *adjective*
= ofnadwy

awfully *adverb*
= ofnadwy o°, uffernol o°, andros o°,
sobor o°
awfully good = ofnadwy o °dda

awkward *adjective*
= lletchwith

axe *noun*
= bwyall, bwyell (*plural* bwyeill, bwyelli)
feminine

Bb

baby *noun*
= baban (*plural* -od) *masculine*, babi (*plural* -s) *masculine*

baby carriage *noun* (*US*)
= pram (*plural* -iau) *masculine*

babysit *verb*
= gwarchod (*plant*)

bachelor *noun*
= hen °lanc

back
1 *adverb*
= yn ôl
come back = dewch yn ôl
I'll be back in a moment = bydda i'n ôl toc
back to front = y tu ôl ymlaen
2 *noun*
= cefn (*plural* -au) *masculine*
to turn one's back on someone = cefnu ar° rywun
3 *verb*
= cefnogi

back benches *plural noun*
= y meinciau cefn *plural*

back door *noun*
= drws cefn (*plural* drysau cefn) *masculine*

background *noun*
= cefndir (*plural* -oedd) *masculine*

backpack *noun*
= gwarbac (*plural* -iau) *masculine*

back seat *noun*
= sedd °gefn (*plural* seddau cefn) *feminine*, sedd ôl (*plural* seddau ôl) *feminine*

backside *noun*
= pen-ôl (*plural* penolau) *masculine*

backwards *adverb*
= yn wysg + [*possessive adjective*] + cefn

> **!** *This expression varies depending on who it refers to:*
> **he went backwards** = aeth e yn wysg ei °gefn
> **she went backwards** = aeth hi yn wysg ei ʰchefn
> **I went backwards** = es i yn wysg 'y ⁿnghefn

bacon *noun*
= cig moch, bacwn

bad *adjective*
• (*general senses*)
= drwg
• (*serious*)
= difrifol
a bad accident = damwain °ddifrifol
• (*poor quality*)
= gwael
bad Welsh = Cymraeg gwael
• (*ill*)
= gwael, sâl
I feel bad = dw i'n teimlo'n °wael
= dw i'n teimlo'n sâl
bad luck = anlwc *masculine*
as bad as... = cynddrwg âʰ...

badge *noun*
= bathodyn (*plural* -nau) *masculine*

badger *noun*
= mochyn daear (*plural* moch daear) *masculine*

badly *adverb*
• (*not well*)
= yn °ddrwg, yn °wael
he did the work badly = mi naeth y gwaith yn °wael
• (*seriously*)
= yn °ddifrifol
he was badly injured = cafodd ei anafu'n °ddifrifol
• (*very much, urgently*)
= wir
I badly need this = dw i wir angen hwn

badminton *noun*
= badminton

bad-tempered *adjective*
he is very bad-tempered = mae e'n °ddrwg iawn ei °dymer
she is very bad-tempered = mae hi'n °ddrwg iawn ei tymer/ʰthymer

bag *noun*
= bag (*plural* -iau) *masculine*, sach (*plural* -au) *feminine*

baggage *noun*
= bagiau *plural*

bake *verb*
= pobi, crasu

baker *noun*
= pobydd (*plural* -ion) *masculine*

bakery *noun*
= popty (*plural* poptai) *masculine*, siop
°fara (*plural* siopau bara) *feminine*

balance *noun*
• (*equilibrium*)
= cydbwysedd *masculine*
to lose one's balance = colli
cydbwysedd
• (*weighing device*)
= clorian *feminine*
in the balance = yn y °fantol

balcony *noun*
= balconi (*plural* balconïau) *masculine*

bald *adjective*
= moel, penfoel

ball *noun*
= pêl (*plural* peli) *feminine*

ballet *noun*
= bale *masculine*

balloon *noun*
= balŵn (*plural* -s *or* balwnau) *masculine
or feminine*

ban *verb*
= gwahardd
**to ban someone from doing
something** = gwahardd rhywun rhag
gwneud rhywbeth

banana *noun*
= banana (*plural* -s) *feminine*

band *noun*
• (*for holding together*)
= rhwymyn *plural* -nau) *masculine*
• (*of musicians*)
= band (*plural* -iau) *masculine*

bandage *noun*
= rhwymyn (*plural* -nau) *masculine*

Band-Aid ® *noun*
= plastr (*plural* -au) *masculine*

bang
1 *noun*
• (*sound*)
= clep (*plural* -iau) *feminine*
• (*blow*)
= ergyd (*plural* -ion) *feminine or
masculine*
2 *verb*
= curo, taro
he banged on the door = mi °gurodd e
ar y drws
the door banged shut = mi °gaeodd y
drws yn °glep

bangs *plural noun* (*US = fringe*)
= rhimyn *masculine*

bank *noun*
• (*financial institution*)
= banc (*plural* -iau) *masculine*
• (*side of river*)
= glan (*plural* -nau) *feminine*

bank account *noun*
= cyfri(f) banc (*plural* cyfrifon banc)
masculine

bank holiday *noun*
= gŵyl banc (*plural* gwyliau banc)
feminine

bank manager *noun*
= rheolwr banc (*plural* rheolwyr banc)
masculine

baptize *verb*
= bedyddio

bar *noun*
• (*place, rod*)
= bar (*plural* -iau) *masculine*
behind bars = yn y carchar
• (*piece*)
= darn (*plural* -au) *masculine*
a bar of soap = darn o sebon

barbecue *noun*
= barbeciw (*plural* -iau) *masculine*

bard *noun*
= bardd (*plural* beirdd) *masculine*

barely *adverb*
= prin

> **!** **prin** *is usually followed by a* 'that...'
> *clause:*
> **I barely remember them** = prin ⁿmod
> i'n cofio nhw
> **we barely know him** = prin bod ni'n
> nabod e
> *but some speakers use an ordinary
> main verb:*
> = prin dw i'n cofio nhw, prin dyn ni'n
> nabod e

bargain *noun*
= bargen (*plural* bargeinion) *feminine*

bark *verb*
= cyfarth

barn *noun*
= (y)sgubor (*plural* -iau) *feminine*

barrel *noun*
= casgen (*plural* -ni) *feminine*

barrier *noun*
- (*physical*)
  = atalfa (*plural* atalfeydd) *feminine*
- (*obstacle*)
  = rhwystr (*plural* -au) *masculine*

base
1 *noun*
- (*foundation*)
  = sail (*plural* seiliau) *feminine*, sylfaen (*plural* sylfeini) *feminine*
- (*bottom*)
  = gwaelod (*plural* -ion) *masculine*
- (*root*)
  = bôn
2 *verb*
  = seilio
  to be based on something = bod yn seiliedig ar° rywbeth

baseball *noun*
  = pêl °fas *feminine*

basement *noun*
  = seler (*plural* -i) *feminine*

basic *adjective*
- (*fundamental*)
  = sylfaenol
- (*simple*)
  = syml

basically *adverb*
  = yn y bôn

> ! yn y bôn *generally comes first in the sentence.*
> **he is basically against the idea** = yn y bôn, mae e yn erbyn y syniad

basin *noun*
  = powlen (*plural* -ni) *feminine*, dysgl (*plural* -au) *feminine*

basis *noun*
  = sail (*plural* seiliau) *feminine*, sylfaen (*plural* sylfeini) *feminine*

basket *noun*
  = basged (*plural* -i) *feminine*

basketball *noun*
  = pêl-fasged *feminine*

bat *noun*
- (*animal*)
  = ystlum (*plural* -od) *masculine*
- (*sport*)
  = bat (*plural* -iau) *masculine or feminine*

bath *noun*
  = bath (*plural* -s) *masculine*

bathroom *noun*
  = stafell molchi (*plural* stafelloedd molchi) *feminine*

> ! *The qualifying word* **molchi** (*from* **ymolchi**) *is not susceptible to the soft mutation that would be expected after the feminine singular* **stafell**.

battery *noun*
  = batri (*plural* -s) *masculine*

battle *noun*
- (*fight*)
  = brwydr (*plural* -au) *feminine*
- (*competition*)
  = gornest (*plural* -au) *feminine*

bay *noun*
  = bae (*plural* -au) *masculine*

be *verb*
  = bod

> ! *See* **bod** *on the Welsh-English side for the various forms and regional variations of this verb.*

  we are happy = dyn ni'n hapus
  she will be here = bydd hi fan hyn
- (*exist*)
  = bod
  there is/are... = mae...
  is/are there...? = oes...?
  there isn't/aren't... = does dim...
- (*health, weather, etc*)
  = bod
  to be ill = bod yn sâl
  it's hot = mae'n °boeth
- (*describing a visit, or travel*)
  = bod
  have you been to Italy? = °fuoch chi yn yr Eidal?
- (*identification*)
  = bod (*present tense* ydy/yw)
  who is that? = pwy ydy/yw hwnna?
  what is this? = beth ydy/yw hwn?
- (*time, measurement*)
  = bod
  what time is it? = faint o'r gloch ydy/yw hi?
- (*expressing future*)
  the visitors are to leave at three = mae'r ymwelwyr i °fod i °adael am °dri

• (*passive*)
= cael
milk is delivered daily = mae llaeth yn cael ei °ddosbarthu °bob dydd

beach *noun*
= traeth (*plural* -au) *masculine*

beak *noun*
= pig (*plural* -au) *masculine or feminine*

beam *noun*
• (*wooden*)
= trawst (*plural* -iau) *masculine*
• (*of light*)
= pelydryn (*plural* pelydrau) *masculine*

beans *noun*
= ffa *plural*
runner beans = ffa dringo
baked beans = ffa pob

bear
1 *noun*
= arth (*plural* eirth) *feminine*
2 *verb*
• (*carry*)
= cario, cludo
• (*suffer, stand*)
= diodde(f)

beard *noun*
= barf (*plural* -au) *feminine*

bearded *adjective*
= barfog

beat *verb*
• (*hit*)
= bwrw, curo
• (*defeat*)
= curo, trechu
• (*eggs etc*)
= curo

beat up
to beat someone up = rhoi (*stem* rhoi-, rhodd-) curfa i °rywun

beautiful *adjective*
= hardd, prydferth

beauty *noun*
= harddwch *masculine*, prydferthwch *masculine*

because
1 *conjunction*
= achos (+ '*that...*' *clause*), oherwydd (+ '*that...*' *clause*), am °fod ..., gan °fod ...

because he is late = achos °fod e'n hwyr
= oherwydd °fod e'n hwyr
= am °fod e'n hwyr
= gan °fod e'n hwyr
2 because of *preposition*
= oherwydd, o achos
because of the war = oherwydd y rhyfel
= o achos y rhyfel

become *verb*
= dod (yn°), mynd (yn°)
it has become clear that... = mae hi wedi dod yn amlwg °fod...
things are becoming worse = mae pethau'n mynd yn °waeth

! *Welsh often uses derived verbs for 'become + adjective', e.g.* **tywyllu** *'become dark',* **oeri** *'become cold'*

bed *noun*
= gwely (*plural* -au) *masculine*
to go to bed = mynd i'r gwely

! *The definite article is needed in Welsh for 'to bed'* **i'r gwely** *and 'out of bed'* **o'r gwely**

bedroom *noun*
= stafell °wely (*plural* stafelloedd gwely) *feminine*

bee *noun*
= gwenynen (*plural* gwenyn) *feminine*

beef *noun*
= cig eidion *masculine*

beer *noun*
= cwrw (*plural* -au) *masculine*

beetroot *noun*
= betysen (*plural* betys) *feminine*

before
1 *conjunction*
= cyn
before we arrived = cyn inni °gyrraedd
before Alun goes = cyn i Alun °fynd
2 *preposition*
• (*time*)
= cyn
before Christmas = cyn Nadolig
before ten o'clock = cyn deg o'r °gloch
• (*in front of*)
= o °flaen

to appear before the court =
ymddangos gerbron y llys

3 *adverb*
(*previously*)
= o'r blaen, gynt

beg *verb*
= cardota

beggar *noun*
= cardotyn (*plural* cardotwyr) *masculine*

begin *verb*
= dechrau (*stem* dechreu-), cychwyn
(*stem* cychwynn-)
to begin doing something = dechrau
gwneud rhywbeth

beginner *noun*
= dechreuwr (*plural* dechreuwyr)
masculine

beginning *noun*
= dechrau (*plural* dechreuadau
dechreuon), *masculine*, cychwyn
masculine
at the beginning = ar y dechrau
at the beginning of the war = ar
°ddechrau'r rhyfel
a new beginning = dechrau newydd

behalf *noun*
on behalf of = ar °ran, dros°
on behalf of the council = ar °ran y
cyngor
on our behalf = ar ein rhan ni

behave *verb*
= ymddwyn (*stem* ymddyg-)
to behave badly = ymddwyn yn °ddrwg
to behave well = ymddwyn yn °dda

behaviour *noun*
= ymddygiad *masculine*

behind *preposition*
= tu cefn i°, tu ôl i°

beige *adjective*
= llwydfelyn (*feminine* llwydfelen)

Belgium *noun*
= Gwlad Belg *feminine*

belief *noun*
= cred (*plural* -au) *feminine*, credo (*plural*
-au) *feminine*, coel (*plural* -ion) *feminine*

believe *verb*
= credu*
to believe in something = credu yn^n
rhywbeth

I believe he's gone to London = dw i'n
credu °fod e wedi mynd i °Lundain

belittle *verb*
= bychanu

bell *noun*
= cloch (*plural* clychau) *feminine*

belly *noun*
= bol (*plural* boliau) *masculine*, bola
(*plural* bolâu) *masculine*

belong *verb*
• (*be the property of*)
= perthyn* (i°)
that belongs to me = mae hwnna'n
perthyn i mi
that belonged to me = roedd hwnna'n
perthyn i mi
• (*be a member of*)
= bod yn aelod o°
do you belong to the squash club? =
wyt ti'n aelod o'r clwb sboncen?

belongings *noun*
= pethau *plural*

below
1 *adverb*
= isod
see below = gweler isod
2 *preposition*
(*underneath*)
= dan°, o dan°

belt *noun*
= gwregys (*plural* -au) *masculine*

bench *noun*
= mainc (*plural* meinciau) *feminine*
to sit on the back benches = eistedd ar
y meinciau cefn

bend
1 *noun*
(*in road*) = tro (*plural* -adau) *masculine*,
troad (*plural* -au) *masculine*
2 *verb*
= plygu
bend down
= plygu

beneath *preposition*
= dan°, o dan°

benefit
1 *noun*
• (*general sense*)
= lles *masculine*
for the benefit of = er lles
of benefit = o °les

• (*state payment*)
= budd-dâl (*plural* budd-daliadau)
masculine
2 *verb*
to benefit from something = elwa o°
rywbeth

bereavement *noun*
= profedigaeth *feminine*

berry *noun*
= mwyaren (*plural* mwyar) *feminine*

beside *preposition*
= wrth och(o)r, wrth ymyl, yn ymyl, ar
°bwys (*South*)
beside the road = wrth ochor y ffordd
= wrth ymyl y ffordd
beside him = wrth ei ochor (e)
beside her = wrth ei hochor (hi)
beside them = wrth eu hochor (nhw)
beside the sea = ar °lan y môr
beside the river = ar °lan yr afon

best *adjective*
= gorau
this is the best one = hwn ydy'r un
gorau
= hon ydy'r un °orau
to do your level best = gwneud eich
gorau glas
the very best = y gorau oll
best of all = yn °well na dim

bet *verb*
= mentro, betio
I bet he's gone already = mi
°fentra/°fetia i °fod e wedi mynd yn
°barod

betray *verb*
= bradychu

better
1 *adjective*
= gwell
this one is better than that one = mae
hwn yn °well na hwnna
to get better = gwella
to be better than something (*superior*)
= rhagori ar° rywbeth
2 *adverb*
= well
I'd better go = well i mi °fynd

between *preposition*
= rhwng
between you and me = rhyngddat ti a fi

> **!** *This preposition is unusual in having
> no mutation after it:*
> **rhwng Cymru ac Iwerddon** =
> between Wales and Ireland

beyond *preposition*
= tu hwnt i°, tu draw i°

biased *adjective*
= unochrog

bicycle *noun*
= beic (*plural* -iau) *masculine*

big *adjective*
= mawr

> **!** *mawr has irregular related forms:*
> **as big, so big** = cymaint
> **bigger** = mwy
> **biggest** = mwya(f)

bike *noun*
= beic (*plural* -iau) *masculine*
racing bike = beic rasio (*plural* beiciau
rasio) *masculine*

bilingual *adjective*
= dwyieithog

bilingualism *noun*
= dwyieithrwydd *masculine*

bill *noun*
= bil (*plural* -iau) *masculine*

billiards *noun*
= biliards *feminine or masculine*

billion *numeral*
= biliwn *feminine*

bin *noun*
= bin (*plural* -iau) *masculine or feminine*
rubbish bin = bin sbwriel (*plural* biniau
sbwriel) *masculine or feminine*

bin liner *noun*
= sach sbwriel (*plural* sachau sbwriel)
feminine

bind *verb*
= clymu, rhwymo
to bind something to something =
clymu rhywbeth wrth° rywbeth

biology *noun*
= bioleg *feminine*, bywydeg *feminine*

bird *noun*
= aderyn (*plural* adar) *masculine*

> **!** *Singular often* **deryn** *in speech.*

biro ® *noun*
= beiro (*plural* -s) *masculine*

birth *noun*
= genedigaeth (*plural* -au) *feminine*, geni *verbnoun*
date of birth = dyddiad geni
place of birth = man geni
congratulations on the birth of your daughter = llongyfarchiadau ar °enedigaeth eich merch
to give birth to = geni

birth control *noun*
= atal cenhedlu *verbnoun*

birthday *noun*
= penblwydd (*plural* -i) *masculine*
Happy Birthday! = Penblwydd Hapus!

biscuit *noun*
= bisgeden (*plural* bisgedi) *feminine*

bishop *noun*
= esgob (*plural* -ion) *masculine*

bit *noun*
• (*small quantity*)
= ychydig, tipyn, braidd, peth
I've only got a bit (*a little*) = dim ond ychydig sy gen i
can I have a bit of that cheese? (*some*) = °ga i ychydig o'r caws 'na?
I think there's a bit left (*some*) = dw i'n meddwl °fod peth ar ôl
• (*rather*)
= bach, braidd, tipyn
he's a bit shy = mae e bach yn swil
= mae e braidd yn swil
= mae e °dipyn yn swil
• (*every bit + comparative*)
= yr un mor°
she's every bit as clever as him = mae hi yr un mor °ddeallus ag e
• (*piece*)
= darn (*plural* -au) *masculine*, tamaid (*plural* tameidiau) *masculine*
can I have a bit of that cheese? = °ga i °ddarn o'r caws 'na?

> **!** **ychydig**, **tipyn** and **tamaid** are true quantity words, and require **o°** when used with a following noun—**ychydig o °gaws** 'a bit of cheese', 'a little cheese'

bite *verb*
= cnoi, brathu

to bite one's nails = cnoi'ch ewinedd

bitter *adjective*
= chwerw

black *adjective*
= du (*plural occasionally* duon *in set phrases*)

blackberries *plural noun*
= mwyar duon *plural*

blackboard *noun*
= bwrdd du (*plural* byrddau du) *masculine*

blackcurrant *noun*
= cyransen °ddu (*plural* cyrains duon) *feminine*

bladder *noun*
= pledren (*plural* -ni, -nau) *feminine*

blade *noun*
= llafn (*plural* -au) *masculine*
blade of grass = glaswelltyn (*plural* glaswellt) *masculine*, gwelltyn (*plural* gwellt) *masculine*

blame
1 *noun*
= bai *masculine*
to put the blame on someone = beio rhywun
= rhoi (*stem* rhoi-, rhodd-) 'r bai ar °rywun
2 *verb*
to blame someone = beio rhywun
= rhoi (*stem* rhoi-, rhodd-) 'r bai ar °rywun
you are to blame = ti sy ar °fai

blank *adjective*
= gwag

blanket *noun*
= blanced (*plural* -i) *feminine*

blast
1 *noun*
• (*of air*)
= chwythiad (*plural* -au) *masculine*
• (*explosion*)
= ffrwydriad (*plural* -au) *masculine*
2 *verb*
= ffrwydro, tanio

blaze *noun*
= ffagl (*plural* -au) *feminine*

bleach *noun*
= cannydd (*plural* canyddion) *masculine*

bleed *verb*
= gwaedu
his leg was bleeding = roedd ei °goes yn gwaedu

bless *verb*
= bendithio
bless you! (*response to sneeze*) = bendith!

blind
1 *adjective*
= dall (*plural* deillion *when referring to people*)
2 *verb*
= dallu
3 *noun*
(*on window*)
= cysgodlen (*plural* -ni) *feminine*, bleind (*plural* -s) *masculine*

blink *verb*
= amrantu

blister *noun*
= swigen (*plural* swigod) *feminine*

blizzard *noun*
= lluwchwynt (*plural* -oedd) *masculine*, storm eira (*plural* stormydd eira) *feminine*

block
1 *noun*
= bloc (*plural* -iau) *masculine*
2 *verb*
= blocio

blood *noun*
= gwaed *masculine*

blood bank *noun*
= banc gwaed (*plural* banciau gwaed) *masculine*

bloody *adjective*
• (*literal sense*)
= gwaedlyd
• (*curse or intensifier*)
= diawledig, cythraul
bloody thing! = y peth diawledig 'ma!

bloom
1 *noun*
= blodyn (*plural* blodau) *masculine*
2 *verb*
= blodeuo

blossom
1 *noun*
= blodyn (*plural* blodau) *masculine*

2 *verb*
= blodeuo

blouse *noun*
= blows (*plural* -ys) *masculine or feminine*

blow
1 *verb*
= chwythu
2 *noun*
= ergyd (*plural* -ion, -iau) *feminine or masculine* (*also figurative*), trawiad (*plural* -au) *masculine*

blow away
= chwythu i ffwrdd

blow down
= chwythu i lawr

blow out
= chwythu allan

blow up
• (*explode*)
= ffrwydro
• (*inflate*)
= chwythu

blue *adjective*
= glas (*plural* gleision *very rare*)

blunt *adjective*
• (*opposite of sharp*)
= di-awch
• (*direct*)
= plaen

blush *verb*
= gwrido, cochi, mynd yn °goch

board *noun*
= bwrdd (*plural* byrddau) *masculine*
on board (*ship*) = ar °long

boarding school *noun*
= ysgol °breswyl (*plural* ysgolion preswyl) *feminine*

boast *verb*
= ymffrostio

boat *noun*
= cwch (*plural* cychod) *masculine*, bad (*plural* -au) *masculine*

> **!** **cwch** *is the general term for a small vessel, while* **bad** *is restricted to certain senses, e.g.* **bad achub** = lifeboat

body *noun*
= corff (*plural* cyrff) *masculine*
dead body = corff marw *masculine*

bog *noun*
= cors (*plural* -ydd) *feminine*

boil *verb*
= berwi

boiled egg *noun*
= ŵy wedi'i °ferwi (*plural* wyau wedi'u berwi) *masculine*

boiler *noun*
= boeler (*plural* -i) *masculine*

boiling *adjective*
= berwedig

bolt
1 *noun*
= bollt (*plural* -iau) *feminine*
2 *verb*
= bolltio

bomb
1 *noun*
= bom (*plural* -iau) *masculine or feminine*
2 *verb*
= bomio

bone *noun*
= asgwrn (*plural* esgyrn) *masculine*

bonnet *noun*
= boned (*plural* -i, -au) *feminine*

book
1 *noun*
= llyfr (*plural* -au) *masculine*
2 *verb*
= bwcio

booking *noun*
= bwcio *verbnoun*

booklet *noun*
= llyfryn (*plural* -nau) *masculine*

bookshop *noun*
= siop °lyfrau (*plural* siopau llyfrau) *feminine*

boost
1 *noun*
= hwb
2 *verb*
= hybu, rhoi (*stem* rhoi-, rhodd-) hwb i°

boot *noun*
• (*footwear*)
= esgid (*plural* -iau) *feminine*
• (*of car*)
= cist (*plural* -iau) *feminine*

border
1 *noun*
• (*frontier*)
= ffin (*plural* -iau) *feminine*
to cross the border = mynd dros y ffin
• (*edge*)
= ymyl (*plural* -on) *masculine or feminine*
2 *verb*
= ymylu
to border on something = ymylu ar° rywbeth

bore *verb*
• (*make bored*)
= diflasu
• (*bore a hole in*)
= tyllu
he bored a hole in the wood = mi °dyllodd e'r pren

bored *adjective*
I am bored with it = dw i wedi diflasu arno

boring *adjective*
= diflas

born
in **be born:**
when were you born? = pryd °gest ti dy °eni?
= pryd °gawsoch chi'ch geni?
I was born in 1942 = °ges i ⁿngeni ym 1942

borrow *verb*
= benthyg
can I borrow your bike? = °ga i °fenthyg dy °feic?
borrowed word = gair benthyg (*plural* geiriau benthyg) *masculine*

boss *noun*
= pennaeth (*plural* penaethiaid) *masculine*

both
1 *adjective*
= y °ddau° (*masculine, masculine + feminine*), y °ddwy° (*feminine*)
both cars = y °ddau °gar
both lorries = y °ddwy lori
both my sons = y °ddau °fab sy gen i
2 *pronoun*
= y °ddau° (*masculine, masculine + feminine*), y °ddwy° (*feminine*)
we/us both = (*also*) ni'n dau/dwy;

you both = (*also*) chi'ch dau/dwy;
they/them both = (*also*) ill dau/dwy
you are both right = mae'r ᵒddau
ohonoch chi'n iawn, dych chi'n iawn
chi'ch dau
we want them both = dyn ni eisiau'r
ᵒddau
we both want them = dyn ni eisiau nhw
ni'n dau
they were both soaked = fe ᵒgaethon
nhw eu gwlychu ill dau

bother
1 *noun*
= trafferth (*plural* -ion) *feminine*
2 *verb*
= poeni, pryderu
don't bother me! = gad ᵒlonydd i mi!
don't bother phoning = paid mynd i'r
trafferth o ffonio
to be bothered about something =
poeni amᵒ rywbeth
I'm not bothered = dw i ᵒddim yn poeni
= dim ots gen i, dim ots 'da fi

bottle *noun*
= potel (*plural* -i) *feminine*

bottle bank *noun*
= banc poteli (*plural* banciau poteli)
masculine

bottle-opener *noun*
= agorwr poteli (*plural* agorwyr poteli)
masculine

bottom *noun*
• (*lowest part*)
= gwaelod (*plural* -ion) *masculine*
• (*of hill*)
= troed *masculine or feminine*
• (*part of body*)
= pen ôl (*plural* penolau) *masculine*

bounce *verb*
= bowndio, bownsio
the cheque bouned = mi naeth y siec
ᵒfownsio, mi ᵒgafodd y siec ei gwrthod

bound *adjective*
it's bound to happen = mae'n rhwym o
ᵒddigwydd
= mae'n siwr o ᵒddigwydd

boundary *noun*
= ffin (*plural* -iau) *feminine*

bow¹ *noun*
• (*knot*)
= cwlwm (*plural* cylymau) *masculine*,
clwm (*plural* clymau) *masculine*

• (*weapon*)
= bwa (*plural* bwâu) *masculine*

bow² *verb*
= plygu

bowl *noun*
= padell (*plural* -i, -au) *feminine*, powlen
(*plural* -ni) *feminine*, dysgl (*plural* -au)
feminine

bowling *noun*
= bowlio *verbnoun*

box *noun*
= blwch (*plural* blychau) *masculine*, bocs
(*plural* -ys) *masculine*

boxer *noun*
= paffiwr (*plural* paffwyr) *masculine*

boxing *noun*
= paffio *verbnoun*

boy *noun*
= bachgen (*plural* bechgyn) *masculine*

boyfriend *noun*
= cariad (*plural* -on) *masculine*

bra *noun*
= bra (*plural* -s) *masculine*

bracelet *noun*
= breichled (*plural* -au, -i) *feminine*

braid *noun* (*US*)
= plethen (-ni) *feminine*

brain *noun*
= ymennydd (*plural* ymenyddiau)
masculine

brake
1 *noun*
= brêc (*plural* -s) *masculine*
2 *verb*
= brecio

branch *noun*
= cangen (*plural* canghennau) *feminine*

brand-new *adjective*
= newydd sbon

brandy *noun*
= brandi *masculine*

brave *adjective*
= dewr

bread *noun*
= bara *masculine*
bread and butter = bara menyn
masculine

breadth noun
= lled (*plural* -au) *masculine*
the length and breadth of Wales = ar hyd a lled Cymru
within a hair's breadth = o ᵒfewn trwch blewyn

break
1 *noun*
• (*fracture*)
= toriad (*plural* -au) *masculine*
• (*interval*)
= egwyl (*plural* -iau, ion) *feminine*, saib (*plural* seibiau) *masculine*
• (*holiday*)
= gwyliau *plural*
2 *verb*
= torri
he broke his arm = mi ᵒdorrodd e ei ᵒfraich

break down
= torri i lawr
the car has broken down = mae'r car wedi torri i lawr

break into
= torri i mewn iᵒ

break out
= torri allan

break up
• (*destroy*)
= chwalu
• (*separate*)
= gwahanu, ysgaru

breakfast noun
= brecwast (*plural* -au) *masculine*

breast noun
• (*of woman*)
= bron (*plural* -nau) *feminine*
• (*chest*)
= brest *feminine*

breath noun
= anadl (*plural* -au, -iadau) *feminine or masculine*

breathe verb
= anadlu

breathe in
= anadlu i mewn

breathe out
= anadlu allan

breather noun
• (*pause*)
= seibiant (*plural* seibiau, seibiannau) *masculine*

breed verb
= bridio, meithrin

breeze noun
= awel (*plural* -on) *feminine*

Breton noun
• (*language*)
= Llydaweg *feminine*
• (*man*)
= Llydäwr (*plural* Llydaw-wyr) *masculine*
• (*woman*)
= Llydawes (*plural* -i, -au) *feminine*

brew verb
= bragu

bribe
1 *noun*
= cildwrn (*plural* cildyrnau) *masculine*
2 *verb*
to bribe someone = rhoi (*stem* rhoi-, rhodd-) cildwrn i ᵒrywun

brick noun
= bricsen (*plural* brics, briciau) *feminine*

bride noun
= priodferch (*plural* -ed) *feminine*

bridegroom noun
= priodfab (*plural* priodfeibion) *masculine*

bridge noun
= pont (*plural* -ydd) *feminine*

bridleway noun
= llwybr (*plural* -au) ceffyl *masculine*

brief adjective
= byr (*feminine* ber, *plural* byrion)

briefs plural noun
= dillad isa(f) *plural*

bright adjective
= disglair, gloyw, llachar
bright blue = glas llachar

brilliant adjective
• (*shining*)
= disglair, gloyw, llachar
• (*intelligent*)
= disglair

bring verb
= dod âʰ
why don't you bring the children? = pam na ᵒddoi di â'r plant?
I've brought you a present = dw i wedi dod ag anrheg i ti

bring about
= (*cause*) achosi

bring back
to bring something back = dod â[h] rhywbeth yn ôl

bring up
= magu
where were you brought up? = lle °gaethoch chi'ch magu?
I was brought up in London = °ges i y' magu yn Llundain

Britain *noun*
= Prydain *feminine*
Great Britain = Prydain °Fawr

British *adjective*
= Prydeinig
the British Isles = yr Ynysoedd Prydeinig

broad *adjective*
= llydan

broadcast
1 *verb*
= darlledu
2 *noun*
= darllediad (*plural* -au) *masculine*

broaden *verb*
= lledu, ehangu

brochure *noun*
= llyfryn (*plural* -nau) *masculine*, taflen (*plural* -ni) *feminine*

broil *verb*
= grilio

broke *adjective*
• (*without money*)
= heb arian, heb yr un °geiniog

broken *adjective*
= wedi'i °dorri (*masculine*), wedi'i [h]thorri/torri (*feminine*), wedi'u torri (*plural*)
a broken window = ffenest wedi'i [h]thorri/torri

bronze *noun and adjective*
= efydd *masculine*

brook *noun*
= nant (*plural* nentydd) *feminine*, ffrwd (*plural* ffrydiau) *feminine*

brother *noun*
= brawd (*plural* brodyr) *masculine*

brother-in-law *noun*
= brawd-yng-nghyfraith (*plural* brodyr-yng-nghyfraith) *masculine*

brown *adjective*
= brown

bruise
1 *noun*
= clais (*plural* cleisiau) *masculine*
2 *verb*
= cleisio

brush
1 *noun*
= brws (*plural* -ys, -iau) *masculine*
2 *verb*
= brwsio

bubble *noun*
= swigen (*plural* swigod) *feminine*

bucket *noun*
= bwced (*plural* -i) *feminine*

budgerigar, budgie *noun*
= byji (*plural* -s) *masculine*

budget
1 *noun*
= cyllideb (*plural* -au) *feminine*
2 *verb*
= cyllidebu, neilltuo arian

build *verb*
= adeiladu, codi
when was this house built? = pryd °gafodd y tŷ 'ma ei °godi?

builder *noun*
= adeiladwr (*plural* adeiladwyr) *masculine*

building *noun*
= adeilad (*plural* -au) *masculine*

built-in *adjective*
= gosodedig

bulb *noun*
= bylb (*plural* -iau) *masculine*

bulge
1 *noun*
= chwydd (*plural* -au) *masculine*
2 *verb*
= chwyddo

bulky *adjective*
= swmpus, trwchus

bull *noun*
= tarw (*plural* teirw) *masculine*

bullet noun
= bwled (*plural* -i) *masculine or feminine*

bulletin noun
= bwletin (*plural* -au) *masculine*

bully
1 noun
= bwli (*plural* -s, bwlïaid) *masculine*
2 verb
= bwlio

bump
1 noun
= ergyd (*plural* -ion, -iau) *feminine or masculine*, cnoc (*plural* -iau) *feminine*
2 verb
= taro, cnocio

bump into
to bump into something = taro yn erbyn rhywbeth
to bump into someone (*meet by chance*) = cwrdd â[h] rhywun yn annisgwyl

bunch noun
bunch of flowers = tusw (*plural* -au) *masculine*, bwnsiad (*plural* bwnsieidiau) *masculine*

bunk beds noun
= gwelyau bync *plural*

bunk off verb
(*miss school*)
= mitsio

burden noun
= baich (*plural* beichiau) *masculine*

bureaucracy noun
= biwrocratiaeth (*plural* -au) *feminine*

burger noun
= byrgyr (*plural* -s) *masculine*, eidionyn (*plural* eidionod) *masculine*

burglar noun
= lleidr tŷ (*plural* lladron tai) *masculine*

burglar alarm noun
= larwm lladron (*plural* larymau lladron) *masculine*

burglary noun
= lladrad (*plural* -au) *masculine* yn y tŷ, i °dŷ

burn verb
= llosgi

burn down
the house burnt down = mi °losgodd y tŷ 'n ulw
= mi naeth y tŷ °losgi'n ulw

burning adjective
= (*fervent*) tanbaid
burning issue = pwnc llosg (*plural* pynciau llosg) *masculine*

burnt adjective
= wedi'i °losgi (*masculine*),
= wedi'i llosgi (*feminine*),
= wedi'u llosgi (*plural*)
a burnt cake = cacen wedi'i llosgi

burst verb
= rhwygo, ffrwydro

burst into
she burst into tears = naeth hi °ddechrau wylo

burst out
they burst out laughing = naethon nhw °ddechrau rhuo chwerthin

bury verb
= claddu

bus noun
= bws (*plural* bysiau) *masculine*

bus conductor noun
= tocynnwr (*plural* tocynwyr) *masculine*; tocynwraig (*plural* tocynwragedd) *feminine*

bus driver noun
= gyrrwr bws (*plural* gyrwyr bysiau) *masculine*

bush noun
= llwyn (*plural* -i) *masculine*

business noun
• (*commerce*)
= masnach *feminine*
• (*firm*)
= cwmni (*plural* cwmnïau) *masculine*, busnes (*plural* -au) *masculine*
local business = cwmnïau lleol, busnesau lleol
• (*affair, concern*)
= busnes (*plural* -au) *masculine*
mind your own business! = paid busnesa!
that's my business = 'y [n]musnes i ydy hwnna

businessman noun
= dyn busnes (plural dynion busnes) masculine

businesswoman noun
= merch °fusnes (plural merched busnes) feminine

bus station noun
= gorsaf °fysiau (plural gorsafoedd bysiau) feminine

bus stop noun
= safle bysiau (plural safleoedd bysiau) masculine

busy adjective
= prysur

> ! '...busy ... -ing' is usually expressed by **wrthi'n** + verbnoun:
> **they're busy filling in the forms** = maen nhw wrthi'n llenwi'r ffurflenni

but conjunction
= ond

butcher noun
= cigydd (plural -ion) masculine

butter noun
= menyn masculine

butterfly noun
= pili-pala (plural pili-palod) masculine; iâr °fach yr ha(f) (plural ieir bach yr ha(f)) masculine

> ! There is a wide range of terms for this insect—see **pili-pala** on the Welsh-English side for more.

button noun
= botwm (plural botymau) masculine

buy verb
= prynu
to buy something from someone = prynu rhywbeth gan °rywun

buzz verb
= suo

by preposition
• (location)
= wrth°, wrth och(o)r, wrth ymyl
by the road = wrth ochor y ffordd
• (past)
= heibio
to go by = mynd heibio (i°)

• (agent)
= gan°
arrested by the police = wedi'i arestio gan yr heddlu
• (by means of)
= â[h]
to pay by cheque = talu â siec
• (author, etc)
a play by Shakespeare = drama gan Shakespeare
• (method)
= drwy°, trwy°
by breaking a window = drwy °dorri ffenest
• (transport)
= ar°, gyda[h]
by bus = ar y bws, gyda'r bws
by car = gyda'r car
• (time)
by ten o'clock = erbyn deg o'r °gloch
by now = erbyn hyn

by-election noun
= is-etholiad (plural -au) masculine

bypass
1 noun
= ffordd osgoi (plural ffyrdd osgoi) feminine
2 verb
= mynd heibio i°

Cc

cab *noun*
- (*of vehicle*)
  = caban (*plural* -au) *masculine*
- (*taxi*)
  = tacsi (*plural* -s) *masculine*

cabbage *noun*
= bresychen (*plural* bresych) *feminine*

cable *noun*
= cebl (*plural* -au) *masculine*

cable tv *noun*
= teledu cebl *masculine*

cafe *noun*
= caffi (*plural* -s) *masculine*

cake *noun*
= cacen (*plural* -nau, -ni) *feminine*, teisen (*plural* -nau, -ni) *feminine*

calculator *noun*
= cyfrifiannell (*plural* cyfrifianellau) *feminine*

calendar *noun*
= calendr (*plural* -au) *masculine*

calf *noun*
= llo (*plural* -i, -eau) *masculine*

call
1 *noun*
- (*action of calling*)
  = galwad (*plural* -au)
- (*also phonecall*)
  = caniad (*plural* -au)
  to give someone a call = rhoi (*stem* rhoi-, rhodd-) caniad i° rywun
2 *verb*
= galw (*stem* galw-)

call off (*postpone*)
= gohirio

call round
= galw draw, galw heibio

calm
1 *adjective*
= tawel, llonydd
2 *noun*
= tawelwch *masculine*, llonyddwch *masculine*
3 *verb*
= tawelu, llonyddu

camcorder *noun*
= camera fideo (*plural* camerâu fideo) *masculine*

camel *noun*
= camel (*plural* -od) *masculine*

camera *noun*
= camera (*plural* camerâu) *masculine*

camp
1 *noun*
= gwersyll (*plural* -oedd) *masculine*
2 *verb*
(*go camping*)
= gwersylla

campaign
1 *noun*
= ymgyrch (*plural* -oedd) *masculine or feminine*
2 *verb*
= ymgyrchu
to campaign for something = ymgyrchu dros° rywbeth

campsite *noun*
= gwersyllfa (*plural* gwersyllfeydd) *feminine*

can¹ *noun*
= tun (*plural* -iau) *masculine*

can ² *verb*
- (*be able*)
  = gallu, medru
  can I help you? = °alla i'ch helpu chi?

> **! gallu** *is the standard and Southern word,* **medru** *more common in the North. The two words are largely, though not entirely, interchangeable - see Welsh-English entries for details; see also* **cannot**.

- (*be allowed*)
  = cael
  can I decide later?—yes = °ga i °benderfynu wedyn?—cewch

canal *noun*
= camlas (*plural* camlesi *or* camlesydd) *feminine*

cancel *verb*
= dileu

Cancer *noun*
= y Cranc *masculine*

cancer *noun*
= canser (*plural* -au) *masculine*

he's got cancer = mae e'n diodde o/gan °ganser

candidate *noun*
= ymgeisydd (*plural* ymgeiswyr) *masculine*

candle *noun*
= cannwyll (*plural* canhwyllau) *masculine*

candy *noun* (*US*)
= melysion *plural*

cannot (can't)
= methu; (*South also*) ffili, ffaelu
I can't understand this = dw i'n methu deall hyn
I can't swim = °alla i °ddim nofio

> **!** **gallu** and **medru** in the negative can also be used for 'cannot'
> **dw i °ddim yn gallu/medru deall hyn, °alla i °ddim deall hyn, °fedra i °ddim deall hyn** = I cannot understand this
> ⇒**can**

canoe *noun*
= canŵ (*plural* -au) *masculine*

canoeing *noun*
= canŵio *masculine*, mynd ar °ganŵ

can-opener *noun*
= agorwr tuniau (*plural* agorwyr tuniau) *masculine*

can't
= **cannot**

canteen *noun*
= ffreutur (*plural* -iau) *masculine*

cap *noun*
• (*hat*)
= cap (*plural* -iau) *masculine*
• (*lid*)
= caead (*plural* -au) *masculine*

capable *adjective*
= galluog
to be capable of doing something = bod yn °alluog i °wneud rhywbeth

capital *noun*
• (*city*)
= prifddinas (*plural* -oedd) *feminine*
• (*finance*)
= cyfalaf *masculine*

capital city *noun*
= prifddinas (*plural* -oedd) *feminine*

capitalism *noun*
= cyfalafiaeth *feminine*

capitalist *noun*
= cyfalafwr (*plural* cyfalafwyr) *masculine*

Capricorn *noun*
= yr °Afr *feminine*

captain *noun*
= capten (*plural* capteiniaid) *masculine*

capture *verb*
= dal (*stem* dali-), cipio

car *noun*
• (*automobile*)
= car (*plural* ceir) *masculine*, modur (*plural* -on) *masculine*
• (*US : carriage on train*)
= cerbyd (*plural* -au) *masculine*

caravan *noun*
= carafan (*plural* -au) *feminine*

card *noun*
= cerdyn (*plural* cardiau) *masculine*

cardphone *noun*
= ffôn cerdyn (*plural* ffonau cerdyn) *masculine*

care
1 *noun*
= gofal
to take care of someone = gofalu am° rywun
2 *verb*
(*bother*)
= becso, poeni
I don't care = dim ots gen i, dim ots 'da fi
to care about something = poeni am° rywbeth
to care for someone = gofalu am° rywun

career *noun*
= gyrfa (*plural* -oedd) *feminine*

careful *adjective*
= gofalus
be careful! = bydd yn °ofalus!
= pwylla!

careless *adjective*
= difeddwl, diofal

car ferry *noun*
= fferi °geir (*plural* fferïau ceir) *feminine*

carnival *noun*
= carnifal (*plural* -au) *masculine*

car park *noun*
= maes parcio (*plural* meysydd parcio) *masculine*

carpenter *noun*
= saer (*plural* seiri) *masculine*

carpet *noun*
= carped (*plural* -i) *masculine*

car phone *noun*
= ffôn car (*plural* ffonau car) *masculine*

carriage *noun*
(*of train*)
= cerbyd (*plural* -au) *masculine*

carrot *noun*
= moronen (*plural* moron) *feminine*

carry *verb*
= cario, cludo

carry on
= mynd ymlaen, parhau
to carry on doing something = parhau i °wneud rhywbeth

carry out
(*fulfil*)
= cyflawni, gweithredu

cartoon *noun*
= cartŵn (*plural* cartwnau) *masculine*

case
1 *noun*
• (*legal etc*)
= achos (*plural* -ion) *masculine*
• (*suitcase*)
= cist (*plural* -iau) *feminine*, cês (*plural* cesys) *masculine*
2 in case *conjunction*
= rhag ofn

> **!** **in case someone comes** = rhag ofn i rywun °ddod,
> = rhag ofn bod rhywun yn dod
> *This phrase uses a typical construction involving* **i°** *before the subject and a mutated verbnoun following.*

in any case = beth bynnag

cash
1 *noun*
= arian *masculine*, arian parod

2 *verb*
to cash a cheque = newid (*stem* newidi-) siec

cash desk *noun*
= desg arian (*plural* desgiau arian) *feminine*

cashpoint *noun*
= arianbwynt (*plural* -iau) *masculine*

cassette *noun*
= casét (*plural* casetiau) *masculine*

cassette player *noun*
= chwaraewr casetiau (*plural* chwaraewyr casetiau) *masculine*

cassette recorder *noun*
= recordydd casetiau (*plural* recordyddion casetiau) *masculine*

castle *noun*
= castell (*plural* cestyll) *masculine*

casual *adjective*
casual clothes = dillad hamdden
casual work = gwaith dros °dros

cat *noun*
= cath (*plural* -od) *feminine*

catch *verb*
= dal (*stem* dali-)
to catch a bus = dal bws
he's caught a cold = mae e wedi dal annwyd

catch up
= dal (*stem* dali-)
he caught up with us in the end = fe °ddaliodd e ni yn y diwedd

caterpillar *noun*
= lindysen (*plural* lindys) *feminine*, Siani °flewog (*plural* Sianis blewog) *feminine*

cathedral *noun*
= eglwys °gadeiriol (*plural* eglwysi cadeiriol) *feminine*

cattle *noun*
= gwartheg *plural*

cauliflower *noun*
= blodfresychen (*plural* blodfresych) *feminine*

cause
1 *noun*
= achos (*plural* -ion) *masculine*
to contribute to good causes = cyfrannu at° achosion da

2 *verb*
= achosi, peri
what caused the fire? = beth achosodd
y tân?, beth oedd achos y tân?
to cause someone to do something =
achosi/peri i° rywun °wneud rhywbeth

caution *noun*
= gofal *masculine*, pwyll *masculine*

cautious *adjective*
= gofalus

cave *noun*
= ogof (*plural* -âu, -eydd) *feminine*

CD *noun*
= crynoddisg (*plural* -iau) *masculine*

CD player *noun*
= peiriant crynoddisgiau (*plural*
peiriannau crynoddisgiau) *masculine*

cease *verb*
= peidio
to cease doing something = peidio
gwneud rhywbeth

ceasefire *noun*
= cadoediad (*plural* -au) *masculine*

ceaseless *adjective*
= dibaid, diderfyn

ceiling *noun*
= nenfwd (*plural* nenfydau) *masculine*

celebrate *verb*
= dathlu

celery *noun*
= seleri *masculine*

cell *noun*
= cell (*plural* -au) *feminine*

cellar *noun*
= seler (*plural* -au *or* -i) *feminine*

cello *noun*
= cello (*plural* -s) *masculine*, soddgrwth
(*plural* soddgrythau) *masculine*

Celt *noun*
= Celt (*plural* -iaid) *masculine*

Celtic *adjective*
= Celtaidd
the Celtic languages = yr ieithoedd
Celtaidd *plural*

cement *noun*
= sment *masculine*

cement mixer *noun*
= corddwr sment (*plural* corddwyr
sment) *masculine*

cemetery *noun*
= mynwent (*plural* -ydd) *feminine*

centenary *noun*
= canmlwyddiant (*plural*
canmlwyddiannau) *masculine*

centimetre *noun*
= sentimedr (*plural* -au) *masculine*,
centimedr (*plural* -au) *masculine*

central *adjective*
= canolog
central region = canolbarth (*plural* -au)
masculine
central England = canolbarth Lloegr

central heating *noun*
= gwres canolog *masculine*

centre *noun*
• (*middle point*)
= canol (*plural* -au) *masculine*
in the centre of town = yng ⁿnghanol y
°dre
• (*place for activities*)
= canolfan (*plural* -nau) *feminine*

century *noun*
= canrif (*plural* -oedd) *feminine*
the twentieth century = yr ugeinfed
°ganrif
the twenty-first century = yr unfed
°ganrif ar hugain
at the turn of the century = ar °droad y
°ganrif

certain *adjective*
= sicr, siŵr, siwr
to know something for certain =
gwybod rhywbeth i sicrwydd
to a certain extent = i °raddau

certainly *adverb*
= yn sicr, yn sicr iawn

certainty *noun*
= sicrwydd *masculine*

certificate *noun*
= tystysgrif (*plural* -au) *feminine*

certify *verb*
= tystio
this is to certify that . . . = hyn i °dystio
°fod. . ., hyn a °dystia °fod. . .

chain *noun*
= cadwyn (*plural* -i, -au) *feminine*

chainsaw *noun*
= llif gadwyn (*plural* llifiau cadwyn) *feminine*

chair *noun*
= cadair (*plural* cadeiriau) *feminine*

chairman *noun*
= cadeirydd (*plural* -ion) *masculine*

chairwoman *noun*
= cadeiryddes (*plural* -au) *feminine*

challenge
1 *noun*
= her (*plural* -iau) *feminine*
2 *verb*
= herio

champagne *noun*
= siampên *masculine*

champion *noun*
= pencampwr (*plural* pencampwyr) *masculine*
= pencampwraig (*plural* pencampwragedd) *feminine*

championship *noun*
= pencampwriaeth (*plural* -au) *feminine*

chance *noun*
• (*opportunity*)
= cyfle (*plural* -oedd) *masculine*, siawns (*plural* -iau) *feminine or masculine*
to have a chance to do something = bod â'r cyfle i °wneud rhywbeth
• (*accident*)
= damwain (*plural* damweiniau) *feminine*
by chance = yn °ddamweiniol
= drwy lwc
= drwy °ddamwain
• (*possibility*)
is there any chance he'll come? = ydy hi'n °bosib y daw e?

change
1 *noun*
• (*alteration*)
= newid (*plural* -iadau) *masculine*
for a change = am newid
• (*money*)
= arian mân
have you got change for five pounds? = oes gynnoch chi newid pum punt? (*North*), oes newid pum punt 'da chi? (*South*)

2 *verb*
• (*alter*)
= newid (*stem* newidi-)
to change one's mind = ailfeddwl
• (*exchange*)
= cyfnewid (*stem* cyfnewidi-)
• (*change clothes*)
= newid dillad

changeable *adjective*
= newidiol

changing room *noun*
= stafell newid (*plural* stafelloedd newid) *feminine*

channel *noun*
= sianel (*plural* -i) *feminine*
television channel = sianel °deledu (*plural* sianeli teledu) *feminine*
to change channels = troi (*stem* troi-, trodd-) i sianel arall, newid sianel
the English Channel = y Sianel *feminine*

chapter *noun*
= pennod (*plural* penodau) *feminine*

characteristic
1 *adjective*
= nodweddiadol
2 *noun*
= nodwedd (*plural* -ion) *feminine*

charge
1 *noun*
• (*money*)
= tâl (*plural* taliadau) *masculine*
• (*accusation*)
= cyhuddiad (*plural* -au) *masculine*
• **in charge**
= mewn gofal, mewn awdurdod
2 *verb*
• (*money*)
= codi, gofyn (*stem* gofynn-)
• (*with a crime*)
= cyhuddo
to charge someone with something = cyhuddo rhywun o° rywbeth

charming *adjective*
= swynol, hudol

charter flight *noun*
= ehediad siarter (*plural* ehediadau siarter) *masculine*

chase *verb*
= rhedeg (*stem* rhed-) ar ôl
chase him! = rhedwch ar ei ôl!

chat
1 *noun*
= sgwrs (*plural* sgyrsiau) *masculine*,
ymddiddan (*plural* -ion) *masculine*
to have a chat with someone = cael
sgwrs âʰ rhywun, sgwrsio âʰ rhywun
2 *verb*
= sgwrsio
to chat with someone = sgwrsio âʰ
rhywun

cheap *adjective*
• (*not expensive*)
= rhad
• (*of poor quality*)
= o ansawdd gwael

cheat
1 *verb*
= twyllo
2 *noun*
= twyllwr (*plural* twyllwyr) *masculine*

check
1 *noun*
(*US: cheque*)
= siec (-iau) *feminine*
2 *verb*
= sicrhau, gwirio

check in
(*to hotel*)
= cofrestru

check out
(*of hotel*)
= ymadael (*stem* ymadaw-)

checkbook *noun*
(*US: chequebook*)
= llyfr siec (*plural* llyfrau siec) *masculine*

checkers *noun*
(*US = draughts*)
= drafftiau *plural*

checkout *noun*
= desg ºdalu (*plural* desgiau talu)
feminine

checkup *noun*
= archwiliad (*plural* -au) *masculine*

cheek *noun*
• (*part of face*)
= boch (*plural* -au) *feminine*
• (*insolence*)
= haerllugrwydd *masculine*

cheeky *adjective*
= haerllug

cheer *noun*
to give someone three cheers = rhoi
(*stem* rhoi-, rhodd-) tair hwrê iº rywun
cheers! = iechyd da!

cheerful *adjective*
= llawen, siriol

cheese *noun*
= caws *masculine*

chef *noun*
= sieff (*plural* -s) *masculine*

chemist *noun*
(*pharmacist*)
= fferyllydd (*plural* fferyllwyr)
masculine

chemistry *noun*
= cemeg *feminine*

chemist's *noun*
(*shop*)
= fferyllfa (*plural* fferyllfeydd) *feminine*

cheque *noun*
= siec (*plural* -iau) *feminine*
blank cheque = siec ºwag (*plural* sieciau
gwag) *feminine*
traveller's cheque = siec ºdeithio (*plural*
sieciau teithio) *feminine*
to pay by cheque = talu â siec

cheque book *noun*
= llyfr siec (*plural* llyfrau siec) *masculine*

cheque card *noun*
= cerdyn siec (*plural* cardiau siec)
masculine

chess *noun*
= gwyddbwyll *feminine*

chest *noun*
= brest *feminine*

chestnut
1 *adjective* (*colour*)
= castan
2 *noun*
= castan (*plural* -au) *feminine*

chew *verb*
= cnoi

chewing gum *noun*
= gwm cnoi *masculine*

chick *noun*
= cyw (*plural* -ion) *masculine*

chicken *noun*
= cyw (*plural* -ion) *masculine*, cyw iâr
(*plural* cywion ieir)

chickenpox *noun*
= y °frech ieir *feminine*

chief
1 *adjective*
= prif°, penna(f)

> **!** **prif°** *always precedes the noun it refers to, and always causes soft mutation where possible*—**prif °reswm** chief reason

2 *noun*
= pennaeth (*plural* penaethiaid) *masculine*

chiefly *adverb*
= yn °benna(f), gan amla

child *noun*
= plentyn (*plural* plant) *masculine*

> **!** *A diminutive plural* **plantos** *is used of small children, especially when addressing them:*
> **dewch, °blantos!** = come (along), children!

childminder *noun*
= gofalwr plant (*plural* gofalwyr plant) *masculine*
= gofalwraig plant (*plural* gofalwragedd plant) *feminine*

chilling *adjective*
= iasoer

chilly *adjective*
= oer

chimney *noun*
= simnai (*plural* simneiau) *feminine*

chin *noun*
= gên (*plural* genau) *feminine*

chip *noun*
= sglodyn (*plural* sglodion) *masculine*
silicon chip = sglodyn silicon (*plural* sglodion silicon)

chips *plural noun*
• (*British : French fries*)
= sglodion *plural*
fish and chips = pysgod a sglodion
• (*US : crisps*)
= creision *plural*

chocolate *noun*
= siocled (*plural* -i) *masculine*

choice *noun*
= dewis (*plural* -ion) *masculine*

we had no choice = doedd gynnon ni °ddim dewis (*North*), doedd dim dewis 'da ni (*South*)
the choice is yours = chi sy â'r dewis

choir *noun*
= côr (*plural* corau) *masculine*

choke *verb*
= tagu

choose *noun*
= dewis (*stem* dewisi-), dethol

chore *noun*
= tasg (*plural* -au) *feminine*

christen *verb*
= bedyddio

christening *noun*
= bedydd (*plural* -iadau) *masculine*

Christian *adjective*
= Cristnogol

Christian name *noun*
= enw bedydd (*plural* enwau bedydd) *masculine*

Christmas *noun*
= (y) Nadolig, Dolig
Merry Christmas! = Nadolig Llawen!

> **!** **Dolig** *is a very common spoken variant of* **Nadolig**, *sometimes even found in writing.*

Christmas card *noun*
= cerdyn Nadolig (*plural* cardiau Nadolig) *masculine*

Christmas carol *noun*
= carol Nadolig (*plural* carolau Nadolig) *feminine*

Christmas cracker *noun*
= clecar Nadolig (*plural* clecars Nadolig) *masculine or feminine*

Christmas Day *noun*
= Dydd Nadolig *masculine*

Christmas Eve *noun*
= Noswyl Nadolig *feminine*

Christmas tree *noun*
= coeden Nadolig (*plural* coed Nadolig) *feminine*

church *noun*
= eglwys (*plural* -i) *feminine*; llan (*plural* -nau) *feminine*

cider *noun*
= seidr (*plural* -au) *masculine*

cigar *noun*
= sigâr (*plural* sigarau *or* sigars) *feminine*

cigarette *noun*
= sigarét (*plural* sigarets) *feminine*

cinders *noun*
= lludw *masculine*, ulw *masculine*

cinema *noun*
= sinema (*plural* sinemâu) *masculine or feminine*

circle *noun*
= cylch (*plural* -au, -oedd) *masculine*

circumstances *plural noun*
= amgylchiadau *plural*
under the circumstances = o dan yr amgylchiadau

circus *noun*
= syrcas (*plural* -au) *feminine*

citizen *noun*
= dinesydd (*plural* dinasyddion) *masculine*

city *noun*
= dinas (*plural* -oedd) *feminine*

civilized *adjective*
= gwareiddiedig

civil servant *noun*
= gwas sifil (*plural* gweision sifil) *masculine*

claim
1 *noun*
• (*assertion*)
= honiad (*plural* -au) *masculine*
• (*demand*)
= cais (*plural* ceisiadau) *masculine*
2 *verb*
• (*assert*)
= honni
• (*demand*)
= hawlio

clap *verb*
to clap someone = rhoi (*stem* rhoi-, rhodd-) clap i °rywun
to clap one's hands = curo dwylo

clarinet *noun*
= clarinét (*plural* clarinetau) *masculine*

clash *verb*
= gwrthdàro

class *noun*
= dosbarth (*plural* -iadau) *masculine*
Welsh class = dosbarth (*plural* dosbarthiadau) Cymraeg *masculine*
night class = dosbarth (*plural* dosbarthiadau) nos *masculine*

classical *adjective*
= clasurol
classical music = cerddoriaeth °glasurol *feminine*

classroom *noun*
= stafell °ddosbarth (*plural* stafelloedd dosbarth) *feminine*

claw *noun*
= crafanc (*plural* crafangau) *feminine*

clay *noun*
= clai *masculine*

clean
1 *adjective*
= glân
2 *verb*
• = glanhau
• = llnau (*colloquial*)

clear
1 *adjective*
• (*general senses*)
= eglur, clir
• (*obvious*)
= amlwg
• (*free from obstruction*)
= clir
to make something clear to someone
= egluro rhywbeth i° rywun
2 *verb*
= clirio

clear up
= clirio

clever *adjective*
= deallus; clyfar (*colloquial*)

client *noun*
= cleient (*plural* -iaid) *masculine*

cliff *noun*
= clogwyn (*plural* -i) *masculine*, gallt (*plural* gelltydd) *feminine*

climate *noun*
= hinsawdd (*plural* hinsoddau) *feminine*

climb *verb*
= dringo

to climb a tree = dringo coeden
to climb down = disgyn (*stem* disgynn-)

climbing *noun*
= dringo *verbnoun*

clinic *noun*
= clinig (*plural* -au) *masculine*

cloakroom *noun*
= stafell °gotiau (*plural* stafelloedd
cotiau) *feminine*

clock *noun*
= cloc (*plural* -iau) *masculine*

close¹
1 *adjective*
• (*near*)
= agos
a close contest = cystadleuaeth agos
• (*sultry*)
= trymaidd, mwll
• (*in detail*)
= manwl
2 *adverb*
(*nearby*)
= yn ymyl, ar °bwys
close to the road = yn ymyl y ffordd

close²
2 *verb*
= cau (*stem* cae-)
close the door! = caewch y drws!
the shop closes at five = mae'r siop yn
cau am °bump

closed *adjective*
= ar °gau
the shop is closed = mae'r siop ar °gau

> **!** *This expression, like all those
> beginning with* **ar°** *and denoting a
> temporary state, is not preceded by*
> **yn°** *in sentences with* **bod**. *Compare
> the above example with:*
> **the shop is big** = mae'r siop *yn* °fawr

closely *adverb*
(*in detail*)
= yn °fanwl
to look closely at something = edrych
yn °fanwl ar° rywbeth

closer *adjective*
= agosach, nes
come closer = dewch yn nes

cloth *noun*
• (*material*)
= brethyn *masculine*

• (*item*)
= lliain (*plural* llieiniau) *masculine*

clothes *noun*
= dillad *plural*

cloud *noun*
= cwmwl (*plural* cymylau) *masculine*

cloudy *adjective*
= cymylog

clown *noun*
= clown (*plural* -s, -iaid) *masculine*

club *noun*
= clwb (*plural* clybiau) *masculine*

clue *noun*
I haven't got a clue = does gen i °ddim
syniad (*North*), does dim clem 'da fi
(*South*)

clumsy *adjective*
= lletchwith

co- *prefix*
= cyd-°

coach *noun*
• (*bus*)
= bws (*plural* bysiau) *masculine*
coach station = gorsaf °fysiau (*plural*
gorsafoedd bysiau) *feminine*
• (*trainer*)
= hyfforddwr (*plural* hyfforddwyr)
masculine
= hyfforddwraig (*plural*
hyfforddwragedd) *feminine*

coal *noun*
= glo *masculine*

coalition *noun*
= clymblaid (*plural* clymbleidiau)
feminine

coalminer *noun*
= glöwr (*plural* glowyr) *masculine*

coast *noun*
= arfordir (*plural* -oedd) *masculine*
on the coast = ger y glannau

coat *noun*
= côt (*plural* cotiau) *feminine*

coat hanger *noun*
= cambren côt (*plural* cambrenni
cotiau) *masculine*

cobweb *noun*
= gwe pry copyn (*plural* gweoedd pryfed
cop) *feminine* (*North*), gwe corryn (*plural*
gwe corynnod) *feminine* (*South*)

cock *noun*
= ceiliog (*plural* -od) *masculine*

cocoa *noun*
= coco *masculine*

coconut *noun*
= cneuen °goco (*plural* cnau coco) *feminine*

cod *noun*
= penfras (*plural* penfreision) *masculine*

coffee *noun*
= coffi *masculine*

coffee machine *noun*
= peiriant coffi (*plural* peiriannau coffi) *masculine*

coffin *noun*
= arch (*plural* eirch) *feminine*

coin *noun*
= darn arian (*plural* darnau arian) *masculine*, pisin, pisyn (*plural* pisiau) *masculine*

coincidence *noun*
= cyd-ddigwyddiad (*plural* -au) *masculine*

cold
1 *adjective*
= oer
to get/grow cold
(*weather*) = oeri
(*person*) = mynd yn oer
2 *noun*
• (*coldness*)
= oerfel *masculine*
• (*illness*)
= annwyd (*plural* anwydau) *masculine*
I've got a cold = mae annwyd arna i

> ! This expression, denoting a temporary physical state, uses **ar°** + person.

collaborate *verb*
= cydweithio, cydweithredu

collaboration *noun*
= cydweithrediad (*plural* -au) *masculine*, cydweithredu *masculine*

collapse *verb*
= syrthio, cwympo, dymchwel

collar *noun*
= coler (*plural* -i) *feminine* (North), *masculine* (South)

colleague *noun*
= cydweithiwr (*plural* cydweithwyr) *masculine*

collect *verb*
= casglu

collection *noun*
= casgliad (*plural* -au) *masculine*

college *noun*
= coleg (*plural* -au) *masculine*

collide *verb*
= gwrthdaro
to collide with something = gwrthdaro â[h] rhywbeth

colour
1 *noun*
= lliw (*plural* -iau) *masculine*
what colour do you want? = pa °liw dych chi eisiau?
2 *verb*
= lliwio

colour in
= lliwio

coloured *adjective*
= lliwiog

colour film *noun*
= ffilm °liw (*plural* ffilmiau lliw) *feminine*

colourful *adjective*
= lliwgar

colour tv *noun*
= teledu lliw *masculine*

comb
1 *noun*
= crib (*plural* -au) *feminine or masculine*
2 *verb*
= cribo

come *verb*
= dod (*irregular*), dŵad (North)

come across
to come across something = dod o hyd i° rywbeth, dod ar °draws rhywbeth

come back
= dod yn ôl

come from
  to come from something (*derive from*)
  = tarddu o° rywbeth

come in
  = dod i mewn
  come in! = ty'd/dere/dewch i mewn!

come on
  come on! = ty'd ymlaen! dere 'mlaen!,
  dewch ymlaen!

come out
  = dod allan

comfortable *adjective*
  = cyfforddus

comforter *noun*
  (*US: duvet, quilt*) = cwilt (*plural* -iau)
  masculine

comic strip *noun*
  = stribed comig (*plural* stribedi comig)
  masculine

commentary *noun*
  = sylwebaeth (*plural* -au) *feminine*

commerce *noun*
  = masnach *feminine*, busnes *masculine*

commercial
1 *adjective*
  = masnachol
2 *noun*
  (*on TV*)
  = hysbyseb (*plural* -ion) *feminine*

commit *verb*
  **to commit oneself to doing
  something** = ymrwymo i °wneud
  rhywbeth

commitment *noun*
  = ymrwymiad (*plural* -au) *masculine*

committee *noun*
  = pwyllgor (*plural* -au) *masculine*

common *adjective*
  = cyffredin
  what have they got in common? =
  beth sy gynnyn nhw'n °gyffredin?
  the House of Commons = Tŷ 'r
  Cyffredin *masculine*

communicate *verb*
  = cyfathrebu

communicative *adjective*
  = cyfathrebol

community *noun*
  = cymuned (*plural* -au) *feminine*

compact disc *noun*
  = crynoddisg (*plural* -iau) *masculine*

company *noun*
  = cwmni (*plural* cwmnïau) *masculine*
  to keep someone company = cadw
  (*stem* cadw-) cwmni i° rywun

company secretary
  = ysgrifennydd cwmni *masculine*

compare *verb*
  = cymharu (â°)

> **!** *The phrase for* **compared with/to**
> *varies in Welsh depending on the
> subject:*
> **compared with** = o'i °gymharu â°
> (*masculine*)
> = o'i ʰchymharu â° (*feminine*)
> = o'u cymharu â° (*plural*)
> **he's tall compared with his brother**
> = mae e'n °dal o'i °gymharu â'i °frawd
> **she's tall compared with her
> brother** = mae hi'n °dal o'i ʰchymharu
> â'i brawd

compartment *noun*
  = adran (*plural* -nau) *feminine*

compass *noun*
  = cwmpawd (*plural* -au) *masculine*
  points of the compass = pwyntiau'r
  cwmpawd

compel *verb*
  = gorfodi

compete *verb*
  = cystadlu

competent *adjective*
  = galluog, medrus
  to be competent to do something =
  medru gwneud rhywbeth

competition *noun*
  = cystadleuaeth (*plural* cystadleuthau)
  feminine

competitive *adjective*
  = cystadleuol

complain *verb*
  = cwyno, achwyn
  **to complain about something to
  someone** = cwyno/achwyn am°
  rywbeth wrth° rywun

complaint *noun*
  = cwyn (*plural* ion) *feminine*

complete
1 *adjective*
= cyflawn, llwyr
complete beginner = dechreuwr llwyr *masculine*
2 *verb*
= cwblhau

completely *adverb*
= yn llwyr, yn hollol, yn °gyfangwbwl
I completely agree = dw i'n cytuno'n llwyr

> **!** 'completely...' used with an adjective is **cwb(w)l°**—this word precedes the adjective and causes soft mutation:
> **completely unnecessary** = cwbwl °ddiangen

complex *adjective*
= cymhleth

complicated *adjective*
= cymhleth

compliment
1 *noun*
to pay someone a compliment = talu teyrnged i° rywun, canmol rhywun
to send compliments to someone = danfon cyfarchion at° rywun
2 *verb*
to compliment someone = canmol rhywun

comprehensive *adjective*
• (*including much*)
= cynhwysfawr
• (*type of school*)
= cyfun

comprehensive school *noun*
= ysgol °gyfun (*plural* ysgolion cyfun) *feminine*

compromise *verb*
= cyfaddawdu

compulsory *adjective*
= gorfodol

computer *noun*
= cyfrifiadur (*plural* -on) *masculine*

computer game *noun*
= gêm °gyfrifiadur (*plural* gemau cyfrifiadur) *feminine*

computer programmer *noun*
= rhaglennydd cyfrifiaduron (*plural* rhaglenwyr cyfrifiaduron) *masculine*

computer studies *noun*
= cyfrifiadureg *feminine*

concentrate *verb*
= canolbwyntio
to concentrate on something = canolbwyntio ar° rywbeth
to concentrate on doing something = canolbwyntio ar °wneud rhywbeth

concern *verb*
• (*with regard to, about*)
= ymwneud â[h], ymdrin â[h]
• (*worry*)
= poeni
I'm concerned = dw i'n poeni

concerning *preposition*
• (*about*)
= ynghylch, ynglŷn â[h]
• (*as regards*)
= o °ran; parthed
to be concerning... = ymwneud â[h]...

concert *noun*
= cyngerdd (*plural* cyngherddau) *masculine*

concert hall *noun*
= neuadd °gyngerdd (*plural* neuaddau cyngerdd) *feminine*

conclusion *noun*
• (*end*)
= diwedd (*plural* -au) *masculine*, terfyniad (*plural* -au) *masculine*
• (*assumption, decision*)
= casgliad (*plural* -au) *masculine*

concrete *noun and adjective*
= concrid *masculine*

condemn *verb*
= condemnio

condition *noun*
• (*state*)
= cyflwr (*plural* cyflyrau) *masculine*
• (*stipulation*)
= amod (*plural* -au) *masculine or feminine*
conditions (*terms*)
= telerau *plural*

condom *noun*
= condom (*plural* -au) *masculine*

conductor *noun*
• (*on bus*)
= tocynnwr (*plural* tocynwyr) *masculine*
= tocynwraig (*plural* tocynwragedd) *feminine*

- (of orchestra)
= arweinydd (*plural* -ion, arweinwyr) *masculine*

conference *noun*
= cynhadledd (*plural* cynadleddau) *feminine*
to hold a conference = cynnal (*stem* cynhali-) cynhadledd

confidence *noun*
= ffydd *feminine*, hyder *masculine*, ymddiriedaeth *feminine*
to have confidence in someone = bod â[h] ffydd yn[n] rhywun
to speak to someone in confidence = siarad â[h] rhywun yn °gyfrinachol

confident *adjective*
= hyderus, ffyddiog

confidential *adjective*
= cyfrinachol

confirm *verb*
= cadarnhau

confiscate *verb*
= cymryd (*stem* cymer-)

conflict *noun*
= gwrthdaro *verbnoun*

conflicting *adjective*
(*not in agreement, inconsistent*)
= anghyson

confuse *verb*
- (*mix up, fail to distinguish*)
= cymysgu
- (*put someone in confusion*)
= drysu, rhoi mewn penbleth

confused *adjective*
= mewn penbleth

confusion *noun*
= penbleth *feminine or masculine*

congratulate *verb*
= llongyfarch

congratulations *noun*
= llongyfarchiadau *plural*

connect *verb*
= cysylltu

connection *noun*
= cysylltiad (*plural* -au) *masculine*

conquer *verb*
= gorchfygu, trechu

conscientious *adjective*
= cydwybodol

conscious *adjective*
= ymwybodol
to be conscious of something = bod yn ymwybodol o° rywbeth

consciousness *noun*
= ymwybyddiaeth (*plural* -au) *feminine*

consent
1 *noun*
= cydsyniad *masculine*
2 *verb*
to consent to do something = cydsynio i °wneud rhywbeth

consequently *adverb*
= o °ganlyniad

> **!** o °ganlyniad *generally comes first in the sentence:*
> **it is consequently impossible at the moment** = o °ganlyniad mae'n amhosib ar hyn o bryd

Conservative
1 *adjective*
= Ceidwadol
2 *noun*
= Ceidwadwr (*plural* Ceidwadwyr) *masculine*

consider *verb*
= ystyried (*stem* ystyri-)

considerate *adjective*
= ystyriol
to be considerate to someone = bod yn ystyriol o° rywun

consideration *noun*
= ystyriaeth (*plural* -au) *feminine*

consistent *adjective*
= cyson

consonant *noun*
= cytsain (*plural* cytseiniaid) *feminine*

constant *adjective*
= diderfyn, dibaid, parhaol

construct *verb*
= adeiladu

consult *verb*
= ymgynghori
to consult someone about something
= ymgynghori â[h] rhywun ynglŷn â[h] rhywbeth

consultative *adjective*
= ymgynghorol

consumer *noun*
= defnyddiwr (*plural* defnyddwyr) *masculine*
= defnyddwraig (*plural* defnyddwragedd) *feminine*

consumption *noun*
= traul (*plural* treuliau) *feminine*
fuel consumption = traul tanwydd *feminine*

contact
1 *noun*
= cyswllt
to keep/stay in contact = cadw mewn cyswllt
2 *verb*
= cysylltu
to contact someone = cysylltu â[h] rhywun

contact lens *noun*
= lens °gyswllt (*plural* lensys cyswllt) *feminine*, lens °gyffwrdd (*plural* lensys cyffwrdd) *feminine*

contain *verb*
= cynnwys *(*stem* cynhwys-), dal *(*stem* dali-)

contaminate *verb*
= llygru

contamination *noun*
= llygredd *masculine*, heintiad *masculine*

contemporary
1 *adjective*
= cyfoes
2 *noun*
= cyfoeswr (*plural* cyfoeswyr) *masculine*
= cyfoeswraig (*plural* cyfoeswragedd) *feminine*

contend *verb*
• (*fight*)
= ymladd, dadlau
• (*assert*)
= honni
• (*face up to*)
= ymdopi
to contend with difficulties = ymdopi ag anawsterau

content *adjective*
= bodlon

to be content to wait = bod yn °fodlon aros
to be content with something = bod yn °fodlon ar° rywbeth

contents *noun*
= cynnwys *masculine*

contest *noun*
• (*competition*)
= cystadleuaeth (*plural* cystadleuthau) *feminine*
• (*fight*)
= gornest (*plural* -au) *feminine*

continent *noun*
= cyfandir (*plural* -oedd) *masculine*

continuation *noun*
= parhad *masculine*

continue *verb*
• (*still do something*)
= dal (*stem* dali-)
he continues to claim that... = mae e'n dal i honni °fod...
• (*last*)
= para; parhau (*formal*)
to continue for two years = para am °ddwy °flynedd

continuing *adjective*
= parhaol

continuous *adjective*
= parhaol

contraception *noun*
= atal cenhedlu *verbnoun*

contraceptive
1 *adjective*
= atal cenhedlu
2 *noun*
= gwrthgenhedlyn (*plural* gwrthgenhedlion) *masculine*

contract *noun*
= cytundeb (*plural* -au) *masculine*

contradict *verb*
= gwrthddweud (*stem* gwrthddwed-)

contrary *adverb*
contrary to = yn °groes i°
they acted contrary to our wishes = mi °weithredon nhw'n °groes i'n dymuniadau

contribute *verb*
= cyfrannu

to contribute to something = cyfrannu at° rywbeth

contribution noun
= cyfraniad (plural -au) masculine

control
1 noun
= rheolaeth
under control = (o) dan °reolaeth
2 verb
= rheoli

controversial adjective
= dadleuol

convenient adjective
= cyfleus

conversation noun
= sgwrs (plural sgyrsiau) feminine, ymddiddan (plural -ion) masculine

converse verb
= sgwrsio, ymddiddan

convince verb
= argyhoeddi

cook
1 noun
= cogydd (plural -ion) masculine
= cogyddes (plural -au) feminine
2 verb
= coginio

cooker noun
= popty (plural poptai) masculine

cookie noun (US)
= bisgeden (plural bisgedi) feminine

cooking noun
= coginio verbnoun

cool adjective
• (temperature)
= eitha oer, braidd yn oer
• (calm)
stay cool! = paid cynhyrfu! peidiwch cynhyrfu!

co-operate verb
= cydweithredu, cydweithio

cope verb
= ymdopi
to cope with something = ymdopi â^h rhywbeth

copper noun and adjective
(metal)
= copor masculine

copy
1 noun
= copi (plural copïau) masculine
2 verb
= copio

cork noun
• (material)
= corc masculine
• (in bottle)
= corcyn (plural cyrc) masculine

corkscrew noun
= tynnwr corcyn masculine

corn noun
• (British: wheat)
= ŷd masculine
• (US: maize)
= india-corn masculine

corner noun
= cornel (plural -i) feminine

cornflakes plural noun
= creision ŷd plural

Cornish
1 adjective
(of Cornwall)
= o °Gernyw
2 noun
(language)
= Cernyweg feminine

Cornwall noun
= Cernyw feminine

corpse noun
= corff (plural cyrff) masculine
= corff marw (plural cyrff marw) masculine, celain (plural celanedd) feminine

correct
1 adjective
= cywir
2 verb
= cywiro

correction noun
= cywiriad (plural -au) masculine

correspond verb
• (write)
= gohebu
to correspond with someone = gohebu â^h rhywun
• (be equivalent of)
= cyfateb

to correspond to something = cyfateb
i° rywbeth

corresponding *adjective*
= cyfatebol

corridor *noun*
= coridor (*plural* -au) *masculine*

cost
1 *noun*
= cost (*plural* -au) *feminine*
2 *verb*
= costio
what do these cost? = faint mae'r
rhain yn °gostio?, beth ydy pris y
rhain?

costly *adjective*
= drud

cost of living *noun*
= costau byw *plural*

costume *noun*
= gwisg (*plural* -oedd) *feminine*

cosy *adjective*
= clyd, cysurus

cot *noun*
= cot (*plural* -iau) *masculine*

cottage *noun*
= bwthyn (*plural* bythynnod) *masculine*

cotton *noun and adjective*
= cotwm *masculine*

cotton wool *noun*
= gwlân cotwm *masculine*

couch *noun*
= soffa (*plural* -s) *feminine*

cough
1 *noun*
= peswch *masculine*
she's got a cough = mae peswch arni
hi

> **!** *This expression, denoting a
> temporary physical state, uses* **ar°** +
> *person.*

2 *verb*
= pesychu

could *verb*
• (*was able*)
I couldn't see the sign = o'n i °ddim yn
gallu gweld yr arwydd
she couldn't speak English = doedd hi
°ddim yn gallu siarad Saesneg

• (*would be able*)
we could help you = gallen ni'ch helpu
chi
I couldn't do the work now = °allwn i
°ddim gwneud y gwaith nawr
could you shut the window? = °allech
chi °gau'r ffenest?
• (*possibility*)
you could be right = gallet ti °fod yn
iawn, efallai °fod ti'n iawn

council *noun*
= cyngor (*plural* cynghorau) *masculine*

count *verb*
• (*calculate*)
= cyfri(f)
• (*be valid*)
= cyfri(f)
• (*say numbers*)
= rhifo
• (*depend*)
to count on someone = dibynnu ar°
rywun

counter *noun*
= cownter (*plural* -i) *masculine*

counter- *prefix*
= gwrth°-

counteract *verb*
= gwrthweithio

counterattack
1 *noun*
= gwrthymosodiad (*plural* -au)
masculine
2 *verb*
= gwrthymosod

counterproductive *adjective*
= gwrthgynhyrchol

countless *adjective*
= diri(f)

country *noun*
• (*nation, land*)
= gwlad (*plural* gwledydd) *feminine*
• (*not town*)
= cefn gwlad *masculine*

countryside *noun*
= cefn gwlad *masculine*

county *noun*
• (*Welsh county*)
= sir (*plural* -oedd) *feminine*
• (*elsewhere*)
= swydd (*plural* -i) *feminine*

couple noun
= cwp(w)l (plural cyplau) masculine
a couple of things = cwpwl o °bethau

courage noun
= dewrder masculine

courageous adjective
= dewr

course noun
= cwrs (plural cyrsiau) masculine
a Welsh course = cwrs Cymraeg
a beginners' course = cwrs dechreuwyr
of course = wrth °gwrs, wrth °reswm

court noun
= llys (plural -oedd) masculine
Magistrates' Court = Llys Ynadon masculine
Crown Court = Llys y °Goron masculine

court case noun
= achos (plural -ion) llys masculine

cousin noun
(male)
= cefnder (plural cefndyr) masculine
(female)
= cyfnither (plural -oedd) feminine

cover
1 noun
• (general)
= gorchudd (plural -ion) masculine
• (of book)
= clawr (plural cloriau) masculine
2 verb
= gorchuddio

cow noun
= buwch (plural buchod) feminine

coward noun
= cachgi (plural cachgwn) masculine

cowboy noun
= cowboi (plural -s) masculine

crab noun
= cranc (plural -od) masculine

crack
1 noun
• (sound)
= clec (plural -iau) feminine
• (split)
= crac (plural -iau) feminine or masculine
2 verb
• (sound)
= clecian (stem cleci-)

• (split)
= cracio

cradle noun
= crud (plural -au or -iau) masculine

craft noun
= crefft (plural -iau) feminine, celfyddyd (plural -au) feminine

cramp noun
= cramp masculine

crane noun
(machine)
= craen (plural -iau) masculine

crash
1 noun
• (collision)
= gwrthdrawiad (plural -au) masculine
• (sound)
= trwst (plural trystau) masculine, clec (plural -iau) feminine
2 verb
= mynd yn erbyn, gwrthdaro
the two cars crashed = aeth y °ddau °gar yn erbyn ei gilydd
to crash a car into a tree = gyrru car i °goeden/ yn erbyn coeden

crate noun
= cawell (plural -au, -i or cewyll) masculine

crawl
1 verb
• (baby)
= cropian (stem cropi-)
• (animals, traffic)
= ymlusgo
2 noun
• (swimming stroke)
= ymlusgo verbnoun

crayon noun
= creon (plural -s) masculine

crazy adjective
= gwallgo(f)

cream
1 adjective
(colour)
= hufen, lliw hufen
2 noun
= hufen masculine

create verb
= creu

creative *adjective*
= creadigol

crèche *noun*
= meithrinfa (*plural* meithrinfeydd) *feminine*

credence *noun*
= coel
to give something credence = rhoi (*stem* rhoi-, rhodd-) coel ar° rywbeth

credit *noun*
= credyd

credit card *noun*
= cerdyn credyd (*plural* cardiau credyd) *masculine*
do you take credit cards? = dych chi'n derbyn cardiau credyd?

crib *noun*
= cot (*plural* -iau) *masculine*

cricket *noun*
(*game*)
= criced

crime *noun*
= trosedd (*plural* -au) *masculine*
to commit a crime = troseddu, cyflawni trosedd

criminal
1 *adjective*
= troseddol
2 *noun*
= troseddwr (*plural* troseddwyr) *masculine*
= troseddwraig (*plural* troseddwragedd) *feminine*

crisis *noun*
= argyfwng (*plural* argyfyngau) *masculine*

crisps *plural noun*
= creision *plural*

critical *adjective*
• (*disparaging*)
= beirniadol
• (*crucial*)
= pwysig, allweddol

criticism *noun*
= beirniadaeth (*plural* -au) *feminine*

criticize *verb*
= beirniadu
to criticize someone severely = beirniadu rhywun yn hallt

crockery *noun*
= llestri *plural*

crocodile *noun*
= crocodeil (*plural* -od) *masculine*

crooked *adjective*
• (*twisted, bent*)
= cam
• (*criminal*)
= troseddol, anonest

cross
1 *adjective*
= crac, dig
to get cross = mynd yn °grac
2 *noun*
= croes (*plural* -au) *feminine*
3 *verb*
= croesi
to cross the road = croesi'r ffordd

cross out
= dileu

crossroads *noun*
= croesffordd (*plural* croesffyrdd) *feminine*

crossword *noun*
= croesair (*plural* croeseiriau) *masculine*

crow *noun*
= brân (*plural* brain) *feminine*

crowd
1 *noun*
= torf (*plural* -eydd) *feminine*
2 *verb*
everyone crowded in = naeth pawb °dyrru i mewn

crown *noun*
= coron (*plural* -au) *feminine*

crucial *adjective*
= allweddol

cruel *adjective*
= creulon

cruelty *noun*
= creulondeb (*plural* -au) *masculine*

cruise *noun*
= mordaith (*plural* mordeithiau) *feminine*

crush *verb*
= gwasgu

crutch *noun*
= bagl (*plural* -au) *feminine*

cry
1 *noun*
= galwad (*plural* -au) *masculine*, cri (*plural* crïau) *feminine*
2 *verb*
• (*weep*)
= crio, llefain, wylo
• (*shout*)
= crio, gweiddi, bloeddio

cub *noun*
= cenau (*plural* cenawon) *masculine*, cenawes (*plural* -au) *feminine*
lion cub = cenau llew

cuckoo *noun*
= cog (*plural* -au) *feminine*

cucumber *noun*
= cucumber (*plural* -au) *masculine*

cuddle *verb*
= anwesu

cuff *noun*
= cyffsen (*plural* cyffs) *feminine*

cul-de-sac *noun*
= ffordd °bengaead (*plural* ffyrdd pengaead) *feminine*

culprit *noun*
= troseddwr (*plural* troseddwyr) *masculine*
= troseddwraig (*plural* troseddwragedd) *feminine*

cultural *adjective*
= diwylliannol

culture *noun*
= diwylliant (*plural* diwylliannau) *masculine*

cup *noun*
• (*vessel*)
= cwpan (*plural* -au) *masculine or feminine*
• (*cupful*)
= cwpanaid, panaid

cupboard *noun*
= cwpwrdd (*plural* cypyrddau) *masculine*

curb *noun* (*US*)
= ymyl palmant (*plural* ymylon palmant) *masculine or feminine*

cure
1 *noun*
(*medicine*)
= moddion *plural*

there's no cure for it = does dim moddion yn ei erbyn
2 *verb*
= gwella
to cure someone of a cold = gwella annwyd rhywun

curious *adjective*
• (*strange*)
= rhyfedd, od
• (*inquisitive*)
= chwilfrydig

curly *adjective*
= cyrliog

currency *noun*
= arian, arian cyfredol *masculine*

current *adjective*
• (*contemporary*)
= cyfoes
current affairs = materion cyfoes
• (*issue of periodical etc*)
= cyfredol

curry *noun*
= cyrri (*plural* cyrïau) *masculine*

curse
1 *noun*
= melltith (*plural* -ion) *feminine*
2 *verb*
• (*put a curse on*)
= melltithio
• (*swear*)
= rhegi

curtain *noun*
= llen (*plural* -ni) *feminine*
to draw the curtains = tynnu'r llenni

cushion *noun*
= clustog (*plural* -au) *feminine*

custard *noun*
= cwstard *masculine*

custom *noun*
= arfer (*plural* -ion) *masculine or feminine*

customer *noun*
= cwsmer (*plural* -iaid) *masculine*

customs *noun*
= tollau *plural*

customs officer *noun*
= swyddog tollau (*plural* swyddogion tollau) *masculine*

cut
1 *verb*
- (*general senses*)
  = torri
  she's had her hair cut = mae hi wedi cael torri ei gwallt
- (*injure with knife*)
  = agor
  he has cut his finger = mae e wedi agor ei ºfys

> **!** Note that **mae e wedi torri ei ºfys** would mean he has broken his finger, the primary meaning of the word.

2 *noun*
= toriad (-au) *masculine*

cute *adjective*
= annwyl

cutlery *noun*
= cyllyll a ffyrc *plural*

CV *noun*
= braslun bywyd (*plural* brasluniau bywyd) *masculine*

cycle
1 *noun*
= beic (*plural* -iau) *masculine*
2 *verb*
= beicio

cycle lane *noun*
= llwybr beiciau (*plural* llwybrau beiciau) *masculine*, lôn ºfeiciau (*plural* lonydd beiciau) *feminine*

cycling *noun*
= beicio *verbnoun*

cyclist *noun*
= beiciwr (*plural* beicwyr) *masculine*
= beicwraig (*plural* beicwragedd) *feminine*

cynical *adjective*
= sinicaidd

Dd

dad *noun*
= tad; (*referring to one's own father*) ºnhad

daddy *noun*
= ºnhad

daffodil *noun*
= cenhinen ºBedr (*plural* cennin Pedr) *feminine*

daily
1 *adjective*
= beunyddiol, ºbob dydd
2 *adverb*
(*every day*)
= ºbob dydd

dairy *noun*
= llaethdy (*plural* llaethdai) *masculine*

daisy *noun*
= llygad y dydd (*plural* llygaid y dydd) *masculine*

damage
1 *noun*
= difrod *masculine*, niwed (*plural* niweidiau) *masculine*
£500 worth of damage was caused = achoswyd gwerth £500 o ºddifrod
damages = iawndal *masculine*
to award damages = dyfarnu iawndal
2 *verb*
= niweidio

damp *adjective*
= llaith; gwlyb

dance
1 *noun*
- (*activity*)
  = dawns (*plural* -iau) *feminine*
- (*social function*)
  = dawns (*plural* -feydd) *feminine*
2 *verb*
= dawnsio

dancer *noun*
= dawnsiwr (*plural* dawnswyr) *masculine*
= dawnswraig (*plural* dawnswragedd) *feminine*

dancing *noun*
= dawnsio *verbnoun*

danger *noun*
= peryg(l) (*plural* peryglon) *masculine*
to be in danger = bod mewn peryg

dangerous *adjective*
= peryglus

dare *verb*
• (*general senses*)
= meiddio, mentro
you wouldn't dare! = °feiddiet ti °ddim!
don't you dare! = paid ti â meiddio!
to dare to do something = mentro
gwneud rhywbeth
• (*challenge*)
= herio
to dare someone to do something =
herio rhywun i °wneud rhywbeth

daring *adjective*
= beiddgar

dark
1 *adjective*
= tywyll
to get dark = tywyllu
2 *noun*
= tywyllwch *masculine*

darken *verb*
= tywyllu

darkness *noun*
= tywyllwch *masculine*

darling
1 *noun*
= cariad *masculine and feminine*
2 *adjective*
= annwyl

darts *noun*
= dartiau *or* darts *plural*

date *noun*
• (*on calendar*)
= dyddiad (*plural* -au) *masculine*
what date is it today? = beth ydy'r
dyddiad heddiw?
• (*appointment*)
= apwyntiad (*plural* -au) *masculine*

daughter *noun*
= merch (*plural* -ed) *feminine*

daughter-in-law *noun*
= merch-yng-nghyfraith (*plural*
merched-yng-nghyfraith) *feminine*

dawn *noun*
= gwawr (*plural* -iau, -oedd) *feminine*

day *noun*
• (*period of 24 hours*)
= diwrnod (*plural* -au) *masculine*

> **!** *A special system of mutations
> applies when* **diwrnod** *is used after
> numbers—see Welsh-English entry
> for details.*

• (*opposite of night*)
= dydd (*plural* -iau) *masculine*
day after day = °ddydd ar ôl dydd
the day after/the next day = y diwrnod
wedyn, trannoeth
once a day = unwaith y dydd
all day = trwy'r dydd
every day = °bob dydd
during the day = yn ystod y dydd
two days (*period of time*) = deuddydd
I was there for two days = o'n i yno am
°ddeuddydd
three days (*period of time*) = tridiau

> **!** *The distinction in meaning between*
> **dydd** *and* **diwrnod** *is not always
> clear-cut.*

day-to-day *adjective*
= beunyddiol, °bob dydd

daybreak *noun*
= gwawr (*plural* -iau, -oedd) *feminine*
at daybreak = yn y bore glas, gyda'r
°wawr

day care centre *noun*
= meithrinfa (*plural* meithrinfeydd)
feminine

daylight *noun*
= golau dydd *masculine*

dazzle *verb*
= dallu

dead
1 *adjective*
= marw, wedi marw
he is dead = mae e wedi marw
2 *noun*
the dead = y meirw *plural*

deaf *adjective*
= byddar

deal *noun*
• **to make a deal with someone** = taro
bargen âʰ rhywun
• **a great deal of money** = llawer iawn o
arian

deal with *verb*
= delio â^h, trin, ymdrin â^h

dear *adjective*
• (*beloved*)
= annwyl

> ! *Also used as a greeting in letters,
> where it precedes the noun and
> causes soft mutation except on
> proper names:* **Annwyl °Olygydd**
> Dear Editor, *but* **Annwyl Dafydd** Dear
> Dafydd.

• (*expensive*)
= drud, costus
• (*term of endearment*)
= bach

dearth *noun*
= prinder (*plural* -au) *masculine*, diffyg
(*plural* -ion) *masculine*

death *noun*
= marwolaeth (*plural* -au) *masculine*,
angau (*plural* angheuoedd, angheuau)
(*formal*) *masculine*

death penalty *noun*
= cosb marwolaeth *feminine*

debate
1 *noun*
= dadl (*plural* -euon) *feminine*,
trafodaeth (*plural* -au) *feminine*
2 *verb*
= dadlau, trafod

debit
1 *noun*
= debyd (*plural* -au) *masculine*
direct debit = debyd uniongyrchol
2 *verb*
= debydu

debit card *noun*
= cerdyn debyd (*plural* cardiau debyd)
masculine

debt *noun*
= dyled (*plural* -ion) *feminine*

decade *noun*
= degawd (*plural* -au) *masculine*

decaffeinated *adjective*
= digaffein, heb °gaffein

deceive *verb*
= twyllo

December *noun*
= mis Rhagfyr, Rhagfyr *masculine*
see also **January**

decide *verb*
= penderfynu
to decide to do something =
penderfynu gwneud rhywbeth
she decided to go = mi °benderfynodd
hi °fynd

decision *noun*
= penderfyniad (*plural* -au) *masculine*
to make a decision = penderfynu

decisive *adjective*
= penderfynol

deck *noun*
• (*of ship*)
= bwrdd (*plural* byrddau) *masculine*
• (*of cards*)
= pecyn (*plural* -nau) *masculine*

deckchair *noun*
= cadair °blygu (*plural* cadeiriau plygu)
feminine

declare *verb*
= datgan, cyhoeddi

decorate *verb*
= addurno

decorations *plural noun*
= addurniadau *plural*

decrease *verb*
= lleihau, gostwng

deep *adjective*
= dwfn

deer *noun*
= carw (*plural* ceirw) *masculine*

defeat *verb*
= trechu, curo

defect *noun*
= diffyg (*plural* -ion) *masculine*, gwall
(*plural* -au) *masculine*, nam (*plural* -au)
masculine

defective *adjective*
= diffygiol, gwallus, â nam

defence *noun*
= amddiffyniad (*plural* -au) *masculine*
Ministry of Defence = Gweinyddiaeth
Amddiffyn

defend *verb*
= amddiffyn
to defend someone from something =
amddiffyn rhywun rhag rhywbeth

definite *adjective*
= pendant, penodol

definitely *adverb*
= yn °bendant, yn °ddi-os

! *These phrases generally come at the end of the sentence, not in the middle:*
she'll definitely have to go = bydd rhaid iddi °fynd yn °bendant, bydd rhaid iddi °fynd—mae hynny'n °bendant

definition *noun*
= diffiniad (*plural* -au) *masculine*

defy *verb*
= herio

degree *noun*
= gradd (*plural* -au) *feminine*
to a great degree = i °raddau helaeth

delay
1 *noun*
= oediad (*plural* -au) *masculine*, oedi *verbnoun*
without further delay = heb oedi rhagor
2 *verb*
= oedi

delete *verb*
= dileu

deliberate *adjective*
= bwriadol, pwrpasol

deliberately *adverb*
= o °fwriad, yn °fwriadol, o °bwrpas, yn °bwrpasol

delicious *adjective*
= hyfryd

delighted *adjective*
= wrth [*possessive adjective*] bodd

! *This expression varies depending on person:*
I'm delighted = dw i wrth 'y ⁿmodd
he's delighted = mae e wrth ei °fodd
she's delighted = mae hi wrth ei bodd
they're delighted = maen nhw wrth eu bodd(au)
It is not *preceded by* **yn°** *when used with the verb* **bod**.

deliver *verb*
= dosbarthu, danfon

demand *verb*
= hawlio, mynnu
to demand something from someone = hawlio rhywbeth gan° rywun
to demand to do something = mynnu gwneud rhywbeth

democracy *noun*
= democratiaeth (*plural* -au) *feminine*

democratic *adjective*
= democrataidd

demolish *verb*
= chwalu, dymchwel

demonstrate *verb*
= profi, dangos, esbonio

demonstration *noun*
• (*proof*)
= prawf (*plural* profion) *masculine*
• (*explanation*)
= esboniad (*plural* -au) *masculine*
• (*protest gathering*)
= gwrthdystiad (*plural* -au) *masculine*

denim *noun*
= denim *masculine*
denims (*jeans*) = trowsus denim *masculine*

dense *adjective*
• (*impenetrable*)
= trwchus
• (*stupid*)
= twp

dentist *noun*
= deintydd (*plural* -ion) *masculine*
to go to the dentist's = mynd at y deintydd

deny *verb*
= gwadu

depart *verb*
= ymadael (*stem* ymadaw-)

department *noun*
= adran (*plural* -nau) *feminine*

department store *noun*
= siop adrannol (*plural* siopau adrannol) *feminine*

departure *noun*
= ymadawiad (*plural* -au) *masculine*

depend *verb*
= dibynnu
to depend on someone = dibynnu ar°
rywun
that depends = mae hynny'n dibynnu

deposit *noun (money put down)*
= blaendal (*plural* blaendaliadau)
masculine

depressed *adjective*
= isel [*possessive adjective*] ysbryd

> **!** *This expression varies depending
> on person:*
> **she's rather depressed** = mae hi
> braidd yn isel ei hysbryd
> **he's depressed** = mae e'n isel ei
> ysbryd
> **I'm depressed** = dw i'n isel 'yn ysbryd

depressing *adjective*
= digalon

deprive *verb*
= amddifadu
to deprive someone of something =
amddifadu rhywun o° rywbeth

depth *noun*
= dyfnder

deputy *noun*
= dirprwy (*plural* -on) *masculine*

derivation *noun*
= tarddiad (*plural* -au) *masculine*

derive *verb*
= tarddu
this word derives from Latin = mae'r
gair 'ma'n tarddu o'r Lladin

describe *verb*
= disgrifio

description *noun*
= disgrifiad (*plural* -au) *masculine*

desert *noun*
= anialwch (*plural* anialychau)
masculine, diffeithwch (*plural*
diffeithychau) *masculine*

deserve *verb*
= haeddu

deserving *adjective*
= teilwng

design
1 *noun*
• (*pattern, way something is designed*)
= cynllun (*plural* -iau) *masculine*
• (*subject of study*)
= cynllunio *verbnoun*
2 *verb*
= cynllunio

desist *verb*
= peidio
to desist from doing something =
peidio gwneud rhywbeth

> **!** *In more formal styles* **peidio** *is
> followed by* **â**, *but this is optional in
> speech.*

desk *noun*
= desg (*plural* -iau) *feminine*

despair
1 *noun*
= anobaith *masculine*
2 *verb*
= anobeithio

desperate *adjective*
• (*serious*)
= difrifol, peryglus
• (*in despair*)
= anobeithiol
• (*keen*)
= taer

despite *preposition*
= er gwaetha(f)
despite the difficulties = er gwaetha'r
anawsterau
despite him = er ei °waetha

dessert *noun*
= pwdin (*plural* -s) *masculine*

destiny *noun*
= tynged (*plural* tynghedau) *feminine*

destroy *verb*
= dinistrio, distrywio, difetha, chwalu

detached *adjective*
detached house = tŷ sengl (*plural* tai
sengl) *masculine*

detail *noun*
= manylyn (*plural* manylion) *masculine*
to go into something in detail =
manylu ar° rywbeth

detailed *adjective*
= manwl

details *plural noun*
= manylion *plural*
to go into details = manylu

detective *noun*
= ditectif (*plural* -s) *masculine*

determined *adjective*
= penderfynol
to be determined to go = bod yn °benderfynol o °fynd

develop *verb*
= datblygu

development *noun*
= datblygiad (*plural* -au) *masculine*

devil *noun*
= diawl (*plural* -iaid) *masculine*, cythraul (*plural* cythreuliaid) *masculine*

devote *verb*
= (*set aside*) neilltuo
to devote time to something = neilltuo amser i° rywbeth
to devote oneself to something = ymroddi i° rywbeth

dew *noun*
= gwlith *masculine*

diagram *noun*
= diagram (*plural* -au) *masculine*

dial *verb*
= deialu
to dial a wrong number = camddeialu

dialect *noun*
= tafodiaith (*plural* tafodieithoedd) *feminine*

dialling code *noun*
= côd deialu (*plural* codau deialu) *masculine*

dialling tone *noun*
= sain °ddeialu (*plural* seiniau deialu) *feminine*

diamond *noun*
= diamwnt (*plural* -au) *masculine*

diaper (*US*) *noun*
= cewyn (*plural* -nau) *masculine*

diary *noun*
= dyddiadur (*plural* -on) *masculine*

dice *noun*
= deisiau *plural*

dictionary *noun*
= geiriadur (*plural* -on) *masculine*

die¹ *verb*
= marw
he died = bu °farw
he is dying = mae e'n marw

> ! *Note the difference between* **bu °farw** *he died,* **mae e wedi marw** *he is dead, and* **mae e'n marw** *he is dying.*

I'm dying to see it = dw i'n ysu am ei °weld e

die² *noun*
= deis (*plural* -iau) *masculine*

diet *noun*
= deiet (*plural* -au) *masculine*
to go on a diet = mynd ar °ddeiet
to be on a diet = bod ar °ddeiet

difference *noun*
= gwahaniaeth (*plural* -au) *masculine*
what's the difference between ..? = beth ydy'r gwahaniaeth rhwng ...?
it makes no difference to me = dim ots gen i (*North*)
= dim ots 'da fi (*South*)

> ! *Although the vast majority of nouns ending in* **-aeth** *are feminine,* **gwahaniaeth** *is masculine.*

different *adjective*
= gwahanol

> ! **gwahanol** *follows the noun it refers to in this sense; when it precedes the noun, it means 'various'.*

difficult *adjective*
= anodd

difficulty *noun*
= anhawster (*plural* anawsterau) *masculine*

dig *verb*
= palu, cloddio

dig up
• (*plants*)
= dadwreiddio
• (*objects*)
= datgloddio, datgladdu

diligent *adjective*
= ymroddgar

dim adjective
- (of light etc)
  = gwan, aneglur
- (stupid)
  = twp

dinghy noun
= dingi (plural -s) masculine

dining room noun
= stafell °fwyta (plural stafelloedd bwyta) feminine

dinner noun
= cinio, swper

dip verb
- (in liquid)
  = trochi
- (headlights)
  = gostwng (stem gostyng-)

direct adjective
= uniongyrchol

direct debit noun
= debyd uniongyrchol masculine

direction noun
= cyfeiriad (plural -au) masculine
in the direction of... = yng ⁿnghyfeiriad...
= tuag at°...

directions noun
(instructions)
= cyfarwyddiadau plural

directly adverb
- (straight)
  = yn syth
- (at once)
  = ar unwaith, yn syth

director noun
= cyfarwyddwr (plural cyfarwyddwyr) masculine
= cyfarwyddwraig (plural cyfarwyddwragedd) feminine

dirt noun
= baw masculine

dirty adjective
= bud(u)r, brwnt

dis- prefix
= af°-, anⁿ-, an°-

disabled adjective
= anabl

disadvantage noun
= anfantais (plural anfanteision) feminine

disadvantaged adjective
= (o) dan anfantais

disagree verb
= anghytuno
to disagree with someone about something = anghytuno âʰ rhywun am° rywbeth, anghytuno â rhywun ynglŷn âʰ rhywbeth

disagreeable adjective
= annymunol

disappear verb
= diflannu

disappoint verb
= siomi

disappointed adjective
= siomedig, wedi [possessive adjective] siomi
we were disappointed = fe °gawson ni'n siomi (action)
= o'n ni wedi'n siomi (state)

disappointing adjective
= siomedig

disappointment noun
= siom (plural -au) feminine or masculine

disapprove verb
= anghymeradwyo

disaster noun
= trychineb (plural -au) masculine or feminine

disastrous adjective
= trychinebus

discipline noun
= disgyblaeth feminine

disco noun
= disgo (plural -s) masculine

disconnect verb
= datgysylltu

discourage verb
- (make downhearted)
  = digalonni
- (persuade not to)
  = perswadio i °beidio
  to discourage someone from doing something = perswadio rhywun i °beidio gwneud rhywbeth

discover verb
= darganfod (stem darganfydd-)

discovery noun
= darganfyddiad (plural -au) masculine

discriminate *verb*
to discriminate against someone =
  dangos anffafriaeth i° rywun

discrimination *noun*
- (*in someone's favour*)
  = ffafriaeth *feminine*
- (*against someone*)
  = anffafriaeth *feminine*

discuss *verb*
  = trafod

discussion *noun*
  = trafodaeth (*plural* -au) *feminine*
  a discussion about politics =
  trafodaeth ar °wleidyddiaeth

disease *noun*
- (*illness*)
  = clefyd (*plural* -au, -on) *masculine*
- (*infection*)
  = haint (*plural* heintiau) *masculine*

disgrace *noun*
  = gwarth *masculine*

disgraceful *adjective*
  = gwarthus

disguise
1 *noun*
  = cuddwisg (*plural* -oedd) *feminine*
2 *verb*
- (*with clothes*)
  = cuddwisgo
- (*conceal*)
  = cuddio

disgusting *adjective*
  = ffiaidd, ysglyfaethus

dish *noun*
  = dysgl (*plural* -au) *feminine*

dishes *noun*
  = llestri *plural*
  to do the dishes = golchi'r llestri

dishonest *adjective*
  = anonest

dishwasher *noun*
  = peiriant golchi llestri (*plural*
  peiriannau golchi llestri) *masculine*

dislike *verb*
  I dislike him = dw i °ddim yn hoff
  ohono fe, dw i °ddim yn leicio *or* hoffi
  fe

I dislike dogs = dw i °ddim yn hoff o
  °gŵn, dw i °ddim yn leicio/hoffi cŵn,
  °gas gen i °gŵn

dismiss *verb*
- (*from job*)
  = diswyddo
- (*treat as unimportant*)
  = diystyru

disobedient *adjective*
  = anufudd

disobey *verb*
  = anufuddhau

disorganised *adjective*
  = anhrefnus, anniben

display *verb*
  = arddangos
  pay and display car park = maes parcio
  talu ac arddangos

dispute
1 *noun*
  = dadl (*plural* -euon) *feminine*
2 *verb*
- (*argue*)
  = dadlau
- (*challenge*)
  = herio

dissatisfied *adjective*
  = anfodlon
  to be dissatisfied with something =
  bod yn anfodlon â^h rhywbeth / ar°
  rywbeth

dissertation *noun*
  = traethawd (*plural* traethodau)
  masculine

distance *noun*
  = pellter (*plural* -au, -oedd) *masculine*
  in the distance = yn y pellter, ymhell
  to keep one's distance = cadw draw

distant *adjective*
  = pell

distinct *adjective*
- (*different*)
  = gwahanol
- (*definite*)
  = penodol, pendant

distinguish *verb*
  to distinguish between A and B =
  gwahaniaethu rhwng A a B

distract *verb*
 to distract someone from his work =
 tynnu sylw rhywun oddiar ei °waith

distressed *adjective*
 = gofidus

distressing *adjective*
 = gofidus

distribute *verb*
• (*hand out*)
 = dosbarthu
• (*share*)
 = rhannu

district
1 *adjective*
 = rhanbarthol
2 *noun*
• (*general senses*)
 = ardal (*plural* -oedd) *feminine*, cylch
 (*plural* -oedd) *masculine*
• (*administrative*)
 = rhanbarth (*plural* -au) *masculine*

disturb *verb*
 = aflonyddu, rhwystro

dive *verb*
 = penllamu, plymio

diversion *noun*
 (*for traffic*)
 = gwyriad (*plural* -au) *masculine*

divert *verb*
 diverted traffic = traffig osgoi

divide *verb*
• = rhannu
 to divide thirty by six = rhannu trideg â
 chwech
• = ymrannu
 the road divides = mae'r ffordd yn
 ymrannu

divorce
1 *noun*
 = ysgariad (*plural* -au) *masculine*
2 *verb*
 = ysgaru, cael ysgariad
 they are getting divorced = maen
 nhw'n mynd i ysgaru, maen nhw'n
 mynd i °gael ysgariad
 they are divorced = maen nhw wedi
 ysgaru, maen nhw wedi cael
 ysgariad

DIY *needs posp*
 DIY shop = siop crefftau'r cartref
 (*plural* siopau crefftau'r cartref)
 feminine
 DIY enthusiast = crefftwr cartref (*plural*
 crefftwyr cartref) *masculine*

dizzy *adjective*
 I feel dizzy = mae ⁿmhen i'n troi
 he felt dizzy = roedd ei °ben e'n troi

do *verb*

> **!** *This verb has a very wide range of
> meanings and uses in English. A
> frequent and important use is as an
> auxiliary in various circumstances,
> and particular care is needed to
> make the right choice in Welsh in
> each case.*

• (*general senses*)
 = gwneud (*irregular*)
 to do the shopping = gwneud y gwaith
 siopa
 he's doing his homework = mae'n
 gwneud ei °waith cartre
 do as you please = gwnewch fel y
 mynnoch chi
 do your best = gwna dy °orau
 they'll do it later = nân nhw fe wedyn
 they didn't do anything = naethon nhw
 °ddim byd
• (*in present tense negatives and
 questions*)
 do you speak Welsh? = dych chi'n
 siarad Cymraeg?
 I don't live there now = dw i °ddim yn
 byw yno bellach
• (*in past tense negatives and
 questions*)
 did you see them? = °welest ti nhw?, nest
 ti °weld nhw?, ddaru ti °weld nhw?
 (*North*)
 she didn't come = °ddaeth hi °ddim,
 naeth hi °ddim dod, ddaru hi °ddim
 dŵad (*North*)
• (*in prohibitions*)
 don't shout like that! = paid gweiddi fel
 'ny!
 don't wait for us = peidiwch aros
 amdanon ni
 don't be angry = paid bod yn °grac
 don't worry = peidiwch poeni
• (*in tags and short answers*)
 Dafydd phoned, didn't he? = mi
 ffoniodd Dafydd, on'do?

she speaks Welsh, doesn't she? = mae hi'n siarad Cymraeg, on'd ydy?
'I like them'—'so do I' = 'dw i'n hoffi nhw'—'a finnau'
'I don't like this'—'neither do I' = 'dw i °ddim yn hoffi hwn'—'na finnau'
'will you come?'—'I might do' = '°ddoi di?'—'efallai'
• (idioms)
  something to do with computers = rhywbeth yn ymwneud â ʰchyfrifiaduron
  that has nothing to do with me = does a nelo hynny â fi
  they can do without it = mi °allan nhw °fyw hebddi

do up
• (garment)
  = cau (stem cae-)
• (renovate)
  = adnewyddu

dock noun
= doc (plural -iau) masculine

doctor noun
= meddyg (plural -on) masculine, doctor (plural -iaid) masculine
to go to the doctor's = mynd at y meddyg

document noun
= dogfen (plural -ni, -nau) feminine

documentary noun
(programme)
= rhaglen °ddogfennol (plural rhaglenni dogfennol) feminine

dog noun
= ci (plural cŵn) masculine

dole noun
on the dole = ar y clwt

doll noun
= dol (plural -iau) feminine, doli (plural -s) feminine

dollar noun
= doler (plural -i) feminine

dolphin noun
= dolffin (plural -od) masculine

domino noun
= dominô (plural -s) masculine
to play dominoes = chwarae (stem chwarae-) dominôs

donate verb
= rhoi (stem rhoi-, rhodd-) yn anrheg
donated by ... = rhoddedig gan° ...

donation noun
= rhodd (plural -ion) feminine

donkey noun
= asyn (plural -nod) masculine

don't
= paid... (singular), peidiwch... (plural); paid âʰ..., peidiwch âʰ...
don't wait for us = paid aros amdanon ni, paid ag aros amdanon ni
don't lose the money = paid colli'r arian, paid â ʰcholli'r arian
don't sit there = peidiwch eistedd fan 'na, peidiwch ag eistedd fan 'na

> **!** The versions with **â** are more formal in style, except in the emphatic construction **paid ti â ...!**, 'don't you...!', where it is normal even in speech.

door noun
= drws (plural drysau) masculine
there's someone at the door = mae rhywun wrth y drws

doorbell noun
= cloch drws (plural clychau drysau) feminine

dormitory noun
= (y)stafell °gysgu (plural (y)stafelloedd cysgu) feminine

dose noun
= dogn (plural -au) masculine

double adjective
= dwb(w)l
to play doubles = chwarae (stem chwarae-) mewn parau

double bass noun
= bas dwb(w)l (plural basau dwb(w)l) masculine, basgrwth (plural basgrythau) masculine

double bed noun
= gwely dwbwl (plural gwelyau dwbwl) masculine

double-decker noun
= bws deulawr (plural bysiau deulawr) masculine

double room *noun*
= stafell °ddwbwl (*plural* stafelloedd dwbwl) *feminine*

doubt
1 *noun*
= amheuaeth (*plural* amheuon) *feminine*
there's no doubt about it = does dim dwywaith amdani
no doubt he'll be along later = mi °ddaw nes ymlaen, mae'n °debyg, mae'n °debyg y daw e nes ymlaen
without a doubt = yn °ddi-os
= heb os nac onibai
2 *verb*
= amau (*stem* amheu-)

dough *noun*
= toes *masculine*

doughnut *noun*
= toesen (*plural* -ni) *feminine*

down *adverb*
= lawr, i lawr
he ran down the road = fe °redodd e (i) lawr y ffordd
prices have gone down = mae prisiau wedi mynd (i) lawr
down there = lawr fan 'na
down here = lawr fan hyn

> ! **lawr** *and* **i lawr** *are interchangeable, with* **i lawr** *the more formal of the two.*

downstairs *adverb*
= (i) lawr y grisiau, (i) lawr staer

dozen *noun*
= dwsin (*plural* -au) *masculine*
a dozen eggs = dwsin o wyau
dozens (*indeterminate number*) = ugeiniau

> ! *When used with a following noun, this noun, either singular or plural, requires* **o°.**

draft *noun* (*US*)
there's a draft here = mae hi'n tynnu fan hyn

drag *verb*
= llusgo, tynnu

dragon *noun*
= draig (*plural* dreigiau) *feminine*
the Red Dragon = y Ddraig Goch

drain *noun*
= ffos (*plural* -ydd) *feminine*, draen (*plural* dreiniau) *feminine*

drama *noun*
= drama (*plural* dramâu) *feminine*

dramatic *adjective*
= dramatig

drapes *plural noun* (*US*)
= llenni *plural*

draught *noun*
there's a draught here = mae hi'n tynnu fan hyn

draughts *plural noun*
(*game*)
= drafftiau *plural*

draw
1 *verb*
• (*pull*)
= tynnu
to draw the curtains = tynnu'r llenni
• (*with pencil*)
= tynnu
to draw a map = tynnu map
• (*attract*)
= denu
to draw someone's attention to something = tynnu sylw rhywun at° rywbeth
2 *noun*
• (*raffle etc*)
= tyniad (*plural* -au) *masculine*
• (*drawn game*)
= gêm °gyfartal (*plural* gemau cyfartal) *feminine*
• (*attraction*)
= atyniad (*plural* -au) *masculine*

draw back
• (*retreat*)
= tynnu'n ôl
• **to draw back the curtains** = tynnu'r llenni

draw up
• (*plans*)
= llunio
• (*of car*)
= stopio

drawer *noun*
= drôr (*plural* -s or droriau) *masculine or feminine*

drawing *noun*
= darlun (*plural* -iau) *masculine*

dread *verb*
= ofni

dreadful *adjective*
= ofnadwy, dychrynllyd, erchyll

dream
1 *noun*
= breuddwyd (*plural* -ion) *masculine or feminine*
a bad dream = hunllef (*plural* -au) *feminine*
2 *verb*
= breuddwydio
to dream about something = breuddwydio am° rywbeth

drench *verb*
= gwlychu
we got drenched = fe °gaethon ni'n gwlychu

dress
1 *noun*
• (*item of clothing*)
= ffrog (*plural* -iau) *feminine*
• (*costume*)
= gwisg (*plural* -oedd) *feminine*
2 *verb*
= gwisgo

dress up
= gwisgo

dressed *adjective*
to be dressed in something = gwisgo rhywbeth

dressing gown *noun*
= gŵn llofft (*plural* gynau llofft) *masculine*

drill
1 *noun*
= dril (*plural* -iau) *masculine*
2 *verb*
= tyllu, drilio

drink
1 *noun*
= diod (*plural* -ydd) *feminine*
can I buy you a drink? = °ga i °brynu diod i chi?
2 *verb*
= yfed (*stem* yf-)
he drank too much = mi yfodd e °ormod

drive
1 *verb*
• (*car etc*)
= gyrru
I don't like driving = dw i °ddim yn hoffi gyrru

• (*impel*)
= ysgogi
what drives him? = beth sy'n ysgogi fe?
2 *noun*
to go for a drive = mynd am °dro yn y car

drive away
= gyrru i ffwrdd (*North*), gyrru bant (*South*)

driver *noun*
= gyrrwr (*plural* gyrwyr) *masculine*

driving licence *noun*
= trwydded °yrru (*plural* trwyddedau gyrru) *feminine*

drizzle
1 *noun*
= glaw mân *masculine*
2 *verb*
= bwrw glaw mân

drop
1 *noun*
= diferyn (*plural* diferion) *masculine*
2 *verb*
= gollwng (*stem* gollyng-), cwympo
you've dropped your gloves = dych chi wedi cwympo'ch menig

drop by
= galw heibio

drop in
to drop in on someone = galw heibio i° rywun

drop off
• (*fall*)
= syrthio, cwympo
• (*set down from car etc*)
I'll drop you off here = na i °adael chi fan hyn
• (*go to sleep*)
= mynd i °gysgu

drop out
• (*withdraw*)
= tynnu'n ôl
• (*give up*)
= rhoi (*stem* rhoi-, rhodd-) 'r gorau i°

drought *noun*
= sychder (*plural* -au) *masculine*

drown *verb*
= boddi

drug *noun*
= cyffur (*plural* -iau) *masculine*

drug addict *noun*
= caeth i °gyffuriau (*plural* caethion i °gyffuriau) *masculine*
= caethes i °gyffuriau (*plural* caethesau i °gyffuriau) *feminine*

drug addiction *noun*
= caethiwed i °gyffuriau *masculine*

druggist *noun* (*US*)
= fferyllydd (*plural* fferyllwyr) *masculine*

drugstore *noun* (*US*)
= fferyllfa (*plural* fferyllfeydd) *feminine*

drum *noun*
= drwm (*plural* drymiau) *masculine*

drunk
1 *adjective*
= meddw, wedi meddwi
blind drunk = meddw °gaib, meddw'n racs
to get drunk = meddwi, mynd yn °feddw
2 *noun*
= meddwyn (*plural* meddwon) *masculine*

dry
1 *adjective*
= sych
2 *verb*
= sychu

duck
1 *noun*
= hwyaden (*plural* hwyaid) *feminine*
2 *verb*
= gostwng (*stem* gostyng-) pen

due *adjective*
• (*for payment*)
= dyledus
• (*proper, fair*)
= teg
• **when is the bus due?** = pryd mae'r bws i °fod i °gyrraedd?
• **due to something** (*because of*) = oherwydd rhywbeth, o achos rhywbeth

dull *adjective*
= diflas

dumb *adjective*
• (*unable to speak*)
= mud
• (*US: stupid*)
= twp

dump *noun*
• (*for rubbish etc*)
= tomen (*plural* -ni) *feminine*
• (*pejorative: place*)
= twll o °le *masculine*

dune *noun*
= twyn (*plural* -i) *masculine*

during *preposition*
= yn ystod
during the war = yn ystod y rhyfel

dusk *noun*
= cyfnos (*plural* -au) *masculine*
at dusk = gyda'r nos, gyda'r cyfnos

dust
1 *noun*
= llwch *masculine*
2 *verb*
= tynnu llwch, dwstio

dustbin *noun*
= bin sbwriel (*plural* biniau sbwriel) *masculine*

dustman *noun*
= dyn y biniau (*plural* dynion y biniau) *masculine*

dustpan *noun*
= rhaw °lwch (*plural* rhawiau llwch) *feminine*, padell °lwch (*plural* padellau llwch) *feminine*

dusty *adjective*
= llychlyd

duty *noun*
• (*obligation*)
= dyletswydd (*plural* -au) *feminine*
to be on duty = bod ar °ddyletswydd
• (*tax*)
= toll *feminine*

duty-free *adjective*
= di-°doll

duvet *noun*
= duvet (*plural* -s) *masculine*, cwilt (*plural* -iau) *masculine*

dwelling *noun*
= preswylfa (*plural* preswylfeydd) *feminine*

dye
1 *noun*
= lliw (*plural* -iau) *masculine*
2 *verb*
= lliwio

Ee

each

1 *adjective*
= pob
each room = pob stafell
each one is different = mae pob un yn
°wahanol

2 *pronoun*
= pob un
each of them has a car = mae gan °bob
un ohonyn nhw °gar
twenty pence each = ugain ceiniog yr
un

3 each other *pronoun*

> **!** *There is a special phrase for* **each
> other** *depending on who it refers to:*
> ei gilydd (*referring to 'them'*)
> ein gilydd (*referring to 'us'*)
> eich gilydd (*referring to 'you'*)
> **they hate each other** = maen nhw'n
> casáu ei gilydd
> **we'll help each other** = nawn ni
> helpu'n gilydd
> **did you recognise each other?** =
> naethoch chi adnabod eich gilydd?

eager *adjective*
= awyddus, taer

eagle *noun*
= eryr (*plural* -od) *masculine*

ear *noun*
= clust (*plural* -iau) *feminine or
masculine*
I'm all ears = dw i'n °glustiau i gyd

earache *noun*
she's got earache = mae gynni hi
°bigyn yn y °glust (*North*), mae clust
°dost 'da hi (*South*)

earlier *adverb*
= °gynt

early *adjective*
= cynnar

earmark *verb*
= clustnodi

earn *verb*
= ennill (*stem* enill-)

earring *noun*
= clustdlws (*plural* clustdlysau)
masculine

earth *noun*
• (*planet*)
= daear *feminine*, byd *masculine*
• (*soil*)
= pridd *masculine*

earthquake *noun*
= daeargryn (*plural* -fâu *or* -feydd)
masculine or feminine

easier *adjective*
= haws
it's easier this way = mae'n haws
ffordd hyn
easier said than done = haws dweud
na gwneud

> **!** *This is the standard, and irregular,
> formation from* **hawdd** *easy—some
> speakers use a regular form*
> **hawddach**, *and a combined form*
> **hawsach** *is also common.*

easily *adverb*
= yn hawdd

east

1 *adverb*
to go east = mynd i'r dwyrain, mynd
tua'r dwyrain

2 *noun*
= dwyrain *masculine*
in the east of Wales = yn ⁿnwyrain
Cymru
to the east of here = i'r dwyrain o fan
hyn
the Middle East = y Dwyrain Canol
the Far East = y Dwyrain Pell

Easter *noun*
= (y) Pasg *masculine*
Happy Easter! = Pasg Hapus!
Easter Sunday = Sul y Pasg
Easter Monday = Llun y Pasg

Easter egg *noun*
= ŵy Pasg (*plural* wyau Pasg) *masculine*

easterly *adjective*
= dwyreiniol, o'r dwyrain

easy *adjective*
= hawdd, rhwydd
it's easy to forget = mae'n hawdd
anghofio

it's not easy to get work here = dydy hi
°ddim yn hawdd i °gael gwaith fan hyn

eat *verb*
= bwyta
eat out = mynd allan i °fwyta

EC *noun*
= y °Gymuned Ewropeaidd *feminine*

echo *noun*
= atsain (*plural* atseiniau) *feminine*

economic *adjective*
= economaidd

economics *noun*
= economeg *feminine*

economize *verb*
= cynilo

economy *noun*
= economi (*plural* economïau) *feminine
or masculine*

edge *noun*
• (*general*)
= ymyl (*plural* -on) *masculine or feminine*
on the edge of town = ar ymyl(on) y
°dre
• (*of knife etc*)
= min *masculine*

educate *verb*
= addysgu
he was educated in Wales = cafodd ei
addysg yng ⁿNghymru

education *noun*
= addysg *feminine*

effect *noun*
= effaith (*plural* effeithiau) *feminine*
to have an effect on something =
effeithio ar° rywbeth

effective *adjective*
= effeithiol

efficient *adjective*
= effeithiol

effort *noun*
= ymdrech (*plural* -ion) *masculine or
feminine*
to make an effort = ymdrechu

egg *noun*
= ŵy (*plural* wyau) *masculine*

eggcup *noun*
= cwpan ŵy (*plural* cwpanau ŵy)
masculine or feminine

eight *numeral*
= wyth
eight cats = wyth cath, wyth o °gathod
eight pounds (*money*) = wyth
punt/°bunt
eight days = wyth ⁿniwrnod/diwrnod
eight years = wyth ⁿmlynedd
eight years old = wyth ⁿmlwydd oed
at eight o'clock = am wyth o'r °gloch
I have eight = mae gen i wyth (*North*),
mae wyth 'da fi (*South*)

eighteen *numeral*
= deunaw, undeg wyth
eighteen pounds = deunaw punt,
undeg wyth o °bunnoedd

eighteenth *adjective*
= deunawfed (*precedes noun*)
the eighteenth book = y deunawfed
llyfr
the eighteenth year = y °ddeunawfed
°flwyddyn
on the eighteenth of September = ar y
deunawfed o °Fedi

eighth *adjective*
= wythfed (*precedes noun*)
the eighth month = yr wythfed mis
the eighth year = yr wythfed
°flwyddyn

eighty *numeral*
= wythdeg
eighty apples = wythdeg o afalau
eighty years = wythdeg o °flynyddoedd
eighty years old = wythdeg oed

eisteddfod *noun*
= eisteddfod (*plural* -au) *feminine*

either
1 *conjunction*
= naill ai
either tea or coffee = naill ai te neu
°goffi, te ynteu coffi
2 *pronoun*
take either of them = cymerwch naill
ai'r un neu'r llall
3 *adjective*
take either book = cymerwch yr un
llyfr neu'r llall
4 *adverb*
• (*in negative sentences—not ... either*)
= chwaith
I can't see them either = °alla i mo'u
gweld nhw chwaith

elastic band *noun*
= dolen elastig (*plural* dolennau *or* dolenni elastig) *feminine*

elbow *noun*
= penelin (*plural* -oedd) *masculine or feminine*

elder *adjective*
= hŷn

elderly *adjective*
= oedrannus, mewn oed

eldest *adjective*
= hyna(f)

elect *verb*
= ethol

election *noun*
= etholiad (*plural* -au) *masculine*
to win an election = ennill (*stem* enill-) etholiad

electric *adjective*
= trydanol, trydan

electrician *noun*
= trydanwr (*plural* trydanwyr) *masculine*

electricity *noun*
= trydan *masculine*

elegant *adjective*
= cain

element *noun*
= elfen (*plural* -nau) *feminine*
he's in his element = mae e wrth ei °fodd
she's in her element = mae hi wrth ei bodd
I'm in my element = dw i wrth 'y ⁿmodd

elephant *noun*
= eliffant (*plural* -od) *masculine*

elevator *noun* (*US*)
= lifft (*plural* -iau) *feminine*

eleven *numeral*
= unarddeg, undeg un
eleven people = unarddeg o °bobol
at eleven o'clock = unarddeg o'r °gloch
eleven years = un °flwyddyn ar °ddeg, undeg un o °flynyddoedd
eleven years old = blwydd ar °ddeg oed, undeg un ⁿmlwydd oed

I have eleven = mae gen i unarddeg/undeg un (*North*), mae unarddeg/undeg un 'da fi (*South*)

eleventh *adjective*
= unfed ar °ddeg
the eleventh month = yr unfed mis ar °ddeg

else
1 *adverb*
= arall
someone else = rhywun arall
something else = rhywbeth arall
somewhere else = rhywle arall
everyone else = pawb arall
everything else = popeth arall
nothing else = dim byd arall
no-one else = neb arall
2 or else (*otherwise*)
= fel arall

elsewhere *adverb*
= rhywle arall

e-mail
1 *noun*
= e-bost *masculine*
2 *verb*
to e-mail someone = danfon e-bost at° rywun

embarrassed *adjective*
= annifyr

embarrassing *adjective*
= annifyr

embassy *noun*
= llysgenhadaeth (*plural* llysgenadaethau) *feminine*

emergency *noun*
= argyfwng (*plural* argyfyngau) *masculine*
in an emergency = mewn argyfwng

emergency exit *noun*
= allanfa °frys (*plural* allanfeydd brys) *feminine*, dihangfa (*plural* dihangfeydd) *feminine*

emergency services *plural noun*
= gwasanaethau brys

emigrate *verb*
= ymfudo, gadael (*stem* gadaw-) y °wlad
they've emigrated = maen nhw wedi gadael y °wlad

emotion *noun*
= emosiwn (*plural* emosiynau) *masculine*

emotional *adjective*
= emosiynol

emperor *noun*
= ymerawdwr (*plural* ymerawdwyr) *masculine*

emphasis *noun*
= pwyslais *masculine*

emphasize *verb*
= pwysleisio
to emphasize something = pwysleisio rhywbeth, rhoi (*stem* rhoi-, rhodd-) 'r pwyslais ar° rywbeth

employ *verb*
• (*give work to*)
= cyflogi
• (*use*)
= defnyddio

employed *adjective*
to be employed = bod â gwaith
= bod â swydd
to be employed as a driver = gweithio fel gyrrwr

employee *noun*
= cyflogedig (*plural* -ion) *masculine*

employer *noun*
= cyflogwr (*plural* cyflogwyr) *masculine*

employment *noun*
= cyflogaeth *feminine*
to find employment = cael gwaith
= cael swydd

empty
1 *adjective*
= gwag
2 *verb*
= gwacáu

enable *verb*
= galluogi
to enable someone to do something = galluogi rhywun i °wneud rhywbeth

enchant *verb*
= swyno

enchanting *adjective*
= swynol

enclose *verb*
= amgau (*stem* amgae-)
I enclose two tickets = amgaeaf °ddau °docyn

enclosed *adjective*
• (*with letter*)
= amgaeëdig

encourage *verb*
• (*give courage to*)
= calonogi
• (*persuade, urge*)
= annog

end
1 *noun*
• (*final part*)
= diwedd (*plural* -ion) *masculine*, terfyn (*plural* -au) *masculine*
the end of the programme = diwedd y rhaglen
at the end = ar y diwedd
in the end = yn y diwedd
at the end of August = °ddiwedd mis Awst
• (*furthest part*)
= pen *masculine*
the end of the street = pen y stryd
2 *verb*
• (*come to an end*)
= diweddu, dod i °ben
• (*put an end to*)
= rhoi pen/terfyn/diwedd ar°

end up
they ended up in Bangor = aethon nhw i °Fangor yn y diwedd
he ended up a teacher = mi aeth yn athro yn y diwedd

endearing *adjective*
= annwyl

ending *noun*
= diwedd (*plural* -ion) *masculine*

endless *adjective*
• (*without ceasing*)
= dibaid
• (*with no end*)
= diderfyn, di-ben-draw

endlessly *adverb*
= yn °ddiderfyn, yn °ddibaid

enemy *noun*
= gelyn (*plural* -ion) *masculine*

energetic *adjective*
= egnïol

energy *noun*
= egni (*plural* egnïon) *masculine*, ynni *masculine*

engaged *adjective*
- (*to be married*)
  to get engaged = dyweddïo
  they're engaged = maen nhw wedi dyweddïo
- (*phone line*)
  = prysur
  the line is engaged = mae'r lein yn °brysur

engine *noun*
= peiriant (*plural* peiriannau) *masculine*, injan (*plural* -s) *feminine*

engineer *noun*
= peiriannydd (*plural* peirianwyr) *masculine*

England *noun*
= Lloegr *feminine*

English
1 *adjective*
- (*language*)
  = Saesneg
- (*pertaining to England*)
  = Seisnig
2 *noun*
- (*language*)
  = Saesneg
- (*people*)
  = y Saeson *plural*

English-only *adjective*
(*language*) = uniaith Saesneg
an English-only document = dogfen uniaith Saesneg

Englishman *noun*
= Sais (*plural* Saeson) *masculine*

Englishwoman *noun*
= Saesnes (*plural* -au) *feminine*

enjoy *verb*
= mwynhau (*stem* mwynheu-)
to enjoy doing something = mwynhau gwneud rhywbeth
did you enjoy the trip? = naethoch chi °fwynhau'r °daith?

enjoyable *adjective*
= dymunol, hyfryd

enjoyment *noun*
= mwynhad *masculine*

enliven *verb*
= bywiogi

enormous *adjective*
= anferth, enfawr

enough
1 *adverb*
= digon
this isn't big enough = dyw hwn °ddim yn °ddigon mawr
2 *pronoun*
= digon (o°)
enough food = digon o °fwyd
have you got enough? = oes gen ti °ddigon?
that's enough = mae hynny'n °ddigon
not enough (*insufficient*) = annigonol
to have enough of something (*ie in excess*) = syrffedu ar° rywbeth

! **digon** *requires* **o°** *with a following noun.*

enquire *verb*
= ymholi, gofyn (*stem* gofynn-)
I'll enquire over there = na i °ofyn draw fan'na

enquiry *noun*
= ymholiad (*plural* -au) *masculine*
to make enquiries = holi, ymholi

ensure *verb*
= sicrhau

enter *verb*
- (*go in*)
  = mynd i mewn, dod i mewn
- (*compete*)
  = cystadlu
  to enter a race = cystadlu mewn ras

enterprise *noun*
= menter (*plural* mentrau) *feminine*, busnes (*plural* -au) *masculine*

entertain *verb*
= difyrru, adlonni

entertaining *adjective*
= difyr

entertainment *noun*
= adloniant *masculine*

enthusiastic *adjective*
= brwd, brwdfrydig

enthusiasm *noun*
= brwdfrydedd *masculine*

entirely *adverb*
= hollol, cwb(w)l

! *Both these adverbs cause soft mutation of a following adjective:*

entirely unnecessary = hollol/cwbwl
°ddiangen

entrails *plural noun*
= perfedd *masculine*, perfeddion
masculine plural

entrance *noun*
• (*way in*)
= mynedfa (*plural* mynedfeydd) *feminine*
• (*admittance*)
= mynediad *masculine*

entry *noun*
• (*admittance*)
= mynediad *masculine*
• (*in competition*)
= cais (*plural* ceisiadau) *masculine*

envelope *noun*
= amlen (*plural* -ni) *feminine*

environment *noun*
= amgylchedd (*plural* -au) *masculine*,
amgylchfyd (*plural* -oedd) *masculine*

envy
1 *noun*
= cenfigen *feminine*
2 *verb*
to envy someone = bod yn
°genfigennus o° rywun

episode *noun*
= pennod (*plural* penodau) *feminine*

equal *adjective*
= cyfartal

equality *noun*
= cyfartalwch *masculine*, cydraddoldeb
masculine

equally *adverb*
= yr un mor° + *adjective*

> **!** yr un mor° *displaces the* yn° *that*
> *we would expect in* **bod-** *sentences:*
> **he is guilty** = mae e'n euog
> **he is equally guilty** = mae e yr un
> mor euog

equal opportunities *plural noun*
= cyfleoedd cyfartal *plural*

equator *noun*
= cyhydedd (*plural* -au) *masculine*

equipment *noun*
= cyfarpar *masculine*, offer *plural*
translation equipment = cyfarpar
cyfieithu

era *noun*
= cyfnod (*plural* -au) *masculine*, oes
(*plural* -oedd *or* -au) *feminine*

eraser *noun*
= rwber (*plural* -au *or* -i) *masculine*

error *noun*
= gwall (*plural* -au) *masculine*,
camgymeriad (*plural* -au) *masculine*

escalator *noun*
= esgaladur (*plural* -on) *masculine*

escape *verb*
• (*get away*)
= dianc (*stem* dihang-)
to escape from prison = dianc o'r
carchar
• (*avoid*)
= osgoi

especially *adverb*
= yn enwedig, yn arbennig
especially in winter = yn
enwedig/arbennig yn y gaea

> **!** especially + *adjective is usually*
> **arbennig o°** + *adjective:*
> **This one is good** = Mae hwn yn °dda
> **This one is especially good** = Mae
> hwn yn arbennig o °dda

essay *noun*
= traethawd (*plural* traethodau)
masculine

essential *adjective*
= hanfodol

essentially *adverb*
= yn ei hanfod

establish *verb*
= sefydlu

estate *noun*
= stad (*plural* -au) *feminine*, ystad (*plural*
-au) *feminine*

estate agent *noun*
= gwerthwr tai (*plural* gwerthwyr tai)
masculine

estimate
1 *noun*
= amcangyfri(f) (*plural* amcangyfrifon)
masculine
2 *verb*
= amcangyfri(f)

eternal *adjective*
= tragwyddol

ethnic *adjective*
= ethnig

Europe *noun*
= Ewrop *feminine*

European
1 *adjective*
= Ewropeaidd
2 *noun*
= Ewropead (*plural* Ewropeaid)
masculine and feminine

European Union *noun*
= yr Undeb Ewropeaidd *masculine*

evacuate *verb*
• (*building*)
= gwacáu
• (*people*)
= symud allan

even
1 *adverb*
• (*expressing surprise*)
= hyd yn oed
he didn't even reply = naeth e °ddim
ateb hyd yn oed
even Aled knows that = mae hyd yn
oed Aled yn gwybod hynny
• (*with comparisons*)
= fyth
this one is even more expensive = mae
hwn yn °ddrutach fyth

> ! **fyth** *in this use shows a fixed and
> permanent soft mutation.*

• even though
= er (+ *'that...' clause*)
I'll come even though I'm ill = mi °ddo i
er ⁿmod i'n sâl
2 *adjective*
• (*flat*)
= gwastad
• (*equal*)
= cyfartal
even number = eilrif (*plural* -au)
masculine

evening *noun*
= nos, noson, noswaith (*plural*
nosweithiau)
good evening! = noswaith °dda!
in the evening = yn yr hwyr
this evening = heno

tomorrow evening = nos yfory
yesterday evening = neithiwr
all evening = trwy'r noson

event *noun*
= digwyddiad (*plural* -au) *masculine*

eventually *adverb*
= yn y diwedd, yn y pen draw

ever *adverb*
• (*at any time*)
= byth; erioed
have you ever been to Ireland? =
°fuoch chi erioed yn Iwerddon?
we didn't ever see them again = °welon
ni byth mohonyn nhw 'to
he's as lazy as ever = mae e mor °ddiog
ag erioed

> ! **byth** *and* **erioed** *are not
> interchangeable—see Welsh-English
> entries for details of the difference
> between them.*

every *adjective*
= pob (*mutates in adverbial expressions*)
every house is different = mae pob tŷ'n
°wahanol
every day = °bob dydd
every week = °bob wythnos
every year = °bob blwyddyn
every time = °bob tro
every other week = °bob yn ail wythnos
every third week = °bob yn °drydedd
wythnos
two out of every three = dau allan o
°bob tri
every bit as ... as ... = yr un mor° ... âʰ ...
= °lawn mor° ... âʰ ...

everybody *pronoun*
= pawb
everybody else = pawb arall

everyone *pronoun*
= pawb
everyone else = pawb arall

everything *pronoun*
= popeth
everything else = popeth arall

everywhere *adverb*
= ymhobman
everywhere else = ymhobman arall

evidence *noun*
= tystiolaeth (*plural* -au) *feminine*

to give evidence = tystio
to be in evidence = bod yn amlwg
= bod i'w °weld

evil
1 *adjective*
= drwg
2 *noun*
= drygioni *masculine*

exact *adjective*
• (*precise*)
= union
• (*detailed*)
= manwl

exactly *adverb*
= yn union, i'r dim

exaggerate *verb*
= gorliwio

exam *noun*
= arholiad (*plural* -au) *masculine*
to sit/take an exam = sefyll (*stem* sef- *or* saf-) arholiad
to pass an exam = pasio arholiad
to fail an exam = methu arholiad

examine *verb*
= archwilio

example *noun*
= enghraifft (*plural* enghreifftiau) *feminine*, esiampl (*plural* -au) *feminine*
for example = er enghraifft (*abbreviation* e.e.)

exceedingly *adverb*
= dros ben (*follows adjective*)
exceedingly good cakes = cacennau blasus dros ben

excellent *adjective*
= ardderchog, rhagorol, campus

except *preposition*
= heblaw (*or* 'blaw), ac eithrio, ar wahân i°

exchange
1 *noun*
(*place*) = cyfnewidfa (*plural* cyfnewidfeydd) *feminine*
in exchange for something = yn °gyfnewid am° rywbeth
2 *verb*
= cyfnewid (*stem* cyfnewidi-)
to exchange something for something else = cyfnewid rhywbeth am° rywbeth arall

exchange rate *noun*
= cyfradd °gyfnewid (*plural* cyfraddau cyfnewid) *feminine*

excited *adjective*
to get excited = cynhyrfu
to be excited = bod yn llawn cyffro

exciting *adjective*
= cyffrous

exclude *verb*
= cau (*stem* cae-) allan, cadw (*stem* cadw-) allan

excursion *noun*
= gwibdaith (*plural* gwibdeithiau) *feminine*

excuse
1 *noun*
= esgus (*plural* -ion) *masculine*
2 *verb*
= esgusodi
excuse me! = esgusodwch fi!

exercise
1 *noun*
= ymarfer (*plural* -ion) *masculine*
to do exercises = gwneud ymarferion
2 *verb*
= ymarfer

exercise book *noun*
= llyfr (y)sgrifennu (*plural* llyfrau (y)sgrifennu) *masculine*

exert *verb*
to exert oneself = ymdrechu

exhausted *adjective*
I'm exhausted = dw i wedi blino'n lân

exhibition *noun*
= arddangosfa (*plural* arddangosfeydd) *feminine*

exit
1 *noun*
= allanfa (*plural* allanfeydd) *feminine*
2 *verb*
= mynd allan

expand *verb*
= ehangu
to expand on something = ehangu ar° rywbeth

expect *verb*
= disgwyl (*stem* disgwyli-)
to expect to do something = disgwyl gwneud rhywbeth

to expect something to happen = disgwyl i° rywbeth °ddigwydd
they expect us to do the work = maen nhw'n disgwyl inni °wneud y gwaith

expectation *noun*
= disgwyl *masculine*
according to expectations = yn ôl y disgwyl

expense *noun*
• (*cost*)
= cost (*plural* -au) *feminine*
• (*detriment*)
at the expense of something = ar °draul rhywbeth

expense account *noun*
= cyfri(f) treuliau (*plural* cyfrifon treuliau) *masculine*

expenses *plural noun*
= treuliau *plural*, costau *plural*
travelling expenses = treuliau/costau teithio

expensive *adjective*
= drud, costus

experience
1 *noun*
= profiad (*plural* -au) *masculine*
2 *verb*
= profi

experienced *adjective*
= profiadol

experiment
1 *noun*
= arbrawf (*plural* arbrofion) *masculine*
2 *verb*
= arbrofi

expert *noun*
= arbenigwr (*plural* arbenigwyr) *masculine*
a computer expert = arbenigwr mewn cyfrifiaduron

explain *verb*
= esbonio, egluro
to explain something to someone = esbonio/egluro rhywbeth i °rywun

explanation *noun*
= esboniad (*plural* -au) *masculine*

explode *verb*
= ffrwydro

exploit *verb*
• (*use*)
= defnyddio
• (*misuse, treat unfairly*)
= camddefnyddio

explosion *noun*
= ffrwydriad (*plural* -au) *masculine*

explosive
1 *adjective*
= ffrwydrol
2 *noun*
= ffrwydryn (*plural* ffrwydron) *masculine*

export
1 *verb*
= allforio
2 *noun*
• (*object*)
= allforyn (*plural* allforion) *masculine*
• (*action*)
for export only = i'w allforio'n unig

express
1 *adverb*
(*fast*) = ar °frys, yn °gyflym
2 *verb*
= mynegi
to express an opinion = mynegi barn

expression *noun*
• (*of face*)
= golwg (*plural* golygon) *feminine or masculine*
• (*phrase*)
= ymadrodd (*plural* -ion) *masculine*

extend *verb*
• = estyn
to extend an invitation = estyn gwahoddiad
• = ymestyn
the road extended for a mile = roedd y ffordd yn ymestyn am °filltir

extension *noun*
= estyniad (*plural* -au) *masculine*

extensive *adjective*
= helaeth

extent *noun*
to a certain extent = i °raddau
to a great extent = i °raddau helaeth

external *adjective*
= allanol

extinct *adjective*
= darfodedig, wedi marw

extinguish *verb*
= diffodd

extra
1 *adjective*
= ychwanegol
no extra charge = dim tâl ychwanegol
2 *adverb*
= yn ychwanegol
we paid five pounds extra = fe °dalon ni °bum punt yn ychwanegol
extra big = mawr dros ben

extraordinarily *adverb*
= hynod o°
extraordinarily clever = hynod o °ddeallus

extraordinary *adjective*
= rhyfedd, anghyffredin iawn

extreme *adjective*
= eitha(f)

extremely *adverb*
= tu hwnt (*follows adjective*), dros ben (*follows adjective*), i'r eitha (*follows adjective*)
this exercise is extremely difficult = mae'r ymarfer 'ma'n anodd tu hwnt

extrovert
1 *adjective*
= allblyg
2 *noun*
= dyn allblyg *masculine*
= dynes allblyg *feminine*

eye *noun*
= llygad (*plural* llygaid) *masculine*

eyebrow *noun*
= ael (*plural* -iau) *feminine*

eyelash *noun*
= blewyn amrant (*plural* blew amrant) *masculine*

eyelid *noun*
= amrant (*plural* amrantau *or* amrannau) *masculine*

eye shadow *noun*
= colur llygaid *masculine*

eyesight *noun*
= golwg *masculine*

eyewitness *noun*
= llygad-dyst (*plural* -ion) *masculine*

Ff

fable *noun*
= chwedl (*plural* -au) *feminine*

fabulous *adjective*
• (*legendary*)
= chwedlonol
• (*great, marvellous*)
= gwych

face
1 *noun*
= wyneb (*plural* -au) *masculine*
2 *verb*
= wynebu
facing the bank = °gyferbyn i'r banc

face up
to face up to something = wynebu rhywbeth

fact *noun*
= ffaith (*plural* ffeithiau) *feminine*
in fact = a dweud y gwir, mewn gwirionedd

factor *noun*
= ffactor (*plural* -au) *masculine*

factory *noun*
= ffatri (*plural* ffatrïoedd) *feminine*

fade *verb*
• (*lose colour*)
= colli lliw
• (*disappear*)
= diflannu

fail *verb*
= methu, pallu

> **!** *In more formal styles,* **methu** *can be followed by* **â** + *verbnoun, though* **methu** + *verbnoun alone is common.*

to fail an exam = methu arholiad

failure *noun*
= methiant (*plural* methiannau) *masculine*

faint
1 *verb*
= llewygu
2 *adjective*
• (*slight, weak*)
= bychan, gawn

- (*unwell*)
  I feel faint = mae ⁿmhen i'n troi

fair
1 *adjective*
- (*reasonable*)
  = teg
  it's not fair = dydy hi ᵒddim yn ᵒdeg
- (*fair-haired*)
  = gwallt golau
  to have fair hair = bod â gwallt golau
2 *noun*
  = ffair (*plural* ffeiriau) *feminine*

fairly *adverb*
= eitha, goᵒ, gweddol, lled
fairly good = eitha da, go ᵒdda *etc*
to be fairly certain of something = bod yn eitha sicr oᵒrywbeth

> **!** eitha (*no mutation*) is the most common word, while at the other extreme **lled** is very rare in the modern language.

fairy tale *noun*
= chwedl (*plural* -au) *feminine*

faith *noun*
= ffydd
to have faith in someone = bod â ffydd ynⁿ rhywun

faithful *adjective*
= ffyddlon

fall
1 *noun*
- (*action*)
  = cwymp (*plural* -au) *masculine*
- (*US: autumn*)
  = hydre(f) *masculine*
  in the fall = yn yr hydre
2 *verb*
  = syrthio, cwympo (*South*)
  to fall in love with someone = syrthio mewn cariad âⁿ rhywun
  to fall asleep = mynd i ᵒgysgu

fall down
= syrthio, cwympo

fall off
to fall off something = syrthio/cwympo oddiarᵒ rywbeth

fall over
= syrthio, cwympo

fall through
- (*fail*) = methu
- (*go wrong*) = mynd yn chwith

false *adjective*
= ffug

false teeth *plural noun*
= dannedd gosod *plural*

familiar *adjective*
= cyfarwydd

family
1 *adjective*
= teuluol
2 *noun*
= teulu (*plural* -oedd) *masculine*

famine *noun*
= newyn (*plural* -au) *masculine*

famous *adjective*
= enwog, adnabyddus

fan *noun*
- (*machine*)
  = ffan (*plural* -iau) *feminine*
- (*supporter*)
  = cefnogwr (*plural* cefnogwyr) *masculine*

fancy dress party *noun*
= parti gwisg ffansi *masculine*

fantastic *adjective*
- (*strange, unusual*)
  = rhyfedd
- (*great*)
  = gwych

far
1 *adjective*
= pell
the far end = y pen pella(f), y pen draw
2 *adverb*
= yn ᵒbell, ymhell
don't go far = paid mynd yn ᵒbell/ymhell
as far as = hydᵒ
so far (*up till now*) = hyd yma
= hyd yn hyn
not far = nid nepell
far from happy = ᵒddim yn hapus o ᵒbell ffordd
far too big = rhy ᵒfawr o ᵒlawer

fare *noun*
- (*cost of trip*)
  = pris (-iau) *masculine*

- (*food*)
  = bwyd (*masculine*)

Far East noun
= y Dwyrain Pell *masculine*

farm
1 *noun*
= fferm (*plural* -ydd) *feminine*
2 *verb*
= ffermio

farmer noun
= ffermwr (*plural* ffermwyr) *masculine*

farmhouse noun
= ffermdy (*plural* ffermdai) *masculine*,
tŷ fferm (*plural* tai fferm) *masculine*

fart
1 *noun*
= rhechen (*plural* rhechod) *feminine*
2 *verb*
= rhechu

farther adverb
= ymhellach

fascinating adjective
= diddorol iawn

fashion
1 *noun*
= ffasiwn (*plural* ffasiynau) *masculine or feminine*
2 *verb*
(*make, shape*)
= ffurfio, llunio

fashionable adjective
= ffasiynol

fast
1 *adjective*
- (*quick*)
  = cyflym, clou
  this watch is three minutes fast =
  mae'r oriawr 'ma °dri munud yn °fuan
- (*firm*)
  = cadarn
2 *adverb*
- (*quickly*) = yn °gyflym
- (*stuck*)
  = sownd
3 *verb*
= ymprydio

fasten verb
- (*attach*)
  = clymu

to fasten something to something =
clymu rhywbeth wrth° rywbeth
- (*garment*)
  = cau (*stem* cae-)

fat
1 *adjective*
= tew
2 *noun*
(*grease*) = saim *masculine*

fatal adjective
- (*deadly*)
  = marwol
- (*disastrous*)
  = enbyd

fate noun
= tynged (*plural* tynghedau) *feminine*,
ffawd *feminine*

father noun
= tad (*plural* -au) *masculine*

> **! tad** appears as **ⁿhad** when 'Father'
> is used to mean 'my father'

Father Christmas noun
= Siôn Corn *masculine*

father-in-law noun
= tad-yng-nghyfraith (*plural* tadau-yng-
nghyfraith) *masculine*

fatty adjective
= seimllyd, seimlyd

faucet noun (*US*)
= tap (*plural* -iau) *masculine*

fault noun
- (*defect*)
  = diffyg (*plural* -ion) *masculine*, nam
  (*plural* -au) *masculine*
- (*blame*)
  = bai *masculine*
  at fault = ar °fai
  it's your fault = chi sy ar °fai
  whose fault is it? = pwy sy ar °fai?, bai
  pwy ydy hi?

favour noun
= ffafr (*plural* -au) *feminine*
to do someone a favour = gwneud ffafr
i° rywun
will you do me a favour? = nei di ffafr i
mi?
to be in favour of something = bod o
°blaid rhywbeth

favourable *adjective*
= ffafriol

favourite *adjective*
= hoff° (*precedes noun*)
what's your favourite programme? =
beth ydy'ch hoff °raglen?

fax
1 *noun*
= ffacs (*plural* -au) *masculine or feminine*
2 *verb*
= ffacsio

fax machine *noun*
= peiriant ffacs (*plural* peiriannau ffacs)
masculine

fear
1 *noun*
• (*general sense*)
= ofn (*plural* -au) *masculine*
• (*anxiety*)
= pryder (*plural* -on) *masculine*
2 *verb*
= ofni, bod ag ofn
to fear something = ofni rhywbeth
to fear the worst = bod ag ofn rhywbeth

fearful *adjective*
• (*inspiring fear*)
= dychrynllyd
• (*afraid*)
= ofnus

feast *noun*
= gwledd (*plural* -oedd) *feminine*

feat *noun*
= camp (*plural* -au) *feminine*

feather *noun*
= pluen (*plural* plu) *feminine*

feature *noun*
= nodwedd (*plural* -ion) *feminine*

February *noun*
= Chwefror, mis Chwefror *masculine*
see also **January**

fed up *adjective*
= wedi cael llond bol(a)

fee *noun*
= tâl (*plural* taliadau) *masculine*, ffi
(*plural* ffioedd) *feminine*

feeble *adjective*
= gwan

feed *verb*
= bwydo

will you feed the animals? = nei di
°fwydo'r anifeiliaid?

feel *verb*
= teimlo
I feel ill = dw i'n teimlo'n sâl
it feels cold here = mae'n teimlo'n oer
fan hyn
can you feel this? = °ellwch chi
°deimlo hwn?
do you feel like going out? = wyt ti'n
teimlo fel mynd allan?
= oes gen ti awydd mynd allan?
I feel like a cup of tea = hoffwn i °gael
panaid o °de

feeling *noun*
= teimlad (*plural* -au) *masculine*

felt-tip pen *noun*
= pin ffelt (*plural* pinnau ffelt)
masculine

female *adjective*
= benywaidd

feminine *adjective*
= benywaidd

fence *noun*
= ffens (*plural* -ys) *feminine*, sietin
masculine (South)

fencing *noun*
(*sport*) = cleddyfa *verbnoun*, cleddyfaeth
feminine

ferry *noun*
= fferi (*plural* fferïau) *feminine*

festival *noun*
= gŵyl (*plural* gwyliau) *feminine*

fetch *verb*
= nôl, moyn
go and fetch the milk = cer i nôl y
llaeth

fever *noun*
= twymyn *feminine*, gwres *masculine*

> **!** *These terms, when indicating a
> temporary physical state, are used
> with ar° + person:*
> **she's got a fever** = mae gwres arni.

few
1 *adjective*
• (*several*)
a few = ychydig

a few people = ychydig o °bobol
a few pounds = ychydig o °bunnoedd
- (*not many*)
= dim llawer, ychydig iawn
few people = dim llawer o °bobol
= ychydig iawn o °bobol

> **!** *These quantity expressions require* **o°** *before the things or people counted.*

2 *pronoun*
- (*several*)
there are a few left = mae ychydig ar ôl
= mae rhai ar ôl
- (*not many*)
there are few left = dim llawer sy ar ôl
= ychydig iawn sy ar ôl
there are few of us left = dim llawer ohonon ni sy ar ôl
so few = cynlleied
as few as = cynlleied â[h]

fewer
1 *adjective*
fewer shops = llai o siopau
2 *pronoun*
fewer than = llai na[h]
fewer than ten people = llai na deg o °bobol

fewest *adjective*
(*smallest number*)
the fewest people = y nifer isa o °bobol

field *noun*
- (*area of ground*)
= cae (*plural* -au) *masculine*, maes (*plural* meysydd) *masculine*
playing field = maes chwarae (*plural* meysydd chwarae) *masculine*
- (*sphere*)
= maes (*plural* meysydd) *masculine*

fierce *adjective*
- (*heat*))
= ffyrnig
- (*ferocious*)
= gwyllt

fifteen *numeral*
= pymtheg
fifteen apples = pymtheg o afalau
fifteen years = pymtheng °mlynedd
fifteen years old = pymtheng °mlwydd oed
at 2.15 = am chwarter wedi dau
I have fifteen = mae gen i °bymtheg (*North*), mae pymtheg 'da fi (*South*)

fifth *adjective*
= pumed

fifty *numeral*
= hanner can(t), pumdeg
fifty apples = pumdeg o afalau
fifty pounds = hanner can punt
fifty years = hanner can °mlynedd
fifty years old = hanner can °mlwydd oed

> **!** **hanner can(t)** *is the normal term with money, measurements and years—note that, as with* **can(t)**, *the final* **-t** *only appears when the numeral stands on its own without the thing counted. Numbers 51–59 use* **pumdeg** *rather than* **hanner cant— pumdeg un, pumdeg dau** *etc.*

fight
1 *noun*
= brwydr (*plural* -au) *feminine*
2 *verb*
= ymladd, brwydro
to fight against something = ymladd yn erbyn rhywbeth
to fight for something = ymladd dros° rywbeth
to fight someone = ymladd â[h] rhywun

fight back
= ymladd yn ôl

figure *noun*
- (*shape*)
= ffurf (*plural* -iau) *feminine*
- (*person, character*)
= ffigwr *masculine*
- (*number*)
= ffigur (*plural* -au) *masculine*

file
1 *noun*
= ffeil (*plural* -iau) *feminine*
in single file = yn un llinell
2 *verb*
= ffeilio

fill *verb*
= llenwi
to fill in a form = llenwi ffurflen
to fill up the car = llenwi'r car

film
1 *noun*
= ffilm (*plural* -iau) *feminine*
2 *verb*
= ffilmio

filthy *adjective*
= bud(u)r, brwnt

> **!** **budur** *is more common in the North,* **brwnt** *in this meaning in the South.*

final
1 *adjective*
= terfynol
2 *noun*
• (*sport*)
= rownd °derfynol (*plural* rowndiau terfynol) *feminine*

finally *adverb*
• (*in the end*)
= yn y diwedd, o'r diwedd
• (*lastly*)
= yn ola(f)

finance *noun*
= cyllid *masculine*

financial *adjective*
= ariannol

find *verb*
= ffeindio, dod o hyd i°, cael hyd i°
find out
= darganfod (*stem* darganfydd-)

fine
1 *adjective*
• (*weather*)
= braf
it's been fine all week = mae hi wedi bod yn braf trwy'r wythnos
• (*great*)
= gwych
a fine performance = perfformiad gwych *masculine*
• (*OK*)
= iawn
how's your coffee?—fine = sut mae dy °goffi?—iawn
2 *noun*
= dirwy (*plural* -on) *feminine*
to be fined for doing something = cael dirwy am °wneud rhywbeth

finger *noun*
= bys (*plural* -edd) *masculine*

fingernail *noun*
= ewin (*plural* -edd) *masculine or feminine*

fingerprint *noun*
= ôl bys (*plural* olion bysedd) *masculine*

finish
1 *verb*
= gorffen (*stem* gorffenn-), cwpla (*colloquial*), bennu (*colloquial*)
to finish doing something = gorffen gwneud rhywbeth

> **!** *Although* **gorffen** *is the standard term, the alternatives* **cwpla** *and* **bennu***, though not part of the written language, are far more common in speech.*

2 *noun*
= diwedd (*plural* -au) *masculine*

finished *adjective*
(*at an end*)
= ar °ben
we're finished = mae hi ar °ben 'da ni

fir *noun*
= pinwydden (*plural* pinwydd) *feminine*

fire
1 *noun*
= tân (*plural* tanau) *masculine*
to set something on fire = tanio rhywbeth
= rhoi (*stem* rhoi-, rhodd-) rhywbeth ar °dân
to catch fire = mynd ar °dân
to light a fire = cynnau tân
2 *verb*
• (*weapon*)
= tanio, saethu
• (*dismiss*)
= diswyddo

fire alarm *noun*
= rhybudd tân *masculine*

fire brigade *noun*
= brigâd °dân *feminine*

fire engine *noun*
= injan °dân (*plural* injans tân) *feminine*

fire exit *noun*
= allanfa °dân (*plural* allanfeydd tân) *feminine*

fire extinguisher *noun*
= offeryn diffodd tân (*plural* offer diffodd tân) *masculine*

firefighter *noun*
= diffoddwr tân (*plural* diffoddwyr tân) *masculine*
= diffoddwraig °dân (*plural* diffoddwragedd tân) *feminine*

fire station noun
= gorsaf °dân (*plural* gorsafoedd tân) *feminine*

fireworks *plural noun*
= tân gwyllt *masculine*
fireworks display = arddangosfa tân gwyllt *feminine*, sioe tân gwyllt *feminine*

firm
1 *adjective*
= cadarn, pendant
2 *noun*
= cwmni (*plural* cwmnïau) *masculine*

first
1 *adjective*
= cynta(f)
the first book = y llyfr cynta
the first example = yr enghraifft °gynta
this is the first time I've been here = dyma'r tro cynta i mi °fod yma

> ! Unlike other ordinal numerals, **cynta** behaves like a normal adjective and follows the noun it refers to.

2 *adverb*
• (*first of all*)
= °gynta
let's go there first = awn ni yno °gynta

> ! In this adverbial use, the mutation on °**gynta** is fixed.

• (*in the first place*)
= yn °gynta
first, I haven't seen him = yn °gynta, dw i heb °weld e
at first = i °ddechrau
3 *noun*
this one is the first = dyma'r un cynta *masculine*, dyma'r un °gynta *feminine*

first aid noun
= cymorth cynta(f) *masculine*

first class noun
= dosbarth cynta(f) *masculine*

first(ly) *adverb*
= yn °gynta(f)

first name noun
= enw bedydd (*plural* enwau bedydd), enw cynta(f) (*plural* enwau cynta(f)) *masculine*

fish
1 *noun*
= pysgodyn (*plural* pysgod) *masculine*

2 *verb*
= pysgota

fisherman noun
= pysgotwr (*plural* pysgotwyr) *masculine*

fishing noun
= pysgota *verbnoun*

fishing rod noun
= gwialen °bysgota (*plural* gwialenni pysgota) *feminine*

fishmonger's noun
= siop °bysgod (*plural* siopau pysgod) *feminine*

fist noun
= dwrn (*plural* dyrnau) *masculine*

fit
1 *adjective*
• (*healthy*)
= ffit, heini
to keep fit = cadw'n heini
• (*suitable*)
to be fit for something = bod yn addas i° rywbeth
2 *verb*
= ffitio

fit in
• (*find room*)
to fit someone in = gwneud lle i° rywun
• (*integrate*)
= cydfynd

fitness noun
= ffitrwydd *masculine*

fitted kitchen noun
= cegin °osod (*plural* ceginau gosod) *feminine*

five *numeral*
= pump (pum *before singular noun*)
five rooms = pum stafell
= pump o stafelloedd
five pounds (*money*) = pum punt
five days = pum ⁿniwrnod/diwrnod
five years = pum ⁿmlynedd
five years old = pum ⁿmlwydd oed
at five o'clock = am °bump o'r °gloch
I have five = mae gen i °bump (*North*), mae pump 'da fi (*South*)

fix *verb*
• (*mend*)
= trwsio
• (*set*)
= gosod

- (*arrange*)
  = trefnu

flag *noun*
   = baner (*plural* -i) *feminine*

flame *noun*
   = fflam (*plural* -au) *feminine*
   to go up in flames = mynd yn
   °wenfflam

flannel *noun*
   = clwt molchi (*plural* clytiau molchi)
   masculine

flash
1 *noun*
   = fflach (*plural* -iau *or* -iadau) *feminine*
   flash of lightning = mellten *feminine*
   in a flash = mewn fflach
2 *verb*
   = fflachio

flashlight *noun* (*US*)
   = tortsh (*plural* -is) *masculine*

flask *noun*
   = fflasg (*plural* -iau) *feminine*

flat
1 *adjective*
- (*countryside, surface etc*)
  = gwastad
- (*tyre*)
  = fflat
- (*not fizzy*)
  = fflat
2 *noun*
   = fflat (*plural* -iau) *feminine*

flavour *noun*
   = blas (*plural* -au) *masculine*

flaw *noun*
   = nam (*plural* -au) *masculine*, diffyg
   (*plural* -ion) *masculine*

flea *noun*
   = chwannen (*plural* chwain) *feminine*

flee *verb*
   = ffoi
   to flee from something = ffoi rhag
   rhywbeth

fleet *noun*
   = llynges (*plural* -au) *feminine*

flesh *noun*
   = cnawd *masculine*

flexible *adjective*
   = hyblyg, ystwyth

flexitime *noun*
   = oriau hyblyg *plural*
   to work flexitime = gweithio oriau
   hyblyg

flight *noun*
   = hediad (*plural* -au) *masculine*
   flight of stairs = rhes o °risiau (*plural*
   rhesi o °risiau) *feminine*

float *verb*
- (*on water*)
  = nofio
- (*in air*)
  = hofran

flock *noun*
- (*of animals*)
  = praidd (*plural* preiddiau) *masculine*
- (*of birds*)
  = haid (*plural* heidiau) *feminine*

flood *noun*
- (*of water*)
  = llif (*plural* -ogydd) *masculine*
- (*of words, ideas etc*)
  = llifeiriant *masculine*

floor *noun*
   = llawr (*plural* lloriau) *masculine*
   the ground floor = y llawr isa(f)
   masculine
   the first floor
   (*British*) = y llawr cynta(f) *masculine*
   (*US: ground floor*) = y llawr isa(f)
   masculine

floppy disk *noun*
   = disg llipa (*plural* disgiau llipa)
   masculine

florist *noun*
   = gwerthwr blodau (*plural* gwerthwyr
   blodau) *masculine*, gwerthwraig
   blodau (*plural* gwerthwragedd blodau)
   feminine

florist's *noun*
   = siop °flodau (*plural* siopau blodau)
   feminine

flour *noun*
   = blawd *masculine*, fflŵr *masculine*

flow
1 *noun*
- (*general sense*)
  = llif (*plural* -au) *masculine*
- (*tidal*)
  = llanw *masculine*
2 *verb*
   = llifo

flower
1 *noun*
= blodyn (*plural* blodau) *masculine*
2 *verb*
= blodeuo

flu *noun*
= y ffliw
she's got the flu = mae'r ffliw arni (hi)

> **!** *This expression requires* **ar°** + *person because it denotes a temporary physical state.*

fluent *adjective*
= rhugl
he speaks fluent Welsh = mae e'n rhugl yn y °Gymraeg, mae e'n siarad Cymraeg yn rhugl

fluid *noun*
= hylif (*plural* -au) *masculine*

flush *verb*
to flush the toilet = tynnu'r dŵr

flute *noun*
= ffliwt (*plural* -iau) *feminine*

fly
1 *noun*
= pryf (*plural* -ed) *masculine*, cleren (*plural* clêr) *feminine*
2 *verb*
= hedfan

foam *noun*
= ewyn *masculine*

focus
1 *noun*
= canolbwynt (*plural* -iau) *masculine*, ffocws (*plural* ffocysau) *masculine*
2 *verb*
to focus on something = canolbwyntio ar° rywbeth

fog *noun*
= niwl *masculine*

foggy *adjective*
= niwlog

fold
1 *verb*
= plygu
he folded his arms = naeth e °blethu'i °freichiau
2 *noun*
= plyg (*plural* -ion) *masculine*, plygiad (*plural* -au) *masculine*

fold up
= plygu i fyny (*North*), plygu lân (*South*)

folder *noun*
= plygell (*plural* -au) *masculine*

foliage *noun*
= dail *plural*

follow *verb*
= dilyn

follower *noun*
= dilynwr (*plural* dilynwyr) *masculine*

following
1 *adjective*
= canlynol
the following day = y diwrnod wedyn
2 *preposition*
= yn sgîl
following this decision = yn sgîl y penderfyniad 'ma

fond *adjective*
= hoff
to be fond of something/someone = bod yn hoff o° rywbeth/rywun, hoffi/leicio rhywbeth/rhywun

food *noun*
= bwyd (*plural* -ydd) *masculine*

food chain *noun*
= cadwyn °fwyd (*plural* cadwyni bwyd) *feminine*

fool
1 *noun*
= ffŵl (*plural* ffyliaid) *masculine*, twpsyn (*plural* twpsod) *masculine*
2 *verb*
= twyllo

foolish *adjective*
= hurt, twp, ffôl, gwirion

foot *noun*
- (*part of body*)
  = troed (*plural* traed) *masculine or feminine*
- (*unit of measurement*)
  = troedfedd (*plural* -i) *feminine*
  on foot (*walking*) = ar °gerdded

football *noun*
- (*game*)
  = pêl-droed *masculine*
- (*ball*)
  = pêl °droed (*plural* peli troed) *feminine*

footballer noun
= pêl-droediwr (plural pêl-droedwyr) masculine

footpath noun
= llwybr (plural -au) masculine

footprint noun
= ôl troed (plural olion traed) masculine

footstep noun
= sŵn troed (plural sŵn traed) masculine

for preposition
• (general senses)
= i°, ar °gyfer
there's a letter for you here = mae llythyr i ti fan hyn
a present for Sioned = anrheg i Sioned
to work for a company = gweithio i °gwmni
will you open this for me? = nei di agor hwn i mi?
a course for beginners = cwrs ar °gyfer dechreuwyr
this is for you = ar eich cyfer chi mae hwn

> **! i°** and **ar °gyfer** are very similar in meaning—the latter has perhaps slightly more of a sense of 'for the benefit of'.
>   **ar °gyfer** is a compound preposition and so changes its form with pronouns—see entry on the Welsh-English side for details.

• (in favour of)
= o °blaid
who is for the motion? = pwy sy o °blaid y cynnig?
• (on behalf of)
= dros°
I'll sign for them = na i arwyddo drostyn nhw
• (future time)
= am°
how long are you going for? = am faint dych chi'n mynd?
we're going for a fortnight = dyn ni'n mynd am °bythefnos
• (past time)
= ers
we've been here for years = dyn ni fan hyn ers blynyddoedd
• (in exchange for)
= am°

he paid ten pounds for it = fe °dalodd e °ddeg punt amdano fe
how much did you get for the car? = faint °gest ti am y car?
I got a pound for washing the car = °ges i °bunt am °olchi'r car
• (in preparation for)
= at°, ar °gyfer
to save for Christmas = cynilo at y Nadolig

forbid verb
= gwahardd
to forbid someone to do something = gwahardd rhywun rhag gwneud rhywbeth

force
1 noun
• (of people)
= llu (plural -oedd) masculine
the police force = yr heddlu masculine
the armed forces = y lluoedd arfog plural
• (power)
= grym (plural -oedd) masculine, nerth masculine
to use force = defnyddio grym
2 verb
= gorfodi
to force someone to do something = gorfodi rhywun i °wneud rhywbeth

forecast
1 noun
(weather forecast)
= rhagolygon y tywydd plural
2 verb
= rhagweld (stem rhagwel-), darogan

forehead noun
= talcen (plural -nau, -ni) masculine

foreign adjective
• (from overseas)
= estron, tramor
foreign languages = ieithoedd estron
• (strange, alien)
= estron, dieithr

foreigner noun
= estron (plural -iaid) masculine
= estrones (plural -au) feminine

Foreign Secretary noun
= Ysgrifennydd Tramor masculine

foresee verb
= rhagweld (stem rhagwel-)

forest noun
= fforest (plural -ydd) feminine

foretaste noun
= rhagflas (plural -au) masculine

foretell verb
= rhagddweud (stem rhagddwed-)

forever adverb
• (for always)
= am byth
Wales forever! = Cymru am byth!
• (constantly)
= byth a hefyd
he's forever talking about it = mae e
byth a hefyd yn siarad amdano

forewarn verb
= rhagrybuddio

foreword noun
= rhagair (plural rhageiriau) masculine

forget verb
= anghofio
to forget about something = anghofio
am° rywbeth
to forget to do something = anghofio
gwneud rhywbeth

forgive verb
= maddau (stem maddeu-)
to forgive someone = maddau i° rywun
forgive me! = maddeuwch i mi!

fork noun
• (cutlery)
= fforc (plural ffyrc) feminine
• (for digging)
= fforch (plural ffyrch) feminine
• (in road)
= fforchiad (plural -au) masculine

form
1 noun
• (shape)
= ffurf (plural -iau) feminine
• (piece of paper)
= ffurflen (plural -ni) feminine
• (school class)
= dosbarth (plural -au or -iadau)
masculine
2 verb
= ffurfio

formal adjective
= ffurfiol

former adjective
= blaenorol, cynt

formerly adverb
= °gynt, o'r blaen

> **!** **°gynt** has a fixed mutation in this
> adverbial sense.

fortnight noun
= pythefnos (plural -au) masculine or
feminine

fortnightly
1 adjective
= pythefnosol
2 adverb
= °bob pythefnos, yn °bythefnosol

fortunate adjective
= ffodus, lwcus

fortunately adverb
= yn ffodus, wrth lwc

fortune noun
to cost a fortune = costio arian mawr
to tell someone's fortune = dweud
(stem dwed-) fortiwn rhywun

forty numeral
= deugain, pedwardeg
forty apples = deugain o afalau
= pedwardeg o afalau
forty years = deugain ⁿmlynedd
forty pounds (money) = deugain punt
forty years old = deugain ⁿmlwydd
oed

> **!** **deugain** is particularly common
> with money, measurements, and
> years. **pedwardeg** must be used with
> numbers 41–49—**pedwardeg un,** etc.

forward
1 adverb
= ymlaen
2 adjective
• (at the front)
= blaen
• (cheeky)
= haerllug
3 verb
to forward a letter = danfon llythyr
ymlaen

foul
1 adjective
• (repulsive)
= ffiaidd
• (dirty)
= bud(u)r, brwnt

2 *noun*
= ffowl (*plural* -iau) *feminine*
(*trip*) = bagliad (*plural* -au) *masculine*

found *verb*
= sefydlu, seilio

foundation *noun*
= sail (*plural* seiliau) *feminine*, sylfaen
(*plural* sylfeini) *feminine*

foundations *plural noun*
= sylfeini

founder *noun*
= sylfaenydd (*plural* sylfaenwyr)
masculine, sefydlydd (*plural* sefydlwyr)
masculine

fountain *noun*
= ffynnon (*plural* ffynhonnau) *feminine*

four *numeral*
= pedwar *masculine*, pedair *feminine*
four books = pedwar llyfr, pedwar o
ºlyfrau
four rooms = pedair stafell, pedair o
stafelloedd
four pounds (*money*) = pedair punt
four days = pedwar diwrnod
four years = pedair blynedd
four years old = pedair blwydd oed
at four o'clock = am ºbedwar o'r ºgloch
I have four = mae gen i ºbedwar/ºbedair
(*North*), mae pedwar/pedair 'da fi
(*South*)

fourteen *numeral*
= pedwararddeg, undeg pedwar
masculine
= pedairarddeg, undeg pedair *feminine*
fourteen horses = pedwar ceffyl ar
ºddeg, undeg pedwar o ºgeffylau
fourteen cats = pedair cath ar ºddeg,
undeg pedair o ºgathod
fourteen years = pedair blynedd ar
ºddeg, undeg pedair o ºflynyddoedd
fourteen years old = pedair blwydd ar
ºddeg oed

fourteenth *adjective*
= pedwerydd ar ºddeg *masculine*
= pedwaredd ar ºddeg *feminine*

fourth *adjective*
= pedwerydd *masculine*
= pedwaredd *feminine*
the fourth book = y pedwerydd llyfr
the fourth desk = y ºbedwaredd ºddesg

fox *noun*
= llwynog (*plural* -od) *masculine*, cadno
(*plural* -id) *masculine*

fraction *noun*
= ffracsiwn (*plural* ffracsiynau)
masculine

fragile *adjective*
= brau

frame *noun*
= ffrâm (*plural* fframiau) *feminine*

framework *noun*
= fframwaith (*plural* fframweithiau)
masculine

France *noun*
= Ffrainc *feminine*

frank *adjective*
= plaen
to speak frankly = siarad yn ºblaen

freckles *plural noun*
= brychau haul

free
1 *adjective*
• (*general sense*)
= rhydd
to set someone free = rhyddhau
rhywun
• (*gratis*)
= rhad ac am ºddim
2 *verb*
= rhyddhau

freedom *noun*
= rhyddid *masculine*

freeway *noun* (*US*)
= traffordd (*plural* traffyrdd) *feminine*,
priffordd (*plural* priffyrdd) *feminine*

freeze *verb*
= rhewi

freezer *noun*
= rhewgell (*plural* -oedd) *feminine*

freezing *adjective*
= rhewllyd
it's freezing today, isn't it? = mae'n
rhewi heddiw, on'd ydy?

French
1 *adjective*
• (*language*)
= Ffrangeg
• (*pertaining to France*)
= Ffrengig

2 *noun*
(*language*)
= Ffrangeg *feminine*
the French = y Ffrancwyr

French fries *plural noun*
= sglodion *plural*

Frenchman *noun*
= Ffrancwr (*plural* Ffrancwyr) *masculine*

Frenchwoman *noun*
= Ffrances (*plural* -au) *feminine*

frequent
1 *adjective*
= aml, mynych
2 *verb*
= mynychu

frequently *adverb*
= yn aml, yn °fynych

fresh *adjective*
= ffres

Friday *noun*
= dydd Gwener
Friday night = nos °Wener
see also **Monday**

fridge *noun*
= oergell (*plural* -oedd) *feminine*

fried *adjective*
= wedi'i ffrio *singular*, wedi'u ffrio
plural
fried egg = ŵy wedi'i ffrio (*plural* wyau
wedi'u ffrio) *masculine*

friend *noun*
= ffrind (*plural* -iau) *masculine*, cyfaill
(*plural* cyfeillion) *masculine*
to be friends = bod yn ffrindiau
a friend of mine = ffrind i mi

> **!** **cyfaill** *is the preferred standard
> term, but in practice the loanword*
> **ffrind** *is far more common.*

friendly *adjective*
= cyfeillgar

friendship *noun*
= cyfeillgarwch *masculine*

fright *noun*
to have a fright = dychryn
to give someone a fright = dychryn
rhywun

frighten *verb*
= dychryn

frightened *adjective*
= wedi dychryn

frightful *adjective*
= dychrynllyd

fringe *noun*
= rhimyn (*plural* -au) *masculine*
to wear one's hair in a fringe =
gwisgo'ch gwallt yn rhimyn

frog *noun*
= llyffant (*plural* -od, llyffaint)
masculine, broga (*plural* -od) *masculine*

> **!** *Technically,* **llyffant** *is* 'toad', *but
> many speakers do not use* **broga** *and
> call all frogs and toads* **llyffaint**.

from *preposition*
• (*direction*)
= o°
they come from North Wales = maen
nhw'n dod o °Ogledd Cymru
to come back from the office = dod yn
ôl o'r swyddfa
open from nine till five = ar agor o naw
tan/hyd °bump
ten miles from the city centre = deng
milltir o °ganol y °ddinas
• (*with letters etc*)
= oddiwrth°, oddi wrth°
a message from Dafydd = neges
oddiwrth Dafydd
• (*from on something*)
= oddiar°, oddi ar°
to fall from a bike = syrthio oddiar °feic
• (*money etc*)
= gan°
how much did you get from him? =
faint °gest ti gynno fo?
• (*with words like 'prevent', 'stop'*)
= rhag
**to prevent someone from doing
something** = rhwystro rhywun rhag
gwneud rhywbeth
**to stop someone from doing
something** = atal rhywun rhag
gwneud rhywbeth

front
1 *adjective*
= blaen, ffrynt
front row = rhes °flaen (*plural* rhesi
blaen) *feminine*
2 *noun*
= blaen *masculine*

in front of the building = o °flaen yr adeilad
in front of me = o ⁿmlaen (i)

> **!** **o °flaen** is a compound preposition and so changes its form with pronouns—see entry on the Welsh-English side for details.

front door noun
= drws ffrynt (plural drysau ffrynt) masculine

frontier noun
= ffin (plural -iau) feminine

front page noun
= tudalen blaen masculine, tudalen °flaen feminine

front seat noun
= sedd °flaen (plural seddau/seddi blaen) feminine

frost noun
= rhew masculine

frosty adjective
= rhewllyd

frown verb
= cuchio, gwgu
to frown at someone = cuchio/gwgu ar °rywun

frozen adjective
= wedi'i °rewi masculine, wedi'i rhewi feminine, wedi'u rhewi plural
frozen foods = bwydydd wedi'u rhewi

fruit noun
= ffrwyth (plural -au) masculine

frustrate verb
= (plans) llesteirio, rhwystro

frustrated adjective
= rhwystredig

fry verb
= ffrio

frying pan noun
= padell ffrio (plural pedyll/padelli ffrio) feminine

fuel noun
= tanwydd masculine

fulfil verb
= cyflawni

full adjective
• (general sense)
= llawn
• (very crowded)
= dan ei sang
full up = llawn °dop

full stop noun
= atalnod llawn (plural atalnodau llawn) masculine

full-time adjective and adverb
= llawn-amser
to work full-time = gweithio llawn-amser

fumes plural noun
= mwg masculine

fun noun
= hwyl feminine, sbort masculine or feminine, sbri masculine or feminine
what fun! = am sbort!
to have fun = cael hwyl
to make fun of someone = gwneud sbort am °ben rhywun

function
1 noun
• (duty, purpose)
= swyddogaeth (plural -au) feminine
2 verb
= gweithio

fundamental adjective
= sylfaenol

fundamentally adverb
= yn y bôn

funeral noun
= angladd (plural -au) masculine or feminine

funfair noun
= ffair °bleser (plural ffeiriau pleser) feminine

funny adjective
= doniol

fur noun
= ffwr masculine

furious adjective
= ffyrnig, gwyllt

furniture noun
= dodrefn plural, celfi plural

further adverb
= ymhellach

further to your letter.... = ymhellach
i'ch llythyr...

fuss
1 *noun*
= ffwdan *feminine*, helynt *feminine*
to make a fuss about something =
creu helynt am° rywbeth
2 *verb*
= ffwdanu

futile *adjective*
= ofer

future
1 *adjective*
= dyfodol
2 *noun*
= dyfodol
in the near future = yn y dyfodol agos

Gaelic *noun*
(*language*)
= Gaeleg *feminine*
Scottish Gaelic = Gaeleg yr Alban

gain *verb*
= ennill (*stem* enill-)
to gain weight = ennill pwysau

gale *noun*
= storm (*plural* -ydd) *feminine*

gallery *noun*
= oriel (*plural* -au) *feminine*

game *noun*
= gêm (*plural* -au) *feminine*

> **!** *Although feminine, this word does
> not lose its initial* **g-** *by soft mutation,
> either after the word for* 'the' *or in any
> other circumstances where soft
> mutation would be expected. So*
> (**gardd**) **yr °ardd °fawr** the big
> garden, *but* (**gêm**) **y gêm °fawr** —the
> big game.

games *noun*
(*school activity*)
= chwaraeon *plural*, mabolgampau
plural

gang *noun*
= criw (*plural* -iau) *masculine*, giang
(*plural* -au) *feminine*

gap *noun*
= bwlch (*plural* bylchau) *masculine*

garage *noun*
= garej (*plural* -is) *feminine*

garbage (*US*) *noun*
= sbwriel *masculine*

garbage can (*US*) *noun*
= bin sbwriel (*plural* biniau sbwriel)
masculine

garbage collector (*US*) *noun*
= dyn y biniau (*plural* dynion y biniau)
masculine

garden
1 *noun*
= gardd (*plural* gerddi) *feminine*
2 *verb*
= garddio

gardener *noun*
= garddwr (*plural* garddwyr) *masculine*
= garddwraig (*plural* garddwragedd) *feminine*

gardening *noun*
= garddio *verbnoun*

garlic *noun*
= garlleg *masculine*

garment *noun*
= dilledyn (*plural* dillad) *masculine*

gas *noun*
• (*general sense*)
= nwy (*plural* -on) *masculine*
• (*US: petrol*)
= petrol *masculine*

gas station *noun* (*US*)
= gorsaf °betrol (*plural* gorsafoedd petrol) *feminine*

gate *noun*
= llidiart (*plural* llidiardau) *masculine*, giât (*plural* giatiau) *feminine*

gather *verb*
• (*collect*)
= casglu
• (*assemble*)
= ymgynnull (*stem* ymgynnull-)

gay *adjective*
(*homosexual*)
= hoyw

gaze *verb*
= syllu
to gaze at something = syllu ar° rywbeth

GCSE (*acronym for* **General Certificate of Secondary Education**) *noun*
= TGAU (*acronym for* **Tystysgrif °Gyffredinol Addysg Uwch**)

gear *noun*
• (*equipment*)
= offer *plural*
• (*clothes*)
= dillad *plural*
• (*of car*)
= gêr *masculine or feminine*

Gemini *noun*
= yr Efeilliaid *plural*

general
1 *adjective*
= cyffredinol

in general = yn °gyffredinol, fel rheol
2 *noun*
= cadfridog (*plural* -ion) *masculine*

generally *adverb*
= yn °gyffredinol, fel arfer

generation *noun*
= cenhedlaeth (*plural* cenedlaethau) *feminine*

generous *adjective*
= hael

genius *noun*
= athrylith (*plural* -oedd) *masculine*

gentle *adjective*
= caredig, tyner

gentleman *noun*
= bonheddwr (*plural* bonheddwyr) *masculine*

genuine *adjective*
= go iawn

> **!** *This phrase behaves like a true adjective and follows the noun it refers to:* **genuine leather** = lledr go iawn

geography *noun*
= daearyddiaeth *feminine*

germ *noun*
= eginyn (*plural* egin) *masculine*

German
1 *adjective*
= o'r Almaen, yr Almaen
2 *noun*
• (*language*)
= Almaeneg *feminine*
• (*man*)
= Almaenwr (*plural* Almaenwyr) *masculine*
(*woman*)
= Almaenes (*plural* -au) *feminine*

German measles *noun*
= brech °goch yr Almaen *feminine*

Germany *noun*
= yr Almaen *feminine*

> **!** *The word for* **the** *is part of the name of the country in Welsh—***they come from Germany** = maen nhw'n dod o'r Almaen.

get *verb*

> **!** *This verb poses translation problems because of its wide range of meanings in English. When in doubt, decide on an alternative in English and use this to pinpoint the correct choice in Welsh.*

- (*receive*)
  = cael *irregular*

> **! cael** *has irregular forms in the preterite, short future and conditional—see entry on the Welsh-English side for details.*

I got socks for Christmas = °ges i sanau i Nadolig
did you get the message? = °gest ti'r neges?
- (*become*)
  = mynd yn°, dod yn° (*rare*)
  it's getting late = mae'n mynd yn hwyr
  everything got too expensive = aeth popeth yn rhy °ddrud
- (*in passive*)
  = cael
  he got arrested by the police = fe °gafodd e ei arestio gan yr heddlu
  are you getting paid? = wyt ti'n cael dy °dalu?
- (*fetch*)
  = nôl, moyn
  go and get the milk = cer i nôl y llaeth
- (*arrive*)
  = cyrraedd (*stem* cyrhaedd-)
  we got there at nine = naethon ni °gyrraedd yno am naw
- (*prepare*)
  = paratoi
  I'll get dinner = na i °baratoi cinio
- (*catch—illnesses, transport etc*)
  = dal (*stem* dali-)
  I got a cold = nes i °ddal annwyd
  we'll have to get the bus = bydd rhaid inni °ddal y bws

get away (*escape*)
  = dianc (*stem* dihang-)

get back
  (*return*) = dod yn ôl, dychwelyd
  to get something back = cael rhywbeth yn ôl
  I'll get back to you = mi °ddo i'n ôl atoch chi

to get back at someone = talu'r pwyth i° rywun
get down
  = dod i lawr
get in (*car etc*)
  = dod/mynd i mewn i°
get off (*bus etc*)
  = dod/mynd allan o°
get on (*bus etc*)
  = dod/mynd i mewn i°
get out
  = dod/mynd (allan) o°
  get out of my sight! = dos o ⁿngolwg i!
get over (*overcome*)
  = meistroli, trechu
get through
  to get through to someone (*contact*) = cysylltu â⁰ rhywun
  to get through to someone (*make understand*) = gwneud i° rywun °ddeall
get together
  = ymgynnull (*stem* ymgynnull-)
get up (*out of bed*)
  = codi
  when do you get up? = pryd dych chi'n codi?

ghost *noun*
  = ysbryd (*plural* -ion) *masculine*

giant
1 *adjective*
  = anferth
2 *noun*
  = cawr (*plural* cewri) *masculine*

gift *noun*
  = anrheg (*plural* -ion) *feminine*, rhodd (*plural* -ion) *feminine*

ginger
1 *adjective*
  = melyngoch
2 *noun*
  = sinsir *masculine*

girl *noun*
  = merch (*plural* -ed) *feminine*, geneth (*plural* -od) *feminine*

girlfriend *noun*
  = cariad (*plural* -on) *feminine* (*but generally* y cariad)

give *verb*
= rhoi (*stem* rhoi-, rhodd-)
　to give something to someone = rhoi rhywbeth i⁰ rywun

give away
　(*for free*) = rhoi (*stem* rhoi-, rhodd-) yn anrheg

give back
= rhoi (*stem* rhoi-, rhodd-) yn ôl

give in
• (*capitulate*)
= ildio
• (*hand in*)
= rhoi (*stem* rhoi-, rhodd-) i mewn

give out (*distribute*)
= dosbarthu

give up (*abandon*)
= rhoi'r gorau i⁰
　to give up doing something = rhoi'r gorau i⁰wneud rhywbeth

give way (*traffic*)
= ildio

glad *adjective*
= balch
　to be glad to do something = bod yn ⁰falch o ⁰wneud rhywbeth

glade *noun*
= llannerch (*plural* llennyrch) *masculine or feminine*

glance
1 *noun*
= cipolwg (*plural* cipolygon) *masculine*
2 *verb*
　to glance at something = rhoi cipolwg ar⁰ rywbeth

glass *noun*
• (*material*)
= gwydr (*plural* -au) *masculine*
• (*vessel*)
= gwydr (*plural* -au) *masculine*, gwydryn (*plural* -nau) *masculine*
• (*glassful*)
= gwydraid (*plural* gwydreidiau) *masculine*
　will you have a glass of wine? = ⁰gymerwch chi ⁰wydraid o ⁰win?

glasses *plural noun*
= sbectol *feminine* (*singular*)

glove *noun*
= maneg (*plural* menig) *feminine*

glow *verb*
= tywynnu

glowing *adjective*
= llewyrchus

glue
1 *noun*
= glud (*plural* -ion) *masculine*
2 *verb*
= gludo

go *verb*
• (*general senses*)
= mynd (*irregular*)

> **! mynd** *has irregular forms in the preterite, short future, conditional and imperative—see entry on the Welsh-English side for details.*

　where are you going? = lle dych chi'n mynd?
　we're going to England = dyn ni'n mynd i ⁰Loegr
　how are things going? = sut mae pethau'n mynd?
　how did it go? = sut aeth hi?
• (*become*)
= mynd yn⁰
　he went red = mi aeth e'n ⁰goch

go across
= croesi

go ahead
= mynd ymlaen

go away
= mynd i ffwrdd (*North*), mynd bant (*South*)
　go away! = cer o 'ma! cerwch o 'ma!

go back
= mynd yn ôl

go by
= mynd heibio

go down
= mynd i lawr

go in
= mynd i mewn (i⁰)

go off
• (*explode*)
= ffrwydro
• (*go rotten*)
= pydru

go on
• (*go ahead*)
= mynd ymlaen

• (*continue, last*)
= para

go out
= mynd allan (*North*), mynd mas (*South*)

go over
= mynd dros/drosodd

go through
= mynd drwy/drwodd

go up
= mynd i fyny (*North*), mynd lan (*South*)

go with (*match*)
= cydfynd âʰ

goal *noun*
• (*in sport*)
= gôl (*plural* goliau) *feminine*

> **!** *Although feminine, this word does not lose its initial* **g-** *by soft mutation, either after the word for 'the' or in any other circumstances where soft mutation would be expected. So* (**gardd**) **yr °ardd**—*the garden, but* (**gôl**) **y gôl**—*the goal*

• (*aim*)
= nod (*plural* -au) *masculine or feminine*, amcan (*plural* -ion) *masculine*

goalkeeper *noun*
= golwr (*plural* golwyr) *masculine*
= gôl-geidwad (*plural* gôl-geidwaid) *masculine*

goat *noun*
= gafr (*plural* geifr) *feminine*

god *noun*
= duw (*plural* -iau) *masculine*
God knows! = Duw a °ŵyr!
God Almighty! = Duw mawr!, 'rargian!
for God's sake = er mwyn Duw
thank God! = diolch byth!
God forbid! = Duw a'n gwaredo!

goddaughter *noun*
= merch °fedydd (*plural* merched bedydd) *feminine*

goddess *noun*
= duwies (*plural* -au) *feminine*

godfather *noun*
= tad bedydd (*plural* tadau bedydd) *masculine*

godmother *noun*
= mam °fedydd (*plural* mamau bedydd) *feminine*

godson *noun*
= mab bedydd (*plural* meibion bedydd) *masculine*

gold *noun*
= aur *masculine*

goldfish *noun*
= pysgodyn coch (*plural* pysgod coch) *masculine*, pysgodyn aur (*plural* pysgod aur) *masculine*

golf *noun*
= golff *masculine*

> **!** **golff** *word does* not *lose its initial* **g-** *by soft mutation where this mutation would otherwise be expected. So* **what do you know about golf?** = beth wyt ti'n °wybod am° golff?

golf course *noun*
= maes golff (*plural* meysydd golff) *masculine*

good *adjective*
= da
good morning = bore da
good afternoon = prynhawn da
good evening = noswaith °dda
good night = nos da
it's no good shouting = does dim pwynt gweiddi
exercise is good for you = mae ymarfer corff yn gwneud lles
we had a good time = °gaethon ni amser da
it was good to meet you = roedd hi'n °dda cwrdd â chi
so good = cystal
as good as ... = cystal âʰ ...
I'm as good as you = dw i cystal â ti
for good (*forever*) = am byth

good-looking *adjective*
= golygus

goodbye *interjection*
= hwyl!, hwyl °fawr! da boch!
to say goodbye to someone = ffarwelio âʰ rhywun

Good Friday *noun*
= Dydd Gwener y °Groglith *masculine*

goods *noun*
= nwyddau *plural*
heavy goods vehicle = cerbyd (*plural* -au) nwyddau trwm *masculine*

goose *noun*
= gŵydd (*plural* gwyddau) *feminine*

gooseberry *noun*
= eirinen Mair (*plural* eirin Mair) *feminine*

gorilla *noun*
= gorila (*plural* -od) *masculine*

gossip
1 *noun*
• (*talk*)
= clecs *plural*
• (*person*)
= clebrwr (*plural* clebrwyr) *masculine*, cleciwr (*plural* clecwyr) *masculine*
2 *verb*
= clebran, hel clecs

got
⇒**get**
• **have got**:
I have got a car = mae gen i °gar (*North*), mae car 'da fi (*South*)
• **have got to** (*must*)
= rhaid
I have got to go = rhaid i mi °fynd

> **! rhaid** *is not a verb, and requires a different construction from English— see entry on the Welsh-English side for details and more examples.*

govern *verb*
= llywodraethu (ar°)

governing *adjective*
= llywodraethol
governing body = corff llywodraethol *masculine*

government *noun*
= llywodraeth (*plural* -au) *feminine*

governor *noun*
= llywodraethwr (*plural* llywodraethwyr) *masculine*

GP *noun*
= meddyg teulu (*plural* meddygon teulu) *masculine*

grab *verb*
= cipio, gafael (yn ⁿ)

to grab someone by the arm = gafael ym ⁿmraich rhywun

grade *noun*
• (*mark*)
= marc (*plural* -iau) *masculine*
to get good/poor grades = cael marciau da/gwael
• (*US: school class*)
= dosbarth (*plural* -au *or* -iadau) *masculine*

gradually *adverb*
= yn °raddol, °fesul tipyn

gram *noun*
= gram (*plural* -au) *masculine*

grammar *noun*
• (*structure of language*)
= gramadeg (*plural* -au) *masculine or feminine*
• (*book*)
= gramadeg (*plural* -au) *masculine*

grandchild *noun*
= ŵyr (*plural* wyrion) *masculine*
= wyres (*plural* -au) *feminine*

granddaughter *noun*
= wyres (*plural* -au) *feminine*

grandfather *noun*
= taid (*plural* teidiau) *masculine* (*North*), tad-cu (*plural* -od) *masculine* (*South*)

grandmother *noun*
= nain (*plural* neiniau) *feminine* (*North*), mam-gu (*plural* -od) *feminine* (*South*)

grandparents *noun*
his grandparents = ei °daid a'i nain (*North*), ei °deidiau a'i neiniau (*North*), ei °dad-cu a'i °fam-gu (*South*), ei °dad-cuod a'i °fam-guod (*South*)

grandson *noun*
= ŵyr (*plural* wyrion) *masculine*

grant
1 *noun*
= grant (*plural* -iau) *masculine*
2 *verb*
• **he was granted permission** = fe °gafodd e °ganiatâd
• (*acknowledge*)
= cydnabod (*stem* cydnabydd-)
I grant you this is true = dw i'n cydnabod °fod hyn yn °wir

to take something for granted =
cymryd (*stem* cymer-) rhywbeth yn
°ganiataol

grapefruit *noun*
= grawnffrwyth (*plural* -au) *masculine*

grapes *plural noun*
= grawnwin *plural*

grass *noun*
= glaswellt, gwair

grasshopper *noun*
= sioncyn y gwair (*plural* sioncod y
gwair) *masculine*

grateful *adjective*
= diolchgar
I would be grateful if you could.... =
byddwn i'n °ddiolchgar pe gallech
chi° ...

gratis *adjective*
= (yn) rhad ac am °ddim

grave
1 *noun*
= bedd (*plural* -au) *masculine*
2 *adjective*
= difrifol

graveyard *noun*
= mynwent (*plural* -ydd) *feminine*

gray (*US*) *adjective*
= llwyd

graze *verb*
= pori

grazing land *noun*
= porfa (*plural* porfeydd) *feminine*

grease *noun*
= saim *masculine*

greasy *adjective*
= seimllyd, seimlyd

great *adjective*
• (*big*)
= mawr
a great success = llwyddiant mawr
• (*splendid*)
= gwych
that's great! = mae hynny'n °wych!

Great Britain *noun*
= Prydain °Fawr *feminine*

great grandfather *noun*
= hendaid (*plural* hendeidiau)
masculine (*North*), hen °dad-cu (*plural* -
od) *masculine* (*South*)

great grandmother *noun*
= hen nain (*plural* hen neiniau) *feminine*
(*North*), hen °fam-gu (*plural* -od) *feminine*
(*South*)

greedy *adjective*
= barus, trachwantus

green *adjective*
• (*basic term*)
= gwyrdd (*feminine* gwerdd)
• (*of vegetation sometimes*)
= glas

greenhouse *noun*
= tŷ gwydr (*plural* tai gwydr) *masculine*

greenhouse effect *noun*
= effaith tŷ gwydr *feminine*

greeting *noun*
= cyfarchiad (*plural* cyfarchion)
masculine
Season's Greetings = Cyfarchion y
Tymor

grey *adjective*
= llwyd

greyhound *noun*
= milgi (*plural* milgwn) *masculine*

grill *verb*
= grilo, brwylio

grin
1 *noun*
= gwên (*plural* gwenau) *feminine*
2 *verb*
= gwenu

grind *verb*
= malu

groan *verb*
= ochneidio

grocer *noun*
= groser (*plural* -iaid) *masculine*
grocer's = siop groser
(*plural* siopau groseriaid) *feminine*

grocery *noun*
= siop groser (*plural* siopau groseriaid)
feminine

ground *noun*
= llawr *masculine*, daear *feminine*, tir
masculine
to burn to the ground = llosgi'n ulw

ground floor *noun*
= llawr isa(f) *masculine*

grounds *plural noun*
(*reason*) = achos *masculine*, sail *feminine*
on the grounds of something = o achos rhywbeth, oherwydd rhywbeth, ar sail rhywbeth

group
1 *noun*
= grŵp (*plural* grwpiau) *masculine*

> **!** **grŵp** *does not lose its initial* **g-** *by soft mutation in any circumstances where soft mutation would be expected. So* (**gorsaf**) *many stations* = **llawer o° orsafoedd**, *but* (**grŵp**) *many groups* = **llawer o° grwpiau**

2 *verb*
= grwpio

grove *noun*
= llwyn (*plural* -i) *masculine*

grow *verb*
• (*general sense*) = tyfu
(*of person*) = tyfu, prifio
• (*become*)
= mynd yn°
he has grown old = mae e wedi mynd yn hen
• (*increase*)
= cynyddu

grow up
= tyfu, prifio

growth *noun*
= twf *masculine*, tyfiant *masculine*, cynnydd *masculine*

grumble *verb*
= cwyno, achwyn

guarantee
1 *noun*
= gwarant (*plural* -au) *feminine*
2 *verb*
= gwarantu

guard
1 *noun*
= gwarchodwr (*plural* gwarchodwyr) *masculine*, ceidwad (*plural* ceidwaid) *masculine*
2 *verb*
= gwarchod

guard dog *noun*
= ci gwarchod (*plural* cŵn gwarchod) *masculine*

guess
1 *noun*
= amcan (*plural* -ion) *masculine*
2 *verb*
= dyfalu

guest *noun*
• (*general sense*)
= gwestai (*plural* gwesteion) *masculine*
• (*invitee*)
= gwestai (*plural* gwesteion) *masculine*, gwahoddedig (*plural* -ion) *masculine*

guesthouse *noun*
= gwesty (*plural* gwestai) *masculine*

guide
1 *noun*
• (*person*)
= arweinydd (*plural* -ion) *masculine*, arweinyddes (*plural* -au) *feminine*
• (*book*)
= arweinlyfr (*plural* arweinlyfrau) *masculine*
2 *verb*
= arwain (*stem* arweini-), tywys

guidebook *noun*
= teithlyfr (*plural* -au) *masculine*, arweinlyfr (*plural* -au) *masculine*

guide dog *noun*
= ci tywys (*plural* cŵn tywys) *masculine*

guided tour *noun*
= taith (*plural* teithiau) dan arweiniad *feminine*

guideline *noun*
= canllaw (*plural* -iau) *feminine or masculine*

guilty *adjective*
= euog
to feel guilty = teimlo'n euog

guinea pig *noun*
= mochyn cwta (*plural* moch cwta) *masculine*

guitar *noun*
= gitâr (*plural* gitarau) *masculine*

> **!** **gitâr** *does not lose its initial* **g-** *by soft mutation in any circumstances where soft mutation would be expected.*

gulf *noun*
= gwlff (*plural* gylffau) *masculine*

> **! gwlff** does not lose its initial **g-** by soft mutation in any circumstances where soft mutation would be expected.

gum noun
- (substance)
  = gwm masculine
- (of teeth)
  = cig y dannedd masculine

gun noun
- (general term)
  = gwn (plural gynnau) masculine

> **! gwn** does not normally lose its initial **g-** by soft mutation in circumstances where soft mutation would be expected.

- (hand-weapon only)
  = dryll (plural -iau) masculine

guts plural noun
= perfedd, perfeddion plural
he's got guts = mae e'n °ddewr, mae gynno fo iau (North)

gym noun
= campfa (plural campfeydd) feminine

gymnasium noun
= campfa (plural campfeydd) feminine

gymnastics noun
= gymnasteg feminine

gynaecologist noun
= gynecolegwr (plural gynecolegwyr) masculine
= gynecolegwraig (plural gynecolegwragedd) feminine

gynaecology noun
= gynecoleg feminine

gypsy noun
= sipsi (plural sipsiwn) masculine and feminine

Hh

habit noun
= arfer (plural -ion) masculine or feminine
to get into the habit of doing something = mynd i'r arfer o °wneud rhywbeth

hail noun
= cenllysg plural (North), cesair plural (South)
it's hailing = mae'n bwrw cenllysg/cesair

hair noun
- (on head)
  = gwallt masculine
- (single)
  = blewyn (plural blew) masculine
  he's having his hair cut = mae e'n cael torri ei °wallt
  you've had your hair cut! = ti wedi cael torri dy °wallt!
  she's got black hair = mae gynni hi °wallt du (North), mae gwallt du 'da hi (South)

hairbrush noun
= brws gwallt (plural brwsys gwallt) masculine

haircut noun
you've had a haircut! = dych chi wedi cael torri'ch gwallt!

hairdresser noun
= dynes trin gwallt (plural merched trin gwallt) feminine
= dyn trin gwallt (plural dynion trin gwallt) masculine

hairdryer noun
= peiriant (plural peiriannau) sychu gwallt masculine

hairstyle noun
= steil gwallt feminine

half noun
= hanner (plural hanerau, haneri) masculine
to cut an apple in half = torri afal yn ei hanner
half a pound of cheese = hanner pwys o °gaws

half of them speak Welsh = mae
hanner ohonyn nhw'n siarad Cymraeg
one-and-a half pounds = pwys a
hanner
two-and-a-half pounds = dau °bwys a
hanner

> **!** *In telling the time, 'half past...' is*
> *always* **hanner <u>awr</u> wedi**—*in contrast*
> *to* **chwarter wedi** *'a quarter past...'*
> **it's half past three** = mae'n hanner
> awr wedi tri

half-brother *noun*
= hanner brawd (*plural* hanner brodyr)
masculine

half-hour *noun*
= hanner awr *feminine*

half-sister *noun*
= hanner chwaer (*plural* hanner
chwiorydd) *feminine*

half term *noun*
= hanner tymor *masculine*

hall *noun*
• (*for meetings etc*)
= neuadd (*plural* -au) *feminine*
• (*in house*)
= cyntedd (*plural* -au) *masculine*

ham *noun*
= cig moch *masculine*
ham sandwich = brechdan (*plural* -au)
cig moch

hamburger *noun*
= eidionyn (*plural* eidionod) *masculine*,
hambyrgyr (*plural* -s) *masculine or
feminine*

hammer *noun*
= morthwyl (*plural* -ion) *masculine*

hamster *noun*
= bochdew (*plural* -ion) *masculine*,
llygoden °fochog (*plural* llygod bochog)
feminine

hand
1 *noun*
• (*part of body*)
= llaw (*plural* dwylo) *feminine*
to hold someone's hand = dal llaw
rhywun
• (*of clock*)
= bys (*plural* -edd) *masculine*

to give someone a hand = rhoi (*stem*
rhoi-, rhodd-) help llaw i° rywun,
helpu rhywun
on the other hand... = ar y llaw arall...
(both) hands up! = dwylo i fyny!
2 *verb*
to hand someone something = rhoi
(*stem* rhoi-, rhodd-) rhywbeth i
°rywun
to hand something in = rhoi (*stem*
rhoi-, rhodd-) rhywbeth i mewn
to hand out (*distribute*) = dosbarthu

handbag *noun*
= bag (*plural* -iau) llaw *masculine*

handball *noun*
(*game*) = pêl-law *feminine*

handbook *noun*
= llawlyfr (*plural* -au) *masculine*

handbrake *noun*
= brêc llaw *masculine*

handicapped *adjective*
= dan anfantais

handkerchief *noun*
= cadach (*plural* -au) *masculine*, hances
(*plural* -i) *feminine*

handle
1 *noun*
= braich (*plural* breichiau) *feminine*, coes
(*plural* -au) *masculine*, dolen (*plural* -ni)
feminine
2 *verb*
• (*deal with*)
= delio â^h
• (*feel, touch*)
= teimlo

handrail *noun*
= canllaw (*plural* -iau) *masculine or
feminine*

handsome *adjective*
= golygus

handwriting *noun*
= ysgrifen *feminine*, llawysgrifen
feminine

hang *verb*
• (*general sense*)
= hongian
to hang something on the wall =
hongian rhywbeth ar y wal

to be hanging on the wall = hongian ar y wal
- (*execute*)
= crogi

hang around
= loetran

hang on
= (*wait*) dal (*stem* dali-)
hang on a moment! = daliwch eiliad!

hang on to
- (*keep hold of*)
= dal (*stem* dali-) gafael yn^n rhywbeth
- (*keep*)
= cadw (*stem* cadw-)

hang up
- (*clothes etc*)
he hung his coat up = mi °roddodd e ei °gôt ar yr hoel
- (*phone*)
= rhoi (*stem* rhoi-, rhodd-) 'r ffôn i lawr
he hung up = mi °roddodd e'r ffôn i lawr

hang-gliding *noun*
= barcuta *verbnoun*

happen *verb*
= digwydd
what's happening? = beth sy'n digwydd?
what happened? = beth °ddigwyddodd?
what has happened? = beth sy wedi digwydd?
what happened to you? = beth °ddigwyddodd i ti?
as it happens = fel mae'n digwydd
as happens = fel sy'n digwydd

happiness *noun*
= llawenydd *masculine*, hapusrwydd *masculine*

happy *adjective*
- (*general sense*)
= hapus, balch
Happy Birthday! = Penblwydd Hapus!
Happy New Year! = Blwyddyn Newydd °Dda!
Happy Christmas! = Nadolig Llawen!
Happy Easter! = Pasg Hapus!
- (*satisfied*)
= bodlon
to be happy with something = bod yn °fodlon ar° rywbeth

harbour *noun*
= porthladd (*plural* -oedd) *masculine*, harbwr (*plural* -s) *masculine*

hard
1 *adjective*
- (*firm, solid*)
= caled
- (*difficult*)
= anodd, caled
2 *adverb*
to work hard = gweithio'n °galed
to try hard = gwneud ymdrech, ymdrechu
to be hard at it doing something = bod wrthi'n gwneud rhywbeth

hardback *noun*
= llyfr clawr caled (*plural* llyfrau clawr caled) *masculine*

hard-boiled *adjective*
a hard-boiled egg = ŵy wedi'i °ferwi'n °galed (*plural* wyau wedi'u berwi'n °galed) *masculine*

hardly *adverb*
- (*scarcely*)
= prin
they can hardly stay here = prin y gallan nhw aros fan hyn
we hardly know him = prin bod ni'n nabod e

> **! prin** *is generally followed by a* 'that...' *clause.*

- (*with pluperfect*)
hardly had he gone than ... = roedd e newydd °fynd pan°...

hardware *noun*
(*computers*)
= caledwedd *feminine or masculine*

hard-working *adjective*
= gweithgar

hare *noun*
= ysgyfarnog (*plural* -od) *feminine*, sgwarnog (*plural* -od) *feminine*

harm
1 *noun*
= niwed *masculine*
there's no harm in asking = waeth inni °ofyn (*North*), man a man inni °ofyn (*South*)
it won't do you any harm = neith hi °ddim drwg i ti

2 *verb*
= niweidio

harmful *adjective*
= niweidiol

harmless *adjective*
= diniwed

harp *noun*
= telyn (*plural* -au) *feminine*
to play the harp = canu'r °delyn

harpist *noun*
= telynor (*plural* -ion) *masculine*
= telynores (*plural* -au) *feminine*

harsh *adjective*
= garw, llym

harvest *noun*
= cynhaea(f) (*plural* cynaeafau)
masculine

hat *noun*
= het (*plural* -iau) *feminine*

hatch *verb*
= deor

hate *verb*
= casáu
I hate doing my homework = °gas gen i
°wneud ⁿngwaith cartre

hateful *noun*
= cas

hatred *noun*
= casineb *masculine*

have *verb*

> **!** *This verb poses translation
> problems because of its wide range
> of meanings in English. When in
> doubt, decide on an alternative in
> English and use this to pinpoint the
> correct choice in Welsh.*

• (*possess*) *no equivalent verb in Welsh*
I have got a new car = mae gen i °gar
newydd (*North*), mae car newydd 'da fi
(*South*)
have you got children? = oes gynnoch
chi °blant? (*North*), oes plant 'da chi?
(*South*)
we haven't got time = does gynnon ni
°ddim amser (*North*), does dim amser
'da ni (*South*)
• (*eat, drink*)
= cael (*irregular*)

I had eggs for breakfast = °ges i wyau i
°frecwast
• (*get, receive*)
= cael (*irregular*)
did you have any letters today? = °gest
ti °lythyrau heddiw?
• (*take*)
= cymryd (*stem* cymer-)
I'll have a dozen of these = °gymera i
°ddwsin o'r rheina
I'll have a glass of red wine = °gymera i
°wydraid o °win coch
what will you have? = beth °gymeri di?
• (*hold a function*)
= cynnal (*stem* cynhali-)
we're having a party tomorrow = dyn
ni'n cynnal parti yfory
• (*illness*)
Sioned has got a cold = mae annwyd
ar Sioned
I've got a headache = mae pen tost 'da
fi (*South*)
= mae gen i °gur (yn) ⁿmhen i (*North*)
• (*spend time*)
= cael (*irregular*), treulio
we had a pleasant week in Spain =
°dreulion ni wythnos °ddymunol yn
Sbaen
• (*get something done*)
= cael (*irregular*)
we're having the video fixed = dan ni'n
cael trwsio'r peiriant fideo
• (*auxiliary*)
we have arrived = dyn ni wedi cyrraedd
have you spoken to them? = wyt ti
wedi siarad â nhw?
• **have to** (*must*)
= rhaid, gorfod
we have to go now = rhaid inni °fynd
nawr, dan ni'n gorfod mynd nawr
do you have to wait? = oes rhaid i chi
aros?

hay *noun*
= gwair *masculine*

hay fever *noun*
= clefyd y gwair *masculine*

hazelnut *noun*
= cneuen °gyll (*plural* cnau cyll) *feminine*

he *pronoun*
= e, fe, o (*North*), fo (*North*), yntau,
fothau (*North*)
he's coming next week = mae e'n dod
wythnos nesa

there he is! = dyna/dacw fe!
he didn't write the letter = dim fe
sgrifennodd y llythyr

> **!** For details on the expanded forms
> **yntau** and **fothau**, see the entries on
> the Welsh-English side.

head
1 noun
• (part of body)
  = pen (plural -nau) masculine
• (chief)
  = pennaeth (plural penaethiaid)
  masculine
2 verb
• (be in charge of)
  = arwain (stem arweini-)
• (in football)
  = penio

head for
= anelu at°

headache noun
= pen tost, cur (yn y) pen (North)
I've got a headache = mae gen i °gur
(yn) ⁿmhen i (North)
= mae pen tost 'da fi (South)

headlamp, headlight noun
= lamp °flaen (plural lampau blaen)
feminine, golau blaen (plural goleuadau
blaen) masculine

headline noun
= pennawd (plural penawdau)
masculine

headphones plural noun
= clustffonau plural

headquarters pluralnoun
= pencadlys masculine or feminine

headteacher noun
= prifathro (plural prifathrawon)
masculine
= prifathrawes (plural -au) feminine

health noun
= iechyd masculine
good health! = iechyd da!
to be in good health = bod mewn
iechyd da
to have health problems = bod â
p(h)roblemau iechyd

healthy adjective
= iach

heap
1 noun
= pentwr (plural pentyrrau) masculine
2 verb
= pentyrru

hear verb
= clywed (stem clyw-)
I can't hear you = °alla i mo'ch clywed
chi
have you heard the news? = °glywsoch
chi'r newyddion?, dych chi wedi
clywed y newyddion?

> **!** **clywed** frequently, though
> optionally, adds an **-s-** between stem
> and plural preterite endings: **°glywest
> ti?** = did you hear?, _but_ **°glywoch chi**
> or **°glywsoch chi?** = did you hear?

hear about
= clywed (stem clyw-) am°

hear from:
have you heard from Aled? = wyt ti
wedi clywed gan/oddiwrth Aled?
you'll be hearing from my solicitors =
bydd ⁿnghyfreithwyr yn cysylltu â chi

hear of:
I've never heard of him = dw i erioed
wedi clywed amdano (fe)

heart noun
= calon (plural -nau) feminine
to lose heart = digalonni
to learn something by heart = dysgu
rhywbeth ar °gof
in the heart of London = yng ⁿnghanol
Llundain

heart attack noun
= trawiad (plural -au) ar y °galon
masculine

hearth noun
= aelwyd (plural -ydd) feminine

heat
1 noun
= gwres masculine
2 verb
= twymo, cynhesu

heater noun
= twymydd (plural -ion) masculine

heath noun
= rhos (plural -ydd) feminine

heating *noun*
= gwres *masculine*

heatwave *noun*
= gwres mawr (*plural* gwresogydd mawr) *masculine*

heave *verb*
• (*lift*)
= codi
• (*pull*)
= tynnu
• (*be very full of people*)
= berwi

heaven *noun*
= nefoedd *plural*
good heavens! = nefoedd °wen!
for heaven's sake! = neno'r nefoedd!

heavily *adverb*
to sleep heavily = cysgu'n °drwm
to rain heavily = bwrw glaw'n °drwm

heavy *adjective*
= trwm

hedge *noun*
= gwrych (*plural* -oedd) *masculine*, clawdd (*plural* cloddiau) *masculine*, sietyn (*plural* -nau) *masculine*

> ! Words for **'hedge'** vary widely from region to region.

hedgehog *noun*
= draenog (*plural* -od) *masculine*

heel *noun*
= sawdl (*plural* sodlau) *masculine or feminine*
Achilles' heel = sawdl Achil
to be on someone's heels = bod ar sodlau rhywun

hefty *adjective*
• (*kick, punch etc*)
= sylweddol
• (*book, document etc*)
= swmpus

height *noun*
• (*general sense*)
= uchder (*plural* -au) *masculine*
to be afraid of heights = ofni uchderau
• (*of person*)
= taldra *masculine*
what height are you? = beth ydy'ch taldra?

helicopter *noun*
= hofrennydd (*plural* hofrenyddion) *masculine*

hell *noun*
• = uffern *feminine*
• = (*as intensifier*) uffern, cythraul, coblyn, diawl
it's a hell of a thing = mae'n °goblyn o °beth
what the hell are you doing? = beth uffern/°gythraul wyt ti'n °wneud?
who the hell are you? = pwy uffern wyt ti?
go to hell! = cer i °gythraul/°ddiawl!
to work like hell = gweithio fel y diawl

hellish *adjective*
= uffernol
hellish expensive = uffernol o °ddrud
= andros o °ddrud

hello *exclamation*
= s'mae (*North*), siwmae! (*South*), shwmae! (*South*), hylo!

helm *noun*
at the helm = wrth y llyw

helmet *noun*
= helm (*plural* -au) *feminine*

help
1 *noun*
= cymorth *masculine*, help *masculine*
2 *verb*
= helpu, cynorthwyo
can I help you? = °alla i'ch helpu chi?
I can't help it = °alla i °ddim peidio
I can't help laughing = °alla i °ddim peidio (â) chwerthin
help yourselves! = helpwch eich hun! (*North*), helpwch eich hunain! (*South*)

helpful *adjective*
to be helpful to someone = bod o °gymorth i° rywun

helping *noun*
= platiad (*plural* plateidiau) *masculine*

helpless *adjective*
= digymorth

hen *noun*
= iâr (*plural* ieir) *feminine*

her
1 *pronoun*
• (*object pronoun*)
= hi, hithau

I know her = dw i'n nabod hi
catch her! = daliwch hi!
don't help her! = paid helpu hi!
• = ei[h] ... (hi) (*as object of verbnoun*)
  I can't hear her = °alla i mo'i [h]chlywed hi
  what about helping her? = beth am ei helpu hi?
• (*to her*)
  = iddi (hi), ati (hi)
  give her the book = rhowch y llyfr iddi (hi)
  I'll write her a letter = na i sgrifennu ati (hi)
2 *adjective*
  = ei[h] ... (hi); *after* i°: 'w[h]...(hi)
  her car = ei [h]char (hi)
  her shoes = ei sgidiau hi
  give them to her brother = rhowch nhw i'w brawd hi

> ! *For details on the expanded form* **hithau**, *see entry on the Welsh-English side.*

herb *noun*
= sawr-lysieuyn (*plural* sawr-lysiau) *masculine*

herd *noun*
= gyr (*plural* -roedd) *masculine*, buches (*plural* -au *or* -i) *feminine*

here *adverb*
• (*location or motion*)
  = yma ('ma), fan hyn, fan'ma, fam'ma
  who lives here? = pwy sy'n byw yma/fan hyn (etc)?
  is there anyone here? = oes unrhywun yma/fan hyn (etc)?

> ! **yma** *is the preferred standard term, while the regional variants* **fan hyn**, **fan'ma** *and* **fam'ma** *are all far more common in speech.*

• (*pointing out*)
  = dyma°
  here comes the bus = dyma'r bws
  here's Dafydd = dyma Dafydd
  here is the city centre = dyma °ganol y °ddinas

heritage *noun*
= etifeddiaeth *feminine*, treftadaeth *feminine*

hers *pronoun*
this is hers = hi (sy) biau hwn

our house is big but hers is small = mae'n tŷ ni'n °fawr ond mae un hi'n °fach

herself *pronoun*
= ei hunan (*South*), ei hun (*North*)
she'll do the work herself = neith hi'r gwaith ei hun(an)
she's by herself = mae hi ar °ben ei hun(an)

hesitate *verb*
= petruso, oedi

hi *exclamation*
= s'mae (*South*), siwmae! (*South*), shwmae! (*South*), hylo!

hiccups *plural noun*
I've got hiccups = mae'r ig arna i
= mae'r igian arna i

> ! *This expression denoting a temporary physical state uses* **ar°** + *person.*

hidden *adjective*
= cudd

hide *verb*
= cuddio

high *adjective*
= uchel
high school (*secondary school*) = ysgol uwchradd (*plural* ysgolion uwchradd) *feminine*

highland *noun*
= ucheldir (*plural* -oedd) *masculine*
the Highlands = Ucheldiroedd yr Alban

highlights *plural noun*
(*of performance etc*) = uchafbwyntiau *plural*

highrise block *noun*
= tŵr fflatiau (*plural* tyrau fflatiau) *masculine*

high season *noun*
= adeg °brysur (*plural* adegau prysur) *feminine*

high tide *noun*
= penllanw *masculine*

highway *noun*
= priffordd (*plural* priffyrdd) *feminine*

hijack

1 *noun*
= herwgipiad (*plural* -au) *masculine*
2 *verb*
= herwgipio

hike

1 *noun*
= crwydr (*plural* -au) *masculine*, heic (*plural* -iau) *feminine*
2 *verb*
= heicio, crwydro

hill *noun*
= bryn (*plural* -iau) *masculine*, rhiw (*plural* -iau) *feminine*

him *pronoun*

• (*object pronoun*)
= e, fe, o (*North*), fo (*North*), yntau, fothau (*North*)
I haven't seen him = dw i heb °weld e
we'll go with him = awn ni gyda fe
do you know him? = dych chi'n nabod e?
will you help him? = newch chi helpu fe?
• = ei° ... (e/fe) (*as object of verbnoun*)
do you want to see him? = dych chi eisiau ei °weld e?
what about supporting him? = beth am ei °gefnogi (fe)?
• (*to him*)
= iddo (fe), ato (fe)
give him the message = rhowch y neges iddo (fe)
did you show him the map? = nest ti °ddangos y map iddo (fe)?
I wrote him a letter = nes i sgrifennu ato (fe)

> **!** *For details on the expanded forms* **yntau** *and* **fothau**, *see the entries on the Welsh-English side.*

himself *pronoun*
= ei hunan (*South*), ei hun (*North*)
he did the work himself = naeth e'r gwaith ei hun(an)
he is by himself = mae e ar °ben ei hun(an)

hinder *verb*
= llesteirio

hindrance *noun*
= llesteiriant *masculine*

hip *noun*
= clun (*plural* -iau) *feminine*

hippopotamus, hippo *noun*
= hipopotamws (*plural* hipopotamysau) *masculine*

hire

1 *verb*
= llogi
2 *noun*
on hire = ar °log
for hire = i'w °logi (*masculine*)
= i'w llogi (*feminine*)
= i'w llogi (*plural*)
car-hire company = cwmni llogi ceir (*plural* cwmnïau llogi ceir) *masculine*

his

1 *adjective*
= ei° ... (hi); *after* i°: 'w° ... (e/fe)
his car = ei °gar (e)
his shoes = ei sgidiau fe
give them to his brother = rhowch nhw i'w °frawd e
2 *pronoun*
this is his = fe (sy) biau hwn
our house is big but his is small = mae'n tŷ ni'n °fawr ond mae un fe'n °fach

historical *adjective*
= hanesyddol

history *noun*
= hanes (*plural* -ion) *masculine*

hit

1 *verb*
= curo, taro (*stem also* traw-), bwrw
2 *noun*
• (*blow*)
= ergyd (*plural* -ion) *feminine or masculine*
• (*success: song, film etc*)
= llwyddiant (*plural* llwyddiannau) *masculine*

hit back
= taro'n ôl

hitch *noun*
without a hitch = yn °ddidrafferth

hitchhike *verb*
= bodio

hitchhiker *noun*
= bodiwr (*plural* bodwyr) *masculine*

hoarse *adjective*
= cryg

hobby *noun*
= hobi (*plural* -s or hobïau) *masculine*

hockey *noun*
= hoci *masculine*

hold
1 *verb*
• (*most senses*)
= dal (*stem* dali-)
to hold hands = dal dwylo
to hold the line = dal y lein
• (*function*)
= cynnal (*stem* cynhali-)
the meeting will be held tomorrow = cynhelir y cyfarfod yfory
• (*keep, detain, save*)
= cadw
to hold a seat for someone = cadw sedd i° rywun
2 *noun*
• (*grip*)
= gafael (*plural* -ion) *feminine*
• (*of ship*)
= howld (*plural* -iau) *feminine*

hold on:
hold on a moment! = daliwch eiliad!

hold on to:
to hold on to something = dal (*stem* dali-) gafael ynⁿ rhywbeth

hold up
(*delay*) = dal (*stem* dali-), rhwystro, atal

hole *noun*
= twll (*plural* tyllau) *masculine*

holiday *noun*
= gwyliau *plural*
a month's holiday = mis o °wyliau

holidays *plural noun*
= gwyliau *plural*

home
1 *noun*
= cartre(f) (*plural* cartrefi) *masculine*
to make a home for oneself = ymgartrefu
make yourself at home! = gwna dy hun yn °gartrefol!
he lives at home = mae e'n byw gartre
to feel at home = teimlo'n °gartrefol
2 *adverb*
• (*homewards*)
= adre
on the way home = ar y ffordd adre
we took them home = aethon ni â nhw adre

• (*at home*)
= gartre
are they home this evening? = ydyn nhw gartre heno?

> **!** *The distinction between* **adre** *(motion) and* **gartre** *(location) is often disregarded in speech, with either word being used for both meanings according to region.*

homeless *adjective*
= digartre(f)

homesick *adjective*
I'm homesick = mae hiraeth arna i

homework *noun*
= gwaith cartre(f) *masculine*

homosexual
1 *adjective*
= cyfunrhywiol
2 *noun*
= gwrywgydiwr (*plural* gwrywgydwyr) *masculine*
= lesbiad (*plural* lesbiaid) *feminine*

honest *adjective*
= gonest
to be honest, I'm not sure = a dweud y gwir, dw i °ddim yn siwr
I'll be there in a minute, honest! = bydda i 'na mewn munud, wir i ti!

honestly *adverb*
= yn °onest

honey *noun*
= mêl *masculine*

honeymoon *noun*
= mis mêl (*plural* misoedd mêl) *masculine*

honour *noun*
= anrhydedd (*plural* -au) *masculine or feminine*
on my (word of) honour = ar 'yn llw

hood *noun*
• (*of garment*)
= cwf(w)l (*plural* cyflau) *masculine*
• (*US: bonnet of car*)
= boned (*plural* -i, -au) *feminine or masculine*

hoof *noun*
= carn (*plural* -au) *masculine*

hook *noun*
= bach (*plural* -au) *masculine*

hooligan *noun*
= hwligan (*plural* -iaid) *masculine*

hoover®
1 *noun*
= hwfer (*plural* -s, hwfrau) *masculine*,
sugnwr llwch *masculine*
2 *verb*
= hwfro

hop *verb*
= hopian, neidio

hope
1 *noun*
= gobaith (*plural* gobeithion) *masculine*
2 *verb*
= gobeithio
I hope you're feeling better = gobeithio
bod chi'n teimlo'n °well
we hope to be there later = dyn ni'n
gobeithio bod yno nes ymlaen
I hope so = gobeithio

hopefully *adverb*
(*I/we hope*)
= gobeithio

hopeless *adjective*
• (*without hope*)
= diobaith
• (*useless, futile*)
= anobeithiol

horizon *noun*
= gorwel (*plural* -ion) *masculine*

horn *noun*
= corn (*plural* cyrn) *masculine*

horoscope *noun*
= horosgop (*plural* -au) *masculine*

horrible *adjective*
= erchyll, ofnadwy

horrid *adjective*
= ffiaidd, ofnadwy

horror *noun*
= arswyd *masculine*

horror film *noun*
= ffilm arswyd (*plural* ffilmiau arswyd)
feminine

horse *noun*
= ceffyl (*plural* -au) *masculine*

horseman *noun*
= marchog (*plural* -ion) *masculine*

horseriding *noun*
= marchogaeth *verbnoun*

horseshoe *noun*
= pedol (*plural* -au) *feminine*

hospital *noun*
= ysbyty (*plural* ysbytai) *masculine*
to take someone to hospital = mynd â[h]
rhywun i'r ysbyty
three people were taken to hospital =
aethpwyd â tri o °bobol i'r ysbyty
to be in hospital = bod yn yr ysbyty

> **!** **'to hospital'** *and* **'in hospital'**
> *always require the word for* **'the'** *in*
> *Welsh.*

host *noun*
• (*large number of people*)
= llu (*plural* -oedd) *masculine*
• (*at party etc*)
= gwahoddwr *masculine*,
gwahoddwraig *feminine*

hostage *noun*
= gwystl (*plural* -on) *masculine*
to take/hold someone hostage =
cymryd (*stem* cymer-)/dal (*stem* dali-)
rhywun yn °wystl

hostel *noun*
= llety (*plural* -au) *masculine*, hostel
(*plural* -au or -i) *feminine*

hostess *noun*
= gwahoddwraig *feminine*

hostile *adjective*
= gelyniaethus

hot *adjective*
• = poeth, twym
it's too hot here = mae'n rhy °boeth fan
hyn
• (*spicy etc*)
= poeth

hot air balloon *noun*
= balŵn awyr poeth (*plural* balwnau
awyr poeth) *masculine or feminine*

hot dog *noun*
= ci poeth (*plural* cŵn poeth) *masculine*

hotel *noun*
= gwesty (*plural* gwestai) *masculine*

hour *noun*
= awr (*plural* oriau) *feminine*

I've been here for hours = dw i fan hyn ers oriau

an hour and a half = awr a hanner

60 miles an hour = chwedeg mya (milltir yr awr)

house noun
= tŷ (*plural* tai) *masculine*

terraced house = tŷ teras

semi-detached house = tŷ semi

detached house = tŷ sengl

housewife noun
= gwraig tŷ (*plural* gwragedd tŷ) *feminine*

housework noun
= gwaith tŷ *masculine*

housing development noun
= (y)stad °dai (*plural* (y)stadau tai) *feminine*

housing estate noun
= (y)stad °dai (*plural* (y)stadau tai) *feminine*

hovercraft noun
= hofrenfad (*plural* -au) *masculine*

how adverb
• (*in what way*)

= sut; ffordd (*colloquial*), fel (*rare*)

how are the family these days? = sut mae'r teulu dyddiau 'ma?

how did you get here? = sut dest ti fan hyn?

it depends how he's feeling = mae'n dibynnu sut mae'n teimlo

how do you know? = ffordd ych chi'n gwybod?

funny how these things happen = rhyfedd fel mae'r pethau 'ma'n digwydd

• (*+ adjective*)

= pa mor° ...?, mor° ...

how big? = pa mor °fawr?

did you see how expensive it was? = °welest ti mor °gostus oedd e?

• (*exclamations*)

= 'na° ...!

how kind! = 'na °garedig!

how pretty! = 'na °bert!

however adverb
• (*nevertheless*)

= er hynny, serch hynny

• (*in whatever way*)

= °fodd bynnag, sut bynnag

however they do it... = sut bynnag maen nhw'n gwneud e...

• (*+ adjective*)

= er mor°

however expensive it is... = er mor °ddrud yw e

how many
= faint, sawl

1 *adjective*

how many children have you got? = faint o °blant sy 'da chi?, sawl plentyn sy 'da chi?

how many people are going? = faint o °bobol sy'n mynd?

> **!** *This quantity expression requires* **o°** *before the people or things counted.*

2 *pronoun*

how many would you like? = faint hoffech chi?

how many are coming? = faint sy'n dod?

how many is he inviting? = faint mae'n gwahodd?

I don't care how many are here = dim ots gen i faint sy 'ma

how much
= faint

1 *adjective*

how much cheese do you want? = faint o °gaws dych chi eisiau?

how much money have you got? = faint o arian sy 'da chi?

> **!** *This quantity expression requires* **o°** *before the people or things counted.*

2 *pronoun*

how much is that? = faint ydy hwnna?

how much would you like? = faint hoffech chi?

how much is needed? = faint sy angen?

huge adjective
= anferth, enfawr, aruthrol

human
1 *adjective*

= dynol

2 *noun*

= bod dynol (*plural* bodau dynol) *masculine*

human being noun
= bod dynol (*plural* bodau dynol) *masculine*

hundred *numeral*
  = cant, (*before singular nouns*) can
  a hundred = cant
  a hundred and one = cant ag un
  a hundred and sixty-four = cant
    chwedeg pedwar
  a hundred people = cant o °bobol
  a hundred miles = can milltir
  a hundred pounds = can punt, cant o
    °bunnoedd
  a hundred apples = cant o afalau
  a hundred years = can ⁿmlynedd
    = cant o °flynyddoedd
  a hundred years old = cant oed

hunger *noun*
- (*day-to-day*)
  = eisiau bwyd *masculine*
- (*starvation*)
  = newyn *masculine*

hungry *adjective*
  I'm hungry = mae eisiau bwyd arna i

  > ! *This expression denoting a*
  > *temporary physical state uses* **ar°** +
  > *person.*

hunt
  1 *verb*
  = hela
  2 *noun*
  = helfa (*plural* helfeydd) *feminine*

hurdle *noun*
  = clwyd (*plural* -i, -au) *feminine*

hurray *noun and exclamation*
  = hwrê *feminine*

hurry *verb*
  = brysio
  to be in a hurry = bod ar °frys
  hurry up! = brysia!, brysiwch!

hurt *verb*
- (*be hurting*)
  = rhoi dolur
  my arm hurts = mae ⁿmraich i'n rhoi
    dolur
- (*do physical damage to*)
  = brifo
  he's hurt his leg = mae e wedi brifo ei
    °goes
  did you hurt yourself? = °gest ti
    °ddolur?

husband *noun*
  = gŵr (*plural* gwŷr) *masculine*

hygiene *noun*
  = glendid *masculine*, glanweithdra
  masculine

hygienic *adjective*
  = glanwaith

hypocrisy *noun*
  = rhagrith *masculine*

hypocrite *noun*
  = rhagrithiwr (*plural* rhagrithwyr)
  masculine

hypocritical *adjective*
  = rhagrithiol

Ii

I *pronoun*
= i, fi, mi; innau, finnau, minnau
here I am = dyma fi
I'm responsible for this = fi sy'n °gyfrifol am hyn
she drives but I don't = mae hi'n gyrru ond dw i °ddim
I saw this film last week = °weles i'r ffilm 'ma wythnos diwetha
I have to go now = rhaid i mi °fynd nawr

> ! *The basic forms* **i, fi** *and* **mi** *are by and large not interchangeable—see entries on the Welsh-English side for details. Similarly for the much less frequently occurring emphatic forms* **innau, finnau** *and* **minnau**—*see entries on the Welsh-English side for more details on these.*

ice *noun*
= iâ *masculine*, rhew *masculine*

ice cream *noun*
= hufen iâ *masculine*

ice hockey *noun*
= hoci iâ *or* hoci rhew *masculine*

ice rink *noun*
= rinc iâ (*plural* rinciau iâ) *masculine or feminine*, llawr iâ (*plural* lloriau iâ) *masculine*

ice-skate
1 *noun*
= esgid sglefrio (*plural* sgidiau sglefrio) *feminine*
2 *verb*
= sglefrio ar iâ / °rew

ice-skating *noun*
= sglefrio ar iâ *or* sglefrio ar °rew *verbnoun*

icing *noun*
= eisin *masculine*

idea *noun*
= syniad (*plural* -au) *masculine*, amcan (*plural* -ion) *masculine*
what a good idea! = 'na syniad da!

I've no idea = does gen i °ddim syniad (*North*)
= does dim clem 'da fi (*South*)

ideal *adjective*
= delfrydol
to be ideal for someone = bod yn °ddelfrydol i° rywun

idealistic *adjective*
= delfrydol

identity *noun*
= hunaniaeth (*plural* -au) *feminine*

identity card *noun*
= cerdyn adnabod (*plural* cardiau adnabod) *masculine*

identity crisis *noun*
= argyfwng hunaniaeth *masculine*

idiot *noun*
= twpsyn *masculine*

if *conjunction*

> ! *Welsh uses different words for* **'if'**, *and different constructions, depending on whether the condition stated is open (possible but not certain) or closed (hypothetical). See* **If** *box for more details and examples.*

- (*open conditions*)
= os
if you see him, let me know = os gweli di fo, rho °wybod i mi
if he's ill, we'd better not go = os ydy e'n sâl, well inni °beidio mynd
if he's ill tomorrow, we'll ... = os bydd e'n sâl yfory, byddwn ni'n ...
- (*closed conditions*)
= pe, t-
if I saw her, I'd ... = pe byddwn i'n gweld hi, byddwn i'n ...
= taswn i'n gweld hi, byddwn/baswn i'n ...
if he were here, ... = pe byddai fe fan hyn ...
if you could help, ... = pe gallech chi helpu, ...
- (*indirect questions*)
= a° (*often silent*)

> ! *This use of* 'if' *in English to mean* 'whether' *has nothing to do with open or closed conditions. In this case it is translated by* **a°**.

If

Welsh has two words for if—**os** for open conditions, where the likelihood or not of fulfilment is more balanced ('If he is here, I will tell him'); and **pe** for closed or hypothetical conditions which are not regarded as likely to be fulfilled ('If he were here, I would tell him'), They are distinguished in English by the verb in the other half of the sentence (future or imperative with open conditions; conditional with closed conditions).

OPEN CONDITIONS

The sequences of tenses for open conditions in Welsh and English differ:
(English)   *if* + present, future/imperative
(Welsh)   **os** + future (sometimes present), future/imperative
os bydd y trên yn hwyr, byddwn ni'n colli'r gêm = *if the train is late, we'll miss the game*
os eith popeth yn °ddidrafferth...
= *if everything goes without a hitch...*
(literally: *'if everything will go...'*)
Note the difference between the following, both corresponding to present in English:
os ydy Gwenith yn sâl, gadewch inni aros tan yfory = *if Gwenith is ill* (i.e right now), *let's wait till tomorrow*
os bydd Gwenith yn sâl, bydd rhaid inni ailfeddwl = *if Gwenith is ill (tomorrow), we'll have to think again*
Other tense sequences are, however, possible so long as the criterion of open condition is maintained:
os aethon nhw ddoe, yna mae'n rhy hwyr, on'd ydy? = *if they went yesterday, then it's too late, isn't it?*
In the 3rd person singular present tense, **os** is always followed by **ydy**, not **mae**. Negatives with **os** (i.e clauses involving 'if...not...' in English) use **os na°** (or ʰ), **os nad** before original vowels:
os nad ydyn nhw'n °barod, gadewch inni °fynd hebddyn nhw = *if they're not ready, let's go without them*

os na °fydd gynnoch chi °ddigon o amser... = *if you don't have enough time...*
os na °ddôn nhw, be' nawn ni? = *if they don't come, what shall we do?*

CLOSED CONDITIONS

The sequences of tenses for closed conditions in Welsh and English also differ:
(English)   *if* + past (really a subjunctive), conditional
(Welsh)   **pe** + conditional, conditional
pe generally combines with the conditional of ⇒**bod**, which has two main variants:

pe baswn i	**pe byddwn i**	if I were
pe baset ti	**pe byddet ti**	if you were
pe basai fe/hi	**pe byddai fe/hi**	if he/she were
pe basen ni	**pe bydden ni**	if we were
pe basech chi	**pe byddech chi**	if you were
pe basen nhw	**pe bydden nhw**	if they were

In addition, the following variants occur widely in speech in various areas:

pe bawn i	pe tawn i	tawn i	pe taswn i	taswn i
pe baet ti	pe taet ti	taet ti	pe taset ti	taset ti
pe bai fe/hi	pe tai fe/hi	tai fe/hi	pe tasai fe/hi	tasai fe/hi
pe baen ni	pe taen ni	taen ni	pe tasen ni	tasen ni
pe baech chi	pe taech chi	taech chi	pe tasech chi	tasech chi
pe baen nhw	pe taen nhw	taen nhw	pe tasen nhw	tasen nhw

The abbreviated variant **taswn i** etc is very common—in this case the **pe** has been dropped, but its presence is understood. Note that all of the above have in common the unreality set of endings that we also see in other hypothetical verb uses such as ⇒**dylwn i** etc 'ought/should', **gallwn i** etc (⇒**gallu**) 'could/would be able' and **hoffwn i/leiciwn i** etc (⇒**hoffi**, ⇒**leicio**) 'would like'.
pe byddai'r lleill fan hyn, gallen ni °ddechrau = *if the others were here, we could start*

If continued

taswn i'n °gyfoethog, 'swn i °ddim yn aros yn y swydd 'ma = *if I were rich, I wouldn't stay in this job*

pe bai hi yno, byddai rhaid esbonio iddi, on' byddai? = *if she were there, it would have to be explained to her, wouldn't it?*

byddai'r cyngor yn cytuno pe byddai'r arian ar °gael = *the council would agree if the money were available*

'sai hynny'n iawn efallai petai pawb yn cydweithio = *that would be OK perhaps if everybody cooperated*

pe bydden nhw'n colli'r bws, byddai rhaid inni °fynd i'w nôl nhw = *if they missed the bus, we'd have to go and fetch them*

(*compare:* os byddan nhw'n colli'r bws, bydd rhaid inni °fynd i'w nôl nhw = *if they miss the bus, we'll have to go and fetch them (open condition)*)

pe baen ni'n methu, fe °fydden ni'n trio eto = *if we failed, we would try again*

Note also the set phrase **fel petai** 'as it were':

mae hi wedi mynd drwy'r °felin, fel petai = *she's been through the mill, as it were*

pe can also be used with other unreality verbs, notably **gallwn i** etc:

'swn i'n helpu pe gallwn i = *I would help if I could*

Using the unreality endings on ordinary verbs in place of the construction **bod-**conditional + verbnoun (i.e saying **pe syrthiet ti** for **pe baset ti'n syrthio** 'if you fell') is very unusual in the modern language, and so therefore is the use of **pe** with ordinary verbs.

---

go and ask if they're ready = cer i °ofyn (a) ydyn nhw'n °barod

I don't know if they'll come = dw i °ddim yn gwybod (a) °ddôn nhw

ignite *verb*
= cynnau, tanio

ignorant *adjective*
= anwybodus

ignore *verb*
= anwybyddu

ill *adjective*
= sâl, gwael, tost
I feel ill = dw i'n teimlo'n sâl/°wael/°dost

illegal *adjective*
= anghyfreithlon

illness *noun*
= salwch *masculine*, gwaeledd *masculine*

illustration *noun*
• (*picture*)
= darlun (*plural* -iau) *masculine*, llun (*plural* -iau) *masculine*
• (*example*)
= enghraifft (*plural* enghreifftiau) *feminine*

imagination *noun*
= dychymyg (*plural* dychmygion) *masculine*

imagine *verb*
• (*use imagination*)
= dychmygu
• (*suppose*)
= tybio

imitate *verb*
= efelychu

immediately *adverb*
= ar unwaith, yn syth, yn °ddi-oed, yn y °fan

immense *adjective*
= aruthrol

immerse *verb*
to immerse something in something = trochi rhywbeth yn^n rhywbeth
to immerse oneself = ymdrochi

immigrant *noun*
= mewnfudwr (*plural* mewnfudwyr) *masculine*, dyn dŵad (*plural* dynion dŵad) *masculine*
= gwraig °ddŵad (*plural* gwragedd dŵad) *feminine*

= pobol °ddŵad *plural*

immigration *noun*
= mewnfudiad (*plural* -au) *masculine*,
mewnfudo *verbnoun*

immovable *adjective*
• (*most senses*)
= ansymudol
• (*stuck*)
= sownd

impatient *adjective*
= diamynedd

impel *verb*
= ysgogi

impolite *adjective*
= anghwrtais

import
1 *verb*
= mewnforio
2 *noun*
= mewnforyn (*plural* mewnforion)
masculine

importance *noun*
= pwysigrwydd *masculine*

important *adjective*
= pwysig, o °bwys
it's important = mae'n °bwysig
= mae o °bwys
it's important that they come = mae'n
°bwysig bod nhw'n dod
important people = pobol o °bwys

impossible *adjective*
= amhosib(l)
it's impossible to say at the moment =
mae'n amhosib dweud ar hyn o °bryd

impress *verb*
to be impressed by something = cael
argraff °dda o° rywbeth

impression *noun*
= argraff (*plural* -ion) *feminine*
to make an impression on someone =
gwneud argraff ar °rywun

impressive *adjective*
= trawiadol

imprison *verb*
= carcharu

improve *verb*
= gwella

improvement *noun*
= gwelliant (*plural* gwelliannau)
masculine

in
1 *preposition*

> **!** There are two words in Welsh for
> location **'in'** a place—one is used with
> specific nouns, and the other with
> non-specific nouns. For more details
> on the difference, and more
> examples, see entries on the Welsh-
> English side.

• (*with specific nouns*)
= yn[n]
in the room = yn y stafell
in Wales = yng [n]Nghymru
in your garden = yn eich gardd chi
• (*with non-specific nouns*)
= mewn
in a room = mewn stafell
in other countries = mewn gwledydd
eraill
• (*at the end of a period of time*)
= ymhen
we'll be back in half an hour = byddwn
ni yn ôl ymhen hanner awr
2 *adverb*
= i mewn
come in! = dewch i mewn!
in we go! = i mewn â ni!
she's not in = dyw hi °ddim i mewn

inadequate *adjective*
= annigonol

inch *noun*
= modfedd (*plural* -i) *feminine*

incident *noun*
= digwyddiad (*plural* -au) *masculine*

incidentally *adverb*
= gyda llaw

include *verb*
= cynnwys (*stem* cynhwys-)

including *preposition*
= gan °gynnwys

income *noun*
= incwm (*plural* incymau) *masculine*

income tax *noun*
= treth incwm *feminine*

incompetent *adjective*
= analluog, anghymwys

inconsiderate *adjective*
= anystyriol

to be inconsiderate of someone = bod yn anystyriol o° rywun

inconvenient *adjective*
= anghyfleus
I hope that's not inconvenient for you
= gobeithio °fod hynny °ddim yn anghyfleus i chi

incorrect *adjective*
= anghywir

increase
1 *noun*
= cynnydd *masculine*, twf *masculine*
2 *verb*
• (*become larger*)
= cynyddu, tyfu, codi
• (*make larger*)
= codi

increasing *adjective*
= cynyddol

incredible *adjective*
= anhygoel
that's incredible! = mae hynny'n anhygoel!

independence *noun*
= annibyniaeth *feminine*

independent *adjective*
= annibynnol

index *noun*
= mynegai (*plural* mynegeion) *masculine or feminine*

indicate *verb*
• (*point to*)
= dangos
• (*make known*)
= mynegi
• (*give signal in car*)
= rhoi (*stem* rhoi-, rhodd-) arwydd

indifferent *adjective*
• (*uninterested*)
= difater
• (*mediocre*)
= canolig

indigestion *noun*
I've got indigestion = mae diffyg traul arna i

> ! *This expression denoting a temporary physical state uses* **ar°** + *person.*

individual
1 *adjective*
= unigol, neilltuol
2 *noun*
= unigolyn (*plural* unigolion) *masculine*

indoor *adjective*
= dan °do

indoor pool *noun*
= pwll dan °do (*plural* pyllau dan °do) *masculine*

indoors *adverb*
= yn y tŷ, tu °fewn

industrial *adjective*
= diwydiannol

industrial estate *noun*
= ystad °ddiwydiannol (*plural* ystadau diwydiannol) *feminine*

industry *noun*
= diwydiant (*plural* diwydiannau) *masculine*

inevitable *adjective*
= anochel, diosgoi

infant school *noun*
= ysgol plant bach (*plural* ysgolion plant bach) *feminine*

infection *noun*
= haint (*plural* heintiau) *masculine or feminine*, heintiad (*plural* au) *masculine*

inflation *noun*
= chwyddiant *masculine*

influence
1 *noun*
= dylanwad (*plural* -au) *masculine*
2 *verb*
= dylanwadu
to influence someone/something = dylanwadu ar° rywun/rywbeth

inform *verb*
= rhoi gwybod i°, hysbysu
to inform someone of something = rhoi gwybod i° rywun am° rywbeth
= hysbysu rhywun o° rywbeth
will you keep me informed? = newch chi °adael i mi °wybod beth sy'n digwydd?
they informed the authorities = fe °roddon nhw °wybod i'r awdurdodau

informal *adjective*
= anffurfiol

information noun
= gwybodaeth feminine

information desk noun
= desg °wybodaeth (plural desgiau gwybodaeth) feminine

information technology noun
= technoleg gwybodaeth feminine

infrequent adjective
= anaml

ingredients plural noun
= cynhwysion plural

inhabitants noun
= trigolion plural (no singular)

inherit verb
= etifeddu

inheritance noun
= etifeddiaeth (plural -au) feminine

injection noun
= pigiad (plural -au) masculine, chwistrelliad (plural -au) masculine

injure verb
= anafu

injured adjective
= wedi'i anafu masculine
= wedi'i hanafu feminine
= wedi'u hanafu plural

injury noun
= anafiad (plural -au) masculine

ink noun
= inc (plural -iau) masculine

innings noun
(cricket)
= batiad (plural -au) masculine

innocent adjective
• (not guilty)
= dieuog
• (harmless)
= diniwed

innumerable adjective
= diri(f)

inoculate verb
= brechu

inoculation noun
= brechiad (plural -au) masculine

inquire verb
= holi, ymholi

to inquire about something = holi or ymholi ynglŷn â^h rhywbeth

inquiry noun
• (request for information)
= ymholiad (plural -au) masculine
to make inquiries about something = holi or ymholi ynglŷn â^h rhywbeth
• (investigation)
= ymchwiliad (plural -au) masculine

insect noun
= pry(f) (plural pryfed) masculine; (technical term) trychfilyn (plural trychfilod) masculine

inside
1 preposition
= (y) tu °fewn i°, (y) tu mewn i°
inside the building = tu °fewn i'r adeilad
2 noun
= tu °fewn, tu mewn
on the inside of something = tu °fewn or mewn i° rywbeth
3 adverb
= i mewn
come inside! = dewch i mewn!
4 adjective
= o'r tu °fewn or mewn
inside information = gwybodaeth o'r tu °fewn or mewn
inside out = (y) tu mewn allan

insist verb
= mynnu
to insist on doing something = mynnu gwneud rhywbeth

inspect verb
= archwilio

inspector noun
= arolygydd (plural -ion) masculine, arolygwr (plural arolygwyr) masculine

inspiration noun
= ysbrydoliaeth feminine

inspire verb
= ysbrydoli, ennyn
to inspire confidence in someone = ennyn hyder yn^n rhywun

instalment noun
• (payment)
= rhandaliad (plural -au) masculine
• (of serial etc)
= pennod (plural penodau) feminine

instantly *adverb*
= ar unwaith, yn syth, yn y °fan, yn °ddi-oed

instead *adverb*
instead of = yn lle
instead of him = yn ei °le
instead of us = yn ein lle
instead of you = yn dy °le
instead of the manager = yn lle'r rheolwr

> **!** **yn lle** *is a compound preposition and so changes its form with pronouns—see entry on the Welsh-English side for details.*

Dafydd was ill but Ieuan came instead
= roedd Dafydd yn sâl ond daeth Ieuan yn ei °le
Sioned was ill but Medi came instead
= roedd Sioned yn sâl ond daeth Medi yn ei lle

institute *noun*
= sefydliad (*plural* -au) *masculine*
Women's Institute = Sefydliad y Merched *masculine*

institution *noun*
= sefydliad (*plural* -au) *masculine*

instructions *plural noun*
= cyfarwyddiadau *plural*

instrument *noun*
(*musical*)
= offeryn (*plural* -nau) *masculine*

insufferable *adjective*
= annioddefol

insufficient *adjective*
= annigonol

insult
1 *noun*
= sarhad (*plural* -au) *masculine*
2 *verb*
= sarhau

insulting *adjective*
= sarhaus

insurance *noun*
= yswiriant (*plural* yswiriannau) *masculine*
comprehensive insurance = yswiriant cynhwysfawr *masculine*
third party insurance = yswiriant trydydd person *masculine*

life insurance = yswiriant bywyd *masculine*
to take out insurance on something = yswirio rhywbeth

insure *verb*
• (*take out insurance on*)
= yswirio
• (*make sure*)
= sicrhau

intelligent *adjective*
= deallus

intend *verb*
= bwriadu
to intend to do something = bwriadu gwneud rhywbeth

intense *adjective*
= dwys

intensive care *noun*
= gofal dwys *masculine*

intention *noun*
= bwriad (*plural* -au) *masculine*

interest *noun*
• (*general sense*)
= diddordeb (*plural* -au) *masculine*
to take an interest in something = ymddiddori yn[n] rhywbeth
• (*on loan etc*)
= llog (*plural* -au) *masculine*

interested *adjective*
to be interested in something = ymddiddori yn[n] rhywbeth, bod â diddordeb yn[n] rhywbeth

interesting *adjective*
= diddorol

interfere *verb*
to interfere with something = ymyrryd â[h] rhywbeth
to interfere in something (*meddle*) = busnesa yn[n] rhywbeth
don't interfere! = paid busnesa!

interference *noun*
= ymyrraeth *feminine*

intermission *noun*
= egwyl (*plural* -ion) *feminine*

internal *adjective*
= mewnol

international *adjective*
= rhyngwladol

Internet noun
= Rhyngrwyd feminine

interpret verb
- (translate)
  = cyfieithu
- (situation etc)
  = dehongli

interpreter noun
= cyfieithydd (plural cyfieithwyr) masculine
= cyfieithwraig (plural cyfieithwragedd) feminine

interrupt verb
= torri ar °draws
to interrupt someone = torri ar °draws rhywun
they interrupted him = naethon nhw °dorri ar ei °draws
don't interrupt me! = paid torri ar ⁿnhraws!

interval noun
- (in show, play etc)
  = egwyl (plural -ion) feminine
- (spell)
  = ysbaid (plural ysbeidiau) masculine or feminine
  sunny intervals = ysbeidiau heulog
  at regular intervals = °bob hyn a hyn

interview
1 noun
= cyfweliad (plural -au) masculine
2 verb
to interview someone = cyfweld âʰ rhywun

intimidate verb
= bygwth (stem bygyth-), dychryn

intimidating adjective
= bygythiol

into preposition
= i°
to go into the garden = mynd i'r °ardd
to translate a book into Welsh = cyfieithu llyfr i'r °Gymraeg
- (where motion is particularly emphasized)
  = i mewn i°
  come into the dining room = dewch i mewn i'r stafell °fwyta

introduce verb
= cyflwyno

may I introduce my brother (to you)? = °ga i °gyflwyno ⁿmrawd (i chi)?

introduction noun
- (in book etc)
  = rhagarweiniad (plural -au) masculine
- (of person, legislation etc)
  = cyflwyniad (plural -au) masculine

introductory adjective
= rhagarweiniol

introvert
1 adjective
= mewnblyg
2 noun
= dyn mewnblyg masculine, dynes °fewnblyg feminine

invade verb
to invade a country = goresgyn gwlad

invent verb
= dyfeisio

invention noun
= dyfais (plural dyfeisiau, dyfeisiadau) feminine

invest verb
= buddsoddi
to invest time/money in something = buddsoddi amser/arian ynⁿ rhywbeth

investigate verb
to investigate something = ymchwilio i° rywbeth

investigation noun
= ymchwiliad (plural -au) masculine

investment noun
- (sum of money)
  = buddsoddiad (plural -au) masculine
- (act of investing)
  = buddsoddi verbnoun

invisible adjective
= anweladwy

invitation noun
= gwahoddiad (plural -au) masculine

invite verb
= gwahodd
to invite someone to do something = gwahodd rhywun i °wneud rhywbeth

involved adjective
- (complex)
  = cymhleth

- (*connected*)
  = cysylltiedig (**â**ʰ with)

iota *noun*
  there's not an iota of truth in it = does dim mymryn o °wir ynddi

Ireland *noun*
  = Iwerddon *feminine*

Irish
1 *adjective*
  = Gwyddelig, o Iwerddon
2 *noun*
  = (*language*) Gwyddeleg
  the Irish = y Gwyddelod

Irishman *noun*
  = Gwyddel (*plural* -od) *masculine*

Irishwoman *noun*
  = Gwyddeles (*plural* -au) *feminine*

iron
1 *noun*
  = (*metal, for clothes*) haearn (*plural* heyrn) *masculine*
2 *verb*
  = smwddio

irrelevant *adjective*
  = amherthnasol

irresponsible *adjective*
  = anghyfrifol

island *noun*
  = ynys (*plural* -oedd) *feminine*

isolate *verb*
  = ynysu

isolated *adjective*
  = ynysedig

issue *noun*
- (*matter, subject*)
  = mater (*plural* -ion) *masculine*, pwnc (*plural* pynciau) *masculine*
- (*of magazine*)
  = rhifyn (*plural* -nau) *masculine*

it *pronoun*

> **!** *Welsh has no word corresponding to* 'it'—*in abstract senses the feminine* **hi** *is used, in concrete senses* **e/o** *or* **hi** *depending on gender.*

- (*abstract*)
  = hi
  how did it go? = sut aeth hi?

it's cold here = mae hi'n oer fan hyn
  what about it? = beth amdani (hi)?
  it was a disappointment = roedd hi'n siom
- (*concrete*)
  masculine: = e, fe, o (*North*), fo (*North*); *feminine*: = hi (*depends on gender of thing referred to*)
- = eiº ...(e/fe) (*masculine*), eiʰ ...(hi) (*feminine*) (*as object of verbnoun*)
  I can't see it = °alla i mo'i °weld e
  = °alla i mo'i gweld hi

IT *abbreviation* (**Information Technology**) *noun*
  = TG (*abbreviation of* Technoleg Gwybodaeth)

itch *verb*
- (*irritate*)
  = cosi
- (*yearn*)
  = ysu
  I was itching to tell her = o'n i'n ysu am °ddweud wrthi

itchy *adjective*
  = coslyd

its *adjective*
  = eiº ... (e/fe) *masculine*, eiʰ ... (hi) *feminine*
  (*after* iº) 'wº ... (e/fe) *masculine*, 'wʰ ... (hi) *feminine*

itself *pronoun*
  = ei hun (*North*), ei hunan (*South*)
  the dog hurt itself = naeth y ci °frifo ei hun/ei hunan
  the car itself wasn't damaged = ʰchafodd y car ei hun/ei hunan °ddim difrod

J j

jacket noun
= siaced (*plural* -i) *feminine*

jail
1 *noun*
= carchar (*plural* -au) *masculine*
2 *verb*
= carcharu
to jail someone for life = carcharu rhywun am oes

jam noun
• (*food*)
= jam *masculine*
• (*traffic*)
= tagfa (*plural* tagfeydd) *feminine*

January noun
= mis Ionawr, Ionawr *masculine*

> **!** **in January** = ym mis Ionawr, yn^n Ionawr
> **every January** = ^{o}bob mis Ionawr
> **on the tenth of January** = ar y degfed o (^{o}fis) Ionawr
> **by the tenth of January** = erbyn y degfed o (^{o}fis) Ionawr
> **by January** = erbyn (mis) Ionawr
> **next/last January** = mis Ionawr nesa/diwetha
> **(in) late January** = yn hwyr ym mis Ionawr
> **(in) early January** = yn ^{o}gynnar ym mis Ionawr
> **at the beginning of January** = ^{o}ddechrau mis Ionawr
> **at the end of January** = ^{o}ddiwedd mis Ionawr
> **for the remainder of January** = am ^{o}weddill mis Ionawr
> **till January** = tan (^{o}fis) Ionawr
> **throughout January** = trwy gydol mis Ionawr

jar noun
= jar (*plural* -iau) *feminine*

jaw noun
= gên (*plural* genau) *feminine*

jazz noun
= jazz *masculine*

JCB noun
= Jac codi baw

jealous adjective
= cenfigennus
to be jealous of someone = bod yn ^{o}genfigennus o^o/wrth^o rywun

jeans plural noun
= jîns *plural*

jeer verb
= gwawdio

jelly noun
= jeli (*plural* jelïau) *masculine*

Jesus noun
= (yr) Iesu *masculine*

jet noun
= jet (*plural* -iau) *feminine*

jewellery noun
= gemau *plural*, gemwaith *masculine*

Jew noun
= Iddew (*plural* -on) *masculine*

Jewish adjective
= Iddewig

jigsaw puzzle noun
= pos jig-so (*plural* posau jig-so) *masculine*

job noun
• (*work*)
= swydd (*plural* -i) *feminine*
to look for a job = chwilio am swydd
• (*task*)
= tasg (*plural* -au) *feminine*, jobyn *masculine*

jogging noun
= loncian *verbnoun*

join verb
• (*bring together*)
= uno
• (*become a member*)
= ymuno â^h, ymaelodi yn^n
I've joined the squash club = dw i wedi ymuno â'r clwb sboncen
= dw i wedi ymaelodi yn y clwb sboncen

join in
= ymuno â^h

jointly adverb
= ar y cyd

joke
1 *noun*
= jôc (*plural* -s) *feminine*

2 *verb*
= jocio, gwneud jôc

jot *noun*
there's not a jot of truth in it = does dim mymryn o °wir ynddi

journalist *noun*
= newyddiadurwr (*plural* newyddiadurwyr) *masculine*
= newyddiadurwraig (*plural* newyddiadurwragedd) *feminine*

journey *noun*
= taith (*plural* teithiau) *feminine*

joy *noun*
= llawenydd *masculine*

judge
1 *noun*
= barnwr (*plural* barnwyr) *masculine*
2 *verb*
• (*act as judge*)
= barnu
• (*in competition*)
= beirniadu

judgment *noun*
• (*sentence*)
= dyfarniad (*plural* -au) *masculine*
• (*opinion*)
= barn (*plural* -au) *feminine*

judo *noun*
= jwdo *masculine*

jug *noun*
= jwg (*plural* jygiau) *masculine or feminine*

juice *noun*
= sudd (*plural* -ion) *masculine*

July *noun*
= mis Gorffennaf, Gorffennaf *masculine*
see also **January**

jump *verb*
= neidio
to jump over something = neidio dros° rywbeth
to jump off something = neidio oddiar° rywbeth

jumper *noun*
(*garment*)
= siwmper (*plural* -i) *feminine*

jump rope *noun*
= cortyn neidio (*plural* cyrt neidio) *masculine*

June *noun*
= mis Mehefin, Mehefin *masculine*
see also **January**

junior *adjective*
= iau

junior high school *noun* (US)
= ysgol uwchradd iau (*plural* ysgolion uwchradd iau) *feminine*

junior school *noun*
= ysgol plant iau (*plural* ysgolion plant iau) *feminine*

jury *noun*
= rheithgor (*plural* -au) *masculine*

just¹ *adverb*

> ! This adverb poses translation problems because of its wide range of meanings in English. When in doubt, decide on an alternative in English and use this to pinpoint the correct choice in Welsh.

• (*just now: with present tense in Welsh, present perfect in English*)
= newydd°
they've just come back = maen nhw newydd °ddod yn ôl
have you just arrived? = wyt ti newydd °gyrraedd?
we had just left = o'n ni newydd °adael

> ! Compare 'he has gone' = **mae e wedi mynd** *and* 'he has just gone' = **mae e newydd °fynd—newydd** *replaces* **wedi**, *and it is wrong to say* *mae e newydd wedi mynd, *or, indeed,* *mae e jyst wedi mynd.

• (*just now: with preterite tense in Welsh, past in English*)
= gynnau
what did he just say? = be' wedodd e gynnau?
• (*about to*)
= ar °fin
I was just going to phone you = o'n i ar °fin eich ffonio (chi)
• (*immediately*)
= yn union
just before Christmas = yn union cyn y Nadolig
• (*exactly*)
= yn union
that's just what I said = 'na'n union be' wedes i

- (*barely*)
  = o'r braidd
  he just escaped = o'r braidd y
  dihangodd e
- (*only*)
  = dim ond, yn unig
  just a week ago = dim ond wythnos yn
  ôl
  = wythnos yn unig yn ôl
- (*in comparisons*)
  = yr un (mor° ... âʰ ...), °lawn (mor° ...
  âʰ ...)
  this one is just as big as that one =
  mae hwn yr un mor °fawr â hwnna
  I'm just as cross as you = dw i °lawn
  mor °grac â ti

just² *adjective*
= cyfiawn

justice *noun*
= cyfiawnder *masculine*, tegwch
masculine

justification *noun*
= cyfiawnhad *masculine*

justify *verb*
- (*give justification for*)
  = cyfiawnhau
- (*align*)
  = unioni

Kk

kangaroo *noun*
= cangarŵ (*plural* -od) *masculine*

karate *noun*
= carate *masculine*

keen *adjective*
- (*eager*)
  = awyddus
- (*enthusiastic*)
  = brwd
  to be keen on something = bod yn hoff
  o° rywbeth

keep *verb*
- (*retain*)
  = cadw
  he keeps sheepdogs = mae'n cadw
  cŵn defaid
  how are you keeping? = sut dych chi'n
  cadw?
- (*stay*)
  = cadw
  keep quiet! = cadwch yn °dawel!
- (*other uses*)
  to keep someone waiting = gwneud i°
  rywun aros
  = cadw rhywun yn aros
  **to keep someone from doing
  something** = rhwystro rhywun rhag
  gwneud rhywbeth

keep away
(*keep one's distance*) = cadw draw

keep back
= cadw yn ôl

keep on
(*continue*) = dal (*stem* dali-)
  to keep (on) doing something = dal i
  °wneud rhywbeth
  = para i °wneud rhywbeth

keep out
= cadw allan (*North*), cadw mas (*South*)

keep up
- (*maintain*)
  = cynnal (*stem* cynhali-)
- (*not fall behind*)
  I couldn't keep up with them = o'n i
  °ddim yn medru dal i fyny â nhw
  (*North*), o'n i °ddim yn gallu dal lan â
  nhw

kerb *noun*
= ymyl palmant (*plural* ymylon palmant) *masculine or feminine*

kettle *noun*
= tegell (*plural* -i, -au) *masculine*

key
1 *noun*
= agoriad (*plural* -au) *masculine* (*North*), allwedd (*plural* -au, -i) *feminine* (*South*)
2 *adjective*
= allweddol

keyhole *noun*
= twll clo (*plural* tyllau clo) *masculine*

kick
1 *verb*
= cicio
2 *noun*
= cic (*plural* -iau) *feminine*

kick out
= cicio allan (*North*), cicio mas (*South*)

kid *noun*
• (*child*)
= plentyn (*plural* plant) *masculine*

> **!** *A plural term of endearment*
> **plantos** *also exists.*

• (*goat*)
= gefryn (*plural* -nod) *masculine*, gafran (*plural* -nod) *feminine*

kidnap *verb*
= herwgipio

kill *verb*
= lladd

killer *noun*
= lladdwr (*plural* lladdwyr) *masculine* (*murderer*)
= llofrudd (*plural* -ion) *masculine*

kilogram *noun*
= cilogram (*plural* -au) *masculine*

kilometre *noun*
= cilomedr (*plural* -au) *masculine*

kind
1 *adjective*
= caredig
2 *noun*
= math (*plural* -au) *masculine or feminine*
what kind of book? = pa °fath o °lyfr?
= sut °lyfr?

kindness *noun*
= caredigrwydd *masculine*

king *noun*
= brenin (*plural* brenhinoedd) *masculine*

kingdom *noun*
= teyrnas (*plural* -oedd) *feminine*
the United Kingdom = y °Deyrnas Unedig

kiss
1 *noun*
= cusan (*plural* -au) *feminine or masculine*, sws (*plural* -us) *feminine*
to give someone a kiss = rhoi (*stem* rhoi-, rhodd-) cusan/sws i° rywun
2 *verb*
= cusanu

kitchen *noun*
= cegin (*plural* -au) *feminine*

kite *noun*
= barcud, barcut (*plural* barcutiaid) *masculine*

kitten *noun*
= cath °fach (*plural* cathod bach) *feminine*

knee *noun*
= pen-glin (*plural* pengliniau) *masculine*

kneel down *verb*
= penlinio, penglinio

knife *noun*
= cyllell (*plural* cyllyll) *feminine*

knight *noun*
= marchog (*plural* -ion) *masculine*

knit *verb*
= gwau, gweu

knock
1 *verb*
= taro
2 *noun*
= cnoc (*plural* -iau) *feminine*, ergyd (*plural* -ion) *feminine*

knock down:
he was knocked down by a car = cafodd ei °daro gan °gar

knock out:
to knock someone out = llorio rhywun

knot noun
= cwlwm (*plural* clymau, cylymau)
masculine

know verb

> **!** *There are two verbs for* **know** *in Welsh—one denoting knowledge of facts, etc; the other denoting acquaintance with people or places. Both express states rather than actions, and therefore cannot be used in the preterite—where English uses a past tense, the Welsh verbs use the imperfect.*

- (*fact etc*)
= gwybod (*irregular*)
he thinks he knows everything = mae'n meddwl °fod e'n gwybod popeth
does he know about the meeting? = ydy e'n gwybod am y cyfarfod?
I knew that = o'n i'n gwybod hynny
who knows? = pwy a °wŷr?
God knows! = Duw a °wŷr!
..., you know = ..., °wyddost ti (*North*) ..., °wyddoch chi (*North*), ..., timod (*South*), ..., chimod (*South*)
to let someone know = rhoi (*stem* rhoi-, rhodd-) gwybod i° rywun
to know how to do something = medru gwneud rhywbeth

> **!** ⇒**Gwybod** *box on the Welsh-English side*

- (*person, place etc*)
= nabod
do you know them? = wyt ti'n nabod nhw?
do you know London = wyt ti'n nabod Llundain?
I knew them = o'n i'n nabod nhw

knowledge noun
= gwybodaeth *feminine*

label
1 *noun*
= label (*plural* -i) *masculine or feminine*
2 *verb*
= labelu

laboratory noun
= labordy (*plural* labordai) *masculine*

labour
1 *noun*
= llafur *masculine*
the Labour Party = y °Blaid °Lafur *feminine*
to be in labour (*giving birth*) = bod ar esgor
2 *verb*
= llafurio

lace noun
- (*of shoe*)
= carrai (*plural* careiau) *feminine*
to tie one's laces = clymu'ch careiau
- (*material*)
= les *feminine*

lack
1 *noun*
= diffyg (*plural* -ion) *masculine*, prinder *masculine*
because of a lack of resources = oherwydd diffyg adnoddau
2 *verb*
he lacks confidence = does gynno fo °ddim hyder (*North*), does dim hyder 'da fe (*South*)

lad noun
= llanc (*plural* -iau) *masculine*, hogyn (*plural* hogiau) *masculine* (*North*)

ladder noun
= ysgol (*plural* -ion) *feminine*

lady noun
= boneddiges (*plural* -au) *feminine*

lake noun
= llyn (*plural* -noedd) *masculine*
the Lake District = Ardal y Llynnoedd *feminine*

lamb noun
- (*animal*)
= oen (*plural* ŵyn) *masculine*

• (*meat*)
= cig oen *masculine*

lamp *noun*
= lamp (*plural* -au) *feminine*

lampshade *noun*
= lamplen (*plural* -ni) *feminine*

land
1 *noun*
• (*opposite of sea*)
= tir *masculine*
• (*country*)
= gwlad (*plural* gwledydd) *feminine*
2 *verb*
= glanio

landlady *noun*
• (*of rented accommodation*)
= perchnoges (*plural* -au) *feminine*
• (*of pub*)
= tafarnwraig (*plural* tafarnwragedd) *feminine*

landlord *noun*
• (*of rented accommodation*)
= perchennog (*plural* perchnogion) *masculine*
• (*of pub*)
= tafarnwr (*plural* tafarnwyr) *masculine*

landscape *noun*
= tirlun (*plural* -iau) *masculine*

lane *noun*
= lôn (*plural* lonydd) *feminine*

language *noun*
= iaith (*plural* ieithoedd) *feminine*
to speak a language = siarad iaith
native language = mamiaith *feminine*
body language = iaith y corff *feminine*
what languages do you speak? = pa ieithoedd dych chi'n siarad?
what language is this in? = ym ⁿmha iaith mae hwn?

language laboratory *noun*
= laberdy iaith (*plural* labordai iaith) *masculine*

lap *noun*
= glin (*plural* -iau) *masculine*, gliniau *plural*

large *adjective*
= mawr

largely *adverb*
= i °raddau helaeth

lass *noun*
= hogen (*plural* genod) *feminine*, hogan (*plural* genod) *feminine* (*North*)

last
1 *adjective*
• (*most recent*)
= diwetha(f)
last week = wythnos diwetha (*not* *wythnos °ddiwetha*)
last month = mis diwetha
last night = neithiwr
the night before last = echnos
last year = llynedd
• (*last in series*)
= ola(f)
that's the last time I saw her = dyna'r tro ola i mi °weld hi
at last = o'r diwedd
2 *adverb*
= yn ola(f)
he came last = daeth e'n ola
3 *verb*
= (*continue*) para; parhau (*formal*)
how long does it last? = am faint mae'n para?

late *adjective*
• (*in the day*)
= hwyr
• (*not on time*)
= hwyr
• (*deceased*)
= diweddar (*precedes noun*)
the late Mr Jones = y diweddar Mr Jones

later *adverb*
= nes ymlaen, wedyn
I'll see you later = °wela i di wedyn/nes ymlaen
later on = nes ymlaen, wedyn
sooner or later = yn hwyr neu'n hwyrach

latest *adjective*
• (*most recent, up-to-date*)
= diweddara(f)
the latest headlines = y penawdau diweddara
by five o'clock at the latest = erbyn pump o'r °gloch man pella *or* °fan °bella

Latin *noun*
= Lladin

Latin America *noun*
= America Ladin *feminine*

Latin American

1 *adjective*
= Lladin-Americanaidd

2 *noun*
= Lladin-Americanwr (*plural* Lladin-Americanwyr) *masculine*
= Lladin-Americanes (*plural* -au) *feminine*
= Lladin-Americaniad (*plural* Lladin-Americaniaid) *masculine and feminine*

laugh *verb*
= chwerthin (*stem* chwardd-, chwerth-)
to laugh at something/someone = chwerthin am ᵒben rhywbeth/rhywun

laughable *adjective*
= chwerthinllyd

launch

1 *verb*
= lansio

2 *noun*
= lansiad (*plural* -au) *masculine*, lansio *verbnoun*

laundry *noun*
• (*clothes*)
= dillad golchi *plural*
to do the laundry = golchi'r dillad
• (*place*)
= golchdy (*plural* golchdai) *masculine*

law *noun*
• (*institution*)
= cyfraith (*plural* cyfreithiau) *feminine*
to study law = astudio'r ᵒgyfraith
to break the law = torri'r ᵒgyfraith
that's against the law = mae hynny yn erbyn y ᵒgyfraith, mae hynny'n anghyfreithlon
• (*statute*)
= deddf (*plural* -au) *feminine*

lawn *noun*
= lawnt (*plural* -iau, -ydd) *feminine*

lawnmower *noun*
= peiriant torri lawnt/glaswellt *masculine*

lawyer *noun*
= cyfreithiwr (*plural* cyfreithwyr) *masculine*
= cyfreithwraig (*plural* cyfreithwragedd) *feminine*

lay *verb*
• (*put*)
= rhoi (*stem* rhoi-, rhodd-) i lawr, gosod

to lay something on the floor = rhoi (*stem* rhoi-, rhodd-) rhywbeth ar y llawr
to lay the table = gosod y bwrdd
• (*eggs*)
= dodwy

lay down
• (*set down*)
= rhoi (*stem* rhoi-, rhodd-) i lawr
• (*establish*)
= gosod

lay off
• (*workers*)
= danfon adre (o'r gwaith)
• (*desist*)
= peidio

lazy *adjective*
= diog

lead¹
noun
(*metal*)
= plwm *masculine*

lead ²

1 *noun*
• = blaen *masculine*
in the lead = ar y blaen
• (*for dogs*)
= tennyn (*plural* tenynnau) *masculine*

2 *verb*
• (*general sense*)
= arwain (*stem* arweini-)
• (*in race, match etc*)
= bod ar y blaen
• (*guide*)
= tywys
• (*roads etc*)
= mynd iᵒ
where does this road lead? = i lle mae'r ffordd 'ma'n mynd?

leader *noun*
= arweinydd (*plural* arweinwyr) *masculine*

leaf *noun*
= deilen (*plural* dail) *feminine*

leaflet *noun*
= taflen (*plural* -ni) *feminine*

leak

1 *noun*
= twll (*plural* tyllau) *masculine*

2 *verb*
= gollwng (*stem* gollyng-)

lean¹ *verb*
= pwyso
to lean on something/someone =
pwyso ar° rywbeth/rywun
to lean against something/someone =
pwyso yn erbyn rhywbeth/rhywun

lean back
= pwyso yn ôl

lean forward
= pwyso ymlaen

lean² *adjective*
= main, tenau

leap *verb*
= neidio, llamu

leap year *noun*
= blwyddyn naid (*plural* blynyddoedd
naid) *feminine*

learn *verb*
= dysgu
to learn Welsh = dysgu Cymraeg
**how long have you been learning
Welsh?** = ers pryd dych chi'n dysgu
Cymraeg?
I've been learning for two years = dw
i'n dysgu ers dwy °flynedd
to learn how to drive = dysgu gyrru

learner *noun*
= dysgwr (*plural* dysgwyr) *masculine*
= dysgwraig (*plural* dysgwragedd)
feminine
learner driver = dysgwr gyrru (*plural*
dysgwyr gyrru) *masculine*
= dysgwraig gyrru (*plural* dysgwragedd
gyrru) *feminine*

leash *noun*
= tennyn (*plural* tenynnau) *masculine*

least *adjective*
= lleia(f)
that was the least we ever got = dyna'r
lleia °gawson ni erioed
it was the least I could do = dyna'r lleia
gallwn i °wneud
at least = o °leia(f)

> **!** This phrase tends to go at the end of
> the sentence:
> **at least he wasn't injured** = ʰchafodd
> e mo'i anafu, o leia
> **there are at least a hundred here** =
> mae cant fan hyn o leia

not in the least = dim o °gwbwl

leather *noun*
= lledr *masculine*

leave *verb*
• (*most senses*)
= gadael (*stem* gadaw-)
to leave school = gadael yr ysgol
to leave early = gadael yn °gynnar
to leave a book on the table = gadael
llyfr ar y bwrdd
leave him alone! = gad °lonydd iddo
(fe)!
she left the room = naeth hi °adael y
stafell
• (*especially of vehicles*)
= ymadael (*stem* ymadaw-)
trains leaving every hour = trenau'n
ymadael °bob awr

> **!** *ymadael* is a rather formal term, and
> many speakers use **gadael** in this
> sense as well.

• (*put off*)
= gadael, gohirio
to leave something till tomorrow
= gadael/gohirio rhywbeth
tan yfory
• (*remain*)
there's nothing left = does dim byd ar ôl
how much is left? = faint sy ar ôl?

leave behind
= gadael ar ôl

leave out
= gadael allan (*North*), gadael mas
(*South*)

leave over
= gadael yn °weddill, gadael yn ôl
with ten left over = gyda deg yn
°weddill

lecture *noun*
= darlith (*plural* -oedd) *feminine*

leek *noun*
= cenhinen (*plural* cennin) *feminine*

left
1 *noun*
= chwith
on the left = ar y chwith
to the left = i'r chwith
2 *adjective*
= chwith
her left hand = ei llaw chwith
3 *adverb*
to turn left = troi (*stem* troi-, trodd-) i'r
chwith

left-handed *adjective*
= llawchwith

left-wing *adjective*
= asgell chwith

leg *noun*
= coes (*plural* -au) *feminine*

legal *adjective*
• (*lawful*)
= cyfreithlon
• (*pertaining to the law*)
= cyfreithiol

legend *noun*
= chwedl (*plural* -au) *feminine*

leisure *noun*
= hamdden

leisure centre *noun*
= canolfan hamdden (*plural* canolfannau hamdden) *feminine*

lemon *noun*
= lemon (*plural* -au) *masculine*

lend *verb*
= benthyca, rhoi (*stem* rhoi-, rhodd-) benthyg i°
to lend someone something = rhoi benthyg rhywbeth i° rywun

length *noun*
= hyd (*plural* -au) *masculine*
the length and breadth of Wales = ledled Cymru
at length (*finally*) = o'r diwedd

lens *noun*
= lens (*plural* -ys) *feminine*

Leo *noun*
= y Llew *masculine*

leopard *noun*
= llewpard (*plural* -iaid) *masculine*

less
1 *adverb*
= llai
this one is less expensive = mae hwn yn llai drud
less money = llai o arian
less work = llai o °waith

> **!** This quantity expression requires **o°** with a following noun.

2 *pronoun*
= llai
it costs less = mae'n costio llai

I read less these days = dw i'n darllen llai dyddiau 'ma
less than half an hour = llai na hanner awr
more or less = mwy na °lai
less and less = llai a llai; lleilai

lessen *verb*
• (*become less, smaller*)
= mynd yn llai, lleihau
• (*make less, smaller*)
= lleihau

lesson *noun*
= gwers (*plural* -i) *feminine*

let¹ *verb*
• (*allow*)
= gadael (*stem* gadaw-)
let me think = gad/gadewch i mi °feddwl
let's go! = gad/gadewch inni °fynd!
= awn ni!
to let someone do something = gadael i° rywun °wneud rhywbeth

let down
to let someone down = gadael rhywun i lawr

let go
to let go of something = gollwng (*stem* gollyng-) rhywbeth

let in
to let someone in = gadael rhywun i mewn

let off
to let off fireworks = tanio tân gwyllt

let²
verb
(*property*)
= gosod

letter *noun*
• (*correspondence*)
= llythyr (*plural* -on, -au) *masculine*
to write someone a letter = ysgrifennu llythyr at° rywun
to send someone a letter = anfon/danfon/hala llythyr at° rywun
• (*of alphabet*)
= llythyren (*plural* -nau) *feminine*

letterbox *noun*
• (*for posting letters*)
= blwch llythyrau (*plural* blychau llythyrau) *masculine*

• (*in door*)
= twll llythyrau (*plural* tyllau llythyrau) *masculine*

lettuce *noun*
= letysen (*plural* letys) *feminine*

level
1 *adjective*
= gwastad
2 *noun*
• (*of course etc*)
= safon (*plural* -au) *feminine*
• (*of noise, income etc*)
= lefel (*plural* -au) *feminine*
• (*floor*)
= llawr (*plural* lloriau) *masculine*

liar *noun*
= celwyddgi (*plural* celwyddgwn) *masculine*

liberal *adjective*
= rhyddfrydig

Liberal *adjective*
the Liberal Democrats = y Democratiaid Rhyddfrydol

liberate *verb*
= rhyddhau

liberty *noun*
= rhyddid *masculine*

Libra *noun*
= y °Glorian *feminine*, y °Fantol *feminine*

librarian *noun*
= llyfrgellydd (*plural* llyfrgellwyr) *masculine*

library *noun*
= llyfrgell (*plural* -oedd) *feminine*

licence *noun*
= trwydded (*plural* -au) *feminine*

license *verb*
= trwyddedu

license number *noun* (*US*)
= rhif car *masculine*

license plate *noun* (*US*)
= plât rhifau (*plural* platiau rhifau) *masculine*

lick *verb*
= llyfu

lid *noun*
= caead (*plural* -au) *masculine*

lie¹
1 *noun*
(*untruth*)
= celwydd (*plural* -au. clwyddau) *masculine*
to tell lies = dweud (*stem* dwed-, wed-) clwyddau
2 *verb*
= dweud celwydd (*plural* -au)

lie² *verb*
= gorwedd
to lie down on the bed = gorwedd ar y gwely
he was lying on the floor = roedd e'n gorwedd ar y llawr

lie around
= gorwedd o °gwmpas

lie down
= gorwedd (i lawr)

life *noun*
• (*general sense*)
= bywyd (*plural* -au) *masculine*
• (*lifetime, lifespan*)
= oes
life imprisonment = carchar am oes
for the rest of his life = am °weddill ei oes

lifeboat *noun*
= bad (*plural* -au) achub *masculine*

lifestyle *noun*
= ffordd o °fyw (*plural* ffyrdd o °fyw) *feminine*, dull o °fyw (*plural* dulliau o °fyw) *masculine*

lift
1 *noun*
• (*elevator*)
= lifft (*plural* -iau) *masculine or feminine*
• (*ride in car etc*)
= lifft (*plural* -iau) *masculine or feminine*
2 *verb*
= codi

lift up
= codi

light
1 *adjective*
• (*not heavy*)
= ysgafn
• (*not dark*)
= golau
light blue = glas golau
2 *noun*
= golau (*plural* goleuadau) *masculine*

to switch on a light = rhoi (*stem* rhoi-, rhodd-) golau ymlaen
to switch off a light = diffodd golau
the lights are red = mae'r golau'n °goch
have you got a light? = °ga i °dân?
3 *verb*
• (*fire, match etc*)
= cynnau
• (*illuminate*)
= goleuo

light bulb *noun*
= bylb golau (*plural* bylbiau golau) *masculine*

lighten *verb*
= ysgafnhau

lighthouse *noun*
= goleudy (*plural* goleudai) *masculine*

lightning *noun*
= mellt *plural*
bolt/flash of lightning = mellten *feminine*

like
1 *preposition*
= fel; megis (*formal*)
people like us = pobol fel ni

! **megis** *is entirely restricted to writing and never heard in unaffected speech.*

who is he like? = i °bwy mae'n °debyg?
2 *noun*
I've never seen his like = weles i erioed mo'i °debyg
3 *verb*
= leicio, hoffi
would you like a drink? = leiciech *or* hoffech chi °ddiod?
I like apples = dw i'n leicio/hoffi afalau
I'd like to come = leiciwn *or* hoffwn i °ddod
does she like swimming? = ydy hi'n leicio *or* hoffi nofio?

! **hoffi** *is the preferred standard term nowadays, but the loanword* **leicio** *is by far the more common with native speakers.*

likelihood *noun*
= tebygolrwydd *masculine*
in all likelihood = yn ôl pob tebyg

likely *adjective*
= tebyg, tebygol
to be likely to do something = bod yn °debyg *or* °debygol o °wneud rhywbeth

limit
1 *noun*
= terfyn (*plural* -au) *masculine*
2 *verb*
= cyfyngu

limited *adjective*
= cyfyngedig
Jones & Son Ltd = Jones a'i °Fab Cyf.

limp
1 *adjective*
= llipa

limp
2 *verb*
= hercian

line
1 *noun*
• (*general, electric, phone etc*)
= llinell (*plural* -au) *feminine*
• (*railway*)
= lein (*plural* -iau) *feminine*
• (*string, cord*)
= llinyn (*plural* -nau) *masculine*
• (*US: queue*)
= rhes (*plural* -i) *feminine*, ciw (*plural* -iau) *masculine*
2 *verb*
a path lined with flowers = llwybr â blodau ar °bob ochr

linguistic *adjective*
= ieithyddol

link
1 *noun*
= cysylltiad (*plural* -au) *masculine*
to have links with Wales = bod â ʰchysylltiadau â ʰChymru
2 *verb*
= cysylltu
the two cases are linked = mae cysylltiad rhwng y °ddau achos, mae'r °ddau achos yn °gysylltiedig

lion *noun*
= llew (*plural* -od) *masculine*

lip *noun*
= gwefus (*plural* -au) *feminine*

lipstick *noun*
= minlliw (*plural* -iau) *masculine*

list

1 *noun*
 = rhestr (*plural* -au) *feminine*
2 *verb*
 = rhestru

listen *verb*
 = gwrando (*stem* gwrandaw-)
 to listen to someone/something =
 gwrando arº rywun/rywbeth
 listen! = gwranda!/gwrandewch!

literal *adjective*
 = llythrennol

literally *adverb*
 = yn llythrennol

literature *noun*
• (*writing, works*)
 = llenyddiaeth (*plural* -au) *feminine*
• (*literary tradition*)
 = llên *feminine*

litre *noun*
 = litr (*plural* -au) *masculine*

litter *noun*
 = (y)sbwriel *masculine*

little

1 *adjective*
• (*small*) = bach, bychan
• (*in quantity*)
 little food = dim llawer o ºfwyd, ychydig
 iawn o ºfwyd
 a little food = ychydig o ºfwyd, tipyn *or*
 tamaid o ºfwyd, peth bwyd

> **!** These quantity expressions (*except*
> **peth**) require **oº** with a following noun.

2 *pronoun*
 I only ate a little = dim ond ychydig nes
 i ºfwyta
 as little as possible = cynlleied ag sy'n
 ºbosib(l)
 little by little = fesul tipyn, ºbob yn
 ºdipyn
3 *adverb*
 a little deaf = braidd yn ºfyddar,
 ychydig yn º fyddar

live¹ *verb*
 = byw*
 she lives in Cardiff = mae hi'n byw yng
 ⁿNghaerdydd
 we lived in Wales = o'n ni'n byw yng
 ⁿNghymru

> **!** **byw** *denotes a state rather than an
> action, and so cannot be used in the
> preterite—where English uses a past
> tense, the imperfect must be used in
> Welsh.*

live² *adjective*
 = byw
 a live broadcast = darllediad/telediad
 byw
 a live programme = rhaglen ºfyw

livelihood *noun*
 = bywoliaeth *feminine*

lively *adjective*
 = bywiog

liven up *verb*
 = bywiogi

living *noun*
 = bywioliaeth *feminine*
 to make/earn a living = ennill (*stem*
 enill-) bywoliaeth

living room *noun*
 = stafell ºfyw (*plural* stafelloedd byw)
 feminine

load

1 *noun*
 = llwyth (*plural* -i) *masculine*, baich
 (*plural* beichiau) *masculine*
 loads of money = llawer iawn o arian,
 hen ºddigon o arian
 that's a load of rubbish! = sothach
 llwyr ydy hwnna!
2 *verb*
 = llwytho

loaf *noun*
 = torth (*plural* -au) *feminine*

loan *noun*
 = benthyciad (*plural* -au) *masculine*

lobster *noun*
 = cimwch (*plural* cimychod, cimychiaid)
 masculine

local *adjective*
 = lleol
 local shop = siop ºleol (*plural* siopau
 lleol) *feminine*

locally *adverb*
 = yn lleol
 they live locally = maen nhw'n byw yn
 yr ardal

locate *verb*
- (*position, situate*)
  = lleoli
  the museum is located in the centre of town = mae'r amgueddfa wedi'i lleoli yng ⁿghanol y ᵒdre
- (*find*)
  = ffeindio, dod o hyd iᵒ

location *noun*
= lleoliad (*plural* -au) *masculine*

lock
1 *noun*
= clo (*plural* -eon) *masculine*
2 *verb*
= cloi; rhoi (*stem* rhoi-, rhodd-) dan ᵒglo
to lock a room = cloi stafell, rhoi stafell dan ᵒglo

lock in:
to lock someone in = cloi rhywun i mewn

locker *noun*
= cloer (*plural* -iau) *masculine or feminine*

locker room *noun*
= stafell newid (*plural* stafelloedd newid) *feminine*

locked *adjective*
= ar ᵒglo

log *noun*
= boncyff (*plural* -ion) *masculine*

logical *adjective*
= rhesymegol

London *noun*
= Llundain *feminine*

lonely *adjective*
= unig

long
1 *adjective*
= hir
how long is the garden? = beth ydy hyd yr ᵒardd? (*dimension*)
a long time ago = amser maith yn ôl
2 *adverb*
before long = cyn hir, cyn bo hir
long before the war = ymhell cyn y rhyfel
don't be long! = paid bod yn hir!
not long ago = ychydig o amser yn ôl
as long as you don't complain = ar yr amod ᵒfod ti ᵒddim yn cwyno

how long are you going for? = am faint dych chi'n mynd? (*time in future*)
how long have you been here? = ers pryd dych chi fan hyn? (*time in past*)
3 *verb*
to long for something = hiraethu amᵒ rywbeth

longing *noun*
= hiraeth *masculine*

long-sighted *adjective*
a long-sighted man = dyn hir ei ᵒolwg
a long-sighted woman = dynes hir ei golwg

look
1 *noun*
- (*glance*)
  = cipolwg *masculine*
  can I have a look? = ᵒga i ᵒgipolwg?
- (*appearance*)
  = golwg *feminine*, gwedd *feminine*
  the new-look Fiesta = y Fiesta ar ei newydd ᵒwedd
2 *verb*
= edrych, sbio

> **!** **edrych** *is the standard general term, while* **sbio** *is a widespread Northern alternative. But while* **edrych amᵒ** *is sometimes used for* **chwilio amᵒ** *'look for',* **sbio** *cannot be used in this way.*

to look at something = edrych arᵒ rywbeth
look! = (e)drych(a)! (e)drychwch! = sbia! / sbiwch!
to look through a window = edrych drwy ffenest
it looks like rain = mae golwg glaw arni
I know him to look at = dw i'n nabod e o'i ᵒolwg

look after
to look after something/someone = gofalu amᵒ rywbeth/rywun

> **!** **edrych ar ôl** *is also used, but is considered wrong by some.*

look down on
= edrych i lawr arᵒ

look for:
to look for something = chwilio amᵒ rywbeth

look forward:
  to look forward to something = edrych ymlaen at° rywbeth
  to look forward to doing something = edrych ymlaen at °wneud rhywbeth

look onto
  = edrych allan ar° (*North*), edrych mas ar° (*South*)

look out
  look out! = gofal!, pwylla!

look up:
  to look up a word = chwilio am °air

loose *adjective*
• (*most senses*)
  = rhydd
• (*of clothes etc*)
  = llac

lord *noun*
  = arglwydd (*plural* -i) *masculine*

lorry *noun*
  = lori (*plural* lorïau) *feminine*
  coal lorry = lori °lo (*plural* lorïau glo) *feminine*

lorry driver *noun*
  = gyrrwr lori (*plural* gyrwyr lorïau) *masculine*

lose *verb*
• (*mislay*)
  = colli
• (*not win*)
  = colli

loss *noun*
  = colled (*plural* -ion) *feminine*

lost *adjective*
  = ar °goll
  Sioned is lost = mae Sioned ar °goll

> ! *This adjective phrase does not use* **yn** *to link it to the verb* 'to be'.

lot *pronoun*
  = llawer, llawer iawn, lot, lot °fawr
  a lot of things = llawer o °bethau, lot o °bethau
  I'll take the lot = °gymera i 'r cwb(w)l/cyfan
  not a lot = dim llawer, dim lot
  he's lots happier = mae'n hapusach o °lawer, mae'n llawer hapusach, mae'n lot hapusach

> ! *This quantity expression requires* **o°** *with a following noun.*

lottery *noun*
  = loteri (*plural* loterïau) *feminine*

loud *adjective*
  = uchel
  speak louder! = siaradwch yn uwch!
  not too loud! = dim yn rhy uchel!

loudspeaker *noun*
  = corn siarad (*plural* cyrn siarad) *masculine*

lounge *noun*
  = lolfa (*plural* lolfeydd) *feminine*

louse *noun*
  = lleuen (*plural* llau) *feminine*

love
1 *noun*
  = cariad *masculine*
2 *verb*
  = caru
  they love each other = maen nhw'n caru ei gilydd
  to love doing something = bod yn hoff iawn o °wneud rhywbeth

lovely *adjective*
  = hyfryd, braf
  it's lovely to be here again = mae'n braf bod yma eto

low *adjective*
  = isel
  prices are low here = mae prisiau'n isel fan hyn

lower
1 *adjective*
  = is
  the water is lower today = mae'r dŵr yn is heddiw
2 *verb*
  = gostwng (*stem* gostyng-)

low season *noun*
  = adeg °dawel (*plural* adegau tawel) *feminine*

low tide *noun*
  = trai *masculine*

loyal *adjective*
  = ffyddlon

luck *noun*
  = lwc *feminine*
  good luck! = pob llwyddiant!
  = pob lwc!

luckily *adverb*
= wrth lwc, drwy lwc

lucky *adjective*
= lwcus

ludicrous *adjective*
= chwerthinllyd

luggage *noun*
= bagiau *plural*

lunch *noun*
= cinio *masculine*
to have lunch = cael cinio

lunchtime *noun*
= amser cinio *masculine*

lungs *plural noun*
= ysgyfaint *plural*

luxurious *adjective*
= moethus

luxury
1 *noun*
= moeth (*plural* -au) *masculine*
2 *adjective*
= moethus

Mm

machine *noun*
= peiriant (*plural* peiriannau) *masculine*

machinery *noun*
= peirianwaith *masculine*

mad *adjective*
• (*crazy*)
= gwallgo(f), lloerig
to go mad = mynd yn °wallgo(f)
to be mad about something/someone
= dwli ar° rywbeth/rywun
• (*US: angry*)
= crac, dig   .

magazine *noun*
= cylchgrawn (*plural* cylchgronau)
masculine

magic
1 *noun*
= hud *masculine*
2 *adjective*
= hud, hudol

magistrate *noun*
= ynad (*plural* -on) *masculine*
magistrate's court = llys ynadon (*plural*
llysoedd ynadon) *masculine*

magnet *noun*
= magned (*plural* -au) *masculine*

magnificent *adjective*
= ardderchog, ysblennydd

maiden name *noun*
= enw morwynol *masculine*

mail *noun*
= post *masculine*

mailbox *noun* (*US*)
= blwch post (*plural* blychau post)
masculine

mailman *noun* (*US*)
= dyn post (*plural* dynion post)
masculine, postmon (*plural* postmyn)
masculine

main *adjective*
= prif°

> **! prif°** *always precedes the noun it
> refers to and causes soft mutation.*

main course *noun*
= prif saig (*plural* prif seigiau) *feminine*, prif °gwrs (*plural* prif °gyrsiau) *masculine*

mainly *adverb*
= yn °benna(f)

main road *noun*
= priffordd (*plural* priffyrdd) *feminine*

maintain *verb*
= cynnal (*stem* cynhali-), cadw (*stem* cadw-)

major *adjective*
• (*most important*)
= prif°

> **! prif°** *precedes the noun it refers to and causes soft mutation.*

• (*important*)
= pwysig

majority *noun*
= mwyafrif (*plural* -oedd) *masculine*, y rhan °fwya(f) *feminine*
an overwhelming majority = mwyafrif llethol

make *verb*
• (*general senses*)
= gwneud

> **! gwneud** *is irregular in the preterite, short future, conditional and imperative—see Welsh-English side for details and more examples.*

to make a phone call = gwneud galwad ffôn
to make room = gwneud lle
to make someone angry = gwneud rhywun yn °grac
made in Wales = gwnaed/gwnaethpwyd yng ⁿNghymru
• (*prepare*)
= paratoi
to make lunch = paratoi cinio
• (*compel*)
= gwneud, gorfodi
to make someone do something = gwneud i° rywun °wneud rhywbeth, gorfodi rhywun i °wneud rhywbeth
• (*create*)
= creu
• (*earn*)
= ennill (*stem* enill-)

she makes £500 a week = mae hi'n ennill pum cant o °bunnoedd yr wythnos
• (*other uses*)
to make something clear = esbonio rhywbeth, amlygu rhywbeth
to make the most of something = manteisio ar° rywbeth

make do
to make do with something = bodloni ar° rywbeth

make out
• (*distinguish*)
= canfod
• (*understand*)
= deall

make up
• (*fabricate*)
= ffugio, dyfeisio
• (*compensate*)
to make it up to someone = gwneud iawn i° rywun

make-up *noun*
= colur (*plural* -on) *masculine*

male
1 *adjective*
= gwrywaidd
2 *noun*
= gwryw (*plural* -iaid, -od) *masculine*

man *noun*
= dyn (*plural* -ion) *masculine*, gŵr (*plural* gwŷr) *masculine*

manage *verb*
• (*control*)
= rheoli
• (*cope*)
= ymdopi
• (*succeed*)
= llwyddo
to manage to do something = llwyddo i °wneud rhywbeth

manager *noun*
= rheolwr (*plural* rheolwyr) *masculine*

manageress *noun*
= rheolwraig (*plural* rheolwragedd) *feminine*

manner *noun*
= dull (*plural* -iau) *masculine*, ffordd (*plural* ffyrdd) *feminine*, modd (*plural* -au) *masculine*

manners *plural noun*
= cwrteisi *masculine*
bad manners = anghwrteisi *masculine*
good manners = cwrteisi *masculine*

mansion *noun*
= plasty (*plural* plastai) *masculine*

manual
1 *noun*
(*book*) llawlyfr (*plural* -au) *masculine*
2 *adjective*
manual labour = gwaith dwylo *masculine*

manufacture
1 *noun*
= (*make*) gwneuthuriad *masculine*
2 *verb*
= gwneud, cynhyrchu

manuscript *noun*
= llawysgrif (*plural* -au) *feminine*

Manx *noun*
(*language*)
= Manaweg *feminine*

many
1 *adverb*
= llawer
many applicants = llawer o ymgeiswyr
how many people? = faint o °bobol?
too many books = gormod o °lyfrau
so many papers = cymaint o °bapurau
= cynifer o °bapurau
many thanks = llawer o °ddiolch
as many toys as possible =
cymaint/cynifer o °deganau ag sy'n °bosib

! *This quantity expression requires* **o°**
with a following noun.

2 *pronoun*
= llawer
have you got many left? = oes llawer
'da chi ar ôl? (*South*), oes gynnoch chi
°lawer ar ôl? (*North*)
there are so many here! = mae
cymaint/cynifer fan hyn!

map *noun*
= map (*plural* -au) *masculine*

marble *noun*
• (*material*)
= marmor (*plural* -au) *masculine*
• (*glass ball*)
= marblen (*plural* marblis) *feminine*

march
1 *verb*
= gorymdeithio
2 *noun*
= gorymdaith (*plural* gorymdeithiau)
feminine

March *noun*
= mis Mawrth, Mawrth *masculine*
see also **January**

margarine *noun*
= marjarîn *masculine*

marginal *adjective*
= ymylol

mark
1 *noun*
• (*on paper etc*)
= marc (*plural* -iau) *masculine*
• (*grade*)
= marc (*plural* -iau) *masculine*
• (*trace, stain*)
= ôl (*plural* olion) *masculine*
2 *verb*
• (*correct*)
= marcio
• (*make a mark*)
= nodi

marker *noun*
= marciwr (*plural* marcwyr) *masculine*

market *noun*
= marchnad (*plural* -oedd) *feminine*
job market = marchnad swyddi (*plural*
marchnadoedd swyddi) *feminine*

marketing *noun*
= marchnata *verbnoun*

marmalade *noun*
= marmalêd *masculine*

marriage *noun*
= priodas (*plural* -au) *feminine*

married *adjective*
= priod
are you married? = dych chi'n °briod?
to get married to someone = priodi
rhywun, priodi â^h rhywun

marry *verb*
= priodi

marsh *noun*
= cors (*plural* -ydd) *feminine*

marvellous *adjective*
= gwych, bendigedig, penigamp

masculine *adjective*
= gwrywaidd

mashed potatoes *noun*
= tatws stwnsh *plural*

mask *noun*
= mwgwd (*plural* mygydau) *masculine*,
masg (*plural* -iau) *masculine*

mason *noun*
= saer (*plural* seiri) *masculine*

mass
1 *adjective*
(*relating to the masses*) = torfol
2 *noun*
• (*church service*)
= offeren *feminine*
• (*physical*)
= màs *masculine*
• (*of people*)
= torf (*plural* -eydd) *feminine*, llu (*plural* -oedd) *masculine*

massive *adjective*
= enfawr, anferth

mass media *noun*
= cyfryngau torfol *plural*

mast *noun*
= hwylbren (*plural* -au) *masculine*, mast (*plural* -iau) *masculine*

master
1 *noun*
= meistr (*plural* -i) *masculine*
2 *verb*
= meistroli

mat *noun*
= mat (*plural* -iau) *masculine*

match
1 *noun*
• (*game*)
= gêm (*plural* -au) *feminine*
• (*matchstick*)
= matsien (*plural* matsis) *feminine*
2 *verb*
• (*correspond*)
= cyfateb
three matching numbers = tri rhif yn cyfateb, tri rhif cyfatebol
• (*go together*)
= cydfynd â^h
the curtains don't match the carpet = dyw'r llenni ºddim yn cydfynd â'r carped

matchbox *noun*
= bocs matsis (*plural* bocsys matsis) *masculine*

mate *noun*
(*friend*) = ffrind (*plural* -iau) *masculine*

material *noun*
= deunydd (*plural* -iau) *masculine*, defnydd (*plural* -iau) *masculine*

math *noun* (*US*)
= mathemateg *feminine*

mathematics *noun*
= mathemateg *feminine*

maths *noun*
= mathemateg *feminine*

matter
1 *noun*
• (*material*)
= deunydd (*plural* -iau) *masculine*, defnydd (*plural* -iau) *masculine*
reading matter = deunydd darllen *masculine*
• (*idiomatic uses*)
for that matter = o ºran hynny
what's the matter? = beth sy'n bod?
what's the matter with him = beth sy'n bod arno (fe)?
2 *verb*
does it matter? = ydy hi'n ºbwysig?
it doesn't matter = does dim ots

mattress *noun*
= matres (*plural* -i) *masculine or feminine*

maximum
1 *adjective*
= ucha(f), mwya(f)
2 *noun*
= uchafswm (*plural* uchafsymiau) *masculine*

May *noun*
= mis Mai, Mai *masculine*
see also **January**

may *verb*

> **!** *This verb has no exact equivalent in Welsh. Where it indicates possibility, phrasings with* **efallai** (*'perhaps'*) *are used. Where it indicates permission,* **cael** *is the best option.*

• (*possibility : generally phrased using* efallai *in Welsh*)

they may be able to come = efallai y gallan nhw °ddod

you may be right = efallai °fod ti'n iawn

he may have gone already = efallai °fod e wedi mynd yn °barod

• (*be allowed*)
= cael

may I come in? = °ga i °ddod i mewn?

you may call round tomorrow = fe °gewch chi °alw heibio yfory

may we contribute? = °gawn ni °gyfrannu?

maybe *adverb*
= efallai (*colloquial* ella (*North*), falle (*South*)), hwyrach (*North*)

maybe they'll come tomorrow = efallai y dôn nhw yfory

maybe he's ill = efallai °fod e'n sâl

maybe they left early = efallai bod nhw wedi gadael yn °gynnar, efallai iddyn nhw °adael yn °gynnar

mayor *noun*
= maer (*plural* meiri) *masculine*

mayoress *noun*
= maeres (*plural* -au) *feminine*

me *pronoun*
• (*object pronoun*)
= i, fi; mi (*rare*)

come with me = dewch 'da fi

phone me = ffonia fi

don't help me! = paid helpu fi!

write to me = ysgrifenna ata i

who's there?—me! = pwy sy'na?—fi!

it's me! = fi sy 'ma!

• (*to me*)
= i mi, i fi, ata i

she gave me a present = rhoddodd hi anrheg i mi

will you send me a letter? = nei di hala llythyr ata i?

• (*as object of verbnoun*)
= 'n/ⁿ ... i/fi

can you hear me? = °elli di ⁿghlywed i?

meagre *adjective*
= pitw

meal *noun*
= pryd o °fwyd *masculine*

mean
1 *adjective*
• (*unkind, nasty*)
= cas

don't be mean to her = paid bod yn °gas wrthi (hi)

• (*stingy*)
= crintach

2 *verb*
• (*signify*)
= meddwl, golygu

what does this word mean? = beth mae'r gair 'ma'n °olygu?, beth mae'r gair 'ma'n °feddwl?, beth ydy ystyr y gair 'ma?

• (*imply*)
= meddwl

what do you mean? = beth dych chi'n °feddwl?

• (*intend*)
= bwriadu

I mean to go there = dw i'n bwriadu mynd yno

• (*to have as a result*)
= golygu, meddwl

this means we'll be late = mae hyn yn golygu *or* meddwl y byddwn ni'n hwyr

meaning *noun*
= ystyr (*plural* -on) *masculine or feminine*

what is the meaning of this word? = beth ydy ystyr y gair 'ma?, beth mae'r gair 'ma'n °feddwl?

means *noun*
• (*way*)
= modd (*plural* -au) *masculine*, ffordd (*plural* ffyrdd) *feminine*

a means of earning money = modd *or* ffordd o ennill arian

• (*method*)
= dull (*plural* -iau) *masculine*

by means of something = drwy° rywbeth

meant: to be meant to *verb*
= i °fod i°

he is meant to go tonight = mae e i °fod i °fynd heno

what are we meant to do? = beth dyn ni i °fod i °wneud?

meantime *noun*
= cyfamser *masculine*

in the meantime = yn y cyfamser

meanwhile *adverb*
= yn y cyfamser

measles *noun*
= y °frech °goch *feminine*

they've got measles = mae'r °frech °goch arnyn nhw

! *This expression denoting a temporary physical state uses* **ar°** + *person.*

---

measure

1 *noun*
- (*for measuring*)
  = mesur (*plural* -au) *masculine*
- (*act, step*)
  = mesur (*plural* -au) *masculine*
2 *verb*
  = mesur, mesuro

measurement *noun*
   to take someone's measurements = mesur rhywun
   to take the measurements of a room = mesur stafell

meat *noun*
   = cig *masculine*

mechanic *noun*
   = mecanydd (*plural* -ion) *masculine*

mechanical *adjective*
   = mecanyddol

mechanism *noun*
   = mecanwaith (*plural* mecanweithiau) *masculine*

medal *noun*
   = medal (*plural* -au) *feminine*

media *noun*
   = cyfryngau *plural*
   the mass media = y cyfryngau torfol

medical *adjective*
   = meddygol

medicine *noun*
   = moddion *plural*

Mediterranean *noun*
   the Mediterranean (Sea) = Môr y Canoldir *masculine*

medium

1 *adjective*
   = canolig
2 *noun*
   = cyfrwng (*plural* cyfryngau) *masculine*
   through the medium of Welsh = drwy °gyfrwng y °Gymraeg

meet *verb*
- (*most senses*)
  = cwrdd â^h, cyfarfod (â^h)

to meet someone = cwrdd â^h rhywun = cyfarfod (â^h) rhywun
   have you met my wife? = dych chi wedi cwrdd â ^ngwraig?
- (*fetch, collect*)
  = casglu
  I'll meet you from the station = na i °gasglu chi o'r °orsaf

meeting *noun*
   = cyfarfod (*plural* -ydd) *masculine*

melon *noun*
   = melon (*plural* -au) *masculine*

melt *verb*
   = toddi

member *noun*
   = aelod (*plural* -au) *masculine*
   to become a member of a club = ymaelodi mewn clwb
   to become a member of the club = ymaelodi yn y clwb
   a member of staff = aelod staff (*plural* aelodau staff) *masculine*
   Member of the (Welsh) Assembly = Aelod Cynulliad (*plural* Aelodau Cynulliad) *masculine*

membership *noun*
   = aelodaeth *feminine*

membership card *noun*
   = cerdyn aelodaeth (*plural* cardiau aelodaeth) *masculine*

membership fee *noun*
   = tâl aelodaeth (*plural* taliadau aelodaeth) *masculine*

memory *noun*
- (*faculty*)
  = cof (*plural* -ion) *masculine*
  he's got a good memory = mae gynno fo °gof da (*North*), mae cof da 'da fe (*South*)
- (*reminiscence*)
  = atgof (*plural* -ion) *masculine*

menace

1 *noun*
   = bygythiad (*plural* -au) *masculine*
2 *verb*
   = bygwth (*stem* bygyth-)

menacing *adjective*
   = bygythiol

mend *verb*
   = trwsio

I'll have to have the car mended = bydd rhaid i mi °gael trwsio'r car

mental *adjective*
= meddyliol

mention *verb*
= sôn (*stem* soni-) am°
I've already mentioned that = dw i wedi sôn am hynny'n °barod
I'm cold, not to mention wet = dw i'n oer, heb sôn am °wlyb

menu *noun*
= bwydlen (*plural* -ni) *feminine*

mercy *noun*
= trugaredd *masculine or feminine*

merry *adjective*
= llawen
Merry Christmas! = Nadolig Llawen!

mess *noun*
• (*disorder*)
= llanast *masculine*
look at this mess! = edrych ar y llanast 'ma!
• (*botch*)
= cawl *masculine*
I've made a mess of it = dw i wedi gwneud cawl ohoni

message *noun*
= neges (*plural* -au, -euon) *feminine*

messenger *noun*
= negesydd (*plural* -on) *masculine*

metal *noun*
= metel (*plural* -au, -oedd) *masculine*

method *noun*
= dull (*plural* -iau) *masculine*

metre *noun*
= medr (*plural* -au) *masculine*

microphone *noun*
= meicroffon (*plural* -au) *masculine*

microwave (oven) *noun*
= meicrodon (*plural* -nau) *feminine*, popty meicrodon (*plural* poptai meicrodon) *masculine*

midday *noun*
= canol dydd, hanner dydd

middle *noun*
• = canol (*plural* -au) *masculine*
in the middle of the town = yng °nghanol y °dre

I'm in the middle of doing this = dw i ar °ganol gwneud hyn
• (*middle region*)
= canolbarth (*plural* -au) *masculine*

middle-aged *adjective*
= canol oed

middle-class *adjective*
= dosbarth canol
middle-class values = gwerthoedd dosbarth canol

middle class *noun*
the middle class(es) = y dosbarthiadau canol *plural*

Middle East *noun*
= y Dwyrain Canol *masculine*

middling *adjective*
= canolig

midland *noun*
the Midlands = Canolbarth Lloegr

midnight *noun*
= canol nos, hanner nos

midwife *noun*
= bydwraig (*plural* bydwragedd) *feminine*

might *verb*

> ! *This verb has no exact equivalent in Welsh. Where it means 'may', phrasings with* **efallai** *('perhaps') or* **mae'n °bosib** *(it's possible) are used. For 'might have...',* **gallu/medru + °fod wedi** *is the usual equivalent, while a special construction is used for 'might as well...'.*

• (*may: generally phrased using efallai or mae'n °bosib in Welsh*)
he might come later = efallai y daw e wedyn
she might be right = efallai bod hi'n iawn
we might miss the bus = mae'n bosib y collwn ni'r bws
they might have gone = efallai bod nhw wedi mynd
• (*could have: indicating something that could have happened but didn't*)
they might have been killed = mi °allen nhw °fod wedi cael eu lladd
she might have warned us = gallai hi °fod wedi'n rhybuddio ni
• **might as well ...**
= waeth i° + °*verbnoun*, man a man i° + °*verbnoun*

we might as well go = waeth inni °fynd
= man a man inni °fynd
she might as well give up = waeth iddi
°roi'r gorau iddi
= man a man iddi °roi'r gorau iddi

mild *adjective*
= mwyn

mile *noun*
= milltir (*plural* -oedd) *feminine*
sixty miles an hour = chwedeg millitr
yr awr

military *adjective*
= milwrol

milk
1 *noun*
= llefrith (*North*) *masculine*, llaeth
(*South*) *masculine*
2 *verb*
= godro

milkman *noun*
= dyn llefrith/llaeth (*plural* dynion
llefrith/llaeth) *masculine*

milkshake *noun*
= ysgytlaeth *masculine*

mill *noun*
= melin (*plural* -au) *feminine*

million *numeral*
= miliwn (*plural* miliynau) *feminine*
eight million people = wyth miliwn o
°bobol
twenty million pounds = ugain miliwn
o °bunnoedd

> **!** *This numeral always requires* **o°** +
> *plural noun.*

millionaire *noun*
= miliwnydd (*plural* -ion) *masculine*

mince *noun*
= cig mân *masculine*

mind
1 *noun*
= meddwl *masculine*
to change one's mind = ailfeddwl
to make up one's mind = penderfynu
2 *verb*

> **!** *This verb has numerous idiomatic
> uses in English and care should be
> taken in finding the appropriate
> translation in Welsh.*

I don't mind = does gen i °ddim ots
= dim ots gen i, dim ots 'da fi
I wouldn't mind a cup of tea = byddai'n
°dda cael panaid
I wouldn't mind coming = °fyddwn i
°ddim yn malio dod
mind your own business! = paid
busnesa!
do you mind? = oes gen ti ots?, oes ots
'da ti?
never mind! = ta waeth!, dim ots!
mind the steps! = gwyliwch y grisiau!
nothing against her, mind = dim byd
yn ei herbyn, cofia

mine¹ *pronoun*
that's mine = fi (sy) biau hwnna
his garden's bigger than mine = mae ei
°ardd e'n °fwy na 'n un i
his marks were better than mine =
roedd ci °farciau fe'n °well na 'n rhai i
the yellow book is mine = fi (sy) biau'r
llyfr melyn

mine²
1 *noun*
• (*general term*)
= mwynglawdd (*plural* mwyngloddiau)
masculine
• (*coal*)
= glofa (*plural* glofeydd) *feminine*, pwll
glo (*plural* pyllau glo) *masculine*
2 *verb*
= cloddio

miner *noun*
• (*general term*)
= cloddiwr (*plural* cloddwyr) *masculine*,
mwyngloddiwr (*plural* mwyngloddwyr)
masculine
• (*coal miner*)
= glöwr (*plural* glowyr) *masculine*

mineral *noun*
= mwyn (*plural* -au) *masculine*

mineral water *noun*
= dŵr mwynol *masculine*

minimum
1 *adjective*
= lleia(f), isa(f)
2 *noun*
= lleiafswm (*plural* lleiafsymiau)
masculine, isafswm (*plural* isafsymiau)
masculine

minister *noun*
= gweinidog (*plural* -ion) *masculine*

minor *adjective*
- (*insignificant*)
  = mân
- (*lesser*)
  = llai, lleia(f)

minority *noun*
= lleiafrif (*plural* -oedd) *masculine*
minority language = iaith °leiafrifol
(*plural* ieithoedd lleiafrifol) *feminine*

mint *noun*
- (*plant*)
  = mint, mintys *masculine*
- (*sweet*)
  = mint (*plural* -s) *masculine*

minus *preposition*
- (*in subtraction*)
  = namyn
  six minus two is four = chwech namyn
  dau ydy pedwar
- (*numbers*)
  = minws
  minus ten degrees Celsius = minws
  deg gradd Celsius
- (*without*)
  = heb°
  **he got his wallet back minus the
  money** = fe °gafodd e ei waled yn ôl
  heb yr arian

minute *noun*
= munud (*plural* -au) *masculine* (*North*),
feminine (*South*)
I'll be back in ten minutes = bydda i yn
ôl ymhen deng munud
at the last minute = ar y °funud ola(f)
wait a minute! = aros/arhoswch °funud!
at the minute = ar hyn o °bryd

> **!** *Although the gender of* **munud**
> *varies from region to region, it is
> always feminine in the expression* **ar y
> °funud ola(f).**

minutes *noun*
to take the minutes = cofnodi

miracle *noun*
= gwyrth (*plural* -iau) *feminine*

miraculous *adjective*
= gwyrthiol

mirror *noun*
= drych (*plural* -au) *masculine*

mis- *prefix*
= cam°-

misbehave *verb*
= camymddwyn

misbehaviour *noun*
= camymddygiad *masculine*,
camymddwyn *verbnoun*

miserable *adjective*
- (*wretched*)
  = truan, truenus
- (*downhearted*)
  = digalon
  to feel miserable = teimlo'n °ddigalon
- (*weather etc*)
  = diflas

misfortune *noun*
- (*single event*)
  = anffawd (*plural* anffodion) *feminine*
- (*state*)
  = anlwc *feminine*

mishap *noun*
= anffawd (*plural* anffodion) *feminine*

mislead *verb*
= camarwain (*stem* camarweini-)

misleading *adjective*
= camarweiniol

miss
1 *verb*
- (*fail to catch, be late for*)
  = colli
  to miss the bus = colli'r bws
  to miss an opportunity = colli cyfle
- (*fail to hit*)
  = methu
  to miss the target = methu'r nod
- (*a person*)
  = colli, gweld eisiau
  we'll miss you = byddwn ni'n colli chi,
  byddwn ni'n gweld eich eisiau
2 *noun*
= methiant (*plural* methiannau)
masculine

missile *noun*
= taflegryn (*plural* taflegrau) *masculine*

missing *adjective*
= ar °goll
the document is missing = mae'r
°ddogfen ar °goll

> **!** *This adjective phrase does not use*
> **yn** *to link it to the verb* 'to be'.

mist *noun*
= niwl (*plural* -oedd) *masculine*

mistake *noun*
- (*misunderstanding, error*)
  = camgymeriad (*plural* -au) *masculine*
  to make a mistake = gwneud
  camgymeriad
- (*written error etc*)
  = gwall (*plural* -au) *masculine*
  this document is full of mistakes =
  mae'r °ddogfen 'ma'n °wallus

mistletoe *noun*
  = uchelwydd *masculine*

mistreat *verb*
  = camdrin (*stem* camdrini-)

misty *adjective*
  = niwlog

misunderstand *verb*
  = camddeall

misunderstanding *noun*
  = camddealltwriaeth (*plural* -au)
  feminine

mix *verb*
  = cymysgu
  to mix something with something
  else = cymysgu rhywbeth âʰ rhywbeth
  arall
  oil and water don't mix = dydy olew a
  dŵr °ddim yn cymysgu
  he mixes well = mae e'n cymysgu'n
  °dda

mix up
  to mix someone up with someone
  else = cymysgu rhwng rhywun a
  rhywun arall
  to mix two things up = cymysgu dau
  °beth

mixed *adjective*
  = cymysg
  mixed feelings = teimladau cymysg
  plural
  mixed school = ysgol °gymysg (*plural*
  ysgolion cymysg) *feminine*

mixture *noun*
  = cymysgedd (*plural* -au) *masculine*

moan *verb*
  = ochneidio

mobile *adjective*
  = symudol

mobile phone *noun*
  = ffôn symudol (*plural* ffonau symudol)

masculine, ffôn cludo (*plural* ffonau
cludo) *masculine*

model *noun*
  = model (*plural* -au) *masculine*

modern *adjective*
  = modern, cyfoes

mole *noun*
- (*animal*)
  = twrch daear (*plural* tyrchod daear)
  masculine (*North*), gwadd, gwadden
  (*plural* gwaddod) *feminine* (*South*)
- (*on skin*)
  = man geni (*plural* mannau geni)
  masculine

mom *noun* (*US*)
  = mam *feminine*

moment *noun*
  = eiliad (*plural* -au) *feminine* or
  masculine, munud (*plural* -au)
  masculine or *feminine*, moment (*plural*
  - au) *feminine*
  at the moment = ar hyn o °bryd, ar y
  °foment
  wait a moment! = arhoswch
  eiliad/°funud!

mommy *noun* (*US*)
  = mam *feminine*

Monday *noun*
  = dydd Llun

> **!** **(on) Monday night** = nos °Lun
> **on Monday** = °ddydd Llun
> **on Mondays** = ar °ddydd Llun
> **on Monday nights** = ar nos °Lun
> **every Monday** = °bob dydd Llun
> **Monday morning** = bore (dydd) Llun
> **on Monday morning** = °fore dydd
> Llun
> **Monday afternoon** = pnawn dydd
> Llun
> **last Monday** = dydd Llun diwetha
> **next Monday** = dydd Llun nesa,
> = dydd Llun sy'n dod
> **from Monday till Wednesday** = o
> °ddydd Llun tan/hyd °ddydd Mercher
> **by Monday** = erbyn dydd Llun
> **a week Monday** = wythnos i °ddydd
> Llun

money *noun*
  = arian *masculine*, pres *masculine*
  (*North*)

monkey *noun*
= mwnci (*plural* mwncïod) *masculine*

monoglot *adjective*
= uniaith

monolingual *adjective*
= uniaith

monotonous *adjective*
= undonog

monster *noun*
= anghenfil (*plural* angenfilod) *masculine*

month *noun*
= mis (*plural* -oedd) *masculine*
two months = deufis
every month = °bob mis
every other month = °bob yn ail °fis
last month = (y) mis diwetha
this month = (y) mis yma
next month = (y) mis nesa
I'll be back in a month = bydda i yn ôl ymhen mis

monthly
1 *adjective*
= misol
2 *noun*
(*magazine*)
= misolyn (*plural* misolion) *masculine*

monument *noun*
= cofeb (*plural* -au) *feminine*

mood *noun*
= tymer (*plural* tymherau) *feminine*, hwyl (*plural* -iau) *feminine*
she's in a good mood = mae hi mewn tymer °dda, mae hwyl °dda arni (hi)
she's in a bad mood = mae hi mewn tymer °ddrwg, mae hwyl °ddrwg arni (hi)
to be in the mood for dancing = bod mewn hwyl dawnsio

moody *adjective*
= oriog

moon *noun*
= lleuad (*plural* -au) *feminine*
full moon = lleuad °lawn (*plural* lleuadau llawn)
new moon = lleuad newydd (*plural* lleuadau newydd)

moor *noun*
= rhos (*plural* -ydd) *feminine*

moped *noun*
= moped (*plural* -au) *masculine*

moral
1 *adjective*
= moesol
2 *noun*
(*of story*) = gwers (*plural* -i) *feminine*, moeswers (*plural* -i) *feminine*

morals *plural noun*
= moesau *plural*

more
1 *pronoun*
= mwy, rhagor
we need more = dyn ni angen mwy
I did more than you = nes i °fwy na ti
there are more here today than yesterday = mae mwy fan hyn heddiw na ddoe
2 *adjective*
• (*in addition*)
= rhagor, mwy, chwaneg, chwanag (*colloquial*)
would you like some more coffee? = hoffech chi °ragor o °goffi?, hoffech chi °fwy o °goffi?, hoffech chi chwaneg o °goffi?

> **!** *All these quantity expressions require* **o°** *with a following noun.*

3 *adverb*
• (*in comparisons*)
= mwy (*with longer words*), -ach (*with shorter words*)
more expensive = mwy costus = drutach
this one is more dangerous = mae hon yn °fwy peryglus
that one is more beautiful = mae honna'n harddach
• (*time*)
= bellach, mwyach (*both with negative verb*)
he doesn't live here any more = dydy e °ddim yn byw yma bellach
• (*in excess of, over*)
= mwy, dros°
more than a thousand people = mwy na mil o °bobol = dros °fil o °bobol
the more..., the more... = mwya yn y byd..., mwya yn y byd...

morning *noun*
= bore (*plural* -au) *masculine*

good morning = bore da!
three o'clock in the morning = tri o'r
  °gloch yn y bore
this morning = (y) bore 'ma
tomorrow morning = bore fory
yesterday morning = bore ddoe

most
1 *pronoun*
  = y rhan °fwya(f), mwyafrif (*plural* -oedd)
  masculine
  most will come back = bydd y rhan
    °fwya'n dod yn ôl
  I like most of it = dw i'n leicio'r rhan
    °fwya ohoni
  at the most = ar y mwya(f)
2 *adverb*
  = mwya (*with longer words*), -a(f) (*with
  shorter words*)
  most expensive = mwya costus,
    druta(f)
  this one is the most dangerous = hon
    ydy'r un °fwya peryglus, hwn ydy'r un
    mwya peryglus
  that one is the most beautiful = honna
    ydy'r un hardda(f)
  most of all = yn anad dim
3 *adjective*
  = y rhan °fwya(f)
  most children watch television =
    mae'r rhan °fwya o °blant yn gwylio'r
    teledu

mostly *adverb*
  = rhan amla(f), gan amla(f), gan
  °fwya(f)/mwya(f)

moth *noun*
  = gwyfyn (*plural* -od *or* gwyfod)
  masculine, pry'r °gannwyll (*plural*
  pryfed y °gannwyll) *masculine*

mother *noun*
  = mam (*plural* -au) *feminine*

mother-in-law *noun*
  = mam-yng-nghyfraith *feminine*

mother tongue *noun*
  = mamiaith *feminine*

motion *noun*
• (*movement*)
  = symudiad (*plural* -au) *masculine*,
  symud *verbnoun*
• (*in debate*)
  = cynnig (*plural* cynigion) *masculine*

motor *noun*
  = motor (*plural* -au) *masculine*

motorbike *noun*
  = beic modur (*plural* beiciau modur)
  masculine

motorcyclist *noun*
  = motorbeiciwr (*plural* motorbeicwyr)
  masculine

motorist *noun*
  = modurwr (*plural* modurwyr)
  masculine

motor racing *noun*
  = rasio ceir *verbnoun*

motorway *noun*
  = priffordd (*plural* priffyrdd) *feminine*,
  traffordd (*plural* traffyrdd) *feminine*

mountain *noun*
  = mynydd (*plural* -oedd) *masculine*
  to climb a mountain = dringo mynydd
  to make a mountain out of a molehill =
    gwneud môr a mynydd o° rywbeth

mountain bike *noun*
  = beic mynydd (*plural* beiciau mynydd)
  masculine

mountaineering *noun*
  = mynydda *verbnoun*

mountainous *adjective*
  = mynyddig

mourning *noun*
  = galar *masculine*
  to be in mourning for someone =
    galaru am° rywun

mouse *noun*
  = llygoden (*plural* llygod) *feminine*

moustache *noun*
  = mwstash (*plural* -is) *masculine*

mouth *noun*
• (*part of face*)
  = ceg (*plural* -au) *feminine*
  shut your mouth! = cau dy °geg!
• (*of river*)
  = aber (*plural* -oedd) *feminine*

movable *adjective*
  = symudol

move *verb*
  = symud
  don't move! = paid symud!
  to move the car = symud y car
  to move house = symud tŷ

to move someone to do something = ysgogi rhywun i °wneud rhywbeth

move away (*to another area*) = mynd i ffwrdd i °fyw

move back (*into an area*) = dod yn ôl i °fyw

move forward = symud ymlaen

move in = symud i mewn

move out = symud allan (*North*), symud mas (*South*)

move over = symud

could you move over? = °allet ti symud?

movement *noun*
- (*act or result of moving*) = symudiad (*plural* -au) *masculine*
- (*organization*) = mudiad (*plural* -au) *masculine*

movie *noun* = ffilm (*plural* -iau) *feminine*

at the movies = yn y sinema

movie theater *noun* (*US*) = sinema (*plural* sinemâu) *masculine or feminine*

mow *verb* = pladurio

MP *noun* = Aelod Seneddol (*plural* Aelodau Seneddol) *masculine*, AS

mph *abbreviation* = mya (milltir yr awr)

Mr *noun* = y Br (*abbreviation of* Bonwr)

Mrs *noun* = y Fns (*abbreviation of* °Foneddiges)

much
1 *adverb*
- (*a lot*) = llawer, (*also* o °lawer *with adjectives*), lot

this work is much too hard = mae'r gwaith 'ma'n llawer rhy °galed, mae'r gwaith 'ma'n rhy °galed o °lawer

I don't read much = dw i °ddim yn darllen llawer

we haven't got much time = does dim llawer o amser 'da ni (*South*), does gynnon ni °ddim llawer o amser (*North*)

not much = dim llawer

how much? = faint (o°)?

how much bread did you buy? = faint o °fara °brynest ti?

too much = gormod (o°)

I've spent too much money = dw i wedi gwario gormod o arian

so much = cymaint (o°)

there was so much noise = roedd cymaint o sŵn

! **llawer** *is the preferred standard term, but the loanword* **lot** *is very common in speech. Welsh has special words for* 'how much', 'too much' *and* 'so much', *none of which use the word* **llawer**.

The quantity expressions **llawer, lot, faint, gormod** *and* **cymaint** *all require* **o°** *with a following noun.*

- (*often*) = yn aml

we don't go out much = dyn ni °ddim yn mynd allan yn aml

too much = gormod, °ormod

you talk too much = ti'n siarad gormod

so much = cymaint, °gymaint

2 *pronoun* = llawer, lot

is there much left? = oes llawer ar ôl?

he didn't eat much = naeth e °ddim bwyta llawer

how much? = faint?

how much is this? = faint ydy hwn?

too much = gormod

she drank too much = naeth hi yfed gormod

so much = cymaint

there was so much to see = roedd cymaint i'w °weld

mud *noun* = baw *masculine*

mug
1 *noun*
- (*cup*) = mwg (*plural* mygiau) *masculine*

- (*fool*)
  = ffŵl (*plural* ffyliaid) *masculine*
2 *verb*
  (*attack*)
  = mygio

mugger *noun*
= mygiwr (*plural* mygwyr) *masculine*

muggy *adjective*
= mwll, trymaidd

multiply *verb*
- (*general sense*)
  = lluosogi
- (*maths*)
  = lluosi

mum *noun*
= mam

mummy *noun*
= mam

mumps *noun*
= clwy'r pennau *masculine*
he's got mumps = mae clwy'r pennau
arno (fe)

> **!** *This expression denoting a
> temporary physical state uses* **ar°** +
> *person.*

murder
1 *noun*
  = llofruddiaeth (*plural* -au) *feminine*
2 *verb*
  = llofruddio

murderer *noun*
= llofrudd (*plural* -ion) *masculine*

murderess *noun*
= llofruddes (*plural* -au) *feminine*

muscle *noun*
= cyhyr (*plural* -au) *masculine*

museum *noun*
= amgueddfa (*plural* amgueddfeydd)
feminine

mushroom *noun*
= madarchen (*plural* madarch) *feminine*

music *noun*
= cerddoriaeth *feminine*

> **!** *The loanword* **miwsig** *is common in
> speech and more informal writing
> styles.*

musical *adjective*
= cerddorol

musical instrument *noun*
= offeryn cerdd (*plural* offerynnau
cerdd) *masculine*

musician *noun*
= cerddor (*plural* -ion) *masculine*
= cerddores (*plural* -au) *feminine*

Muslim
1 *noun*
  = Moslem (*plural* -iaid) *masculine and
  feminine*
2 *adjective*
  = Moslemaidd

must *verb*
- (*obligation*)
  = rhaid, gorfod
  we must go now – rhaid inni °fynd
  nawr, dyn ni'n gorfod mynd nawr
  must you shout like that? = oes rhaid i
  ti °weiddi felly?
  they mustn't miss the bus = rhaid
  iddyn nhw °beidio colli'r bws
- (*supposition*)
  = rhaid
  you must be tired = rhaid °fod ti'n
  °flinedig
  they must have arrived by now = rhaid
  bod nhw wedi cyrraedd erbyn hyn

> **!** **rhaid** *is the usual term for* 'must', *but
> is not a verb, and furthermore uses
> different constructions for the two
> English senses.* **gorfod** *is a verb, but
> is restricted to the* 'obligation' *sense
> of the word. See Welsh-English
> entries for more details and
> examples.*

mustache *noun* (*US*)
= mwstash (*plural* -is) *masculine*

mustard *noun*
= mwstard *masculine*

mutate *verb*
  (*grammar*)
  = treiglo

mutation *noun*
  (*grammar*)
  = treiglad (*plural* -au) *masculine*
  soft mutation = treiglad meddal
  masculine

aspirate mutation = treiglad llaes
masculine
nasal mutation = treiglad trwynol
masculine
to wrongly apply a mutation =
camdreiglo

mute *adjective*
= mud

mutton *noun*
= cig dafad *masculine*

my *adjective*
= 'n ... (i/fi); ^{n} ... (i/fi); fy^n ... (*formal written*)
my children = ^{n}mhlant (i)
my shoes = 'n sgidiau (fi)
my dog = ^{n}nghi (fi)
my room = 'n stafell (i)

> **!** *The form* **fy** *is largely confined to the written language, where it is the norm. Systematic use of it in speech sounds affected.*

myself *pronoun*
= 'n hun (*North*), 'n hunan (*South*)
I'll go there myself = a i yno 'n hun(an)
I hurt myself = nes i ^{o}frifo 'n hun(an)
by myself (*on my own*) = ar ^{o}ben 'n
hun(an), ar ^{n}mhen 'n hun(an)
I'm working for myself = dw i'n
gweithio ar 'n liwt 'n hun(an)

mysterious *adjective*
= rhyfedd, rhyfeddol

mystery *noun*
= dirgelwch (*plural* dirgelion) *masculine*

Nn

nail *noun*
• (*on finger*)
= ewin (*plural* -edd) *masculine*
• (*metal*)
= hoelen, hoel (*plural* hoelion) *feminine*

nail polish *noun*
= lliw ewinedd (*plural* lliwiau ewinedd)
masculine

naked *adjective*
= noeth
stark naked = noethlymun

name *noun*
= enw (*plural* -au) *masculine*
what's your name? = beth ydy'ch enw
chi?
my name is Aled = Aled dw i
= Aled ydy'r enw
first name = enw cynta (*plural* enwau
cynta) *masculine*

namely *adverb*
= sef

napkin *noun*
= napcyn (*plural* -au) *masculine*

nappy *noun*
= cewyn (*plural* -nau) *masculine*

narrow *adjective*
= cul

narrow-minded *adjective*
a narrow-minded man = dyn cul ei
^{o}feddwl
a narrow-minded woman = dynes cul ei
meddwl

nasty *adjective*
• (*person*)
= cas, ffiaidd
• (*cold*)
= drwg
• (*moment*)
= annymunol

nation *noun*
= cenedl (*plural* cenhedloedd) *feminine*
the United Nations = y Cenhedloedd
Unedig

national *adjective*
= cenedlaethol

nationalism *noun*
= cenedlaetholdeb *masculine*

nationalist *noun*
= cenedlaetholwr (*plural* cenedlaetholwyr) *masculine*
= cenedlaetholwraig (*plural* cenedlaetholwragedd) *feminine*

nationality *noun*
= cenedligrwydd *masculine*

native
1 *adjective*
= brodorol
native language = mamiaith *feminine*
2 *noun*
= brodor (*plural* -ion) *masculine*
= brodores (*plural* -au) *feminine*
he's a native of Pwllheli = brodor o °Bwllheli ydy e

natural *adjective*
= naturiol

naturally *adverb*
• (*general senses*)
= yn naturiol
• (*of course*)
= wrth °gwrs

nature *noun*
= natur (*plural* -oedd) *feminine*

naughty *adjective*
= drwg

navy *noun*
= llynges (*plural* -au) *feminine*
to join the navy = ymuno â'r llynges, mynd i'r llynges

navy blue *adjective*
= glas tywyll

near
1 *adjective*
• (*general sense*)
= agos
the school is quite near = mae'r ysgol yn eitha agos
to get near to something = agosáu/nesáu at° rywbeth
to come nearer = dod yn nes
the nearest shops = y siopau agosa
2 *preposition*
= yn agos i°, yn ymyl, gerllaw, ar °bwys (*South*)
they live near the hospital = maen nhw'n byw yn agos i'r ysbyty

! **ar °bwys** *is a compound preposition and so changes its form with pronouns—see entry on the Welsh-English side for details.*

• (*with geographical locations*)
= ger
they live near Cardiff = maen nhw'n byw ger Caerdydd
3 *adverb*
= yn agos, yn ymyl, ar °bwys, gerllaw
do you live near? = dych chi'n byw'n agos?, dych chi'n byw ar °bwys?, dych chi'n byw yn ymyl?, dych chi'n byw gerllaw?

nearby *adverb*
= yn agos, yn ymyl, gerllaw, ar °bwys
do you live nearby? = dych chi'n byw'n agos?, dych chi'n byw ar °bwys?, dych chi'n byw yn ymyl?, dych chi'n byw gerllaw?

nearly *adverb*
= bron
I nearly fell = roedd bron i mi syrthio
they've nearly finished = maen nhw bron â gorffen
it's nearly four o'clock = mae hi bron yn °bedwar o'r °gloch
very nearly = bron iawn

near-sighted *adjective*
= byrolwg

neat *adjective*
= twt, taclus

necessary *adjective*
= angenrheidiol

neck *noun*
= gwddf (*colloquial* gwddw) (*plural* gyddfau) *masculine*

necklace *noun*
= cadwyn (*plural* -i) *feminine*, mwclis *plural* (*North*)

need
1 *verb*
• (*require*)
= angen; (*in combination with verb also:*) eisiau
I need money = dw i angen arian
do you need help? = oes angen help arnoch chi?, dych chi angen help?
do they need telling? = oes angen/eisiau dweud wrthyn nhw?

support is needed = mae angen cefnogaeth, mae rhaid wrth °gefnogaeth

> **!** **angen** and **eisiau** are both used as verbnouns except that they do not have the usual **yn** to link them to the verb 'to be'.

• (*have to*)
= rhaid
you'll need to come early = bydd rhaid i chi °ddod yn °gynnar
2 *noun*
= angen (*plural* anghenion) *masculine*, eisiau (*no plural*) *masculine*

needle *noun*
= nodwydd (*plural* -au) *feminine*

negative
1 *adjective*
= negyddol
2 *noun*
(*photographic*)
= negatif (*plural* -au) *masculine*

neglect
1 *verb*
= esgeuluso
2 *noun*
= esgeulustod *masculine*

negotiate *verb*
• (*discuss*)
= trafod
• (*get through, overcome*)
= goresgyn

negotiations *plural noun*
= trafodaethau *plural*

neighbour *noun*
= cymydog (*plural* cymdogion) *masculine*

neither
1 *conjunction*
she speaks neither English nor Welsh = dydy hi °ddim yn siarad Saesneg na ᶜChymraeg (chwaith)
he has neither car nor bike = does gynno fo °ddim car na beic (chwaith) (*North*), does dim car na beic 'da fe (*South*)
'I don't watch TV'—'neither do I' = 'dw i °ddim yn gwylio'r teledu'—'na finnau (chwaith)'
2 *adjective*
neither man is right = dydy'r un o'r dynion (°ddim) yn iawn

3 *pronoun*
neither of them is coming = dydy'r un ohonyn nhw (°ddim) yn dod

nephew *noun*
= nai (*plural* neiaint) *masculine*

nerve *noun*
= nerf (*plural* -au) *feminine or masculine*
nerves (*nervousness*) = nerfusrwydd *masculine*
to get on someone's nerves = mynd ar nerfau rhywun
her nerves are bad = un nerfus ydy hi

nervous *adjective*
= nerfus

nervousness *noun*
= nerfusrwydd *masculine*

nest *noun*
= nyth (*plural* -od) *masculine or feminine*

net
1 *noun*
= rhwyd (*plural* -i, -au) *feminine*
the Net = y Rhyngrwyd *feminine*
2 *verb*
= rhwydo

netball *noun*
= pêl-rwyd *masculine*

network *noun*
= rhwydwaith (*plural* rhwydweithiau) *masculine*

neutral *adjective*
= niwtral

neutralize *verb*
= niwtraleiddio

never *adverb*
= byth;
= erioed
they never agree = dydyn nhw byth yn cytuno
we'll never see them again = °welwn ni byth mohonyn nhw eto
I've never seen such a mess = °weles i erioed y °fath llanast
we've never been to Italy = °fuon ni erioed yn yr Eidal
never again = byth eto

> **!** **byth** and **erioed** are not interchangeable—their use depends broadly on the tense of the verb in the

sentence. See entries on the Welsh-English side for more details and examples.

never mind = ta waeth, dim ots
never mind about that = ta waeth am hynny, dim ots am hynny

nevertheless *adverb*
= serch hynny

new *adjective*
= newydd
brand new = newydd sbon

newborn baby *noun*
= baban newydd ei °eni *masculine*

newcomer *noun*
= newydd-ddyfodiad (*plural* newydd-ddyfodiaid) *masculine*

news *noun*
• (*information, events*)
= newyddion *plural*
have you heard the news? = dych chi wedi clywed y newyddion
news programme = rhaglen newyddion (*plural* rhaglenni newyddion) *feminine*
• (*of a person*)
= hanes *masculine*
what's the news on Dafydd (*what's he been up to*)? = beth ydy hanes Dafydd?

newsagent *noun*
= gwerthwr papurau newydd (*plural* gwerthwyr papurau newydd) *masculine*

newsagent's *noun*
= siop °bapurau (*plural* siopau papurau) *feminine*

newscaster *noun*
= darlledwr newyddion (*plural* darlledwyr newyddion) *masculine*
= darlledwraig newyddion (*plural* darlledwragedd newyddon) *feminine*

newspaper *noun*
= papur newydd (*plural* papurau newydd) *masculine*

newsreader *noun*
= darlledwr newyddion (*plural* darlledwyr newyddion) *masculine*
= darlledwraig newyddion (*plural* darlledwragedd newyddon) *feminine*

New Year *noun*
= y °Flwyddyn Newydd *feminine*
Happy New Year! = Blwyddyn Newydd °Dda!

New Year's Day *noun*
= Dydd Calan *masculine*

New Year's Eve *noun*
= Nos °Galan *feminine*

next
1 *adjective*
= nesa
when does the next train leave? = pryd mae'r trên nesa'n ymadael?
next week = wythnos nesa
the next day = y diwrnod wedyn, trannoeth
next door = drws nesa
who's next? = pwy sy nesa?
me next! = fi nesa!
2 *adverb*
• (*in the past*)
= wedyn, ar ôl hynny
what happened next = beth °ddigwyddodd wedyn?
• (*now*)
= nawr, nesa
what shall we do next? = be' nawn ni nawr *or* nesa?
• (*future*)
= y tro nesa
when you're next in Cardiff... = y tro nesa i ti °fod yng ⁿNghaerdydd ...

next door *adverb*
= drws nesa

nice *adjective*
• (*pleasant, agreeable*)
= hyfryd, neis, dymunol
how nice! = 'na neis!, 'na hyfryd!
• (*personality*)
= annwyl, dymunol
• (*weather*)
= braf

nickname *noun*
= llysenw (*plural* -au) *masculine*

niece *noun*
= nith (*plural* -oedd) *feminine*

night *noun*
• (*opposite of day*)
= nos (*plural* -au) *feminine*
good night! = nos da!

to stay the night = aros (*stem* arhos-) dros nos
all night = trwy'r nos
every night = °bob nos
overnight = dros nos
to become night = nosi
last night = neithiwr
the night before last = echnos
the night after = y noson wedyn
• (*evening*)
= noson (*plural* nosweithiau) *feminine*, noswaith (*plural* nosweithiau) *feminine*
a night in the pub = noson yn y °dafarn

nightclub *noun*
= clwb nos (*plural* clybiau nos) *masculine*

nightdress *noun*
= coban (*plural* -au) *feminine*

nightmare *noun*
= hunlle(f) (*plural* hunllefau) *feminine*

nil *numeral*
= dim

nine *numeral*
= naw
nine people = naw o °bobol
nine days = naw ⁿniwrnod
nine years = naw ⁿmlynedd
nine years old = naw ⁿmlwydd oed
at nine o'clock = am naw o'r °gloch
I have nine = mae gen i naw (*North*), mae naw 'da fi (*South*)

nineteen *numeral*
= pedwararbymtheg, undeg naw *masculine*
= pedairarbymtheg, undeg naw *feminine*
nineteen horses = pedwar ceffyl ar °bymtheg, undeg naw o °geffylau
nineteen cats = pedair cath ar °bymtheg, undeg naw o °gathod
nineteen years = pedair blynedd ar °bymtheg, undeg naw o °flynyddoedd
nineteen years old = pedair blwydd ar °bymtheg oed, undeg naw ⁿmlwydd oed

ninety *numeral*
= nawdeg
ninety apples = nawdeg o afalau
ninety years = nawdeg o °flynyddoedd
ninety years old = nawdeg oed

ninth *adjective*
= nawfed

no
1 *adverb*

> ! *How to say* **'no'** *to a question in Welsh depends on the phrasing of the question itself. For this reason there are numerous equivalents.*

• (*with tenses other than past*)
= na / nag + *verb of question*
'are you coming?'—'no' = 'wyt ti'n dod?'—'nag ydw'
'were they late?'—'no' = 'oedden nhw'n hwyr?'—'nag oedden'
'will she be here?'—'no' = '°fydd hi yma?'—'na °fydd'
• (*with past tenses*)
= naddo
'did you see him?'—'no' = '°welest ti fe?'—'naddo'
• (*in focused questions*)
= nage
'is she Welsh?'—'no' = 'Cymraes yw hi?'—'nage'
2 *adjective*
= dim
no smoking = dim ysmygu
there's no food left = does dim bwyd ar ôl

nobody *pronoun*
= neb
there's nobody here = does neb fan hyn
I saw nobody = °weles i neb
nobody else = neb arall

nod *verb*
= amneidio, nodio
he nodded his head = mi nodiodd e ei °ben
= mi amneidiodd e â'i °ben
to nod to someone = nodio ar° rywun

noise *noun*
= sŵn (*plural* synau) *masculine*
to make a noise = gwneud sŵn, (*constantly*) = cadw sŵn

noisy *adjective*
= swnllyd

non-alcoholic *adjective*
= dialcohol, heb alcohol

none *pronoun*
= dim un, dim yr un

none of them understands = dydy'r un
ohonyn nhw (°ddim) yn deall
there is none left = does dim ar ôl
there are none left = does dim ar ôl
I've got none = does gynna i °ddim
(*North*), does gen i °ddim (*North*), does
dim 'da fi (*South*)

nonsense *noun*
= lol *feminine*, sothach *masculine*
to talk nonsense = malu awyr
= siarad lol

noon *noun*
= canol dydd, hanner dydd

no-one *pronoun*
= neb
there's no-one here = does neb fan hyn
I saw no-one = °weles i neb
no-one else = neb arall

nor *conjunction*
= na[h]
'I don't understand'—'nor do I' = 'dw i
°ddim yn deall'—'na finnau (chwaith)'
(*for* **neither ... nor...**, ⇨**neither**)

normal *adjective*
= normal

normality *noun*
= normalrwydd *masculine*

normalize *verb*
= normaleiddio

normally *adverb*
= fel arfer, fel rheol

north
1 *adjective*
= gogledd
the north wind = gwynt y gogledd
we live in North Wales = dyn ni'n byw
yng [n]Ngogledd Cymru
2 *adverb*
to go north = mynd i'r gogledd, mynd
tua'r gogledd
3 *noun*
= gogledd *masculine*
to the north of Cardiff = i'r gogledd o
°Gaerdydd
they come from the North of England
= maen nhw'n dod o °Ogledd Lloegr

northeast *noun*
= gogledd-°ddwyrain *masculine*

northerly *adjective*
= gogleddol, o'r gogledd

northern *adjective*
= gogleddol, gogledd

northwest *noun*
= gogledd-°orllewin *masculine*

nose *noun*
= trwyn (*plural* -au) *masculine*
**to stick one's nose in someone's
business** = busnesa

nosebleed *noun*
= gwaedlif (*plural* -au, -oedd) o'r trwyn
masculine

nosey, nosy *adjective*
= busneslyd

not *adverb*
• (*general senses*)
= dim

> **!** This is the universal word for
> negating verbs in the living
> language—it follows the subject and
> is therefore practically always
> encountered with soft mutation—
> °**ddim**. (*In formal written Welsh an
> entirely different way of negating
> verbs is used.*) The unmutated from
> **dim** is found when words other than
> verbs are negated.

I'm not coming = dw i °ddim yn dod
'is she here?'—'I hope not' = 'ydy hi
fan hyn?'—'gobeithio dim'
not tomorrow = dim yfory
not me = dim fi
not at all = dim o °gwbwl
• (*with* rhaid)
= peidio
you must not forget = rhaid i ti °beidio
anghofio
• **....or not?** = ...neu °beidio?
are they coming or not? = ydyn nhw'n
dod neu °beidio?

note
1 *noun*
• (*short message, informal letter*)
= nodyn (*plural* nodion) *masculine*
• (*record*)
= nodiad (*plural* -au) *masculine*
to make a note of something = nodi
rhywbeth
to take notes = cymryd (*stem* cymer-)
nodiadau
• (*money*)
= papur *masculine*

five pound note = papur pum punt (*plural* papurau pum punt) *masculine*
• (*in music*)
= nodyn (*plural* nodau) *masculine*
2 *verb*
= nodi
to note something down = nodi rhywbeth

notebook *noun*
= nodiadur (*plural* -on) *masculine*

nothing *pronoun*
= dim byd, dim
nothing has changed = does dim (byd) wedi newid
there's nothing left = does dim (byd) ar ôl
I saw nothing = ºweles i ºddim byd
that has nothing to do with us = does a nelo hynny ºddim â ni

notice
1 *noun*
• (*sign*)
= arwydd (*plural* -ion) *masculine*, rhybudd (*plural* -ion) *masculine*
• (*attention*)
= sylw *masculine*
to take notice of something = sylwi arº rywbeth
to draw something to someone's notice = tynnu sylw rhywun atº rywbeth
to take no notice of something/someone = anwybyddu rhywbeth/rhywun
• (*warning*)
= rhybudd (*plural* -ion) *masculine*
to do something without notice = gwneud rhywbeth yn ºddirybudd
at short notice = ar ºfyr ºrybudd
to give notice to someone = rhoi (*stem* rhoi-, rhodd-) rhybudd iº rywun
2 *verb*
= sylwi
to notice something = sylwi arº rywbeth

noticeable *adjective*
= amlwg

notice board *noun*
= hysbysfwrdd (*plural* hysbysfyrddau) *masculine*

novel *noun*
= nofel (*plural* -au) *feminine*

novelist *noun*
= nofelydd (*plural* nofelwyr) *masculine*
= nofelwraig (*plural* nofelwragedd) *feminine*, nofeles (*plural* -au) *feminine*

November *noun*
= mis Tachwedd, Tachwedd *masculine*
see also **January**

now *adverb*
• (*general sense*)
= nawr, rŵan (*North*)
we have to go now = rhaid inni ºfynd nawr
I'm phoning her now = dw i'n ffonio hi nawr
• (*indicating change from previously*)
= bellach
he's unemployed now = mae'n ºddiwaith bellach
we don't send cards now = dyn ni ºddim yn danfon cardiau bellach
• (*idiomatic phrases*)
up till now = hyd yma, hyd yn hyn
by now = erbyn hyn
now and then = o ºbryd i'w gilydd
right now = ar unwaith

> **!** **nawr** and **rŵan** are interchangeable regional variants; **bellach** on the other hand has a much more restricted sense as indicated above.

nowhere *adverb*
= nunlle, nunman

nuclear *adjective*
= niwcliar

nude *adjective*
= noeth

nuisance *noun*
what a nuisance! = 'na ºddiflas!
these flies are a nuisance = mae'r clêr 'ma'n ºboen

numb *adjective*
= dideimlad, fferllyd

number *noun*
• (*figure*)
= rhif (*plural* -au) *masculine*
odd number = odrif (*plural* -au) *masculine*
even number = eilrif (*plural* -au) *masculine*

Numbers

THE NUMBERS 1–10

These present few problems other than mutations:

1	**un** masculine,	5	**pum(p)**
	un° feminine	6	**chwe(ch)**
2	**dau**° masculine,	7	**saith**
	dwy° feminine	8	**wyth**
3	**tri**ʰ masculine,	9	**naw**
	tair feminine	10	**deg**
4	**pedwar** masculine,		
	pedair feminine		

Note that 1, 2, 3 and 4 have separate forms for use with masculine and feminine nouns, eg **dau °fachgen** 'two boys', **dwy °ferch** 'two girls'; **pedwar bwrdd** 'four tables', **pedair desg** 'four desks'.

Numbers 5 and 6 have short forms **pum** and **chwe** when immediately followed by a noun, but full forms **pump** and **chwech** in all other cases: **pum afal** 'five apples', **chwe afal** 'six apples', but **pump o afalau** 'five apples', **chwech o afalau** 'six apples'; **dw i wedi prynu pump** 'I've bought five', **dw i wedi prynu chwech** 'I've bought six'.

These numbers tend to be followed by a singular noun—**pedwar llyfr** 'four books', **naw ceiniog** 'nine pence'—but the higher ones (and generally all numbers higher than this) are also found with **o**° + plural noun—**naw o °geiniogau**. It is difficult to give hard-and-fast rules for this point.

THE TEENS

There are two parallel sets of numbers—the original one based on the vigesimal (20) system, and an artificial decimal-based set:

	original	decimal
11	**unarddeg**	**undeg un**
12	**deuddeg**	**undeg dau**
13	**triarddeg**	**undeg tri**
14	**pedwararddeg**	**undeg pedwar**
	original	decimal
15	**pymtheg**	**undeg pump**
16	**unarbymtheg**	**undeg chwech**
17	**dauarbymtheg**	**undeg saith**
18	**deunaw**	**undeg wyth**
19	**pedwararbymtheg**	**undeg naw**
20	**ugain**	**dauddeg**

The original teens that include **-ar-** may also be written as three words: **un ar ddeg** etc; when used with a noun they are split in any case: **tri bwrdd ar ddeg** 'thirteen tables', **dwy °ddesg ar °bymtheg** 'seventeen desks'. The decimal teens simply use **o**° + plural noun: **undeg trl o °fyrddau, undeg saith o °ddesgiau**.

THE DECIMAL SYSTEM

Promoted officially, but the original system lives on with native speakers, and **unarddeg, deuddeg, pymtheg, deunaw** and **ugain** are at least as common everywhere as their decimal counterparts. The decimal term **dauddeg** 'twenty' is easily confused with **deuddeg** 'twelve' in the original system, while **ugain** is both distinctive and in common use.

Above twenty the decimal system is in common use nowadays, but with some of the old system numbers (in brackets) still widely found:

21	**dauddeg un**
22	**dauddeg dau**
30	**trideg**
31	**trideg un**
40	**pedwar deg** (**deugain**—used particularly for money and years)
41	**pedwardeg un**
50	**pumdeg** (**hanner can(t)**)
51	**pumdeg un**
60	**chwedeg**
70	**saithdeg**
80	**wythdeg**
90	**nawdeg**

continued overleaf

Numbers continued

HUNDREDS

Like **pump** and **chwech**, **cant** has a shortened form **can** when a singular noun immediately follows—**can punt** or **cant o °bunnoedd** 'a hundred pounds'. This is true for **hanner cant** 'fifty' as well.

200	**dau °gant**	600	**chwe ʰchant**
300	**tri ʰchant**	700	**saith cant**
400	**pedwar cant**	800	**wyth cant**
500	**pum cant**	900	**naw cant**

THOUSANDS AND MILLIONS

The words for 'thousand' **mil** and 'million' **miliwn** are nouns, both feminine, and are always followed by **o°**: **mil o °bobol** 'a thousand people', **dwy °fil o °bunnoedd** 'two thousand pounds', **miliwn o °flynyddoedd** 'a million years'.

ORDINALS

Ordinal numbers behave like adjectives except that they all (apart from **ail°** 'second') precede the noun. Those for 'third' and 'fourth' have separate masculine and feminine forms.

1st	**cynta(f)**
2nd	**ail°**
3rd	**trydydd, trydedd**
4th	**pedwerydd, pedwaredd**
5th	**pumed**
6th	**chweched**
7th	**seithfed**
8th	**wythfed**
9th	**nawfed**
10th	**degfed**
11th	**unfed ar °ddeg**
12th	**deuddegfed**

• (*quantity*)
 = nifer (*plural* -oedd) *masculine or feminine*, sawl (+ *singular*)
 there are a number of people outside
 = mae nifer o °bobol tu allan
 there are a number left = mae sawl un ar ôl

> **!** nifer *requires* **o°** *with a following plural noun, while* **sawl** *on the other hand is followed directly by the singular:* **a number of books** = nifer o °lyfrau *or* sawl llyfr.

• (*issue of periodical*)
 = rhifyn (*plural* -nau) *masculine*

numberplate *noun*
 = plât rhif (*plural* platiau rhif) *masculine*

numerous *adjective*
 = niferus

nun *noun*
 = lleian (*plural* -od) *feminine*

nurse *noun*
 = nyrs (*plural* -ys) *feminine*

nursery *noun*
 = meithrinfa (*plural* meithrinfeydd) *feminine*

nursery school *noun*
 = ysgol °feithrin (*plural* ysgolion meithrin) *feminine*

nursing home *noun*
 = cartre(f) nyrsio (*plural* cartrefi nyrsio) *masculine*

nurture *verb*
 = meithrin, magu

nut *noun*
 = cneuen (*plural* cnau) *feminine*

Oo

oak *noun*
= derwen (*plural* derw) *feminine*

oar *noun*
= rhwyf (*plural* -au) *feminine*

oath *noun*
= llw (*plural* -on) *masculine*
to swear an oath = tyngu llw

obedient *adjective*
= ufudd

obey *verb*
= ufuddhau
to obey someone = ufuddhau i° rywun

object
1 *noun*
= gwrthrych (*plural* -au) *masculine*, peth (*plural* -au) *masculine*
2 *verb*
= gwrthwynebu, gwrthod
to object to something = gwrthwynebu rhywbeth
to object to doing something = gwrthod gwneud rhywbeth

objection *noun*
= gwrthwynebiad (*plural* -au) *masculine*
I have no objection = does gen i °ddim gwahaniaeth, does gen i °ddim byd yn erbyn

oblige *verb*
= gorfodi
to oblige someone to do something = gorfodi rhywun i °wneud rhywbeth
to be obliged to do something = gorfod gwneud rhywbeth
we were obliged to leave = o'n ni'n gorfod gadael, oedd rhaid inni °adael

> **!** *Obligation can be expressed either by the verbnoun* **gorfod** *or, more commonly, by the non-verbal* **rhaid**— *see entries on Welsh-English side for details and more examples.*

I'm much obliged = diolch yn °fawr

obstacle *noun*
= rhwystr (*plural* -au) *masculine*

obtain *verb*
= cael

> **!** **cael** *is irregular in the preterite, short future and conditional—see entry on the Welsh-English side for details and examples.*

obvious *adjective*
= amlwg

obviously *adverb*
= yn amlwg

occasion *noun*
= achlysur (*plural* -on) *masculine*
on several occasions = sawl gwaith
on that occasion = y tro 'na, °bryd hynny
on every occasion = °bob tro, ar °bob achlysur
on occasion = weithiau, o °bryd i'w gilydd

occasional *adjective*
= ambell° (*precedes noun*)

occasionally *adverb*
= weithiau, o °bryd i'w gilydd

occupation *noun*
= galwedigaeth (*plural* -au) *feminine*
what's your occupation? = beth ydy'ch gwaith (chi)?

occupational *adjective*
= galwedigaethol

occupy *verb*
• (*take possession of*)
= meddiannu
to occupy someone's time = llenwi amser rhywun
this seat is occupied = dydy'r sedd 'ma °ddim yn rhydd

occur *verb*
• (*happen*)
= digwydd
• (*come to mind*)
it occurred to him that . . . = fe °ddaeth (y syniad) i'w °feddwl °fod. . .

ocean *noun*
= môr (*plural* moroedd) *masculine*
the Atlantic Ocean = Môr Iwerydd
the Pacific Ocean = y Môr Tawel

o'clock *adverb*
= o'r °gloch

it's three o'clock = mae'n ºdri o'r ºgloch
at ten o'clock = am ºddeg o'r ºgloch

October *noun*
= mis Hydre(f), Hydre(f) *masculine*
see also **January**

octopus *noun*
= octopws (*plural* octopysau) *masculine*

odd *adjective*
• (*strange*)
= rhyfedd, od
• (*opposite of* **even**)
= od
odd number = odrif (*plural* -au)
masculine

odour *noun*
= oglau (*plural* ogleuon) *masculine*,
gwynt (*plural* -oedd) *masculine* (*South*)

of *preposition*

> **!** *In its main use in English, 'of' has no equivalent in Welsh—it is simply not translated in cases of one noun dependent on another (genitive relationship), such as 'the middle of the town'* **canol y ºdre**. *Using* **o** *and saying* *y canol o'r ºdre *is wrong. This use of 'of' is by far the most common, so more often than not the word 'of' will not correspond to anything in Welsh. For* **oº** *to be needed, there has to be some idea of quantity, or singling out. Otherwise, various words correspond to the different senses.*

• (*not translated in genitive relationships*)
the middle of the town = canol y ºdre
the capital of Wales = prifddinas
Cymru
the top of the mountain = copa'r
mynydd
• (*in quantity expressions*)
= oº
a pound of cheese = pwys o ºgaws
two bottles of milk = dwy ºbotel o
ºlefrith
plenty of time = digon o amser
a packet of crisps = pecyn o ºgreision
• (*singling out*)
= oº
there are five of them left = mae pump
ohonyn nhw ar ôl
• (*about, concerning*)
= amº

we talked of the future = naethon ni
siarad am y dyfodol
• (*US: when telling the time*)
it's a quarter of nine = mae hi'n
chwarter i naw

off *adverb*
• (*general senses*)
= i ffwrdd, bant (*South*)
I'm off! = i ffwrdd â fi, bant â fi!
off we go! = i ffwrdd â ni, bant â ni!
it's miles off = mae'n ºfilltiroedd i
ffwrdd/bant
• (*from on*)
= oddiarº, oddi arº
he fell off his chair = mi syrthiodd
oddiar ei ºgadair
to turn something off = diffodd
rhywbeth, troi (*stem* troi-, trodd-)
rhywbeth i ffwrdd
to take one's clothes/shoes off =
tynnu'ch dillad/sgidiau

offence *noun*
• (*insult*)
to take offence at something = digio
wrthº rywbeth
to cause offence to someone = digio
rhywun
• (*crime*)
= trosedd (*plural* -au) *masculine*

offend *verb*
= digio

offer
1 *noun*
= cynnig (*plural* cynigion) *masculine*
2 *verb*
= cynnig (*stem* cynigi-)
to offer someone something = cynnig
rhywbeth iº rywun
to offer to do something = cynnig
gwneud rhywbeth

office *noun*
= swyddfa (*plural* swyddfeydd) *feminine*

office block *noun*
= block swyddfeydd (*plural* blociau
swyddfeydd) *masculine*

officer *noun*
= swyddog (*plural* -ion) *masculine*

office worker *noun*
= gweithiwr swyddfa (*plural* gweithwyr
swyddfa) *masculine*, gweithwraig

swyddfa (*plural* gweithwragedd swyddfa) *feminine*

official
1 *adjective*
= swyddogol
2 *noun*
= swyddog (*plural* -ion) *masculine*

often *adverb*
= yn aml, yn °fynych
most often = gan amla(f)

oil *noun*
= olew (*plural* -au, -on) *masculine*

oil rig *noun*
= llwyfan olew (*plural* llwyfannau olew) *masculine or feminine*

okay
1 *adjective*
• (*in order*)
= iawn
is it okay for them to come? = ydy hi'n iawn iddyn nhw °ddod?
• (*health*)
= iawn, go lew, gweddol
are you okay? = wyt ti'n iawn/go lew/°o lew?
2 *adverb*
• (*signifying compliance or agreement*)
= iawn, o'r gorau
'will you shut the door?'—'okay' = 'nei di °gau'r drws?'—'iawn/o'r gorau'

> **!** *For practically all instances of* 'okay', **iawn** *is a safe translation. The alternatives* **go lew, o'r gorau** *etc. are restricted to one sense only as shown above.*

old *adjective*
= hen°

> **!** hen° *precedes the noun it refers to, causing soft mutation, unless some other qualifying word (e.g.* **iawn** *'very') is also present.*

an old man = hen °ddyn
a very old man = dyn hen iawn
how old are you = faint oed dych chi? = beth ydy'ch oedran (chi)?
she's ten years old = mae hi'n °ddeng ⁿmlwydd oed
he's older than me = mae e'n hŷn/henach na fi
Dafydd is the oldest = Dafydd ydy'r hyna/hena

old-fashioned *adjective*
= hen ffasiwn
old-fashioned clothes = dillad hen ffasiwn *plural*

old people's home *noun*
= cartre(f) henoed (*plural* cartrefi henoed) *masculine*, cartre(f) hen °bobol (*plural* cartrefi hen °bobol) *masculine*

olive *noun*
= olif (*plural* -au) *feminine*

olive oil *noun*
= olew olewydd *masculine*

Olympic Games *plural noun*
= Chwaraeon Olympaidd *plural*

omelette *noun*
= omled (*plural* -au) *masculine or feminine*

on
1 *adverb*
= ymlaen
come on! = dewch ymlaen!
to carry on = mynd ymlaen, cario ymlaen
to go on (last) = para
later on = nes ymlaen
is the radio on? = ydy'r radio ymlaen?
what's on (television)? = beth sy ymlaen?
will you turn it on? = nei di °droi fe ymlaen?
from Monday on = o °ddydd Llun ymlaen
2 *preposition*
• (*location*)
= ar°
it's on the table = mae e ar y bwrdd
to fall on the floor = syrthio *or* cwympo ar y llawr
on the left = ar y chwith
• (*transport*)
to go on the bus = mynd ar y bws
to go on the train = mynd ar y trên, mynd gyda'r trên
• (*media*)
on the television = ar y teledu
on the radio = ar y radio
on the news = ar y newyddion
on video = ar fideo
• (*about*)
= am°
a book on Wales = llyfr am °Gymru

a programme on unemployment =
rhaglen am °ddiweithdra
• (*time*)
on Saturday = °ddydd Sadwrn
on Saturdays = ar °ddydd Sadwrn
on the seventh of December = ar y
seithfed o °fis Rhagfyr

once
1 *adverb*
= unwaith
once a week = unwaith yr wythnos
more than once = mwy nag unwaith,
droeon
once upon a time = un tro
once more = unwaith yn rhagor,
unwaith eto
once again = unwaith eto
at once = ar unwaith, yn syth
2 *conjunction*

> **!** In this use, **unwaith** is followed by a
> 'that. . .' clause.

once they have gone = unwaith bod
nhw wedi mynd
once we've decided = unwaith bod ni
wedi penderfynu

one
1 *numeral*
= un *masculine*, un° *feminine*
one boy = un bachgen
one girl = un °ferch
the one . . ., the other . . . = y naill. . ., y
llall. . .
one by one = fesul un
one year = un °flwyddyn
one year old = blwydd oed
at one o'clock = am un o'r °gloch
2 *pronoun*
• (*referring to noun*)
= un *masculine*, un° *feminine*, rhai *plural*
I prefer the blue one = well gen i'r un
glas
I prefer the blue ones = well gen i'r rhai
glas
did you buy one? = °brynoch chi un?
your one is better = mae'ch un chi'n
°well
• (*meaning 'you' or 'people'*)
= ti, chi
one never knows = ti *or* chi byth yn
gwybod

one another *pronoun*
= (*referring to 'them'*) = ei gilydd

= (*referring to 'us'*) ein gilydd
= (*referring to 'you'*) eich gilydd
they hate one other = maen nhw'n
casáu ei gilydd
we'll help one other = nawn ni helpu'n
gilydd
did you recognise one other? =
naethoch chi adnabod eich gilydd?

oneself *pronoun*
= eich hun (*North*), eich hunan (*South*)

one-way street *noun*
= heol unffordd (*plural* heolydd
unffordd) *feminine*

one-way ticket *noun*
= tocyn unffordd (*plural* tocynnau
unffordd) *masculine*

onion *noun*
= nionyn (*plural* nionod) *masculine*

only
1 *adjective*
= unig° (*precedes noun*)
the only man left = yr unig °ddyn ar ôl
this is the only one I've got = dyma'r
unig un sy gen i
2 *adverb*
• (*general sense*)
= yn unig, dim ond (*colloquial* 'mond)

> **!** **yn unig** follows the word qualified,
> and is rather more formal, while the
> less formal **dim ond** precedes.

only five pounds = pum punt yn unig,
dim ond pum punt
I only asked = dim ond gofyn nes i
only just = newydd°
I've only just arrived = dw i newydd
°gyrraedd

onto *preposition*
= ar°

open
1 *adjective*
• (*not closed*)
= ar agor, agored
when are you open? = pryd dych chi ar
agor?
the shop is open = mae'r siop ar agor,
mae'r siop yn agored

> **!** The adjective phrase **ar agor**, like all
> similar phrases with **ar**, does not use
> **yn** to link it to the verb **bod** to be—so

> not **mae'r siop yn ar agor. But **agored** is a normal adjective and does require the* **yn**.

- (*frank*)
  = agored
- (*undecided*)
  = agored
  = heb ei °benderfynu *masculine*, heb ei penderfynu/ʰphenderfynu *feminine*, heb eu penderfynu *plural*

2 *verb*
  = agor
  when do you open? = pryd dych chi'n agor?

3 *noun*
  out in the open (*outdoors*)
  = yn yr awyr agored
  (*not in secret*)
  = yn agored

opener *noun*
  = agorydd (*plural* -ion) *masculine*

opening
1 *noun*
  = agoriad (*plural* -au) *masculine*
- (*hole*)
  = agoriad (*plural* -au) *masculine*; twll (*plural* tyllau) *masculine*

2 *adjective*
  opening hours = oriau agor *plural*
  opening night = noson °gynta(f) *feminine*

openly *adverb*
  = yn agored

> ! *Although* 'open' *is either* **ar agor** *or* **agored**, *only* **agored** *can be used for the adverb.*

open-minded *adjective*
  = â meddwl agored

opera *noun*
  = opera (*plural* operâu) *feminine*

operate *verb*
- (*be/put in operation*)
  = gweithredu
- (*perform surgery*)
  = llaw-drin (*stem* llaw-drini-)
  to operate on someone = llaw-drin rhywun

operation *noun*
- (*action*)
  = gweithred (*plural* -oedd) *feminine*
- (*surgical*)
  = llawdriniaeth (*plural* -au) *feminine*, triniaeth °lawfeddygol

operator *noun*
- (*on phone*)
  = cysylltydd (*plural* cysylltwyr) *masculine*
- (*person operating something*)
  = gweithredwr (*plural* gweithredwyr) *masculine*

opinion *noun*
  = barn (*plural* -au) *feminine*, tyb (*plural* -iau) *feminine*
  what is your opinion? = beth ydy'ch barn?
  in my opinion = yn 'y ⁿmarn i

opponent *noun*
  = gwrthwynebwr (*plural* gwrthwynebwyr) *masculine*
  = gwrthwynebwraig (*plural* gwrthwynebwragedd) *feminine*

opportunity *noun*
  = cyfle (*plural* -oedd) *masculine*
  to get the opportunity to visit someone = cael y cyfle i ymweld âʰ rhywun

oppose *verb*
  = gwrthwynebu

opposite
1 *adjective*
  = cyferbyn
2 *preposition*
  = gyferbyn âʰ/iᵒ
  opposite the bank = gyferbyn â'r banc, gyferbyn i'r banc

opposition *noun*
- (*general sense*)
  = gwrthwynebiad (*plural* -au) *masculine*
- (*political party*)
  = gwrthblaid (*plural* gwrthbleidiau) *feminine*

optician *noun*
  = optegydd (*plural* optegwyr) *masculine*

optimism *noun*
  = optimistiaeth *feminine*

optimist *noun*
  = optimydd (*plural* -ion) *masculine*

optimistic *adjective*
  = optimistaidd

option noun
I don't have any option, do I? = does gen i °ddim dewis, nag oes?

or conjunction
- (general sense)
= neu°
tea or coffee = te neu °goffi
once or twice a week = unwaith neu °ddwywaith yr wythnos
come now or you'll be late = dewch nawr neu mi °fyddwch chi'n hwyr
- (indicating two mutually exclusive alternatives)
= neu°, ynteu, ta
today or tomorrow? = heddiw ta yfory?
- (in negative sentences)
= na^h
I can't come today or tomorrow = °alla i °ddim dod heddiw na yfory

oral adjective
- (of mouth)
= geneuol
- (spoken)
= llafar

orange
1 adjective
= (colour) oren
2 noun
= oren (plural -nau) masculine or feminine

orange juice noun
= sudd oren masculine

orchard noun
= perllan (plural -nau) feminine

orchestra noun
= cerddorfa (plural cerddorfeydd) feminine

order
1 noun
- (command)
= gorchymyn (plural gorchmynion) masculine
to give someone an order = gorchymyn (stem gorchmynn-) i° rywun
- (for goods, service)
= archeb (plural -ion) feminine
- (system, orderliness)
= trefn feminine
out of order = allan o °drefn
in order (in correct sequence) = mewn trefn; (tidy) = taclus

- **in order** (expressing purpose)
= er mwyn
in order for him to go = er mwyn iddo (fe) °fynd
in order to arrive on time = er mwyn cyrraedd yn °brydlon

> ! **er mwyn** uses i° + person + °verbnoun.

2 verb
- (give command)
= gorchymyn (stem gorchmynn-)
to order someone to do something = gorchymyn i° rywun °wneud rhywbeth
- (place an order)
= archebu

orderly adjective
= trefnus

ordinary adjective
= cyffredin

organ noun
= organ (plural -au) feminine

organization noun
= corff (plural cyrff) masculine, mudiad (plural -au) masculine

organize verb
= trefnu

organizer noun
- (person)
= trefnydd (plural -ion) masculine
- (notebook)
= trefniadur (plural -on) masculine

oriental adjective
= dwyreiniol, o'r dwyrain

original adjective
= gwreiddiol

originally adverb
= yn °wreiddiol
where do you come from originally? = o lle dych chi'n dod yn °wreiddiol?

ornament noun
= addurniad (plural -au) masculine

orphan noun
= plentyn amddifad (plural plant amddifad) masculine

ostrich *noun*
= estrys (*plural* -iaid, -od) *masculine or feminine*

other

1 *adjective*
= arall *singular*, eraill *plural*
the other book = y llyfr arall
the other books = y llyfrau eraill
the other one = yr un arall
the other ones = y rhai eraill
what about the other one? = beth am yr un arall?
what about the other ones? = beth am y rhai eraill?

2 *pronoun*
= llall *singular*, lleill *plural*
what about the other? = beth am y llall?
what about the others? = beth am y lleill?
some . . ., others . . . = rhai . . ., (rhai) eraill . . .
someone or other = rhywun neu'i gilydd

otherwise *adverb*
= fel arall

ought *verb*
= dylwn i *etc*

> **!** *This verb appears only with 'unreality' or hypothetical endings in Welsh. An* **-s-** *can optionally be inserted before these endings, so* **dylwn i** *or* **dylswn i, dylech chi** *or* **dylsech chi**, *etc. The verbnoun for the action dependent on it immediately follows the subject, and therefore has soft mutation.*

I ought to go = dylwn i °fynd
ought you to say something? = °ddylset ti °ddweud rhywbeth?
they oughtn't go = °ddylen nhw °ddim mynd
we ought to have agreed = dylen ni °fod wedi cytuno
you ought not have shouted = °ddylet ti °ddim °fod wedi gweiddi

our *adjective*
= ein . . . (ni)
our children = ein plant (ni)
this is our car = dyma'n car (ni)
all our CDs are gone = mae'n crynoddisgiau i gyd wedi mynd

ours *pronoun*
that's ours = ni (sy) biau hwnna
his garden's bigger than ours = mae ei °ardd e'n °fwy na 'n hun ni
their marks were better than ours = roedd eu marciau nhw'n °well na 'n rhai ni
the yellow book is ours = ni (sy) biau'r llyfr melyn

ourselves *pronoun*
= ein hun (*North*), ein hunain (*South*)
we'll go there ourselves = awn ni yno 'n hun(ain)
we hurt ourselves = naethon ni °frifo 'n hun(ain)
by ourselves (*on our own*) = ar °ben 'n hun(ain), ar ein pennau'n hun(ain)

out *adverb*
• (*general senses*)
= allan; mas (*South*)
come out! = dewch allan/mas!
we're going out tonight = dyn ni'n mynd allan/mas heno
the book will be out soon = bydd y llyfr allan/mas cyn bo hir
he came out of the shop = daeth e allan/mas o'r siop
keep out! = cadwch allan/mas!
out we go! = allan/mas â ni!
the lights are out = mae'r goleuadau wedi'u diffodd
he is out this evening = mae e allan/mas heno
we're out of bread = does gynnon ni °ddim bara ar ôl (*North*), does dim bara ar ôl 'da ni (*South*)
to walk out of the room = cerdded (*stem* cerdd-) allan/mas o'r stafell
to get out of the city = dianc (*stem* dihang-) o'r °ddinas
to take something out of something = cymryd (*stem* cymer-) rhywbeth allan/mas o° rywbeth
• (*outside*)
= tu allan, tu mas *or* tu °fas (*South*)
it's cold out = mae hi'n oer tu allan

outdoor *adjective*
= awyr agored, allanol
outdoor activities = gweithgareddau awyr agored

outdoors *adverb*
= tu allan (i'r tŷ)

outer space *noun*
= y gofod *masculine*

outline
1 *noun*
= braslun (*plural* -iau) *masculine*
2 *verb*
= amlinellu, rhoi braslun o°

outlook *noun*
• (*forecast*)
= rhagolygon *plural*
• (*view, attitude*)
= golwg (*plural* golygon) *feminine or masculine*, agwedd (*plural* -au) *feminine*

outside
1 *adjective*
= tu allan, allanol
2 *adverb*
= tu allan
let's go outside = awn ni tu allan
3 *preposition*
• (*opposite of inside*)
= tu allan i°
outside the hall = tu allan i'r neuadd
• (*in front of*)
= o °flaen
outside the school = o °flaen yr ysgol

oven *noun*
= popty (*plural* poptai) *masculine*

over
1 *adverb*
• (*to one's home*)
= draw
why don't you come over? = pam na °ddoi di draw?
• (*finished*)
= drosodd, ar °ben
the performance is over = mae'r perfformiad drosodd, mae'r perfformiad ar °ben
• (*remaining*)
= ar ôl, yn °weddill
six for us and one over = chwech inni ac un yn °weddill, chwech inni ac un ar ôl
2 *preposition*
• (*general location or motion*)
= dros°
to go over a bridge = mynd dros °bont
over the road = dros y ffordd
over there = acw, fan acw, draw fan'na
• (*more than*)
= dros°

over a thousand people = dros °fil o °bobol
• (*during*)
= yn ystod, dros°
over the last three years = yn ystod y tair blynedd diwetha
over the weekend = dros y Sul
• (*above*)
= uwchben
there was a helicopter over the building = roedd hofrennydd uwchben yr adeilad
• (*covering*)
= dros°
all over the place = dros y lle i gyd
all over Wales = dros °Gymru °gyfan, ledled Cymru

over- *prefix*
= gor°-

overdo *verb*
= gorwneud

overdose *noun*
= gorddos (*plural* -au) *masculine*

overdraft *noun*
= gorddrafft (*plural* -iau) *masculine*

overeat *verb*
= gorfwyta, bwyta gormod

overhead projector *noun*
= uwchdaflunydd (*plural* -ion) *masculine*

overleaf *adverb*
= drosodd

overload *verb*
= gorlwytho

overtake *verb*
= mynd heibio; goddiweddyd (*formal*)
to overtake someone = mynd heibio i° rywun, goddiweddyd rhywun (*formal*)

overthrow *verb*
= dymchwel

overweight *adjective*
= rhy °drwm

overwhelming *adjective*
= llethol
overwhelming majority = mwyafrif llethol *masculine*

overwork *verb*
= gorweithio

owe *verb*

> **!** *This is expressed in Welsh by an idiomatic phrase with* **ar°** *and* **i°**:
> **how much do I owe you?** = faint sy arna i i chi?
> **you owe me ten pounds** = mae arnoch chi °ddeg punt i mi

owl *noun*
= tylluan (*plural* -od) *feminine*, gwdihŵ (*plural* -iaid) *feminine (South)*

own

1 *adjective*
= hun (*North*), hunan *singular*, hunain *plural* (*South*)

> **!** *For* 'my own car' *Welsh says* 'my car myself'—*the Northern term* **hun** *is invariable, while singular* **hunan** *in the South changes to* **hunain** *in the plural.*

my own car = °nghar 'n hun (*South*: hunan)
your own car = dy °gar dy hun (*South*: hunan)
our own car = ein car ein hun (*South*: hunain)
is it her own work? = ei gwaith ei hun ydy e? (*South*: hunan)
on my own (*alone*) = ar °ben 'n hun (*South*: hunan)
on their own = ar °ben eu hun (*South*: hunain)
he's got a house of his own = mae gynno fo °dŷ ei hun (*North*), mae tŷ ei hunan 'da fe (*South*)

2 *verb*
= biau
who owns this field? = pwy (sy) biau'r cae 'ma?
we own this = ni (sy) biau hwn
they owned them = nhw oedd biau nhw

own up
= cyfadde(f)
to own up to something = cyfadde(f) rhywbeth

owner *noun*
= perchennog (*plural* perchnogion) *masculine*

ox *noun*
= ych (*plural* -en) *masculine*

oxygen *noun*
= ocsigen *masculine*

oyster *noun*
= wystrysen (*plural* wystrys) *feminine*

ozone layer *noun*
= haen osôn *feminine*

Pp

Pacific *noun*
the Pacific = y Môr Tawel *masculine*

pack
1 *noun*
= pecyn (*plural* -nau) *masculine*, paced (*plural* -i) *masculine*
2 *verb*
= pacio

pack up
= pacio

package *noun*
= paced (*plural* -i) *masculine*, pecyn (*plural* -nau) *masculine*

packed *adjective*
(*of a room*)
= dan ei sang, llawn °dop

packet *noun*
= pecyn (*plural* -nau) *masculine*, paced (*plural* -i) *masculine*
a packet of crisps = pecyn o °greision

paddle
1 *verb*
• (*boat*)
= rhodli, rhwyfo
• (*go for a paddle*)
= padlo
2 *noun*
to go for a paddle = padlo, mynd i °badlo

page *noun*
= tudalen (*plural* -nau) *masculine or feminine*
on page six = ar °dudalen chwech

pain *noun*
= dolur (*plural* -iau) *masculine*, poen (*plural* -au) *masculine or feminine*

painful *adjective*
• (*general sense*)
= poenus
• (*sore*)
= tost
is it painful? = ydy hi'n rhoi dolur?

paint
1 *noun*
= paent (*plural* -iau) *masculine*
2 *verb*
= paentio; (*picture, also:*) darlunio

paintbrush *noun*
= brws paent (*plural* brwsiau paent) *masculine*

painter *noun*
• (*artist*)
= arlunydd (*plural* arlunwyr) *masculine*
= arlunwraig (*plural* arlunwragedd) *feminine*
• (*decorator*)
= paentiwr (*plural* paentwyr) *masculine*

painting *noun*
• (*picture*)
= llun (*plural* -iau) *masculine*
• (*act of painting*)
= paentio *verbnoun*

pair *noun*
= pâr (*plural* parau) *masculine*
do this in pairs = gwnewch hyn mewn parau

pajamas *plural noun* (*US*)
= pyjamas *plural*

palace *noun*
= palas (*plural* -au) *masculine*

pale *adjective*
= gwelw, llwyd
to go pale = gwelwi
pale blue = glas golau

pan *noun*
(*for cooking*)
= padell (*plural* -au, -i) *feminine*

pancake *noun*
= crempog (*plural* -au) *feminine*

panties *plural noun*
= pantis *plural*

pantihose *noun*
= trowsanau *plural*

pants *plural noun*
• (*British*)
= trôns (*plural* tronsiau) *masculine*
• (*US: trousers*) = trowsus *masculine*

paper *noun*
• (*material*)
= papur (*plural* -au) *masculine*
• (*newspaper*)
= papur (*plural* -au) *masculine*, papur newydd (*plural* papurau newydd) *masculine*

paperback *noun*
= llyfr clawr meddal *masculine*

parachute *noun*
= parasiwt (*plural* -iau) *masculine*

parachuting *noun*
= parasiwtio *verbnoun*

parade *noun*
• (*avenue*)
= rhodfa (*plural* rhodfeydd) *feminine*
• (*procession*)
= gorymdaith (*plural* gorymdeithiau) *feminine*

paragliding *noun*
= paragleidio *verbnoun*

paralysed *adjective*
= parlysedig

parcel *noun*
= parsel (*plural* -i) *masculine*

pardon *verb*
= maddau (*stem* maddeu-)
pardon?, I beg your pardon? = mae'n °ddrwg gen i?, eto?
pardon me
(*apologizing*)
= mae'n °ddrwg gen i
(*interrupting*)
= maddeuwch i mi

parent *noun*
= rhiant (*plural* rhieni) *masculine and feminine*

parish *noun*
= plwyf (*plural* -i, -ydd) *masculine*

parishioner *noun*
= plwyfolyn (*plural* plwyfolion) *masculine*

park
1 *noun*
= parc (*plural* -au, -iau) *masculine*
2 *verb*
= parcio
no parking = dim parcio

parking lot *noun* (*US*)
= maes parcio (*plural* meysydd parcio) *masculine*

parliament *noun*
= senedd (*plural* -au) *feminine*
Member of Parliament = Aelod Seneddol *masculine*
• (*Westminster*)
= San Steffan

parrot *noun*
= parot (*plural* -iaid) *masculine*

part *noun*
= rhan (*plural* -nau) *feminine*
• (*general sense*)
part of a book = rhan o °lyfr
it's part of the job = mae'n rhan o'r swydd
from what part of Wales? = o °ba °ran o °Gymru?
in part = mewn rhan
to take part in something = cymryd (*stem* cymer-) rhan yn[n] rhywbeth
• (*for a car etc*)
= rhan (*plural* -nau) *feminine*, darn (*plural* -au) *masculine*
• (*in a play, film*)
= rhan (*plural* -nau) *feminine*, rôl (*plural* rolau) *feminine*

partial *adjective*
= rhannol

partially *adverb*
= yn rhannol

participate *verb*
= cymryd (*stem* cymer-) rhan yn[n] rhywbeth

particular *adjective*
• (*specific*)
= penodol, arbennig
on that particular day = ar y diwrnod penodol/arbennig 'na
• (*special*)
= arbennig, neilltuol
in particular = yn arbennig
of particular interest = o °ddiddordeb arbennig
• (*fussy*)
= ffwdanus

particularly *adverb*
particularly heavy/important = arbennig o °drwm/°bwysig

partisan *adjective*
(*biased*)
= unochrog

partly *adverb*
= yn rhannol

partner *noun*
• (*general senses*)
= partner (*plural* -iaid) *masculine*
= partneres (*plural* -au) *feminine*
• (*in relationship*)
= cymar (*plural* cymheiriaid) *masculine and feminine*

part-time
1 *adjective*
= rhan-amser
2 *adverb*
I work part-time = dw i'n gweithio rhan-amser

party *noun*
• (*social function*)
= parti (*plural* -s) *masculine*
• (*political party*)
= plaid (*plural* pleidiau) *feminine*
the Conservative Party = y °Blaid °Geidwadol
the Labour Party = y °Blaid °Lafur
the Liberal Party = y °Blaid °Ryddfrydol

pass *verb*
• (*go past*)
= mynd heibio i°, pasio
I passed him = es i heibio iddo (fe)
• (*give*)
= estyn (*stem* estynn-)
will you pass the salt? = newch chi estyn yr halen?
• (*exam*)
= pasio
• (*time*)
= treulio

pass around:
to pass something around = estyn rhywbeth o °law i °law

pass on:
to pass something on = pasio rhywbeth ymlaen

passage *noun*
• (*long narrow space*)
= cyntedd (*plural* -au) *masculine*
• (*in text*)
= rhan (*plural* -nau) *feminine*, darn (*plural* -au) *masculine*

passenger *noun*
= teithiwr (*plural* teithwyr) *masculine*
= teithwraig (*plural* teithwragedd) *feminine*

passport *noun*
= trwydded °deithio (*plural* trwyddedau teithio) *feminine*, pasport (*plural* -au, -iau) *masculine*

past
1 *adjective*
• (*former*)
= cynt, o'r blaen

• (*last*)
= diwetha(f)
the past three months = y tri mis diwetha
2 *adverb*
= heibio
to go past = mynd heibio
3 *noun*
= gorffennol
in the past = yn y gorffennol
4 *preposition*
• (*motion*)
= heibio i°
we walked past the museum = cerddon ni heibio i'r amgueddfa
• (*in telling the time*)
= wedi
at ten past three = am °ddeng munud wedi tri

pasta *noun*
= pasta *masculine*

pastry *noun*
• (*baked*)
= crwst *masculine*
• (*uncooked*)
= toes *masculine*

pasture *noun*
= porfa (*plural* porfeydd) *feminine*

patch *noun*
= clwt (*plural* clytiau) *masculine*

path *noun*
= llwybr (*plural* -au) *masculine*

patience *noun*
= amynedd *masculine or feminine*

patient
1 *adjective*
= amyneddgar
2 *noun*
= claf (*plural* cleifion) *masculine*

patrol car *noun*
= car patrôl (*plural* ceir patrôl) *masculine*

patronising *adjective* (*attitude*)
= nawddoglyd

pattern *noun*
= patrwm (*plural* patrymau) *masculine*

pause
1 *noun*
= saib (*plural* seibiau) *masculine*

2 *verb*
= oedi, petruso

pavement *noun*
= palmant (*plural* palmentydd, palmantau) *masculine*

paw *noun*
= pawen (*plural* -nau) *feminine*

pawn *noun*
(*chess piece*)
= gwerinwr (*plural* gwerinwyr) *masculine*

pay
1 *noun*
(*salary*)
= cyflog (*plural* -au) *masculine*
2 *verb*
• (*give money*)
= talu
to pay someone for something = talu rhywun am° rywbeth
this work pays well = mae'r gwaith 'ma'n talu'n °dda
• (*give*)
to pay attention to something = cymryd (*stem* cymer-) sylw o °rywbeth
to pay someone a visit = ymweld (*stem* ymwel-) â[h] rhywun
to pay someone a compliment = talu teyrnged i °rywun

pay back
= talu yn ôl

payable *adjective*
= taladwy

payment *noun*
= tâl (*plural* taliadau) *masculine*, taliad (*plural* -au) *masculine*

PE
(*abbreviation of* **Physical Education**)
= AG (*abbreviation of* Addysg °Gorfforol)

pea *noun*
= pysen (*plural* pys) *feminine*

peace *noun*
• (*general sense*)
= heddwch *masculine*
• (*stillness or calm, also:*)
= tawelwch *masculine*, llonydd *masculine*
to leave someone in peace = gadael (*stem* gadaw-) llonydd i° rywun

peaceful *adjective*
= tawel

peach *noun*
= eirinen °wlanog (*plural* eirin gwlanog) *feminine*

peacock *noun*
= paun (*plural* peunod) *masculine*

peak *noun*
• (*summit*)
= copa (*plural* -on) *feminine or masculine*
• (*high point*)
= anterth *masculine*
it was at its peak before the war = roedd e ar ei anterth cyn y rhyfel
• (*of cap*)
= pig (*plural* -au) *masculine or feminine*

peanut *noun*
= cneuen °ddaear (*plural* cnau daear) *feminine*

pear *noun*
= gellygen (*plural* gellyg) *feminine*

pearl *noun*
= perl (*plural* -au) *masculine*

pebble *noun*
= carreg °gron (*plural* cerrig crynion) *feminine*

pedestrian *noun*
= cerddwr (*plural* cerddwyr) *masculine*
= cerddwraig (*plural* cerddwragedd) *feminine*

pedestrian crossing *noun*
= croesfan cerddwyr (*plural* croesfannau cerddwyr) *masculine or feminine*

peel *verb*
= tynnu croen, digroeni, crafu
to peel an apple = tynnu croen afal

pen *noun*
= pen ysgrifennu (*plural* pennau ysgrifennu) *masculine*

> **!** *More informal alternatives are* **pen sgrifennu** *and* **pen sgwennu**—*in all cases the second element is needed to distinguish from* **pen** *'head'.*

penalize *verb*
= cosbi

penalty *noun*
• (*punishment*)
= cosb (*plural* -au) *feminine*

• (*in football*)
  = cic °gosb (*plural* ciciau cosb) *feminine*

pencil *noun*
= pensil (*plural* -iau) *masculine*

pencil sharpener *noun*
= hogydd pensil *masculine*

penetrate *verb*
= treiddio

penetrating *adjective*
= treiddgar

penfriend *noun*
= ffrind llythyru (*plural* ffrindiau llythyru) *masculine*

penguin *noun*
= pengwin (*plural* -iaid) *masculine*

peninsula *noun*
= penrhyn (*plural* -ion) *masculine*

penknife *noun*
= cyllell °boced (*plural* cyllyll poced) *feminine*

penny *noun*
= ceiniog (*plural* -au) *feminine*

pension *noun*
= pensiwn (*plural* pensiynau) *masculine*

pensioner *noun*
= pensiynwr (*plural* pensiynwyr) *masculine*
= pensiynwraig (*plural* pensiynwragedd) *feminine*

people *noun*
= pob(o)l *feminine*
they are very nice people = maen nhw'n °bobol neis iawn
there are a lot of people here = mae llawer o °bobol fan hyn
three people = tri o °bobol
other people = pobol eraill

> ! *In some areas* **bobol** *is treated as the unmutated form, giving* °**fobol** *under soft mutation—this usage is regarded by many as substandard.*

pepper *noun*
= pupur *masculine*

per *preposition*
= y, yr, 'r *definite article*
twenty pounds per week = ugain punt yr wythnos

forty miles per hour = deugain milltir yr awr

per cent *noun*
= y cant
twenty per cent = ugain y cant

perfect
1 *adjective*
• (*without fault*)
  = perffaith
• (*ideal*)
  = delfrydol
• (*as exclamation*)
  = i'r dim!
2 *verb*
= perffeithio

perfection *noun*
= perffeithrwydd *masculine*

perfectly *adverb*
• (*without fault*)
  = yn °berffaith
• (*completely*)
  = yn hollol
  it's perfectly legal = mae'n °gwbwl °gyfreithlon

perform *verb*
= perfformio

performance *noun*
= perfformiad (*plural* -au) *masculine*

performer *noun*
= perfformiwr (*plural* perfformwyr) *masculine*
= perfformwraig (*plural* perfformwragedd) *feminine*

perfume *noun*
= sent (*plural* -iau) *masculine*

perhaps *adverb*
= efallai (*colloquial* ella (*North*), falle (*South*)), hwyrach (*North*)

> ! *All these words are generally followed by a 'that...' clause when they begin the sentence.*

perhaps he is ill = efallai °fod e'n sâl
perhaps they'll come later = efallai (y) dôn nhw wedyn
perhaps they have gone = efallai bod nhw wedi mynd
perhaps she won't be here = efallai na °fydd hi yma
perhaps it wasn't cold enough = efallai nad oedd hi'n °ddigon oer

period noun
- (of time)
= cyfnod (plural -au) masculine, oes (plural -au, -oedd) feminine, adeg (plural -au) feminine
- (menstrual cycle)
= misglwyf (plural -au) masculine
I'm having my period = mae'r misglwyf arna i

> ! This expression denoting a temporary physical state uses **ar°** + person.

- (US: full stop)
= atalnod llawn (plural atalnodau llawn) masculine

permanent adjective
= parhaol

permission noun
= caniatâd masculine
to get permission to do something = cael caniatâd i °wneud rhywbeth
to give someone permission = rhoi (stem rhoi, rhodd-) caniatâd i° rywun
to have permission = bod â ʰchaniatâd

permit
1 verb
= caniatáu
to permit someone to do something = caniatáu i° rywun °wneud rhywbeth
2 noun
= trwydded (plural -au) feminine

perplexity noun
= penbleth feminine

person noun
= person (plural -au) masculine

> ! Often, especially in the plural, this word is not translated:
> **enough room for ten persons** = digon o °le i °ddeg
> or is translated by **dyn** or **merch** as appropriate:
> **he's a kind person** = mae'n °ddyn caredig iawn

personal adjective
= personol

personality noun
= personoliaeth (plural -au) feminine

personally adverb
= yn °bersonol

perspire verb
= chwysu

persuade verb
= perswadio
to persuade someone to do something = perswadio rhywun i °wneud rhywbeth

pessimism noun
= pesimistiaeth feminine

pessimist noun
= pesimist (plural -iaid) masculine

pessimistic adjective
= pesimistaidd

pet noun
= anifail anwes (plural anifeiliaid anwes) masculine

petrol noun
= petrol masculine

petrol station noun
= gorsaf °betrol (plural gorsafoedd petrol) feminine

pet shop noun
= siop anifeiliaid (plural siopau anifeiliaid) feminine

pharmacist noun
= fferyllydd (plural fferyllwyr) masculine

pharmacy noun
= fferyllfa (plural fferyllfeydd) feminine

pheasant noun
= ffesant (plural -od) masculine

phone
1 noun
= ffôn (plural ffonau) masculine
to answer the phone = ateb y ffôn
the phone is ringing = mae'r ffôn yn canu
he's on the phone = mae e ar y ffôn
2 verb
= ffonio
to phone someone about something = ffonio rhywun am° rywbeth

phone book noun
= llyfr ffôn (plural llyfrau ffôn) masculine

phone booth noun
= ciosg ffôn (plural ciosgau ffôn) masculine

phone call noun
= galwad ffôn (*plural* galwadau ffôn) masculine, caniad (*plural* -au) masculine

phone card noun
= cerdyn ffôn (*plural* cardiau ffôn) masculine

phone number noun
= rhif ffôn (*plural* rhifau ffôn) masculine

photo noun
= llun (*plural* -iau) masculine, ffoto (*plural* -s) masculine
to take a photo = tynnu llun

photocopier noun
= llun-gopïwr (*plural* llun-gopiwyr) masculine, peiriant ffotogopïo (*plural* peiriannau ffotogopïo) masculine

photocopy verb
= llun-gopïo, ffotogopïo

photograph
1 noun
= llun (*plural* -iau) masculine, ffoto (*plural* -s) masculine
she's having her photograph taken = mae hi'n cael tynnu ei llun
2 verb
= tynnu llun

photographer noun
= ffotograffydd (*plural* ffotograffwyr) masculine

physical adjective
= corfforol

physics noun
= ffiseg feminine

piano noun
= piano (*plural* -s) masculine

pick verb
• (*choose*)
= dewis
• (*collect fruit*)
= casglu

pick on
to pick on someone
= pigo ar° rywun

pick up
to pick something up = codi rhywbeth
to pick someone up from the station = casglu rhywun o'r °orsaf

picnic noun
= picnic (*plural* -s) masculine

picture noun
= llun (*plural* -iau) masculine
to draw a picture = tynnu llun
to take a picture = tynnu llun

piece noun
• (*general senses*)
= darn (*plural* -au) masculine
• (*bit*)
= tamaid (*plural* tameidiau) masculine

> **!** Both **darn** and **tamaid** are quantity expressions and require **o°** with a following noun:
> **a piece of paper** = darn o °bapur
> **a piece of cheese** = tamaid o °gaws

• (*coin*)
= pisin (*plural* pisiau) masculine
a ten pence piece = pisin deg ceiniog

pierce verb
= treiddio

pig noun
= mochyn (*plural* moch) masculine

pigeon noun
= colomen (*plural* -nod) feminine

pile
1 noun
= pentwr (*plural* pentyrrau) masculine
2 verb
= pentyrru

pilgrim noun
= pererin (*plural* -ion) masculine

pilgrimage noun
= pererindod (*plural* -au) feminine

pill noun
= pilsen (*plural* pils) feminine

pillow noun
= clustog (*plural* -au) feminine, gobennydd (*plural* gobenyddiau) masculine

pilot noun
= peilot (*plural* -iaid) masculine

pin
1 noun
= pin (*plural* -nau) masculine
2 verb
= pinio

pinball *noun*
= pinbel *feminine*

pinch
1 *verb*
• *(with fingers)*
= pinsio
• *(steal)*
= dwyn (*stem* dyg-), bachu
2 *noun*
a pinch of salt = pinsiaid o halen
masculine

pine *noun*
= pinwydden (*plural* pinwydd) *feminine*

pineapple *noun*
= pîn-afal (*plural* -au) *masculine*

pink *adjective*
= pinc

pint *noun*
= peint (*plural* -iau) *masculine*

pipe *noun*
• *(for gas, water etc)*
= pibell (*plural* -au, -i) *feminine*
• *(for smoking)*
= pibell (*plural* -au, -i) *feminine*, pib
(*plural* -au) *feminine*

pipeline *noun*
in the pipeline (*planned*) = ar y gweill

pirate *noun*
= môr-leidr (*plural* môr-ladron)
masculine

Pisces *noun*
= y Pysgod *plural*

pitch *noun*
(field)
= cae (*plural* -au) *masculine*, maes (*plural*
meysydd) *masculine*
football pitch = cae pêl-droed
rugby pitch = maes rygbi

pity *noun*
• *(a shame)*
= trueni *masculine*
what a pity! = 'na °drueni!, 'na °biti!
it's a pity you're not coming = °drueni
°fod ti °ddim yn dod
• *(compassion)*
= tosturi *masculine*

place *noun*
• *(general senses)*
= lle (*plural* -fydd, -oedd) *masculine*
this is the best place to buy fish =
dyma'r lle gorau i°brynu pysgod

in place of = yn lle
all over the place = dros y lle i gyd
in the first place = yn y lle cynta(f)
to win first place = ennill (*stem* enill-) y
lle cynta(f)
to take someone's place = cymryd
(*stem* cymer-) lle rhywun

> **! lle** also means (in some parts of
> Wales) 'where?'—see entries on the
> Welsh-English and English-Welsh
> sides for more details.

• *(mainly in set phrases)*
= man (*plural* -nau) *masculine or
feminine*
in places = mewn mannau
place of birth = man geni
• *(spot)*
= llecyn (*plural* -nau) *masculine*
this is a nice place! = dyma °lecyn
hyfryd!

plague *noun*
= pla (*plural* plâu) *masculine*

plain *adjective*
• *(unadorned, simple)*
= plaen
• *(clear)*
= eglur, amlwg
it's plain to see = mae'n amlwg

plait *noun*
= plethen *feminine*, plethyn *masculine*
(*plural* plethi, *plural* plethau)

plan
1 *noun*
= cynllun (*plural* -iau) *masculine*
2 *verb*
• *(design)*
= cynllunio
• *(organize)*
= trefnu
to plan a trip = trefnu taith
• *(intend)*
to plan to do something = bwriadu
gwneud rhywbeth

plane *noun*
= awyren (*plural* -nau) *feminine*

planet *noun*
= planed (*plural* -au) *feminine*

planned *adjective*
= (*scheduled for later; in preparation*) ar
y gweill

plant
1 *noun*
= planhigyn (*plural* planhigion) *masculine*
2 *verb*
= plannu

plaster *noun*
(*medical*) = plastr (*plural* -au) *masculine*

plastic *adjective and noun*
= plastig

plate *noun*
= plât (*plural* platiau) *masculine*

platform *noun*
= platfform (*plural* -au) *masculine*

play
1 *noun*
= drama (*plural* dramâu) *feminine*
2 *verb*
(*games, most musical instruments*)
= chwarae (*stem* chwarae-)
to play with friends = chwarae gyda ffrindiau
to play football = chwarae pêl-droed
to play cards = chwarae cardiau
to play the piano = chwarae'r piano
to play the harp = canu'r °delyn

player *noun*
= chwaraewr (*plural* chwaraewyr) *masculine*
= chwaraewraig (*plural* chwaraewragedd) *feminine*

playground *noun*
= maes chwarae (*plural* meysydd chwarae) *masculine*

plead *noun*
= pledio
to plead guilty = pledio'n euog

pleasant *adjective*
= hyfryd, dymunol, difyr

please
1 *adverb*
= os gweli di'n °dda, os gwelwch yn °dda

> **!** *These phrases are the preferred standard usage for* 'please' *but differ from the English expression in that they cannot come first in the sentence:*
> **please come in** = dewch i mewn os gwelwch yn °dda

please wait here = arhoswch fan hyn os gwelwch yn °dda
> *The loanword* **plîs** *is very common in speech, though regarded by some as substandard.*

2 *verb*
= plesio, mynnu
there's no pleasing everyone = does dim plesio pawb
do as you please = gwnewch fel y mynnoch

pleased *adjective*
= balch
I was pleased to hear the news = o'n i'n °falch o °glywed y newyddion

pleasure *noun*
= pleser (*plural* -au) *masculine*
it was a great pleasure for me = oedd yn °bleser mawr i mi

plenty *pronoun*
= digon
I have plenty of time = mae gen i °ddigon o amser

> **!** **digon** *is a quantity expression and requires* **o°** *with a following noun.*

plug *noun*
= plwg (*plural* plygiau) *masculine*
to pull out a plug = tynnu plwg
plug in:
to plug something in = plygio rhywbeth i mewn

plum *noun*
= eirinen (*plural* eirin) *feminine*

plumber *noun*
= plymer (*plural* -iaid) *masculine*

plural *adjective*
= lluosog

plus *preposition*
• (*addition*)
= â[h]
two plus six is eight = dau â chwech ydy wyth
• (*with temperatures*)
= plws
between minus ten and plus five = rhwng minws deg a plws pump

pocket *noun*
= poced (*plural* -i) *feminine*

pocket money noun
= arian poced masculine

poem noun
= cerdd (plural -i) feminine

poet noun
= bardd (plural beirdd) masculine

point
1 noun
• (general senses)
= pwynt (plural -iau) masculine
point of view = safbwynt (plural -iau) masculine
turning point = trobwynt (plural -iau) masculine
high point = uchafbwynt (plural -iau) masculine
three point eight = tri pwynt wyth
• (remark)
= sylwad (plural -au) masculine
to make a point = gwneud sylwad
• (purpose)
= pwynt
there's no point shouting = does dim pwynt gweiddi
to be on the point of doing something (about to) = bod ar °fin gwneud rhywbeth
• (sharp end)
= blaen (plural -au) masculine
2 verb
= pwyntio
to point at something = pwyntio at° rywbeth

point out:
to point something out to someone = tynnu sylw rhywun at °rywbeth
to point out something (indicate) = dangos rhywbeth
to point out that... = tynnu sylw at y ffaith °fod...

poison
1 noun
= gwenwyn (plural -au) masculine
2 verb
= gwenwyno

pole noun
• (rod)
= polyn (plural polion) masculine
• (geographic)
= pegwn (plural pegynau) masculine
the North Pole = Pegwn y Gogledd
the South Pole = Pegwn y De

police noun
= heddlu masculine

policeman noun
= plismon (plural plismyn) masculine, heddwas (plural heddweision) masculine

police station noun
= gorsaf heddlu (plural gorsafoedd heddlu) feminine

policewoman noun
= plismones (plural -au) feminine

policy noun
= polisi (plural polisïau) masculine

polish verb
= sgleinio

polite adjective
= cwrtais

political adjective
= gwleidyddol

politician noun
= gwleidydd (plural -ion) masculine

politics noun
= gwleidyddiaeth feminine

poll noun
= arolwg (plural arolygon) masculine
opinion poll = arolwg barn (plural arolygon barn) masculine, pôl piniwn (plural polau piniwn) masculine

pollute verb
= llygru

pollution noun
= llygredd masculine

pond noun
= pwll (plural pyllau) masculine, llyn (plural -oedd) masculine

pony noun
= merlyn (plural merlod) masculine

ponytail noun
= cynffon merlen feminine

pony-trekking noun
= merlota verbnoun

pool noun
• (of liquid)
= pwll (plural pyllau) masculine

swimming pool = pwll nofio (*plural* pyllau nofio) *masculine*
pool of blood = pwll o °waed
• (*game*)
= pŵl *masculine*

poor *adjective*
• (*not rich*)
= tlawd
• (*of bad quality*)
= gwael
• (*deserving of pity*)
= truan
poor you! = °druan ohonot ti!

popular *adjective*
= poblogaidd

population *noun*
= poblogaeth (*plural* -au) *feminine*

pork *noun*
= cig moch *masculine*

porridge *noun*
= uwd *masculine*

port *noun*
• (*harbour*)
= porthladd (*plural* -oedd) *masculine*
• (*opposite of starboard*)
= y llaw chwith
• (*wine*)
= port *masculine*

porter *noun*
= porthor (*plural* -ion) *masculine*

portrait *noun*
= llun (*plural* -iau) *masculine*, portread (*plural* -au) *masculine*

positive *adjective*
• (*not negative*)
= cadarnhaol
• (*sure*)
= sicr, siwr, pendant

possession *noun*
= meddiant *masculine*

possibility *noun*
• (*fact of being possible*)
= posibilrwydd
the possibility of being injured = y posibilrwydd o °gael eich anafu
• (*opportunity, possible thing*)
= posibiliad (*plural* -au) *masculine*
an unpleasant possibility = posibiliad annymunol

possible *adjective*
= posib(l)
is it possible to speak to him? = ydy hi'n °bosib siarad ag e?, oes modd siarad ag e?

post
1 *noun*
• (*letters*)
= post
has the post come yet? = ydy'r post wedi cyrraedd?
• (*situation, job*)
= swydd (*plural* -i) *feminine*
to look for a new post = chwilio am° swydd newydd
2 *verb*
= postio, rhoi (*stem* rhoi-, rhodd-) yn y post
will you post this for me? = nei di °roi hwn yn y post i mi?

postbox *noun*
= blwch post (*plural* blychau post) *masculine*

postcard *noun*
= cerdyn post (*plural* cardiau post) *masculine*

postcode *noun*
= côd post (*plural* codau post) *masculine*

poster *noun*
= poster (*plural* -i) *masculine*

postman *noun*
= dyn post (*plural* dynion post) *masculine*, postmon (*plural* postmyn) *masculine*

post office *noun*
• (*building*)
= swyddfa °bost (*plural* swyddfeydd post) *feminine*
• (*organization*)
= Swyddfa'r Post *feminine*

postpone *verb*
= gohirio
to postpone a meeting = gohirio cyfarfod

pot *noun*
= pot (*plural* -iau) *masculine*

potato *noun*
= taten (*plural* tatws) *feminine*

pottery *noun*
- (*product*)
  = crochenwaith *masculine*
- (*place of production*)
  = crochendy (*plural* crochendai)
  masculine

pound *noun*
- (*currency*)
  = punt (*plural* punnoedd, punnau)
  feminine
  two pounds (£2) = dwy °bunt
  a hundred pounds (£100) = can punt
  = cant o °bunnoedd
  a million pounds = miliwn o
  °bunnoedd
- (*weight*)
  = pwys (*plural* -au) *masculine*
  two pounds of cheese = dau °bwys o
  °gaws

> **!** **pwys** *is a quantity expression and
> requires* **o°** *with a following noun.*

pour *verb*
- (*general*)
  = tywallt, tollti, arllwys
- (*flow*)
  the water was pouring in = roedd y dŵr
  yn llifo i mewn
- (*rain*)
  it's pouring = mae'n tollti'r glaw
  (*North*), mae'n arllwys y glaw (*South*),
  mae'n bwrw hen °wragedd a ffyn

poverty *noun*
  = tlodi *masculine*

powder *noun*
  = powd(w)r *masculine*
  washing powder = powd(w)r golchi
  masculine

power *noun*
- (*general senses*)
  = grym (*plural* -oedd) *masculine*, nerth
  (*plural* -oedd) *masculine*
- (*political*)
  = grym (*plural* -oedd) *masculine*
  to come to power = dod i °rym
- (*authority*)
  = pŵer (*plural* pwerau) *masculine*
  the great powers = y pwerau mawr
- (*electric power, etc*)
  = pŵer *masculine*
- (*energy*)
  = ynni *masculine*

- (*ability*)
  = gallu (*plural* -oedd) *masculine*, pŵer
  (*plural* pwerau) *masculine*

power cut *noun*
  = toriad trydan (*plural* toriadau trydan)
  masculine

powerful *adjective*
  = pwerus, grymus

power station *noun*
  = pwerdy (*plural* pwerdai) *masculine*

practical *adjective*
  = ymarferol

practice *noun*
- (*general sense*)
  = ymarfer (*plural* -ion) *masculine*
- (*doctor's, dentist's etc*)
  = gweithgylch (*plural* -oedd) *masculine*

practise *verb*
  = ymarfer
  to practise doing something = ymarfer
  gwneud rhywbeth

praise
1 *verb*
  = canmol
2 *noun*
  = canmoliaeth *feminine*

pram *noun*
  = pram (*plural* -iau) *masculine*

prawn *noun*
  = corgimwch (*plural* corgimychiaid)
  masculine

pray *verb*
  = gweddïo

prayer *noun*
  = gweddi (*plural* gweddïau) *feminine*

preach *verb*
  = pregethu

preacher *noun*
  = pregethwr (*plural* pregethwyr)
  masculine

precaution *noun*
  = rhagofal (*plural* -on) *masculine*

precious *adjective*
  = gwerthfawr

precise *adjective*
  = manwl

precisely *adverb*
(*exactly*)
= yn °gwmws

> **!** yn °gwmws is usually spelt **yn °gymwys** in formal writing.

pre-eminent *adjective*
= rhagorol

preface *noun*
= rhagair (*plural* rhageiriau) *masculine*, rhagymadrodd (*plural* -ion) *masculine*

prefer *verb*
I prefer tea to coffee = well gen i °de na ʰchoffi (*North*), well 'da fi °de na ʰchoffi (*South*)
she prefers to read books = well gynni hi °ddarllen llyfrau (*North*), well 'da hi °ddarllen llyfrau (*South*)
which do you prefer? = p'un sy'n °well gen ti/'da ti?

pregnancy *noun*
= beichiogrwydd *masculine*

pregnant *adjective*
= beichiog

prejudice *noun*
= rhagfarn (*plural* -au) *feminine*

prejudiced *adjective*
= rhagfarnllyd

preparation *noun*
= paratoad (*plural* -au) *masculine*, paratoi *verbnoun*
to make preparations = paratoi *verbnoun*
the food is in preparation = mae'r bwyd yn cael ei °baratoi

prepare *verb*
= paratoi
(*oneself*) = ymbaratoi
to prepare to do something = paratoi i °wneud rhywbeth
to prepare for an exam = ymbaratoi ar °gyfer arholiad

prepared *adjective*
= parod
to be prepared for something = bod yn °barod am° rywbeth
to be prepared to do something = bod yn °barod i °wneud rhywbeth

prescription *noun*
(*medical*)
= cyfarwyddeb (*plural* -au) *feminine*

present
1 *adjective*
= presennol
to be present = bod yn °bresennol
the present price = y pris ar hyn o °bryd
2 *noun*
• (*time now*)
= presennol
for the present = am y tro
at present = ar hyn o °bryd
• (*gift*)
= anrheg (*plural* -ion) *feminine*
to give someone a present = rhoi (*stem* rhoi-, rhodd-) anrheg i° rywun
3 *verb*
• (*introduce*)
= cyflwyno
may I present Mr Jones? = °ga i °gyflwyno Mr Jones?
• (*on TV or radio*)
= cyflwyno
to present a programme = cyflwyno rhaglen
• (*give*)
= rhoi (*stem* rhoi-, rhodd-)
to present someone with a clock = rhoi cloc i °rywun
to present a prize to someone = gwobrwyo rhywun

presently *adverb*
• (*soon*)
= maes o law, cyn bo hir, yn y man
• (*at the moment*)
= ar hyn o °bryd

preserve *verb*
= cadw

presidency *noun*
• (*of state*)
= arlywyddiaeth *feminine*
• (*of union, club etc*)
= llywyddiaeth *feminine*

president *noun*
• (*of state*)
= arlywydd (*plural* -ion) *masculine*
• (*of union, club etc*)
= llywydd (*plural* -ion) *masculine*

press
1 *noun*
(*newspapers*)
= gwasg *feminine*
2 *verb*
= gwasgu

press conference *noun*
= cynhadledd i'r °wasg (*plural*
cynadleddau i'r °wasg) *feminine*

press release *noun*
= datganiad i'r °wasg (*plural*
datganiadau i'r °wasg) *masculine*

pressure *noun*
= pwysau *plural*
to bring pressure on someone = dwyn
(*stem* dyg-) pwysau ar° rywun, pwyso
ar° rywun
under pressure = dan °bwysau

pretend *verb*
= esgus
to pretend to do something = esgus
gwneud rhywbeth

pretty
1 *adjective*
= pert, tlws
2 *adverb*
= eitha, go°
that's pretty good = mae hynny'n eitha
da
there are pretty few left = go ychydig sy
ar ôl

> **!** **eitha** (*no mutation*) *is the general
> term—practically always the right
> choice—while* **go°** *is less common;*
> **go ychydig** *is a set phrase.*

prevent *verb*
= rhwystro, atal
**to prevent someone (from) doing
    something** = rhwystro *or* atal rhywun
rhag gwneud rhywbeth

previous *adjective*
= o'r blaen, blaenorol, cynt
the previous day = y diwrnod o'r
blaen

previously *adverb*
= °gynt

price *noun*
= pris (*plural* -iau) *masculine*

price cut *noun*
= gostyngiad (*plural* -au) *masculine*

prick *verb*
= pigo
to prick one's finger = pigo'ch bys

prickly *adjective*
(*touchy*)
= pigog

pride *noun*
= balchder *masculine*

priest *noun*
= offeiriad (*plural* offeiriaid) *masculine*

primary *adjective*
• (*main*)
= prif°

> **!** **prif°** *always precedes the noun and
> causes soft mutation.*
> **the primary reason for this** = y prif
> °reswm am hyn

• (*school*)
= cynradd

primary school *noun*
= ysgol °gynradd (*plural* ysgolion
cynradd) *feminine*

primary school teacher *noun*
= athrawes ysgol °gynradd (*plural*
athrawesau ysgol °gynradd) *feminine*
= athro ysgol °gynradd (*plural* athrawon
ysgol °gynradd) *masculine*

prime minister *noun*
= prif °weinidog *masculine*

prince *noun*
= tywysog (*plural* -ion) *masculine*

princess *noun*
= tywysoges (*plural* -au) *feminine*

principal
1 *adjective*
= prif°

> **!** **prif°** *always precedes the noun and
> causes soft mutation.*
> **the principal reason for this** = y prif
> °reswm am hyn

2 *noun*
• (*of institution or department*)
= pennaeth (*plural* penaethiaid)
masculine
• (*of school, college, etc*)
= prifathro (*plural* prifathrawon)
masculine
= prifathawes (*plural* -au) *feminine*

principality *noun*
= tywysogaeth (*plural* -au) *feminine*

principle *noun*
= egwyddor (*plural* -ion) *feminine*
basic principles = sylfeini *plural*

print
1 *noun*
• (*of photo etc*)
= print (*plural* -iau) *masculine*
• (*trace*)
= ôl (*plural* olion) *masculine*
2 *verb*
= argraffu
to print a book = argraffu llyfr

priority *noun*
= blaenoriaeth (*plural* -au) *feminine*

prison *noun*
= carchar (*plural* -au) *masculine*
to send someone to prison = carcharu
rhywun, anfon rhywun i °garchar, rhoi
(*stem* rhoi-, rhodd-) rhywun yn y
carchar

prisoner *noun*
= carcharor (*plural* -ion) *masculine*
= carcharores (*plural* -au) *feminine*
they took him prisoner = fe °gymeron
nhw fe'n °garcharor

privacy *noun*
= preifatrwydd *masculine*

private *adjective*
= preifat

privatize *verb*
= preifateiddio

prize *noun*
= gwobr (*plural* -au) *feminine*
to give/award someone a prize =
gwobrwyo rhywun

probability *noun*
= tebygolrwydd *masculine*
in all probability = yn ôl pob tebyg

probably *adverb*
= mae'n °debyg

> **!** *This phrase must either begin the
> sentence and be followed by a 'that...'
> clause, or be tagged on at the end; it
> cannot be put in the middle as in
> English*:
> **he probably won't come** = mae'n
> °debyg na °ddaw e,
> °ddaw e °ddim, mae'n °debyg

they're probably late = mae'n °debyg
bod nhw'n hwyr,
maen nhw'n hwyr, mae'n °debyg
it's probably her fault = mae'n
°debyg mai hi sy ar °fai,
hi sy ar °fai, mae'n °debyg

problem *noun*
• (*general sense*)
= problem (*plural* -au) *feminine*
to solve a problem = datrys problem
• (*difficulty, hitch*)
= trafferth (*plural* -ion) *feminine*
are you having problems? = wyt ti'n
cael trafferth(ion)?
**to manage to do something without
problems** = llwyddo i °wneud
rhywbeth yn °ddidrafferth

process
1 *noun*
= process (*plural* -au) *masculine or
feminine*
2 *verb*
= prosesu

produce
1 *noun*
= cynnyrch (*plural* cynhyrchion)
masculine
2 *verb*
= cynhyrchu

product *noun*
= cynnyrch (*plural* cynhyrchion)
masculine

production *noun*
= cynhyrchiad (*plural* -au) *masculine*

profession *noun*
= galwedigaeth (*plural* -au) *feminine*,
proffesiwn (*plural* proffesiynau)
masculine

professional
1 *adjective*
= proffesiynol
2 *noun*
= gweithiwr proffesiynol (*plural*
gweithwyr proffesiynol) *masculine*
= gweithwraig °broffesiynol (*plural*
gweithwragedd proffesiynol)
feminine

professor *noun*
= athro (*plural* athrawon) *masculine*

profit
1 noun
- (monetary)
  = elw masculine
- (advantage)
  = mantais feminine, budd masculine, lles masculine

2 verb
  = elwa

to profit from something = elwa o° rywbeth, manteisio ar° rywbeth, cael budd/lles o° rywbeth

profitable adjective
- (yielding profit)
  is the business profitable? = ydy'r busnes yn gwneud/dwyn elw?
- (advantageous)
  = manteisiol, buddiol, o °fudd, o °les

program
1 noun
  = rhaglen (plural -ni) feminine
  computer program = rhaglen °gyfrifiadur (plural rhaglenni cyfrifiadur) feminine

2 verb
  = rhaglennu

programme noun
  = rhaglen (plural -ni) feminine
  television programme = rhaglen °deledu (plural rhaglenni teledu) feminine
  a programme about Wales = rhaglen am °Gymru

progress
1 noun
- (course)
  = cwrs masculine, datblygiad masculine
- (in learning etc)
  = cynnydd
  they are making progress = maen nhw'n gwneud cynnydd

2 verb
- (proceed)
  = mynd ymlaen
  work is progressing = mae'r gwaith yn mynd yn ei °flaen
- (build on achievement)
  = gwneud cynnydd

prohibit verb
  = gwahardd

to prohibit someone from doing something = gwahardd rhywun rhag gwneud rhywbeth

project noun
  = prosiect or project (plural -au) masculine, cynllun (plural -iau) masculine

projector noun
  = taflunydd (plural -ion) masculine
  overhead projector = uwchdaflunydd (plural -ion) masculine

promise
1 noun
  = addewid (plural -ion) masculine or feminine
  to keep a promise = cadw (stem cadw-) addewid
  to break a promise = torri addewid
  to show promise = bod yn addawol

2 verb
  = addo (stem addaw-)
  to promise to do something = addo gwneud rhywbeth
  to promise something to someone = addo rhywbeth i° rywun

promote verb
- (boost, advertise)
  = hybu
- (elevate)
  = dyrchafu

pronoun noun
  = rhagenw (plural -au) masculine

pronounce verb
  = ynganu
  am I pronouncing that right? = ydw i'n ynganu hynny'n iawn?

pronunciation noun
  = ynganiad (plural -au) masculine

proof noun
  = prawf (plural profion) masculine

proper adjective
- (right, correct)
  = iawn, cywir
- (appropriate)
  = priodol
- (genuine)
  = go iawn

properly adverb
  = yn iawn, yn °gywir

property noun
= eiddo
whose property is this? = eiddo pwy ydy hwn?

prophecy noun
= proffwydoliaeth (*plural* -au) *feminine*

prophesy verb
= proffwydo

prophet noun
= proffwyd (*plural* -i) *masculine*

proposal noun
• (*offer*)
= cynnig (*plural* cynigion) *masculine*
• (*intention*)
= bwriad (*plural* -au) *masculine*

proprietor noun
= perchennog (*plural* perchnogion) *masculine*

prose noun
= rhyddiaith *feminine*

prospective adjective
= darpar°

> **!** darpar° *precedes the noun and causes soft mutation:*
> **prospective parliamentary candidate** = darpar ymgeisydd seneddol

prospect noun
there's no prospect of her agreeing = does dim gobaith y bydd hi'n cytuno
what are the prospects? = beth ydy'r rhagolygon?

protect verb
= amddiffyn
to protect someone from something = amddiffyn rhywun rhag rhywbeth

protest
1 noun
= protest (*plural* -iadau) *masculine*, gwrthdystiad (*plural* -au) *masculine*
under protest = dan °brotest
2 verb
= protestio, gwrthdystio
to protest against something = protestio yn erbyn rhywbeth

protester noun
= protestiwr (*plural* protestwyr) *masculine*

proud adjective
• (*with a feeling of pride*)
= balch
to be proud of something = bod yn °falch o° rywbeth
• (*arrogant*)
= ffroenuchel

prove verb
= profi

provide verb
= darparu

provided conjunction
= ar yr amod
provided (that) you stay here = ar yr amod bod chi'n aros fan hyn
provided (that) we don't have to see him = ar yr amod na °fydd rhaid inni ei °weld e

province noun
= talaith (*plural* taleithiau) *feminine*

psychiatrist noun
= seiciatrydd (*plural* -ion) *masculine*

psychological adjective
= seicolegol

psychologist noun
= seicolegydd (*plural* seicolegwyr) *masculine*

psychology noun
= seicoleg *feminine*

pub noun
= tafarn (*plural* -au) *feminine*
to go to the pub = mynd i'r °dafarn

public
1 adjective
= cyhoeddus
2 noun
= cyhoedd *masculine*
not open to the public = °ddim ar agor i'r cyhoedd
in public = yn °gyhoeddus

public holiday noun
= gŵyl °gyhoeddus (*plural* gwyliau cyhoeddus) *feminine*

publicity noun
= cyhoeddusrwydd *masculine*

public transport noun
= cludiant cyhoeddus *masculine*

publish verb
= cyhoeddi

pudding noun
= pwdin (*plural* -au) *masculine*

puddle noun
= pwll (*plural* pyllau) *masculine*

pull verb
= tynnu
to pull down a building =
tynnu/chwalu adeilad
to pull a tooth out = tynnu dant

pull over, pull up (*in a car*)
= stopio

pullover noun
= pwlofer (*plural* -s, -i) *masculine or feminine*, siwmper (*plural* -i) *feminine*

pump
1 noun
= pwmp (*plural* pympiau) *masculine*
2 verb
= pwmpio

pumpkin noun
= pwmpen (*plural* -ni) *feminine*

punch
1 noun
= (*blow*) pwniad (*plural* -au) *masculine*
2 verb
= pwnio

punctual adjective
= prydlon

punctuality noun
= prydlondeb *masculine*

punctually adverb
= yn °brydlon

puncture noun
= twll (*plural* tyllau) *masculine*

punish verb
= cosbi

punishment noun
= cosb (*plural* -au) *feminine*

pupil noun
= disgybl (*plural* -ion) *masculine*

puppy noun
= ci bach (*plural* cŵn bach) *masculine*

purchase verb
= prynu

pure adjective
= pur

purple adjective
= piws; porffor (*formal*)

purpose noun
= amcan (*plural* -ion) *masculine*, pwrpas (*plural* -au) *masculine*, bwriad (*plural* -au) *masculine*
on purpose = o °fwriad, o °bwrpas
= yn °fwriadol, yn °bwrpasol

purposeful adjective
• (*deliberate*)
= bwriadol, pwrpasol
• (*decisive*)
= penderfynol

purse noun
• (*for money*)
= pwrs (*plural* pyrsau) *masculine*
• (*US: handbag*)
= bag llaw (*plural* bagiau llaw) *masculine*

push verb
• (*general sense*)
= gwthio
to push past someone = gwthio heibio i °rywun
to push someone down the stairs =
gwthio rhywun i lawr y grisiau
push off! = cer o 'ma!
= bacha hi!
to push something through = gwthio rhywbeth drwodd
• (*sell drugs*)
= gwerthu cyffuriau

pushchair noun
= cadair °wthio (*plural* cadeiriau gwthio) *feminine*

pusher noun
(*seller of drugs*)
= gwerthwr cyffuriau (*plural* gwerthwyr cyffuriau) *masculine*

put verb
• (*most general senses*)
= rhoi (*stem* rhoi-, rhodd-), gosod
to put something down = rhoi rhywbeth i lawr
to put something on the table = rhoi rhywbeth ar y bwrdd

put away:
to put the toys away = rhoi'r teganau ar °gadw

put back

to put something back = rhoi rhywbeth yn ôl

to put the clocks back = troi (*stem* troi-, trodd-)'r clociau yn ôl

put off

• (*postpone*)

= gohirio

to put off a meeting = gohirio cyfarfod

• (*switch off*)

= diffodd

to put the television off = diffodd y teledu

put on:

to put on clothes = gwisgo dillad

he put on his shirt = gwisgodd e ei °grys

• (*switch on*)

= troi (*stem* troi-, trodd-) ymlaen

to put the television on = troi'r teledu ymlaen

• (*gain*)

to put on weight = ennill (*stem* enill-) pwysau

• (*stage*)

to put on a play = llwyfannu drama

put out

• (*extinguish*)

= diffodd

to put out the lights = diffodd y goleuadau

• (*place outside*)

= rhoi (*stem* rhoi-, rhodd-) allan

to put the cat out = rhoi'r °gath allan

put up

• (*on wall etc*)

to put up a sign = rhoi arwydd i fyny

• (*suffer*)

to put up with something = diodde(f) rhywbeth

• (*give accommodation*)

to put someone up = rhoi llety i° rywun

puzzle *noun*

= pos (*plural* -au) *masculine*

pyjamas *plural noun*

= pyjamas *plural*

qualification *noun*

= cymhwyster (*plural* cymwysterau) *masculine*

qualified *adjective*

= â ʰchymwysterau

quality *noun*

= ansawdd (*plural* ansoddau) *masculine or feminine*

= safon (*plural* -au) *feminine*

of good quality = o ansawdd da/°dda

of poor quality = o ansawdd gwael/°wael

quantity *noun*

• (*countable things*)

= nifer (*plural* -oedd) *masculine or feminine*

a large quantity of books = nifer °fawr o °lyfrau

• (*uncountable things*)

= maint (*plural* meintiau) *masculine*

a small quantity of cheese = maint bychan o °gaws

quarrel

1 *noun*

= cweryl (*plural* -on, -au) *masculine*, ffrae (*plural* -au, -on) *feminine*

2 *verb*

= cweryla, ffraeo

quarter

1 *noun*

= chwarter (*plural* -i) *masculine*

a quarter of an hour = chwarter awr

to cut something in quarters = torri rhywbeth yn chwarteri

at a quarter to three = am chwarter i °dri

! *Note the difference between* **chwarter wedi naw** 'a quarter past nine' *and* **hanner <u>awr</u> wedi naw** 'half past nine'.

---

2 *pronoun*

a quarter of them are absent = mae chwarter ohonyn nhw'n absennol

quay *noun*

= cei (*plural* -au *or* -oedd) *masculine*

queen *noun*
= brenhines (*plural* breninesau) *feminine*

question

1 *noun*
= cwestiwn (*plural* cwestiynau) *masculine*
to ask someone a question = gofyn (*stem* gofynn-) cwestiwn i° rywun, holi rhywun
question and answer session = sesiwn holi ac ateb
it's a question of principle = mae'n °fater o egwyddor

2 *verb*
= holi
to question someone = holi rhywun

queue

1 *noun*
= cwt (*plural* cytau) *feminine*, ciw (*plural* -iau) *masculine*, rhes (*plural* -i) *feminine*
to stand in a queue = sefyll mewn cwt/ciw
to jump the queue = neidio'r °gwt/ciw

2 *verb*
= aros (*stem* arhos-)/sefyll (*stem* saf-, sef-) mewn ciw/cwt

quick *adjective*
= cyflym; sydyn (*North*), clou (*South*)

> **!** **sydyn** and **clou** are found in speech only, where they are however widespread; **cyflym** is the standard term.

it's quicker by train = mae'n °gyflymach ar y trên
come quick! = dewch yn °glou!

quickly *adverb*
• (*fast*)
= yn °gyflym; yn sydyn (*North*), yn °glou (*South*)
• (*hastily*)
= ar °frys
• (*without delay*)
= yn °ddi-oed

quiet

1 *adjective*
= tawel, llonydd
to go quiet = tawelu
keep quiet! = cadwch yn °dawel!
be quiet! = byddwch yn °dawel!

2 *noun*
= tawelwch *masculine*

quieten down *verb*
= tawelu

quietly *adverb*
= yn °dawel

quit *verb*
• (*leave*)
= gadael (*stem* gadaw-)
• (*give up*)
= rhoi (*stem* rhoi-, rhodd-) 'r gorau i°
to quit a job = rhoi'r gorau i swydd
• (*stop*)
= peidio, rhoi'r gorau i°
to quit smoking = peidio ysmygu
= rhoi'r gorau i ysmygu
• (*resign*)
= ymddiswyddo

quite *adverb*
• (*rather*)
= eitha
I quite like Chinese food = dw i'n eitha hoff o °fwyd Tseinaidd
it's quite early = mae'n eitha cynnar
quite a few people = cryn nifer o °bobol
quite a bit of money = cryn °dipyn o arian
• (*completely*)
= hollol°, cwbwl°
I'm quite certain = dw i'n hollol sicr
that's quite different = mae hynny'n hollol °wahanol
that was quite unnecessary = roedd hynny'n °gwbwl °ddiangen
quite! (*agreement*) = yn hollol!
= yn llwyr!
• (*exactly*)
= yn union
I don't know quite what it means = dw i °ddim yn gwybod yn union beth mae'n °feddwl

quiz *noun*
= cwis (*plural* -iau) *masculine*

quotation *noun*
• (*from a book*)
= dyfyniad (*plural* -au) *masculine*
• (*price for work*)
= pris (*plural* -iau) *masculine*

quote

1 *noun*
= dyfyniad (*plural* -au) *masculine*

2 *verb*
= dyfynnu

Rr

rabbit *noun*
= cwningen (*plural* cwningod) *feminine*

rabies *noun*
= y °gynddaredd *feminine*

race[1]
1 *noun*
(*contest*)
= ras (*plural* -ys) *feminine*
horse race = ras °geffylau (*plural* rasys ceffylau) *feminine*
2 *verb*
= rasio
to race someone = rasio yn erbyn rhywun
I'll race you! = rasia i di!

race[2] *noun*
(*people*)
= hil (*plural* -ion, -iau) *feminine*

racehorse *noun*
= ceffyl rasio (*plural* ceffylau rasio) *masculine*

racetrack *noun*
= rhedfa rasio (*plural* rhedfeydd rasio) *feminine*

racism *noun*
= hiliaeth *feminine*

racist
1 *adjective*
= hiliol
2 *noun*
= hilydd (*plural* -ion, hilwyr) *masculine*

racket *noun*
• (*for sport*)
= raced (*plural* -i) *feminine*
• (*noise*)
= twrw *masculine*
to make a racket = codi twrw

radiation *noun*
= ymbelydredd *masculine*

radiator *noun*
= rheiddiadur (*plural* -on) *masculine*

radical *adjective*
• (*political*)
= radicalaidd
• (*basic: disagreement, advances etc*)
= sylfaenol

radio *noun*
= radio (*plural* -s) *masculine or feminine*
to listen to the radio = gwrando (*stem* gwrandaw-) ar y radio

radio station *noun*
= gorsaf radio (*plural* gorsafoedd radio) *feminine*

rage *noun*
= cynddaredd *feminine*
to fly into a rage = cynddeiriogi, gwylltio

raid
1 *noun*
= ymosodiad (*plural* -au) *masculine*
2 *verb*
= ymosod ar°
to raid a bank = ymosod ar °fanc
the police raided the building = ymosododd yr heddlu ar yr adeilad

rail *noun*
• (*handrail*)
= canllaw (*plural* -iau) *feminine*
• (*for train etc*)
= cledren (*plural* cledrau) *feminine*
to go by rail = mynd ar y trên

railway *noun*
= rheilffordd (*plural* rheilffyrdd) *feminine*

railway line *noun*
= rheilffordd (*plural* rheilffyrdd) *feminine*

railway station *noun*
= gorsaf °reilffordd (*plural* gorsafoedd rheilffordd) *feminine*, stesion (*plural* -s) *feminine*

> **!** *gorsaf is the standard term, while the loanword* **stesion** *is common with native speakers.*

rain
1 *noun*
= glaw (*plural* -ogydd) *masculine*
it looks like rain = mae golwg glaw arni
2 *verb*
= bwrw glaw, glawio, bwrw
it's raining = mae'n bwrw (glaw), mae'n glawio

rainbow noun
= enfys (plural -au) feminine

raincoat noun
= côt °law (plural cotiau glaw) feminine

raise verb
• (lift up)
= codi
• (increase)
= codi
• (bring up: children)
= magu
where were you raised? = lle °gest ti dy °fagu?
= lle °gawsoch chi'ch magu?
• (voice)
to raise one's voice = codi'ch llais
• (objection)
to raise an objection = gwrthwynebu, codi gwrthwynebiad

ram noun
= maharen (plural meheryn) masculine, hwrdd (plural hyrddod) masculine (South)

range noun
• (selection)
= dewis masculine, detholiad (plural -au) masculine
• (mountains)
a range of mountains = cadwyn o °fynyddoedd feminine
• (for cooking)
= popty (plural poptai) masculine

rape
1 verb
= treisio
2 noun
= trais, trais rhywiol

rare adjective
• (scarce)
= prin
• (infrequent)
= anaml
• (lightly cooked)
= gwaedlyd

rarely adverb
= yn anaml

rash noun
= brech (plural -au) feminine

rasher noun
= tafell (plural -i, -au, tefyll) feminine, sleisen (plural sleisys) feminine

raspberry noun
= mafonen (plural mafon) feminine

rat noun
= llygoden °fawr (plural llygod mawr) feminine

rate noun
= cyfradd (plural -au) feminine, graddfa (plural graddfeydd) feminine
basic rate = cyfradd sylfaenol
rate of interest = cyfradd llog
rate of exchange = cyfradd/graddfa °gyfnewid

rather adverb
• (in preferences)
= °well
I'd rather go tomorrow = (basai'n) °well gen i °fynd yfory (North), (byddai'n) °well 'da fi °fynd yfory (South)
would you rather wait? = °fasai'n °well gen ti aros? (North), °fyddai'n °well 'da ti aros? (South)
• (in comparisons)
= yn hytrach (na[h])
come tomorrow rather than today = dewch yfory yn hytrach na heddiw
• (fairly)
= braidd
it's rather hot = mae hi braidd yn °boeth

raw adjective
• (general)
= crai
raw materials = defnyddiau crai
• (wound)
= cignoeth
• (meat etc)
= amrwd

ray noun
= pelydryn or pelydr (plural pelydrau) masculine
a ray of hope = llygedyn o °obaith

razor noun
= rasel (plural -i) feminine, raser (plural -au) feminine (South)
safety razor = rasel °ddiogel (plural raseli diogel)
electric razor = rasel °drydan (plural raseli trydan)

razor blade noun
= llafn rasel (plural llafnau rasel) masculine

re- *prefix*
= ail°-

reach *verb*
• (*general*)
= cyrraedd (*stem* cyrhaedd-)
when did they reach the town? = pryd
°gyrhaeddon nhw'r °dre?
to reach a decision = dod i
°benderfyniad
I can't reach the shelf = °alla i °ddim
cyrraedd y silff
the letter didn't reach him =
ʰchafodd/°gafodd e mo'r llythyr
• (*on phone*)
you can reach me on this number =
gellwch chi °gysylltu â fi ar y rhif yma

reach out
he reached out = estynnodd e ei
°fraich

react *verb*
• (*to chemicals, medicines etc*)
= adweithio
• (*respond*)
= ymateb
to react to something = ymateb i°
rywbeth

read *verb*
= darllen
to read something to someone =
darllen rhywbeth i° rywun
can you read Welsh? = °ellwch chi
°ddarllen Cymraeg?
to read through something = darllen
drwy °rywbeth

read out
= darllen yn uchel

readiness *noun*
= parodrwydd *masculine*

reading *noun*
= darlleniad (*plural* -au) *masculine*

ready *adjective*
= parod
to be ready to do something = bod yn
°barod i °wneud rhywbeth
to be ready for something = bod yn
°barod am° rywbeth, bod yn °barod ar
°gyfer rhywbeth

! *The related phrase* **yn °barod** *is an
adverb in its own right meaning*
'already'.

to get something ready = paratoi
rhywbeth

real *adjective*
• (*actual, not imagined*)
= gwir°

! *gwir° precedes the noun it refers to
and causes soft mutation.*

• (*genuine*)
= go iawn

reality *noun*
= gwirionedd (*plural* -au) *masculine*
in reality = mewn gwirionedd

realize *verb*
= sylweddoli
I hadn't realized = o'n i heb sylweddoli

really *adverb*
• (*actually*)
= mewn gwirionedd
it was my fault really = fi oedd ar °fai,
mewn gwirionedd
• (*with adjective*)
= gwirioneddol°, gwir°, reit° (*colloquial*)
it's really heavy = mae'n °wirioneddol
°drwm
• (*interjection*)
= °wir!

rear
1 *adjective*
= cefn, ôl
rear wheel = olwyn °gefn (*plural*
olwynion cefn), olwyn ôl (*plural*
olwynion ôl)
rear seat = sedd °gefn (*plural* seddau
cefn), sedd ôl (*plural* seddau ôl)
2 *verb*
(*bring up*)
= magu

rear-view mirror *noun*
= drych ôl (*plural* drychau ôl) *masculine*

reason *noun*
= rheswm (*plural* rhesymau) *masculine*
a reason for doing something =
rheswm dros °wneud rhywbeth
for no reason = heb °reswm
for this reason = o achos hyn, o'r
herwydd, oherwydd hyn
for that reason = o achos hynny
= oherwydd hynny

reasonable *adjective*
= rhesymol

reassure *verb*
= tawelu meddwl
I reassured him = nes i °dawelu ei °feddwl

rebroadcast *verb*
= ailddarlledu

receipt *noun*
= derbynneb (*plural* derbynebau, derbynebion) *feminine*
to get a receipt for something = cael derbynneb am° rywbeth

receive *verb*
= derbyn (*stem* derbyni-), cael
to receive something from someone = derbyn *or* cael rhywbeth gan° rywun

> **!** **cael** *is irregular in the preterite, short future and conditional—see entry on the Welsh-English side for details.*

recent *adjective*
= diweddar

recently *adverb*
= yn °ddiweddar

reception *noun*
• (*in hotel, hospital etc*)
= derbynfa (*plural* derbynfeydd) *feminine*
• (*formal event*)
= derbyniad (*plural* -au) *masculine*

receptionist *noun*
= croesawydd (*plural* -ion) *masculine*
= croesawferch (*plural* -ed) *feminine*
= derbynnydd (*plural* derbynyddion) *masculine*
= derbynyddes (*plural* -au) *feminine*

recipe *noun*
= rysáit (*plural* ryseitiau) *feminine*
to follow a recipe = dilyn (*stem* dilyn-) rysáit

recognize *verb*
• (*person*)
= adnabod (*stem* adnabydd-)
to recognize someone by something = adnabod rhywun o° rywbeth

> **!** *In the literary language,* **adnabod** *is used for* **nabod** *'know' in the sense of 'be acquainted with', but in the living language these two verbs are distinct.*

• (*fact*)
= cydnabod (*stem* cydnabydd-)

recommence *verb*
= ailddechrau (*stem* ailddechreu-)

recommend *verb*
= cymeradwyo
what do you recommend? = beth dych chi'n °gymeradwyo?

record
1 *noun*
• (*disc*)
= record (*plural* -iau) *feminine*
to play a record = chwarae (*stem* chwarae-) record
• (*in sport*)
= record (*plural* -iau) *feminine*
to break a record = torri record
• (*note, memorandum*)
= cofnod (*plural* -ion) *masculine*
to make a record of something = gwneud cofnod o° rywbeth
2 *verb*
= recordio

recorder *noun*
• (*machine*)
= recordydd (*plural* -ion) *masculine*
• (*musical instrument*)
= recorder (*plural* -s) *masculine*

record player *noun*
= chwaraewr recordiau (*plural* chwaraewyr recordiau) *masculine*

recover *noun*
• (*from illness*)
= gwella
• (*retrieve*)
= ailffeindio, cael yn ôl

rectangle *noun*
= pedrongl (*plural* -au) *feminine*

recycle *verb*
= ailgylchu
recycling centre = canolfan ailgylchu (*plural* canolfannau ailgylchu) *feminine*

red *adjective*
= coch
to go red
= mynd yn °goch, cochi
(*blush*)
= gwrido, cochi

red-haired *adjective*
= pengoch, gwalltgoch

reduce *adjective*
= gostwng (*stem* gostyng-), lleihau
to reduce prices = gostwng prisiau
reduce speed now = arafwch nawr

reduction *noun*
= gostyngiad (*plural* -au) *masculine*,
lleihad (*plural* -au) *masculine*

redundant *adjective*
he was made redundant = mi °gafodd e
ei °ddiswyddo

refectory *noun*
= ffreutur (*plural* -iau) *feminine*

refer *adjective*
= cyfeirio
to refer to something = cyfeirio at°
rywbeth
I refer to your letter ... = cyfeiriaf at eich
llythyr ... (*formal*)

referee *noun*
• (*in sport*)
= dyfarnwr (*plural* dyfarnwyr)
masculine
• (*for applicant*)
= canolwr (*plural* canolwyr) *masculine*,
cefnogwr (*plural* cefnogwyr) *masculine*

reference *noun*
= cyfeiriad (*plural* -au) *masculine*
to make reference to something =
cyfeirio at° rywbeth
to give someone as a reference = enwi
rhywun fel canolwr

reference book *noun*
= cyfeirlyfr (*plural* -au) *masculine*

reflect *verb*
= adlewyrchu

reflection *noun*
= adlewyrchiad (*plural* -au) *masculine*

refreshing *adjective*
• (*renewing*)
= adnewyddol
• (*reviving*)
= adfywiol

refreshments *plural noun*
= lluniaeth *masculine*

refrigerator *noun*
= oergell (*plural* -oedd) *feminine*

refuge *noun*
= lloches (*plural* -au) *feminine*

to seek/take refuge from something =
ymochel rhag rhywbeth
to give someone refuge = llochesu
rhywun

refugee *noun*
= ffoadur (*plural* -iaid) *masculine*
= ffoadures (*plural* -au) *feminine*

refuse[1] *verb*
= gwrthod, nacáu (*colloquial* cau), pallu
(*South*)
to refuse to do something = gwrthod
gwneud rhywbeth
to refuse someone something =
gwrthod rhywbeth i° rywun
the car refuses to go = mae'r car yn
pallu mynd

refuse[2] *noun*
(*rubbish*)
= sbwriel *masculine*

regarding *preposition*
= ynghylch, ynglŷn â[h], parthed (*formal*)

! *Only in very formal written styles is*
parthed *encountered, and certainly
never in unaffected speech.*

regards *plural noun*
(*at end of letter*)
= cofion
as regards = o °ran
as regards the rest of the family = o
°ran gweddill y teulu

region *noun*
= ardal (*plural* -oedd) *feminine*,
rhanbarth (*plural* -au) *masculine*, bro
(*plural* bröydd) *feminine*

regional *adjective*
= rhanbarthol

register
1 *noun*
= cofrestr (*plural* -au, -i) *feminine*
2 *verb*
= cofrestru

registration number *noun*
• (*general*)
= rhif cofrestru (*plural* -au cofrestru)
masculine
• (*car*)
= rhif car *masculine*

regret *verb*
= edifaru, difaru (*colloquial*)

to regret doing something = edifaru gwneud rhywbeth

regular adjective
- (conforming to pattern or type) = rheolaidd
  regular verbs = berfau rheolaidd
- (consistent, habitual) = cyson

regularly adverb
- (all senses) = yn rheolaidd
- (consistently, habitually—also:) = yn °gyson
  to do something regularly = gwneud rhywbeth yn rheolaidd/yn °gyson

rehearsal noun
= ymarfer (plural -ion) masculine

rehearse verb
= ymarfer

reincarnation noun
= ailymgnawdoliad (plural -au) masculine

reject verb
= gwrthod

related adjective
to be related to someone = perthyn i° rywun
are they related to you? = ydyn nhw'n perthyn i ti?

relation noun
- (relationship, related person) = perthynas (plural perthnasau) feminine
  in relation to something = mewn perthynas/cysylltiad â ͪ rhywbeth
  they are my relations = maen nhw'n perthyn i mi
  to visit one's relations = ymweld (stem ymwel-) â'ch perthnasau
- (link) = cysylltiad (plural -au) masculine

relationship noun
= perthynas (plural perthnasau) feminine, cysylltiad (plural -au) masculine

relative noun
he's a relative of mine = mae e'n perthyn i mi
those are his relatives = dyna ei °berthnasau

relax verb
= ymlacio

relaxed adjective
= wedi ymlacio

relay race noun
= ras °gyfnewid (plural rasys cyfnewid) feminine

release
1 noun
- (announcement) = datganiad (plural -au) masculine
  press release = datganiad i'r °wasg
- (from prison etc) = rhyddhad masculine, rhyddhau verbnoun
  a new release (record) = record newydd
  (film) = ffilm newydd
2 verb
- (liberate) = rhyddhau
- (put on the market) = rhyddhau
- (let go of) = gollwng (stem gollyng-)

relevant adjective
= perthnasol

reliable adjective
= dibynadwy

relieved adjective
you'll be relieved to know that ... = bydd yn rhyddhad i chi °wybod °fod ...

religion noun
= crefydd (plural -au) feminine

religious education, RE noun
= addysg °grefyddol feminine

rely verb
= dibynnu
to rely on someone/something = dibynnu ar° rywun/rywbeth

remain verb
= aros (stem arhos-)

remainder noun
= gweddill (plural -ion) masculine

remark
1 noun
= sylwad (plural -au) masculine
2 verb
- (make observation) = gwneud sylwad

to remark on something = gwneud sylwad ar° rywbeth
- (*notice*)
  = sylwi

remarkable *adjective*
  = hynod

remarkably *adverb*
  = hynod o°
  remarkably clever = hynod o °ddeallus

remember *verb*
  = cofio
  do you remember them? = wyt ti'n cofio nhw?
  to remember to do something = cofio gwneud rhywbeth
  remember me to your parents = cofiwch fi at eich rhieni

remind *verb*
  = atgoffa
  to remind someone of something = atgoffa rhywun o° rywbeth
  to remind someone to do something = atgoffa rhywun i °wneud rhywbeth

remote control *noun*
  (*device*)
  = teclyn (*plural* -au) pell-reolaeth *masculine*

remove *verb*
- (*get rid of*)
  = cael gwared
  to remove something = cael gwared ar° rywbeth/ â^h rhywbeth
- (*move*)
  = symud
- (*delete*)
  = dileu

renew *verb*
  = adnewyddu

renowned *adjective*
  = enwog, adnabyddus
  to be renowned for something = bod yn enwog am° rywbeth

rent
1 *noun*
  = rhent (*plural* -i) *masculine*
2 *verb*
  = rhentu
  to rent a bike = rhentu beic

rental *noun*
  car rental company = cwmni llogi ceir (*plural* cwmnïau llogi ceir) *masculine*

repair *verb*
  = trwsio, atgyweirio, cyweirio
  to have something repaired = cael trwsio rhywbeth

repeat
1 *noun*
  (*programme*)
  = ailddarllediad (*plural* -au)
2 *verb*
- (*say again*)
  = ailadrodd, ailddweud
  could you repeat (that)? = °allech chi ailadrodd (hynny)?
- (*programme*)
  = ailddarlledu

replace *verb*
- (*substitute*)
  = disodli
- (*put back*)
  = ailosod, rhoi (*stem* rhoi-, rhodd-) yn ôl

reply
1 *noun*
  = ateb (*plural* -ion) *masculine*
2 *verb*
  = ateb
  to reply to someone = ateb rhywun

report
1 *noun*
  = adroddiad (*plural* -au) *masculine*
2 *verb*
- (*make report*)
  = adrodd
- (*bring to notice*)
  = rhoi (*stem* rhoi-, rhodd-) gwybod, hysbysu
  to report a crime to the police = rhoi gwybod i'r heddlu am °drosedd, hysbysu'r heddlu am °drosedd

reporter *noun*
  = gohebydd (*plural* -ion, gohebwyr) *masculine*

represent *verb*
  = cynrychioli

representative *noun*
  = cynrychiolydd (*plural* cynrychiolwyr) *masculine*

republic *noun*
  = gweriniaeth (*plural* -au) *feminine*

reputation *noun*
  = enw *masculine*

request

1 *noun*
= cais (*plural* ceisiadau) *masculine*
2 *verb*
= gofyn (*stem* gofynn-)
to request someone to do something
= gofyn i° rywun °wneud rhywbeth
to request something from someone =
gofyn rhywbeth gan° rywun

requirement *noun*
= angen (*plural* anghenion) *masculine*,
gofyn (*plural* -ion) *masculine*
to meet someone's requirements =
bodloni anghenion rhywun

rescue

1 *verb*
= achub
2 *noun*
= achub *verbnoun*, achubiad (*plural* -au)
masculine

research

1 *noun*
= ymchwil *feminine or masculine*
2 *verb*
= ymchwilio

resemble *verb*
he resembles his father = mae e'n
°debyg i'w °dad

resent *verb*
to resent someone for something =
bod yn °ddig wrth° rywun o achos
rhywbeth

reservation *noun*
• (*of seat*)
= sedd °gadw (*plural* seddi cadw, seddau
cadw) *feminine*
• (*of room*)
= stafell °gadw (*plural* stafelloedd cadw)
feminine

reserve *verb*
to reserve something for someone =
rhoi rhywbeth ar °gadw i° rywun,
neilltuo rhywbeth i° rywun
to reserve a room = bwcio *or* sicrhau
stafell
all rights reserved = cedwir pob hawl
(*formal*)

residence *noun*
(*domicile*)
= preswylfa
hall of residence = neuadd °breswyl
(*plural* neuaddau preswyl) *feminine*

resign *verb*
= ymddiswyddo

resist *verb*
• (*oppose*)
= gwrthwynebu
• (*refrain from*)
I can't resist saying this = °alla i °ddim
peidio dweud hyn

resolute *adjective*
= penderfynol

resources *plural noun*
= adnoddau *plural*

respect

1 *noun*
= parch
to have respect for someone = bod â
ʰpharch/parch (tuag) at° rywun,
parchu rhywun
out of respect for someone = o °barch
at °rywun
2 *verb*
= parchu

respectable *adjective*
• (*person, behaviour*)
= parchus
• (*amount*)
= sylweddol

respond *verb*
• (*react*)
= ymateb
to respond to someone/something =
ymateb i° rywun/rywbeth
he responded by walking out =
cerdded allan oedd ei ymateb
• (*answer*)
= ateb

response *noun*
• (*reaction*)
= ymateb (*plural* -ion) *masculine*
a response to someone/something =
ymateb i° rywun/rywbeth
her response was to say nothing =
dweud dim oedd ei hymateb
• (*answer*)
= ateb (*plural* -ion) *masculine*

responsibility *noun*
= cyfrifoldeb (*plural* -au) *masculine*
this is your responsibility = chi sy'n
°gyfrifol am hyn

responsible *adjective*
= cyfrifol

to be responsible for something = bod yn °gyfrifol am° rywbeth
to be responsible for doing something = bod yn °gyfrifol am °wneud rhywbeth

rest
1 *noun*
- (*relaxation, recuperation*)
  = gorffwys *masculine*
- (*interval*)
  = seibiant (*plural* seibiannau) *masculine*
- (*remainder*)
  = gweddill *masculine*
  what about the rest? = beth am y gweddill?
2 *verb*
  = gorffwys

restart *verb*
= ailddechrau (*stem* ailddechreu-), ailgychwyn (*stem* ailgychwynn-)

restaurant *noun*
= tŷ bwyta (*plural* tai bwyta) *masculine*

result *noun*
= canlyniad (*plural* -au) *masculine*
as a result of something = o °ganlyniad i° rywbeth
football results = canlyniadau pêl-droed

resumé (*US*) *noun*
= braslun bywyd (*plural* brasluniau bywyd) *masculine*

retire *verb*
= ymddeol
he retired last year = naeth e ymddeol llynedd

retired *adjective*
= wedi ymddeol
he is retired = mae e wedi ymddeol

retirement *noun*
= ymddeoliad *masculine*

return *verb*
- (*come back*)
  = dod yn ôl, dychwelyd (*stem* dychwel-)
- (*go back*)
  = mynd yn ôl, dychwelyd (*stem* dychwel-)
  to return to school = mynd yn ôl i'r ysgol
  to return to work = mynd yn ôl i'r gwaith

> **!** **dod** and **mynd** are irregular in the preterite, short future, conditional and imperative—see entries on the Welsh-English side for details.
>
> **dychwelyd** is a formal and official word not normally encountered in speech.

- (*give back*)
  = rhoi (*stem* rhoi-, rhodd-) yn ôl, dychwelyd (*stem* dychwel-)
- (*send back*)
  = danfon/anfon/hala yn ôl

return ticket *noun*
= tocyn dwyffordd (*plural* tocynnau dwyffordd) *masculine*

reveal *verb*
= datgelu

revenge *noun*
= dial *masculine*
to take revenge on someone for something = dial (*verbnoun*) ar° rywun am° rywbeth

reverend *adjective*
= parchedig

revolution *noun*
= chwyldro (*plural* -adau) *masculine*
the Industrial Revolution = y Chwyldro Diwydiannol
the French Revolution = y Chwyldro Ffrengig

revolutionary
1 *adjective*
= chwyldroadol
2 *noun*
= chwyldroadwr (*plural* chwyldroadwyr) *masculine*
= chwyldroadwraig (*plural* chwyldroadwragedd) *feminine*

reward
1 *noun*
= gwobr (*plural* -au) *feminine*
2 *verb*
to reward someone for something = gwobrwyo rhywun am° rywbeth
= rhoi (*stem* rhoi-, rhodd-) gwobr i° rywun am° rywbeth

rewind *verb*
= ailddirwyn

rhinoceros, rhino *noun*
= rhinoseros (*plural* -od, -iaid) *masculine*

rhythm *noun*
= rhythm (*plural* -au) *masculine*

rib *noun*
= asen (*plural* -nau) *feminine*

ribbon *noun*
= rhuban *or* ruban (*plural* -au) *masculine*

rice *noun*
= reis *masculine*

rich *adjective*
= cyfoethog

riches *plural noun*
= cyfoeth *masculine*

rid *verb*
to get rid of something = cael gwared ar° rywbeth/â° rhywbeth, gwaredu rhywbeth

> **!** **cael** *is irregular in the preterite, short future and conditional—see entry on the Welsh-English side for details.*

ride
1 *verb*
• (*general senses*)
  = reidio
  to ride a bike = reidio beic, reidio ar °gefn beic
• (*on horseback*)
  = marchogaeth, reidio
  to ride a horse = reidio ceffyl, reidio ar °gefn ceffyl, marchogaeth
  he rides well = mae e'n °farchog da
2 *noun*
  = reid (*plural* -iau) *feminine*, tro (*plural* -eon) *masculine*

rider *noun*
• (*on horse*)
  = marchog (*plural* -ion) *masculine*
• (*on bike*)
  = beiciwr (*plural* beicwyr) *masculine*

ridiculous *adjective*
= chwerthinllyd

riding *noun*
= marchogaeth *verbnoun*

rifle *noun*
= reiffl (*plural* -au *or* -s) *feminine*

right
1 *adjective*
• (*opposite of left*)
  = de

her right hand = ei llaw °dde
• (*correct*)
  = iawn, cywir
  you are right = dych chi'n iawn
  this is the right way = dyma'r ffordd iawn
  that's right = mae'n hynny'n iawn
  to do the right thing = gwneud y peth iawn
2 *adverb*
  to turn right = troi (*stem* troi-, trodd-) i'r °dde

> **!** *There is a distinction between* **i'r °dde** *'to the right' and* **i'r de** *'to the South'. When* **de** *means 'right', it always has soft mutation after the words for 'the'.*

3 *noun*
• (*opposite of left*)
  = de *feminine*
  on the right = ar y °dde
  to the right = i'r °dde
• (*entitlement*)
  = hawl (*plural* -iau) *feminine or masculine*
  human rights = hawliau dynol

right-handed *adjective*
= llawdde

right-wing *adjective*
= asgell °dde

ring
1 *noun*
• (*on finger*)
  = modrwy (*plural* -au) *feminine*
  wedding ring = modrwy °briodas
  ring finger = bys modrwy *masculine*
• (*circle*)
  = cylch (*plural* -oedd) *masculine*
• (*phone call*)
  = caniad (*plural* -au) *masculine*
  give me a ring = rho °ganiad i mi
2 *verb*
  = canu
  the bells are ringing = mae'r clychau'n canu
  will you ring the bell? = nei di °ganu'r °gloch?
  will you ring me? = nei di °roi caniad i mi?

rinse *verb*
= strelio

rip

1 *verb*
= rhwygo
2 *noun*
= rhwyg (*plural* -au) *feminine*, rhwygiad (*plural* -au) *masculine*

ripe *adjective*
= aeddfed

rise

1 *verb*
• (*general senses*)
= codi, mynd i fyny

> **!** **mynd** *is irregular in the preterite, short future, conditional and imperative—see entry on the Welsh-English side for details.*

• (*sun*)
= codi
2 *noun*
= codiad (*plural* -au) *masculine*

risk

1 *noun*
= peryg(l) (*plural* peryglon) *masculine*
at risk = mewn peryg(l)
2 *verb*
• (*chance*)
= mentro
she won't risk coming out = °fydd hi °ddim yn mentro dod allan
• (*put at risk*)
= peryglu
to risk one's life = peryglu'ch bywyd

rival

1 *adjective*
= cystadleuol
2 *noun*
= cystadleuwr (*plural* cystadleuwyr) *masculine*

river *noun*
= afon (*plural* -ydd) *feminine*

riverbank *noun*
= glan afon (*plural* glannau afon) *feminine*

road *noun*
= heol (*plural* heolydd) *feminine*, ffordd (*plural* ffyrdd) *feminine*

> **!** **hewl** *is a common variant of* **heol** *in many areas.*

road sign *noun*
= arwydd ffordd (*plural* arwyddion ffyrdd) *masculine*

roadworks *plural noun*
= gwaith ar y ffordd

roar *verb*
= rhuo

roast

1 *verb*
= rhostio
2 *adjective*
roast meat = cig rhost

rob *verb*
= dwyn (*stem* dyg-), lladrata
to rob someone of something = dwyn rhywbeth oddiar°/oddi ar° rywun

robber *noun*
= lleidr (*plural* lladron) *masculine*

robbery *noun*
= lladrad (*plural* -au) *masculine*

robin *noun*
= robin °goch *masculine*

robot *noun*
= robot (*plural* -iaid) *masculine*

rock *noun*
• (*material*)
= carreg *feminine*
• (*a stone*)
= carreg (*plural* cerrig) *feminine*
• (*music*)
= roc

rock climbing *noun*
= dringo creigiau *verbnoun*

rocket *noun*
= roced (*plural* -i, -au) *feminine*

rocking chair *noun*
= cadair siglo (*plural* cadeiriau siglo) *feminine*

role *noun*
= rôl (*plural* rolau) *feminine*, rhan (*plural* -nau) *feminine*
to play a role = chwarae (*stem* chwarae-) rhan/rôl

roll

1 *noun*
• (*bread, of film*)
= rholyn (*plural* rholion) *masculine*

- (list of names)
  to call the roll (US) = galw'r enwau
2 verb
= rholio
roll around
= rholio o °gwmpas
roll over
= rholio drosodd
roll up
  to roll up one's sleeves = torchi'ch llewys

roller coaster noun
= ffigar-êt masculine

roller-skate
1 noun
= esgid °rolio (plural esgidiau rholio) feminine
2 verb
= troed-rolio

roller-skating noun
= rhôl-sglefrio verbnoun

Roman
1 adjective
= Rhufeinig
2 noun
= Rhufeiniwr (plural Rhufeinwyr, Rhufeiniaid) masculine

romantic adjective
= rhamantus

Rome noun
= Rhufain feminine

roof noun
= to (plural -eau, -eon) masculine

rook noun
- (bird)
  = ydfran (plural ydfrain) feminine
- (chess piece)
  = castell (plural cestyll) masculine

room noun
- (in house)
  = stafell (plural -oedd) feminine, ystafell (plural -oedd) feminine

> **!** Although **ystafell** is the standard written form, **stafell** is far more common in speech, and increasingly in writing.

living room = stafell °fyw (plural stafelloedd byw)
bedroom = stafell °wely (plural stafelloedd gwely)
dining room = stafell °fwyta (plural stafelloedd bwyta)
bathroom = stafell molchi (plural stafelloedd molchi)
- (space)
  = lle masculine
  is there enough room? = oes digon o °le?
  there's room for three = mae lle i °dri
  to make room for someone = gwneud lle i° rywun

root noun
= gwreiddyn, gwraidd (plural gwreiddiau) masculine
  to be at the root of something = bod wrth °wraidd rhywbeth

rope noun
= rhaff (plural -au) feminine

rose noun
= rhosyn (plural -nau) masculine

rosy adjective
= gwridog, rhosynnaidd

rot
1 noun
= pydredd masculine
2 verb
= pydru

rotten adjective
= wedi pydru
  to go rotten = pydru

rough adjective
- (not smooth)
  = garw
- (approximate)
  = bras
- (not gentle)
  = garw, cas
- (difficult)
  = anodd

roughly adverb
= (approximately) yn °fras, tua[h]
  roughly half an hour = tua hanner awr

round
1 adjective
= crwn
2 adverb
  to come round (visit) = dod draw
  to call round = galw (stem galw-) heibio
  all year round = trwy °gydol y °flwyddyn

round the corner = rownd y °gornel
to go round and round = mynd rownd a rownd
3 *preposition*
= o °gwmpas, o amgylch, (*occasionally*) am°

> **!** **o °gwmpas** and **o amgylch** are compound prepositions and so change their form when used with pronouns—see entries on the Welsh-English side for details.

round the town = o °gwmpas/o amgylch y °dre
round a table = o °gwmpas/o amgylch bwrdd
put a bandage round his head = rho °rwymyn am ei °ben
4 *noun*
(*of golf, boxing, drinks*)
= rownd (*plural* -iau) *feminine*
the final round = y rownd °derfynol

roundabout *noun*
• (*at road junction*)
= trogylch (*plural* -oedd) *masculine*
• (*at fair*)
= ceffylau bach *plural*

route *noun*
= ffordd (*plural* ffyrdd) *feminine*

routine *noun*
= trefn *feminine*
the daily routine = y °drefn °feunyddiol

row¹
1 *noun*
(*line*)
= rhes (*plural* -i) *feminine*
a row of houses = rhes o °dai
six days in a row = chwe diwrnod yn °olynol
2 *verb*
(*boat*)
= rhwyfo

row² *noun*
(*argument*)
= ffrae (*plural* -au, -on) *feminine*

rowing *noun*
= rhwyfo *verbnoun*

rowing boat *noun*
= cwch rhwyfo (*plural* cychod rhwyfo) *masculine*

royal *adjective*
= brenhinol

rub *verb*
= rhwbio

rub out:
to rub something out (*erase*) = dileu rhywbeth

rubber *noun*
• (*eraser*)
= rwber (*plural* -i) *masculine*
• (*material*)
= rwber *masculine*

rubber band *noun*
= dolen elastig (*plural* dolennau *or* dolenni elastig) *feminine*

rubbish *noun*
• (*refuse*)
= sbwriel *masculine*
• (*nonsense*)
= sothach *plural*
this is all rubbish = sothach ydy hwn i gyd
don't talk rubbish! = paid siarad lol!

rubbish bin *noun*
= bin sbwriel (*plural* biniau sbwriel) *masculine*

rucksack *noun*
= sach °deithio (*plural* sachau teithio) *feminine*

rude *adjective*
• (*impolite*)
= anghwrtais
to be rude to someone = bod yn anghwrtais wrth° rywun
• (*obscene*)
= anweddus

rug *noun*
= carped (*plural* -i) *masculine*, ryg (*plural* -iau) *feminine*

rugby *noun*
= rygbi *masculine*

ruin
1 *noun*
(*ruined building*)
= adfail *masculine*
to go to ruin = adfeilio
2 *verb*
= difetha, dinistrio

ruins *plural noun*
= adfeilion *plural*

the building is in ruins = mae'r adeilad yn adfeilion

rule
1 *noun*
= rheol (*plural* -au) *feminine*
as a rule = fel rheol
that is against the rules = mae hynny yn erbyn y rheolau
2 *verb*
= rheoli, llywodraethu

ruler *noun*
• (*implement*)
= pren mesur (*plural* prennau mesur) *masculine*
• (*person*)
= rheolwr (*plural* rheolwyr) *masculine*, llywodraethwr (*plural* llywodraethwyr) *masculine*

rumour *noun*
= sôn *masculine*, si (*plural* sïon) *masculine*
there's a rumour that ... = mae sôn/si bod ...

run
1 *verb*
= rhedeg (*stem* rhed-)
to run after someone = rhedeg ar ôl rhywun
to run a business = rhedeg busnes
to run on unleaded petrol = rhedeg ar °betrol diblwm
to run a competition = rhedeg cystadleuaeth
the river runs to the sea = mae'r afon yn rhedeg/llifo i'r môr
the buses run every hour = mae'r bysiau'n rhedeg °bob awr
to run for office = sefyll (*stem* sef-, saf-) am swydd
he's running a temperature = mae gwres arno (fe)
in the long run = yn y pen draw
2 *noun*
• **go for a run** = rhedeg
• **on the run** = ar ffo
• (*cricket*)
= rhediad (*plural* -au) *masculine*

run about, run around
= rhedeg o °gwmpas

run away, run off
= rhedeg i ffwrdd, ffoi

runner *noun*
= rhedwr (*plural* rhedwyr) *masculine*

= rhedwraig (*plural* rhedwragedd) *feminine*

rural *adjective*
= gwledig

rush
1 *verb*
• (*general senses*)
= rhuthro
to rush into the shop = rhuthro i (mewn i) 'r siop
to rush dinner = rhuthro drwy °ginio
• (*hurry*)
= brysio
she was rushed to hospital = aethpwyd â hi ar °frys i'r ysbyty
don't rush me! = paid â ⁿngwthio i!
2 *noun*
to be in a rush = bod ar °frys
to do something in a rush = gwneud rhywbeth ar °frys

rush hour *noun*
= oriau brys *plural*

rust *noun*
= rhwd *masculine*

rusty *adjective*
= rhydlyd, wedi rhydu

sack
1 *noun*
= sach (*plural* -au) *masculine or feminine*
to give someone the sack = diswyddo rhywun
2 *verb*
(*dismiss*)
= diswyddo

sad *adjective*
= trist

saddle *noun*
= cyfrwy (*plural* -au) *masculine*

sadness *noun*
= tristwch *masculine*

safe
1 *adjective*
= diogel, saff
to make something safe = diogelu rhywbeth
to keep something safe = cadw rhywbeth yn °ddiogel
2 *noun*
= coffor (*plural* coffrau) *masculine*, sêff (*plural* -s) *feminine*

safeguard *verb*
= diogelu

safety *noun*
= diogelwch *masculine*

Sagittarius *noun*
= y Saethydd *masculine*

sail
1 *verb*
= hwylio
2 *noun*
= hwyl (*plural* -iau) *feminine*

sailing *noun*
to go sailing = hwylio

sailing boat *noun*
= cwch hwyliau (*plural* cychod hwyliau) *masculine*

sailor *noun*
= llongwr (*plural* llongwyr) *masculine*

saint *noun*
= sant (*plural* seintiau *or* saint) *masculine*
= santes (*plural* -au) *feminine*

sake *noun*
for the sake of = er mwyn
for his sake = er ei °fwyn e
for God's sake = neno'r Tad, er mwyn Duw

salad *noun*
= salad (*plural* -au) *masculine*

salary *noun*
= cyflog (*plural* -au) *masculine*

sale *noun*
• (*in shop*)
= arwerthiant *masculine*
the sale begins tomorrow = mae'r arwerthiant yn dechrau yfory
• **for sale**
= ar °werth
the building is for sale = mae'r adeilad ar °werth

> **!** *The adjective phrase **ar °werth**, like all similar phrases with **ar**, does not use **yn** to link it to the verb **bod** 'to be'—so not *mae'r adeilad yn ar °werth.*

sales assistant *noun*
= dyn siop (*plural* dynion siop) *masculine*, merch siop (*plural* merched siop) *feminine*

salesman *noun*
= gwerthwr (*plural* gwerthwyr) *masculine*

saleswoman *noun*
= gwerthwraig (*plural* gwerthwragedd) *feminine*

salmon *noun*
= eog (*plural* -iaid) *masculine*

salt *noun*
= halen *masculine*

salty *adjective*
= hallt

same
1 *adjective*
= yr un, yr un° (*feminine singular*)
the same book as me = yr un llyfr â fi
they go to the same school = maen nhw'n mynd i'r un ysgol
people are the same everywhere = mae pobol yr un ymhobman
the same one = yr un un

the same ones = yr un rhai
exactly the same thing = yn union yr un peth

2 *pronoun*
= yr un peth
I'll have the same = °gymera i'r un peth
we'll do the same as them = nawn ni'r un peth â nhw
'Merry Christmas!'—'the same to you!' = 'Nadolig Llawen!'—'a chithau!'

3 *adverb*
= yr un °fath
I feel the same as you = dw i'n teimlo'r un °fath â ti
we'll go all the same = awn ni ta beth

sand *noun*
= tywod (*plural* -ydd) *masculine*

sandal *noun*
= sandal (*plural* -au) *feminine*

sandwich *noun*
= brechdan (*plural* -au) *feminine*
cheese sandwich = brechdan °gaws (*plural* brechdanau caws)

Santa Claus *noun*
= Siôn Corn *masculine*

sardine *noun*
= sardîn (*plural* -s) *masculine*

satellite *noun*
• (*planetoid*)
= lleuad (*plural* -au) *feminine*
• (*artificial*)
= lloeren (*plural* -nau) *feminine*
satellite television = teledu lloeren *masculine*
satellite dish = soser °loeren (*plural* soseri lloeren) *feminine*, dysgl °loeren (*plural* dysglau lloeren) *feminine*

satisfactory *adjective*
= boddhaol

satisfied *adjective*
= bodlon
to be satisfied with something = bod yn °fodlon ar° rywbeth

Saturday *noun*
= dydd Sadwrn, Sadwrn
Saturday night = nos Sadwrn
see also **Monday**

sauce *noun*
= sôs (*plural* sosys) *masculine*, saws (*plural* -iau) *masculine*

saucepan *noun*
= sosban (*plural* -au, sosbenni) *feminine*

saucer *noun*
= soser (*plural* -i) *feminine*

sausage *noun*
= selsigen (*plural* selsig) *feminine*, sosej (*plural* -is) *feminine*

save *verb*
• (*rescue*)
= achub
to save someone's life = achub bywyd rhywun
• (*time, money*)
= arbed
this will save time = bydd hyn yn arbed amser
that will save me five pounds = bydd hynny'n arbed pum punt i mi
• (*keep*)
= cadw
to save something till tomorrow = cadw rhywbeth tan yfory
• (*spare*)
= arbed
to save someone doing something = arbed i° rywun °wneud rhywbeth
• (*budget, save up*)
= cynilo

savings *plural noun*
= cynilion *plural*

saw *noun*
= llif (*plural* -iau) *feminine*
chainsaw = llif °gadwyn (*plural* llifiau cadwyn) *feminine*

saxophone *noun*
= sacsoffon (*plural* -au) *masculine*

say *verb*
• (*general senses*)
= dweud (*stem* dwed-, dywed-, wed-), deud (*stem* deud-, dud-) (*North*), gweud (*stem* gwed- or wed-) (*South*)

> **! dweud** *is the standard form of the verbnoun, less common in informal speech than* **deud** *and* **gweud***.

to say something to someone = dweud rhywbeth wrth° rywun
he says he can't go = mae e'n dweud °fod e °ddim yn gallu mynd
what did you say? = beth °ddwedest ti?
= be' wedest ti?

that's what I said = dyna beth °ddwedes i
= 'na be' wedes i
what does the message say? = beth mae'r neges yn °ddweud?
it says here that ... = mae'n dweud fan hyn bod ...
five or six, I would say = pump neu chwech, wedwn i
..., as they say = ..., fel maen nhw'n dweud
that is to say = sef
• (with quoted speech)
= meddai etc
'Here I am!' she said = 'Dyma fi!' meddai hi
'Go away,' said Aled and Dafydd = 'Cer o 'ma,' meddai Aled a Dafydd
'It's late,' they said = 'Mae'n hwyr,' meddai nhw/medden nhw
so they say = meddai nhw/medden nhw
= ..., chadal nhwthau (North)

> ! **meddai** etc. is used only with quoted words or sentiments—see entry on the Welsh-English side for more information and examples.

scale noun
= graddfa (plural graddfeydd) feminine
on a large scale = ar °raddfa °fawr
on a small scale = ar °raddfa °fechan

scales plural noun
(weighing machine)
= clorian feminine

scandal noun
= sgandal (plural -au) feminine, gwarth masculine

scandalous adjective
= gwarthus

scarce adjective
= prin
to become scarce = mynd yn °brin
= prinhau

scarcely adverb
= prin
I can scarcely remember = prin y galla i °gofio, prin ⁿmod i'n gallu cofio

> ! This adverb usually starts the sentence and is followed by a 'that...' clause—see entry on Welsh-English side for further examples.

scarcity noun
= prinder (plural -au) masculine

scare
1 verb
= dychryn
2 noun
= dychryn (plural -iadau) masculine

scare away:
to scare someone away from somewhere = dychryn rhywun o °rywle

scared adjective
= wedi dychryn, ofnus

scarf noun
= sgarff (plural -iau) feminine

scatter verb
= gwasgaru

scenery noun
• (view)
= golygfa (plural golygfeydd) feminine
• (landscape)
= tirlun (plural -iau) masculine
• (for a play)
= golygfeydd plural

scheme noun
= cynllun (plural -iau) masculine

school noun
= ysgol (plural -ion) feminine
at school = yn yr ysgol
from school = o'r ysgol
to go to school = mynd i'r ysgol
to attend school = mynychu ysgol

> ! Phrases like 'at school', 'to school' etc. require the word for 'the' in Welsh.

schoolboy noun
= bachgen ysgol (plural bechgyn ysgol) masculine
school bus noun = bws ysgol (plural bysiau ysgol)

schoolgirl noun
= merch ysgol (plural merched ysgol) feminine

schoolwork noun
= gwaith ysgol masculine

science noun
• (general sense)
= gwyddoniaeth feminine

to study science = astudio gwyddoniaeth
- (*particular field*)
= gwyddor (*plural* -au) *feminine*
natural sciences = gwyddorau naturiol

scientific *adjective*
= gwyddonol

scientist *noun*
= gwyddonydd (*plural* gwyddonwyr) *masculine*

scissors *noun*
pair of scissors = siswrn (*plural* sisyrnau) *masculine*

score
1 *noun*
= sgôr (*plural* sgorau) *feminine*
2 *verb*
= sgorio

Scorpio *noun*
= y Sgorpion *masculine*

Scot *noun*
= Albanwr (*plural* Albanwyr) *masculine*
= Albanes (*plural* -au) *feminine*

Scotland *noun*
= yr Alban *feminine*

> ! *The word for* 'the' *is part of the name of the country in Welsh*—**they come from Scotland** = maen nhw'n dod o'r Alban.

Scottish *adjective*
= o'r Alban, Albanaidd

Scottish Gaelic *noun*
= Gaeleg yr Alban

scrape *verb*
= rhathu

scratch
1 *verb*
= crafu
to scratch oneself on something = cael crafiad gan ºrywbeth
2 *noun*
= crafiad (*plural* -au) *masculine*

scratchcard *noun*
= cerdyn datgelu (*plural* cardiau datgelu) *masculine*

scream
1 *verb*
= sgrechian
2 *noun*
= sgrech (*plural* -au) *feminine*

screen
1 *noun*
= sgrîn (*plural* sgriniau) *feminine*
2 *verb*
- (*film*)
= dangos
- (*check*)
= sgrinio

screw
1 *noun*
= sgriw (*plural* -iau) *feminine*
2 *verb*
= sgriwio

sea *noun*
= môr (*plural* moroedd) *masculine*
by the sea = ar ºlan y môr
the North Sea = y Môr Tawch
the Irish Sea = Môr Iwerddon
the Mediterranean Sea = Môr y Canoldir

seagull *noun*
= gwylan (*plural* -od) *feminine*

seal
1 *noun*
- (*animal*)
= morlo (*plural* -i) *masculine*
- (*on package*)
= sêl (*plural* seliau) *feminine*
2 *verb*
= selio

search *verb*
= chwilio
to search for something = chwilio amº rywbeth
to search something = chwilio rhywbeth

seashell *noun*
= cragen (*plural* cregyn) *feminine*

seasick *adjective*
= sâl môr

seaside *noun*
by/at the seaside = ar ºlan y môr

season *noun*
= tymor (*plural* tymhorau) *masculine*

season ticket *noun*
= tocyn tymor (*plural* tocynnau tymor) *masculine*

seat *noun*
= sedd (*plural* -i, -au) *feminine*
to take a seat = eistedd
front seat = sedd °flaen (*plural* seddi blaen)
back seat = sedd °gefn (*plural* seddi cefn)
safe seat = sedd °ddiogel (*plural* seddi diogel)
marginal seat = sedd ymylol (*plural* seddi ymylol)

seatbelt *noun*
= gwregys diogelwch (*plural* gwregysau diogelwch) *masculine*

second
1 *adjective*
= ail°

> **!** **ail°** *always precedes the noun it qualifies, and causes soft mutation.*

this is the second time I've called = dyma'r ail °dro i mi °alw
every second day = °bob yn ail °ddiwrnod
to have second thoughts = ailfeddwl
2 *noun*
= eiliad (*plural* -au) *feminine or masculine*
wait a second = arhoswch eiliad
3 *adverb*
= yn ail
to come second = dod yn ail

secondary *adjective*
• (*less important*)
= eilradd

secondary school *noun*
= ysgol uwchradd (*plural* ysgolion uwchradd) *feminine*

second-hand *adjective*
= ail-law
second-hand books = llyfrau ail-law

secret
1 *adjective*
= cyfrinachol, cudd
to keep something secret = cadw rhywbeth yn °gyfrinach
in secret = yn °gyfrinachol
2 *noun*
= cyfrinach (*plural* -au) *feminine*
to tell someone a secret = dweud cyfrinach wrth° rywun

secretary *noun*
= ysgrifenyddes (*plural* -au) *feminine*
= ysgrifennydd (*plural* ysgrifenyddion) *masculine*

secure
1 *adjective*
= diogel
2 *verb*
= diogelu, sicrhau
to secure someone's release = cael rhyddhau rhywun

security *noun*
• (*safety*)
= diogelwch *masculine*
• (*financial guarantee*)
= gwarant (*plural* -au) *feminine*

security forces *plural noun*
= lluoedd diogelwch *plural*

see *verb*
= gweld (*stem* gwel-)
..., you see = ..., °weli di, ..., °welwch chi
see you! = °wela i di/chi!
see you tomorrow = °wela i di/chi yfory
I'll go and see = a i i °weld
what can you see? = beth °welwch chi?
I see (*I understand*) = gwela i
to see someone home = mynd âʰ rhywun adre, hebrwng (*stem* hebryng-) rhywun adre

seek *verb*
• (*look for*)
= chwilio
to seek something = chwilio am° rywbeth
• (*try*)
= ceisio, trio
to seek to do something = ceisio/trio gwneud rhywbeth

seem *verb*
= ymddangos, edrych
it seems you are right = mae'n ymddangos bod chi'n iawn
everything seems okay = mae popeth yn edrych yn iawn
she seems sad = mae golwg °drist arni (hi)

> **!** **ymddangos** *is normal in impersonal uses involving 'it...' and a following 'that...' clause, but is usually avoided in other cases—*mae hi'n ymddangos yn °drist *sounds odd for*

'she seems sad', *which is better
rendered by the noun* **golwg** *(see
third example above) or* **edrych**. *See
entries on the Welsh-English side for
more examples.*

seize *verb*
= cipio

seldom *adverb*
= yn anaml

select
1 *verb*
= dewis, dethol
2 *adjective*
= dethol
a select few = ychydig o °bobol
°ddethol

selection *noun*
= dewis *masculine*, detholiad (*plural* -au)
masculine

self-aware *adjective*
= hunanymwybodol

self-confidence *noun*
= hunanhyder *masculine*

self-confident *adjective*
= hunanhyderus

self-destructive *adjective*
= hunanddinistriol

self-employed *adjective*
= hunangyflogedig

self-expression *noun*
= hunanfynegiant *masculine*

self-respect *noun*
= hunanbarch *masculine*

self-service *noun*
= hunanwasanaeth *masculine*
a self-service canteen = ffreutur
hunanwasanaeth

selfish *adjective*
= hunanol

sell *verb*
= gwerthu

semester *noun*
= tymor (*plural* tymhorau) *masculine*

semi-detached *adjective*
semi-detached house = tŷ semi (*plural*
tai semi) *masculine*

send *verb*
= anfon, danfon, hela, hala

> **!** *All these terms are broadly
> synonymous, with little to choose
> between them. Note that they all use
> **i°** with places or establishments, but
> **at°** with people.*

to send someone something = anfon
rhywbeth at° rywun
to send something to somewhere =
anfon rhywbeth i° rywle
to send someone a letter = anfon
llythyr at° rywun
to send someone to do something =
anfon rhywun i °wneud rhywbeth

senior *adjective*
= hŷn

sense
1 *noun*
• *(faculty)*
= synnwyr (*plural* synhwyrau)
masculine
common sense = synnwyr cyffredin
the five senses = y pum synnwyr
sense of humour = synnwyr digrifwch
masculine
• *(reason)*
= pwyll *masculine*
that would make sense = byddai
hynny'n °ddoeth
• *(sanity)*
he's out of his senses = mae e o'i
°go(f), mae e'n °wallgo(f)
• *(consciousness)*
to come to one's senses = dod atoch
chi'ch hun(an)
• *(sensation)*
= teimlad (*plural* -au) *masculine*
• *(meaning)*
= ystyr (*plural* -on) *feminine*
to make sense of something = deall
rhywbeth
in what sense? = ym ⁿmha ystyr?
in the true sense of the word = yng
ⁿngwir ystyr y gair
2 *verb*
= synhwyro, teimlo

sensible *adjective*
(reasonable, wise)
= synhwyrol

sensitive *adjective*
= teimladwy, sensitif

sentence
1 noun
- (grammatical)
  = brawddeg (plural -au) feminine
- (judicial)
  = dedfryd (plural -au) feminine
  a life sentence = dedfryd am oes

2 verb
  = dedfrydu
  to sentence someone to three years' imprisonment = dedfrydu rhywun i °dair blynedd o °garchar

separate
1 adjective
  = gwahanol, ar wahân
2 verb
- (come apart)
  = gwahanu, ymrannu
- (pull/keep apart)
  = gwahanu
  they'll have to be separated = bydd rhaid (eu) gwahanu nhw
- (of a couple)
  = gwahanu, ymwahanu
  they separated last year = naethon nhw °wahanu/ymwahanu llynedd

separated adjective
  (of couple)
  = wedi gwahanu

separately adverb
  = ar wahân

September noun
  = Medi, mis Medi
  see also **January**

serial noun
  = cyfres (plural -i) feminine

series noun
  = cyfres (plural -i) feminine

serious adjective
- (not minor or unimportant)
  = difrifol
  a serious accident = damwain °ddifrifol feminine
- (in earnest)
  = o °ddifri(f)
  are you serious? = dych chi o °ddifri?

seriously adverb
  = o °ddifri(f)
  I want to talk seriously now = dw i am siarad o °ddifri nawr

sermon noun
  = pregeth (plural -au) feminine

serve verb
  = gwasanaethu
  are you being served? = ydy/oes rhywun yn helpu chi?
  = ydy/oes rhywun yn delio â chi?
  breakfast is served from eight till nine = darperir brecwast o wyth tan naw

service noun
  = gwasanaeth (plural -au) masculine

> **!** A masculine noun despite the ending **-aeth** which is usually a sign of feminine.

  bus service = gwasanaeth bysiau
  the service here is poor = mae'r gwasanaeth fan hyn yn °wael

service station noun
  = gorsaf °betrol (plural gorsafoedd petrol) feminine

serviette noun
  = napcyn (plural -au) masculine

set
1 noun
  = set (plural -iau) feminine
  a set of keys = set o allweddi
  a set of books = set o °lyfrau
2 verb
- (general senses)
  = gosod, rhoi (stem rhoi-, rhodd-)
  to set a price = gosod pris
  to set the alarm = gosod y larwm
  to set an exam = gosod arholiad
  to set homework = gosod/rhoi gwaith cartre(f)
  to set an example = gosod esiampl
  to set the table = gosod y bwrdd
  to set fire to something = rhoi rhywbeth ar dân
  to set someone free = rhyddhau rhywun
  the film is set in Wales = mae'r ffilm wedi'i lleoli yng ⁿNghymru
- (sun)
  = machlud
  before the sun sets = cyn i'r haul °fachlud

set off
- (leave)
  = gadael (stem gadaw-)
- (cause to explode etc)
  = tanio

to set off an alarm = cychwyn (*stem* cychwynn-) larwm

set up
- (*establish*)
= sefydlu
- (*organise*)
= trefnu

settle *verb*
to settle an argument = torri dadl
to settle a question = datrys cwestiwn
nothing is settled yet = does dim byd wedi'i °benderfynu hyd yma
to settle in an area = ymgartrefu/ymsefydlu mewn ardal

settle down
= setlo

settle in
(*to a new home*)
= ymgartrefu

settled *adjective*
(*weather etc*)
= sefydlog

seven *numeral*
= saith
seven days = saith ⁿniwrnod
seven years = saith ⁿmlynedd
seven years old = saith ⁿmlwydd oed
at seven o'clock = am saith o'r °gloch
I have seven = mae gen i saith (*North*), mae saith 'da fi (*South*)

seventeen *numeral*
= dauarbymtheg *or* undeg saith *masculine*
= dwyarbymtheg *or* undeg saith *feminine*
seventeen horses = dau °geffyl ar °bymtheg, undeg saith o °geffylau
seventeen cats = dwy °gath ar °bymtheg, undeg saith o °gathod
seventeen years = dwy °flynedd ar °bymtheg, undeg saith o °flynyddoedd
seventeen years old = dwy °flwydd ar °bymtheg oed, undeg saith ⁿmlwydd oed

seventh *adjective*
= seithfed

> **!** **seithfed** *precedes the noun.*

seventy *numeral*
= saithdeg
seventy apples = saithdeg o afalau

seventy years = saithdeg o °flynyddoedd
seventy years old = saithdeg oed

several
1 *adjective*
= amryw° (*precedes noun*), sawl (*precedes singular noun*)

> **!** **amryw°** and **sawl** both precede the noun they refer to but behave differently—**amryw°** takes a plural and causes soft mutation, **sawl** takes a singular and causes no mutation.

several books = amryw °lyfrau
= sawl llyfr
several times = °droeon
2 *pronoun*
I've got several = mae amryw/sawl un 'da fi

severe *adjective*
- (*serious*)
= difrifol
- (*harsh*)
= llym, hallt

sew *verb*
= gwnïo

sewing machine *noun*
= peiriant gwnïo (*plural* peiriannau gwnïo) *masculine*

sex *noun*
= rhyw (*plural* -iau) *masculine or feminine*
to have sex with someone = cael rhyw âʰ rhywun, cael cyfathrach °rywiol âʰ rhywun

shade *noun*
= cysgod (*plural* -ion) *masculine*
to sit in the shade of something = eistedd dan °gysgod rhywbeth

shadow *noun*
= cysgod (*plural* -ion) *masculine*
to cast a shadow over something = taflu cysgod dros° rywbeth

shake *verb*
- (*tremble*)
= crynu
he was shaking with fright = roedd e'n crynu gan ofn
the walls were shaking = roedd y waliau'n crynu

- (*bottle, fist etc*)
  = ysgwyd, siglo (*South*)
  he shook his head = mi siglodd e ei
  °ben
  to shake someone's hand = ysgwyd
  llaw rhywun
  to shake hands with someone =
  ysgwyd llaw â^h rhywun

shall *verb*

> **!** There is no verb in Welsh directly
> corresponding to this auxiliary—its
> main use in English is for making
> suggestions, and for this there are
> various phrasings available in Welsh.

shall I open the window? = dych chi
eisiau i mi agor y ffenest?, beth am i
mi agor y ffenest?
shall we go out? = beth am inni °fynd
allan?

shame *noun*
- (*feeling*)
  = cywilydd *masculine*
- (*pity*)
  it's a shame he's not here = °drueni
  °fod e °ddim yma
  what a shame! = 'na °drueni!

shampoo *noun*
= siampŵ (*plural* -s) *masculine*

shape *noun*
= ffurf (*plural* -iau) *feminine*, siâp (*plural*
siapiau) *masculine*
to be in good shape = bod yn heini,
bod mewn cyflwr da
in the shape of a circle = ar ffurf cylch

share
1 *noun*
= cyfran (*plural* -nau) *feminine*
to have shares in something = dal
(*stem* dali-) cyfrannau ynⁿ rhywbeth
2 *verb*
= rhannu
to share a flat with someone = rhannu
fflat â^h rhywun

shark *noun*
= morgi (*plural* morgwn) *masculine*,
siarc (*plural* -od) *masculine*

sharp *adjective*
- (*blade, point etc*)
  = minog, miniog
- (*sudden*)
  = sydyn

- (*intelligent*)
  = siarp
- (*severe*)
  = hallt
- (*in taste*)
  = egr

shave *verb*
= siafio

shaver *noun*
= siafiwr (*plural* siafwyr) *masculine*

she *pronoun*
= hi; hithau
she'll be there = bydd hi yno
there she is! = dyna/dacw hi!
here she comes! = dyma hi'n dod!

> **!** For details on the expanded form
> hithau, see entry on the Welsh-
> English side.

sheep *noun*
= dafad (*plural* defaid) *feminine*

sheepdog *noun*
= ci defaid (*plural* cŵn defaid) *masculine*

sheet *noun*
- (*on bed*)
  = cynfas (*plural* -au) *feminine*
- (*of paper*)
  = dalen (*plural* -nau) *feminine*
- (*with writing on it*)
  = taflen (*plural* -ni) *feminine*

shelf *noun*
= silff (*plural* -oedd) *feminine*

shell *noun*
= cragen (*plural* cregyn) *feminine*

shelter *noun*
- (*refuge*)
  = lloches (*plural* -au) *feminine*
- (*cover*)
  = cysgod *masculine*
  to take shelter from something =
  cysgodi rhag rhywbeth

shield
1 *noun*
= tarian (*plural* -au) *feminine*
2 *verb*
= gwarchod, cysgodi

shilling *noun*
= swllt (*plural* sylltau) *masculine*

shin *noun*
= crimog (*plural* -au) *feminine*

shine *verb*
- (*give out light*)
  = disgleirio
- (*sun, moon*)
  = tywynnu, disgleirio
- (*torch etc*)
  to shine a light at someone = cyfeirio
  golau at° rywun
- (*polish*)
  = sgleinio

shining *adjective*
= disglair, llewyrchus

ship
1 *noun*
= llong (*plural* -au) *feminine*
merchant ship = llong °fasnach (*plural*
llongau masnach)
passenger ship = llong °deithwyr
(*plural* llongau teithwyr)
warship = llong °ryfel (*plural* llongau
rhyfel)
2 *verb*
- (*transport goods etc*)
  = anfon/danfon mewn llong

shirt *noun*
= crys (*plural* -au) *masculine*

shit
1 *noun*
= cachu *masculine*
2 *verb*
= cachu

shiver *verb*
= crynu

shock
1 *noun*
- (*general senses*)
  = sioc (*plural* -iau) *feminine*
  to give someone a shock = rhoi (*stem*
  rhoi-, rhodd-) sioc i° rywun
  to get a shock = cael sioc
  to be in shock = bod mewn llewyg/sioc
  an electric shock = sioc °drydanol
  (*plural* siociau trydanol) *feminine*
- (*blow, impact*)
  = ergyd (*plural* -ion) *feminine or
  masculine*
2 *verb*
  to shock someone = rhoi (*stem* rhoi-,
  rhodd-) sioc i° rywun

shocked *adjective*
I was shocked = °ges i sioc

! cael (*preterite* °**ges i**) *is used in
expressions of this type because the
emphasis is on the receiving of the
shock.*

shoe *noun*
- (*general sense*)
  = esgid (*plural* -iau, sgidiau) *feminine*
- (*for horse*)
  = pedol (*plural* -au) *feminine*

shoelace *noun*
= carrai (*plural* careiau) *feminine*

shoot *verb*
- (*general sense*)
  = saethu
  to shoot someone = saethu rhywun
  he was shot in the leg = cafodd e ei
  saethu yn ei °goes
- (*rush*)
  = rhuthro
  he shot past = rhuthrodd e heibio
- **to shoot a film** = gwneud ffilm

shop
1 *noun*
= siop (*plural* -au) *feminine*
2 *verb*
= siopa

shop assistant *noun*
= dyn siop (*plural* dynion siop)
masculine
= merch siop (*plural* merched siop)
feminine

shopper *noun*
= siopwr (*plural* siopwyr) *masculine*
= siopwraig (*plural* siopwragedd)
feminine

shopkeeper *noun*
= dyn siop (*plural* dynion siop)
masculine
= gwraig siop (*plural* gwragedd siop)
feminine

shoplifter *noun*
= siopleidr (*plural* siopladron)
masculine
shoplifters will be prosecuted =
erlynir siopladron

shopping *noun*
to do the shopping = gwneud y gwaith
siopa

shopping cart *noun* (*US*)
= troli siopa (*plural* troliau siopa) *masculine*

shopping centre *noun*
= canolfan siopa (*plural* canolfannau siopa) *masculine or feminine*

shopping mall *noun* (*US*)
= canolfan siopa (*plural* canolfannau siopa) *masculine or feminine*

shopping trolley *noun*
= troli siopa (*plural* troliau siopa) *masculine*

shop window *noun*
= ffenest siop (*plural* ffenestri siopau) *feminine*

shore *noun*
= glan (*plural* -nau) *feminine*

short *adjective*
• (*not long, not tall*)
= byr

> **!** This adjective has a feminine form **ber**. It also has a plural form **byrion**, largely restricted now to set phrases.

to have short hair = bod â gwallt byr
at short notice = ar °fyr °rybudd
in short = yn °fyr, mewn gair
• (*scarce*)
= prin
to be short of something = bod yn °brin o° rywbeth
to be in short supply = bod yn °brin

shortage *noun*
= prinder *masculine*
a shortage of materials = prinder o °ddefnyddiau

short cut *noun*
= llwybr llygad (*plural* llwybrau llygad) *masculine*

shorten *verb*
= byrhau

shorthand *noun*
= llaw-fer *feminine*

shortly *adverb*
= cyn (bo) hir, yn y man, nes ymlaen, toc

> **!** *toc* is not part of the standard, still less of the written, language, but is widespread in informal speech. It resists soft mutation, even though it is an adverb.

shorts *noun*
= trowsus byr *masculine*

short-sighted *adjective*
= byrolwg

shot *noun*
• (*from a gun*)
= ergyd (*plural* -ion) *feminine or masculine*
• (*attempt*)
= cynnig (*plural* cynigion) *masculine*
to have a shot at something = rhoi (*stem* rhoi-, rhodd-) cynnig ar° rywbeth
• (*in football*)
= cic (*plural* -iau) *feminine*
• (*in tennis, golf*)
= trawiad (*plural* -au) *masculine*

should *verb*
= dylwn i *etc*

> **!** *This verb appears only with 'unreality' or hypothetical endings in Welsh. An* **-s-** *can optionally be inserted before these endings, so* **dylwn i** *or* **dylswn i, dylech chi** *or* **dylswn i, dylech chi** *or* **dylsech chi**, *etc. The verbnoun for the action dependent on it immediately follows the subject, and therefore has soft mutation.*

we should go now = dylen ni °fynd nawr
should I tell them? = °ddylwn i °ddweud wrthyn nhw?
she should have asked = dylai hi °fod wedi gofyn
you shouldn't have come = °ddylet ti °ddim °fod wedi dod
the letter should have arrived by now = dylai'r llythyr °fod wedi cyrraedd erbyn hyn

shoulder *noun*
= ysgwydd (*plural* -au) *feminine*

shout
1 *noun*
= cri (*plural* -au) *masculine or feminine*
2 *verb*
= gweiddi, bloeddio
to shout at someone = gweiddi ar° rywun
to shout something = gweiddi rhywbeth

shovel *noun*
= rhaw (*plural* -iau) *feminine*

show

1 *noun*
= sioe (*plural* -au) *feminine*

2 *verb*
- (*general sense*)
= dangos
  to show someone something = dangos
  rhywbeth i° rywun
  **to show someone how to do
  something** = dangos i° rywun sut i
  °wneud rhywbeth
  to show someone where something is
  = dangos i° rywun lle mae rhywbeth
- (*broadcast*)
= darlledu
  the programme was shown last night
  = cafodd y rhaglen ei darlledu
  neithiwr

show off
= ymffrostio, brolio'ch hun(an)

show round
(*guide*)
= tywys

show up
(*arrive*)
= cyrraedd (*stem* cyrhaedd-)
- (*be found*)
= dod i'r golau

shower *noun*
(*all senses*)
= cawod (*plural* -ydd) *feminine*

showjumping *noun*
= neidio ceffylau *verbnoun*

shriek

1 *noun*
= sgrech (*plural* -iadau) *feminine*

2 *verb*
= sgrechian

shrimp *noun*
= berdysen (*plural* berdys) *feminine*

shrink *verb*
= mynd yn llai, lleihau

> **!** *mynd* is irregular in the preterite,
> short future and conditional—see
> entry on the Welsh-English side for
> details.

shut

1 *adjective*
= ar °gau
  the shop is shut = mae'r siop ar °gau

> **!** *The adjective phrase* **ar °gau**, *like all
> similar phrases with* **ar**, *does not use*
> **yn** *to link it to the verb* **bod** 'to be'—so
> not **mae'r siop yn ar °gau. Note also
> the difference between* **mae'r siop ar
> °gau** *and* **mae'r siop yn cau** 'the
> shop is shutting/shuts'.

2 *verb*
= cau (*stem* cae-)
  to shut something down = cau
  rhywbeth i lawr
  to shut someone out = cau rhywun
  allan
  shut up! = cau dy °geg!

shy *adjective*
= swil

sick *adjective*
- (*nauseous*)
  to feel sick = eisiau chwydu
  to be sick (*vomit*) = chwydu
- (*ill*)
= sâl, gwael
- (*fed up*)
  I'm sick of this = dw i wedi cael llond
  bol ar hyn

sickness *noun*
= salwch *masculine*, gwaeledd
masculine

side

1 *noun*
- (*all senses*)
= och(o)r (*plural* ochrau) *feminine*

> **!** *The spelling* **ochr** *is standard and
> literary; the spelling* **ochor** *reflects
> pronunciation and is becoming more
> common in writing as well.*

a building with a garden on the side =
  adeilad â gardd ar/wrth ei ochor
by the side of the road = wrth ochor y
  ffordd
by the side of the river = ar °lan yr afon
she's lying on her side = mae hi'n
  gorwedd ar ei hochor
on all sides = ar °bob ochor
on both sides = ar y °ddwy ochor
side by side = ochor wrth ochor
to/on one side = o'r neilltu
to set something to one side = neilltuo
  rhywbeth

2 *verb*
  to side with someone = cymryd (*stem*
  cymer-) ochor rhywun

side-effect noun
= sgîl-effaith (plural sgîl-effeithiau) feminine

sidewalk noun (US)
= palmant (plural palmentydd, palmantau) masculine

sigh
1 noun
= ochenaid (plural ochneidiau) feminine
2 verb
= ochneidio

sight noun
= golwg masculine
in sight = o °fewn golwg
out of sight = allan o °olwg
get out of my sight! = dos o ⁿngolwg i!
to have good sight = gweld (stem gwel-) yn °dda
to catch sight of something = cael cipolwg ar° rywbeth

sightseeing noun
to go sightseeing = gweld (stem gwel-) y golygfeydd
to go sightseeing in Blaenau Ffestiniog = gweld golygfeydd Blaenau Ffestiniog

sign
1 noun
= arwydd (plural -ion) masculine
2 verb
= arwyddo, llofnodi
sign here, please = arwyddwch or llofnodwch fan hyn os gwelwch yn °dda

signal
1 noun
• (most senses)
= arwydd (plural -ion) masculine
• (trace)
there was no sign of them = doedd dim golwg ohonyn nhw
2 verb
= rhoi (stem rhoi-, rhodd-) arwydd

signature noun
= llofnod (plural -au, -ion) masculine

significant adjective
• (meaningful)
= arwyddocaol
this is a significant development = mae hyn yn °ddatblygiad arwyddocaol

• (important, appreciable)
= sylweddol, pwysig
a significant improvement = gwelliant sylweddol

signpost noun
= arwyddbost (plural arwyddbyst) masculine

silence noun
= tawelwch masculine, distawrwydd masculine

silent adjective
= tawel, distaw

silk
1 noun
= sidan masculine
2 adjective
= sidan

silly adjective
= hurt, gwirion, ffôl
don't be silly! = paid bod yn hurt!

silver noun & adjective
= arian masculine

similar adjective
= tebyg
to be similar to something = bod yn °debyg i° rywbeth

similarity noun
= tebygrwydd masculine

simple adjective
= syml

simplicity noun
= symledd masculine

simplify verb
= symleiddio

simply adverb
• (general sense)
= yn syml
• (as intensifier)
= yn °wirioneddol
it's simply awful! = mae'n °wirioneddol ofnadwy!

sin
1 noun
= pechod (plural -au) masculine
2 verb
= pechu
to sin against someone = pechu yn erbyn rhywun

since

1 *preposition*
= ers
since last year = ers llynedd
since last week = ers wythnos diwetha
since Tuesday = ers dydd Mawrth
we've lived here since the war = dyn ni'n byw yma ers y rhyfel

> ! Note the present tense used in the last example because the situation continues into the present.

2 *conjunction*
• (*time*)
= ers

> ! This time conjunction uses the normal construction **i°** + *subject* + *verbnoun*, with the tense of the verb not specified. The subject of the sentence in Welsh causes soft mutation, here of the verbnoun.

since they left = ers iddyn nhw °adael
since the meeting ended = ers i'r cyfarfod °ddod i °ben
• (*because*)
= gan °fod, am °fod
since no-one agrees = gan °fod neb yn cytuno
since the money is missing = gan °fod yr arian ar °goll
3 *adverb*
= ers hynny
I haven't seen them since = dw i heb °weld nhw ers hynny

sincere *adjective*
= diffuant

sincerely *adverb*
yours sincerely = yr eiddoch yn °gywir, yn °ddiffuant

sing *verb*
= canu

singer *noun*
= canwr (*plural* canwyr, cantorion) *masculine*
= cantores (*plural* -au) *feminine*

singing *noun*
= canu *verbnoun*

single *adjective*
• (*most senses*)
= sengl
every single one of them = pob un ohonyn nhw

every single thing = pob dim
not a single one = (dim) yr un
• (*unmarried*)
= di-briod, sengl

single bed *noun*
= gwely sengl (*plural* gwelyau sengl) *masculine*

single-parent family *noun*
= teulu un rhiant (*plural* teuluoedd un rhiant) *masculine*

single room *noun*
= stafell sengl (*plural* stafelloedd sengl) *feminine*

single ticket *noun*
(*one-way*)
= tocyn sengl (*plural* tocynnau sengl) *masculine*, tocyn unffordd (*plural* tocynnau unffordd) *masculine*

singular

1 *adjective*
= unigol
2 *noun*
= unigol
what's the singular of this word? = beth ydy unigol y gair 'ma?

sink

1 *noun*
= sinc (*plural* -iau) *feminine*
2 *verb*
= suddo

sister *noun*
= chwaer (*plural* chwiorydd) *feminine*

sister-in-law *noun*
= chwaer-yng-nghyfraith (*plural* chwiorydd-yng-nghyfraith) *feminine*

sit *verb*
= eistedd

sit back
= eistedd yn ôl

sit down
= eistedd

sit up:
he sat up = cododd e ar ei eistedd
she sat up = cododd hi ar ei heistedd

sitting room *noun*
= lolfa (*plural* lofeydd) *feminine*
= stafell °fyw (*plural* stafelloedd byw) *feminine*

situated *adjective*
= wedi'i °leoli *masculine*, wedi'i lleoli *feminine*, wedi'u lleoli *plural*

situation *noun*
• (*general sense*)
= sefyllfa (*plural* -oedd) *feminine*
the situation is worsening = mae'r sefyllfa'n gwaethygu
• (*location*)
= safle (*plural* -oedd) *masculine*, lleoliad (*plural* -au) *masculine*
to live in a quiet situation = byw mewn lleoliad tawel

six *numeral*
= chwech, chwe[h]

> **! chwe** *is used with a directly following singular noun,* **chwech** *in all other cases. Some regions use* **chwech** *in all cases. The aspirate mutation after* **chwe** *(as elsewhere) is not consistently applied except on words beginning* **c-**.

six horses = chwe [h]cheffyl *or* chwech o °geffylau
six days = chwe diwrnod
six years = chwe blynedd
six years old = chwe blwydd oed
at six o'clock = am °chwech o'r °gloch
I have six = mae gen i chwech (*North*), mae chwech 'da fi (*South*)

sixteen *numeral*
= unarbymtheg, undeg chwech
sixteen horses = un ceffyl ar °bymtheg, undeg chwech o °geffylau
sixteen cats = un °gath ar °bymtheg, undeg chwech o °gathod
sixteen years = un °flwyddyn ar °bymtheg, undeg chwech o °flynyddoedd
sixteen years old = blwydd ar °bymtheg oed, undeg chwe blwydd oed

sixteenth *adjective*
= unfed ar °bymtheg, undeg chweched

sixth *adjective*
= chweched

> **! chweched** *precedes the noun.*

sixth form = chweched dosbarth

sixty *numeral*
= chwedeg

sixty apples = chwedeg o afalau
sixty years = chwedeg o °flynyddoedd
sixty years old = chwedeg oed

size *noun*
= maint (*plural* meintiau) *masculine*
what size is it? = beth ydy ei °faint?
= pa mor °fawr ydy e?

skateboard *noun*
= sgrialfwrdd (*plural* sgrialfyrddau) *masculine*

skates *plural noun*
= sgidiau sglefrio *plural*

skating *noun*
= sglefrio

skating rink *noun*
= rinc sglefrio (*plural* rinciau sglefrio) *masculine or feminine*, llawr sglefrio (*plural* lloriau sglefrio) *masculine*

skeleton *noun*
= sgerbwd (*plural* sgerbydau) *masculine*

sketch
1 *noun*
= braslun (*plural* -iau) *masculine*
2 *verb*
= braslunio

ski
1 *noun*
= sgi (*plural* sgïau) *feminine*
2 *verb*
= sgïo

skiing *noun*
= sgïo *verbnoun*

skilful *adjective*
= medrus

skill *noun*
= medr (*plural* -au) *masculine*

skin *noun*
= croen (*plural* crwyn) *masculine*

skinny *adjective*
= tenau, main

skip
1 *noun*
(*for rubbish*)
= sgip (*plural* -iau) *masculine or feminine*
2 *verb*
= prancio, sgipio

skipping rope *noun*
= cortyn neidio (*plural* cyrt neidio) *masculine*

skirt *noun*
= sgert (*plural* -iau) *feminine*

skive *verb*
= mitsio

skull *noun*
= penglog (*plural* -au) *feminine*

sky *noun*
= awyr *feminine*
in the sky = yn yr awyr

skydiving *noun*
= nenblymio

skyscraper *noun*
= nendwr (*plural* nendyrau) *masculine*

slap
1 *noun*
= slapen, slap (*plural* slapiau) *feminine*
2 *verb*
= slapio

slate *noun*
• (*material*)
= llechfaen *masculine*
• (*piece for roofing etc*)
= llechen (*plural* llechi) *feminine*

sledge *noun*
= sled (*plural* -i or -iau) *feminine*

sleep
1 *noun*
= cwsg *masculine*
to go to sleep = mynd i °gysgu
to go back to sleep = mynd yn ôl i °gysgu
2 *verb*
= cysgu
sleep tight! = cysga'n °dawel!, cysgwch yn °dawel!

sleep in
(*sleep late*)
= cysgu'n hwyr

sleeping bag *noun*
= sach °gysgu (*plural* sachau cysgu) *feminine*

sleepy *adjective*
= cysglyd

sleet
1 *noun*
= eirlaw *masculine*
2 *verb*
it's sleeting = mae'n bwrw eirlaw

sleeve *noun*
= llawes (*plural* llewys) *feminine*
to roll up one's sleeves = torchi'ch llewys

slender *adjective*
= main

slice
1 *noun*
= tafell (*plural* -i, -au, tefyll) *feminine*, sleisen (*plural* sleisys) *feminine*
2 *verb*
= tafellu

slide
1 *noun*
• (*in playground*)
= llithren (*plural* -nau) *feminine*
• (*photographic, scientific*)
= sleid (*plural* -iau) *feminine*
2 *verb*
= llithro

slight *adjective*

> **!** *For this adjective Welsh generally uses the quantity expressions* **tipyn** *or* **ychydig** *'a little'/'a bit'—these must be followed by* **o°** *before the noun.*

he's got a slight cold = mae tipyn o annwyd arno (fe)
slight nervousness = tipyn *or* ychydig o nerfusrwydd

slightly *adverb*

> **!** *For this adverb Welsh generally uses the quantity expressions* **tipyn** *or* **ychydig** *'a little'/'a bit' followed by* **yn°** *and the adjective qualified.*

slightly better = tipyn *or* ychydig yn °well
slightly too big = tipyn *or* ychydig yn rhy °fawr

slim
1 *adjective*
= main
2 *verb*
I'm slimming = dw i wrthi'n colli pwysau

slip

1 *verb*
= llithro
to slip someone's mind = mynd o °feddwl rhywun

2 *noun*
• (*mistake*)
= camgymeriad (*plural* -au) *masculine*
a slip of the tongue = llithriad tafod (*plural* llithriadau tafod) *masculine*
• (*of paper*)
= slip (*plural* -iau) *masculine*

slipper *noun*
= sliper (*plural* -i) *feminine*

slippery *adjective*
= llithrig

slot machine *noun*
= peiriant ceiniogau (*plural* peiriannau ceiniogau) *masculine*

slow *adjective*
= araf

slow down
= arafu

slowly *adverb*
= yn araf

slug *noun*
= gwlithen (*plural* gwlithod) *feminine*

sly *adjective*
= cyfrwys

small *adjective*
• (*little*)
= bach, bychan

> **!** **bach** *has a number of irregular forms:*
> **smaller** = llai
> **smallest** = lleia(f)
> **so small** = cynlleied
> **as small as ...** = cynlleied â^h
> **bychan** *has a feminine form* **bechan**.

• (*insignificant*)
= mân

smaller *adjective*
= llai

smallest *adjective*
= lleia(f)

smallholding *noun*
= tyddyn (*plural* -nau, -nod) *masculine*

smallpox *noun*
= y °frech °wen
he's got smallpox = mae'r °frech °wen arno

smart *adjective*
• (*presentable*)
= taclus, twt
• (*US: clever*)
= deallus

smash *verb*
to smash into something = taro yn erbyn rhywbeth
to smash something = torri rhywbeth yn °ddarnau

smell

1 *noun*
= oglau (*plural* ogleuon)
2 *verb*
• (*use sense of smell*)
= ogleuo, clywed oglau
to smell something = ogleuo rhywbeth, clywed oglau rhywbeth
• (*to give off nice smell*)
= ogleuo (*North*), gwynto (*South*)
this flower smells nice = mae'r blodyn 'ma'n ogleuo'n °dda
• (*stink*)
= drewi

smelly *adjective*
= drewllyd

smile

1 *noun*
= gwên (*plural* gwenau) *feminine*
2 *verb*
= gwenu
to smile at someone = gwenu ar° rywun

smoke

1 *noun*
= mwg *masculine*
2 *verb*
= (y)smygu, smocio

smoking *noun*
= (y)smygu, smocio *verbnoun*

smooth *adjective*
= llyfn

smother *verb*
= mygu

snack
1 *noun*
= tamaid (*plural* tameidiau) i aros pryd *masculine*
2 *verb*
= cael tamaid i aros pryd

snail *noun*
= malwen *or* malwoden (*plural* malwod) *feminine*

snake *noun*
= neidr (*plural* nadredd, nadroedd) *feminine*

snapshot *noun*
= ciplun (*plural* -iau) *masculine*

snatch *verb*
= cipio

sneakers *plural noun*
= (e)sgidiau dal adar *plural*

sneeze *verb*
= tisian

snob *noun*
= crechyn (*plural* crachach) *masculine*, snob (*plural* -iaid) *masculine*

snobbery *noun*
= snobyddiaeth *feminine*

snobbish *adjective*
= snobyddlyd, snoblyd

snooker *noun*
= snwcer *masculine*

snore *verb*
= chwyrnu

snow
1 *noun*
= eira (*plural* -oedd) *masculine*
2 *verb*
= bwrw eira
it's snowing = mae'n bwrw eira

snowball *noun*
= pelen eira (*plural* peli eira) *feminine*

snowdrift *noun*
= lluwch (*plural* lluwchfeydd) *feminine*

snowflake *noun*
= pluen eira (*plural* plu eira) *feminine*, fflochen eira (*plural* fflochennau eira *or* fflochenni eira) *feminine*

snowman *noun*
= dyn eira (*plural* dynion eira) *masculine*

so
1 *adverb*
• (*to such an extent*)
= mor°

> **!** *mor° displaces yn° in sentences with the verb* **bod** *'to be'—compare:*
> **it's hard** = mae e'n °galed
> **it's so hard** = mae e mor °galed (*not* *mae e'n mor °galed.*)
>   *Some common words have special irregular forms for 'so...' that do not involve* **mor°**—*e.g.* **cymaint**.

it's so heavy = mae e mor °drwm
they speak so fast = maen nhw'n siarad mor °gyflym
it's so much lighter = mae e °gymaint ysgafnach
so many = cymaint, cynifer
so few = cynlleied
so much = cymaint
so little = cynlleied
I have so much work = mae gen i °gymaint o °waith (*North*), mae cymaint o °waith 'da fi (*South*)
there are so few people = mae cynlleied o °bobol
• (*also*)
= hefyd
I'm late and so are you = dw i'n hwyr, a ti hefyd
'I speak French'—'so do I' = 'dw i'n siarad Ffrangeg'—'a finnau'
• (*other uses*)
so you're not coming? = felly ti °ddim yn dod?
I don't think so = dw i °ddim yn meddwl
so they say = meddai/medden nhw
and so on = ac yn y blaen
2 *conjunction*
(*so that*)
= fel

> **!** *This conjunction is followed by a 'that...' clause in Welsh.*

so (that) we can see = fel y gallwn ni °weld, fel bod ni'n gallu gweld
so (that) we won't be late = fel na °fyddwn ni'n hwyr
so as not to miss the plane = rhag (ofn) inni °golli'r awyren

soak *verb*
= gwlychu

we got soaked = fe °gawson ni'n gwlychu

soap *noun*
= sebon (*plural* -au) *masculine*

soap opera *noun*
= opera sebon (*plural* operâu sebon) *feminine*

sober *adjective*
= sob(o)r

so-called *adjective*
= honedig

soccer *noun*
= pêl-droed *feminine*

social *adjective*
= cymdeithasol

social security *noun*
= nawdd cymdeithasol *masculine*

social studies *noun*
= astudiaethau cymdeithasol *plural*

social worker *noun*
= gweithiwr cymdeithasol (*plural* gweithwyr cymdeithasol) *masculine*
= gweithwraig °gymdeithasol (*plural* gweithwragedd cymdeithasol) *feminine*

socialism *noun*
= sosialaeth *feminine*

socialist *noun*
= sosialydd (*plural* sosialwyr) *masculine*

socialize *verb*
= cymdeithasu

society *noun*
= cymdeithas (*plural* -au) *feminine*

sock *noun*
= hosan (*plural* sanau) *feminine*

> ! *The original plural* **hosanau** *is never heard.*

sofa *noun*
= soffa (*plural* -s) *feminine*

soft *adjective*
• (*not hard*)
= meddal
• (*not harsh*)
= tyner
• (*not strict*)
= meddal, maddeugar

soft drink *noun*
= diod ysgafn (*plural* diodydd ysgafn) *feminine*

software *noun*
= meddalwedd *masculine or feminine*

soil *noun*
= pridd *masculine*

soldier *noun*
= milwr (*plural* milwyr) *masculine*

sole
1 *adjective*
= unig°

> ! **unig°**—*in this sense—precedes the noun it refers to and causes soft mutation. When it follows the noun it means 'lonely'.*

2 *noun*
(*of shoe*)
= gwadn (*plural* -au) *feminine or masculine*

solely *adverb*
= yn unig

solicitor *noun*
= cyfreithiwr (*plural* cyfreithwyr) *masculine*
= cyfreithwraig (*plural* cyfreithwragedd) *feminine*

solution *noun*
(*to problem*)
= datrysiad (*plural* -au) *masculine*, datrys *verbnoun*

solve *verb*
= datrys

solvent *noun*
= toddydd (*plural* -ion) *masculine*

some
1 *adjective*

> ! *This adjective has a number of different senses in English, and care must be taken in deciding how to translate it in Welsh.*

• (*an amount of or a quantity of—not translated in Welsh*)
I've bought some apples = dw i wedi prynu afalau
would you like some coffee? = leiciech chi °goffi?

I need some money = dw i angen arian
there's some cheese left = mae caws ar ôl
- (*certain*)
  = rhai (+ *plural*)
  some people work from home = mae rhai pobol yn gweithio oddi gartre
- (*certain amount—with uncountable things*)
  = peth
  there is some cheese left = mae peth caws ar ôl
- (*some.. or other*)
  = rhyw° (+ *singular*)
  some man is waiting for you = mae rhyw °ddyn yn aros amdanoch chi
  some politician or other = rhyw °wleidydd neu'i gilydd
2 *pronoun*
  = rhai
  some are here, others are over there = mae rhai fan hyn, mae eraill draw fan'na
  have you got some? = oes gynnoch chi °rai? (*North*), oes rhai 'da chi? (*South*)
  some of my friends = rhai o'n ffrindiau (*but not always translated*):
  have some more! = cymerwch °ragor!

somebody *pronoun*
  = rhywun
  somebody famous = rhywun enwog

somehow *adverb*
  = °rwysut, °ryw ffordd

someone *pronoun*
  = rhywun
  someone famous = rhywun enwog

something *pronoun*
  = rhywbeth
  something interesting = rhywbeth diddorol

sometime *adverb*
  = °rywbryd, °rwydro

sometimes *adverb*
  = weithiau, ambell °dro

somewhere *adverb*
  = °rywle, yn rhywle

son *noun*
  = mab (*plural* meibion) *masculine*

song *noun*
  = cân (*plural* caneuon) *feminine*, cerdd (*plural* -i) *feminine*

son-in-law *noun*
  = mab-yng-nghyfraith (*plural* meibion-yng-nghyfraith) *masculine*

soon *adverb*
  = yn °fuan, maes o law, nes ymlaen, cyn (bo) hir, toc

  > ! *All these terms are broadly interchangeable (except in set phrases), though **toc** in particular is very informal and does not appear in the written language.*

  see you soon! = °wela i di cyn hir!
  we'll soon be home = byddwn ni gartre cyn hir
  out soon! (*product*) = allan yn °fuan!
  get well soon = gwella'n °fuan
  the sooner the better = gorau po °gynta(f)
  as soon as possible = cyn °gynted ag y bo modd
  as soon as you have finished = cyn °gynted ag y byddi di wedi gorffen

sophisticated *adjective*
  = soffistigedig

sore *adjective*
  = tost

  > ! **tost** *is used generally for aches and pains affecting a particular part of the body - so **pen tost** 'headache', **stumog °dost** 'stomach ache'.*

sorry
1 *exclamation*
  = mae'n °ddrwg gen i (*North*), mae'n °ddrwg 'da fi (*South*), mae'n °flin 'da fi (*South*)
2 *adjective*
- (*when apologizing*)
  I'm sorry I'm late = mae'n °ddrwg gen i ⁿmod i'n hwyr
- (*when expressing regret*)
  I'm sorry you can't come = mae'n °ddrwg gen i °fod ti °ddim yn gallu dod, mae'n °ddrwg gen i na °elli di °ddod
- (*feeling pity*)
  I'm sorry for her = mae'n °ddrwg gen i drosti (hi), dw i'n teimlo drosti (hi)
  to feel sorry for oneself = teimlo'n °ddigalon

sort
1 *noun*
  = math (*plural* -au) *masculine*

what sort of bird is that? = path °fath o aderyn ydy hwnna?

all sorts of people = pob math o °bobol

nothing of the sort = dim byd o'r °fath (*note mutation!*)

I sort of think we should = rhyw °feddwl dw i y dylen ni

2 *verb*

to sort papers = trefnu papurau

sort out

• (*solve*)

to sort a problem out = datrys problem

• (*organize*)

to sort out documents = trefnu *or* didoli dogfenni

• (*deal with*)

I'll sort it out = mi °ddelia i â hynny

sound

1 *noun*

= sŵn *masculine*, sain (*plural* seiniau) *feminine*

2 *verb*

= swnio

that sounds strange = mae hynny'n swnio'n rhyfedd

sounds familiar = swnio'n °gyfarwydd

soup *noun*

= cawl (*plural* -iau) *masculine*

sour *adjective*

= sur, egr

to go/turn sour = mynd yn sur/egr

source *noun*

• (*general senses*)

= ffynhonnell (*plural* ffynonellau) *feminine*

they are looking for the source of the river = maen nhw'n chwilio am ffynhonnell yr afon

the source of the information = ffynhonnell y °wybodaeth

we can't reveal our sources = °allwn ni °ddim datgelu'n ffynonellau

• (*derivation*)

= tarddiad (*plural* -au) *masculine*

south

1 *adjective*

= de

to work in south Wales = gweithio yn ⁿNe Cymru

2 *adverb*

= i'r de

to go south = mynd i'r de

to live south of Bangor = byw i'r de o °Fangor

! *There is a distinction between* **i'r °dde** *'to the right' and* **i'r de** *'to the South'. When* **de** *means 'right', it always has soft mutation after the words for* 'the'; *when it means* 'South' *it never does.*

3 *noun*

= de

to the south of Bangor = i'r de o °Fangor

in the south of the country = yn ⁿne'r °wlad

South America *noun*

= De America

South Africa *noun*

= De Affrica

southeast *noun*

= de-°ddwyrain *masculine*

southerly *adjective*

= deheuol, o'r de

southern *adjective*

= deheuol, o'r de

southwest *noun*

= de-°orllewin *masculine*

souvenir *noun*

= cofrodd (*plural* -ion) *feminine*

space *noun*

• (*room*)

= lle (*plural* llefydd, lleoedd) *masculine*

to make space for someone = gwneud lle i° rywun

• (*interval of time*)

= ysbaid (*plural* ysbeidiau) *masculine or feminine*

• (*gap*)

= bwlch (*plural* bylchau) *masculine*

to leave spaces = gadael (*stem* gadaw-) bylchau

• (*outer space*)

= gofod *masculine*

creatures from space = creaduriaid o'r gofod

• (*area of land*)

= lle (*plural* llefydd, lleoedd) *masculine*

an open space = lle agored

spacecraft *noun*

= llong °ofod (*plural* llongau gofod) *feminine*

spade *noun*
= rhaw (*plural* -iau) *feminine*

spare *adjective*
= sbâr

spare part *noun*
= darn sbâr (*plural* darnau sbâr)
masculine

spare room *noun*
= stafell sbâr (*plural* stafelloedd sbâr)
feminine

spare time *noun*
= oriau hamdden *plural*

sparse *adjective*
= prin, pitw

speak *verb*
= siarad
**to speak to someone about
something** = siarad â^h rhywun am^o
rywbeth
do you speak Welsh? = dych chi'n
siarad Cymraeg?
can I speak to ...? = ^{o}ga i siarad â^h ...?
who's speaking? = pwy sy'n siarad?

> **! siarad** 'speak', 'talk' *should not be
> confused with* **dweud** 'say', 'tell'.

speak up
= siarad yn uwch

speaker *noun*
= siaradwr (*plural* siaradwyr) *masculine*

special *adjective*
= arbennig
special offer = cynnig arbennig (*plural*
cynigion arbennig) *masculine*

specialist *noun*
= arbenigwr (*plural* arbenigwyr)
masculine

speciality *noun*
= arbenigedd (*plural* -au) *masculine*

specially *adverb*
= yn arbennig, yn enwedig

species *noun*
= rhywogaeth (*plural* -au) *feminine*, math
(*plural* -au) *masculine*

specific *adjective*
= penodol

spectacles *plural noun*
= sbectol *feminine singular*
to wear spectacles = gwisgo sbectol

spectator *noun*
= gwyliwr (*plural* gwylwyr) *masculine*

speech *noun*
• (*formal address*)
= araith (*plural* areithiau) *feminine*
to make/give a speech = rhoi (*stem*
rhoi-, rhodd-) araith, areithio
• (*faculty*)
= lleferydd *masculine or feminine*

speed
1 *noun*
= cyflymder (*plural* -au) *masculine*
to pick up speed = cyflymu
what speed were you doing? = pa mor
^{o}gyflym o'ch chi'n mynd?
2 *verb*
= gyrru'n rhy ^{o}gyflym, brysio
you're speeding = dych chi'n gyrru'n
rhy ^{o}gyflym

speed up
= cyflymu

speed limit *noun*
= cyfyngiad cyflymder (*plural*
cyfyngiadau cyflymder) *masculine*

spell
1 *noun*
• (*interval of time*)
= ysbaid (*plural* ysbeidiau) *masculine or
feminine*, sbel (*plural* -iau) *feminine*
sunny spells = ysbeidiau heulog
• (*enchantment*)
= swyn (*plural* -ion) *masculine*
2 *verb*
= sillafu
how do you spell that? = sut dych chi'n
sillafu hynny?
how is that spelt? = sut mae sillafu
hynny?

spelling *noun*
= sillafu *verbnoun*

spend *verb*
• (*money*)
= gwario
• (*time*)
= treulio
to spend time doing something =
treulio amser yn gwneud rhywbeth

spider noun
= pry(f) copyn (plural pryfed cop) masculine, copyn (plural -nod) masculine

spill verb
= gollwng (stem gollyng-)

spin verb
• (wool)
= nyddu
• (turn)
= troi, troelli
my head is spinning = mae ⁿmhen i'n troi

spinach noun
= pigoglys masculine

spine noun
= asgwrn cefn masculine

spirit noun
• = ysbryd (plural -oedd) masculine
• (ghost)
= ysbryd (plural -ion) masculine

spiritual adjective
= ysbrydol

spit verb
= poeri

spite noun
in spite of = er gwaetha(f)
in spite of the weather = er gwaetha'r tywydd
in spite of him = er ei ᵒwaetha

! **er gwaetha** is a compound preposition and so changes its form with pronouns.

she did that out of spite = naeth hi hynny o ᵒran gwenwyn

spiteful adjective
= sbeitlyd

splendid adjective
= bendigedig, campus

split
1 verb
= hollti
to split something in two = hollti rhywbeth yn ᵒddau
2 noun
• (in material etc)
= hollt (plural -au) feminine

• (disagreement)
= rhwygiad (plural -au) masculine

spoil verb
• (damage, wreck)
= difetha
the rain spoilt our holiday = naeth y glaw ᵒddifetha'n gwyliau
• (go rotten)
= pydru
these apples have spoilt = mae'r afalau 'ma wedi pydru
• (a child)
= difetha, sbwylio

spoken adjective
= llafar
spoken language = iaith ᵒlafar

sponge noun
= sbwnj (plural -is) masculine or feminine, sbwng (plural sbyngau) masculine

sponsor
1 noun
= noddwr (plural noddwyr) masculine
2 verb
= noddi

spoon noun
= llwy (plural -au) feminine

spoonful noun
= llwyaid feminine, llond llwy masculine

sport noun
= chwaraeon plural

sports centre noun
= canolfan chwaraeon (plural canolfannau chwaraeon) feminine

sports club noun
= clwb chwaraeon (plural clybiau chwaraeon) masculine

spot
1 noun
• (mark)
= smotyn (plural smotiau) masculine
• (place)
= llecyn (plural -nau) masculine
2 verb
(notice)
= sylwi
to spot something = sylwi arᵒ rywbeth

sprain verb
= sigo

spread *verb*
= taenu, lledaenu
to spread butter thick = taenu menyn yn °drwchus
to spread things out on the floor = taenu pethau ar y llawr

spring
1 *noun*
• (*season*)
= gwanwyn *masculine*
in the spring = yn y gwanwyn
all spring = trwy gydol y gwanwyn
• (*of water*)
= ffynhonnell (*plural* ffynonellau) *feminine*
• (*of mattress, chair etc*)
= sbring (*plural* -iau, -s) *masculine*
2 *verb*
= neidio
to spring to one's feet = neidio ar eich traed
to spring to someone's mind = dod i °feddwl rhywun

spy
1 *noun*
= ysbïwr (*plural* ysbiwyr) *masculine*
2 *verb*
= ysbïo
to spy on someone = ysbïo ar° rywun

square
1 *adjective*
= sgwâr
2 *noun*
• (*geometric shape*)
= sgwâr (*plural* sgwar(i)au) *feminine or masculine*, petryal (*plural* -au) *masculine*
• (*in town*)
= sgwâr, maes (*plural* meysydd) *masculine*

squash
1 *noun*
(*game*)
= sboncen *feminine*
2 *verb*
= gwasgu

squeak
1 *verb*
= gwichian (*stem* gwichi-)
2 *noun*
= gwich (*plural* -iau) *feminine*, gwichiad (*plural* -au) *masculine*

squeeze *verb*
= gwasgu

squirrel *noun*
= gwiwer (*plural* -od) *feminine*

stab *verb*
= trywanu

stability *noun*
= sefydlogrwydd *masculine*

stable
1 *adjective*
= sefydlog
2 *noun*
= stabl (*plural* -au) *feminine*

stadium *noun*
= stadiwm (*plural* stadia) *feminine*

staff *noun*
• (*workforce*)
= staff *masculine*
we have three hundred staff = mae gynnon ni °dri ʰchant o °weithwyr, mae tri ʰchant o °weithwyr 'da ni
• (*rod*)
= ffon (*plural* ffyn) *feminine*

stage
1 *noun*
= llwyfan (*plural* -nau) *masculine or feminine*
2 *verb*
(*put on stage*)
= llwyfannu

stain
1 *noun*
= staen (*plural* -iau) *masculine*
2 *verb*
= staenio

stairs *plural noun*
= grisiau *plural*, staer *feminine*
to fall down the stairs = syrthio lawr y grisiau

stall *noun*
(*at fair etc*)
= stondin (*plural* -au) *feminine*

stamp
1 *noun*
• (*on envelope*)
= stamp (*plural* -iau) *masculine*
first class stamp = stamp dosbarth cynta(f)
second class stamp = stamp ail °ddosbarth
book of stamps = llyfryn o stampiau

• (*on document, passport*)
  = stamp (*plural* -iau) *masculine*
2 *verb*
  = stampio

stamp collecting *noun*
  = casglu stampiau *verbnoun*

stand *verb*
• (*general senses*)
  = sefyll (*stem* saf-, sef-)
  to be standing = sefyll
  to stand as a candidate = sefyll fel
  ymgeisydd
  to make a stand against something =
  gwneud safiad yn erbyn rhywbeth
  to stand trial = sefyll eich prawf
• (*put*)
  = gosod
  he stood the bottle on the table = fe
  °ososdd e'r °botel ar y bwrdd
• (*bear, suffer*)
  = diodde(f)
  I can't stand dogs = °alla i °ddim
  diodde cŵn
  they can't stand waiting = °allan nhw
  °ddim diodde aros

stand back
  = sefyll draw, sefyll yn ôl

stand for
  what does this letter stand for? = beth
  mae'r llythyren 'ma'n °olygu?

stand out
• (*be prominent*)
  = bod yn amlwg, sefyll allan
• (*insist on getting*)
  to stand out for something = mynnu
  cael rhywbeth

stand up
• (*get to one's feet*)
  = codi (ar eich traed), sefyll (ar eich
  traed)
• (*support*)
  to stand up for someone = cefnogi
  rhywun

standard
1 *adjective*
  = safonol
2 *noun*
• (*level*)
  = safon (*plural* -au) *feminine*
  the standard of the class is low = mae
  safon y dosbarth yn isel
• (*flag*)
  = baner (*plural* -i) *feminine*

standpoint *noun*
  = safbwynt (*plural* -iau) *masculine*

stapler *noun*
  = staplydd (*plural* -ion) *masculine*

star
1 *noun*
• (*in space*)
  = seren (*plural* sêr) *feminine*
  shooting star = seren °wib (*plural* sêr
  gwib)
• (*celebrity*)
  = seren (*plural* sêr) *feminine*
2 *verb*
  to star in a film = chwarae (*stem*
  chwarae-)'r °brif °ran mewn ffilm

stare *verb*
  = syllu
  to stare at someone/something = syllu
  ar° rywun/rywbeth

start
1 *noun*
• (*beginning*)
  = dechrau (*plural* dechreuadau)
  masculine, cychwyn *verbnoun*
  at the start of the week = °ddechrau'r
  wythnos
  from the very start = o'r cychwyn
  cynta(f)
• (*sudden movement*)
  to wake up with a start = deffro'n
  sydyn
2 *verb*
• (*begin*)
  = dechrau (*stem* dechreu-), cychwyn
  (*stem* cychwynn-)
  to start doing something = dechrau
  gwneud rhywbeth
  to start work = dechrau gwaith
• (*start out*)
  = cychwyn (*stem* cychwynn-)
  to start (out) on a journey = cychwyn
  ar °daith
• (*cars, machines etc*)
  = cychwyn (*stem* cychwynn-)
  the car won't start = neith y car °ddim
  cychwyn
• (*put into action*)
  = cychwyn (*stem* cychwynn-)
  start your machines! = cychwynnwch
  eich peiriannau!
• (*establish*)
  to start a business = sefydlu busnes

start off
  to start off on a journey = cychwyn ar
    °daith

start over (*US*)
  = ailddechrau, ailgychwyn

starve *verb*
• (*be in danger of dying*)
  = newynu, llwgu
  to be starving = newynu, llwgu
• (*be feeling very hungry*)
  I'm starving! = dw i bron â llwgu!

state *noun*
• (*condition*)
  = cyflwr (*plural* cyflyrau) *masculine*
  to be in a bad state = bod mewn cyflwr
    gwael
• (*country*)
  = gwlad (*plural* gwledydd) *feminine*
• (*province*)
  = talaith (*plural* taleithiau) *feminine*
  the United States = yr Unol °Daleithiau

statement *noun*
  = datganiad (*plural* -au) *masculine*
  to make a statement = gwneud
    datganiad

station *noun*
  = gorsaf (*plural* -oedd) *feminine*, stesion
  (*plural* -s) *feminine*

  > ! **gorsaf** is the standard term, while
  > the loanword **stesion** is common with
  > native speakers.

statistics *noun*
• (*set of figures*)
  = ystadegau *plural*
• (*academic subject*)
  = ystadegaeth *feminine*

statue *noun*
  = cerflun (*plural* -iau) *masculine*

statute *noun*
  = deddf (*plural* -au) *feminine*

stay *verb*
  = aros (*stem* arhos-)
  we stayed there for a month = arhoson
    ni yno am °fis, naethon ni aros yno am
    °fis

stay away
  = cadw (*stem* cadw-) draw, aros draw

stay in
  = aros i mewn

stay out
  = aros allan

stay up
  = aros ar eich traed

steady *adjective*
• (*firm*)
  = cadarn
• (*regular*)
  = cyson

steak *noun*
  = stêc (*plural* steciau, stêcs) *feminine*

steal *verb*
  = dwyn (*stem* dyg-)
  to steal something from someone =
    dwyn rhywbeth oddiar°/oddi ar°
    rywun

steam *noun*
  = stêm *masculine*, ager *masculine*

steel *noun*
  = dur *masculine*

steep *adjective*
  = serth

steering wheel *noun*
  = olwyn °lywio (*plural* olwynion llywio)
  feminine

step
1 *noun*
• (*movement*)
  = cam (*plural* -au) *masculine*
  to take a step = cymryd (*stem* cymer-)
    cam
  step by step = fesul cam
• (*stair*)
  = gris (*plural* -iau) *masculine*
• (*measure*)
  to take steps to prevent something =
    cymryd camau i °rwystro rhywbeth
2 *verb*
  = camu

stepbrother *noun*
  = llysfrawd (*plural* llysfrodyr) *masculine*

stepfather *noun*
  = llystad (*plural* -au) *masculine*

stepmother *noun*
  = llysfam (*plural* -au) *feminine*

stepsister *noun*
  = llyschwaer (*plural* llyschwiorydd)
  feminine

stereo *noun*
= stereo (*plural* -s) *feminine*

stereotype *noun*
= ystrydeb (*plural* -au) *masculine*

stereotyped *adjective*
= ystrydebol

steward *noun*
= stiward (*plural* -iaid) *masculine*

stewardess *noun*
= stiwardes (*plural* -au) *feminine*

stick
1 *noun*
= ffon (*plural* ffyn) *feminine*
2 *verb*
• (*with glue, tape etc*)
= gludo
  to stick something to something =
  gludo rhywbeth wrth° rywbeth
• (*adhere*)
= glynu
  to stick to something/someone =
  glynu wrth° rywbeth/rywun
  stick to him! = glynwch wrtho!
• (*put in*)
= plannu, rhoi (*stem* rhoi-, rhodd-)
  to stick something in something =
  plannu *or* rhoi rhywbeth ynⁿ
  rhywbeth
• (*fail to move*)
  the window is stuck = mae'r ffenest yn
  sownd

stick at
(*persevere*)
  stick at it! = dal/daliwch ati!

sticker *noun*
= sticer (*plural* -i) *masculine*, glynyn
  (*plural* glynion) *masculine*

sticky tape *noun*
= tâp gludiog *masculine*

stiff *adjective*
• (*inflexible, not supple, hard to move*)
= anhyblyg, anystwyth
• (*after sport etc*)
= stiff
  to have stiff legs = coesau stiff

still
1 *adjective*
• (*quiet*)
= tawel

  to sit still = eistedd yn °dawel
• (*unmoving*)
= llonydd
  to keep still = aros (*stem* arhos-) yn
  llonydd
2 *adverb*
= yn dal (i° / yn°), o hyd
  they're still arguing = maen nhw'n dal
  i °ddadlau
  they're still here = maen nhw'n dal fan
  hyn
  = maen nhw fan hyn o hyd
  I'm still cross = dw i'n dal yn °grac
  it's still too heavy = mae e'n dal yn rhy
  °drwm

> **!** *The usual way to indicate the
> continuation of an action or state is
> with* **dal**, *linked to a following
> verbnoun by* **i°**, *or to a following
> adjective (or noun) by* **yn°**.
> *Sometimes a longer alternative* **dal i
> °fod yn** + *verbnoun,* **dal i °fod yn°** +
> *adjective is encountered. And some
> areas dispense with the preceding* **yn**
> *These various usages can be seen in
> the examples that follow:*
> **mae pobl yn dal i °ddefnyddio'r
> afonydd fel tomennydd sbwriel** =
> people are still using the rivers as
> rubbish tips
> **er gwaetha popeth sy wedi
> digwydd, dw i'n dal yn °fodlon
> helpu** = despite everything that's
> happened, I'm still willing to help
> **ydyn nhw'n dal i °fod yn cerdded i'r
> °dre °bob dydd?** = are they still
> walking into town every day?
> **maen nhw'n dal i °fod yn °grac** =
> they're still angry
> **mae e dal yn y carchar** = he's still in
> prison

stimulate *verb*
= symbylu

sting
1 *noun*
= pigiad (*plural* -au) *masculine*
2 *verb*
= pigo

stink *verb*
= drewi

stinking *adjective*
= drewllyd

stir
1 *verb*
- (*liquid*)
  = cynhyrfu
- (*move*)
  = symud
  no-one was stirring = doedd neb yn symud
2 *noun*
  to cause a stir = creu cynnwrf

stitch
1 *noun*
  = pwyth (*plural* -au, -i) *masculine*
2 *verb*
  = pwytho, gwnïo

stomach *noun*
  = stumog (*plural* -au) *feminine*

stomach ache *noun*
  I've got stomachache = mae stumog °dost 'da fi

stone *noun*
- (*substance*)
  = carreg *feminine*
- (*pebble; in fruit*)
  = carreg (*plural* cerrig) *feminine*

stop
1 *noun*
  = safle (*plural* -oedd) *masculine*
  bus stop = safle bysiau (*plural* safleoedd bysiau)
2 *verb*
- (*desist, cease*)
  = peidio
  to stop doing something = peidio gwneud rhywbeth

> **!** *peidio* *can also be used with* **â**ʰ + *verbnoun*: peidio â gwneud rhywbeth

- (*prevent*)
  to stop someone doing something = atal rhywun rhag gwneud rhywbeth
- (*come to a halt*)
  = stopio
  the cars stopped = stopiodd y ceir

store *noun*
- (*storeroom, depot, warehouse*)
  = storfa (*plural* storfeydd) *feminine*, stordy (*plural* stordai) *masculine*
- (*US: shop*)
  = siop (*plural* -au) *feminine*

storekeeper *noun* (*US*)
  = dyn siop (*plural* dynion siop) *masculine*
  = gwraig siop (*plural* gwragedd siop) *feminine*

storey *noun*
  = llawr (*plural* lloriau) *masculine*
  top storey (*in house*) = llofft *feminine*
  on the second storey = ar yr ail °lawr

storm *noun*
  = storm (*plural* -ydd) *feminine*

stormy *adjective*
  = stormus

story *noun*
  = stori (*plural* storïau, straeon) *feminine*, hanes (*plural* -ion) *masculine*

straight
1 *adjective*
  = syth
2 *adverb*
  = yn syth
  he went straight back = aeth e'n syth yn ôl

straight away *adverb*
  = yn syth, ar unwaith
  I'll come straight away = mi °ddo i'n syth, mi °ddo i ar unwaith

strange *adjective*
  = rhyfedd, od
  how strange! = 'na °ryfedd!

stranger *noun*
  = dieithryn (*plural* dieithriaid) *masculine*

strangle *verb*
  = tagu

straw *noun*
- (*material*)
  = gwellt *masculine*
- (*drinking straw*)
  = gwelltyn *masculine*

strawberry *noun*
  = mefusen (*plural* mefus) *feminine*

stream *noun*
  = nant (*plural* nentydd) *feminine*, ffrwd (*plural* ffrydiau) *feminine*

street *noun*
  = heol (*plural* -ydd) *feminine*, stryd (*plural* -oedd) *feminine*

streetlamp *noun*
= golau stryd (*plural* goleuadau stryd) *masculine*

strength *noun*
= nerth (*plural* -oedd) *masculine*, cryfder (*plural* -au) *masculine*

stress
1 *noun*
• (*pressure*)
= pwysau *plural*
she's under stress = mae hi dan °bwysau
• (*emphasis in word*)
= pwyslais (*plural* pwysleisiau) *masculine*
2 *verb*
= pwysleisio

stressful *adjective*
= ingol

stretch *verb*
= estyn (*stem* estynn-), ymestyn (*stem* ymestynn-)
to be stretched out = ymestyn

strict *adjective*
= llym

strike
1 *noun*
• (*industrial dispute*)
= streic (*plural* -iau) *feminine*
to go on strike = mynd ar streic, streicio
• (*attack*)
air strike = cyrch awyr (*plural* cyrchoedd awyr) *masculine*, ymosodiad o'r awyr (*plural* ymosodiadau o'r awyr) *masculine*
2 *verb*
• (*hit*)
= curo, taro (*stem also* traw-), bwrw
• (*go on strike*)
= streicio, mynd ar streic

striking *adjective*
= trawiadol

string *noun*
= llinyn (*plural* -nau) *masculine*

strip
1 *noun*
= stribedyn (*plural* stribedi) *masculine*, stribed (*plural* stribedi) *masculine or feminine*

2 *verb*
• (*remove*)
= tynnu
• (*remove clothes*)
= tynnu dillad, dinoethi

striped *adjective*
= streipog, streipiog

stroke
1 *noun*
= trawiad (*plural* -au) *masculine*
to have a stroke = cael trawiad
on the stroke of ten = ar °ben deg o'r °gloch
2 *verb*
= anwesu

strong *adjective*
= cryf

> **!** **cryf** *has a feminine form* **cref**; *also a plural form* **cryfion** *found mostly in set phrases.*

strong winds = gwyntoedd cryfion
a strong English accent = acen °gref Saesneg

structure *noun*
= strwythur (*plural* -au) *masculine*

struggle
1 *noun*
= brwydr (*plural* -au) *feminine*, ymdrech (*plural* -ion) *feminine*
a struggle for freedom = brwydr am °ryddid
2 *verb*
= brwydro, ymdrechu

stubborn *adjective*
= styfnig

stuck *adjective*
(*immovable, immobile*)
= sownd
to be stuck in something = bod yn sownd ynⁿ rhywbeth

student *noun*
= myfyriwr (*plural* myfyrwyr) *masculine*
= myfyrwraig (*plural* myfyrwragedd) *feminine*

studio *noun*
= stiwdio (*plural* -s) *feminine*

study
1 *verb*
= astudio

to study something at university =
astudio rhywbeth yn y °brifysgol
2 *noun*
• (*room*)
= astudfa (*plural* astudfeydd) *feminine*
• (*act or result of studying*)
= astudiaeth *feminine*
to make a close study of the facts =
gwneud astudiaeth °fanwl o'r
ffeithiau, astudio'r ffeithiau'n
°fanwl

stuff *noun*
= stwff *masculine*

stuffy *adjective*
(*close*)
= mwll, trymaidd

stumble *verb*
= baglu

stumbling block *noun*
= maen tramgwydd (*plural* meini
tramgwydd) *masculine*

stun *verb*
= syfrdanu
I was stunned by the news = °ges i 'n
syfrdanu gan y newyddion

stupid *adjective*
= twp, hurt, gwirion, ffôl

stupidity *noun*
= twpdra *masculine*

style *noun*
• (*way of dressing, behaving*)
= steil (*plural* -iau) *masculine*
• (*method, manner*)
= dull (*plural* -iau) *masculine*

stylish *adjective*
= ffasiynol, steilus

subject *noun*
• (*topic*)
= pwnc (*plural* pynciau) *masculine*,
testun (*plural* -au) *masculine*
• (*academic*)
= pwnc (*plural* pynciau) *masculine*
• (*grammatical*)
= goddrych (*plural* -au) *masculine*

submarine *noun*
= llong °danfor (*plural* llongau tanfor)
feminine

subscribe *verb*
= tanysgrifio

to subscribe to a magazine =
tanysgrifio i °gylchgrawn

subscription *noun*
= tanysgrifiad
**to take out a subscription to
something** = tanysgrifio i° rywbeth

substantial *adjective*
= sylweddol

subtitle *noun*
= isdeitl (*plural* -au) *masculine*
with subtitles = gydag isdeitlau

suburb *noun*
= maestref (*plural* -i) *feminine*

subway *noun*
• (*British: underpass*)
= isffordd (*plural* isffyrdd) *feminine*
• (*US: underground*)
= rheilffordd danddaear(ol) (*plural*
rheilffyrdd tanddaear(ol)) *feminine*

succeed *verb*
• (*be successful*)
= llwyddo
to succeed in doing something =
llwyddo i °wneud rhywbeth
• (*follow*)
= dilyn, olynu

success *noun*
= llwyddiant (*plural* llwyddiannau)
masculine
to be a success = llwyddo, bod yn
llwyddiant

successful *adjective*
= llwyddiannus

such
1 *adjective*
= y °fath°, ffasiwn° (*precedes noun*),
felly (*follows noun*)
such a man = y °fath °ddyn
= dyn felly
such things = y °fath °bethau
= pethau felly
there's no such thing as ... = does y
°fath °beth âʰ ...
2 *adverb*
= mor°
such a big machine = peiriant mor
°fawr
such a big garden = gardd mor °fawr
such heavy books = llyfrau mor
°drwm

such a lot (of) ... = cymaint o° ...
such a little ... = cynlleied o° ...
such as (*like*) = fel; megis (*formal*)

> **!** **megis** *is very formal and does not belong to the spoken language.*

suck *verb*
= sugno

sudden *adjective*
= sydyn

suddenly *adverb*
= yn sydyn

suffer *verb*
= diodde(f)
to suffer from something = diodde(f) gan° rywbeth

sufficient *adjective*
= digonol

sugar *noun*
= siwg(w)r *masculine*

suggest *verb*
= awgrymu
to suggest something to someone = awgrymu rhywbeth i° rywun

suggestion *noun*
= awgrym (*plural* -iadau) *masculine*
to make a suggestion = gwneud awgrym

suicidal *adjective*
= hunanddinistriol

suicide *noun*
= hunanladdiad (*plural* -au) *masculine*
he committed suicide = mi °laddodd e ei hun

suit
1 *noun*
= siwt (*plural* -iau) *feminine*
2 *verb*
• (*go well with*)
= gweddu
red suits you = mae coch yn gweddu i ti
• (*be convenient*)
= bod yn °gyfleus
when it suits you = pan °fydd hi'n °gyfleus i chi

suitable *adjective*
= addas
to be suitable for something = bod yn addas i° rywbeth, gweddu i° rywbeth

suitcase *noun*
= cês dillad (*plural* cesys dillad) *masculine*

sulk *verb*
= pwdu

sultry *adjective*
(*weather*)
= mwll, trymaidd

sum *noun*
• (*of money etc*)
= swm (*plural* symiau) *masculine*
• (*total*)
= cyfanswm (*plural* cyfansymiau) *masculine*

summary *noun*
= crynodeb (*plural* -au) *masculine*

summer *noun*
= ha(f) *masculine*
in summer = yn yr ha(f)
through the summer = trwy °gydol yr ha(f)
summer holiday = gwyliau'r ha(f) *plural*

summery *adjective*
= hafaidd

summit *noun*
• (*of mountain*)
= copa (*plural* -on) *feminine or masculine*
• (*meeting*)
= uwchgyfarfod (*plural* -ydd) *masculine*

sun *noun*
= haul
the sun is rising = mae'r haul yn codi
the sun is setting = mae'r haul yn machlud
to lie in the sun = gorwedd dan yr haul

sunbathe *verb*
= torheulo

sunburn *noun*
= llosg haul *masculine*

sunburnt *adjective*
they got sunburnt = cawson nhw eu llosgi yn yr haul

Sunday *noun*
= dydd Sul, Sul
Sunday night = nos Sul
see also **Monday**

sunglasses *plural noun*
= sbectol haul *feminine*

sunshade *noun*
= cysgodlen (*plural* -ni) *feminine*

sunny *adjective*
= heulog

sunrise *noun*
= codiad yr haul
at sunrise = ar °godiad yr haul

sunset *noun*
= machlud (*plural* -au) *masculine*
at sunset = ar °fachlud yr haul

sunshine *noun*
= heulwen *feminine*
in the sunshine = yn yr heulwen
= yn llygad yr haul

suntan *noun*
= lliw haul *masculine*
to get a suntan = cael lliw haul

suntanned *adjective*
= â lliw haul

suntan oil *noun*
= olew torheulo *masculine*

super *adjective*
super! = gwych!

superior *adjective*
to be superior to something (*better*)
= rhagori ar° rywbeth, bod yn °well na^h
rhywbeth

supermarket *noun*
= archfarchnad (*plural* -oedd) *feminine*,
uwchfarchnad (*plural* -oedd) *feminine*

superstitious *adjective*
= ofergoelus

supper *noun*
= swper (*plural* -au) *masculine or
feminine*
to have supper = cael swper

supple *adjective*
= ystwyth

supply
1 *noun*
= cyflenwad (*plural* -au) *masculine*,
darpariaeth (*plural* -au) *feminine*
2 *verb*
= cyflenwi, darparu

support
1 *verb*
• (*give support to*)
= cefnogi

• (*maintain, keep*)
= cynnal (*stem* cynhali-)
2 *noun*
= cefnogaeth *feminine*

supporter *noun*
= cefnogwr (*plural* cefnogwyr)
masculine

supportive *adjective*
= cefnogol
to be supportive of something = bod
yn °gefnogol o° rywbeth
= cefnogi rhywbeth

suppose *verb*
= tybio
they'll come tomorrow, I suppose = mi
°ddôn nhw yfory, °dybiwn i
= mi °ddôn nhw yfory, mae'n °debyg
do you suppose he's gone? = wyt ti'n
meddwl efallai °fod e wedi mynd?
I suppose so = mae'n °debyg
= am °wn i

supposed *adjective*
• (*alleged*)
= tybiedig
• (*meant to*)
= i °fod i°
I was supposed to go yesterday = o'n i
i °fod i °fynd ddoe
you're not supposed to do that = dych
chi °ddim i °fod i °wneud hynny
where are we supposed to sit? = lle
dyn ni i °fod i eistedd?
he is supposed to have gone abroad =
mae e wedi mynd tramor, medden
nhw

sure *adjective*
= siŵr, sicr
to know something for sure = gwybod
rhywbeth i sicrwydd
I'm sure he went = dw i'n siŵr iddo
°fynd
are you sure? = wyt ti'n siŵr?
to make sure that ... = gwneud yn siŵr
°fod ...
he's sure to win = mae e'n siŵr o ennill

surely *adverb*
• (*supposition*)
= rhaid
surely they've gone? = rhaid bod nhw
wedi mynd
• (*certainly*)
= yn sicr

we'll surely ask = byddwn ni'n gofyn
yn sicr
= yn sicr byddwn ni'n gofyn

surf *verb*
= syrffio

surface
1 *noun*
= wyneb (*plural* -au) *masculine*, arwyneb
(*plural* -au) *masculine*
2 *verb*
= dod i'r wyneb, codi i'r wyneb

surfboard *noun*
= bwrdd syrffio (*plural* byrddau syrffio)
masculine

surgeon *noun*
= llawfeddyg (*plural* -on) *masculine*

surgery *noun*
• (*action*)
= llawfeddygaeth *feminine*,
llawdriniaeth *feminine*
• (*place*)
= meddygfa (*plural* meddygfeydd)
feminine

surgical *adjective*
= llawfeddygol

surname *noun*
= cyfenw (*plural* -au) *masculine*

surprise
1 *noun*
• (*event, being amazed*)
= syndod
to get a surprise = cael syndod, synnu
to take someone by surprise = dal
(*stem* dali-) rhywun yn annisgwyl
• (*gift, treat*)
= syrpreis (*plural* -ys) *masculine*
2 *verb*
= synnu
to be surprised = cael (eich) synnu
we were surprised by the news =
cawson ni'n synnu gan y newyddion

surprised *adjective*
to be surprised (*state*) = synnu
I'm surprised to see you = dw i'n
synnu'ch gweld chi
he was surprised when you came in =
fe °gafodd ei synnu pan °ddest ti i
mewn

surrender *verb*
= ildio; rhoi (*stem* rhoi-, rhodd-) 'r gorau
iddi

surround *verb*
= amgylchynu, cwmpasu
they were surrounded by soldiers =
roedd milwyr o'u cwmpas

surroundings *plural noun*
• (*general senses*)
= amgylchoedd *plural*
• (*of town*)
= cyffiniau *plural*

survey
1 *noun*
= arolwg (*plural* arolygon) *masculine*
2 *verb*
= arolygu

survive *verb*
= goroesi

suspect *verb*
= amau
**to suspect someone of doing
something** = amau i° rywun °wneud
rhywbeth
I suspect that he knows = dw i'n amau
°fod e'n gwybod

suspicious *adjective*
= amheus, drwgdybus
to be suspicious of someone = amau
rhywun

swallow *verb*
= llyncu

swan *noun*
= alarch (*plural* elyrch) *masculine*

swap *verb*
= cyfnewid (*stem* cyfnewidi-)
to swap something for something else
= cyfnewid rhywbeth am° rywbeth
arall
to swap places with someone = newid
(*stem* newidi-) lle â^h rhywun

swear *verb*
• (*bad language*)
= rhegi
• (*say on oath*)
= tyngu
to swear an oath = tyngu llw

swearword *noun*
= rheg (*plural* -feydd) *feminine*

sweat
1 *noun*
= chwys

2 *verb*
= chwysu

sweater *noun*
= siwmper (*plural* -i) *feminine*

sweatshirt *noun*
= crys chwys (*plural* crysau chwys)
masculine

sweep *verb*
= sgubo

sweet
1 *adjective*
• (*taste*)
= melys
• (*endearing, cute*)
= annwyl
2 *noun*
• (*confectionery*)
= losin (*plural* -s) *feminine*
• (*pudding*)
= pwdin (*plural* -au) *masculine*

sweets *plural noun*
= melysion *plural*, fferins *plural*, losin(s)
plural

swim *verb*
= nofio
to go swimming/for a swim = mynd i
nofio

swimmer *noun*
= nofiwr (*plural* nofwyr) *masculine*
= nofwraig (*plural* nofwragedd) *feminine*

swimming *noun*
= nofio *verbnoun*

swimming pool *noun*
= pwll nofio (*plural* pyllau nofio)
masculine
open air swimming pool = pwll nofio
awyr agored
indoor swimming pool = pwll nofio
dan °do

swimsuit *noun*
= gwisg nofio (*plural* gwisgoedd nofio)
feminine

swing
1 *noun*
• (*in playground*)
= siglen (*plural* -ni) *feminine*
• (*of share of votes etc*)
= gwyriad (*plural* -au) *masculine*
2 *verb*
= siglo

switch
1 *noun*
= switsh (*plural* -is) *masculine*
2 *verb*
• (*operate switch*)
= switsio
• (*exchange*)
= cyfnewid (*stem* cyfnewidi-)

switch off
= diffodd, troi (*stem* troi-, trodd-) i
ffwrdd

switch on
= rhoi (*stem* rhoi-, rhodd-) ymlaen, troi
(*stem* troi-, trodd-) ymlaen

syllable *noun*
= sillaf (*plural* -au) *feminine*

sympathetic *adjective*
= cydymdeimladol

sympathy *noun*
= cydymdeimlad (*plural* -au) *masculine*
to have sympathy for someone =
cydymdeimlo â° rhywun

synonymous *adjective*
= cyfystyr
to be synonymous with something =
bod yn °gyfystyr â° rhywbeth

syringe *noun*
= chwistrell (*plural* -au *or* -i) *feminine*

system *noun*
= cyfundrefn (*plural* -au) *feminine*,
system *or* sustem (*plural* -au) *feminine*

Tt

table *noun*
= bwrdd (*plural* byrddau) *masculine*,
bord (*plural* -ydd) *feminine* (*South*)

tablet *noun*
= tabled (*plural* -i) *feminine*
to take tablets = cymryd (*stem* cymer-)
tabledi

table tennis *noun*
= tenis bwrdd *masculine*

tackle *verb*
• (*deal with, approach*)
to tackle a problem = ymgodymu â
ᵸphroblem / problem
• (*in football, rugby etc*)
= taclo

tail *noun*
= cynffon (*plural* -au) *feminine*

take *verb*

> **!** This verb has a very wide range of
> senses and uses in English, and care
> should therefore be taken in
> identifying meaning before finding the
> Welsh equivalent.

• (*most senses*)
= cymryd (*stem* cymer-)
do you take sugar? = dych chi'n
cymryd siwgwr?
take the first street on the left =
cymerwch y stryd °gynta ar y
chwith
how long will it take? = faint o amser
°fydd hi'n cymryd/°gymryd?
it takes two hours to get there = mae'n
cymryd dwy awr i °gyrraedd yno
to take a book off a shelf = cymryd
llyfr oddiar silff
to take a taxi = cymryd tacsi, mynd
mewn tacsi
• (*take hold of*)
= cydio ynⁿ
to take someone's arm = cydio ym
ⁿmraich rhywun
• (*accompany*)
= mynd âʰ
to take the children to school = mynd
â'r plant i'r ysgol

> **!** **mynd** is irregular in the preterite,
> short future, conditional and
> imperative—see entry on the Welsh-
> English side for details.

• (*accept*)
= derbyn (*stem* derbyni-)
to take traveller's cheques = derbyn
sieciau teithio
• (*carry with one*)
= mynd âʰ
to take something to someone = mynd
âʰ rhywbeth i° rywun
• (*cope with, suffer*)
I can't take the pain = °alla i °ddim
diodde'r poen
• (*other uses*)
to take a seat = eistedd
to take an exam = gwneud / sefyll
arholiad
to take a decision = gwneud
penderfyniad, penderfynu
to take aim at something = anelu at°
rywbeth

take apart
= datod, datgymalu

take down:
to take something down (*note*) =
nodi

take hold:
to take hold of something =
cydio/gafael ynⁿ rhywbeth

take off
• (*clothes*)
= tynnu
• (*plane*)
= mynd i'r awyr

take part:
to take part in something = cymryd
(*stem* cymer-) rhan ynⁿ rhywbeth

take place
= digwydd

tale *noun*
= stori (*plural* storïau, straeon)
feminine
= hanes (*plural* -ion) *masculine*

talent *noun*
= dawn (*plural* doniau) *feminine*, talent
(*plural* -au) *feminine*

talented *adjective*
= dawnus, talentog

talk

1 *noun*
- *(rumour)*
  = sôn *verbnoun*, si *(plural* sïon)
  masculine
  there is talk that ... = mae (rhyw) sôn
  bod...
- *(conversation, address)*
  = sgwrs *(plural* sgyrsiau) *feminine*
  to have a talk with someone = cael
  sgwrs â^h rhywun
  to give a talk about something = rhoi
  sgwrs am° rywbeth
- *(plural: discussions)*
  = trafodaethau *plural*
  to have talks about something = cael
  trafodaethau am° rywbeth

2 *verb*
  = siarad
  to talk to someone = siarad â^h rhywun
  to talk on the phone = siarad ar y ffôn
  to talk about something = siarad am°
  rywbeth, sôn *(stem* soni-) am° rywbeth
  I talked to them about the trip = nes i
  siarad â nhw am y °daith
  talking of Dafydd, where is he? = sôn
  am Dafydd, lle mae e?
  talk about hypocrisy! = sôn am
  °ragrith!
  to talk nonsense = siarad lol

> **!** siarad 'talk', 'speak' *should not be*
> *confused with* **dweud** 'say', 'tell'.

talkative *adjective*
  = siaradus

tall *adjective*
- *(of people)*
  = tal
  how tall are you? = pa mor °dal wyt ti?,
  beth ydy dy °daldra?
  six foot tall = chwe throedfedd o °daldra
- *(of things)*
  = uchel

tallness *noun*
  = taldra *masculine*

tame *adjective*
  = dof

tan *noun*
  = lliw haul *masculine*

tank *noun*
  = tanc *(plural* -iau) *masculine*

tanned *adjective*
  = â lliw haul

tantamount *adjective*
  = cyfystyr
  to be tantamount to something = bod
  yn °gyfystyr â^h rhywbeth

tap

1 *noun*
  = tap *(plural* -iau) *masculine*
2 *verb*
  = tapio

tape

1 *noun*
  = tâp *(plural* tapiau) *masculine*
  sticky tape = tâp gludiog *masculine*
2 *verb*
(record)
  = tapio

tape measure *noun*
  = tâp mesur *(plural* tapiau mesur)
  masculine

tape recorder *noun*
  = recordydd tâp *(plural* recordyddion
  tâp) *masculine*

target

1 *noun*
  = targed *(plural* -au) *masculine*
2 *verb*
  = targedu

tart *noun*
- *(cake)*
  = tarten *(plural* -nau *or* -ni) *feminine*
- *(prostitute)*
  = putain *(plural* puteiniaid) *feminine*

task *noun*
  = tasg *(plural* -au) *feminine*
  to carry out a task = cyflawni tasg

taste

1 *noun*
- *(flavour)*
  = blas *masculine*
  this has an odd taste = mae blas
  rhyfedd ar hwn
- *(good taste in something)*
  = chwaeth
  bad taste = diffyg chwaeth
  she's got taste = mae hi'n chwaethus
2 *verb*
  = blasu

to taste of something = blasu o°
rywbeth
to taste something = blasu rywbeth,
cael blas ar° rywbeth

tasty adjective
= blasus

Taurus noun
= y Tarw masculine

tax noun
= treth (plural -i) feminine
council tax = treth y cyngor
income tax = treth incwm
poll tax = treth y pen
value added tax (V.A.T.) = treth ar
°werth (T.A.W.)
tax year = blwyddyn °drethi (plural
blynyddoedd trethi) feminine

taxi noun
= tacsi (plural -s) masculine

taxi rank noun
= safle tacsis (plural safleoedd tacsis)
masculine

taxpayer noun
= trethdalwr (plural trethdalwyr)
masculine

tea noun
• (drink)
= te masculine
cup of tea = panaid (o °de) feminine or
masculine
• (meal)
= swper (masculine or feminine)

teach verb
= dysgu
to teach French = dysgu Ffrangeg
to teach someone to do something =
dysgu rhywun i °wneud rhywbeth

> **!** **dysgu** also means 'learn'—where
> ambiguity could arise, 'teach...' is
> expressed as **dysgu... fel**
> **athro/athrawes**.

teacher noun
= athro (plural athrawon) masculine
= athrawes (plural -au) feminine

team noun
= tîm (plural timau) masculine

teapot noun
= tebot (plural -iau) masculine

tear[1]
noun
= deigryn (plural dagrau) masculine
to shed tears = wylo dagrau
he was in tears = roedd e yn ei
°ddagrau
she was in tears = roedd hi yn ei
dagrau

tear[2]
1 verb
= rhwygo
to tear something out of something =
torri rhywbeth allan o° rywbeth
2 noun
rhwyg (plural -iadau) feminine

tear off:
to tear something off = tynnu
rhywbeth

tear up:
to tear something up = rhwygo
rhywbeth

teaspoon noun
= llwy °de (plural llwyau te) feminine

teatime noun
= amser swper masculine

technical adjective
= technegol

technology noun
= technoleg (plural -au) feminine

teenager noun
= plentyn yn ei arddegau (plural plant
yn eu harddegau) masculine

teens plural noun
= arddegau plural

telephone noun
= ffôn (plural ffonau) masculine

telephone call noun
= galwad ffôn (plural galwadau ffôn)
masculine, caniad (plural -au) masculine

telephone directory noun
= llyfr ffôn (plural llyfrau ffôn)
masculine

telescope noun
= telesgop (plural -au) masculine

television noun
• (medium)
= teledu masculine

• (*set*)
= set °deledu (*plural* setiau teledu) *feminine*
television programme = rhaglen °deledu (*plural* rhaglenni teledu) *feminine*
on television = ar y teledu

tell *verb*
= dweud (*stem* dwed-, dywed-, wed-), deud (*stem* deud-, dud-) (*North*), gweud (*stem* gwed-) (*South*)

> **!** **dweud** 'tell', 'say' *should not be confused with* **siarad** 'speak', 'talk'.

• (*say to*)
to tell someone = dweud wrth° rywun
did you tell your parents? = wedest ti wrth dy °rieni?
to tell lies = dweud celwyddau
to tell someone about something = dweud wrth° rywun am° rywbeth, sôn (*stem* soni-) wrth° rywun am° rywbeth
to tell the time = dweud yr amser
don't tell anyone = paid dweud wrth neb

• (*give order*)
to tell someone to do something = dweud wrth° rywun am °wneud rhywbeth
I told you not to = wedes i wrthoch chi am °beidio

• (*distinguish*)
to tell the difference between... = dweud y gwahaniaeth rhwng...
to tell two things apart = gwahaniaethu rhwng dau °beth

tell off:
to tell someone off = rhoi (*stem* rhoi-, rhodd-) pryd o °dafod i° rywun

temper *noun*
= tymer *feminine*
don't lose your temper = paid colli dy °dymer
to be in a bad temper = bod mewn tymer °ddrwg

temperature *noun*
• (*general sense*)
= tymheredd (*plural* tymereddau) *masculine*
• (*fever*)
= gwres
he's got a temperature = mae gwres arno (fe)

> **!** *This expression denoting a temporary physical state uses* **ar°** + *person.*

temporary *adjective*
= dros °dro
a temporary job = swydd dros °dro

ten *numeral*
= deg, deng
ten minutes = deng munud
ten days = deng ⁿniwrnod
ten years = deng ⁿmlynedd
ten miles = deng milltir *or* deg milltir
ten books = deg o °lyfrau
ten windows = deg o ffenestri
ten years old = deng ⁿmlwydd oed
at ten o'clock = am °ddeg o'r °gloch
at ten to five = am °ddeng munud i °bump
I have ten = mae gen i °ddeg (*North*), mae deg 'da fi (*South*)

> **!** *The variant form* **deng** *appears before* **m-, ⁿm-, ⁿn-** *with time words and a few others.*

tend *verb*
= tueddu
to tend to do something = tueddu i °wneud rhywbeth
he tends to come very late = mae e'n tueddu i °ddod yn hwyr iawn

tendency *noun*
= tuedd (*plural* -iadau) *feminine*
to have a tendency to do something = tueddu i °wneud rhywbeth

tennis *noun*
= tenis *masculine*

tennis ball *noun*
= pêl °denis (*plural* peli tenis) *feminine*

tennis court *noun*
= cwrt tenis (*plural* cyrtiau tenis) *masculine*

tennis racket *noun*
= raced °denis (*plural* racedi tenis) *feminine*

tense *adjective*
= tyn

tension *noun*
= tyndra *masculine*

tent *noun*
= pabell (*plural* pebyll) *feminine*

tenth *adjective*
= degfed

> **!** **degfed** *precedes the noun it refers to.*

the tenth book = y degfed llyfr *masculine*
the tenth desk = y ᵒddegfed ᵒddesg *feminine*

term *noun*
• (*of school etc*)
= tymor (*plural* tymhorau) *masculine*
• (*period*)
= cyfnod (*plural* -au) *masculine*
short term = cyfnod byr
in the short term = am y tro
long term = cyfnod hir
long-term implications = goblygiadau cyfnod hir
in the long term = yn y tymor hir, yn y pendraw
• (*plural: conditions*)
= amodau *plural*
in terms of ... = yn ⁿnhermau...
to come to terms with something = dod i ᵒdelerau âʰ rhywbeth
• (*plural: payment arrangements*)
= telerau *plural*

terrible *adjective*
= ofnadwy

terribly *adverb*
terribly heavy = trwm ofnadwy, trwm uffernol, ofnadwy o ᵒdrwm, uffernol o ᵒdrwm

terrified *adjective*
to be terrified of something = dychryn rhag rhywbeth

terror *noun*
= arswyd *masculine*

terrorism *noun*
= terfysgaeth *feminine*

terrorist *noun*
= terfysgwr (*plural* terfysgwyr) *masculine*

test
1 *noun*
= prawf (*plural* profion) *masculine*
driving test = prawf gyrru (*plural* profion gyrru) *masculine*

eye test = prawf llygaid (*plural* profion llygaid) *masculine*
2 *verb*
= profi
to test someone's patience = trethu amynedd rhywun

testify *verb*
= tystio

text *noun*
= testun (*plural* -au) *masculine*

textbook *noun*
= gwerslyfr (*plural* -au) *masculine*

than
1 *preposition*
= naʰ, nag (*before vowels*)
to be stronger than a horse = bod yn ᵒgryfach na ʰcheffyl
more valuable than gold = mwy gwerthfawr nag aur
2 *conjunction*
= nag, nag y ...
she's younger than I thought = mae hi'n iau nag o'n i'n ᵒfeddwl
he's quicker than I would be = mae e'n ᵒgyflymach nag y byddwn i

thank *verb*
= diolch
to thank someone for doing something = diolch iᵒ rywun am ᵒwneud rhywbeth
thank you = diolch (i ti/chi)
thank you very much = diolch yn ᵒfawr (iawn) (i ti/chi)
thank you for your help = diolch am eich cymorth

thankful *adjective*
= diolchgar

thanks *plural noun*
= diolch
many thanks = llawer o ᵒddiolch
heartfelt thanks = diolch o ᵒgalon
thanks for the coffee = diolch am y coffi

that

> **!** *This word has a very wide range of senses and uses in English, and care should therefore be taken in identifying meaning before finding the Welsh equivalent.*

1 *adjective*

> **!** *In the living language 'that...' is expressed not by an adjective as in English but by placing the word for 'the' before the noun and* **'na** *after it. The literary and formal language uses a different method that is not part of everyday usage.*

= y ... 'na

= y ... hwnnw *masculine* (*formal*), y ... honno *feminine* (*formal*)

that boy = y bachgen 'na (*formal*: y bachgen hwnnw)

that girl = y °ferch 'na (*formal*: y °ferch honno)

that shirt is dearer = mae'r crys 'na'n °ddrutach (*formal*: y crys hwnnw)

2 *pronoun*

- (*most senses*)
  = hwnna *or* hwnnw *masculine*
  = honna *or* honno *feminine*
  = hynny (*abstract or non-concrete*)

> **!** *Unlike the situation with the adjective 'that' above, these pronouns are appropriate for all styles of the written and spoken language.*

what is that? = beth ydy hwnna?
who is that? = pwy ydy hwnna?
= pwy ydy honna?
that is disgraceful = mae hynny'n °warthus
like that = fel hynny, fel 'ny, fel 'na
after that = wedi hynny, wedi 'ny
that is (i.e.) = hynny yw (h.y.)

- (*in pointing out*)
  = dyna°, 'na°
  that is the manager = dyna'r rheolwr
  that's kind! = 'na °garedig!

- (*used as relative pronoun: which, who*)
  = (a)°
  the letter that came yesterday = y llythyr (a) °ddaeth ddoe
  = sy(dd)
  the man that lives next door = y dyn sy'n byw drws nesa
  = y
  the books that I brought = y llyfrau (y) des i â nhw
  the house that we will live in = y tŷ y byddwn ni'n byw ynddo

3 *conjunction*

> **!** *The conjunction 'that' (introducing clauses) has a number of different forms in Welsh, depending on what type of word starts the clause. See entries on the Welsh-English side for further information.*

- (*with present tense verb 'to be'*)
  = bod/°fod/ⁿmod *etc*
  I'm sorry that I'm late = mae'n °ddrwg gen i ⁿmod i'n hwyr
  I think that he's ill = dw i'n meddwl °fod e'n sâl

- (*with other verb forms*)
  = y
  I think we'll be late = dw i'n meddwl y byddwn ni'n hwyr
  I think that we should go = dw i'n meddwl y dylen ni °fynd

- (*past tense*)
  = i°
  I'm sure they went this morning = dw i'n siwr iddyn nhw °fynd bore 'ma, dw i'n siwr bod nhw wedi mynd bore 'ma

- (*focused clauses*)
  = mai, taw, na
  I think that you are right = dw i'n meddwl mai (/taw/na) ti sy'n iawn

- (*that ... not ...*)
  = naʰ/°, nad (*before original vowels*)
  I hope that he's not here = gobeithio °fod e °ddim yma, gobeithio nad ydy e yma
  I hope that we won't be late = gobeithio na °fyddwn ni'n hwyr
  I'm sure that we shouldn't go = dw i'n siwr na °ddylen ni °fynd

- (*that ... not ...—focused*)
  = nad, mai nid
  I'm sure that he's not responsible = dw i'n siwr nad (*or* mai nid) fe sy'n °gyfrifol

thaw *verb*
= toddi

the *definite article*

> **!** *The word for 'the' in Welsh varies depending solely on what type of letter/sound is next to it.*

= y (*before consonants*)
= yr (*before vowels and* h-)

= 'r (*after vowels—takes precedence over other two options*)
the shop = y siop
to the shop = i'r siop
the museum = yr amgueddfa
to the museum = i'r amgueddfa

! Although the words for 'the' do not themselves vary for gender, feminine singular nouns undergo soft mutation after them:
the son (mab) = y mab
the daughter (merch) = y °ferch
the sons = y meibion
the daughters = y merched

---

theatre *noun*
= theatr (*plural* -au) *feminine*

their *adjective*
= eu ... (nhw) (*no mutation, but prefixes h- to vowels*)
their car = eu car nhw
their school = eu hysgol nhw
to their ... = i'w ... (nhw)
to their car = i'w car nhw
to their school = i'w hysgol nhw

! The 'echoing' pronoun **nhw** is optional but usual.

---

theirs *pronoun*
this is theirs = nhw (sy) biau hwn
our car is big but theirs is small = mae'n car ni'n °fawr ond mae un nhw'n °fach

them *pronoun*
• (*object pronoun*)
= nhw, nhwthau
I haven't seen them = dw i heb °weld nhw
we'll go with them = awn ni gyda nhw
do you know them? = dych chi'n nabod nhw?
will you help them? = newch chi helpu nhw?
• = eu...(nhw) (*as object of verbnoun*)
do you want to see them? = dych chi eisiau eu gweld nhw?
what about supporting them? = beth am eu cefnogi (nhw)?
• (*to them*)
= iddyn nhw, atyn nhw
give them the message = rhowch y neges iddyn nhw

did you show them the map? = nest ti °ddangos y map iddyn nhw?
I wrote them a letter = nes i sgrifennu atyn nhw
• (*with* ill)
the two of them/both of them = ill dau/dwy
the three of them = ill tri

theme *noun*
= thema (*plural* themâu) *feminine*

themselves *pronoun*
= eu hun (*North*), eu hunain (*South*)
they didn't hurt themselves = naethon nhw °ddim brifo eu hun(ain)
they told me themselves = wedon nhw wrtha i eu hun(ain)
by themselves (*on their own*) = ar °ben eu hun(ain), ar eu pennau eu hunain (*formal*)

then *adverb*
• (*at that time*)
= °bryd hynny, °bryd 'ny
I was living in Cardiff then = o'n i'n byw yng ⁿNghaerdydd °bryd 'ny
• (*after, next*)
= wedyn, yna (*can only start sentence or phrase*)
then I came back = wedyn/yna fe °ddes i yn ôl
what did you do then? = be' nest ti wedyn?
and then ... = ac wedyn...
now and then = o °bryd i'w gilydd
then again, perhaps he's right = eto i gyd, efallai °fod e'n iawn
• (*in that case*)
= yna (*starts sentence*), felly
then you should have said
you should have said, then = yna dylet ti °fod wedi dweud
= dylet ti °fod wedi dweud, felly
• (*tag*)
= 'te, 'ta (*North*), felly
alright, then = iawn, 'te
what happened to you, then? = be' °ddigwyddodd i ti, 'te?
now, then = nawr 'te, rwan 'ta
are you goint, then? = wyt ti'n mynd, 'te?
= wyt ti'n mynd, felly?

therapist *noun*
= therapydd (*plural* -ion) *masculine*

therapy *noun*
= therapi (*plural* therapïau) *masculine*
speech therapy = therapi lleferydd

there *adverb*
• (*general location*)
= yna, fan'na, 'na
who lives there? = pwy sy'n byw yna/fan'na?
who's there? = pwy sy 'na?
• (*in the distance*)
= acw, fan acw, fan'cw
they live there = maen nhw'n byw acw/fan acw/fan'cw
• (*out of sight*)
= yno
I've got family there = mae gen i °deulu yno (*North*), mae teulu 'da fi yno (*South*)
• (*in pointing out*)
= dyna°, dacw°, 'co° (*South*)
there's the bus = dyna'r bws
there's Snowdon = dacw'r Wyddfa
there are the children = dyna'r plant, dacw'r plant
• **there is, there are**
not translated or = 'na°
there is cheese in the fridge = mae caws yn yr oergell, mae 'na °gaws yn yr oergell
there are too many people here = mae gormod o °bobol fan hyn, mae 'na °ormod o °bobol fan hyn

therefore *adverb*
= felly, o °ganlyniad

thermometer *noun*
= thermomedr (*plural* -au) *masculine*

these
1 *adjective*
= y ... 'ma, y ... hyn (*formal*)

> **!** *In the living language* 'these...' *is expressed not by an adjective as in English but by placing the word for* 'the' *before the noun and* **'ma** *after it. The literary and formal language uses a different method that is not part of everyday usage.*

these books = y llyfrau 'ma (*formal:* y llyfrau hyn)
these desks = y desgiau 'ma (*formal:* y desgiau hyn)

2 *pronoun*
• (*general use*)
= (y) rhain
what about these? = beth am y rhain?
how much are these? = faint ydy'r rhain?
these are expensive = mae'r rhain yn °ddrud
(*but:* **these things are expensive** = mae'r pethau 'ma'n °ddrud)
• (*in pointing out*)
= dyma°
these are the children = dyma'r plant

they *pronoun*
= nhw, nhwthau
they're coming next week = maen nhw'n dod wythnos nesa
they arrived yesterday = fe °gyrhaeddon nhw ddoe, naethon nhw °gyrraedd ddoe
they will come tomorrow = fe °ddôn nhw yfory
there they are! = dyna/dacw nhw!
they didn't write the letter = dim nhw sgrifennodd y llythyr

> **!** *For details on the expanded form* **nhwthau**, *see entry on the Welsh-English side.*

thick *adjective*
• (*general senses*)
= trwchus, tew
• (*liquid*)
= tew
• (*stupid*)
= twp

thief *noun*
= lleidr (*plural* lladron) *masculine*

thieve *verb*
= lladrata

thigh *noun*
= clun (*plural* -iau) *feminine*

thin *adjective*
= tenau, main
to get thin = mynd yn °denau

thing *noun*
= peth (*plural* -au) *masculine*
I've got things to do = mae gen i °bethau i'w gwneud
can I leave my things here? = °ga i °adael ⁿmhethau fan hyn?
the thing is, ... = y peth ydy, ...

not a thing = dim (byd)
I can't hear a thing = dw i'n clwyed dim

think *verb*
• (*have an opinion*)
= meddwl (*stem* meddyli-), credu (*South*)
what do you think about it? = beth
dych chi'n ᵒfeddwl amdani?
I think it's unfair = dw i'n meddwl bod
hi ᵒddim yn ᵒdeg
'will they come?'—'I don't think so' =
'ᵒddôn nhw?'—'dw i ᵒddim yn meddwl'
• (*reflect*)
= meddwl (*stem* meddyli-)
think before answering = meddyliwch
cyn ateb
to think of someone = meddwl amᵒ
rywun
to think about doing something =
meddwl am ᵒwneud rhywbeth
to think again (*have second thoughts*) =
ailfeddwl

> **!** *When quoting someone's thought,
> the preterite* **meddyliodd** *is used, but
> generally 'thought' is translated by the
> imperfect. Compare:*
> **'It's too late,' thought Aled** = 'Mae'n
> rhy hwyr,' meddyliodd Aled
> **he thought that Wales won
> yesterday** = roedd e'n meddwl mai
> Cymru erillodd ddoe

• (*remember*)
= cofio
I can't think of his name = dw i ᵒddim
yn cofio ei enw

third
1 *adjective*
= trydydd (*masculine*), trydedd
(*feminine*)

> **!** **trydydd, trydedd** *precedes the
> noun it refers to.*

the third man = y trydydd dyn
masculine
the third station = y ᵒdrydedd ᵒorsaf
feminine
he came third = daeth e'n ᵒdrydydd
she came third = daeth hi'n ᵒdrydedd
2 *noun*
(*fraction*)
= traean (*plural* -au) *masculine*

thirst *noun*
= syched *masculine*
to quench one's thirst = torri syched

thirsty *adjective*
I'm thirsty = mae syched arna i
are you thirsty? = oes syched arnat ti?

> **!** *This expression denoting a
> temporary physical state uses* **arᵒ** +
> *person.*

thirteen *numeral*
= triarddeg *or* undeg tri *masculine*
= tairarddeg *or* undeg tair *feminine*
thirteen horses = tri ʰcheffyl ar
ᵒddeg, undeg tri o ᵒgeffylau
thirteen cats = tair cath ar ᵒddeg,
undeg tair o ᵒgathod
thirteen years = tair blynedd ar ᵒddeg,
undeg tair o ᵒflynyddoedd
thirteen years old = tair blwydd ar
ᵒddeg oed

thirteenth *adjective*
= trydydd ar ᵒddeg *masculine*
= trydedd ar ᵒddeg *feminine*

> **!** *The artificial forms* **undeg trydydd,
> undeg trydedd** *are also
> encountered.*

thirty *numeral*
= trideg
thirty apples = trideg o afalau

this
1 *adjective*
= y ... 'ma
= y ... hwn *masculine*, y ... hon *feminine*
(*formal*)

> **!** *In the living language 'this...' is
> expressed not by an adjective as in
> English but by placing the word for
> 'the' before the noun and* **'ma** *after it.
> The literary and formal language uses
> a different method that is not part of
> everyday usage.*

this boy = y bachgen 'ma (*formal:* y
bachgen hwn)
this girl = y ᵒferch 'ma (*formal:* y ᵒferch
hon)
this shirt is dearer = mae'r crys 'ma'n
ᵒddrutach (*formal:* y crys hwn)
2 *pronoun*
• (*general use*)
= hwn *masculine*
= hon *feminine*
= hyn (*abstract or non-concrete*)

> ❗ *Unlike the situation with the adjective 'this' above, these pronouns are appropriate for all styles of the written and spoken language.*

what is this? = beth ydy hwn?
who is this? = pwy ydy hwn?, pwy ydy hon?
how much is this? = faint ydy hwn?, faint ydy hon?
this is disgraceful = mae hyn yn °warthus
is this a problem for you? = ydy hyn yn °broblem i chi?
like this = fel hyn
all this = hyn oll
• (*in pointing out*)
  = dyma°, 'ma°
  this is the town centre = dyma °ganol y °dre
  this is my wife = dyma ⁿngwraig

thorn *noun*
= draenen (*plural* drain) *feminine*

thorough *adjective*
= trylwyr, trwyadl

those

1 *adjective*
= y ... 'na
= y ... hynny (*formal*)

> ❗ *In the living language 'those...' is expressed not by an adjective as in English but by placing the word for 'the' before the noun and* **'na** *after it. The literary and formal language uses a different method that is not part of everyday usage.*

those books = y llyfrau 'na (*formal:* y llyfrau hynny)
those desks = y desgiau 'na (*formal:* y desgiau hynny)
those things are expensive = mae'r pethau 'na'n °ddrud
2 *pronoun*
• (*general use*)
  = (y) rheina, (y) rheiny
  what about those? = beth am y rheina?
  how much are those? = faint ydy'r rheina?
  those are expensive = mae'r rheina'n °ddrud
• (*in pointing out*)
  = dyna°
  those are the children = dyna'r plant

though

1 *conjunction*
• (*general sense*)
  = er

> ❗ **er** *is followed by a 'that ...' clause in the present and future, but by* **i°** + *subject* + °*verbnoun in the past.*

though he is ill = er °fod e'n sâl
though he won't be here = er na °fydd e fan hyn
though I told him = er i mi °ddweud wrtho
• **as though** (*as if*)
  = fel (+ *conditional*)
  as though he were still here = fel tasai fe yma o hyd
2 *adverb*
(*however*)
= er hynny, serch hynny
he won't agree, though = er hynny °fydd e °ddim yn cytuno

thought *noun*
• (*faculty*)
  = meddwl (*plural* meddyliau) *masculine*
• (*idea*)
  = syniad (*plural* -au) *masculine*
• (*intention*)
  = bwriad (*plural* -au) *masculine*

thoughtful *adjective*
• (*reflective*)
  = meddylgar
• (*considerate*)
  = ystyriol
  to be thoughtful of someone = ystyried rhywun, bod yn ystyriol o° rywun

thousand *numeral*
= mil (*plural* -oedd) *feminine*
two thousand pounds = dwy °fil o °bunnoedd
thousands and thousands = miloedd ar °filoedd
about a thousand people = tua mil o °bobol
a hundred thousand = can mil

> ❗ **mil** *and its multiples always require* **o°** + *plural noun.*

thread *noun*
= edau (*plural* edafedd) *feminine*

threat *noun*
= bygythiad (*plural* -au) *masculine*

there is a threat of rain = mae'n bygwth glaw

threaten *verb*
= bygwth (*stem* bygyth-)
to threaten someone with something = bygwth rhywun â'h rhywbeth

threatening *adjective*
= bygythiol

three *numeral*
= tri'h *masculine*, tair *feminine*

> **!** *The aspirate mutation after* **tri** *(as elsewhere) is not consistently applied except on words beginning with* **c-**. *Note that there is no mutation of any kind after the feminine* **tair**.

three brothers = tri brawd
three sisters = tair chwaer
three days = tridiau
we were there for three days = oedden ni yno am °dridiau
the three of them = ill tri
= ill tair
three years = tair blynedd
three years old = tair blwydd oed
at three o'clock = am °dri o'r °gloch
I have three = mae gen i °dri/°dair (*North*), mae tri/tair 'da fi (*South*)

threshold *noun*
= trothwy (*plural* -au) *masculine*
on the threshold of something = ar °drothwy rhywbeth

throat *noun*
= gwddf (*plural* gyddfau) *masculine*
sore throat = gwddf tost

through
1 *preposition*
= drwy°, trwy°

> **!** *drwy°* *is more common in speech,* **trwy°** *in writing.*

to see through the fog = gweld drwy'r niwl
to look through the window = edrych drwy'r ffenest
right through the day = drwy gydol y dydd
all through the night = ar hyd y nos
open April through September = ar agor o °fis Ebrill tan/hyd °fis Medi
2 *adverb*
= drwodd

to come through = dod drwodd
to push something through = gwthio rhywbeth drwodd

throughout *preposition*
= drwy°, trwy°

> **!** *drwy°* *is more common in speech,* **trwy°** *in writing.*

= drwy/trwy gydol (*time only*)
= ledled (*space only*)
throughout the year = drwy'r °flwyddyn, drwy gydol y °flwyddyn
throughout the country = drwy'r °wlad, ledled y °wlad

throw *verb*
= taflu; taflyd (*stem* tafl-) (*used in some areas*)
to throw something at someone = taflu rhywbeth at° rywun

throw away
to throw something away = taflu rhywbeth

throw out
to throw something out = taflu rhywbeth
to throw someone out = taflu rhywun allan/mas

throw up
(*be sick*)
= chwydu

thumb *noun*
= bawd (*plural* bodiau) *feminine or masculine*

thump
1 *verb*
= (*punch*) pwnio
2 *noun*
= cnoc (*plural* -iau) *feminine*, dyrnod (*plural* -iau) *masculine or feminine*

thunder *noun*
= taranau *plural*
thunder and lightning = mellt a 'htharanau

thunderstorm *noun*
= storm °fellt a 'htharanau (*plural* stormydd mellt a 'htharanau) *feminine*

Thursday *noun*
= dydd Iau, Iau
Thursday night = nos Iau
see also **Monday**

ticket *noun*
 = tocyn (*plural* -nau) *masculine*, ticed
 (*plural* -i) *masculine*
 season ticket = tocyn tymor (*plural*
 tocynnau tymor) *masculine*
 one-way ticket = tocyn unffordd (*plural*
 tocynnau unffordd) *masculine*
 return ticket = tocyn dwyffordd (*plural*
 tocynnau dwyffordd) *masculine*

tickle *verb*
 = cosi

tide *noun*
 = llanw (*plural* -au) *masculine*
 high tide = penllanw *masculine*
 low tide = trai *masculine*

tidy
1 *adjective*
• (*room, desk*)
 = taclus, twt
 to keep something tidy = cadw
 rhywbeth yn °daclus
• (*person*)
 = taclus
2 *verb*
 = tacluso
 to tidy (up) a room = tacluso stafell

tie
1 *noun*
• (*item of clothing*)
 = tei (*plural* -s) *masculine or feminine*
• (*in sport: draw*)
 = gêm °gyfartal *feminine*
2 *verb*
 = clymu
 to tie something to something = clymu
 rhywbeth wrth° rywbeth
 to tie a dog to a tree = clymu ci wrth
 °goeden
tie up
 to tie up a parcel = clymu parsel
 to tie someone up = clymu rhywun

tiger *noun*
 = teigr (*plural* -od) *masculine*

tight *adjective*
 = tyn, sownd

tights *plural noun*
 = trywsanau *plural*

tile *noun*
 = teilsen *or* teilen (*plural* teils) *feminine*

till¹
1 *preposition*
 = tan°; hyd° (*especially with specific
 times*)
 till Christmas = tan (y) Nadolig
 till tomorrow! = tan yfory!
 till next week! = tan wythnos nesa!
 from morning till night = o °fore tan nos
 from nine o'clock till five = o naw o'r
 °gloch hyd °bump
 till now = hyd yma, hyd yn hyn
 till then = tan hynny, hyd hynny
2 *conjunction*
• (*present/future reference*)
 = nes

 > **!** **nes** *can be followed either by a 'that
 ...' clause or by* **i°** + *subject* +
 °*verbnoun when reference is to the
 present or future.*

 till they come back = nes bod nhw'n
 dod yn ôl, nes iddyn nhw °ddod yn ôl
 till it's ready = nes bod hi'n °barod, nes
 (y) bydd hi'n °barod
 till we arrive = nes bod ni'n cyrraedd,
 nes inni °gyrraedd
• (*past reference*)
 = nes

 > **!** *When reference is to the past,* **nes** *is
 used with* **i°** + *subject* + °*verbnoun.*

 till we arrived = nes inni °gyrraedd

till² *noun*
 = til (*plural* -iau, -s) *masculine*

timber *noun*
 = coed *masculine*, pren *masculine*

time *noun*

 > **!** *There are a number of Welsh
 equivalents for the various senses
 and uses of this word—see entries on
 the Welsh-English side for more
 examples.*

• (*general*)
 = amser (*plural* -au) *masculine*
 we haven't got time = does gynnon ni
 °ddim amser (*North*), does dim amser
 'da ni (*South*)
 I haven't seen him for some time = dw
 i heb °weld e ers amser
 a long time ago = amser maith yn ôl
 all the time = trwy'r amser
• (*period*)

Telling the Time

Welsh sees time as a clock face, not digitally:

2.00	**dau o'r °gloch**
2.05	**pum munud wedi dau**
2.10	**deng munud wedi dau**
2.15	**chwarter wedi dau**
2.20	**ugain munud wedi dau**
2.25	**pum munud ar hugain wedi dau**
2.30	**hanner awr wedi dau**
2.35	**pum munud ar hugain i °dri**
2.40	**ugain munud i °dri**
2.45	**chwarter i °dri**
2.50	**deng munud i °dri**
2.55	**pum munud i °dri**

Notice that the word **munud** must be included when the number of minutes is stated; and that the word **awr** must be included in 'half past ...'. Also that **i°** 'to' causes soft mutation, while **wedi** 'past' does not.

To ask the time, use:
Faint o'r °gloch ydy hi? (*North*)
Faint o'r °gloch yw hi? (*South*)

To say what the time is, use:
mae'n° ...   *it's ...*
mae'n °ddeng munud i °bedwar = *it's ten to four*
mae hi bron yn° ...   *it's almost ...*
mae hi bron yn °bum munud i °ddau = *it's almost five to two*
mae'n tynnu at° ...   *it's getting on for ...*
mae'n tynnu at chwarter i saith = *it's getting on for a quarter to seven*
mae hi newydd °droi ... = *it's just turned ...*
mae hi newydd °droi pump o'r °gloch = *it's just turned five o'clock*

You may also need:
erbyn = *by*
cyn = *before*
ar ôl = *after*

= adeg (*plural* -au) *feminine*, cyfnod (*plural* -au) *masculine*
at the time of the strike = adeg y streic
the time of the Renaissance = cyfnod y Dadeni
• (*point in time*)
= pryd (*plural* -iau) *masculine*
at the time = ar y pryd
at that time = °bryd hynny
at the same time = ar yr un pryd
from time to time = o °bryd i'w gilydd
at times = ar °brydiau
= ar adegau
it's time we went = mae'n °bryd inni °fynd
to arrive on time = cyrraedd mewn pryd
= cyrraedd yn °brydlon
by the time you leave = erbyn i chi °adael
by the time we arrived = erbyn inni °gyrraedd
• (*number of times*)
= gwaith (*plural* gweithiau) *feminine*
three times = °dairgwaith
a hundred times = cant o °weithiau

three times as big as ... = tairgwaith cymaint â^h ...
how many times? = sawlgwaith?, faint o °weithiau?
• (*sequence*)
= tro (*plural* -eon) *masculine*
the first time = y tro cynta(f)
the second time = yr ail °dro
the third time = y trydydd tro
this is the first time I've been here = dyma'r tro cynta i mi °fod yma
several times = °droeon
this time = (y) tro 'ma
that time = (y) tro 'na
for the time being = am y tro
every time = °bob tro
time and time again = °dro ar ôl tro
• (*other uses*)
in a short time = ymhen ychydig
= cyn (bo) hir
in a week's time = ymhen wythnos
what's the time? = faint o'r °gloch ydy hi?

timetable *noun*
= amserlen (*plural* -ni) *feminine*

tin *noun*
- (*container*)
  = tun (*plural* -iau) *masculine*
  a tin of baked beans = tun o ffa pob
- (*metal*)
  = tun *masculine*

tin-opener *noun*
  = agorwr tuniau (*plural* agorwyr tuniau) *masculine*

tiny *adjective*
  = bychan (*feminine* bechan), mân

tip
1 *noun*
- (*advice*)
  = cyngor (*plural* cynghorion) *masculine*
- (*pile, dump*)
  = tomen (*plural* -ni, -nydd) *feminine*
- (*money*)
  = cildwrn (*plural* cildyrnau) *masculine*
- (*point*)
  = blaen (*plural* -au) *masculine*
2 *verb*
  = tywalltu (*North*), arllwys (*South*), dymchwel

tire *verb*
  = blino

tired *adjective*
  = wedi blino, blinedig

> **!** *These two terms both mean 'tired', but only* **blinedig** *can be used with qualifying words like* **iawn** *'very',* **braidd** *'rather' etc.*

to be tired = bod wedi blino
  = bod yn °flinedig
to be very tired = bod yn °flinedig iawn
to be rather tired = bod braidd yn °flinedig
to get tired of doing something = diflasu ar °wneud rhywbeth
I'm tired of doing this = dw i wedi diflasu ar °wneud hyn

tiresome *adjective*
  = diflas

tiring *adjective*
  = blinedig

tissue *noun*
(*paper handkerchief*)
  = hances °bapur (*plural* hancesi papur) *feminine*

title *noun*
  = teitl (*plural* -au) *masculine*

to *preposition*
- (*many general senses*)
  = i°
  to go to France = mynd i Ffrainc
  to go to school = mynd i'r ysgol
  to give something to someone = rhoi rhywbeth i° rywun
  to show something to someone = dangos rhywbeth i° rywun
  to ask someone to lunch = gwahodd rhywun i °ginio
- (*in telling the time*)
  = i°
  it's twenty to four = mae'n ugain munud i °bedwar
- (*writing or sending things to people*)
  = at°
  will you write to me? = nei di sgrifennu ata i?
  to send a letter to someone = danfon llythyr at° rywun
- (*with certain verbs and adjectives*)
  = wrth°
  to say something to someone = dweud rhywbeth wrth° rywun
  (*but:* **to talk to someone** = siarad âʰ rhywun)
  to be kind to someone = bod yn °garedig wrth° rywun
- (*towards*)
  = tuaʰ
  to look to the east = edrych tua'r dwyrain
- (*as part of English infinitive: purpose*)
  = i°
  we've come to see the doctor = dyn ni wedi dod i °weld y meddyg
- (*in order to*)
  = er mwyn
  I've done this to make things easier = dw i wedi gwneud hyn er mwyn gwneud pethau'n haws
- (*as part of English infinitive: instruction*)
  = am°
  to ask someone to do something = gofyn i °rywun am °wneud rhywbeth
  to tell someone to do something = dweud wrth° rywun am °wneud rhywbeth
- (*as part of English infinitive: verbnoun alone*)
  I want to go = dw i eisiau mynd

they ought to wait = dylen nhw aros
they have to go = rhaid iddyn nhw
°fynd
are you able to see? = dych chi'n gallu
gweld?
I hope to see you = gobeithio'ch gweld
chi
to try to do something = ceisio gwneud
rhywbeth
it's hard to understand why = mae'n
anodd deall pam

toad noun
= llyffant (*plural* -od, llyffaint) *masculine*

> ! **llyfant** *is often used indiscriminately*
> *for* 'frog' *as well as* 'toad'.

toadstool noun
= caws llyffant *masculine*

toast
1 *noun*
• (*food*)
= tost *masculine*
• (*speech*)
= llwncdestun (*plural* -au) *masculine*
2 *verb*
• (*bread*)
= tostio
• (*drink to someone's health*)
= yfed iechyd rhywun

toaster noun
= tostiwr (*plural* tostwyr) *masculine*

today adverb
= heddiw
till today = hyd heddiw
today week = wythnos i heddiw

toe noun
= bys troed (*plural* bysedd troed/traed)
masculine

toffee noun
= toffi *masculine*

together adverb
(*referring to* 'them')
= gyda'i gilydd, efo'i gilydd (*North*)
(*referring to* 'you')
= gyda'ch gilydd, efo'ch gilydd (*North*)
(*referring to* 'us')
= gyda'n gilydd, efo'n gilydd (*North*)
they left together = naethon nhw
°adael gyda'i gilydd, naethon nhw
°adael efo'i gilydd

sit together! = eisteddwch gyda'ch
gilydd!
= eisteddwch efo'ch gilydd!
let's go together = awn ni gyda'n
gilydd
= awn ni efo'n gilydd
together with = ynghyd â[h]

toil
1 *noun*
= llafur *masculine*
2 *verb*
= llafurio

toilet noun
= tŷ bach (*plural* tai bach) *masculine*, lle
chwech (*plural* llefydd chwech)
masculine (*North*)
= toiled (*plural* -au, -i) *masculine* (*formal*)
I want to go to the toilet = dw i eisiau
mynd i'r tŷ bach
is the toilet free? = ydy'r tŷ bach yn
rhydd?

toilet paper noun
= papur toiled *masculine*

tomato noun
= tomato (*plural* -s) *masculine*

tomorrow adverb
= yfory, fory
see you tomorrow! = wela i di/chi
yfory!
till tomorrow! = tan yfory!
tomorrow morning = bore fory
tomorrow afternoon = prynhawn yfory
tomorrow evening/night = nos yfory
the day after tomorrow = °drennydd

ton noun
= tunnell (*plural* tunelli) *feminine*
it weighs a ton! = mae'n pwyso
tunnell!

tone noun
= tôn (*plural* tonau) *feminine*

tongue noun
= tafod (*plural* -au) *masculine*
to stick out one's tongue = rhoi (*stem*
rhoi-, rhodd-) 'ch tafod allan
hold your tongue! = taw!

tonight adverb
= heno

> ! **heno** *is also the normal word for*
> 'this evening'.

too *adverb*
- *(also)*
  = hefyd
  I'll come too = mi °ddo i hefyd
- *(in addition)*
  = hefyd, yn ogystal
  we bought some books too = fe °brynon ni °lyfrau hefyd, fe °brynon ni °lyfrau'n ogystal
- *(more than necessary)*
  = rhy°
  too big = rhy °fawr
  these are too small for me = mae'r rhain yn rhy °fach i mi
  too much = gormod
  too much money = gormod o arian
  this is too much for me = mae hyn yn °ormod i mi
  too many = gormod
  too many people = gormod o °bobol
  to drink too much = goryfed
  to eat too much = gorfwyta
  to work too much = gorweithio

tool *noun*
  = offeryn (*plural* offer) *masculine*, teclyn (*plural* taclau) *masculine*

tooth *noun*
  = dant (*plural* dannedd) *masculine*
  false teeth = dannedd gosod

toothache *noun*
  = y °ddannoedd
  she's got toothache = mae'r ddannoedd arni (hi)

> ! This expression denoting a temporary physical state uses **ar°** + person.

toothbrush *noun*
  = brws dannedd (*plural* brwsys *or* brwsiau dannedd) *masculine*

toothpaste *noun*
  = pâst dannedd *masculine*

top
1 *adjective*
  = ucha(f)
  the top class = y dosbarth ucha
2 *noun*
- *(general senses)*
  = top (*plural* -iau) *masculine*, pen (*plural* -nau) *masculine*
- *(summit)*
  = copa (*plural* -on) *masculine or feminine*, top (*plural* -iau) *masculine*, pen (*plural* -nau) *masculine*
  the top of the hill = pen y bryn
  the top of the mountain = copa'r mynydd
  full to the top = llawn °dop
  at the top of the page = ar °dop y tudalen
  on top of everything else = ar °ben popeth arall
  to get to the top = cyrraedd (*stem* cyrhaedd-) y brig
  to be at the top of the class = bod ar °ben y dosbarth
- *(lid)*
  = caead (*plural* -au) *masculine*

topic *noun*
  = pwnc (*plural* pynciau) *masculine*
  = pwnc trafod (*plural* pynciau trafod) *masculine*

torch *noun*
  = tortsh (*plural* -is) *masculine*

torn *adjective*
  = wedi rhwygo, rhwygedig

tortoise *noun*
  = crwban (*plural* -od) *masculine*

total
1 *adjective*
- *(whole)*
  = cyfan, holl° (*precedes noun*)
- *(complete)*
  = llwyr
2 *noun*
  = cyfanswm (*plural* cyfamsymiau) *masculine*

totally *adverb*
  = yn llwyr, yn °gyfangwb(w)l (*qualifying an adjective*)
  = cwb(w)l°, hollol°
  totally unnecessary = cwbwl °ddiangen

touch *verb*
  = cyffwrdd (*stem* cyffyrdd-)
  to touch something = cyffwrdd â^h rhywbeth
  to get in touch with someone = cysylltu â^h rhywun
  to stay/keep in touch with someone = aros (*stem* arhos-) mewn cyswllt â^h rhywun

touchy *adjective*
= pigog

tough *adjective*
- (*hard, unyielding*)
  = gwydn, caled, garw
- (*severe*)
  = llym, caled
- (*difficult*)
  = anodd, caled

tour
1 *noun*
= taith (*plural* teithiau) *feminine*,
gwibdaith (*plural* gwibdeithiau)
feminine
guided tour = taith dan arweiniad
(*plural* teithiau dan arweiniad)
feminine
2 *verb*
= teithio
to tour the United States = teithio o
°gwmpas yr Unol °Daleithiau

tourism *noun*
= twristiaeth *feminine*

tourist *noun*
= twrist (*plural* -iaid) *masculine*

tourist office *noun*
= canolfan °groeso/croeso (*plural*
canolfannau croeso) *masculine or
feminine*, canolfan °dwristaeth (*plural*
canolfannau twristiaeth) *masculine or
feminine*

toward(s) *preposition*
- (*general sense*)
  = tuag at°; tua^h (*in certain set phrases*)
  to turn towards someone = troi (*stem*
  troi-, trodd-) tuag at° rywun
  towards the north = tua'r gogledd
- (*time expressions: at about*)
  = tua^h
  towards nine o'clock = tua naw o'r
  °gloch
- (*attitude to someone*)
  = wrth°
  to be kind towards someone = bod yn
  °garedig wrth° rywun

towel *noun*
= tywel (*plural* -i) *masculine*, lliain (*plural*
llieiniau) *masculine*

tower *noun*
= twr̂ (*plural* tyrau) *masculine*

tower block *noun*
= blocdwr (*plural* blocdyrau) *masculine*

town *noun*
= tre(f) (*plural* trefi, trefydd) *feminine*
in town = yn y °dre
to go to town = mynd i'r °dre

town hall *noun*
= neuadd y °dre *feminine*

toy *noun*
= tegan (*plural* -au) *masculine*

trace
1 *noun*
= ôl (*plural* olion) *masculine*, trywydd
(*plural* -au) *masculine*
2 *verb*
- (*track down*)
  = olrhain
- (*draw outline*)
  = amlinellu

track
1 *noun*
- (*mark, trail*)
  = ôl (*plural* olion) *masculine*, trywydd
  (*plural* -au) *masculine*
  to be on the wrong track = bod ar y
  trywydd anghywir
  to keep track of someone = dilyn
  trywydd rhywun
- (*path*)
  = llwybr (*plural* -au) *masculine*
- (*for sports*)
  = trac (*plural* -iau) *masculine*
2 *verb*
= olrhain

track down:
to track someone down = dod o hyd i
°rywun

tracksuit *noun*
= siwt °redeg (*plural* siwtiau rhedeg)
feminine, tracsiwt (*plural* -iau) *feminine*

trade *noun*
- (*commerce*)
  = masnach (*plural* -au) *feminine*
- (*job, skill*)
  what is your trade? = beth ydy'ch
  gwaith chi?
  he's a carpenter by trade = saer ydy e
  wrth ei °grefft, mae'n saer wrth ei
  °grefft

tradition *noun*
= traddodiad (*plural* -au) *masculine*

traditional *adjective*
= traddodiadol

traffic *noun*
= traffig *masculine*, trafnidiaeth
feminine
diverted traffic = traffig osgoi

traffic circle *noun* (*US*)
= trogylch (*plural* -oedd) *masculine*

traffic jam *noun*
= tagfa °geir (*plural* tagfeydd ceir)
feminine

traffic lights *noun*
= goleuadau traffig

trailer *noun*
• (*British: behind car, van*)
= ôl-gerbyd (*plural* -au) *masculine*
• (*US: caravan*)
= carafan (*plural* -au) *feminine*

train
1 *noun*
= trên (*plural* trenau) *masculine*
to go by train = mynd ar y trên, mynd
gyda'r trên
2 *verb*
• (*give or undergo training*)
= hyfforddi
to train someone to do something =
hyfforddi rhywun i °wneud rhywbeth
to train as a doctor = hyfforddi i °fod yn
°feddyg
• (*exercise*)
= ymarfer

trainee *adjective*
= dan hyfforddiant
trainee teacher = athro dan
hyfforddiant *masculine*

trainer *noun*
• (*person*)
= hyfforddwr (*plural* hyfforddwyr)
masculine
• (*shoe*)
= esgid ymarfer (*plural* (e)sgidiau
ymarfer) *feminine*

training *noun*
= hyfforddiant *masculine*, hyfforddi
verbnoun

training course *noun*
= cwrs hyfforddi (*plural* cyrsiau
hyfforddi) *masculine*

tramp *noun*
= crwydryn (*plural* crwydriaid)
masculine

trample *verb*
= sathru

tranquil *adjective*
= llonydd, tawel

transfer
1 *noun*
= trosglwyddiad (*plural* -au) *masculine*
2 *verb*
= trosglwyddo
to transfer something from A to B =
trosglwyddo rhywbeth o° A i° B

transform *verb*
= trawsnewid (*stem* trawsnewidi-),
trawsffurfio

translate *verb*
= cyfieithu, trosi
to translate from English into Welsh =
cyfieithu o'r Saesneg i'r °Gymraeg

translation *noun*
= cyfieithiad (*plural* -au) *masculine*,
trosiad (*plural* -au) *masculine*

translator *noun*
= cyfieithydd (*plural* cyfieithwyr)
masculine
= cyfieithwraig (*plural* cyfieithwragedd)
feminine

transmission *noun*
(*broadcast*)
= darllediad (*plural* -au) *masculine*
(*television, also:*)
= telediad (*plural* -au) *masculine*

transplant
1 *noun*
= trawsblaniad (*plural* -au) *masculine*
2 *verb*
= trawsblannu

transport
1 *noun*
= cludiant *masculine*
2 *verb*
= cludo

trap
1 *noun*
= magl (*plural* -au) *feminine*, trap (*plural*
-iau) *masculine*
to set a trap = gosod trap

2 *verb*
= maglu

trash *noun* (*US*)
= sbwriel *masculine*

trash can *noun* (*US*)
= bin sbwriel (*plural* biniau sbwriel) *masculine*

travel *verb*
= teithio
to travel to Germany = teithio i'r Almaen
to travel the world = teithio'r byd

travel agent's *noun*
= asiantaeth °deithio (*plural* asiantaethau teithio) *feminine*

traveller's cheque *noun*
= siec °deithio (*plural* sieciau teithio) *feminine*
do you take traveller's cheques? = dych chi'n derbyn sieciau teithio?

tray *noun*
= hambwrdd (*plural* hambyrddau) *masculine*

tread *verb*
= troedio
to tread on something = sathru/damsgen ar° rywbeth

treasure *noun*
= trysor (*plural* -au) *masculine*

treat *verb*
to treat someone rudely = trin (*stem* trini-) rhywun yn anghwrtais
to treat someone to something = prynu rhywbeth i° rywun
to treat a patient = trin claf

treatment *noun*
= triniaeth (*plural* -au) *feminine*
to get/receive treatment = cael triniaeth

tree *noun*
= coeden (*plural* coed) *feminine*

tremble *verb*
= crynu

trendy *adjective*
= ffasiynol

trial *noun*
• (*law*)
= treial (*plural* -on) *masculine*
to go on trial = mynd i °dreial

• (*test*)
= prawf (*plural* profion) *masculine*, treial (*plural* -on) *masculine*
• (*hardship*)
= profedigaeth (*plural* -au) *feminine*

triangle *noun*
= triongl (*plural* -au) *masculine*

tribe *noun*
= llwyth (*plural* -au) *masculine*

tribulation *noun*
= profedigaeth (*plural* -au) *feminine*

trick
1 *noun*
= tric (*plural* -iau) *masculine*
2 *verb*
= twyllo

trip
1 *noun*
• (*journey*)
= taith (*plural* teithiau) *feminine*
to make/take a trip = teithio
a business trip = taith °fusnes (*plural* teithiau busnes) *feminine*
• (*excursion*)
= gwibdaith (*plural* gwibdeithiau) *feminine*
2 *verb*
(*trip up*)
= baglu

troops *plural noun*
= milwyr *plural*

trouble *noun*
• (*difficulty*)
= trafferth (*plural* -ion) *feminine*, anhawster (*plural* anawsterau) *masculine*, trwbwl *masculine*, helynt (*plural* -ion) *feminine*
to get into trouble = mynd i helynt *or* °drwbwl
• (*bother, effort*)
to go to the trouble of doing something = trafferthu gwneud rhywbeth
• (*discord*)
= helynt (*plural* -ion) *feminine*, trwbwl *masculine*
to look for trouble = chwilio am helynt *or* °drwbwl
• (*problem, drawback*)
= bai *masculine*, drwg *masculine*
the trouble is, he's not here = y bai *or* drwg ydy, dydy e °ddim yma

troublesome *adjective*
= trafferthus

trousers *noun*
= trowsus *masculine singular*

trout *noun*
= brithyll (*plural* -od) *masculine*

truck *noun*
• (*British: railway wagon*)
= tryc (*plural* -iau) *masculine*
• (*US: lorry*)
= lori (*plural* loriau) *feminine*

truck driver *noun* (*US*)
= gyrrwr lori (*plural* gyrwyr loriau) *masculine*

true *adjective*
= gwir
is it true that he's leaving? = ydy hi'n °wir °fod e'n gadael?
to come true = dod yn °wir

truly *adverb*
yours truly = yr eiddoch yn °gywir

trumpet *noun*
= utgorn (*plural* utgyrn) *masculine*, trwmped (*plural* -au) *masculine*

trunk *noun*
• (*box*)
= cist (*plural* -iau) *feminine*
• (*US: car boot*)
= cist (*plural* -iau) *feminine*
• (*of tree*)
= boncyff (*plural* -ion) *masculine*
• (*of elephant*)
= trwnc (*plural* tryncìau) *masculine*

trust
1 *noun*
• (*faith*)
= ymddiriedaeth *feminine*
to have/put trust in someone = ymddiried yn^{n} rhywun
• (*organization*)
= ymddiriedolaeth (*plural* -au) *feminine*
2 *verb*
= ymddiried
to trust someone = ymddiried yn^{n} rhywun

truth *noun*
= gwir *masculine*, gwirionedd *masculine*
to tell the truth = dweud (*stem* dwed-, wed-) y gwir

try
1 *noun*
• (*attempt*)
= ymgais (*plural* ymgeisiadau) *masculine or feminine*
• (*rugby*)
= cais (*plural* ceisiadau) *masculine*
to score a try = sgorio cais
2 *verb*
• (*attempt*)
= ceisio, trio, treial
to try to/and do something = ceisio/trio gwneud rhywbeth
• (*test*)
= profi
do you want to try them? = wyt ti eisiau profi nhw?

try on
(*garment*)
= trio, rhoi (*stem* rhoi-, rhodd-) amdanoch chi

try out:
to try something out = rhoi (*stem* rhoi-, rhodd-) rhywbeth ar °brawf

T-shirt *noun*
= crys-T (*plural* crysau-T) *masculine*

tube *noun*
• (*general senses*)
= tiwb (*plural* -au) *masculine*
• (*underground*)
= rheilffordd °danddaear(ol)

Tuesday *noun*
= dydd Mawrth, Mawrth
Tuesday night = nos °Fawrth
see also **Monday**

tumble-dryer *noun*
= sychdaflwr (*plural* sychdaflwyr) *masculine*

tummy *noun*
= bol (*plural* -iau) *masculine*, bola (*plural* bolâu) *masculine*

tuna *noun*
= tiwna (*plural* -od) *masculine*

tune *noun*
= tôn (*plural* tonau) *feminine*, alaw (*plural* -on) *feminine*

tunnel *noun*
= twnel (*plural* -au, -i) *masculine*

turkey *noun*
= twrci (*plural* twrcïod) *masculine*

turn

1 *noun*

= tro (*plural* -eon) *masculine*, troad
(*plural* -au) *masculine*

at the turn of the century = ar °droad y
°ganrif

to make/take a turn to the left = troi i'r
chwith

it's your turn = dy °dro di ydy hi

2 *verb*

• (*general senses*)

= troi (*stem* troi-, trodd-)

to turn left = troi i'r chwith

to turn the page = troi'r tudalen

to turn a key = troi agoriad (*North*), troi
allwedd (*South*)

• (*become*)

to turn red = mynd yn °goch

turn around

= troi rownd

turn back

= troi yn ôl

turn down:

to turn something down = troi
rhywbeth (i) lawr

turn into:

to turn into something = troi yn°
rhywbeth

**to turn something/someone into
something** = troi rhywbeth/rhywun
yn° rhywbeth

turn off:

to turn something off = diffodd
rhywbeth

= troi rhywbeth i ffwrdd

turn on:

to turn something on = troi rhywbeth
ymlaen

turn over

= troi (drosodd)

turn up

• (*appear, arrive*)

= ymddangos, troi i fyny, troi lan

• (*increase*)

= troi i fyny, troi lan

turning point *noun*

= trobwynt (*plural* -iau) *masculine*

turtle *noun*

= crwban y môr (*plural* crwbanod y môr)
masculine

tutor *noun*

= tiwtor (*plural* -iaid) *masculine*

Welsh tutor = tiwtor Cymraeg

to work as a tutor = tiwtora

TV *noun*

• (*medium*)

= teledu *masculine*

• (*set*)

= set °deledu (*plural* setiau teledu)
feminine

TV programme = rhaglen °deledu
(*plural* rhaglenni teledu) *feminine*

on TV = ar y teledu

twelfth *adjective*

= deuddegfed

> **!** **deuddegfed** *precedes the noun it
> refers to.*

the twelfth month = y deuddegfed mis

the twelfth year = y °ddeuddegfed
°flwyddyn

Twelfth Night = Nos Ystwyll

twelve *numeral*

= deuddeg

twelve cats = deuddeg cath

= deuddeg o °gathod

twelve days = deuddeng niwrnod

twelve o'clock = deuddeg o'r °gloch

twelve years = deuddeng mlynedd

twelve years old = deuddeng mlwydd
oed

at twelve o'clock = am °ddeuddeg o'r
°gloch

I have twelve = mae gen i °ddeuddeg
(*North*), mae deuddeg 'da fi (*South*)

twentieth *adjective*

= ugeinfed

> **!** **ugeinfed** *precedes the noun it
> refers to.*

the twentieth word = yr ugeinfed gair

the twentieth century = yr ugeinfed
°ganrif

twenty *numeral*

= ugain

twenty cars = ugain car

= ugain o °geir

twenty pounds = ugain punt

twenty years = ugain mlynedd

twenty years old = ugain mlwydd oed

at twenty past two = am ugain munud
wedi dau

I have twenty = mae gen i ugain (*North*),
mae ugain 'da fi (*South*)

! An artificial form **dauddeg** *is promoted officially, but is easily confused with* **deuddeg** *'twelve'. In any case, it is hard to see why the real and widely used word* **ugain** *should be abandoned.*

twice *adverb*
= dwywaith, (*but more usually in mutated form:*) °ddwywaith

! *This word usually appears with soft mutation because it is an adverb of time.*

once or twice = unwaith neu °ddwy
I've told him twice = dw i wedi dweud wrtho °ddwywaith
twice as big as . . . = dwywaith °gymaint â^h . . .
to think twice = ailfeddwl

twin *noun*
= gefell (*plural* gefeilliaid) *masculine and feminine*
= gefeilles (*plural* -au) *feminine*
the twins = yr °efeilliaid (*note mutation*)
this is my twin brother = dyma ^ngefell
this is my twin sister = dyma ^ngefeilles

twist *verb*
= troi (*stem* troi-, trodd-)
to twist an ankle = troi pigwrn

two *numeral*
= dau° (*masculine*), dwy° (*feminine*)

! *Both these words cause soft mutation, and both themselves undergo soft mutation after the words for* 'the'.

the two boys = y °ddau °fachgen
the two girls = y °ddwy °ferch
the two of them = ill dau, ill dwy
two years = dwy °flynedd
two years old = dwy °flwydd oed
at two o'clock = am °ddau o'r °gloch
I have two = mae gen i °ddau/°ddwy (*North*), mae dau/dwy 'da fi (*South*)

type
1 *noun*
= (*kind, species*) math (*plural* -au) *masculine*
things of this type = y °fath °bethau
= pethau o'r °fath (*note mutation!*)

what type of flower is it? = pa °fath o °flodyn yw e?
2 *verb*
= teipio

typewriter *noun*
= teipiadur (*plural* -on) *masculine*

typical *adjective*
= nodweddiadol

typist *noun*
= teipydd (*plural* -ion) *masculine*
= teipyddes (*plural* -au) *feminine*

tyre *noun*
= teiar (*plural* -s) *masculine*
to burst a tyre = rhwygo teiar
a flat tyre = teiar fflat

Uu

ugly adjective
= hyll

ultimate adjective
= ola(f), terfynol

ultimately adverb
= yn y diwedd

umbrella noun
= ymbarél (plural ymbarelau, ymbareli)
masculine or feminine

un- prefix
= af⁰-, anⁿ-, an⁰-

unable adjective
= analluog
to be unable to do something =
methu/ffili gwneud rhywbeth
I am unable to say = ⁰alla i ⁰ddim
dweud

unacceptable adjective
= annerbyniol

unbearable adjective
= annioddefol

unbelievable adjective
= anhygoel, anghredadwy

uncertain adjective
= ansicr

uncle noun
= ewythr (plural -od, -edd) masculine

> ! The loanword **wncwl** is found in
> some areas.

uncomfortable adjective
• (shoes, chair, heat)
= anghyfforddus
• (awkward)
= lletchwith
I felt rather uncomfortable there = o'n
i'n teimlo'n lletchwith braidd fan'na

uncommon adjective
= anghyffredin

unconscious adjective
= anymwybodol

under preposition
• (location)
= dan⁰, o dan⁰
to hide under the bed = cuddio (o) dan
y gwely
• (less than)
= llai naʰ
under ten pounds = llai na deg punt
under a month = llai na mis

underground
1 adjective
= tanddaear(ol)
2 noun
(underground railway)
= rheilffordd ⁰danddaear(ol) feminine

underline verb
= tanlinellu

underneath
1 preposition
= dan⁰, o dan⁰
underneath the trees = (o) dan y coed
2 adverb
= oddi dano(dd), oddi tano(dd)
I want to see what's underneath = dw i
am ⁰weld beth sy oddi tano

underpants plural noun
= trôns (plural tronsiau) masculine

undersea adjective
= tanfor

undershirt noun (US)
= fest (plural -iau) feminine

understand verb
= deall
I don't understand = dw i ⁰ddim yn
deall
do you understand? = dych chi'n
deall?

> ! **deall** often uses the imperfect rather
> than the preterite when reference is to
> the past:
> **she understood the situation** =
> roedd hi'n deall y sefyllfa
> **I didn't understand the film** = o'n i
> ⁰ddim yn deall y ffilm
> **did you understand?** = o'ch chi'n
> deall?

understanding
1 noun
• (comprehension)
= dealltwriaeth feminine

• (*agreement*)
= dealltwriaeth *feminine*
to come to an understanding = dod i
°ddealltwriaeth
2 *adjective*
= deallgar, cydymdeimladol

undertake *verb*
= ymgymryd (*stem* ymgymer-),
ymrwymo
to undertake something = ymgymryd
â^h rhywbeth
to undertake to do something =
ymrwymo i °wneud rhywbeth

underwater *adjective*
= tanddwr

underwear *noun*
= dillad isa(f) *plural*

undo *verb*
(*buttons etc*)
= datod, agor

undress *verb*
= tynnu dillad

uneasy *adjective*
= anesmwyth, pryderus

unelected *adjective*
= heb ei ethol *masculine*;
= heb ei hethol *feminine*;
= heb eu hethol *plural*

> **!** See entry for **unopened** for
> examples of this kind of phrase in
> use.

unemployed *adjective*
= diwaith
to be unemployed = bod yn °ddiwaith
= bod heb °waith

unemployment *noun*
= diweithdra *masculine*

unfair *adjective*
= annheg
to be unfair to someone = bod yn
annheg â^h rhywun

unfamiliar *adjective*
= anghyfarwydd

unfortunate *adjective*
= anffodus

unfortunately *adverb*
= yn anffodus, gwaetha'r modd

> **!** Both these expressions must either
> start or end the phrase, and cannot
> come in the middle as can the English
> word:
> **it is unfortunately too late** =
> yn anffodus, mae'n rhy hwyr,
> mae'n rhy hwyr, yn anffodus,
> gwaetha'r modd, mae'n rhy hwyr,
> mae'n rhy hwyr, gwaetha'r modd

unfriendly *adjective*
= anghyfeillgar
to be unfriendly to someone = bod yn
anghyfeillgar â^h rhywun

ungrateful *adjective*
= anniolchgar

unhappy *adjective*
• (*sad*)
= anhapus, trist
• (*not satisfied*)
= anfodlon

unhealthy *adjective*
= afiach

uniform *noun*
school uniform = gwisg ysgol *feminine*
military uniform = gwisg °filwrol
feminine

unintentional *adjective*
= anfwriadol

unintentionally *adverb*
= yn anfwriadol

union *noun*
= undeb (*plural* -au) *masculine*

unique *adjective*
= unigryw

unit *noun*
= uned (*plural* -au) *feminine*

unite *verb*
= uno

united *adjective*
= unedig, unol

United Kingdom *noun*
= y °Deyrnas Unedig *feminine*

United Nations *noun*
= y Cenhedloedd Unedig

United States *noun*
= yr Unol °Daleithiau

United States of America
= Unol °Daleithiau America (*no article*)

universe *noun*
= bydysawd (*plural* bydysodau) *masculine*

university *noun*
= prifysgol (*plural* -ion) *feminine*
to go to university = mynd i'r °brifysgol
to study at university = astudio yn y °brifysgol

> **!** *Phrases like* 'at university', 'to university' *etc. require the word for* 'the' *in Welsh.*

unkind *adjective*
= cas, angharedig
to be unkind to someone = bod yn °gas wrth° rywun

unknown *adjective*
= anhysbys

unlawful *adjective*
= anghyfreithlon

unless *conjunction*
= onibai (+ 'that...' *clause*)

> **!** *This conjunction is followed by a* 'that...' *clause.*
> **unless you agree** = onibai bod chi'n cytuno
> **unless they've decided already** = onibai bod nhw wedi penderfynu'n °barod

unlikely *adjective*
= annhebyg, annhebygol

unload *verb*
= dadlwytho

unlock *verb*
= datgloi

unlucky *adjective*
= anlwcus

unopened *adjective*
= heb ei agor *masculine*;
= heb ei hagor *feminine*;
= heb eu hagor *plural*
an unopened letter = llythyr heb ei agor
an unopened document = dogfen heb ei hagor
unopened letters = llythyrau heb eu hagor

unpack *verb*
= dadbacio

unpleasant *adjective*
= annymunol

unsatisfactory *adjective*
= anfoddhaol

unsolved *adjective*
= heb ei °ddatrys *masculine*
= heb ei datrys *feminine*
= heb eu datrys *plural*

> **!** *See entry for* **unopened** *for examples of this kind of phrase in use.*

unsuccessful *adjective*
= aflwyddiannus, heb °lwyddiant
to be unsuccessful = bod yn aflwyddiannus, bod yn °fethiant

unsuccessfully *adverb*
= yn aflwyddiannus, heb °lwyddiant

unsuitable *adjective*
= anaddas
to be unsuitable for something/someone = bod yn anaddas i° rywbeth/rywun

untidy *adjective*
• (*room etc*)
= anhrefnus, blêr
• (*person's looks*)
= anhrefnus, didoreth (*South*)

until
1 *conjunction*
= nes; hyd (*less frequent*)

> **!** **nes** *can be followed either by a* 'that...' *clause or by* **i°** + *subject* + *°verbnoun when reference is to the present or future. When reference is to the past,* **nes** *is only used with* **i°** + *subject* + *°verbnoun.*

wait until someone comes = arhoswch nes (y) bydd rhywun yn dod, arhoswch nes i° rywun °ddod, arhoswch nes bod rhywun yn dod
until you see the lights = nes bod chi'n gweld y goleuadau, nes (y) gwelwch chi'r goleuadau, nes (y) byddwch chi'n gweld y goleuadau, hyd y gwelwch chi'r goleuadau
until he arrived = nes iddo (fe) °gyrraedd

2 *preposition*
= hyd°, tan°
until Christmas = tan Nadolig
I'm staying until Thursday = dw i'n
aros tan/hyd °ddydd Iau
open from nine until five = ar agor o
naw hyd °bump

unusual *adjective*
= anarferol
it's unusual to see so many people =
mae'n anarferol gweld cymaint o
°bobol

unwilling *adjective*
= amharod
to be unwilling to do something = bod
yn amharod i °wneud rhywbeth

up
1 *adverb*
• (*motion*)
= i fyny (*North*), lan (*South*)
to go up the hill = mynd i fyny'r bryn
= mynd lan y bryn
• (*in idioms*)
what's up? = beth sy'n bod?
what's up with him? = beth sy'n bod
arno (fe)?
time's up = mae'r amser ar °ben
is he up? (*out of bed*) = ydy e wedi
codi?
2 *preposition*
= i fyny (*North*), lan (*South*)
• (*location*)
they live up the hill = maen nhw'n byw
i fyny'r bryn, maen nhw'n byw lan y
bryn

up to *preposition*
= hyd at°
up to three hundred pounds = hyd at
°dri ʰchant o °bunnoedd
up to seventy miles an hour = hyd at
saithdeg milltir yr awr
up to now = hyd yma
= hyd yn hyn
• (*responsibility*)
that's up to me = ⁿnghyfrifoldeb i ydy
hwnna
• (*decision, choice*)
it's up to you = chi sy â'r dewis

upset
1 *adjective*
to get upset = cynhyrfu
to be upset = bod yn llawn cynnwrf

2 *verb*
• (*make upset*)
= cynhyrfu
• (*turn over*)
= dymchwel, troi (*stem* troi-, trodd-)
°drosodd

upside down *adverb*
= °ben i lawr, °ben ucha'n isa

upstairs *adverb*
= i fyny'r grisiau, lan y grisiau, lan
staer, lan llofft

urban *adjective*
= trefol

urgent *adjective*
= brys, pwysig, taer
an urgent call = galwad brys (*plural*
galwadau brys) *masculine*
an urgent message = neges °bwysig
(*plural* negeseuon pwysig) *feminine*

urgently *adverb*
= ar °fyrder

us *pronoun*
• (*object pronoun*)
= ni, ninnau
they haven't seen us = maen nhw heb
°weld ni
he'll come with us = fe °ddaw e gyda ni
do they know us? = ydyn nhw'n nabod
ni?
will you help us? = newch chi helpu ni?
• = ein ...(ni) (*as object of verbnoun*)
does he want to see us? = ydy e eisiau
ein gweld ni?
what about supporting us? = beth am
ein cefnogi (ni)?
• (*to us*)
= inni, aton ni
give us the message = rhowch y neges
inni
she wrote us a letter = naeth hi
sgrifennu aton ni

> **!** *For details on the expanded form*
> **ninnau**, *see entry on the Welsh-*
> *English side.*

USA *noun*
= UDA

use
1 *noun*
= defnydd *masculine*

to make use of something = gwneud defnydd o° rywbeth, defnyddio rhywbeth

to be of no use = bod yn °ddiddefnydd

this thing is no use = dyw'r peth 'ma'n °dda i °ddim

it's no use complaining = does dim pwynt cwyno
= ofer cwyno

2 *verb*
= defnyddio

used *verb*

> **!** *Habitual action in the past is expressed either by the imperfect with* **arfer** *or by the* **byddwn i** *etc. conditional.*

I used to read a lot = o'n i'n arfer darllen llawer

you used not to smoke = o't ti °ddim yn arfer smygu

we used to go for a walk every day = o'n ni'n arfer mynd am °dro °bob dydd, bydden ni'n mynd am °dro °bob dydd

useful *adjective*
= defnyddiol, o °ddefnydd

useless *adjective*
= diddefnydd

this thing is useless = dyw'r peth 'ma'n °dda i °ddim

usual *adjective*
= arferol

as usual = fel arfer

> **!** **fel arfer** *means both* 'as usual' *and* 'usually'—*context generally serves to distinguish the meanings.*

usually *adverb*
= fel arfer, arfer

I usually get up at six = dw i'n codi am chwech fel arfer, dw i'n arfer codi am chwech

we usually went to bed at ten = o'n ni'n mynd i'r gwely am °ddeg fel arfer, o'n ni'n arfer mynd i'r gwely am °ddeg

> **!** **fel arfer** *means both* 'usually' *and* 'as usual'—*context generally serves to distinguish the meanings.*

utter *adjective*
= llwyr

an utter waste of time = gwastraff llwyr o amser

utterly *adverb*
= hollol°

utterly stupid = hollol °dwp

> **!** *This adverb precedes the adjective it qualifies and causes soft mutation.*

Vv

vacant *adjective*
= gwag

vacation *noun*
(*US: holiday*)
= gwyliau *plural*

vaccinate *verb*
= brechu

vaccination *noun*
= brechiad (*plural* -au) *masculine*

vacuum
1 *noun*
= gwactod (*plural* -au) *masculine*
2 *verb*
= hwfro

vacuum cleaner *noun*
= sugnwr llwch (*plural* sugnwyr llwch)
masculine

vague *adjective*
= aneglur

vain *adjective*
• (*unavailing*)
a vain hope = gobaith ofer
in vain = yn ofer
• (*conceited*)
= ffroenuchel

valid *adjective*
= dilys

valley *noun*
= cwm (*plural* cymoedd) *masculine*,
dyffryn (*plural* -noedd) *masculine*, glyn
(*plural* -noedd) *masculine*

valuable *adjective*
= gwerthfawr

value
1 *noun*
= gwerth (*plural* -oedd) *masculine*
to get good value = cael gwerth eich
arian
these things have increased in value =
mae gwerth y pethau 'ma wedi
cynyddu
2 *verb*
• (*set, estimate a value*)
= prisio

• (*appreciate*)
= gwerthfawrogi

valueless *adjective*
= diwerth

van *noun*
= fan (*plural* -iau) *feminine*

vandal *noun*
= fandal (*plural* -iaid) *masculine*

vandalism *noun*
= fandaliaeth *feminine*

vandalize *verb*
= fandaleiddio

vanilla *noun*
= fanila *masculine*

vanish *verb*
= diflannu

various *adjective*
= gwahanol°

> **!** *In this sense,* **gwahanol** *precedes
> the noun it refers to and causes soft
> mutation. When it follows the noun, it
> means* 'different'.

various things = gwahanol °bethau

vary *verb*
= amrywio
to vary from town to town = amrywio o
un °dre i'r llall

vase *noun*
= fâs (*plural* fasys) *feminine*

veal *noun*
= cig llo *masculine*

vegetable *noun*
= llysieuyn (*plural* llysiau) *masculine*

vegetarian
1 *noun*
= llysieuwr (*plural* llysieuwyr) *masculine*
= llysieuwraig (*plural* llysieuwragedd)
feminine
2 *adjective*
vegetarian food = bwyd i °lysieuwyr

vehicle *noun*
= cerbyd (*plural* -au) *masculine*

vein *noun*
= gwythïen (*plural* gwythiennau)
feminine

velvet *adjective and noun*
= melfed *masculine*

venture
1 *noun*
= menter (*plural* mentrau) *feminine*
2 *verb*
= mentro
to venture to do something = mentro gwneud rhywbeth
to venture into town = mentro i'r ºdre

verse *noun*
• (*of song*)
= pennill (*plural* penillion) *masculine*
• (*poetry*)
= barddoniaeth *feminine*

version *noun*
= fersiwn (*plural* fersiynau) *masculine or feminine*

versus *preposition*
= yn erbyn
Wales versus Scotland = Cymru yn erbyn yr Alban

very
1 *adverb*
= iawn

> **!** *In this sense* **iawn** *always follows the adjective it refers to; for its other uses, see entry on the Welsh-English side.*

he's very tired = mae e'n ºflinedig iawn
it's very late = mae hi'n hwyr iawn
she's been very unwell = mae hi wedi bod yn sâl iawn
very much/many = llawer iawn
for the very first time = am y tro cynta erioed
the very last = yr olaf un
2 *adjective*
= (*exact*) unionº

> **!** *In this sense* **union** *precedes the noun it refers to and causes soft mutation.*

this is the very thing = dyma'r union ºbeth

vest *noun*
• (*British: underwear*)
= fest (*plural* -iau) *feminine*
• (*US: waistcoat*)
= gwasgod (*plural* -au *or* -ion) *feminine*

vet *noun*
= milfeddyg (*plural* -on) *masculine*

via *preposition*
= drwyº, trwyº

vicious *adjective*
= cas, llym

victorious *adjective*
= buddugol

victory *noun*
= buddugoliaeth (*plural* -au) *feminine*

video *noun*
= fideo (*plural* -s) *masculine or feminine*

video camera *noun*
= camera fideo (*plural* camerâu fideo) *masculine*

video cassette *noun*
= casét fideo (*plural* casetiau fideo) *masculine*

video game *noun*
= gêm fideo (*plural* gemau fideo) *feminine*

video recorder *noun*
= recordydd fideo (*plural* recordyddion fideo) *masculine*

videotape *noun*
= tâp fideo (*plural* tapiau fideo) *masculine*

view *noun*
• (*sight*)
= golwg (*plural* golygon) *feminine*
• (*scene*)
= golygfa (*plural* golygfeydd) *feminine*
• (*opinion*)
= barn (*plural* -au) *feminine*
point of view = safbwynt (*plural* -iau) *masculine*

village *noun*
= pentre(f) (*plural* pentrefi) *masculine*

vinegar *noun*
= finegr *masculine*

vineyard *noun*
= gwinllan (*plural* -nau *or* -noedd) *masculine*

violence *noun*
= trais *masculine*

violent *adjective*
• (*using violence*)
= treisiol
• (*wild*)
= gwyllt, ffyrnig

violin *noun*
= ffidil (*plural* ffidlau) *feminine*

Virgo *noun*
= y °Forwyn *feminine*

virtue *noun*
= rhinwedd (*plural* -au) *masculine or feminine*
by virtue of something = yn rhinwedd rhywbeth

virtuous *adjective*
= rhinweddol

visit
1 *noun*
= ymweliad (*plural* -au) *masculine*
to pay someone a visit = ymweld â^h rhywun
2 *verb*
= ymweld (*stem* ymwel-)
to visit someone = ymweld â^h rhywun
to visit Wales = ymweld â ^hChymru

visitor *noun*
= ymwelydd (*plural* ymwelwyr) *masculine*

vocabulary *noun*
= geirfa (*plural* -oedd) *feminine*

vocation *noun*
= galwedigaeth (*plural* -au) *feminine*

vocational *adjective*
= galwedigaethol

voice
1 *noun*
= llais (*plural* lleisiau) *masculine*
to give voice to an opinion = lleisio barn
to shout at the top of one's voice = gweiddi nerth eich pen *or* llais
he was shouting at the top of his voice = roedd e'n gweiddi nerth ei °ben *or* °lais
2 *verb*
= lleisio

volleyball *noun*
(*game*)
= pêl-foli *masculine*

voluntary *adjective*
= gwirfoddol

volunteer
1 *noun*
= gwirfoddolwr (*plural* gwirfoddolwyr) *masculine*
= gwirfoddolwraig (*plural* gwirfoddolwragedd) *feminine*

2 *verb*
= gwirfoddoli
to volunteer to do something = gwirfoddoli i °wneud rhywbeth

vomit *verb*
= chwydu

vote
1 *noun*
= pleidlais (*plural* pleidleisiau) *feminine*
2 *verb*
= pleidleisio
to vote for something/someone = pleisleisio dros° rywbeth/rywun
to vote Liberal = pleidleisio dros y Rhyddfrydwyr

vowel *noun*
= llafariad (*plural* llafariaid) *feminine*

Ww

wages *plural noun*
= cyflog *masculine*

waist *noun*
= canol (*plural* -au) *masculine*

waistcoat *noun*
= gwasgod (*plural* -au *or* -ion) *feminine*

wait *verb*
= aros (*stem* arhos-), disgwyl (*stem* disgwyli-)
to wait for someone/something = aros am° rywun/rywbeth, disgwyl rhywun/rhywbeth
to wait for someone to do something = aros i° rywun °wneud rhywbeth, disgwyl i° rywun °wneud rhywbeth
wait a minute! = arhoswch eiliad/°funud!
I couldn't wait to go = o'n i'n ysu am °fynd

waiter *noun*
= gweinydd (*plural* -ion) *masculine*

waiting room *noun*
= stafell aros (*plural* stafelloedd aros) *feminine*

waitress *noun*
= gweinyddes (*plural* -au) *feminine*

wake[1] *verb*
to wake up = deffro, dihuno
to wake someone up = deffro rhywun, dihuno rhywun

wake[2] *noun*
in the wake of = yn sgîl
in the wake of the announcement = yn sgîl y cyhoeddiad

Wales *noun*
= Cymru *feminine*
North Wales = Gogledd Cymru
from North Wales = o °Ogledd Cymru
in North Wales = yng ⁿNgogledd Cymru
Mid Wales = Canolbarth Cymru
from Mid Wales = o °Ganolbarth Cymru
in Mid Wales = yng ⁿNghanolbarth Cymru

South Wales = De Cymru
from South Wales = o °Dde Cymru
in South Wales = yn ⁿNe Cymru

walk
1 *noun*
to go for a walk = mynd am °dro
five minutes' walk from here = pum munud o °waith cerdded o fan hyn
2 *verb*
= cerdded (*stem* cerdd-)
let's walk to town = gad inni °gerdded i'r °dre
to walk the dog = mynd â'r ci am °dro
to walk around town = cerdded o amgylch y °dre
to walk past someone = cerdded heibio i° rywun
walk out:
to walk out on someone = gadael (*stem* gadaw-) rhywun

wall *noun*
= mur (*plural* -iau) *masculine*, wal (*plural* -iau) *feminine*

wallet *noun*
= waled (*plural* -i) *feminine*

wallpaper *noun*
= papur wal *masculine*

walnut *noun*
= cneuen Ffrengig (*plural* cnau Ffrengig) *feminine*

wander *verb*
= crwydro
to wander the streets = crwydro'r strydoedd

want
1 *noun*
= (*lack*) diffyg *masculine*
for want of a better word = yn ⁿniffyg gair gwell
for want of money = oherwydd diffyg arian, yn ⁿniffyg arian
2 *verb*
= eisiau; moyn, mofyn (*South*) (*all with verbs or nouns*)
= am° (*more often with verbs than nouns*)

! **eisiau** *(various pronunciations)*
uses a slightly different construction from the verbnouns **moyn** *and* **mofyn**; **am°** *is rather more restricted in use. See entries on the Welsh-*

English side for more details on usage and examples of these different ways of expressing 'want'.

I want to go home = dw i eisiau mynd adre (*note no* yn), dw i'n moyn mynd adre, dw i am °fynd adre

do you want to come? = wyt ti eisiau dod?, wyt ti'n moyn dod?, wyt ti am °ddod?

we don't want to be late = dyn ni °ddim eisiau bod yn hwyr, dyn ni °ddim yn moyn bod yn hwyr

I wanted to help = o'n i eisiau helpu, o'n i'n moyn helpu, o'n i am helpu

do you want anything else? = dych chi eisiau unrhywbeth arall?, dych chi'n moyn unrhywbeth arall?

I'll want to see you tomorrow = bydda i eisiau'ch gweld chi yfory, bydda i'n moyn eich gweld chi yfory, bydda i am eich gweld chi yfory

support is wanted = mae eisiau/angen cefnogaeth

war *noun*
= rhyfel (*plural* -oedd) *masculine*
the First World War = y Rhyfel Byd Cynta(f)
the Second World War = yr Ail °Ryfel Byd
the Civil War = y Rhyfel Cartre(f)
to declare war on someone = cyhoeddi rhyfel ar° rywun
to go to war = mynd i °ryfel
to wage war = rhyfela

wardrobe *noun*
= cwpwrdd dillad (*plural* cypyrddau dillad) *masculine*

warehouse *noun*
= stordy (*plural* stordai) *masculine*

warm
1 *adjective*
= cynnes, twym (*South*)
to get/become warm = cynhesu
2 *verb*
= cynhesu, twymo

warm up
• (*get warm, make warm*)
= cynhesu, twymo
• (*before sport*)
= ymgynhesu

warn *verb*
= rhybuddio

to warn someone of something = rhybuddio rhywun o° rywbeth
to warn someone against doing something = rhybuddio rhywun rhag gwneud rhywbeth

warning *noun*
= rhybudd (*plural* -ion) *masculine*
without warning = dirybudd
she came without warning = mi °ddaeth hi'n °ddirybudd

warship *noun*
= llong °ryfel (*plural* llongau rhyfel) *feminine*

wash *verb*
(*things*)
= golchi
(*oneself*)
= ymolchi (*colloquial* molchi—*does not mutate*)
to wash the car = golchi'r car
to have a wash = ymolchi

wash up
(*wash the dishes*) = golchi'r llestri

wash basin *noun*
= basn ymolchi (*plural* basnau ymolchi) *masculine*

washing *noun*
• (*clothes to be washed*)
= dillad i'w golchi
• (*action*)
= gwaith golchi *masculine*
to do the washing = golchi'r dillad

washing machine *noun*
= peiriant golchi (*plural* peiriannau golchi) *masculine*

washing-up *noun*
(*dishes*)
= llestri *plural*
to do the washing-up = golchi'r llestri

wasp *noun*
= cacynen (*plural* cacwn) *feminine*
he was stung by a wasp = fe °gafodd ei °bigo gan °gacynen

waste
1 *noun*
• (*squandering*)
= gwastraff
this is a complete waste of time = mae hyn yn °wastraff llwyr o amser

to let food go to waste = gadael (*stem* gadaw-) i °fwyd °fynd yn °wastraff
- (*rubbish*)
= sbwriel *masculine*
2 *verb*
= gwastraffu
to waste time/money = gwastraffu amser/arian

watch
1 *noun*
(*timepiece*)
= oriawr (*plural* oriorau) *feminine*, wats (*plural* -is) *feminine*
this watch has stopped = mae'r oriawr 'ma wedi sefyll
this watch is slow = mae'r oriawr 'ma ar ei hôl
this watch is fast = mae'r oriawr 'ma'n °fuan
2 *verb*
- (*look at*)
= gwylio
to watch television = gwylio'r teledu
to watch someone doing something = gwylio rhywun yn gwneud rhywbeth
- (*take care*)
watch you don't fall! = gwylia °fod ti °ddim yn cwympo!

watch out:
watch out! = pwylla!, gwylia!, gofal!

water
1 *noun*
= dŵr (*plural* dyfroedd) *masculine*
drinking water = dŵr yfed *masculine*
2 *verb*
to water plants = rhoi (*stem* rhoi-, rhodd-) dŵr i °blanhigion

waterfall *noun*
= rhaeadr (*plural* -au, rhëydr) *feminine*

water-skiing *noun*
= sgïo dŵr *verbnoun*

wave
1 *noun*
- (*on water*)
= ton (*plural* -nau) *feminine*
- (*radio etc: wavelength*)
= tonfedd (*plural* -i) *feminine*
short wave radio = radio tonfedd °fer *masculine or feminine*
- (*of the hand*)
= chwifiad (*plural* -au) *masculine*

2 *verb*
= chwifio, siglo
to wave flags = chwifio baneri
to wave to someone = codi llaw ar° rywun

wavelength *noun*
= tonfedd (*plural* -i) *feminine*
to be on the same wavelength as someone = bod ar yr un °donfedd âʰ rhywun

way *noun*
- (*means, method*)
= ffordd (*plural* ffyrdd) *feminine*, dull (*plural* -iau) *masculine*, modd *masculine*
which is the best way to do this? = p'un ydy'r ffordd °orau i °wneud hyn?
way of life = ffordd o °fyw (*plural* ffyrdd o °fyw), dull o °fyw (*plural* dulliau o °fyw)
is there a way we can do this? = oes modd inni °wneud hyn?
- (*the way one does something*)
= ffordd (*plural* ffyrdd) *feminine*
I like the way he writes = dw i'n leicio'r ffordd mae'n sgrifennu
(in) this way = fel hyn, ffordd hyn
(in) that way = fel 'na, fel 'ny, ffordd 'na
- (*road, path*)
= ffordd (*plural* ffyrdd) *feminine*, llwybr (*plural* -au) *masculine*
is this the right way to the library? = ai dyma'r ffordd iawn i'r llyfrgell?
the others are on their way = mae'r lleill ar eu ffordd
it's on the way = mae hi ar y ffordd
I met them on the way back = °gwrddes i â nhw ar y ffordd yn ôl
on the way to Cardiff = ar y ffordd i °Gaerdydd
- (*direction*)
= cyfeiriad (*plural* -au) *masculine*, ffordd (*plural* ffyrdd) *feminine*
which way are you going? = ym ⁿmha °gyfeiriad dych chi'n mynd?
- (*idioms*)
it's a long way away = mae'n °bell
what's his name, by the way? = beth ydy ei enw fe, gyda llaw?
to get one's own way = cael eich ffordd
there's no two ways about it = does dim dwywaith amdani

way out *noun*
= allanfa (*plural* allanfeydd) *feminine*

we *pronoun*
= ni, ninnau
we'll be there = byddwn ni yno
here we are! = dyma ni!
off we go! = ffwrdd/bant â ni!

> **!** *For details on the expanded form*
> **ninnau***, see entry on the Welsh-*
> *English side.*

weak *adjective*
= gwan

weakness *noun*
= gwendid (*plural* -au) *masculine*

wealth *noun*
• (*most senses*)
= cyfoeth *masculine*
• (*abundance*)
– digonedd *masculine*

wealthy *adjective*
= cyfoethog

weapon *noun*
= arf (*plural* -au) *masculine or feminine*

wear
1 *noun*
wear (and tear) = traul *feminine*
2 *verb*
= gwisgo
to wear clothes = gwisgo dillad

wear out:
to wear out shoes = treulio sgidiau
to wear someone out = blino rhywun

weather *noun*
= tywydd *masculine*
what's the weather like today? = sut
mae'r tywydd heddiw?
fine weather = tywydd braf
bad weather = tywydd garw
weather permitting = os bydd hi'n braf

weather forecast *noun*
= rhagolygon y tywydd *plural*

web *noun*
= gwe (*plural* -oedd) *feminine*
the (World Wide) Web = y °we (°fyd-
eang)

wedding *noun*
= priodas (*plural* -au) *feminine*

Wednesday *noun*
= dydd Mercher, Mercher *masculine*

Wednesday night = nos °Fercher
see also **Monday**

week *noun*
= wythnos *feminine*
all week = trwy'r wythnos
every week = °bob wythnos
every other week = °bob yn ail wythnos
last week = wythnos diwetha(f)
this week = wythnos 'ma
next week = wythnos nesa(f)
in a week's time = ymhen wythnos
a week today = wythnos i heddiw

weekend *noun*
= penwythnos (*plural* -au) *masculine*
over the weekend = dros y Sul
to spend the weekend = bwrw'r Sul

weekly
1 *adjective*
= wythnosol
2 *adverb*
(*every week*)
= °bob wythnos, yn wythnosol
3 *noun*
(*magazine etc*)
= wythnosolyn (*plural* wythnosolion)
masculine

weep *verb*
= wylo, llefain, crio

weigh *verb*
= pwyso
how much does it weigh? = faint
mae'n °bwyso?
it weighs too much = mae'n pwyso
gormod
he weighs himself every morning =
mae'n pwyso ei hun(an) °bob bore

weight *noun*
= pwysau *plural*
to put on weight = ennill (*stem* enill-)
pwysau
to lose weight = colli pwysau
what weight is it? = faint mae'n
°bwyso?

weird *adjective*
= rhyfedd

welcome
1 *adjective*
= croeso
welcome to Wales = croeso i °Gymru
welcome to our school = croeso i'n
hysgol ni

welcome back = croeso yn ôl
you're welcome (*answer to thanks*) =
  croeso (i chi)
all (are) welcome = croeso i °bawb
2 *verb*
  = croesawu
to welcome someone = croesawu
  rhywun, rhoi (*stem* rhoi-, rhodd-)
  croeso i° rywun

well

1 *adjective*
  = da, iawn
I'm not feeling well = dw i °ddim yn
  teimlo'n °dda
I hope everyone is well = gobeithio
  °fod pawb yn iawn
to get well = gwella
2 *adverb*
• (*in a good manner*)
  = yn °dda, yn iawn
he speaks Welsh well = mae'n siarad
  Cymraeg yn °dda
he's not eating well = dydy e °ddim yn
  bwyta'n °dda
everything went well = aeth popeth yn
  iawn
• (*at start of sentence*)
  = wel
well, what shall we do? = wel, be' nawn
  ni?
• **as well**
  = hefyd, yn ogystal
the children came as well = daeth y
  plant hefyd
I want to play tennis as well = dw i
  eisiau chwarae tenis yn ogystal
as well as ... = yn ogystal â^h ...
Irish as well as Welsh = Gwyddeleg yn
  ogystal â ^hChymraeg
• **might as well**
  = °waeth, man a man
we might as well go = °waeth inni
  °fynd, man a man inni °fynd

well-known *adjective*
  = enwog, adnabyddus

Welsh

1 *adjective*
• (*Welsh-language*)
  = Cymraeg
a Welsh magazine = cylchgrawn
  Cymraeg
• (*belonging to Wales*)
  = Cymreig

are you Welsh? (*to a man*) = Cymro
  dych chi?
are you Welsh? (*to a woman*) = Cymraes
  dych chi?
2 *noun*
• (*language*)
  = Cymraeg *feminine*, y °Gymraeg
in Welsh = yn °Gymraeg
to translate from English to Welsh =
  cyfieithu o'r Saesneg i'r °Gymraeg
• (*people*)
  = Cymry *plural*

Welsh Assembly *noun*
the Welsh Assembly = y Cynulliad
  masculine

Welsh language *noun*
  = Cymraeg *feminine*, y °Gymraeg

Welsh Office *noun*
the Welsh Office = y Swyddfa °Gymreig
  feminine

Welsh-only *adjective*
(*language*)
  = uniaith °Gymraeg
Welsh-only leaflets = taflenni uniaith
  °Gymraeg

Welshman *noun*
  = Cymro (*plural* Cymry) *masculine*

Welsh-speaking *adjective*
Welsh-speaking Welshman = Cymro
  Cymraeg (*plural* Cymry Cymraeg)
  masculine
non-Welsh-speaking Welshman =
  Cymro di-Gymraeg (*plural* Cymry di-
  Gymraeg) *masculine*
Welsh-speaking area = ardal °Gymraeg
  (*plural* ardaloedd Cymraeg) *feminine*

Welshwoman *noun*
  = Cymraes (*plural* -au) *faminine*

west

1 *adjective*
  = gorllewin
to work in West Wales = gweithio yng
  ⁿNgorllewin Cymru
2 *adverb*
to go west = mynd i'r gorllewin, mynd
  tua'r gorllewin
to live west of Cardiff = byw i'r
  gorllewin o °Gaerdydd
3 *noun*
  = gorllewin
to the west of Carmarthen = i'r
  gorllewin o °Gaerfyrddin

in the west of the country = yng
ⁿngorllewin y ᵒwlad

westerly *adjective*
= gorllewinol, o'r gorllewin
westerly winds = gwyntoedd o'r
gorllewin

western *adjective*
= gorllewinol

wet
1 *adjective*
= gwlyb
to get wet = mynd yn ᵒwlyb
to get wet (*in rain*) = cael eich gwlychu
wet weather = tywydd gwlyb

> **! gwlyb** has comparative forms
> **gwlypach** 'wetter' and **gwlypa(f)**
> 'wettest'.

2 *verb*
= gwlychu

what
1 *pronoun*
• (*general senses*)
= beth (*often* be' *in speech*)
what is this? = beth ydy hwn?
what is happening? = beth sy'n
digwydd
what is Aled doing? = beth mae Aled
yn ᵒwneud?
what is your name? = beth ydy'ch enw
chi?
I don't know what he wants = dw i
ᵒddim yn gwybod beth mae e eisiau
what is this thing for? = at ᵒbeth mae'r
teclyn 'ma? (*note word order!*)
what are you looking for? = am beth
wyt ti'n chwilio? (*note word order!*)
what's the Welsh for 'boring'? = beth
ydy 'boring' yn ᵒGymraeg, sut mae
dweud 'boring' yn ᵒGymraeg?
what if you don't win? = beth os na
enillwch chi?
2 *adjective*
• (*which*)
= paᵒ, pwyᵒ (*South*)
what book did you buy? = pa ᵒlyfr
ᵒbrynest ti?
what clothes were you wearing? = pa
ᵒddillad o't ti'n gwisgo?
what time is it? = faint o'r ᵒgloch ydy
hi?
• (*in exclamations*)
= 'naᵒ . . .! amᵒ . . .!

what a bargain! = 'na ᵒfargen!
what a good idea! = 'na syniad da!
what fun! = am sbort!
what a day! = am ᵒddiwrnod!
• (*the thing that . . .*)
= yr hyn
what is needed is a timetable = yr hyn
sy angen ydy amserlen
we will do what is right = byddwn ni'n
gwneud yr hyn sy'n iawn

whatever
1 *adjective*
= paᵒ . . . bynnag, pwyᵒ . . . bynnag
(*South*)
whatever book she's reading = pa ᵒlyfr
bynnag mae hi'n ᵒddarllen
2 *pronoun*
• (*anything*)
= beth bynnag
whatever you want = beth bynnag dych
chi eisiau

wheat *noun*
= gwenith *masculine*

wheel *noun*
= olwyn (*plural* -ion) *feminine*
steering wheel = olwyn ᵒlywio (*plural*
olwynion llywio) *feminine*

wheelchair *noun*
= cadair olwyn (*plural* cadeiriau olwyn)
feminine

when
1 *adverb*
= pryd
when is your brother going? = pryd
mae'ch brawd yn mynd?
when did you buy those? = pryd
ᵒbrynoch chi'r rheina?
I don't know when the film starts = dw
i ᵒddim yn gwybod pryd mae'r ffilm yn
dechrau
2 *conjunction*
= panᵒ; pryd (*in some areas*)
when I watch television = pan dw i'n
gwylio'r teledu
when I was a child = pan o'n i'n
ᵒblentyn
when they came home = pan
ᵒddaethon nhw adre
when they've gone = pan ᵒfyddan nhw
wedi mynd (*note future!*)

where
1 *adverb*
= lle (*generally does not mutate*), ᵒle, ble

! *All these terms are interchangeable;* **lle** *often resists soft mutation where it would be expected.*

where are you going? = lle dych chi'n mynd?
where do you come from = o lle dych chi'n dod? (*note word order!*)
I don't know where they are = dw i °ddim yn gwybod lle maen nhw
where is the lid? = lle mae'r caead?
I wonder where he lives = 'sgwn i lle mae'n byw, tybed °le mae'n byw
2 *conjunction*
= lle (*generally does not mutate*), °le, ble
that's where it was = dyna lle oedd e
I'll leave the key where you can see it = na i °adael yr agoriad lle gellwch chi °weld e

whether *conjunction*
= (a)°

! **(a)°** *is often silent in normal speech, though the mutation following it is always present.*

go and ask whether they're ready = cer i °ofyn (a) ydyn nhw'n °barod
I don't know whether we should go or not = dw i °ddim yn gwybod (a) °ddylen ni °fynd neu °beidio

which
1 *adjective*
• (*interrogative*)
= pa°, pwy° (*South*)
which book did you buy? = pa °lyfr °brynest ti?
which clothes were you wearing? = pa °ddillad o't ti'n gwisgo?
• (*relative*)
= (a)°
the bus which came late = y bws (a) °ddaeth yn hwyr
the film which we saw = y ffilm (a) °welon ni
(*in combination with present tense*)
= sy(dd)
the bus which leaves at eight = y bws sy'n gadael am wyth
• (*relative with negative verb*)
= na^h/°
the book which I didn't buy = y llyfr na °brynes i
2 *pronoun*
= pa un, p'un *singular*, pa °rai *plural*

which do you want? = p'un wyt ti eisiau
= pa °rai wyt ti eisiau
which is the longest? = p'un ydy'r hira?
which are the cheapest? = pa °rai ydy'r rhata?

while
1 *conjunction*
= wrth; tra

! **wrth** *is followed by* **i**° + *subject* + °*verbnoun;* **tra,** *on the other hand, is followed by a 'that. . .' clause. See entries on the Welsh-English side for further details and examples.*

while walking down the street = wrth °gerdded lawr y stryd
while we were in Spain = wrth inni °fod yn Sbaen, tra oedden ni yn Sbaen
while she was sleeping = wrth iddi (hi) °gysgu, tra oedd hi'n cysgu
while I am here = tra ⁿmod i yma
2 *noun*
all the while = trwy'r amser
for a while = am °gyfnod
for the while = am y tro
for a long while (since) = ers amser maith

whisper
1 *noun*
= sibrwd (*plural* sibrydion) *masculine*
2 *verb*
= sibrwd (*stem* sibryd-)
to whisper something to someone = sibrwd rhywbeth wrth° rywun

whistle
1 *noun*
= chwiban (*plural* -au) *masculine or feminine*
2 *verb*
= chwibanu

white *adjective*
= gwyn

! **gwyn** *has a special feminine form* **gwen;** *also a plural* **gwynion** *confined nowadays to set phrases.*

who *pronoun*
• (*interrogative*)
= pwy

who is that? (*masculine*) = pwy ydy
hwnna?
(*feminine*) = pwy ydy honna?
who is speaking? = pwy sy'n siarad?
who(m) is Aled inviting? = pwy mae
Aled yn °wahodd?
who came yesterday? = pwy °ddaeth
ddoe?
who will be there? = pwy °fydd yno?
who knows? (*rhetorical*) = pwy a °ŵyr?
I don't know who was here = dw i
°ddim yn gwybod pwy oedd fan hyn
• (*relative*)
= (a)°
my friend who lives in Swansea =
ⁿnghyfaill sy'n byw yn Abertawe
the man who(m) we saw = y dyn (a)
°welon ni
(*in combination with present tense*)
= sy(dd)
the family who live next door = y teulu
sy'n byw drws nesa
• (*relative with negative verb*)
= naʰ/°; (*with present*) sy °ddim
someone who shouldn't be here =
rhywun na °ddylai °fod fan hyn
someone who doesn't speak Welsh =
rhywun sy °ddim yn siarad Cymraeg

whole

1 *adjective*
= hollᵒ (*precedes noun*), cyfan

> **!** holl *always precedes the noun it*
> *refers to and causes soft mutation;*
> **cyfan** *always follows the noun.*

the whole time = yr holl amser
the whole year = y °flwyddyn °gyfan
on the whole = ar y cyfan
the whole thing = y cyfan, y cyfan i gyd
2 *noun*
the whole of Wales = Cymru °gyfan
the whole of the school = pawb yn yr
ysgol

whose

no equivalent word in Welsh
1 *adjective*
whose car is this? = car pwy ydy hwn?
whose books are these? = llyfrau pwy
ydy'r rhain?
2 *pronoun*
• (*interrogative*)
whose is this? = pwy (sy) biau hwn?
whose are these? = pwy (sy) biau'r
rhain?

• (*relative*)
the man whose car broke down = y
dyn (y) torrodd ei °gar i lawr

why

= pam

> **!** pam *is followed by a 'that ...' clause*
> *when reference is to the present,*
> *future or negative past. So, for*
> *example,* **pam °fod e yma?** *'why is he*
> *here?' rather than* *pam mae e yma?

1 *adverb*
• (*asking reason*)
why are you here? = pam bod chi fan
hyn?
why aren't they coming? = pam bod
nhw °ddim yn dod?
why did you say that? = pam wedest ti
hynny?
why didn't you say? = pam na wedest
ti?
why not? = pam °lai?
• (*in suggestions*)
why don't you come round later? =
pam na °ddoi di draw wedyn?
2 *conjunction*
that's why he's going = 'na pam °fod
e'n mynd, 'na'r rheswm dros iddo
°fynd

wicket *noun*

= wiced (*plural* -i) *feminine*

wide *adjective*

• (*size*)
= eang, llydan
a wide room = stafell eang
how wide is this room? = beth ydy lled
y stafell 'ma?
to make something wider = ehangu
rhywbeth
• (*range, scope*)
= helaeth, eang
a wide choice of books = dewis
helaeth o °lyfrau

> **!** eang *has comparative forms*
> **ehangach** *'wider' and* **ehanga(f)**
> *'widest'.*

wide-awake *adjective*

= hollol effro, hollol ar °ddihun

widen *verb*

= ehangu

widow *noun*
= gweddw (*plural* -on) *feminine*, gwraig °weddw (*plural* gwragedd gweddw) *feminine*

widowed *adjective*
= gweddw

widower *noun*
= gŵr gweddw (*plural* gwŷr gweddw) *masculine*

width *noun*
= lled (*plural* -au) *masculine*

wife *noun*
= gwraig (*plural* gwragedd) *feminine*

wild *adjective*
= gwyllt
to go wild = mynd yn °wyllt
to drive someone wild = gwylltio rhywun

wildlife *noun*
= bywyd gwyllt *masculine*

will
1 *verb*
• (*future*)
we will be back tomorrow = byddwn ni yn ôl yfory
will they come? = °fyddan nhw'n dod?, °ddôn nhw?
what will we do? = beth nawn ni?
• (*intention*)
I'll phone you = na i ffonio chi
we'll write to them = nawn ni sgrifennu atyn nhw
I'll leave them here = na i °adael nhw fan hyn
• (*in requests and invitations*)
will you shut the door? = nei di °gau'r drws?
=newch chi °gau'r drws?
will you have some tea? = °gymerwch chi °de?
• (*tags*)
we won't be late, will we? = °fyddwn ni °ddim yn hwyr, na °fyddwn?
we'll be late, won't we? = byddwn ni'n hwyr, on' byddwn?
• (*please, wish*)
do what you will = gwnewch fel y mynnoch
2 *noun*
(*wish, testament*)
= ewyllys (*plural* -iau) *feminine or masculine*

willing *adjective*
= bodlon, parod
to be willing to do something = bod yn °fodlon gwneud rhywbeth, bod yn °barod i °wneud rhywbeth

win *verb*
= ennill (*stem* enill-)

wind[1] *noun*
= gwynt (*plural* -oedd) *masculine*
strong winds = gwyntoedd cryfion
a northerly wind = gwynt o'r gogledd

wind[2] *verb*
• (*string etc*)
= troi (*stem* troi-, trodd-)
• (*watch, clock*)
= weindio
• (*roads etc*)
= troelli, ymdroelli

window *noun*
= ffenest (*plural* -ri) *feminine*

windscreen *noun*
= sgrîn °flaen (*plural* sgriniau blaen) *feminine*

windsurfing *noun*
= bordhwylio *verbnoun*

windy *adjective*
= gwyntog

wine *noun*
= gwin (*plural* -oedd) *masculine*
white wine = gwin gwyn
red wine = gwin coch
wine bar = tafarn °win (*plural* tafarnau gwin) *feminine*

wing *noun*
• (*of bird, plane*)
= adain (*plural* adenydd) *feminine*
• (*in politics*)
= asgell (*plural* esgyll) *feminine*
• (*in sport*)
= asgellwr (*plural* asgellwyr) *masculine*

winger *noun*
= asgellwr (*plural* asgellwyr) *masculine*

winter *noun*
= gaea(f) (*plural* gaeafau) *masculine*
all winter = trwy'r gaea
in winter = yn y gaea

wipe *verb*
= sychu

to wipe the dishes = sychu'r llestri
to wipe one's feet = sychu'ch traed

wire *noun*
= gwifren (*plural* gwifrau) *feminine*

wise *adjective*
= doeth, call
I'm none the wiser = dw i °fawr callach

wish
1 *noun*
= dymuniad (*plural* -au) *masculine*
best wishes = dymuniadau gorau
= cofion gorau
to make a wish = gwneud dymuniad
2 *verb*
= dymuno
to wish someone well = dymuno'n
°dda i° rywun
to wish someone Happy Christmas =
dymuno Nadolig Llawen i° rywun
to wish to do something = dymuno
gwneud rhywbeth
I wish I could speak French! = byddai'n
°dda gen i siarad Ffrangeg!

with *preposition*
• (*general senses*)
= gyda^h (colloquial: 'da^h); efo (*North*)

> **!** *The aspirate mutation after* **gyda/'da**
> *(as elsewhere) is not consistently
> applied except on words beginning*
> **c-**.

to go with someone = mynd gyda/efo
rhywun
to stay with friends = aros gyda/efo
ffrindiau
who is with you? = pwy sy gyda/efo chi?
with permission = gyda ^hchaniatâd
with thanks = gyda diolch
with best wishes = gyda dymuniadau
gorau
• (*by means of*)
= â^h

> **!** *The aspirate mutation after* **â** *(as
> elsewhere) is not consistently applied
> except on words beginning* **c-**.

to cut something with a knife = torri
rhywbeth â ^hchyllell
• (*because of*)
= gan°
to shiver with (the) cold = crynu gan yr
oerfel

• (*against*)
= yn erbyn
to fight with someone = ymladd yn
erbyn rhywun
• (*in one's attitude towards*)
= wrth°
to be angry with someone = bod yn
°ddig/°grac wrth° rywun

within *preposition*
• (*location*)
= tu ° fewn i°, tu mewn i°
within the building = tu °fewn i'r
adeilad
• (*time*)
= o °fewn, cyn pen
within a month = o °fewn mis, cyn pen
mis
• (*distance*)
= o °fewn
within a mile of the town centre = o
°fewn milltir o °ganol y °dre

without *preposition*
= heb°
tea without milk = te heb °laeth
he went out without paying = aeth e
allan heb °dalu

wolf *noun*
= blaidd (*plural* bleiddiau, bleiddiaid)
masculine

woman *noun*
= gwraig (*plural* gwragedd) *feminine*,
merch (*plural* -ed) *feminine*, dynes
(merched *or* gwragedd used as plural)
(*North*), menyw (*plural* -od) *feminine*
(*South*)

wonder
1 *noun*
= rhyfeddod (*plural* -au) *masculine*
no wonder you're angry = dim rhyfedd
°fod ti'n °grac
2 *verb*
to wonder about something = meddwl
am° rywbeth
to wonder at something = rhyfeddu at°
rywbeth, synnu at° rywbeth
I wonder = sgwn i (*North*), tybed
(*South*)
I wonder if they'll come or not = 'sgwn
i (a) °ddôn nhw neu °beidio, tybed (a)
°ddôn nhw neu °beidio
I wonder what that is = 'sgwn i beth ydy
hwnna, beth ydy hwnna, 'sgwn i?,

tybed beth yw hwnna, beth yw hwnna, tybed?

I shouldn't wonder = synnwn i °ddim

I wonder if you could help us? = 'sgwn i (a) °fedrech chi helpu ni? (*North*), tybed (a) °allech chi helpu ni? (*South*)

wonderful *adjective*

• (*amazing*)
  = rhyfeddol
• (*great, marvellous*)
  = gwych

wood *noun*

• (*forest*)
  = coed (*plural* -ydd) *masculine*, coedwig (*plural* -oedd) *feminine*
• (*material*)
  = pren *masculine*

wooden *adjective*

= pren

wooden horse = ceffyl pren (*plural* ceffylau pren) *masculine*

wool *noun*

= gwlân *masculine*

word *noun*

= gair (*plural* geiriau) *masculine*

what's the Welsh word for 'quick'? = beth ydy'r gair Cymraeg am 'quick'?

he kept his word = mi °gadwodd ei °air

she broke her word = mi °dorrodd ei gair

I gave him my word = mi °roddes i ⁿngair iddo

to have a word with someone = cael gair âʰ rhywun

I'll have a word with them = °ga i °air â nhw

in a word = mewn gair

in other words = mewn geiriau eraill

for want of a better word = yn ⁿniffyg gair gwell

word of honour = llw (*plural* -on) *masculine*

word processor *noun*

= prosesydd geiriau (*plural* prosesyddion geiriau) *masculine*

work

1 *noun*

= gwaith *masculine*

to go to work = mynd i'r gwaith

to be in work = bod mewn gwaith

! 'to work' *and* 'from work' *always require the word for* 'the' *in Welsh.*

to be hard at work = bod wrthi

to be out of work = bod yn °ddiwaith, bod heb °waith

roadworks = gwaith ar y ffordd

2 *verb*

• (*do work*)
  = gweithio
  to work hard = gweithio'n °galed
  to work from home = gweithio oddi cartre(f)
  to work late = gweithio'n hwyr
  to work for someone = gweithio i° rywun
• (*use, operate*)
  = gweithio
  I don't know how to work this = dw i °ddim yn gwybod sut i °weithio hwn
• (*function*)
  = gweithio
  this isn't working properly = dydy hwn °ddim yn gweithio'n iawn
• (*succeed*)
  = llwyddo, gweithio
  the plan worked = mi °lwyddodd y cynllun, mi °weithiodd y cynllun
  the plan didn't work = roedd yn cynllun yn °fethiant, naeth y cynllun °ddim gweithio

work out

to work something out = gweithio rhywbeth allan/mas

to work out a problem = datrys problem

everything worked out OK = aeth popeth yn iawn yn y diwedd

worker *noun*

= gweithiwr (*plural* gweithwyr) *masculine*

= gweithwraig (*plural* gweithwragedd) *feminine*

working-class *adjective*

= dosbarth gweithiol

workshop *noun*

= gweithdy (*plural* gweithdai) *masculine*

world *noun*

= byd (*plural* -oedd) *masculine*

all over the world = dros y byd (i gyd)

= ledled y byd

the **biggest city in the world** = y °ddinas °fwya yn y byd
to **travel round the world** = teithio o amgylch y byd
what in the world is that? = beth yn y byd ydy hwnna?
the **World Cup** = Cwpan y Byd

world-famous *adjective*
= byd-enwog

worm *noun*
= abwydyn (*plural* abwyd) *masculine*

worried *adjective*
to **be worried about something** = poeni am° rywbeth
to **be very worried** = poeni'n °fawr

worry
1 *noun*
= pryder (*plural* -on) *masculine*, gofid (*plural* -iau) *masculine*
to **have worries about something** = bod â pryderon am° rywbeth, poeni am° rywbeth
2 *verb*
= poeni, gofidio, pryderu; becso (*colloquial*)
don't worry! = paid poeni! *or* paid â poeni! *or* paid â ʰphoeni!
= paid becso!
= peidiwch poeni!
= peidiwch becso!

worse *adjective*
= gwaeth
this book is worse than the others = mae'r llyfr 'ma'n °waeth na'r lleill
to **get worse** = gwaethygu
= mynd yn °waeth
the **weather is going to get worse** = mae'r tywydd yn mynd i °waethygu

worsen *verb*
= gwaethygu, mynd yn °waeth

> **! mynd** *is irregular in the preterite, short future and conditional - see entry on the Welsh-English side for details.*

worst *adjective*
= gwaetha(f)
the **worst hotel in town** = y gwesty gwaetha yn y °dre

this is the worst programme ever = hon ydy'r rhaglen °waetha erioed
the **worst thing would be to tell him** = y peth gwaetha °fyddai dweud wrtho

worth
1 *adjective*
= gwerth
this is worth a hundred pounds = mae hwn yn °werth can punt
it's not worth the trouble = dydy hi °ddim yn °werth y °drafferth
2 *noun*
= gwerth *masculine*
a thousand pounds worth of damage = gwerth mil o °bunnoedd o °ddifrod

worthless *adjective*
= diwerth

worthy *adjective*
= teilwng

would *verb*
• (*hypothetical situations*)
I would go if I could = byddwn i'n mynd pe gallwn i, baswn i'n mynd taswn i'n gallu
I would have gone = byddwn i wedi mynd, baswn i wedi mynd
• (*reported speech*)
he said he would come = wedodd e y byddai fe'n dod, wedodd e y basai fe'n dod
• (*unwillingness*)
she wouldn't help him = doedd hi °ddim am ei helpu fe, doedd hi °ddim yn °fodlon helpu fe
• (*wishes*)
I would like a cup of tea = hoffwn i °banaid (o °de), leiciwn i °banaid (o °de)
would you like some more? = hoffech chi °ragor?, leiciech chi °ragor?, hoffet ti °ragor?, leiciet ti °ragor?
• (*requests*)
would you close the door? = °allech chi °gau'r drws?, newch chi °gau'r drws?, °fyddech chi cystal â ʰchau'r drws?
• (*assumptions*)
she'd be twenty now = ugain ⁿmlwydd oed byddai hi erbyn hyn

wound
1 *noun*
= anafiad (*plural* -au) *masculine*, briw (*plural* -iau) *masculine*

2 *verb*
= anafu, brifo

wrap *verb*
= lapio
to wrap (up) a present = lapio anrheg

wreck
1 *noun*
= dryll llong (*plural* drylliau llongau)
masculine
2 *verb*
• (*ship*)
= dryllio
• (*destroy*)
= dinistrio

wrestling *noun*
= reslo *verbnoun*

wretched *adjective*
= truan, truenus

wrist *noun*
= arddwrn (*plural* arddyrnau)
masculine, garddwrn (*plural*
garddyrnau) *masculine*

write *verb*
= (y)sgrifennu; sgwennu (*colloquial*)
to write to someone = sgrifennu at°
rywun
to write to the Welsh Office =
sgrifennu i'r Swyddfa °Gymreig
to write an essay = sgrifennu
traethawd

write back
= sgrifennu yn ôl

write down:
will you write it down for me? = newch
chi sgrifennu fe lawr i mi?

writing *noun*
= ysgrifen *feminine*

writing pad *noun*
= pad sgrifennu (*plural* padiau
sgrifennu) *masculine*

written *adjective*
(*as opposed to spoken*)
= ysgrifenedig

wrong *adjective*
• (*incorrect*)
= anghywir
this answer is wrong = mae'r ateb
'ma'n anghywir

to go the wrong way = mynd ar y ffordd
anghywir
to dial the wrong number =
camddeialu
• (*person*)
= °ddim yn iawn
you're wrong = dych chi °ddim yn iawn
• (*morally wrong*)
= drwg
it's wrong to tell lies = peth drwg ydy
dweud celwyddau
• (*not as it should be*)
something is wrong here = mae
rhywbeth o'i °le fan hyn
there's something wrong with this =
mae rhywbeth yn bod ar hwn
what's wrong with him? = beth sy'n
bod arno (fe)?
everything went wrong = aeth popeth
yn chwith
= aeth popeth o chwith

Xx   Yy

X-ray *noun*
= pelydr-X (*plural* pelydrau-X) *masculine*
to have an X-ray = cael pelydr-X

> **!** **cael** *is irregular in the preterite,
> short future and conditional—see
> entry on the Welsh-English side for
> details*

yacht *noun*
= cwch hwylio (*plural* cychod hwylio)
masculine, iot (*plural* -iau) *feminine*

yard *noun*
• (*unit of length*)
= llath (*plural* -au) *feminine*, llathen
(*plural* -ni) *feminine*
a hundred yards = can llath
• (*open space*)
= iard (*plural* -iau) *feminine*
• (*US: garden*)
= gardd (*plural* gerddi) *feminine*

yawn *verb*
= ymagor, (*colloquial*) magor (*does not
mutate*), dylyfu gên

year *noun*
• = blwyddyn (*plural* blynyddoedd,
blynyddau (*South*))

> **!** **blwyddyn** *is used where no
> numbers (other than 'one') are
> mentioned*

we sold that field a year ago = fe
°werthon ni'r cae 'na °flwyddyn yn ôl
**she's been living in France for a year
now** = mae hi'n byw yn Ffrainc ers
blwyddyn bellach
we'll see you next year! = °welwn ni
chi °flwyddyn nesa!
he/she died years ago = mae wedi
marw ers blynyddoedd
last year = llynedd
this year = eleni
next year = y °flwyddyn nesa(f)
a year ago = °flwyddyn yn ôl
years ago = °flynyddoedd yn ôl
at the end of the year = °ddiwedd y
°flwyddyn
in a year's time = ymhen blwyddyn
for years (since) = ers blynyddoedd
leap year = blwyddyn naid
Happy New Year! = Blwyddyn Newydd
°Dda!
New Year's Eve = Nos °Galan
New Year's Day = Dydd Calan
• = blynedd

> **!** **blynedd** *is the form used for years
> after numerals—it appears as*

ⁿ**mlynedd** *after 5–10 (though not consistently after 6 and 8), 15 and 20.*

I first saw her four years ago = °bedair blynedd yn ôl °weles i hi °gynta

it's been a dream of hers for three years = fe °fu'n °freuddwyd ganddi ers tair blynedd

my brother doesn't want to spend twenty years in the same job = dyw ⁿmrawd °ddim eisiau treulio ugain ⁿmlynedd yn yr un swydd

two years = dwy °flynedd
three years = tair blynedd
four years = pedair blynedd
five years = pum ⁿmlynedd
six years = chwe blynedd
seven years = saith ⁿmlynedd
eight years = wyth ⁿmlynedd
nine years = naw ⁿmlynedd
ten years = deng ⁿmlynedd
twenty years = ugain ⁿmlynedd
fifty years = hanner can ⁿmlynedd
a hundred years = can ⁿmlynedd
in two years' time = ymhen dwy °flynedd
a two-year contract = cytundeb dwy °flynedd
• = blwydd

> ! **blwydd** *means* 'years old', *and is often followed by* **oed** 'age'; **blwydd** *without a number means* 'one year old'.

we've got a three-year-old daughter = mae gynnon ni °ferch tair (blwydd) oed

what age is your younger daughter?—a year = faint ydy oed eich merch iau?—blwydd

a year old = blwydd oed
two years old = dwy °flwydd oed
three years old = tair blwydd oed *(and so on, with mutations as for* **blynedd** *above)*

he is three years old = mae e'n °dair blwydd oed

a five-year-old child = plentyn pum ⁿmlwydd oed

six months old = hanner blwydd oed
eighteen months old = blwydd a hanner oed

yell

1 *verb*
= gweiddi, bloeddio

2 *noun*
to give a yell = gweiddi, bloeddio

yellow *adjective*
= melyn

> ! *This adjective has a special feminine form* **melen**.

to go yellow = mynd yn °felyn

yes *adverb*

> ! *Saying* **yes** *in Welsh depends on the phrasing of the question—in most cases answering in the affirmative involves repeating or turning around the verb of the question see* **Yes and No** *box for more details*

are you coming?—yes = wyt ti'n dod?—ydw

is she coming?—yes = ydy hi'n dod?—ydy

is it cold?—yes = ydy hi'n oer?—ydy

were you ill?—yes = o't ti'n sâl?—oeddwn

were they home?—yes = oedden nhw gartre?—oedden

will Aled be there?—yes = °fydd Aled yno?—bydd

will they come?—yes = °ddôn nhw?—dôn

is there any cheese?—yes = oes caws?—oes

have you got children?—yes = oes plant 'da chi?—oes

would that be okay?—yes = °fasai hynny'n iawn?—basai

have they gone?—yes = ydyn nhw wedi mynd?—ydyn

would you have told him?—yes = °fyddet ti wedi dweud wrtho?—byddwn

can you help?—yes = °ellwch chi helpu?—galla(f) *singular*–gallwn *plural*

would you like to see?—yes = hoffet/leiciet ti °weld?—hoffwn/leiciwn

can I go now?—yes = °ga i °fynd nawr?—cei *singular*–cewch *plural*

> ! *But in the case of past tense questions, and questions that do not begin with the verb,* **do** *and* **ie** *respectively are used invariably for* 'yes'

did you phone them?—yes = ffonioch chi nhw?—do, naethoch chi ffonio

Yes and No

GENERAL PRINCIPLES

Generally, answering 'yes' in Welsh involves repetition of the verb of the question (usually the verb **bod**):

dych chi'n dod?—ydw =
are you coming?—yes (I am)

dych chi'n dod?—ydyn =
are you coming?—yes (we are)

oedd Dafydd yno?—oedd =
was Dafydd there?—yes (he was)

°fyddan nhw'n °barod?—byddan =
will they be ready?—yes (they will be)

°faset ti'n °fodlon?—baswn =
would you be willing?—yes (I would)

°ddylen ni °fynd?—dylen =
should we go?—yes (we should)

°allech chi °ddod?—gallwn =
could you come?—yes (I could)

Answering 'no' in these circumstances simply requires **na°/ʰ** (**nag** before original vowels):

nag ydw; nag ydyn; nag oedd; na °fyddan; na °faswn; na °ddylen; na °allwn

EXCEPTIONS

There are two main exceptions to this principle:

1 **do** (negative **naddo**) Unlike most affirmative reponses in Welsh, **do** is all-purpose in that it does not vary for person. However, it can only be used in response to neutral (i.e. not focused) questions phrased in the preterite.

°glywoch chi'r newyddion?—do =
did you hear the news?—yes

Many speakers extend this to other tenses referring to the past, notably the perfect in **wedi**. This usage is rejected by the literary language as being inconsistent from the point of view of grammar, with the argument that the initial present tense, **wedi** or no, requires a present tense response. On the deeper level of meaning, however, it seems clear that the primary sense of **do** is past time

rather than preterite tense, and on this basis the widespread use of **do** with the main **wedi**-tense is entirely logical.

ydych chi wedi clywed y newyddion?—ydw *or* **do** =
have you heard the news?—yes

do is the correct response whichever method of forming the preterite is used in the question:

ffonion nhw yn y diwedd? – do
naethon nhw ffonio yn y diwedd? – do
ddaru nhw ffonio yn y diwedd? – do
did they phone in the end? – yes

But if a focused word-order is used, removing the verb from its normal position at the start of the sentence, then the focused affirmative response ⇒**ie** is required:

nhw ffoniodd? – ie
was it they who phoned? – yes

The confirmation tag after an affirmative preterite statement is **on' do**, again regardless of person:

naethon nhw °gytuno, on' do? – do
they agreed, didn't they? – yes

mi aeth popeth yn iawn, on' do? – do
everything went well, didn't it? – yes

2 **ie** (negative **nage**) This word is of much more restricted use in Welsh than 'yes' in English—it is used as an affirmative response only to questions which begin with an element that is not the verb, generally focused questions. Compare:

dych chi'n mynd i °Lanelli heddiw? – ydw
are you going to Llanelli today – yes

i °Lanelli dych chi'n mynd heddiw? – ie
are you going to Llanelli today? – yes
[is it to Llanelli that you're going...?]

heddiw dych chi'n mynd i °Lanelli? – ie
are you going to Llanelli today? – yes
[is it today that you're going to Llanelli?]

In the first example, the question is neutral, with no special emphasis placed

continued overleaf

Yes and No continued

on any particular element, and so the first position in the sentence is occupied by the verb (**dych**)—the response echoes the verb. But in the second and third examples we are singling out a particular piece of information—we know, in example 2, that the person addressed is going somewhere, and the question is really about whether they're going to Llanelli or to somewhere else. In the third example, we know that the person is going to Llanelli, but we want to ask whether this is happening today or some other time. In both these cases, the element in doubt is singled out by being placed at the front of the question, and this removes the option of a response using an echoing verbform. So instead the all-purpose non-verbal **ie** (or

negative ⇒**nage**) is used. Further examples:

Eleri sy'n siarad Ffrangeg? – ie
  is it Eleri that speaks French? – yes
Caerdydd enillodd yn y diwedd 'te? – ie
  it was Cardiff that won in the end, then?
  – yes
gwrthod naethon nhw, felly? – ie
  did they refuse, then? – yes

Notice in the last example that **gwrthod**, though expressing the main action of the sentence, is not grammatically a verb, but a verbnoun (in other words, a type of noun, albeit with verbal meaning)—the verb is **naethon**, and the neutral version of this question would be **naethon nhw °wrthod?** to which the answer 'yes' would be **do**).

nhw?—do, ddaru chi ffonio nhw?—do
did they come?—yes =
  °ddaethon nhw?—do,
  naethon nhw °ddod?—do,
  ddaru nhw °ddod?—do
did Eleri read the book?—yes =
  °ddarllenodd Eleri'r llyfr?—do,
  naeth Eleri °ddarllen y llyfr?—do,
  ddaru Eleri °ddarllen y llyfr?—do
are you Welsh?—yes
  = Cymro dych chi?—ie
was it they that phoned?—yes
  = nhw ffoniodd?—ie
is this one the cheapest?—yes
  = hwn ydy'r un rhata?—ie

yesterday *adverb*
  = ddoe
  the day before yesterday = echdoe
  yesterday morning = bore ddoe
  yesterday afternoon = pnawn ddoe
  yesterday evening = neithiwr

yet *adverb*
• (*time*)
  = eto
  not yet = dim eto
  it's not ready yet = dydy e °ddim yn
    °barod eto

have they arrived yet? = ydyn nhw
  wedi cyrraedd eto?
• (*nevertheless*)
  = eto, eto i gyd, er hynny
  yet I have to agree = eto i gyd mae
    rhaid i mi °gytuno, er hynny mae
    rhaid i mi °gytuno
• (*in comparatives*)
  = fyth
  this one is stronger yet = mae hwn yn
    °gryfach fyth

yield *verb*
(*give way*)
  = ildio

yogurt *noun*
  = iogwrt (*plural* iogyrtiau) *masculine*

yonder *adverb*
• (*location*)
  = acw
  the mountains yonder = y mynyddoedd
    acw
• (*in pointing out*)
  = dacw°

you *pronoun*

  ! *In Welsh there are two basic words
  for 'you': **ti** (**di** in inflected future and*

reinforced commands) used with one person with whom the speaker is on familiar terms, or with a child or animal, and **chi** *for all other cases. As with all the pronouns in Welsh, no distinction is made between subject and object pronouns.*

- *(as subject)*
  = *singular:* ti/di, tithau, *plural:* chi, chithau
  are you okay? = wyt ti'n iawn?
  = dych chi'n iawn?
  did you see the film? = °welest ti'r ffilm?
  = °weloch chi'r ffilm?
  if you (will) see him... = os gweli di fe...
  = os gwelwch chi fe...
  would you like to see? = hoffet ti °weld?
  = hoffech chi °weld?
  you can come if you want = °gei di °ddod os wyt ti eisiau
  = °gewch chi °ddod os dych chi eisiau
  it's you who are responsible = ti sy'n °gyfrifol
  = chi sy'n °gyfrifol
  you paid by cheque = °dalest ti â siec
  = °daloch chi â siec
  it was you who paid = ti °dalodd
  = chi °dalodd
  you wait here = aros di fan hyn
  = arhoswch chi fan hyn
  Happy Christmas!—and you! = Nadolig Llawen!—a tithau!/a chithau!
  there you are! = 'na ti!
  = 'na chdi! (*North*), 'na chi!
- *(as object)*
  = *singular:* ti/di; chdi (*North*), tithau, *plural:* chi, chithau
  I saw you = °weles i ti
  = °weles i chi
  I'll phone you = ffonia i ti/di
  = ffonia i chi
  I'll come with you = mi °ddo i efo chdi (*North*)
  = fe °ddo i gyda ti (*South*)
- = dy° ...(di), eich ... (chi) (*as object of verbnoun*)
  I want to see you = dw i eisiau dy °weld di
  = dw i eisiau'ch gweld chi

- *(to you)*
  = i ti, i chi; atat ti, atoch chi
  did he give you the message? = °roddodd e'r neges i ti?
  = °roddodd e'r neges i chi?
  I'll write you a letter
  = na i sgrifennu atat ti
  = na i sgrifennu atoch chi

  > **!** *For details on the expanded forms* **tithau** *and* **chithau**, *see entries on the Welsh-English side.*

young *adjective*
= ifanc (*plural sometimes* ifainc)
a young man = dyn ifanc
young people = pobol ifanc/ifainc
a younger brother = brawd iau
she's younger than me = mae hi'n iau/ifancach/fengach na fi

> **!** **ifanc** *has a variety of comparative forms—see entry on the Welsh-English side for details and examples.*

your *adjective*
= dy° ...(di), eich ... (chi)
your car = dy °gar (di)
= eich car (chi)
your shoes = dy sgidiau (di)
= eich sgidiau (chi)

yours *pronoun*
this is yours = ti (sy) biau hwn
= chi (sy) biau hwn
where is yours? = lle mae d' un di?
= lle mae'ch un chi?

yourself *pronoun*
= dy hun (*North*), dy hunan (*South*)
= eich hun (*North*), eich hunan (*South*)
did you hurt yourself? = nes ti °frifo dy hun(an)?
= naethoch chi °frifo'ch hun(an)?
you can do the work yourself = gelli di °wneud y gwaith dy hun(an)
= gellwch chi °wneud y gwaith eich hun(an)
are you by yourself? = wyt ti ar °ben dy hun(an)?
= dych chi ar °ben eich hun(an)?

yourselves *pronoun*
= eich hun (*North*), eich hunain (*South*)
did you hurt yourselves? = naethoch chi °frifo'ch hun(ain)?
are you by yourselves? = dych chi ar °ben eich hun(ain)?

youth noun
- (*young age*)
  = ieuenctid *masculine*
- (*young man*)
  = dyn ifanc (*plural* dynion ifanc/ifainc) *masculine*, llanc (*plural* -iau) *masculine*
  the town's youth = pobol ifanc y °dre

youth club noun
= clwb ieuenctid (*plural* clybiau ieuenctid) *masculine*

youth hostel noun
= hostel ieuenctid (*plural* hostelau ieuenctid) *feminine*

youth worker noun
= gweithiwr ieuenctid (*plural* gweithwyr ieuenctid) *masculine*

Zz

zebra noun
= sebra (*plural* -s, -od) *masculine*

zebra crossing noun
= croesfan sebra (*plural* croesfannau sebra) *masculine or feminine*

zenith noun
= anterth *masculine*
his career was at its zenith = roedd ei °yrfa yn ei hanterth

zero numeral
= sero *masculine*
(*in phone numbers*) = dim

zip
1 *noun*
= sip (*plural* -iau) *masculine*
to do up a zip = cau (*stem* cae-) sip
to undo a zip = agor sip
2 *verb*
to zip something up = sipio rhywbeth

zip code noun
= (*US: post code*) côd post (*plural* codau post) *masculine*

zipper noun
(*US*) ⇒**zip 1**

zodiac noun
= sidydd *masculine*
signs of the zodiac = arwyddion y sidydd

zone noun
= ardal (*plural* -oedd) *feminine*

zoo noun
= sŵ (*plural* -au) *masculine or feminine*

Names of countries, regions, and languages

	Country	Language
Albania	**Albania** *feminine*	**Albaneg**
America	**America** *feminine*	
North America	**Gogledd America**	
South America	**De America**	
Central America	**Canolbarth America** *masculine*	
Africa	**Affrica** *feminine*	
South Africa	**De Affrica**	
North Africa	**Gogledd Affrica**	
East Africa	**Dwyrain Affrica**	
West Africa	**Gorllewin Affrica**	
Argentina	**yr Ariannin** *feminine*	
Australia	**Awstralia** *feminine*	
Austria	**Awstria** *feminine*	
the Balkans	**y Balcanau** *plural*	
the Basque Country	**Gwlad y Basg(iaid)** *feminine*; **Euskadi**	**Basgeg**
Belarus	**Belarws** *feminine*	**Belarwsieg**
Belgium	**Gwlad Belg** *feminine*	
Bosnia	**Bosnia** *feminine*	
Brazil	**Brasil** *feminine*	
Britain	**Prydain** *feminine*	
Great Britain	**Prydain ºFawr**	
Brittany	**Llydaw** *feminine*	**Llydaweg**
Bulgaria	**Bwlgaria** *feminine*	**Bwlgareg**
Canada	**Canada** *feminine*	
Catalonia	**Catalwnia** *feminine*	**Catalaneg**
China	**Tsieina** *feminine*	**Tsieineg**
Cornwall	**Cernyw** *feminine*	**Cernyweg**
Croatia	**Croatia** *feminine*	**Croateg**
Czech Republic	**Gweriniaeth y Tsieciaid** *feminine*	**Tsieceg**
Denmark	**Denmarc** *feminine*	**Daneg**
Egypt	**yr Aifft** *feminine*	**Arabeg**
England	**Lloegr** *feminine*	**Saesneg**
Estonia	**Estonia** *feminine*	**Estoneg**
Europe	**Ewrop** *feminine*	
Western Europe	**Gorllewin Ewrop**	
Eastern Europe	**Dwyrain Ewrop**	
the Far East	**y Dwyrain Pell** *masculine*	
Finland	**y Ffindir** *masculine*	**Ffinneg**
France	**Ffrainc** *feminine*	**Ffrangeg**
Germany	**yr Almaen** *feminine*	**Almaeneg**
Greece	**Groeg** *feminine*	**Groeg**

	Country	Language
Hungary	**Hwngari** *feminine*	**Hwngareg**
Iceland	**Gwlad yr Iâ** *feminine*; **Ynys yr Iâ** *feminine*	**Islandeg**
India	**(yr) India** *feminine*	**Hindi**
Ireland	**Iwerddon** *feminine*	**Gwyddeleg**
Israel	**Israel** *feminine*	**Hebraeg**
Italy	**yr Eidal** *feminine*	**Eidaleg**
Japan	**Japan** *feminine*	**Japaneg**
Jordan	**Iorddonen** *feminine*	
Korea	**Corea** *feminine*	**Corëeg**
Latvia	**Latfia** *feminine*	**Latfieg**
Lebanon	**Libanus** *feminine*	
Lithuania	**Llethaw** *feminine*; **Lithwania** *feminine*	**Llethaweg**
Luxembourg	**Lwcsembwrg** *feminine*	
Mexico	**Mecsico** *feminine*	
the Middle East	**y Dwyrain Canol** *masculine*	**Arabeg**
the Netherlands	**yr Iseldiroedd** *plural*	**Iseldireg**
New Zealand	**Seland Newydd** *feminine*	
Norway	**Norwy** *feminine*	**Norwyeg**
Peru	**Perw** *feminine* (*or* **Periw** *feminine*)	
Poland	**(Gwlad) Pwyl** *feminine*	**Pwyleg**
Portugal	**Portiwgal** *feminine*	**Portiwgaleg**
Rumania	**Rwmania** *feminine*	**Rwmaneg**
Russia	**Rwsia** *feminine*	**Rwsieg**
Saudi Arabia	**Sawdi-Arabia** *feminine*	
Scandinavia	**Llychlyn** *masculine* or *feminine*	
Scotland	**yr Alban** *feminine*	**Gaeleg yr Alban**
Serbia	**Serbia** *feminine*	**Serbeg**
Slovakia	**Slofacia** *feminine*	**Slofaceg**
Slovenia	**Slofenia** *feminine*	**Slofeneg**
South Africa	**De Affrica**	**Afrikaans** **Zwlw; Zwlŵeg**
Spain	**Sbaen** *feminine*	**Sbaeneg**
Sudan	**y Swdan** *feminine*	
Sweden	**Sweden** *feminine*	**Swedeg**
Switzerland	**y Swistir** *masculine*	
Thailand	**Gwlad y Thai** *feminine*	**(iaith) Thai**
Turkey	**Twrci** *feminine*	**Twrceg**
Ukraine	**(yr) Wcráin** *feminine*	**Wcreineg**
United States	**yr Unol °Daleithiau** *plural*	
United Kingdom	**y °Deyrnas Unedig** *feminine*	
Soviet Union	**yr Undeb Sofietaidd** *masculine*	
Vietnam	**Fietnam** *feminine*	**Fietnameg**
Wales	**Cymru** *feminine*	**Cymraeg**
West Indies	**Ynysoedd y Caribî** *plural* **India 'r Gorllewin** *feminine*	
former Yugoslavia	**cyn-Iwgoslafia** *feminine*	

Names of towns, cities, etc.

Abergavenny	**Y Fenni**
Ammanford	**Rhydaman**
Anglesey	**Môn; Ynys Môn**
Athens	**Athen**
Bala Lake	**Llyn Tegid**
Bath	**Caerfaddon**
Birkenhead	**Penbedw**
Brecon	**Aberhonddu**
Bridgend	**Pen-y-Bont ar Ogwr**
Bristol	**Bryste**
Builth Wells	**Llanfair-ym-Muallt**
Cambridge	**Caergrawnt**
Canterbury	**Caergaint**
Cardiff	**Caerdydd**
Cardigan	**Aberteifi**
Carlisle	**Caerliwelydd**
Carmarthen	**Caerfyrddin**
Catterick	**Catraeth**
Chepstow	**Casgwent**
Cheshire	**Swydd °Gaerlleon**
Chester	**Caer**
Cornwall	**Cernyw**
Denbigh	**Dinbych**
Devil's Bridge	**Pontarfynach**
Devon	**Dyfnaint**
Dublin	**Dulyn**
Ebbw Vale	**Glynebwy**
Edinburgh	**Caeredin**
Exeter	**Caerwysg**
Fishguard	**Abergwaun**
Glamorgan	**Morgannwg**
Mid Glamorgan	**Morgannwg °Ganol**
South Glamorgan	**De Morgannwg**
West Glamorgan	**Gorllewin Morgannwg**
Glastonbury	**Ynys Afallon**
Gloucester	**Caerloyw**
Haverfordwest	**Hwlffordd**
Hebrides	**Ynysoedd Heledd**
Hereford	**Henffordd**
Herefordshire	**Swydd Henffordd**
Holyhead	**Caergybi**
Isle of Man	**Ynys Manaw**
Isle of Wight	**Ynys Wyth**

Kent	**Caint**
Lampeter	**Llanbedr Pont Steffan**
Lancashire	**Swydd °Gaerhirfryn**
Leicester	**Caerlŷr**
Leicestershire	**Swydd °Gaerlŷr**
Liverpool	**Lerpwl**
Llandaff	**Llandaf**
Llandovery	**Llanymddyfri**
London	**Llundain**
Ludlow	**Llwydlo**
Manchester	**Manceinion**
Menai Bridge	**Porthaethwy**
Milford Haven	**Aberdaugleddau**
Mold	**yr Wyddgrug**
Monmouth	**Trefynwy**
Morriston	**Treforys**
Narberth	**Arberth**
Neath	**Castell Nedd**
Newcastle Emlyn	**Castell Newydd Emlyn**
Newport	**Casnewydd**
Newquay	**Cei Newydd**
Newtown	**y °Dre Newydd**
New York	**Efrog Newydd**
Offa's Dyke	**Clawdd Offa**
Orkney Islands	**Ynysoedd Erch**
Oswestry	**Croesoswallt**
Oxford	**Rhydychen**
Pendine	**Pentywyn**
Port Dinorwic	**y °Felinheli**
Rhayader	**Rhaeadr**
Rome	**Rhufain**
St Asaph	**Llanelwy**
St Davids	**Tŷ °Ddewi**
St Fagans	**Sain Ffagan**
Salisbury	**Caersallog**
Severn	**Hafren**
Shetland Islands	**Ynysoedd Shetland**
Shrewsbury	**Amwythig**
Snowdon	**yr Wyddfa**
Solva	**Solfach**
Somerset	**Gwlad yr Haf**
Strata Florida	**Ystrad Fflur**
Swansea	**Abertawe**
Tenby	**Dinbych-y-Pysgod**
Thames	**Tafwys**
Usk	**Wysg**
Vale of Glamorgan	**Bro Morgannwg**
Welshpool	**y Trallwng**
Winchester	**Caerwynt**

Worcester	**Caerwrangon**
Worcestershire	**Swydd °Gaerwrangon**
Wrexham	**Wrecsam**
Wye	**Gwy**
York	**Efrog**
Yorkshire	**Swydd Efrog**

Also available from Oxford University Press

Oxford Starter French Dictionary
Revised edition
0-19-860715-6

Oxford Starter German Dictionary
Second edition
0-19-860329-0

Oxford Starter Spanish Dictionary
Revised edition
0-19-860716-4

Oxford Starter Russian Dictionary
0-19-860032-1

Oxford Starter Chinese Dictionary
0-19-860258-8

Oxford Starter Japanese Dictionary
0-19-860197-2